Racism *in*
College Athletics

3rd Edition

DANA BROOKS

•

RONALD ALTHOUSE

Editors

Fitness Information Technology
a Division of the International Center
for Performance Excellence
West Virginia University
262 Coliseum, WVU-CPASS
PO Box 6116
Morgantown, WV 26506-6116

Library of Congress Card Catalog Number: 2012949255

ISBN: 978-1-935412-45-8

Cover Design: Bellerophon Productions

Cover Images: Hurdler courtesy of Aspenphoto/Dreamstime.com; basketball player courtesy of djma/Dreamstime.com; football players courtesy of Gordon Parks, Library of Congress Prints and Photographs Division; runner courtesy of Holly Reed Photography; Mark Sanchez courtesy of USC Athletic Department

Production Editor: Matt Brann

Copyeditor: Jennifer Bowman

Typesetter: Craig Hines

Proofreader: Geoffrey Fuller

Indexer: Geoffrey Fuller

Printed by Data Reproductions Corporation

10 9 8 7 6 5 4 3 2 1

Fitness Information Technology
A Division of the International Center for Performance Excellence
West Virginia University
262 Coliseum, WVU-CPASS
PO Box 6116
Morgantown, WV 26506-6116

800.477.4348 (toll free)
304.293.6888 (phone)
304.293.6658 (fax)
Email: fitcustomerservice@mail.wvu.edu
Website: www.fitinfotech.com

Contents

A Personal Statement

EARL FRANCIS LLOYD

Former NBA Player and Coach; Basketball Hall of Fame Inductee

Those who take a hard look at current practices in college athletics will realize the tremendous disparity as it relates to the number of athletes, coaches, directors, head coaches, and assistant coaches. This situation illustrates that racism in college athletics is alive and well.

Athletic participation dominates, but that dominance does not reveal itself in the upper echelon of management in major colleges. The myth still exists that the virile Black athlete is perfect for entertainment but not for administration and leadership. Speaking as a Black former NBA coach, I am aware of the attitude as it relates to the welfare of the Black athlete at the intercolligate level and the professional level. Most of the institutions or organizations that elected to hire Black coaches were not top echelon teams, and their fortunes appeared to be hopeless prior to hiring the Black coach, who is put into a situation that is designed to fail.

Many young Black athletes fall by the wayside because of a culture gap between the player and the coach. Most of the media is composed of White males who evaluate, influence the rule makers, and judge Black males—a culture they know very little about. This is made clear by the reactions to young men "celebrating" after scoring an important goal.

Young players are used for the profit of the school but not given a share of the profits that they have helped bring into the arena. More and more I believe there should be a pay structure for the college athletes.

Young players who have been recruited leave college early to participate on the professional level; I think some effort should be made by the college and the NCAA to entice the young person to return to school after his career. It should at least be an option because not all of those kids make millions of dollars, and a degree would give them a more profitable life. After all, they have brought millions to the college.

I've had coaches say to me, "I need some Black players." When asked what makes his school better than some other school, the coaches replied, "We're near a Black college, so when the player wants to date he can go over there and date." My response to those coaches was, "Why should the player work for your school and not be able to enjoy his school's social life?" Unfortunately, this is still the underlying attitude of many schools even in this day and age.

But change seems to be working itself out . . . hopefully.

Foreword

MINORITIES ARE SEPARATE AND UNEQUAL: A LOOK AT MINORITY HIRING PRACTICES IN COLLEGIATE AND PROFESSIONAL ATHLETICS

FLOYD KEITH

President, Black Coaches & Administrators (Formerly Black Coaches Association)

I was fortunate to be in attendance for Super Bowl XLI in Miami.[1] My emotional tears of joy and pride were mixed with the steady rain that fell upon my face throughout the game as I was blessed to be present for an historic event that was so artfully and taste-fully orchestrated by head football coaches Tony Dungy and Lovie Smith.[2] It was much more than a football game, much more than the utopia of the National Football League, much more than the crowning moment of the ultimate event in our sports world: It was the essence of what individuals of color can accomplish if given the opportunity. How many "Dungys" and "Smiths" have we missed because of the lack of an opportunity, not only in football, but in all sports and professions as well? It is impossible to estimate the millions of young eyes who watched that day and are now able to dream of being Afri-can American head coaches because they could visualize the reality and have tangible evidence![3]

During Super Bowl XLI, the NFL and the accompanying media frenzy exalted the prog-ress of minority coach hires through the success of its Rooney Rule. The rule, which was instituted in 2003, mandates that any NFL team with a head coaching vacancy is required to meaningfully interview at least one minority candidate.[4] The Rooney Rule has resulted in an increase in the number of minority head coaches in the NFL, rising from three to seven in 2006, where African American coaches made up 21.8% of NFL head coaches. The number of NCAA Football Bowl Subdivision (FBS, formerly Division I-A) minority coaches also rose in 2006, but only to five black head coaches out of 119 teams, making up only 4.2% of head coaches.[5] Over the years, the number of minority head coaches has remained relatively consistent in the NFL. Heading into the 2012 season, six of 32 NFL teams (18.8%) were coached by minorities. Of the 120-school NCAA FBS, 19 programs (15.8%) were coached by minority head coaches heading into the 2011 season.

While we have made some progress in the hiring of minority head coaches across the board, there is still much progress to be had. In an effort to address significant issues that pertain directly to the participation and employment of minorities in sports, the Black Coaches & Adminstrators (BCA) implemented the Hiring Report Card for the NCAA football division.[8, 9] While the BCA believes this process has made the hiring practices of

Division I-A (FBS) and Division I-AA (FCS) in football more transparent and accountable, we continue to try to answer the same disturbing questions.[10] If 58% of the players in Division I men's basketball are African American and 25% of the head basketball coaches are of color,[11] why does the 49% of African American players in Division I-A football translate to only 16% in the football coaching ranks?[12] If the trend of only a few annual hires of African American head football coaches continues, in order to reach the equivalent of the current 25% of head basketball coaches in Division I men's basketball, it will take six years, provided all current coaches remain where they are, which is highly unlikely since coaching roles transition every two to five years.

These statistics are hard facts that bring an end to the multitude of subjective conversations stimulated by this ongoing debate. This is not only unacceptable, this is unconscionably wrong. The reality is we are dealing with a social injustice. The 2007 football hiring cycle produced only two hires of color for 33 opportunities.[13] In the eight years of the Hiring Report Card study, however, 52% of all African Americans ever hired were appointed.[14]

The BCA has both a moral and social responsibility to maintain our annual Hiring Report Card for intercollegiate football and the benefit of sport in general. In addition, our Association began conducting similar studies with regard to women's basketball head coach appointments in 2008.[15] As we reflect upon the eight years of our survey, it becomes increasingly obvious that more is needed to correct a problem that is both systematic in nature and wrapped with all of the characteristics of social injustice. We are not sure if public acknowledgement is strong enough to make significant change. Is an NCAA version of the Rooney Rule or a Title VII[16] lawsuit the answer?

Richard Lapchick, director of the University of Central Florida's Institute for Diversity and Ethics in Sport and renowned advocate for the rights of women and minorities in athletics, said, "I think it's pretty clear that embarrassment hasn't been enough. One of the things (the BCA) is thinking about is Title VII lawsuits."[17] Title IX opened doors for NCAA women's athletics;[18] we believe the use of Title VII may be necessary to break the current logjam in intercollegiate hiring. History has shown that in order for any significant progress to be made in eradicating a social injustice, legal action has often been the catalyst for change.

We acknowledge that individual NCAA institutions hire coaches; however, not much seems to be happening to increase diversity among coaches when left in the hands of the individual institutions. As such, the ramifications of a successful claim under the provisions of Title VII would be monumental in scope and impact. The filing of a strong qualifying Title VII case against a visible institution would most certainly change the status quo of collegiate intercollegiate athletic searches. The realization of legal implications with regard to Title VII could be the much needed serum for an injection of equality in the intercollegiate hiring landscape.

Title VII of the Civil Rights Act of 1964, which prohibits employment discrimination based on race, color, religion, sex, or national origin, seems to fit the formula. Under Title VII, it is illegal to discriminate in any aspect of employment, including hiring and firing; compensation, assignment, or classification of employees; transfer, promotion, layoff, or recall; job advertisements; recruitment; fringe benefits; pay, retirement plans and disability leave; or other terms and conditions of employment.[19] Title VII prohibits not only intentional discrimination, but also practices that have the effect of discriminating against individuals because of their race, color, national origin, religion, or sex.[20] Title VII covers all private employers, state and local governments, and education institutions that employ 15 or more individuals, and also private and public employment agencies, labor organizations, and joint labor management committees controlling apprenticeship and training.[21] Any individual who believes that their employment rights have been violated may file a charge of discrimination with the Equal Employment Opportunity Commission (EEOC).[22] In addition, an individual, organization, or agency may file a charge on behalf of another person in order to protect the aggrieved individual's identity.[23]

The merits of bringing a visible Title VII case forward may be more far reaching than the verdict; it might effect change by forcing the NCAA's member institutions to consider a best practices model like the NFL's Rooney Rule.[24] "The BCA and others have argued that the burden should be on the member institutions who have erected barriers against quality opportunities; but under the current system, it is the hardest way to try to rework the system to put the burden on the employer. An NCAA policy similar to the Rooney Rule would put the burden on the employer at all times."[25] Cyrus Mehri in 2007 stated it right: "When you change the process, you will change the outcome."[26] The purpose is to change the set of hiring practices for college sports in America, to bring a person of color into the interview process with the attempt to get significantly more minorities into collegiate coaching positions. This is the point of a Rooney Rule-type of policy, or something similar in nature to Title IX.

In the October 3, 2007, *USA Today*, Steve Wieberg referenced an encouraging effort by Division I-A Athletic Directors Association to respond to years of criticism regarding minority hiring.[27] In a meeting in Texas, the Athletic Director Association revealed their intent to implement a set of standards for best hiring practices that will not be to put this into law but rather will "encourage" schools to adhere to specified acceptable standards that are likely to include the one-minority candidate interview minimum.[28] Dutch Baughman, executive director of the I-A Athletic Directors' Association, feels that "nobody wants to be called out by his peers."[29]

The BCA, the Fritz Pollard Alliance, the NCAA Minority Opportunities and Interest Committee, and the Minority Opportunities Athletic Association must continue to put real pressure on the NCAA to develop a best practice hiring policy that can assist institutions with their hiring policies and procedures and ensure accountability in the process. To do this, there must be ownership taken by the major power brokers within collegiate athletics: athletic directors, university presidents and conference commissioners. Currently, the only tool in place is the BCA Hiring Report Card, but in the past four or five years, this does not seem to be doing the job. The BCA Hiring Report Card has used power of public exposure as its source of accountability. Based upon the hiring results in football over the past four years of the study, we are unsure whether the court of public opinion is strong enough to promote significant changes in the hiring process. I can personally confirm the sincere and sympathetic concerns of key NCAA administrators, prominent athletic directors, and some NCAA college presidents to work with organizations such as the BCA and Fritz Pollard Alliance to address this issue, especially during the past two years. We can only hope the effort to resolve the lack of minority coaches at the collegiate level catches up with the need to end this social injustice. It should not require a wreck to draw a crowd.

ENDNOTES

1. The AFC champion Indianapolis Colts (16-4) defeated the NFC champion Chicago Bears (15-4). The tagline for Super Bowl XLI, was "One Game, One Dream," partially due to the historic marking of the first Black coach to make it to a Super Bowl. See Smith, Dungy are first Black coaches in Super Bowl. (2007, January 27). *ESPN*. Retrieved from http://sports.espn.go.com/nfl/playoffs06/news/story?id = 2738495

2. Tony Dungy is a former professional American football player and coach in the NFL. Dungy was head coach of the Indianapolis Colts from 2002 to 2008. Biography of Tony Dungy, available at http://www.gale.cengage.com /free_resources/bhm/bio/dungy_t.htm. Lovie Smith is the head coach of the Chicago Bears professional football

team. Lovie Smith joined Tony Dungy as the first Black NFL head coach to make it to a Super Bowl. Biography of Lovie Smith, available at http://www.kevo.com/profile/loviesmith/Lovie_Smith_on_Wikipedia

3. *See* Pond Cumming, A. D. (2008). Pushing weight. *Thurgood Marshall Law Review*, *33*(1), 1–34.

4. Maravent, B., & Tario, B. (2007). Leveling the playing field: Can Title VII work to increase minority coaching hires In NCAA athletics? *Florida Bar Journal*, *81*(9), 42–55.

5. Forde, P. (2007). NFL leads colleges in promoting minority coaches. *ESPN*. Retrieved from http://sports.espn.go.com/espn/columns/story?columnist = forde_pat&id = 2735369 Pat Forde writes that "In college football, meanwhile, 10 out of 10 BCS bowl coaches and 62 out of 64 bowl coaches overall were White . . . With the hirings of African American Randy Shannon at Miami and Cuban-born Mario Cristobal at Florida International, the number of minority Division I-A coaches has ballooned to seven. Woo-hoo. That's two out of the 21 hires made to date, not enough to appreciably move the needle toward equality." *Id.*

6. Proxmire, D. C. (2008). Coaching diversity: The Rooney Rule, its application and ideas for expansion. *American Constitution Society for Law and Policy*. Retrieved from http://www.acslaw.org/files/Proxmire%20Issue%20Brief.pdf

7. Diversity study: Number of Black head coaches in FBS falls to four. (2008, November 6). *ESPN*. Retrieved from http://sports.espn.go.com/ncf/news/story?id = 3686028

8. The BCA Hiring Report Card places the hiring process of institutions of higher education in their search for a new head football coach under public scrutiny. *See* Harrison, C. K. (2006). Scoring the hire: Hiring report card and social network analysis for NCAA Division I-A and I-AA football head coaching positions in American higher education. *Black Coaches Association*. Retrieved from http://74.52.140.242/ ~ bcasport/images/pdf/HRCfootball-06.pdf

9. See Black Coaches Association (BCA) releases the 3rd hiring report card for football coaches. (2006). *Black Coaches Association*. Retrieved from http://www.bcasports.org/MiContent.aspx?pn + NewsListings&sss = 1&xid = 1064

10. The Lack of Diversity in Leadership Positions in NCAA Collegiate Sports: Hearings Before the Subcomm. On Commerce, Trade and Consumer Protection of the H. Comm. On Energy and Commerce, 110th Cong. (2007) (testimony of Myles Brand), available at http://energy-commerce.house.gov/cmte_mtgs?110-ctcp_hrg.022807.Brand-testimony.pdf [hereinafter Brand Testimony].

11. See Floyd Keith Statement in *The Big Game In Sport Management and Higher Education: The Hiring Practices of Division I-A and I-AA Head Football Coaches*, ix (2007), available at http://grx.cstv.com/photos/schools/bca/genrel/auto_pdf/07-hiring-report-card.pdf; *See also Hiring Report Card highlights hiring practices for head football coaches in Football Bowl Subdivision and Football Championship Division*, BCA, October 8, 2007, available at http://bcasports.cstv.com/genrel/100807aae.html; See also Keith, F. (2008). *Statement in who you know & who knows you: The hiring process & practice of NCAA FBS & FCS head coaching positions*. Retrieved from http://grfx.cstv.com/photos/schools/bca/genrel/auto_pdf/08-hiring-report-card.pdf

12. Ibid.

13. See *Hiring Report Card highlights hiring practices for head football coaches in Football Bowl Subdivision and Football championship Division*, *supra* note 12.

14. See Richard Lapchick, *"Building Positive Change:" The Black Coaches and Administrators (BCA) Hiring Report Card for NCAA FBS and FCS Football Head Coaching Positions (2010–11)*, BCA, 2011, available at http://www.bcasports.org/images/pdf/bca_fb_hiring_final_11.20.2011.pdf

15. *See* Richard Lapchick, *Scoring the Hire: A Hiring Report Card for NCAA Division I Women's Basketball Head Coaching Positions*, BCA, 2008, available at http://web.bus.ucf.edu/documents/sport/wbbbcareportcard2009 .pdf

16. Title VII of the Civil Rights Act of 1964 prohibits discrimination against by covered employers on the basis of race, color, religion, sex or national origin. See Title VII of the Civil Rights Act of 1964, 42 U.S.C.A. § 2000 et seq. (West 2001) *available at* http://www.eeoc.gov/policy/vii.html

17. Associated Press, *Lack of Black Coaches Lamented at Hearing*, March 1, 2007, available at http://sports.espn.go.com/ncf/news/story?id = 2783335. Dr. Lapchick also produces an annual report called The Racial and Gender Report Card, now produced by the University of Central Florida's Institute for Diversity and Ethics in Sport. Until 1998, the report was known as the Racial Report Card. DeVos Sports Institute, Dr. Lapchick biography, http://www.bus.ucf.edu/faculty/rlapchick/file.axd?file = 2011%2F9%2FBiography + 9.10.11.pdf

18. Secretary Roderick Raynor "Rod" Paige, statement in After year of scrutiny, law's longtime interpretation faces uncertain future (2002) http://www.ncaa.org/wps/ncaa?Content ID = 3344, US Department of Education Secretary Paige announced the formation of the commission to study Title IX.

19. *See* Title VII, *supra* note 18.

20. *Ibid.*

21. *Ibid.*; See also Elizabeth Grossman, *Issues in EEOC Agency Litigation*, 631 PLI/Lit 7, 12 (2000).

22. *Ibid.*

23. *Ibid.*

24. Telephone interview with Temple University Beasley School of Law Professor Jeremi Duru (March 20, 2007). His biography is at www.law.temple.edu/servlet/RetrievePage?site = TempleLaw&page = Faculty_Duru

25. *Ibid.*

26. Cyrus Mehri statement in *Major-college ADs tackle minority hiring*, (2007). Retrieved from http:// www.usatoday.com/sports/college/football/2007-10-02-minority_N.htm

27. Steve Wieberg, *Major-college ADs tackle minority hiring*, USA TODAY, Oct. 3, 2007. Retrieved from http://www.usatoday.com/sports/college/football/2007-10-02-minority_N.htm

28. *Ibid.*

29. *Ibid.*

Acknowledgments

We would like to express appreciation to Fitness Information Technology for its ongoing loyalty, support, and encouragement of this textbook. We thank the nationally recognized scholars for their contribution to this text: Floyd Keith, Angela Lumpkin, Samuel Hodge, Frankie Collins, Robert Bennett III, Delano Tucker, Chevelle Hall, Wardell Johnson, Brandon Martin, Derrick Gragg, Dennis Kramer II, Doris Corbett, Cryshanna Jackson, Robertha Abney, C. Keith Harrison, Bill Sutton, Andre Smith, D. Lyn Dotson, Andrea Dean-Crowley, Emmett Gill, Tina Sloan-Green, Suzanne Malia Lawrence Kirkland, John Singer, Vanessa Ochoa, Michelle Hernandez, and Kenneth Teed. We would also like to thank Mrs. Linda Shaw and Ms. Joanne Pollitt for their secretarial and management contribution to this textbook.

—DANA BROOKS and RONALD ALTHOUSE

Introduction

RONALD ALTHOUSE and DANA BROOKS

Sport has long been an important set of practices and institutions in the African American community, providing many of its leaders with the sites for public resistance and an established institutional context for race-based protest and critiques of post-civil rights racial culture. African Americans have always viewed the sport playing field as a place where they could compete on a level playing field within American society. Even so, for more than a century intercollegiate athletics has been a source of frustration, disappointment, and despair for African Americans as they have struggled against the discrimination that has historically been a part of intercollegiate sport. Sport has been a place of courage and achievement for African American athletes, coaches, and athletic administrators who have been given the chance to play, coach, and administer college sports. Deeds of the past need not be visited upon African Americans in the future, but for full equality and opportunity to be achieved for African American college athletes, coaches, and administrators, a number of still unresolved problems must be addressed.

The widespread interest in the study of racism in college athletics generated by the first two editions of *Racism in College Athletics* created a need for the third edition. The growing literature on this topic and recent social changes prompted us, as editors, to secure original new essays from well-respected authors and scholars in compiling this edition.

Contemporary Sport in the United States

Any discussion of intercollegiate sports must begin at a level much broader than college athletics; it can be understood only within the context of contemporary American society, including the pervasive racism that has been systemic in America for nearly the past 400 years.

Among the various popular cultural practices in American society, sport is the most ubiquitous. Sport is fun! More than 25 million young boys and girls participate in youth sports programs each year; nearly 6 million high school athletes compete in more than 25 different sports; and nearly 500,000 college athletes—more than 420,000 athletes in the NCAA alone—participate competitively for their institutions. Add to those participants the elite-level athletes who represent the United States in international competition, as well as professional athletes, and you have a vast number of athletes engaged in organized sports. Yet the major form of involvement with sports is not as participants, but rather as spectators—the millions who watch sporting events, either by actually attending contests or by viewing them on television.[1]

Beyond participating in sports in various ways, noted sport sociologist George Sage reflects about the zest for sport expressed in the U.S., writing

> Americans invest a great deal of their time and emotions in understanding the intricacies of sports while following their favorite teams and athletes. They are knowledgeable about rules (or at least think they are); they are able to recite 'their' teams' strengths and weaknesses and chances for winning the championship of their league; and they are enthusiastic admirers of certain athletes. Much of this knowledge and enthusiasm is fueled and sustained by the mass media, which cover several thousand hours of sporting events each year. (Sage, 2000, p. 1)

Broadly speaking, in 2005 in the United States, cautiously conservative estimates of the economic scope of the sport industry (i.e., participation, viewing, marketing, but not gambling) range from $44 to $73 billion, with some sport economists projecting as much as $152 billion annually. And these figures do not even include the revenues of various types of mass media dedicated to sports (Humphreys & Ruseski, 2008).

Understanding Sport as a Cultural Practice

In spite of the various ways in which Americans consume sports, they are not encouraged to critically examine for the prevalent attitudes, values, myths, and folklore about this cultural practice. Americans tend to be unaware of the social relations of control in sport, showing a remarkable gullibility about the social context and material conditions underlying sporting practices. Although sports embody specific and identifiable purposes, values, and meanings, sports are typically viewed by both participants and fans as ahistorical and apolitical in nature. Sage (2000) comments that such naiveté is common because "sport and society have traditionally been seen as discrete social phenomena, with sports often thought of as a pristine and isolated activity that is (or should be) uncontaminated by problems and issues of the wider society" (p. 2). Those who have the power and influence in sports have fought attempts to change this image. In large measure, mass media information about sports in American society tends to celebrate sports as "fun and games," not to confront us with questions about social issues. Instead, sport is valorized and Americans are fed a diet of slogans, clichés, and ritualized trivia about sports. Although these can be comforting to the devoted athlete, coach, sport administrator, and fan, they do not come to grips with the social reality of contemporary sport.

It is probably not too much of a stretch to argue that to see sport as cultural practice begins with the awareness that it cannot be examined as if isolated from the social, economic, political, and cultural context in which it is situated. The essence of understanding the social relevance of sport is embedded in its relationship to social class, race, gender, and power. Sport has the potential to wipe out racial barriers and to create new opportunities. The critical issue in this volume is to trace progress toward a society in which race is not supposed to matter.

Racism in American Society

When Americans talk about difference, how do they do so? What visions of order are attractive or appreciated? How does American society deal with cultural inclusion and the recognition of inequalities? History shows, for the most part, that dominant and privileged groups will downplay or dismiss inequalities because they believe they have granted equal cultural recognition to those below them, or at least that those below are offered the chance to assimilate. This is a version of multicultural assimilation—the incorporation of diversity—that is fairly widespread in our contemporary American society. Yet the question remains one of how widely distributed the opportunities are for inclusion across lines of class and, especially, race.

Because this book is about race relations in intercollegiate athletics, it is essential to historically situate and culturally locate racism in American society. To understand the role of racism in college athletics, it must be seen from the larger cultural context in which it is situated. The 2010 U.S. Census reported approximately 42 million African Americans who made up about 13.6% of the total U.S. population ("Black (African-American) History," 2012). A persisting thread running through the garment of the American experience is discrimination against African Americans; racism is rooted deeply in America's history. African Americans are the only racial group that has been subjected to an extended period of slavery; they are the only racial group to have segregation laws passed against them that were supported and fully sanctioned by the Supreme Court (Bell, 1992; Wilson, 1996). Of course, African Americans are not the only minority group in America that has had to struggle for basic civil rights, but theirs has been a unique and insidious heritage of injustice.

Black Africans were brought to colonial America in 1619, soon after the establishment of the English settlement at Jamestown. By the mid-17th century, the slave-based economic system thrived among colonial plantation owners, and at the turn of the 18th century enslaved Black Africans were the principal source of labor and a fundamental component of colonial agricultural and commercial interests. An oppressive racist social structure, with Blacks at the bottom, was institutionalized among slave owners of the agricultural South, and integral to the economies of Northern trading and shipping firms.

By the latter 18th century the dealings between colonists and the British were strained and soon led to revolution, and finally to colonial independence. A system of racism was incorporated into the basic documents of the newly formed United States, with the Declaration of Independence and U.S. Constitution condoning racial subordination and discrimination against African Americans. So, in spite of what was considered an enlightened stance toward human rights by the framers of these documents, their liberal vision of liberties for Whites was not challenged by denying it to African Americans, who totaled 20% of the population when the United States became a new nation. Slavery was sanctioned, black oppression secured, and African Americans were denied all rights of citizenship.

It took a civil war and the passage of the 13th, 14th, and 15th Amendments to the U.S. Constitution in the years immediately following the Civil War to officially end the slavery system. First and foremost, this had been a war about sustaining the "union" among the states, and secondarily about slavery. Although slavery was abolished, by the latter decades of the 19th century, many states passed Jim Crow laws mandating racial segregation in almost all areas of public life. In effect, then, Jim Crow laws legalized White domination, yet encouraged black oppression, and thus left racism essentially intact. A "separate but equal" system replaced slavery and became an even more efficient instrument of domination and subordination than slavery had been.

It was not until 1954 that the "separate but equal" doctrine was successfully challenged when the U.S. Supreme Court in the *Brown v. Board of Education of Topeka* decision ruled that separate schools are inherently unequal, thus setting the stage for desegregation of American schools. This decision set in motion a series of challenges to discrimination against African Americans that came to a head in sweeping civil rights legislation in the mid-1960s. So it has only been in the past 45 years that the civil rights of Black citizens have been protected by law (Wilson, 1996).

In the 1960s African Americans began to experience increases in relative pay levels, racial segregation of schools was unconstitutional, and other anti-discrimination policies were put in effect to outlaw workplace discrimination. While enforcement was targeted on the South, throughout the 1970s and '80s, economic stagnation weakened anti-discrimination policies. African Americans in urban centers suffered particular hardships with the relocation of industries to peripheral areas at the same time that the introduction of new technologies reduced opportunities for employment or surrounded them with jobs for which they were unqualified. In 1990, 11% of African Americans 25 years or older had four years of college or more, versus 22% of Whites (Kaminski & Adams, 1992).

On all major economic indicators—income, wages, unemployment, and poverty—African Americans were worse off in 2007 than they were in 2000 (Austin, 2008). African Americans have not shared in America's prosperity, and the current economic downturn does not bode well for the immediate future. While laws protecting the civil rights of African Americans exist and provide improved conditions in some private and public sectors, domination and subordination of African Americans are still institutionally systemic in American society. Race is still a fundamental determinant of people's position in the social structure. African Americans are still defined as racially different by the White majority and singled out for a broad range of individual and institutionalized discrimination (Rowe & Jeffries, 1996; Orfield & Lee, 2007).

Although that last statement may seem to overstate current conditions, it actually does not. The U.S. Department of Justice reported that 47% of hate crime incidents were motivated by race. According to a report compiled by the FBI's civil rights division, there were 6,628 hate crimes reported in 2010. About 47% of all hate cases were racially motivated, but significantly, 70% of these race-based cases had targeted African Americans. More insidious, about 14% of reported hate crimes occur at schools or colleges and of these crimes, 54% were motivated by race ("FBI," 2011).

On the other hand, America's "tough on crime" policies have been toughest on African Americans. The rate of involvement is massive: The number of males in state and federal prisons increased by 66%; among females, the rate increased by 86%. This does not include the number of men and women on parole or probation. This rate of incarceration occurred during a decline in crime in African American communities. In general, upward mobility is impeded by high incarceration rates (Mauer, 2006; Austin, 2008; Kerby, 2012).

There are widespread perceptions that things are getting better for African Americans, but in fact the economic gap between Whites and Blacks has actually been widening in the past 20 years. It's standard practice among poverty researchers to examine the percent of families and children who are below twice the poverty level. In 2007, 46.5% of all African American families had incomes below twice the poverty level (Austin, 2008). Worse, 60.6% of black children were below twice the poverty level (Bernstein, 2007). The official poverty rate is a minimal measure of the economic well-being of Americans. Given this low bar, a third of African American children are facing economic distress (DeNavas-Walt, 2011).

African American household income was only 62% that of Whites, and it had changed very little since the 1990s (Austin, 2008).The jobless rate for African Americans has consistently been more than twice that of Whites. Not only are African American more likely to be unemployed, but those who are employed are overrepresented in jobs whose pay, power, and prestige are low. Even more disturbing, African American teens have the lowest employment rate among African Americans, and they experienced the largest decline in employment; in 2000 employment was 29.5%, by 2007 it had dropped to 21% (Austin, 2008). Although low educational attainment is one reason for low employment rates, racial discrimination in the marketplace and dysfunctional criminal justice policies also are significant in preventing African Americans from obtaining jobs.

African Americans held no wealth when freed from slavery, and their incomes have prevented any accumulation at the rates that Whites had had. Therefore, if we focus strictly on financial, income-producing assets, African Americans held little wealth, perhaps 10–15%, compared to White households. When we look beyond labor market success we see that big differences in wealth holding do exist, and because wealth is passed from parents to children, the differences found at the mid-20th century continue to have an important impact today. Comparatively few African Americans have moved beyond middle levels of authority and control in private sector American business, and a mere handful are found among the CEOs in the Fortune 500. Out of 17 million U. S. business firms, only 2% are owned by African Americans (Allegretto, 2011)

Although less common today than in the past, token integration in the workplace is more prevalent than demographic balance, even among occupations that are integrated. A greater percentage of African Americans have moved into white-collar and blue-collar manufacturing jobs, and fewer have gone into service and farming. During the last two decades, however, the distribution of occupations among African Americans and Whites has also been tied to unemployment and poverty levels and the hyperghettoization of the inner city (Hurst, 2007).

The relationship between economic success and educational opportunity is deep-seated in our society; indeed, education has served as a super-highway for adult occupational achievement. For African Americans, education has had an embarrassing record. The report by the Civil Rights Project shows that the percentage of African American students in majority-White schools rose from almost zero in 1954 to a peak of 43.5% in 1988 before a steady decline to 27% by the middle of the first decade of the 21st century (Frankenberg, Lee, & Orfield, 2003). Meanwhile, the proportion of African Americans attending majority-minority schools has been increasing over the past decades. In 2005, 73% of African American students were in majority-minority schools, and more than a third (38%) were in intensely segregated schools with 90% to 100% minority enrollment (Jost, 2010a).

By 1995, according to a Century Foundation report, race-preference affirmative action at 146 top-tier colleges accounted for only 6% admissions of African American students. Socioeconomically, 74% of students came from families in the wealthiest quarter of the socioeconomic status scale (SES), and 3% came from families in the bottom quarter (Carnevale & Rose, 2003). Overall, at the K–12 level affirmative action has not generated much forward movement, with little closing of the gap of the past 20 to 30 years. Affirmative action has typically focused on Black students, who are assumed to be academically under-qualified. Faced by the political preferences of Congress and the Supreme Court, affirmative action and quotas have been recast as diversity. Political trends are against it. Observers on both sides see a dim future for affirmative action, mainly because the condition of the public schools in low-income America are chronically deficient.

So, although some African Americans have made gains economically and in educational achievements, barriers remain and these barriers are rooted in institutional patterns and practices of racial discrimination that are deeply ingrained in the structure of American society. Where racism coexists with class stratification, as it does in the United States, the evidence is convincing that it is more basic to social structure and, therefore, the ultimate determinant of inequality between racial minorities and the dominant class. Though some people feel they have little influence, one way to assess political impact is through participation. For African Americans, their relationship started in slavery and confronted them with utter exclusion from the polity. The Civil War to save the union also granted the right to vote—the 15th Amendment—to all citizens, although its extension of this franchise to African Americans was resisted. Blacks were excluded from a right to vote, or faced with limited voting rights until 1965, when President Lyndon Johnson signed the Voting Rights act into law, applying a nationwide prohibition against the denial or abridgement to vote. Data show that during the 1960s—the period of Civil Rights movements—a larger percentage of African Americans voted in national elections than they did in 2000. Since 1984, the percent voting has remained the low-to-mid 50s, and in 2004, about 56% of voting-age African Americans went to the polls in the presidential election (Jost, 2010b).

Among African Americans, historically men have significantly outnumbered women as elected officials; however, women have tended to gain so that about 35% of all elected officials are women. In 2001, there were 9,101 African American elected officials, compared to 1,469 in 1970. But African Americans comprise about 11% of the voting age population. After the 2004 elections, there were 42 African Americans in the House of Representatives, and one in the Senate, Barack Obama (Jost, 2010b). On January 20, 2009, Barack Obama, the first African American ever to serve as the nation's chief executive, was sworn into office as the 44th president of the United States. Spectators came from all over the country and many lands, and the crowd was racially and ethnically diverse. Within weeks the truce was beginning to break down, and partisan division was taking over.

While Obama benefitted from sacrifices of the civil rights generation, his politics differed from the veterans of that movement. African American voters were initially reluctant to support him, but as the campaign wore on, no one forgot that Obama is Black. The exit polls showed that he prevailed among those who considered race a significant factor. His victory did not bring racial enmity to an end, but it did leave America with hope that the end is in sight.

The basic fact is that much inequality and discrimination against African Americans continues, regardless of whether one uses income, employment rates, educational attainment, or political office-holding as measures. African Americans remain among the most disadvantaged groups in American society, and it is racial barriers that block Black achievement, not merely economic or class barriers. Martin Luther King, Jr.'s dream that one day racism would end in America has not been fulfilled. Racism, then, is a salient aspect of the structure of American society. The most important aspect of this form of stratification is that it excludes people of color from equal access to socially valued rewards and resources. They tend to have less wealth, power, and social prestige than do other Americans. Moreover, racism has built-in policies and practices that systematically discriminate against people in employment, housing, politics, education, health care, and many other areas. These conditions result in fewer human resources and diminished life chances for African Americans.

Racism in American Sport

Despite pervasive and systematic discrimination against African Americans throughout history in North America, they have played a continuing and significant role in every era of American sport history, as Lumpkin (Chapter 1) and Hodge, Bennett, and Collins (Chapters 2 and 3) document in their chapters of this new edition. These four authors, along with virtually every contributor to this third edition, are aware of and write within a Critical Race Theory or multicultural theory frame of interpretation.[2] Their analyses suggest that this involvement can be divided roughly into four stages: (1) exclusion before the Civil War, (2) breakthroughs immediately following the Civil War, (3) segregation from the last two decades of the 19th century until after World War II, and (4) integration after World War II.

Broadly viewed, Lumpkin reminds us that the predominant viewpoint among the majority of Americans across the country is that "sports should be praised for accepting minorities, and especially African Americans, more quickly and more equitably than other sectors of society. Many have claimed that performance, not ethnicity or skin color, counted the most in sports." Lumpkin's perspective underscores the ways of thinking and acting that account for the persistence and the perpetuation of racial differences and inequalities because of the color-blind ideals and White normativity that fosters ways of disavowing race and racism in American society.

In the years following the Civil War some African Americans advanced their status economically and socially, but most remained oppressed. Across the nation, many White Americans treated African Americans as if they were inferior psychologically, biologically, and anthropologically. In 1896, the United States Supreme Court *Plessy v. Ferguson* decision affirmed the maintenance of the status quo of separate educational institutions, public accommodations, and transportation and other services. The relegation of African Americans to separate schools, places to live, and subservient jobs allowed White Americans throughout the US to ignore the plight of African Americans and to assume that no one was harmed by a society divided on the basis of race.

Throughout the early decades of the 20th century their oppression continued as they were subjected to allegedly separate but equal treatment. African Americans who were fortunate enough to advance into higher education were segregated into historically Black colleges and universities (HBCUs), most of which were located in the South. With few exceptions, HBCUs formed their own teams and competed against themselves in segregated sports competitions. Athletics gave opportunities, often denied them due to the discrimination they faced in society, to demonstrate manhood. African American male athletes could be aggressive and strong, rather than having to be passive and deferential toward White athletes. Also, sports, and particularly football, became popular and helped generate campus spirit and racial pride. Lumpkin writes that "Female students attending some HBCUs beginning in the 1920s enjoyed the opportunity to participate on basketball and track teams."

In 1912, the Colored College Athletic Association was formed. These segregated athletics organizations sought to standardize rules and facilitate fair competitions. Competitions between athletes attending HBCUs were conducted in relative obscurity except for publicity in the African

Prior to breaking the color barrier in Major League Baseball in 1945, Jackie Robinson faced racial difficulties as a student-athlete at UCLA like many of his fellow Black athletes during that era. Courtesy of National Baseball Hall of Fame Library

American press. Only a few colleges in the North and Midwest would admit an occasional, and usually exceptional, African American student. These athletes had to demonstrate exceptional prowess in sports and strong academic abilities, and acquire the mental toughness required to overcome the racism they experienced. They advocated that through athletic accomplishments, racial pride could be enhanced. Some believed that sports provided platforms for advancing racial equality.

By the end of World War II, most African American athletes still remained marginally visible in HBCUs. Lumpkin writes, "in retrospect, it is deplorable that Southern bigotry and prejudice were so deep-seated that institutions and their coaches refused to allow competitions against African American athletes." African American players were withheld from inter-regional football games as their coaches acquiesced to the demands of Southern segregationists and denied African American players the right to compete—the so called "gentleman's agreement" among coaches in several conferences. This practice of withholding African Americans from competitions also occurred in track and field as well as basketball.

Until about 1945 most African Americans athletes playing at predominantly White colleges played football, at a rate approximately the same as basketball, baseball, and track and field combined. The peak decade for them playing on predominately White teams was the 1920s, which was predictable given the increased popularity of football in public schools and colleges. The numbers dropped somewhat in the 1930s, and then began to pick up again in the post-World War II years.

Hodge and his colleagues (Chapter 2) noted that the second Morrill Act (1890) was the primary genesis of the HBCUs and their growth in America. The authors wrote "it required states with segregated systems of higher education (all White and colored) to provide land-grant institutions for both systems," which led to the establishment of land-grant HBCUs for teaching of agriculture and mechanical arts to African American citizens. Today, HBCUs are mostly four-year private and public liberal arts colleges and universities as well as two- and four-year community colleges, and various business, law, medical, theological, and technical institutions. It was not until 1953 that a predominantly White collegiate athletic association, the National Association of Intercollegiate Athletics (NAIA), even voted to admit HBCUs as members.

Lumpkin contends that in the post-war years the increased commercialization of collegiate sports opened more opportunities for African American males as an untapped resource for talent. Indications are that the African American recruits often felt exploited athletically and were not encouraged to achieve academically nor accepted as social equals. She reminds us that two effects shaped throughout war-time years were free substitution in football due to the shortage of players and recruiting of African American athletes, which were described as an untapped talent pool (Spivey, 1983). She reasons that some coaches began tapping the talent pool of African American athletes to win games. In part, segregation succumbed in college athletics because colleges wanted skilled African American athletes to help them win games (Davis, 1995), and the recruitment of African Americans marked a turning point in race relations in the South.

In the middle of the 20th century on HBCU campuses, athletics and social opportunities for African American athletes thrived. The championships among African American colleges won by several football teams attested to their excellence as coaches built successful programs that allowed African American athletes to display their talents. For example, Jake Gaither won six titles at Florida A&M University between 1945 and 1969, John Merritt at Jackson State University and Tennessee State University won seven titles between 1953 and 1983, and Eddie Robinson at Grambling State University won nine titles between 1941 and 1997. Clarence Gaines's teams at Winston Salem State University won 828 basketball games between 1946 and 1993. Leroy Walker in men's track and field and Ed Temple in women's track and field coached several collegiate and Olympic champions.

By the mid-1950s, most northern colleges had at least token integration, which allowed most institutions outside the South to back away from their "gentleman's agreement" to withhold African Americans. While Jim Crow practices were glaring and flagrant in the South, elsewhere coaches and institutions failed the test for justice and fairness by opening the sport, almost with any qualifications, to anyone who demonstrated physical prowess (Spivey, 1988).

The decade of the 1960s in the United States was a time of turmoil in the fight for civil rights. Between 1948 and 1964, increasing recognition of the outstanding performances of African Americans reflected a dramatic transition in the Olympians who transformed men's basketball. While a single African American first helped the 1948 team win the gold, by 1964, Walt Hazzard (UCLA) was joined by African Americans Jim Barnes (Texas El Paso), Joe Caldwell (Arizona State), Lucius Jackson (Texas-Pan American), and George Wilson (Cincinnati) on the gold medal winning team. Fifteen African American track and field athletes won Olympic gold between 1948 and 1964, and that year Rafer Johnson, the gold medal decathlete from UCLA, became the first African American to carry the United States flag into the stadium at the Opening Ceremonies in Rome.

And, as Lumpkin claims, the walls came tumbling down. Racial conflict and turmoil came to a boil on many campuses. In the midst of the resistance associated with overt and subtle discrimination in accommodations, restaurants, transportation, education, and job opportunities, Harry Edwards initiated the Olympic Project for Human Rights and tried to foment a boycott of the 1968 Olympic Games. He encouraged African American male athletes to boycott in protest of the residual prejudice and discriminatory treatment they experienced on predominantly white campuses where they competed. In the midst of this thrust, Lumpkin reflects that maybe because female athletes were provided with hardly any competitive opportunities in colleges at the time, Edwards fully ignored female athletes in his organizing efforts.

Racial turmoil persisted on many predominantly White campuses during the 1960s and 1970s. Davis (1995) stated that racism exists whenever Whites believe and act as if they are superior to people of color. He emphasized that some White Americans, including members of the electronic and print media, have stereotypically and prejudicially attributed the successes of African American athletes to innate physical skills, rather than to intellect and hard work. The latter two attributes have been most often reserved for White athletes. Illustrations of the disparate treatment experienced by African Americans attending predominantly White institutions (what Hodge and his associates refer to as PW-IHEs, or predominantly White institutions of higher education) have included poor academic support; academic marginalization; harsh discipline; positional stacking based on speed, quickness, and jumping ability; quotas; and social segregation. Observers have stressed that African American athletes seldom sat on the bench, because they either played or were not on the team.

Even after many teams were integrated, African American athletes were subjected to stacking and quotas. *Stacking* was the practice of assigned athletes, typically African Americans, to certain positions and forcing them to compete against each other for a limited number, or quota, of starting or playing positions. Furthermore, African Americans were seldom allowed to play so-called "thinking positions" because White-normativity rendered them incapable of performing well in these cerebral and leadership positions. Although there was considerable record of success already logged at the HBCU associations/conferences, a blatant example of discriminatory treatment was that African Americans were almost never hired as head coaches; for many years, they also were not hired as assistant coaches in football, basketball, or track and field.

Lumpkin reiterates Davis' (1995) concern as to whether African American athletes were objectified as commodities to serve the financial interests of primarily White institutions without a reciprocal commitment to their educational advancement. That is, often institutions and athletics departments did not put the same resources into helping these athletes benefit from their educational opportunities. Likewise, African American athletes lacked a support structure to help them to deal with the challenges of an often hostile or racist social climate on and off campus.

In the wake of the resistance offered on campuses, a glimmer of hope that discriminatory treatment might be addressed and eliminated occurred in one conference. In 1972, the Big Ten Conference appointed an advisory committee to investigate the complaints of African American athletes and associated racial disturbances on several campuses. Several recommendations were implemented. By 1974 the first African American assistant commissioner was hired to systematically address the treatment African American athletes had endured. These proposals were applied to all athletes. Among the proposals, counseling programs were set up at all member institutions to help athletes make progress toward their degrees. All athletes were given a fifth year of financial aid, if needed, to complete their degrees. Educational seminars were conducted to improve communication between White coaches and African American athletes. Lists were developed of qualified African American candidates for coaching, athletic training, officiating, and administrative positions. These actions foreshadowed increased sensitivity toward African American athletes as administrators and coaches began to address the disparate treatment that pioneer African American athletes had endured on the campuses of predominantly white institutions.

Lumpkin and Hodges et al. report that an increased number of highly skilled African Americans athletes chose to attend predominantly White institutions beginning in the 1980s. Their decisions were influenced by seeking exposure through the media, positioning themselves for potential professional careers and taking advantage of better facilities. This migration adversely affected sport teams at HBCUs because many of the schools were unable to sustain high levels of performances in football, basketball, and track and field.

While football, basketball, and track and field teams are fully integrated with a higher-than-representative percentage of African Americans today, this is not the case in other sports, as African Americans today are infrequently members of college teams in sports such as tennis, golf, or wrestling. Whether this is a result of socioeconomic factors, fewer opportunities, or lack of role models, college sports are less fully integrated than many have claimed. Subtle discrimination persists whenever people act based on beliefs that certain sports are for African Americans, while other sports are not.

In recent decades African American athletes have expressed less concern about discrimination in housing, social isolation, or racist treatment by teammates, opponents, and coaches. While overt bigotry was almost eliminated by the beginning of the 21st century, covert discrimination has continued to plague sports and society. A persistent issue has been academic exploitation. This problem occurred whenever African American athletes were encouraged to focus primarily on developing their athletic skills and playing their sports to the detriment of their academic work.

The NCAA and Rules for Eligibility. The NCAA has been criticized for what many have classified as lax academic standards for athletes, which allowed them to do the minimum to maintain eligibility, rather than being serious students seeking to learn and earn degrees. In response, with an implementation date in 1986, the NCAA passed a regulation that based the eligibility of a prospective athlete for receiving an athletic scholarship on having achieved a high school grade point average of at least 2.0 in a college-preparatory core curriculum and attained a minimum score on a standardized admissions test. Some African Americans believed that this rule, which came to be known as Proposition 48, discriminated against minorities because standardized tests were culturally biased. Possibly to diffuse this outcry, the NCAA changed this rule in 1983 (i.e., prior to this rule becoming effective in 1986) to allow an athlete to receive an athletic scholarship while attending an institution, but he or she was not permitted to play or practice during the first year. This partial qualifier, assuming the required grades in the first year of college courses were earned, had three years of varsity eligibility remaining.

Effective in August of 1990, Proposition 42 eliminated the partial qualifier loophole. That is, incoming freshmen had to meet all the requirements of Proposition 48. If a prospective athlete failed to meet this standard, he or she was not eligible for an athletic scholarship at an NCAA institution. Another firestorm erupted as African American coaches like John Thompson of Georgetown University and John Chaney of Temple University claimed that this rule discriminated against African Americans who had attended inadequately funded urban schools or had been disadvantaged educationally. In 2003, the NCAA, in an attempt to eliminate the perceived prejudice, implemented a sliding scale that allowed a higher grade point average to offset a lower score on a standardized test, or vice versa.

The NCAA also has been criticized for its failure to enact rules to emphasize academics over athletics, because it was perceived that some athletes were being exploited to help win games and earn revenues for institutions. These accusations were especially directed at football and basketball, two sports with a high African American presence. The NCAA enacted several requirements associated with athletes making progress toward earning their degrees. For example, after the first year in college, athletes had to have completed 24 hours and achieved at least 90% of the grade point average required for graduation. These credit hours and minimum grades increased incrementally each successive year.

Because many athletes, and a disproportionally higher number of African Americans, had failed to graduate, in 2004 the NCAA initiated the academic progress rate (APR) at the highest competitive level. This new rule has resulted in institutions facing sanctions if athletes failed academically. The APR and other data (such as the graduation success rate [GSR]) have revealed a wide gap between the graduation rates of African American and Caucasian athletes who play football and basketball (Lapchick, 2008, 2011, 2012). Despite numerous academic reforms, some African American athletes continue to feel that they are being exploited. This occurs when their eligibility to compete in their sports has been exhausted, their dreams of playing professionally have been dashed, and they remain dozens of credit hours away from earning a degree.

HBCUs and Sports in the 1980s. Historically, HBCUs contributed an array of elite, talented African American student-athletes (men and women), and many went on to distinguish themselves in various professional endeavors, including sports. Many more remained obscure and unrecognized, an oversight similar to the failure of America to recognize contributions made to building America. One of points of the chapter written by Hodges et al. (Chapter 3) was to describe in some detail the sporting experience of African American student-athletes and, especially, their experiences on HBCU campuses as compared to their White counterparts. Guided by results from a landmark, comprehensive study conducted in 1989 (AIR), the experiences of Black and White student-athletes were compared across various NCAA division levels and the HBCUs, revealing notable differences between the various groups in their ACT/SAT scores, high school GPA, lack of control of their lives, and experiences of racial isolation. Comparing these results with more recent current information, Hodges and his colleagues, not at all surprisingly, found that more African American student-athletes continue to have negative social and educational experiences as compared to their White counterparts. As they see it, race-based stereotypes, perception about fairness, consequences of racial policies and race neutrality, and racial identity are still forceful factors affecting America's conversations about inequality, power, and privilege that affect discourses about diversity and directly impact playing and coaching experiences of African American student-athletes (men and women).

The issues denoted by Hodges and his colleagues are equally of concern to Jackson, whose work on Title IX's impact upon women's participation is focused on HBCU campus (Chapter 8). From a historic perspective, HBCUs are facing very important challenges that will have an impact on the future experiences of young African American men and women who attend these institutions. As talented African American male student-athletes made their great migration to predominantly White college playing fields during the 1980s, the surfeit of talented athletes on HBCU campuses migrated away a few years after women's entitlement was enacted (1972). About 61% of undergraduates are women, 39% are men (Jackson, 2006). This makes compliance under Title IX very difficult. HBCUs must continue to offer a socially and culturally rich environment, thus providing a climate for athletic and academic success, and they need to be attractive for a significant amount of non-black students to enroll. If HBCUs plan and hope to remain a portal by which African American high school boys and girls gain access to higher education, HBCUs must provide an arena by which student-athletes are afforded the opportunity to play sports at the college level, recognizing that not all participants will pursue a professional sports career.

Particularly noteworthy is Hodge et al.'s "Historically Black Colleges and Universities' Athletes and Sport Programs" (Chapter 2), which traces the historical development of HBCUs and their athletic programs in America. As already noted, the Second Morrill Act (1890) was the primary genesis of the growth of HBCUs in America. They assembled a good deal of information about the number of athletic teams (HBCUs) by gender and athletic affiliations. Typically, football teams consisted of almost 47% of all male student-athletes on HBCUs campuses. The highest percentage of female student-athletes participated in track and field (indoor/outdoor, almost 29%) and basketball was almost 24%.

Since the majority of the HBCUs are still located in America's southern states, historical conditions anchored in segregation and racism were imposed on the growth of sport programs between and within HBCU competition. It was surprising to realize that it took the NCAA 10 years after the Brown vs. Board of Education decision to accept HBCU member institutions. One of the unilateral consequences of the Brown decision was an exodus of Black athletes to predominantly White institutions. During all the years since the creation of Civil Rights legislation in the mid-1960s it is noteworthy to realize that although African American men make up half the athletes playing football and basketball on a typical NCAA Division I campus, they make up less than 10% of the entire student body on these same campuses.

A number of factors coincided to contribute to the drain of athletes (i.e., access to scholarships, access to better facilities, name visibility for the student-athletes). Data supports that HBCUs and all NCAA level institutions need to work harder to increase student-athlete graduation rates. With regard to these rates, Why do so many students fail to complete their educational journey? The quality of African American student-athletes' lives after their playing days are over is likely to be related to their college education. Coming from very different backgrounds than their fellow student-athletes and their fellow African American college students, African-American student-athletes may have unique post-athletic career experiences.

Chapter 2 concludes with a discussion of traditionally White campuses (i.e., NAIA) where HBCUs compete, providing an overview of the historical development of the various HBCU athletic conferences, while examining various consequences of association with NCAA member institutions, as well as social and political factors impacting conference status. America's financial crisis does have an effect on the athletic programs located on HBCU campuses. In an attempt to guarantee new sources of revenue, HBCUs are scheduling athletic events with more predominantly White institutions and increasing marketing and promotion.

Limited Opportunities for Leadership

While access to intercollegiate sport has expanded greatly in the past quarter century, opportunities for the upper levels of the sport hierarchy have continued to be much more restricted. These higher levels are far more shielded from scrutiny, so that those who control access to the center of authority and control are apt to use more subtle strategies of maintaining discriminatory practices. Thus, the oppressed group typically has a much more difficult time entering into higher paying and more prestigious positions. Efforts to eliminate discrimination through legislative and judicial system processes tend to produce relatively immediate results, but such results are most noticeable at the lower levels of organized formations.

In the case of intercollegiate athletics, coaching and management jobs are under control of those who presently have powers for determining who gets selected into these leadership positions. Chapter 4, written by Tucker, Hall, and Johnson, examines NCAA member institutions' hiring and retention practices impacting African American men and women. Building on the work of Mintzberg (1973), they focus on three roles of effective sports administrators: informational (spokesperson), interpersonal (leader), and decision-maker (resource allocator). Without question, Black coaches withstood countless challenges during segregation, including the inability to coach at majority institutions. Historically, there have been notable African American coaches who have been showcased for their strength and tenacity, principally at traditional HBCUs. What is striking about the men and women who were leaders and coached sports at the HBCUs is the unique challenges they dealt with recruiting and mentoring their student-athletes.

Abney (Chapter 9) chronicles a similar concern with regard to leadership positions among African American women. Managing inclusion depends on an environment that is respectful and welcoming of diverse experiences. She explains the impact of the *glass ceiling effect* on the ability of African American females to gain access to head coaching and other administrative positions, particularly within NCAA divisions, but also to their slow progress among NAIA and HBCU organization. With the passage of federal legislation (e.g., Title IX, Civil Rights Act of 1991), an increase in the number of women holding leadership positions within college athletics could have been anticipated. Unfortunately, "efforts to assess the effects of the glass ceiling on coaches and athletic administrators can be difficult because hiring and promotion decisions can be subjective, and universities use different criteria in making decisions to hire and promote." Beyond the glass ceiling impact, considerations similar to those encountered among African American men bear on the lack of African American women from holding leadership positions—salary, lack of support, discrimination, lower performance expectations, lack of network ties, and lack of role models. Based on recent information (Acosta & Carpenter, 2010), more women hold positions within administrative ranks at all levels than any time since the mid-1970s. However, the percentage represented by African American women is unclear. Building the ranks of African American women in athletic department decision-making positions will require a change in the organizational mindset.

College sports in the 21st century continue to be governed and coached primarily by White males. Historically and prejudicially, African Americans were perceived as incapable of effectively leading athletics departments and coaching football, basketball, and track and field teams. The advocacy work of the Black Coaches & Administrators (BCA, formerly the Black Coaches Association) and Richard Lapchick's Diversity and Ethics in Sports institute show an appalling lack of people of color and women at the NCAA Division I level, from the director through university presidents, athletic directors, and coaches. Tucker and his colleagues insisted coaching mobility largely depends on networking. But with only about 16% of head coaches in NCAA football who are minority, and the numbers not looking much better for minority coaches in all sports, networking is, at best, a weak option. Tucker and colleagues suggest colleges may want to implement the Rooney Rule, thus requiring colleges to interview at least one minority candidate when filling a head coaching position. This is particularly noteworthy given the more recent practice of some NCAA institutions to adopt the *coach-in-waiting* concept, thus by-passing the search and screen process for new hires.

Recruitment, Retention, and NCAA Rules and Regulations

At the middle of the 20th century, in the wake of the World War II and with the 1954 Supreme Court decision forbidding separate educational facilities, the increasing commercialization of college sports and the demands for winning teams to generate more and more revenue have produced what is called big-time college athletics. Talented African American athletes found it advantageous to play at predominately White colleges because of their greater visibility. Such visibility meant a better opportunity to sign a contract and the catch-on with a professional team at the conclusion of their intercollegiate athletic eligibility. One effect, noted earlier, was depleted athletic programs at HBCUs, forcing them to modify or cancel their programs.

For many who view the mission of higher education as the promotion of scholarship and academic training for careers, such commercialization of big-time, big-media sports (big revenue football and basketball programs) is inherently incompatible with academic achievement. There is little doubt among some observers that the sports-media nexus has pumped out a flow of images promoting Black superstars, and as often as not, it has reinforced pernicious racial stereotypes of Black male athletes and distorted gender stereotypes. Martin, Gragg, and Kramer tackle the historical debate about the relationship between NCAA academic regulations and their effect on participation rates for minority athletes on college campuses in Chapter 5. They present their analysis of the issues and problems within the current situation.

The road to academic reform dates back to the 1944 Sanity Code (elimination of athletic scholarships). The 1.6 Rule (1965) was a further attempt to predict academic success based on a predicted grade point average. In 1982, Proposition 48 was established to have uniform standardization of entrance standards, emphasizing grade point average (GPAs and SAT scores) to project future postsecondary academic success. Opposition against Proposition 48 was made on the grounds that its purpose was to reduce the number of African American college student-athletes. While that may not have been the intent of Proposition 48, numerous African American male athletes were declared ineligible to participate. The rule also had a very negative effect on African Americans who attended HBCUs. By the mid-1990s Proposition 16 was offered to address the voiced concerns. Proposition 16 provided a study scale whereby a student-athlete could offset a low SAT/ACT score with a higher GPA. Unfortunately, both Proposition 48 and 16 continued to have a negative effect on participation rates of African American student-athletes. The courts were not immune to the debate, eventually changing Proposition 16, so that more weight was given to high school GPAs.

Martin et al. reminded the readers of the academic and physical prowess of early African American student-athletes. Today, the African American male college athlete is inundated with images of a highly commercial, profitable college scholarships and professional sports contracts. The entrance to college became a means to professional sports, rather than access to a quality education. According to the authors, the debate between stronger academic requirements, initial high school core course requirements, and continuing eligibility rules for student-athletes remains contested grounds. The implementation of the 40/60/80 rule, graduation success rate (GSR), and the academics ptogress rate (APR) are manifestations of this debate. It appears the ultimate goal of NCAA legislation is to ensure student-athletes, especially minority students, have higher graduation rates.

Parallel to Chapter 5, Corbett's Chapter 6 on academic integrity resonates with those who are deeply concerned with understanding the current academic state of affairs for African American students who are athletes in higher education. Over the past two decades, literature has shown that African American athletes are not taken seriously as students on many of the predominately White college campuses. In fact, their value as a student is of little academic importance. Stereotypes of African American student-athletes as dumb jocks, who are overprivileged, coddled, indolent and out of control, and whose primary incentive to attend college is to participate in sports is often flashed across the media. Corbett claims that the assignment of such a role to African American student-athletes "results in the failure of many colleges and universities to improve support services and take measures necessary to reduce the social isolation of Black athletes" and, as a result, negatively affects their academic performance.

Corbett writes, "I would argue that any serious discourse about the academic plight of the African American in sport is about integrity, dignity, human rights, justice, and honor in the academy." The level of dishonesty and duplicity in collegiate athletics is pervasive. Exploitation in sport is a multifaceted intercollegiate experience, and has fiscal, educational, racial, social, and moral overtones. Reports are rampant about transcript irregularities, the admission of students who are academically underprepared because of lenient admission standards, grade fabrication and forgery, and plummeting graduation rates. African American students who are athletes have been taken advantage of and are especially susceptible to academic abuses.

Although many have supported the NCAA's efforts to address the issue of graduation rates, the BCA has been critical of the NCAA's approach to raise admission standards. BCA members argued that Proposition 16 and Proposition 48 revealed an overall lack of understanding of the African American community, since scholarship reductions eliminate opportunities for Black student-athletes to receive an education and to advance their careers. The BCA's strongest criticism addresses the NCAA's eligibility requirements that allegedly adversely impact African American student-athletes. For BCA and many other observers like Corbett herself, the opposition to Proposition 48 centered on their allegation that it is blatantly racist.

The most recent NCAA reform initiative is the Academic Performance Rating, which dictates that schools must achieve a combined score across several indicators in order to avoid penalties. A 2010 report underscores that many challenges continue to plague institutions whose resources are strained. The NCAA's academic progree rating measures the eligibility, retention rates, and graduation rates for each of the 6,400 plus teams that is a part of Division I (Sander, 2010). The report shows that the financially constrained institutions rank in the bottom 10% of Division I universities in terms of spending per student and tend to have greater difficulty in advancing the academic performance of their students. Elsewhere, current data establishes that the graduation gap between NCAA Black and White student-athletes has increased. Corbett argues that a recent study conducted by the University of Central Florida's Institute for Diversity and Ethics in Sport shows a staggering gap between the graduation rates of African American and White student-athletes.

Corbett believes recent and past occurrences of low graduation rates, academic scandals, and the frequency with which African American athletes leave higher education institutions in mediocre, if not poor academic standing have annihilated the public's faith regarding the educational benefits of sports participation at the collegiate level. Faculty-driven reform has been spearheaded by advocacy bodies such as the Drake Group and the Coalition on Intercollegiate Athletics (COIA). The Drake Group works to support faculty whose job security is threatened for defending academic standards and disseminates information on current issues and controversies in sports. Finding the appropriate balance between intercollegiate athletics and the academic goals of higher education is not an easy task, but it is one that must be achieved so that African American students can experience gains in student learning and academic performance.

Bearing on academic regulation as well as eligibility and participation of student-athletes, often low-income minority women and men, intercollegiate sport programs at two-year colleges seldom attain any media attention and are expected to function with low operating costs. Coaching is not particularly lucrative, often below the average community college faculty salary. Furthermore, reports on minorities—men and women— show that those who earned major posts or coaching positions in community/junior college sport are seriously under-represented. Chapter 7 reflects how intercollegiate "juco" sports were shaped as they adapted to "big-time" collegiate athletics in the context of NCAA policies and its rules.

Junior and community colleges have a long and distinguished history of providing quality and affordable higher education opportunities for Americans, especially for ethnic minorities to gain access to higher education. On a national scale, as "open-door policy" educational institutions, where many entering students may require academic remediation, the community and two-year colleges were established to meet the needs of the local communities and to enhance the technical skills of a diverse work force. At no time has this function been more critical than at the present (Doyle, 2006). In the fall of 2012, community colleges provided access to higher education to about 44 percent of the undergraduate students in America ("Fast facts," 2012).

The number of two-year colleges (public and private) grew from 74 (1915–1916) to 1,195 in 2008, and back to 1132 in 2012 (986 public; 115 independent; 31 tribal), enrolling more eight million students. Demographic data for 2012 shows 39% of students enrolled in community colleges are ages 21 years or younger, some 45% are between 22 and 39 years, and 15% are 40 or more years old. About 44% of all first-time freshmen begin their post-secondary careers at community colleges. Since 2010 nearly 46% of students received some form of financial aid, while less than a fifth (16%) of their revenues is from tuition and fees ("Fast facts," 2012).

Chapter 7, authored by the book's editors, examines the transition from junior/community colleges to four-year institutions. The chapter begins with a discussion about the playing and coaching experiences of ethnic minorities, especially African Americans who attended these institutions. These colleges often provided ethnic minorities the opportunity to play sports and, in some cases, to transfer to four-year institutions to complete their education and improve playing skills. Since 1939, the number of two-year institutions associated with the National Junior College Athletic Association (NJCAA) continued to expand. Some observers, however, have suggested the nation's junior/community colleges act as a feeder to Division I colleges, raising questions about academic accountability and thus, the qualification and transfer of student-athletes into four-year colleges. Those who don't favor sports programs are apt to see junior college sports as a farm system, yielding quick fixes for coaches afflicted with winning at all costs.

Historically, promotion of athletic programs in two-year institutions, much like the evaluation of athletics at four-year campuses, is caught up in issues on the alignment of athletics within the educational mission of the institutions. Castaneda (2004) articulated the internal and external benefits to the student-athletes and the college as a result of intercollegiate athletics at the community college level. Over time and given the influx of freshmen and first-year student-athletes at the community college level, a public outcry was voiced regarding the academic qualifications of these individuals to attend college. In addition, the lay public and sport scholars voiced a concern about the apparent low graduation rates of these students. Anderson and South (2000) stated the junior/community colleges were not governed by Proposition 48 adopted by the NCAA (1986–1987). Given this fact, and an open-door policy at the community college level, we wrote in Chapter 7 that, "No matter which path one chooses to trace the experiences of students in post-secondary of junior colleges, the issues of the student-athletes subsequently transferring from or to other four-year colleges and institutions have been a continuing concern for study about national standards and practices."

Apace with controversial reforms spawned within the NCAA to "level the playing field," community colleges will remain valuable resources to help meet local community workforce demands and will remain significant educational institutions for ethnic minorities to gain access to higher education. Community college coaches and administrators must continue to be cognizant of how NCAA academic standards legislation affects community colleges and be willing to seek internal and external financial support to enhance the mission of the institution, including seeking financial aid for student-athletes, and provide all student-athletes the opportunity to complete their associate's degrees and certification, if appropriate. There are numerous external forces (e.g., Title IX legislation, NCAA legislation) and internal factors (e.g., budget for athletic teams, facilities and equipment, geographical localities of the institution, and mission) that will continue affecting the future community college athletic programs in America.

Gender and Race Intersections
(African American Women and Intercollegiate Sport)

Forty years after the passing of the Educational Amendment Act of 1972, also known as Title IX, gender equity continues as a serious issue for the NCAA. While Title IX has supported opportunities for women in college-sponsored sports, considerable misinformation and significant myths limit improvement. A recent study indicated that only about 40% of program administrators surveyed knew what steps needed to be taken to enforce Title IX (Osbourne, 2010). And women of color have not benefitted as much from Title

IX as White women from the growth of new sport opportunities, although they have shared benefits of improvements in esteem and treatment. The chapters by Jackson and Abney examine the historic impact of Title IX on women's athletics. Jackson (Chapter 8) focuses on an institutional level, within HBCUs, while Abney (Chapter 9) brings forward for consideration the bearing that affirmative action guidelines have had on increasing the number of women, specifically African American women, in athletic administrative and coaching position in intercollegiate sports.

Jackson shows the origin of Title IX legislation, its enforcement cases, and its measure of compliance (proportionality, continuing history and expansion, and interests and abilities) when trying to meet with Title IX requirements on women's athletics. The majority of colleges and universities comply with Title IX by using prong one (i.e., proportionality), which essentially amounts to spending the same *percentage* on their athletic programs as the undergraduate population of the institution, which depends on the ratio of women to men. HBCUs are put at a disadvantage when trying to comply with Title IX because the average undergraduate population for females is 69% as compared to 31% males (Jackson, 2006). Jackson wrote, "The problems facing HBCUs, as compared to other colleges and universities, is that enrollment for males at HBCUs is decreasing and enrollment for females is increasing." As a result of this trend, "In order to meet Title IX compliance, 39% of HBCUs' athletic budgets should go to male athletes and 61% for female athletes." It is impossible for HBCUs to spend almost 70% of their athletic budget on female athletics. Another pressing issue that HBCUs face is that the enrollment for men in higher education overall has decreased and currently there is almost a 2-1 female-to-male ratio.

College administrators are faced with what can be done to increase the number of African American males to attend HBCUs. If this trend is not reversed, Jackson estimates that it will be very difficult for HBCUs to meet Title IX requirements. She reports that many HBCUs are unable to document efforts to expand athletic programs and moreover, may be unable to add programs due to budget constraints and other factors. "Until the recent trends are reversed and more African American males are entering colleges and universities, Title IX compliance will remain an issue for HBCUs," she wrote. On a positive note, "HBCUs can prove compliance with Title IX if they can fully and effectively accommodate the interest and abilities of the underrepresented gender." The key to determining the interests and abilities of individuals is to develop an appropriate instrument and methodology.

Abney (Chapter 9, "The Glass Ceiling Effect for African American Women Coaches and Athletic Administrators") turns our attention to the sociocultural and structural barriers that deny access and opportunities to African American women who aspire to positions as head coaches, college athletic administrators, and administrators in collegiate governing administrations. Managing inclusion depends on an environment that is respectful and welcoming of diverse experiences. She explains explores the impact of the glass-ceiling effect on the ability of African American females to gain access to head coaching and other administrative positions, particularly within NCAA divisions, but also reflects about their slow progress among NAIA and HBCU organization. Building the ranks of African American women in athletic department decision-making positions will require a change in the organizational mind-set.

Abney lays out strategies for change that could be used by various groups in formulating policies and procedures for redressing the inequalities that exists for African American women in sport. Abney's recommendation to increase the potential NCAA pool of applications included strategies to change the employment process and workplace culture (i.e., establish formal mentoring programs, establish support groups, expand recruitment networks, provide staff support, and help establish a career development plan for each employee). Abney believes that positive and proactive measures must be taken by college administrators to ensure African American women are afforded the opportunity to apply for vacant positions. To sustain inclusion, institutions and athletic departments must make the transition to a more multicultural environment—starting at the top and generating a sense of urgency and importance.

Abney trumpets her conclusion, which is that a commitment must be forthcoming from the NCAA to establish a rule (mirroring the Rooney Rule) to ensure that institutions interview at least one African American minority candidate for coaching and athletic administrative positions. Such a ruling would not only constitute an acknowledgement that a problem or glass ceiling exists, but that strategies are being implemented to provide opportunities for minorities to reach and shatter the ceiling.

The African American Student-Athlete and Popular Culture

Sport programs are often targeted specifically toward at-risk minority communities and populations. Here, it is probably not too much of a stretch to argue that intervention programs are aimed at equipping young athletes with the tools for self-improvement and self-management. This brand of development is about the discipline, socialization, and social direction of otherwise problematic groups on the grounds that self-authentication projects generate much needed social capital for disaffected groups. Through bridging and bonding, sport creates access to resources, information, social networks, and opportunity from which marginalized individuals are estranged. In creating these networks, sport-based interventions may be able to engender the "right" environment for individuals to lift themselves out of challenging and marginalized circumstances.

Harrison and Sutton's "Cracking Their World: Utilizing Pop Culture to Impact Academic Success of Today's Student-Athlete" (Chapter 10) offers a refreshing look at the intersection of pop culture, athletic participation, and academic success. Two questions focus attention: Is it possible to create more balance and engagement between the player and his/her academic performance as a student in American higher education? If so, can academic institutions and individual stakeholders find ways to utilize pop culture to improve academic performance?

The authors skillfully articulate the concepts of self-affirmation, and the cultural concepts of cool and cool pose to help us understand and appreciate the African American male culture and media images. In hip hop culture authenticity is everything and weakness is an egregious character flaw. Scholar-Baller claims to be a transformer. It is important to convince African American male student-athletes that staying in school is cool. The authors believe there is the perception that staying in school and studying is "uncool." The authors speak to a need to "crack this world" or break this perceived perception by some African American males.

In an attempt to alter behaviors and perceptions, Harrison and Sutton hail the success of the Scholar-Baller Program as an innovative and culturally relevant approach to academic performance and intellectual recognition through pop culture. The Scholar-Baller Program was implemented on several colleges and community colleges in America. The authors reported a positive effect (i.e., increased GPAs) of this initiative with its primary mission to "increase academic performance and cultural motivation of today's student-athletes with a particular focus of African American male student-athletes." In closing, the authors introduce the concept of *educationalism* to the reader. Harrison and Sutton provided a list of 10 items that are perceived as "cool" and are tied to academic success (e.g., sneakers associated with cool people, being respected for who you are as an individual is cool).

Sport is a powerful social force, but not necessarily a positive one. "By itself," as Coakley has summarized, "the act of playing a sport leads to no regularly identifiable pattern of development or developmental outcomes. Instead, outcomes are related to and dependent on combinations of factors" (Coakley, 1990, p. 14) When it comes to increased performance and cultural motivation of student-athletes, the power of intercollegiate sport is better understood as a kind of "empty form," that is, like any other technology or social practice whose meaning, use, and impact is dependent on the ways in which it is employed and to what ends it is used. The extent to which positive outcomes are achieved in and through intercollegiate sport, like any other level of sport practice, is contingent on various factors: the ends to which the collegiate sport experience is organized and directed, the programming and interventions that are conducted in concert with such practices, and the resources that are devoted to any such initiatives.

Given the visibility of athletic scholarship compared to academic scholarships, gifted athletes have a higher expectation of receiving athletic scholarships. The not-so-gifted know that their chance of receiving an athletic scholarship are smaller, but many know their chances of obtaining one is greater than receiving an academic scholarship. The result is a substantial investment by young African Americans, principally males, in athletic prowess, an investment encouraged by coaches, counselors, and the rest of the athletic complex. There are other features that impact the recruitment and performance of athletes. The incentive for using performance-enhancing substances continues to grow among athletes at all levels of sports, including high school youth and young collegiate adults. If colleges seek to upgrade athletic talent and award scholarships to better athletes, these young athletes have an incentive to resort to such substances.

"Coaching Hip Hop Athletes, Confronting Double Doses of Hyper Masculinity" (Chapter 11) by Smith represents a new departure dealing with the relationship between the hip hop culture and college athletics. Smith suggested that some of America's most talented and highly visible professional athletes are products of hip hop culture (e.g., Allen Iverson, Shaquille O'Neal, and Kobe Bryant). It appears that some athletic departments and businesses are beginning to embrace hip hop for its cultural and economic benefits. Smith argues that it would be wise for college coaches to better understand and appreciate hip hop culture by attending conferences or workshops.

One of the many strengths of this chapter is the discussion of the relationship between sports and hip hop culture and understanding the functional nature of each to society. In hip hop culture authenticity is everything. In the "streets" weakness is victimized; strength is a means of achieving status. In the corporate culture of big-time sports, propped up by media-driven profits, raw hip hop values are mediated. The author's depiction of the relationship between hip hop and hypermasculinity in sports, economics, and power helps the reader to understand why Smith wrote, "Hip hop and sports as distinct social systems are more symmetrical with each other than either of them are with mainstream culture." Part of the symmetry between hip hop and sports includes the way each system develops language, generates esteem, and orders social relationships. Any discussion of hip hop culture and sports would not be complete without the consideration of women in hip hop. According to the author, hip hop transcends gender and begins to build a foundation in which African American women are valued for their "strength."

If faculty are dissatisfied with the academic performance of athletes in revenue-producing sports, then perhaps, weak academic performance results in part from programs that provide little opportunity for many more students. In closing, Smith encourages high school and college coaches to embrace hip hop culture: "Specifically, coaches dealing with hip hop athletes are likely to be more successful, not by feigning understanding and adoption of hip hop music and culture, and certainly not by treating hip hop as a lesser culture, but by respecting its normative order."

Race, Gender, and Fan Support

Althouse, Brooks, Dean-Crowley, and Dotson open Chapter 12 with a brief review of the development of intercollegiate athletics from its humble beginning as activities organized by the student body into a contemporary multimillion dollar commercial enterprise caught up in an "arms race" that is spurred on as colleges and universities attempt to broaden their successes in sports, especially urged on by big-time sports media interests. As such, NCAA institutions and their administrative leaders are constantly seeking funds (e.g., television and bowl receipts, sponsorships, and alumni support) to offset the cost of coaches' salaries, scholarships, travel, meals, equipment purchases, medical costs, lodging, and so on. Commercialization of intercollegiate athletics sees collegiate leagues and teams compete for lucrative media contracts and postseason bowl invitations and manage, much like their professional counterparts, to generate very lucrative returns. While some observers lament such commercialization of big-time revenue football and basketball programs, the sports-media linkage has pumped out a flow of images promoting black superstars, but as often as not, it has reinforced racial stereotypes of Black male athletes and distorted gender stereotypes.

On the issue of sustainability of big-revenue sports, The Knight Commission recently discussed results of a survey of more than 2,000 faculty members about their perceptions of the role of faculty engagement in intercollegiate athletics. There was some considerable dissatisfaction on a number of issues, including their role in the governance of intercollegiate athletics and athletes' academic performance, particularly football and basketball student-athletes, who incur a good deal more of out-of-class demands than other students. If faculty are dissatisfied with the academic performance of athletes in revenue-producing sports, then perhaps, weak academic performance results in part from programs that provide little opportunity for many more students. Current data suggests the cost to conduct big-time athletic programs continues to increase.

From the fans' viewpoint, the most avid of which are alumni, the authors made the argument that many athletic alumni may feel that they have already made significant contributions to their alma mater by playing a sport. That is, an alumnus or alumna may justify his or her feelings in believing that one has already paid one's dues for the benefits that the institutions receive from gate receipts and other pay outs. Some such rationale seemed guided by an *exchange model*, thus, helping each other when there is a positive cost-benefit more commonly benefits from helping outweigh the cost of helping others.

The perceptions about making meager contributions may also be justified when as former athletes, they were isolated from the general student body and class demands because of their rigorous practice and game travel schedules. Postseason appearances in football and men's basketball were identified as being positively correlated with an increase of donations. Bowl game appearances resulted in alumni making higher donations. However, the relative independence of athletic associations and other athletic fundraising groups on college campuses, separated as they often are from institutional advancement offices, provides some insight into this mistaken notion that there is a positive link between the athletic department and the institution when it comes to matters of fundraising. Many big-time athletic programs are run as independent, profit-driven, auxiliary enterprises. The separation and mistrust that exists between academic and athletic communities means that virtually all athletic department fundraising efforts are directed at raising money specifically for sports, rather than for the institution generally.

If we come to terms with the fact that athletic programs clearly fundraise for their own needs, while winking at the overall fundraising goals of colleges and universities, we can begin to understand why the notion of a *spillover benefit* from athletics has been questioned repeatedly. Without full disclosure of the entire institutional fundraising record with a complete breakdown of athletic and general fund donations, the assumed spillover benefit may in fact mask the undermining effect that occurs when athletic fundraising creates a clear competing interest with academic and other educational priorities where limited financial resources exist.

When considering race and gender and the potential of alumni donations, there is limited information. There is some antidotal evidence that indicates former athlete alumni do sometimes give back to their alma mater. For example, Steve Smith donated $2.5 million dollars to Michigan State to be used for the construction of a student-athlete academic center. Carmelo Anthony donated $3.5 million dollars to Syracuse for the construction of a new basketball practice facility. In conclusion, Althouse et al. made it evident that more information is needed to accurately show how ethnic minority athletic alumni make financial donations to their respective alma maters.

In Chapter 13 ("Title IX & Black Female Student-Athletes: Increasing Sports Participation through Shared Advocacy") Gill, Jr. and Sloan-Green provide an excellent discussion of three objectives: (1) the status of African American female collegiate athletics, (2) the impact of demography on African American female athletes, and (3) a critique of the concept of social justice advocacy for Black women in sport.

While Title IX (passed in 1972) has had a positive effect on increasing the number of women participating in high school and college athletics, Gill, Jr., and Sloan-Green insist that "concern remains over the scarcity of Black females in collegiate athletics." Of particular concern to them is a diminished level of African American female student-athletes in what the authors label as "country club sports" (e.g., golf, lacrosse, tennis, and rowing). A review of NCAA race and gender data gives credence, to a degree, to the authors' position that "Black female student-athletes have not benefited to the degree of White female student-athletes." The authors believe shared advocacy should be employed to develop strategies to increase the number of Black females participating in college level athletics and, at the same time, enhance the on- and off-field experiences of Black female student-athletes.

Critical race feminists have criticized Title IX's legacy for disproportionately benefiting white Women rather than women of color. The fact that most litigation and enforcement activity surrounding Title IX has occurred at the college level has meant that women of color, many who are African American, are most often denied access to college opportunities and are largely left out of the law's enforcement. By applying most forcefully at the collegiate level, Title IX has sidelined women and girls who do not make it that far in academic careers. And even for women who make it to college, the growth in women's collegiate sports that Title IX has spurred has quite often involved the addition of sports that have been disproportionately played by White women, such as crew, soccer, field hockey, tennis, golf, and other sport offerings that fewer women of color have had an opportunity to play. Clearly, this resonates strongly with Sloan-Green's years of advocacy and engagement.

Chapter 13 provides an array of Title IX stakeholder advocacy organizations (e.g., Women's Sport Foundation, AAHPERD, Tucker Center for Research on Girls and Women in Sport) committed to promoting social justice and diversity in collegiate athletics. What irks the authors is an absence of this concern from previous discussion among Black females holding leadership positions on the various governing boards where policy, strategies, and priorities are established for the organization. Given this scenario, the authors asked the very important question, "If advocates are aware of the obvious racial disparities in women's sports participation, then why do they overlook this issue in organized conversation, national meetings, and international expert media commentary?"

Gill, Jr., and Sloan-Green provide a ranging discussion of the work of Black feminists in promoting women's issues in America. However, Black females, accordingly, are not proactive in Title IX advocacy efforts. One possible explanation of this lack of advocacy work on behalf of Black feminists may be a desire to de-emphasize sport participation and the expense associated with achieving a quality higher education. The college sports scene is resistant to the racial linkages that reflect Title IX's implicit acceptance of a "White privilege" in sports by applying a sexual equality lens that ignores issues of racial justice, even as it also reflects the law's successes in enhancing the cultural privilege of female athletes.

Looking toward the future, the authors believe stakeholders must answer the question, "What is the magnitude of the disparities among Black and White interscholastic and collegiate female student-athletes?" In an attempt to answer this question, policy makers and other stakeholders should collect a variety of qualitative and quantitative data, then "market" these collected data, forming new alliances between organizations committed to promoting social justice for Black women athletes, as well as engaging in participatory action research (PAR), so as to become more inclusive by specifically advocating for Hispanic women, and finally be willing to create public space at conferences in which a forum is provided to articulate issues facing African American women experiences in college sports. In order to achieve racial and gender equity, Black feminists and White advocates must "step up their game" and engage in shared responsibility when carrying out social justice advocacy.

Racism, Media Exposure, and Stereotyping

In the first edition of *Racism in College Athletics*, Oglesby (1993) called on White Americans to end the denial, disregard, and resistance that they historically used and still use to maintain and sustain racism in our society at large and in sports in particular. She wrote that Whites have the power to make a difference in racial matters and must begin with acknowledging and accepting responsibility for White domination. In order to enhance a multiracial future we need to commit some of our professional work to antiracist activity. Oglesby proposed three steps to be taken: personal, research oriented, and programmatic. The first resolves to pursue historical and cultural understanding through studies, especially African-American studies. The second includes researching various dimensions of race relations in society and sports, while the third proposes engagement in antiracist action programs designed to counter and finally eliminate institutional, cultural, and individual racism. Programs of this kind do exist, and taking first steps can build a path for personal empowerment for Whites as well as African Americans.

Being dedicated by taking steps is the intention of Lawrence in "Whiteness Studies in Sport: A 21st Century Perspective" (Chapter 14). Lawrence provides an overview of race relation theories with a focus on contemporary whiteness theory and whiteness studies in order to sharpen up the concepts of race, racism, and discrimination to better understand "how power, whiteness, White privilege, and the White athlete have had an impact on sports and the sport science literature." Beginning with a critique of our own society's practiced colorblindness and racial complacency, Lawrence contends overt racism and segregation has been replaced with various forms of discrimination associated with race. The phenomenon of overlooking the White athlete is relevant to Whiteness in sport and is explored. And why is there a failure to focus on the large number of sports that the White athlete is overly represented in? The study of White privilege, White supremacy, and the a color-blind media in the context of sports permits the reader to more fully comprehend the interconnectiveness of racial identity, privilege, cultural values, masculinity, gender, nationalism, and dominate cultural beliefs.

Antiracist advocacy begins at the personal level with a desire to learn more about other racial minorities. Hopefully for Lawrence, such advocacy can propel a color-affirming White female to become "committed to building an equitable, racially diverse network of relationships." The chapter unfolds through a series of questions about trends that will affect race relations in a context of global racial diversity: What is the state of global race relations? What is White privilege and how is it manifest in society? Are White athletes an underdog in most sports? How does whiteness impact sports and the sport sciences? Lawrence believes her present journey as a White woman, athlete, and scholar mirrors the journey of a "color-affirming White" who is vested in promoting the concepts of social justice and fairness, especially in college athletics.

Singer's mission in "Stakeholder Management in Big-Time College Sport" (Chapter 15) is to map out a literature and framework that can provide scholars, practitioners, and students who are interested in college sport with a tool for understanding and addressing the educational interests of the African American male athlete in the revenue-producing sports of football and men's basketball at predominantly White institutions of higher education. At the heart of the debate rests the question: To what degree are big-time college athletic programs willing to sacrifice the education experiences of student-athletes, especially African American males, to gain a greater market share on their investment? A common theme throughout this chapter is the perceived contradiction of such terms as *student-athlete* and *educational mission of college athletes*, and Singer suggests that "those who manage sport (i.e., coaches and administrators) must be more concerned with the benefits that prime beneficiaries (student-athletes) receive from the athletic department's existence and operations." Singer understands that stakeholder groups have a vested interest in how things are organized and operated in their programs, but also chastises them not only because of their fiscal gains via the commodification of the African American male body, but also for their disregard of policies and practices that might affect the overall welfare of these athletes.

Most importantly, according to Singer, the African American male athlete himself must take charge of his own educational experiences and interests. College athletics in America has become such a highly commercialized entity that athletes have no voice and very little input into policies that directly influence their educational experiences. Given that individuals' athletic scholarships (i.e., being able to retain it from year to year) depend directly on their ability to perform athletically at the highest levels, along with their ability to remain in favor with the coaching staff, many African American athletes are discouraged from speaking honestly and openly about those things that negatively affect their educational experiences. Again, according to Singer, when you combine these factors with the reality that many African American male athletes seem only to be interested in the pursuit of a professional sports career, and therefore, take very little interest in other areas of personal and professional development during their time on these campuses, one begins to see and understand how forces at the structural and individual levels collide to create the many problems related to the educational experiences of African American male athletes.

Consequently, African American males and all other athletes in these big-time college sports programs must take charge of their educational interests by aligning themselves with programs, coalitions, alliances, and people that will enlighten and provide support for them during their time on campus. One supposes that the lesson learned here is for one to look out for one's own self, for one's own good, but Singer seems to be saying that highly talented athletes in high-powered programs apparently are not aware of what is for their own good; thus they must be set straight. In this sense, the ultimate responsibility lies on the shoulders of athletes to embrace this reality and utilize all of the resources at their disposal to reap the benefits from their experiences as important stakeholders of big-time college sport. There is, after all, a moral duty to provide remedies to eradicate the condition contributing to exploitation of stakeholders (i.e., African-American male student-athletes).

Diversity: Beyond Black and White

Chapter 16 ("From the Turf to the Top: Access to Higher Education by Latino Male College Football Players") by Harrison, Ochoa, and Hernandez turns our focus on the sport experiences of male Latino college football players. Historically, African American and Latino students were confronted by similar social conditions: discrimination, limited resources, health issues, lower high school and college graduation rates when compared to their White counterparts, and access to higher education via the junior/community college route.

As the authors tell Joe Kapp's story as a student-athlete and as someone who enjoys motivating students to succeed in academics and athletics, they attempt to bring a focus to the similarities and differences encountered among minorities in America today. As a 12-year old, when Joe Kapp visited the University of California, Berkeley, he asked a teacher: "What do I have to do to play here?" The teacher responded: "You have to take college prep courses" (Craddock, 2005). Eventually Kapp, born in New Mexico and of Mexican descent, earned a basketball scholarship to attend the University of California, Berkeley, in the late 1950s. As a Golden Bear on the basketball court, Kapp earned honors and his team won the 1959 NCAA championship. On the football field, Kapp distinguished himself as a leader and tough opponent as quarterback of the team (Longoria, 1997). After earning his college degree, he played professionally in the National Football League (NFL) and the Canadian Football League (CFL). Kapp recently established an organization to promote excellence in higher education (Craddock, 2005).

To an extent, by overcoming some barriers, Latinos have gained a level of success in the sport industry. Latino athletes made contributions to boxing, baseball, and professional football. Yet much is still unknown about the academic and athletic experiences of Latino male and female student-athletes. Harrison and his colleagues use the term *Latino* to describe the ethnicity and cultural identity of the student-athletes discussed in this chapter; Latino, as used in their chapter, includes "Mexican Americans, Puerto Ricans, Cubans, and Latin Americans who are linked to U.S. history through immigration, acquisition of lands, or political upheavals" (Macdonald & Garcia, 2003, p. 19).

The principle focus was to examine the role and dilemma of the Latino male student-athlete in the revenue sport of intercollegiate football, examining existing higher education access to and success. Next, there is a historical overview of Latinos in sport. Third, applying critical race theory (CRT), they drafted an exploration of Latino male student-athletes across their social and athletic identities, lending to their appreciation that "when recruiting Latinos, you're not just recruiting the son/daughter, but the whole family." Finally, these authors bring attention to the importance of qualitative research with respect to Latino male football student-athletes, with an eye on the African American male athlete (Jordan & Denson, 1990).

Sports are not immune to the increasing specter of globalization. As colleges and universities attempt to broaden their successes in sports, especially urged on by big-time sports media interests, they look for the best players around the world. In the last chapter (Chapter 17) of this book, "Migration of the International Student-Athlete into the NCAA," Teed considers some of the current consequences of the ever-increasing need to produce and sustain successful teams as collegiate athletic programs turn toward international frontiers to capture potential student-athlete resources. As both sports and intercollegiate success adapt to increasing globalized arenas, the choices made will have substantial influence on the future.

According to a recent NCAA report of international migration, international student-athletes comprise 5.5% of all male athletes and 6.9% of all female athletes at the Division I level in 2008, up from the 2.4% males and 2.4% females in 2000 (DeHass, 2009). Teed wrote, "The ability to maintain a successful athletic program is predicated on the recruitment of high-level talent and successful coaches who work as a part of a very effective management team to produce those blue-chippers who will increase their chances of winning." On the other hand, with regard to the ability to adapt to the environment of a college campus in the United States, the most important stakeholder in international student-athletes' well-being is the student athlete her- or himself. While only limited data exists regarding the college selection process, retention rates, or college satisfaction levels of migrant collegiate athletes, international student athletes do appear to have different motives and perspectives than those of both domestic student-athletes and international students.

Not uncommonly, the international student-athlete has a limited academic relationship with faculty. College curriculum and campus-related decisions are often made for them by staff and advisory units with regard to academic progress, classroom absenteeism, or intentions to return home, all of which affect academic adjustment. Some considerable cultural shock (e.g., weather, diet, westernized culture) emerges between campus culture and culture of the student-athlete's "home world." These student-athletes may possess a heightened sense of adventure and limited commitment to longer term relationships. Specifically, nearly 40% of international students were not highly motivated to complete their degrees in the United States (Popp et. al., 2010).

Pulling Things Together

In the conclusion of this third edition, we feature the major themes of racism and exploitation, as well as the forms and practices of social injustice in college athletics as articulated in the first two editions of our *Racism in College Athletics* text. Within the scope of these key themes we assembled 17 essays to address a range of topics, such as the impact of historical racist legislation on the development and contributions of sports at historically Black colleges and universities; African-American student-athlete recruitment and retention inequality expressed through graduation rates; racial imbalance in coaching and administrative positions; the intersection between racism and sexism; the role for sport in creating cultural identity, tinkering with black identity, and its relationship with the hip hop culture; big business aspects of intercollegiate sports; and the commercialism and internationalization of big-time, big-media sports for youth and particularly African American collegiate men and women.

As globalization matures and penetrates everywhere and as more people throughout the world encounter one another, frequently, in more permanent dealings and relationships, *diversity* and *multicultural differences* will likely grow more pervasive, with increasingly powerful effects in politics and economic practices, and most certainly will bestow a greater salience to symbolic processes—the emotions, meanings, and symbols—that motivate behaviors and personal aspirations. With regard to American society, White Americans can influence ethnic and racial matters, and certainly accept responsibility for the unconscionable White domination that has prevailed into the present day. For sports, responsibility and action must go forward by confronting the reluctance of the White sports establishment to acknowledge and confront racism. In order to enhance a future committed to acceptance and advancement of diversity, everyone needs to commit to giving a meaningful share of their professional work to antiracist activity.

ENDNOTES

1. Some data in this paragraph are drawn from George Sage's introductory chapter included in the second edition of this text.

2. Critical Race Theory shares the current playing field with multicultural social theory and intellectually taps the space occupied by various versions of post-modernist thinking. A number of concerns shared by CRT with multicultural theory are the following: it seeks to be inclusive, and typical analyses are offered on behalf of disempowered groups; it is intended to change social structure and culture, and thus projects gains for the disempowered; and it seeks to disrupt the social as well as the intellectual world, pressing to be diverse and open. With regard to its methods, CRT gives the upper hand to narrative, and regards any "voice" as an act of resistance or confrontation. As a perspective, it is self-critical and critical of other theories and the social world and finally, all happenings are limited to a particular historical, social, cultural context.

Race Theory traces itself back to W.E.B. DuBois' work and forward, principally, to more recent developments from the civil rights impetus. As a principal spokesperson, the popular philosopher, black activist, and pop icon, Cornell West insists that *race does matter*, and that America is a racist society that uses psychic and physical violence to keep black people in line. To some degree, there is the recognition that the momentum from civil rights movement of the 1960s has been lost and that a revival of social activism depends on new ways of thinking.

Racism is endemic to American life, and there is little incentive for whites to deal with racism. Clearly, race is a social construct and as such, it is subjected to manipulation. It leads to skepticism about the law, which can be similarly manipulated. Racial identity is not unidimensional nor fixed, and historically, different minorities have been racialized. Again, the conclusion is that race matters, not only in the legal system but throughout the structures and institutions of society. In the U.S. colorblindness is a smokescreen that allows white Americans to perpetuate racial discrimination, and to grasp at the conclusion that white racism has ended or at least is in real decline. Critical theory of race is committed to the elimination of racial oppression (Mann, 2011; Ritzer, 2010).

REFERENCES

Acosta, R. V., & Carpenter, L. J. (2010). *Women in intercollegiate sport: A longitudinal study thirty-three year update (1977–2010)*. Retrieved from http://www.acostacarpenter.org/

Allegretto, S. A. (2011, March 24). *The state of working America's wealth, 2011: Through volatility and turmoil, the gap widens*. Retrieved from http://www.epi.org/publication/the_state_of_working_americas_wealth_2011/

Anderson, A., & South, D. (2000). Racial differences in collegiate recruitment, retention and graduation rates. In D. Brooks & R. Althouse (Eds.), *Racism in college athletics: The African American athlete's experience* (pp. 155–169). Morgantown, WV: Fitness Information Technology.

Austin, A. (2008, September). *Reversal of fortune: Economic gains of 1990s overturned for African-Americans from 2000–2007*. EPI Briefing Paper #220. Washington, DC: Economic Policy Institute.

Bernstein, J. (2007). Economic opportunity and poverty in America. Testimony to the U.S. House of Representatives, February 13. Retrieved from http//www.epi.org/content.efm/webfeatures-viewpoint-econ-oppty-and-poverty

Black (African-American) History Month: February 2012. (2012, Janurary 4). United States Census Bureau. Retrieved from http://www.census.gov/newsroom/releases/archives/facts_for_features_special_editions/cb12-ff01.html

Carnevale, A. P., & Rose, S. J. (2003, March). *Socio-economic status, race/ethnicity, and selective college admissions*. New York, NY: The Century Foundation.

Castaneda, C. (2004, April). *A national review of intercollegiate athletics in public community colleges*. The Mid-South Partnership for Rural Community Colleges.

Coakley, J. (1990). *Sport in society: Issues and controversies* (4th ed.). Maryland Heights, MO: Times Mirror/Mosby.

Craddock, B. (2005, March 23). Ex Super Bowl star backs college play: Quarterback visits Modesto to promote school among Latinos. *The Modesto Bee*, p. B3.

Davis, T. (1995). The myth of the superspade: The persistence of racism in college athletics. *Fordham Urban Law Journal, 22*, 615–698.

DeHass, D. (2009). 1999–2000—2007–2008 NCAA student-athlete ethnicity report. Indianapolis, IN: National Collegiate Athletic Association.

DeNavas-Walt, C., Proctor, B. D., & Smith, J. C. (2011, September). *Income, poverty, and health insurance coverage in the United States: 2010*. United States Census Bureau. Retrieved from http://www.census.gov/prod/2011pubs/p60-239.pdf

Doyle, W. R. (2006, May/June). Community college transfers and college graduation. *Change, 38*(3), 56–58.

Fast facts. (2012). American Association of Community Colleges. Retrieved from http://www.aacc.nche.edu/ABOUTCC/Pages/fastfacts.aspx

FBI: Hate crimes target Blacks in 70 percent of race-based cases. (2011, November 15). *Huffington Post*. Retrieved from http://www.huffingtonpost.com/2011/11/15/fbi-hate-crimes-target-bl_n_1095465.html

Frankenberg, E., Lee, C., & Orfield, G. (2003). *A multiracial society with segregated scools: Are we losing the dream?* The Civil Rights Project. Retrieved from http://www.civilrightsproject.ucla.edu/news/pressrelease20100204-report.html

Hate crimes on campus (2007, December 9). StateUniversity.com. Retrieved from http://www.stateuniversity.com/blog/permalink/College-Hate-Crimes.html

Humphreys, B. R., & Ruseski, J. E. (2008, August). *The size and scope of the sports industry in the United States*. ASE/NAASE Working Paper Series, No. 0811, North American Association of Sports Economists.

Hurst, C. E. (2007). *Social inequality: Forms, causes, and consequences* (6th ed.). Upper Saddle River, NJ: Pearson.

Jackson, C. (2006) *Measuring the impact of Title IX on women of color* (Doctoral dissertation). Retrieved from http://www.ohiolink.edu

Jordan, J., & Denson, E. (1990). Student services for athletes: A model for enhancing the student-athlete experience. *Journal of Counseling & Development, 69*, 95–97.

Jost, K. (2010a). Racial diversity in public schools: Has the Supreme Court dealt a blow to integration? In *Issues in race, ethnicity, gender, and class: Selections from CQ Researcher* (pp. 71–92). Thousand Oaks, CA: Sage.

Jost, K. (2010b) The Obama presidency: Can Obama deliver the change he promises? In *Issues in race, ethnicity, gender, and class: Selections from CQ Researcher* (pp. 277–307). Thousand Oaks, CA: Sage.

Kaminski, R., & Adams, A. (1992). *Educational attainment in the United States: March 1991 and 1990*. United States Census Bureau. Retrieved from https://www.census.gov/hhes/socdemo/education/data/cps/1991/P20-462.pdf

Kerby, S. (2012, March 17). 1 in 3 Black men go to prison? The 10 most disturbing facts about racial inequality in the U.S. criminal justice system. Retrieved from http://www.alternet.org/story/154587/1_in_3_black_men_go_to_prison_the_10_most_disturbing_facts_about_racial_inequality_in_the__u.s._criminal_justice_system

Lapchick, R. (2008). The 2006–07 racial and gender report card: College sport. Retrieved from http://www.tidesport.org/RGRC/2007/2006-07_CollegeSportRGRC_PR.pdf

Lapchick, R. (2010). The effect of economic downturn on college athletics and athletic departments on issues of diversity and inclusion. *Journal of Intercollegiate Sport, 3*(1), 81–95.

Lapchick, R. (2011). Keeping score when it counts: Assessing the 2011—128 bowl-bound college football teams: Graduation rates improve; Racial gap persists. Retrieved from http://ncasports.org/wp-content/uploads/2011/12/2011-FBS-Bowl-Study1.pdf

Lapchick, R. (2012). *Keeping score when it counts: Graduation success and academic progress rates for 2012 NCAA men's division I basketball tournament teams*. Retrieved from http://ncasports.org/wp-content/uploads/2012/03/2012-Mens-Basketball-Tournament-Teams-Study.pdf

Longoria, M. (1997). *Athletes remembered: Mexicano/Latino professional football players, 1929–1970*. Tempe, AZ: Bilingual Review Press/Editorial Bilingüe.

Macdonald, V., & García, T. (2003). Historical perspectives on Latino access to higher education, 1848–1990. In J. Castellanos & L. Jones (Eds.), *The majority in the minority: Expanding the representation of Latina/o faculty, administrators, and students in higher education*. Sterling, VA: Stylus Publishing.

Mann, D. (2011). *Understanding society: A survey of modern social theory*. New York, NY: Oxford.

Mauer, M. (2006). *Race to incarcerate*. New York, NY: The New York Press.

Mintzberg, H. (1973). *The nature of managerial work*. New York, NY: Harper & Row.

Oglesby, C. (1993). Issues of sport and racism: Where is the white in the rainbow coalition? In D. Brooks & R. Althouse (Eds.), *Racism in college athletics: The African American athlete's experience* (pp. 251–267). Morgantown, WV: Fitness Information Technology.

Orfield, G., & Lee, C. (2007, August). *Historic reversals, accelerating resegregation, and the need for new integration strategies*. Los Angeles, CA: UCLA Civil Rights Project (formerly based at Harvard).

Osbourne, B. (2010). Title IX backlash and intercollegiate athletics. In A. D. P. Cummings & A. M. Lofaso (Eds.), *Reversing the field: Examining commercialization, labor, gender, and race in 21st century sports law* (pp. 217–234). Morgantown, WV: West Virginia University Press.

Popp, N., Love, A., Kim, S., & Hums, M. (2010). Cross cultural adjustments and the international collegiate athletes. *Journal of Intercollegiate Sport, 3*, 163–181.

Ritzer, G. (2010). *Sociological theory* (8th ed.). New York, NY: McGraw Hill.

Rowan, C. T. (1996). *The coming race war*. Boston, MA: Little Brown.

Rowe, A., & Jefferies, J. M. (Eds.). (1996). *The state of black America 1996*. New York, NY: National Urban Leagues.

Sage, G. H. (2000). "Introduction." In D. Brooks & R. Althouse (Eds.), *Racism in college athletics: The African American athlete's experience* (pp. 1–12). Morgantown, WV: Fitness Information Technology.

Sander, L. (2010, June 9). *Athletes' academic performance Improves, but work is still not finished, NCAA says*. Washington, DC: The Chronicle of Higher Education.

Spivey, D. (1988). 'End Jim Crow in sports: The protest at New York University, 1940–1941. *Journal of Sport History, 15*, 282–303.

Wilson, C. A. (1996). *Racism: From slavery to advanced capitalism*. Thousand Oaks, CA: Sage.

Section I: Historical Analysis of Racism in College Sports

Racism in College Athletics opens with four chapters focusing on the story of exclusion of African American athletes, the shaping of Black student-athlete participation at historically Black colleges and universities (HBCUs), the nature of intercollegiate sports at the HBCUs, and the plight of African American coaches in American society. The authors of all four chapters in Section I ask what can be done to reduce the perceived exploitation of African-American student-athletes. In unison, they commonly argue that proposed changes in policies governing NCAA student-athletes must be based on the proposition of the student-athlete concept.

Lumpkin reminds readers in the opening chapter that most African American collegiate athletes competed with each other within HBCUs prior to World War II. After the 1954 Supreme Court ruling in Brown v. Board of Education, a growing number of African American collegiate athletes achieved recognition because of their talents, and did so despite persistent discrimination in the form of Jim Crow laws. This typically lead to the refusal by southern college athletic teams to compete against integrated college teams outside their region, reinforcing an ever-present racial stereotyping, and to this day, the dismally conspicuous lack of African American college head coaches and administrators.

Chapter 2 reveals that the second Morrill Act (1890) was "the primary genius of the growth of HBCUs in America." Today, HBCUs are mostly four-year private and public, liberal arts colleges and universities, as well as two- and four-year community colleges, and various business, law, medical, theological, and technical institutions. The majority of the HBCUs are located in America's southern states. One of the unilateral consequences of the 1954 Brown decision was an exodus of Black athletes to attend predominantly White institutions. A number of factors appear to have contributed to the drain of athletes (e.g., access to scholarships, access to better facilities, and name visibility for the student-athletes).

In a companion piece, Chapter 3 provides a telling description of the sporting experience of African American student-athletes and, especially, their experiences on HBCU campuses as compared to their White counterparts. The HBCUs provided an arena by which student-athletes were afforded the opportunity to play sports at the college level. HBCUs, however, are currently facing some very important challenges that will have an effect on future experiences of Black men and women who attend these institutions, and this chapter offers suggestions about how HBCUs can remain a viable portal by which Black high school boys and girls can gain access to higher education.

The final chapter in this section critiques NCAA member institutions' hiring and retention practices that effect African American men and women relative to NCAA college coaches and administrative positions. As minorities, Black college coaches withstood countless challenges during segregation, including the inability to coach at majority institutions. Today African American coaches continue to struggle with upward mobility. The social justice advocacy work of the Black Coaches & Administrators and dedicated efforts of individuals continue to shed light on equality of hiring practices still in existence on college campuses. Tucker, Hall, and Johnson suggest that colleges may want to implement a version of the NFL's Rooney Rule, thus requiring colleges to interview at least one minority candidate when filling a head coaching position.

CHAPTER 1

Critical Events: Historical Overview of Minorities (Men and Women) in College Sports

ANGELA LUMPKIN

Abstract

African American athletes were largely excluded from predominantly Caucasian institutions of higher education until the second half of the 20th century. The few African American males who initially were allowed to enroll and play on football, basketball, and track and field teams had to excel athletically. African American athletes have been subjected to indignities like racial epithets, discriminatory treatment in housing, food service, and transportation, social isolation, and denial of competitive opportunities when opposing teams from the South. Numerous African American athletes withstood bigotry and prejudice to attain the highest levels in their sports, such as earning All-American recognition, winning Olympic medals, and receiving national honors, especially after they were recruited more by coaches at predominantly Caucasian institutions to help win. Despite becoming dominant forces in football, basketball, and track and field, today, some African Americans are still victimized by academic exploitation and inequitable hiring practices for coaching and athletic administration positions.

Key Terms		
• academic exploitation	•	historically Black colleges and universities
• All-American		
• athletic revolution	• pioneers	
• color barrier	• quotas	
• discrimination	• stacking	

INTRODUCTION

Sports have been praised for accepting minorities, and especially African Americans, more quickly and more equitably than other sectors of society. Many have claimed that performance, not ethnicity or skin color, counted the most in sports. An objective assertion of colorblindness, however, failed to hide the overt and subtle racism that persistently plagued college sports for over a century.

Prior to the 20th century, a very small number of African American males were permitted to integrate sport teams in predominantly Caucasian institutions in the North and Midwest. When an African American male was permitted to enroll, he was inevitably a superb athlete, academically strong, and nonconfrontational to the racism he regularly experienced. These African American pioneers were inevitably subjected to bigotry, second-class status, and social isolation. For most African Americans who were fortunate enough to advance into higher education in the mid- to late-1800s, however, they were segregated into historically Black colleges and universities (HBCUs).

Exploitation of African Americans continued several decades into the 20th century as they were subjected to allegedly separate but equal treatment. Almost all African Americans were excluded from sport facilities, such as tennis courts and golf courses at exclusive clubs, and even denied access to publicly funded swimming pools and parks. The segregated schools and colleges provided to African Americans were inadequately funded for academics as well as athletics. The African American athletes who did compete in sports did so in obscurity with little notice paid to their achievements. Overcoming numerous barriers and prejudicial treatment in a society sharply divided by race, a few African Americans, however, became All-Americans in college sports and Olympians in the first half of the 20th century.

In the post-World War II years, both society and sport began to change. The government that had required African American men to fight and die could no longer ignore the blatant practice of segregation and racism at home. Federal laws and gradual enforcement of these laws made overt discrimination and mistreatment illegal, although resistance to civil rights legislation remained strong in the minds and actions of most Southerners and some others throughout the nation. The increased commercialization of college sports in the post-war years opened more opportunities for African American males, because coaches on primarily Caucasian campuses saw an untapped resource for athletic talents. In most cases, though, the African Americans who were recruited had to endure numerous indignities. Many felt exploited as they performed well athletically, but were not expected and encouraged to achieve academically or accepted as equals socially.

The 1960s and 1970s were especially tumultuous times as some African Americans resented and resisted being exploited. Some African American athletes demanded fair and equitable treatment comparable to their Caucasian teammates. Some African Americans risked, and lost, their athletic scholarships for speaking out against discriminatory treatment. Others focused on their sports and succeeded despite the hardships they had to endure.

An increased number of highly skilled African Americans athletes chose to attend predominantly Caucasian institutions beginning in the 1980s. Their decisions were influenced by seeking exposure through the media, positioning themselves for potential professional careers, and taking advantage of better facilities. This migration adversely affected sport teams at HBCUs that were unable to sustain previously high levels of performances in football, basketball, and track and field.

While football, basketball, and track and field teams are fully integrated with a higher than representative percentage of African Americans today, this is not the case in other sports, as African Americans are infrequent members of college teams in sports such as tennis, golf, or wrestling. Whether this is a result of socio-economic factors, fewer opportunities, or lack of role models, college sports are less fully integrated than many have claimed. Subtle discrimination persists whenever people act based on beliefs that certain sports are for African Americans, while other sports are not.

This chapter will describe numerous critical events that have occurred in the history of college sports that have provided opportunities for African American athletes to excel. Given that the most extensive contributions of African American athletes in colleges have occurred in football, basketball, and track and field, this chapter will focus on these sports. Since college sports, until recent years, have been primarily for males, they will be mostly featured, although some mention of the accomplishments of African American female athletes has been included.

1800s

In the years following the Civil War, while some African Americans advanced their status economically and socially, most remained oppressed throughout the United States. Despite the elimination of slavery and gains made during Reconstruction in the South, pervasive prejudice and discrimination plagued the lives of most African Americans. In the South, racist attitudes, discriminatory biases, and bigotry relegated African Americans to inferior status and segregated lives as Jim Crow laws and practices prevailed. In the North, racism persisted too, as African Americans struggled to achieve equitable treatment and opportunities for economic advancement. Throughout the nation, many Caucasians treated African Americans as if they were inferior psychologically, biologically, and anthropologically. The relegation of African Americans to separate schools, places to live, and subservient jobs allowed Caucasians throughout the country to ignore the plight of African Americans and falsely assume that no one was harmed by a society divided on the basis of race.

In 1896, the United States Supreme Court *Plessy v. Ferguson* decision affirmed the maintenance of the status quo of separate educational institutions, public accommodations, and transportation and other services. This court decision reinforced the actions of Caucasians who resisted accepting African Americans as their equal in all aspects of society. Relegated to the fringes of society, the plight of African Americans disappeared from the consciousness of many Caucasians.

It was in this context that the first African American athletes played on teams at colleges where once they never would have been allowed to enroll. Parents in some African American middle-class families viewed education as essential for upward mobility in society, as they supported their sons in preparing for professions such as medicine and law (Wiggins, 1991). In pushing against their second-class status in society, African Americans sought to foster racial pride and elevate their race through education, which held the key to greater economic benefits.

Only a few colleges in the North and Midwest would admit an occasional, and usually exceptional, African American student. Martin (1993) concluded that the pioneer African American athletes had to demonstrate exceptional prowess in sports, strong academic abilities, good character, and the mental toughness required to overcome the racism they experienced.

The few African Americans who were allowed to enroll at institutions like Harvard University, Amherst College, and Oberlin College were exceptional. (Throughout this chapter, the current name of each institution of higher education, rather than the name at the time, is used so the reader can more easily identify the correct institution.) As beneficiaries of educational opportunities closed to most of their race, Young (1963) argued that many perceived themselves as pioneers who carried the hopes and dreams of others with them. These young men realized that their behaviors and accomplishments could open doors for other African Americans.

Even though a few African American athletes in the late 1800s excelled, they often had to endure biased and stereotypical put-downs, caricatures in the media, and social isolation on almost exclusively Caucasian campuses. African American athletes were cheered for their exploits on the gridiron, according to Davis (1995), but they were inevitably excluded from public accommodations like hotels and restaurants due to Jim Crow laws in the South and prejudicial practices in the North. The corresponding sidebar describes how William Lewis provided an exemplary example of the type of African American student and athlete that a Northern institution would admit.

Some African Americans believed that sports provided platforms for advancing racial equality. They advocated that through athletic accomplishments, racial pride could be enhanced. Journalists, especially in the African American press, applauded the exploits of African American athletes who played on predominantly Caucasian teams in colleges in the North and Midwest. They advanced the thought that these achievements would soften racial prejudices and serve as a vehicle for social change (Miller, 1995).

Moses Walker, who played baseball for Oberlin College and the University of Michigan from 1881–1883, may have been the first African American to compete in athletics at a predominantly Caucasian institution: Oberlin. It is noteworthy that he played two years at Michigan while attending law school. In the 1890s, Francis Gregory at Amherst College and Yale Divinity School, Frank Armstrong at Cornell College (Iowa), and Eu-

WILLIAM LEWIS: Shining Star at Amherst College and Harvard University

Like other African Americans, William Lewis first had to demonstrate his academic abilities to attend a predominantly Caucasian institution, which he did by studying at Virginia State University. A classmate there was William Jackson, who joined him as the first known African Americans to play on a football team at a predominantly Caucasian campus at Amherst College. Lewis was cheered for his athletics prowess, but often excluded or disdained outside of sport. Despite the prejudicial treatment he suffered, Lewis engaged in extracurricular activities, including participation in the Hitchcock Society of Inquiry, a social and literary organization. He was selected as president of this society as a senior. He delivered the class oration at graduation. Lewis, in 1891, was the first African American elected by his teammates to serve as captain of an integrated football team.

After graduation in 1892, Lewis attended Harvard Law School while he continued to play football for two years given the lax eligibility rules, which were tightened after the 1893 season. He was the first African American named to Walter Camp's All-American teams at the center-rush position in 1892 and 1893. He also was Harvard University's first All-American football player. Despite his achievements in football, Lewis remained isolated at Harvard and had to endure racial indignities and repeated antagonistic treatment.

As a tribute to his outstanding knowledge of football and its strategies, Lewis served as an assistant coach at Harvard from 1894 through 1906. To reward him for his services and loyalty (he declined taking a coaching position at Cornell University), Lewis was given an annual salary, thus making him the first African American paid coach. In 1893, Lewis also helped coach the Amherst College football team, as he did in 1894 and occasionally thereafter through 1900 (Bond, 2006; Wiggins, 1991).

gene Gregory at Harvard University also played on their colleges' baseball teams. Track and field athletes at predominantly Caucasian institutions in the 1890s included Napoleon Marshall at Harvard University, Spencer Dickerson at the University of Chicago, and G. C. H. Burleigh at the University of Illinois. The popularity of football in the 1890s probably enabled a few African Americans to have opportunities to play this sport on predominantly Caucasian campuses that they would not have otherwise enjoyed: Howard Lee at Harvard University; William Arthur at Massachusetts Institute of Technology, Alton Washington at Northwestern University, William Washington at Oberlin College, Edward Harvey at the University of Kansas, George Jewett at the University of Michigan, George Flippin at the University of Nebraska, and George Caldwell at Williams College (Ashe, 1988; Kish, 1998; Young, 1963). An interesting trend was revealed at this time as about half of these African Americans in football played the halfback position.

HBCUs

In HBCUs, most of which were located in the South, African Americans engaged in segregated sport competitions despite limited resources. According to Captain (1991), Tuskegee University, Talladega College, Wilberforce University, Morehouse College, and Hampton Institute emphasized athletics soon after their establishment. Morehouse College first played Atlanta University in baseball in 1890. In 1896, these two teams and Morris Brown College and Clark University formed a baseball league. In 1893, Tuskegee University held the first African American college track meet (Ashe, 1988).

In 1892, Johnson C. Smith University played Livingstone College in the first recorded African American college football game (Miller, 1995). In 1894, Howard University and Lincoln University began their football rivalry, while Tuskegee University and Morehouse College began their football teams in 1897. Morgan College, Virginia Union University, Wiley College, Wilberforce University, Talladega College, South Carolina State University, and Claflin University soon began competing in football as well. Miller (1995) reported that most of these teams struggled because their institutions and teams were poorly funded. Ashe (1988) noted that these teams were coached by men such as Howard University's Charles Cook, who had played football at Cornell University and Tuskegee University's Charles Winterwood, who had played football at Beloit College. So, football enjoyed a strong beginning on the campuses of HBCUs.

Athletics gave African American males the opportunities to demonstrate their manhood, often denied to them due to the discrimination they faced in society. African American male athletes could be aggressive and strong, rather than having to be passive and deferential toward Caucasians, according to Miller (1995). Also, on many of these campuses, sports, and particularly football, became popular and helped generate campus spirit and racial pride.

1900–1945

HBCUs

Throughout the early decades of the twentieth century, the United States remained a segregated society. With few notable exceptions, African Americans formed their own teams and competed against themselves. In 1912, the Colored College Athletic Association was formed. It was followed by the establishment of the Southern College Athletic Association, South-Atlantic College Athletic Association, and Southwestern Athletic Conference during the next two decades (Miller, 1995). These segregated athletics organizations

Mordecai Johnson, the first African-American president at Howard University, eliminated athletic scholarships in 1927 in an attempt to place a greater emphasis on academics. Courtesy of Harris & Ewing, Library of Congress Prints and Photographs Division

sought to standardize rules and facilitate fair competitions because there were few, if any, eligibility rules. For example, some players competed for several institutions and while enrolled in preparatory, college, and professional school courses (Ashe, 1988).

With nearly every HBCU sponsoring teams in football, basketball, and track and field, rule violations in athletics were similar to those in predominantly Caucasian institutions in the 1920s and 1930s. Some coaches engaged in unfair recruiting practices and did not comply with eligibility standards. Subsidization of the best athletes occurred. The sportsmanship of athletes and teams was questioned. Miller (1995) suggested that winning had become more important than the welfare of athletes or their education in HBCUs. Some administrators at HBCUs and national leaders like W. E. B. Du Bois sought to deemphasize athletics and focus on promoting strong academic programs. For example, in 1927, Mordecai Johnson, who was the first African American president of Howard University, eliminated athletic scholarships, the training table for athletes, and other types of compensation for athletes (Miller 1995). Mostly, though, such reductions in athletics were resisted by those who thought sport would uplift and cultivate racial pride.

Track and field became a popular sport for African Americans, possibly because it was relatively inexpensive. Henry (Binga) Dismond was a successful quarter-miler at Howard University before competing for the University of Chicago in the early 1900s (Ashe, 1988). Matthew Bullock organized the first African American track meet in the Southeast in 1907 while employed at Morehouse College (Ashe, 1988). Because of their prowess, African Americans were allowed to compete against Caucasian athletes in the Penn Relays, which were sponsored by the University of Pennsylvania, beginning in the 1920s (Miller 1995). Cleveland Abbott organized the first Tuskegee Relays in 1927.

Competitions between athletes attending HBCUs were conducted in relative obscurity except for publicity in the African American press. So, few Caucasians realized the wealth of talent in football, track and field, and basketball that African American athletes displayed. Another reality was that most HBCUs lacked the financial resources for elaborate facilities, large coaching staffs, and the best equipment and uniforms (Martin, 1993). So by the end of World War II, most African American athletes remained marginally visible in HBCUs, and only a few were allowed to play sports alongside Caucasians.

Withholding African American Players from Games

Even though a few African Americans were permitted to compete in athletics on predominantly Caucasian campuses, this did not mean that they were treated fairly. Coaches in institutions in the South maintained exclusionary practices by allowing their teams to play against segregated teams only from the South. Before World War II, according to

---

PAUL ROBESON:
All-Around Outstanding Student

Paul Robeson exemplified academic and athletic excellence. He earned 12 varsity letters in four sports at Rutgers University, was valedictorian of his graduating class, earned Phi Beta Kappa honors, and distinguished himself in drama and other cultural activities. As an outstanding end on the football team from 1915–1918, he was named an All-American in football in 1918. Robeson was withheld from a 1916 game against Washington and Lee University because the team from that southern institution refused to play against an African American. Robeson, despite his outstanding play and earning the respect of his teammates, still had to endure humiliations due to his race and discriminatory treatment on and off campus (Davis, 1995; Wiggins, 1991)

Davis (1995), whenever teams representing institutions from the North or Midwest played teams from the South (which occurred infrequently), coaches for the Southern teams demanded that teams from the North or Midwest leave their African American players at home or not play them in deference to their prejudicial attitudes and bigoted practices. Spivey (1988) argued that racism was egregious when a team representing a Northern college withheld its star player, who was African American, to placate the racism of the opposing team. Paul Robeson's experiences illustrated how despite his outstanding talents and achievements, these were discounted because as an African American he was perceived by some as an unworthy opponent (see corresponding sidebar).

Following are a few other examples of African American players who were withheld from interregional football games as their coaches acquiesced to the demands of Southern segregationists and denied African American players the right to compete. In 1935, University of Minnesota end Dwight Reed was kept out of the homecoming game because Tulane University refused to play against an African American athlete (Ashe, 1988). In 1929, Coach Chuck Meehan of New York University held out star halfback Dave Myers against the University of Georgia and West Virginia Wesleyan College. In 1930, Ohio State University withheld William Bell when the football team traveled to Annapolis to play the United States Naval Academy and again in 1931 in a home game against Vanderbilt University in deference to Southern prejudices. In 1934, the University of Michigan and Georgia Institute of Technology agreed to withhold one player each in their football game so that Michigan's star end, Willis Ward, would not play (Martin, 1993; Wiggins, 1991). In 1937, Wilmeth Sidat-Singh of Syracuse University was withheld from a game against the University of Maryland. In 1939, running back Lou Montgomery was withheld by Boston College from games against the University of Florida and Auburn University. That year, the Cotton Bowl Committee refused to allow Montgomery to play against Clemson University in its post-season bowl game. In 1940, New York University acquiesced to the demands of the University of Missouri that Leonard Bates would not be allowed to play despite protests by New York University students against this discriminatory treatment (Spivey, 1983).

This practice of withholding African Americans from competitions also occurred in track and field and basketball. For example, in 1941, New York University withheld three African American athletes from a track meet against Catholic University. In 1945, Coach Clair Bee withheld two African American basketball players on his Long Island University team when it played the University of Tennessee (Martin, 1993). Yet journalists in Caucasian newspaper seldom mentioned these racist slights in deference to Southern practices. African American journalists gave this practice of withholding African American players from competitions extensive coverage as they lashed out against this denial of the rights of African American athletes.

In retrospect, it is deplorable that Southern bigotry and prejudice were so deep-seated that institutions and their coaches refused to allow competitions against African American athletes. It is equally unthinkable that opposing institutions and coaches acquiesced to their demands and thereby denied competitive opportunities to African American athletes. In sport, where fairness and other values are purported to be taught and practiced, the withholding of African Americans from games during this era of time is a woeful blemish on the lives on those who allowed prejudicial, traditional practices to persist.

Other Discriminatory Practices

Besides being denied opportunities to play, African American athletes had to deal with other discriminatory practices, too. Spivey (1983) argued persuasively that Grantland Rice, who began making the All-American football selections after the death of Walter Camp, discriminated against African Americans. His selections over the next two decades included only six African Americans: Brice Taylor, University of Southern California offensive guard in 1925; Dwight Reed, University of Minnesota end in 1935–1937; Jerome Holland, Cornell University end in 1937–1938; Julius Franks, University of Michigan guard in 1942; Bill Willis, Ohio State University tackle in 1944, and Buddy Young, University of Illinois halfback in 1944. Kenny Washington of the University of California at Los Angeles was the leading rusher in the nation in 1939, but he was not selected as an All-American by Rice (Washington was selected as an All-American by another organization.).

Another illustration of discrimination was the "gentleman's agreement" among coaches in several conferences, such as the Missouri Valley Conference. Because of this unwritten policy, the University of Nebraska dropped out of this conference, as it refused to withhold its African American player from a football game against the University of Kansas (Wiggins, 1991). Similarly, Princeton University, possibly due to that institution's strong tradition of attracting the sons of Southern elite families, excluded African American students long after other institutions had broken the color barrier. Not until 1944 did Arthur Wilson become the first African American to play basketball at Princeton University (Wiggins, 1991).

African American players, despite their athletic prowess, had to endure the indignities of racism on their campuses. Sometimes from bigoted coaches and teammates, they received harsh treatment. While playing games at home and away, they were often subjected to verbal and physical abuse. Even though regularly admitted students, seldom were any African Americans permitted to live on campus. They almost always were excluded from social activities, such as dances. African American athletes, who sometimes were the only minorities on campus, were subjected to racial slurs from other students and lived an isolated existence. Some African American athletes who played in the 1920s and 1930s were recruited for their athletic skills, according to Davis (1995), but they lacked college-preparatory schooling. As victims of academic neglect, many were kept eligible rather than helped to earn degrees.

Some African Americans were victims of brutality from racist opponents. For example, in 1923, Jack Trice, playing in his first game for Iowa State University, suffered a broken collarbone after being ferociously hit again and again by University of Minnesota players. Trice, who continued to play despite the vicious hits, eventually was carried off the field on a stretcher and died soon thereafter from internal bleeding. In 1936, the University of North Carolina played New York University, a team that included Ed Williams, an African American. Williams took a merciless beating from the North Carolina players and was carried off the field unconscious and never played football again (Spivey, 1988).

Male Athletes in Track and Field

The Amateur Athletic Union (AAU) controlled track and field in the early decades of the 20th century, including the Olympic Trials where athletes qualified to compete in the Olympic Games. While some AAU-sanctioned meets excluded African Americans, the Olympic Trials were open to everyone. Seldom, however, did African Americans who attended HBCUs earn an Olympic berth.

George Poage starred in hurdles and running events at the University of Wisconsin in 1903 (Ashe, 1988). Poage competed in the 60-meter dash and won bronze medals in 200-meter hurdles and 400-meter hurdles at the 1904 Olympic Games, thus becoming the first African American to win a medal in the Olympics. John Taylor attended the University of Pennsylvania in 1904, 1907, and 1908 and excelled in the 440-yard dash, winning the Intercollegiate Amateur Athletic Association of American titles in this event all three years (Wiggins, 2004). Taylor won the first gold medal by an African American at the

JESSE OWENS:
Star of the 1936 Olympic Games

Owens attended segregated East Technical High School in Cleveland obtaining a trades-based vocational education. As a result, he was ill-prepared to succeed academically at Ohio State University in the 1930s and was kept eligible for competing on the track and field team by taking courses that did not lead to a degree. Because of his achievements as a track and field athlete while in high school, an Ohio State booster arranged for Owens to get a job as a freight elevator operator in a state government office complex. He was barred from living on campus, one of many racial slights he experienced while in Columbus. Because of his outstanding abilities, he ran special exhibitions as a freshman when he could not compete on the varsity team. He became a star as a sophomore in May of 1935 at the Big Ten Conference Championships when he set three world records and tied another one, in what many track experts consider the greatest performance ever in collegiate track and field history. Not wanting to lose the top draw in its meets when the AAU learned that Owens had been paid for working while he was competing, he received minor sanctions. But the AAU removed his name from consideration for the 1935 Sullivan Award, which annually honors the outstanding amateur athlete in the United States (Dyreson, 2006).

Owens along with nine other African American males and two African American females were members of the 1936 Olympic Games track and field team. Owens won gold medals in the 100-meters, 200-meters, 4 × 100-meter relay, and long jump. While Owens returned home a national hero for having thwarted Adolf Hitler's boast of Aryan supremacy, he never capitalized financially from his celebrity status. One reason was that he was not permitted by the AAU to receive payments for running and maintain his amateur status. Another reason was that as an African American, many doors were shut to him. Despite the discriminatory treatment Owens experienced throughout his life, he refused to allow this to defeat him. Dyreson (2006) concluded that Owens conformed to the societal expectations of a segregated society and persisted to serve as an exemplar of how a member of a minority race could overcome odds to live a successful life.

1908 Olympic Games as a member of the 4 × 400-meter relay team. Sol Butler excelled in track and field, football, and basketball from 1915 to 1918 at Duquesne University. Butler competed in the 1920 Olympic Games in the broad jump, one of three African Americans on the United States' team. Although favored to win, he pulled a tendon and finished seventh (Wiggins, 2004).

African American athletes in track and field achieved high levels of performance in college competitions as well as in the Olympic Games. Ted Cable representing Harvard University was the intercollegiate champion in the hammer throw in 1912 and 1913. Ned Gourdin, also a Harvard University student, won a silver medal in the long jump in the 1924 Olympic Games. The University of Michigan featured two stars in track and field, William Hubbard and Eddie Tolan. Hubbard captured National Collegiate Athletic Association (NCAA) long jump titles in 1923 and 1925, plus the 100-meter title in 1925. He won a gold medal in the long jump in the 1924 Olympics. Tolan won the NCAA 220-yard title in 1931. He captured gold medals in the 100-meters and 200-meters in the 1932 Olympics (National Track and Field Hall of Fame, 2009).

While attending the University of Iowa, Ed Gordon, Jr. won three NCAA titles in the long jump; he also won a gold medal in the long jump in the 1932 Olympic Games. Ralph Metcalfe of Marquette University won three consecutive NCAA 100-meter titles and 200-meter titles from 1932–1934. He also won a silver medal in the 100 meters and bronze medal in the 200 meters in the 1932 Olympic Games and a gold medal in the 4 × 100-meter relay and silver medal in the 100 meters in the 1936 Olympics. Archie Williams won the NCAA 400-meters title in 1936 representing the University of California, Berkeley, and won the same event in the 1936 Olympic Games. Fritz Pollard, Jr., who attended the University of North Dakota, won a bronze medal in the 110-meter hurdles in the 1936 Olympics. David Albritton won an Olympic silver medal in the high jump in 1936 and also won three NCAA high jump titles in 1936–1938 while a student at Ohio State University (National Track and Field Hall of Fame, 2009). Norwood Ewell won consecutive NCAA 100-meter and 200-meter titles in 1940 and 1941 competing for Pennsylvania State University. The star of the 1936 Olympic Games, however, was Jesse Owens as described in the corresponding sidebar.

Female Athletes in Track and Field

Female students attending some HBCUs beginning in the 1920s enjoyed the opportunity to participate on basketball and track teams. For example, Cleveland Abbott added female events to the Tuskegee Relays in 1929 and established the women's track and field team at Tuskegee University. Between 1936 and 1955, the women's track and field teams that he coached won 14 AAU national outdoor titles, including eight consecutively. It should be noted that there were no national intercollegiate championships available to female athletes at this time.

In 1943, Tennessee State University hired Jessie Abbott, Cleveland Abbott's daughter and a recent Tuskegee University graduate, to coach its new track and field team. When Ed Temple began coaching the Tennessee State women's track and field team, he began year-round training, offered summer institutes for Tennessee State and high school students, recruited promising athletes, secured funds for travel to AAU meets, and got work-study jobs for team members since there were no athletic scholarships. Temple insisted that the female track and field athletes at Tennessee State behave in acceptable ways relative to their dress, manners, relationships, and public behaviors (i.e., they had to act feminine). This was often quite a different expectation from many African American women's rural, urban, or working class backgrounds. But the women on the track and field team had no choice than to follow these paternalistic rules if they wanted to compete (Gissendanner, 1996).

Analysis of This Time Period

Football was the most popular sport on college campuses prior to the beginning of the 20th century and through the years of World War II, although most institutions also sponsored track and field and basketball teams. It was these sports that attracted the few African American students who were permitted to join these teams on predominantly Caucasian campuses. Based on an analysis of the extensive information available in the works of Ashe (1988), Wiggins (2004), and Young (1963), no institution had more than a total of seven African Americans on any of its athletic teams during these 46 years. Only twice did an institution have three African Americans on the same team. This occurred at the University of Pennsylvania in track and field during 1919–1921 with Lloyd Granger; Ed Jones, and Dewey Rogers and the University of California at Los Angeles in football in 1938 and 1939 when Ray Bartlett, Kenny Washington, and Woody Strode starred. The norm was a single African American on a team at any one time. This athlete was inevitably was one of the star players, since seldom did an African American sit on the bench. In reviewing the institutions, sports, and decades of the African American athletes who competed for predominantly Caucasian institutions during these years, a few other noteworthy trends emerged.

Private and public institutions were equally likely to allow an outstanding African American athlete to integrate one of its teams. However, private institutions led the way in the first two decades. For example, Fritz Pollard excelled athletically as a halfback at Brown University and earned All-American recognition in 1916. Public institutions were more likely to accept an African American athlete in the 1920s, 1930s, and 1940s than earlier. For example, the large, public institutions in the Big Ten Conference lagged behind in integrating their teams. While the University of Minnesota allowed Bob Marshall to play end on its football team in 1903–1906, it was more likely because of his outstanding athletic prowess than an enlightened acceptance of African Americans as equals. Marshall was named an All-American in football in 1905 and 1906 and also competed on the baseball, track and field, boxing, and ice hockey teams. The University of Minnesota did not have another African American on its football team until the 1930s, when it boasted of three-time All-American end Dwight Reed in 1935–1937. The second African American in this conference to earn All-American recognition occurred in 1921 in recognition of the play of Fred (Duke) Slater for the University of Iowa. Slater was only the second African American football player to play at Iowa. Although Ohio State University did not have its first African American football player until 1940, it had its first All-American in football in 1944 when tackle Bill Willis earned this recognition. Halfback Buddy Young of the University of Illinois was the other All-American in the Big Ten Conference during this time, an honor he received in 1944 and 1947. At the University of Michigan, Julius Franks was named an All-American guard in 1942, while Willis Ward was a star at end.

From 1900 through 1945, most African American athletes in predominantly Caucasian institutions played football, at a rate approximately the same as track and field, basketball, and baseball combined. The peak decade for African Americans playing on athletic teams in predominantly Caucasian institutions was the 1920s, as might have been predicted given the increase in popularity of football. About as many African Americans played in this decade as the two decades preceding it. This number dropped somewhat in the 1930s, possibly due to the economic issues in the United States, and then began to increase.

1946–1965

Persistent Discrimination

Even though African Americans were relegated to second-class status and discriminated against economically and socially, over one million were drafted into the military during World War II to fight for freedoms that most did not enjoy at home. At the same time, the United States continued to segregate African Americans into institutions of higher education or to exclude socially the few who were admitted into predominantly Caucasian institutions. For example, while no Jim Crow laws existed in Kansas, the University of Kansas minimized interactions between Caucasians and African Americans by relegating African American students to the back of classrooms and excluding them from most extracurricular activities. Although John McLendon learned the game of basketball from the inventor, James Naismith, he was not allowed to play basketball at the University of Kansas. Nonetheless, McClendon excelled as a coach as described in the corresponding sidebar.

Segregation continued years after the United States Supreme Court *Brown v. Board of Education* decision in 1954 that required equal educational opportunity. Almost all higher education institutions in the South refused to immediately comply with this federal mandate and persisted in their refusals to allow their Caucasian athletes to play against African Americans. For example, in 1946, the University of Tennessee basketball team refused to play Duquesne University because Chuck Cooper, who was the team's leading scorer, was an African American. Instead, Tennessee forfeited the game (Martin, 1993). In 1956, Mississippi State University withdrew from the championship game of a basketball tournament in Indiana rather than play against an integrated team from the University of Denver. In 1957, Jackson State University (an HBCU in Mississippi) was forced to withdraw from the NCAA small college basketball tournament because it would have had to compete against all-white or mixed teams. The University of Alabama in 1956, Mississippi State University in 1959 and 1961, and Auburn University in 1960 refused to compete in the NCAA men's basketball tournament even though they qualified by winning the Southeastern Conference championship those years (Martin, 1993). In

---

JOHN McCLENDON: Trailblazing Basketball Coach

John McClendon coached North Carolina Central University to eight Colored College Athletic Association titles between 1940 and 1952. During a time when inter-racial athletics competition was illegal in many Southern states, in a clandestine game in 1944 his North Carolina Central University team defeated an all-Caucasian Duke University Medical School team. McClendon was the first coach to win three consecutive National Association of Intercollegiate Athletics (NAIA) titles at Tennessee State University in 1957 to 1959. While his teams competed in these annual national tournaments, they helped integrate hotels and restaurants in Kansas City, Missouri.

McClendon helped popularize basketball as well as open doors for African Americans as a trailblazing coach. As an African American basketball coach, he achieved numerous noteworthy firsts: of a professional team with the Cleveland Pipers in the American Basketball League in 1961; of a United States All-Star team overseas in 1961; at a predominately white institution, Cleveland State University, beginning in 1966; on the staff of the men's basketball team in the 1968 Olympic Games; and of the Denver Rockets in the American Basketball Association in 1969. Despite the fact that his teams (at all levels) won 744 games, when he was inducted into the Naismith Memorial Basketball Hall of Fame in 1979, it was as a contributor, not as coach (Katz, 2007).

1961, the University of Mississippi, which was ranked #2, would not allow its team to play Michigan State University, which was ranked #1, in a post-season football bowl game because the Michigan State team included African American athletes (Paul, McGhee, & Fant, 1984).

In 1946, the Big Six (today's Big XII) Conference authorized its member institutions to ban the use of African American players by opposing teams, even though an unwritten gentleman's agreement had existed prior to this ruling. In 1947, university student leaders at the University of Colorado, Iowa State University, University of Kansas, Kansas State University, and University of Nebraska actively worked to change the Big Six Conference's policy that the home team could determine if an African American on an opposing team would be permitted to play. The conference dropped this policy in 1950 (Martin, 1993).

Integrated teams did not prevent racial stereotyping and discrimination. The actual integration of football, basketball, and track and field teams, given their visibility, may simply have obscured or masked continued racism in sport. Davis (1995) posited that racism was overt prior to World War II and more covert thereafter. While often ignoring the achievements of African American athletes, violence toward them persisted. For example, Johnny Bright playing for Drake University as a single-wing halfback led the nation in total offense in 1949 and 1950. He was not named an All-American either year. Already leading the nation in offense for the third consecutive year in 1951, he became the victim of the most egregious example of unsportsmanlike racism in a game against Oklahoma State University. Wilbanks Smith viciously hit Bright in the face with his fist (there were no face masks on the helmets at that time) breaking Bright's jaw, even though neither of these two players was directly involved with the play at the time. The photo sequence of the attack captured on film shocked viewers by its brutality and left little doubt that racial hatred had triggered the attack. Since Bright, who was drafted by the Philadelphia Eagles, held serious reservations about competing with and against players from the segregated South, he opted for the Canadian Football League and retired as the league's all-time leading rusher.

By the mid-1950s, most northern institutions had at least a token level of integration, which caused problems for rigidly segregated southern institutions because there was less acquiescence to their refusals to allow competitions against African Americans. In a change from the past, now most institutions outside the South refused to withhold African Americans when playing home games and were reluctant to withhold them when playing games in the South. Still, some African American and Caucasian athletes suffered when denied opportunities to play. For example, in 1955 the Georgia governor banned Georgia Institute of Technology from playing in the Sugar Bowl against the University of Pittsburgh because it had an African American player, Bobby Grier. In 1969, the University of Washington withheld all of its thirteen African American players in a game against the University of California at Los Angeles (Martin, 1993).

Jim Crow practices in the South, which were incompatible with Democratic principles and federal law, were glaring and flagrant in sport. In sport, where values like hard work, self-sacrifice, and teamwork were claimed to be taught and respected, coaches and institutions failed the test for justice and fairness because of racial prejudice by opening the field of play to anyone who could demonstrate physical prowess (Spivey, 1988).

Even when many teams were integrated, African American athletes were subjected to stacking and quotas. *Stacking* describes the practice of assigning African Americans to certain positions, such as running back or defensive back in football or center in basketball, so that they would have to compete against each other for only a limited number, or quota, of starting or playing positions. African Americans were seldom allowed to play the so-called thinking positions of quarterback or linebacker in football or guard in basketball because prejudicial attitudes judged them incapable of performing well in these cerebral and leadership positions.

Another example of discriminatory treatment was that African Americans were almost never hired as head coaches; for many years, they also were not hired as assistant coaches in football, basketball, and track and field. While John McClendon and Ed Temple had excelled as coaches, inevitably African Americans were restricted to coaching at HBCUs. Similarly, when public schools were eventually integrated, there was a concomitant loss of jobs by African American coaches and a resultant loss of coaching role models for African American athletes.

Two effects of World War II were free substitution in football due to the shortage of players and the recruiting of African American athletes, which Spivey (1983) described as an untapped talent pool. As college athletics became more commercialized after World War II, Caucasian coaches crossed the color line in sports to recruit African Americans. While the decade of the 1950s did not become a decade when racism was overcome nationally, some coaches in the 1940s began tapping into the talent pool of African American athletes to help their teams win games. That is one reason why segregation in college athletics gradually began to end in the post-World War II years, as institutions wanted skilled African American athletes to help them win games (Davis, 1995). Martin (1993) added that the recruitment of African Americans marked a turning point in race relations in the South.

Breakthroughs in Basketball

Change was coming as illustrated by several firsts or critical events that led to more equitable treatment of African Americans. For example, in 1946 Chuck Cooper played for Duquesne University against Morehead State University in Louisville, Kentucky. This was the first time an African American basketball player had played against an all-Caucasian team from the South. In 1948, the National Association of College Basketball (precursor to the NAIA) eliminated its ban on African American players in its postseason basketball tournament in Kansas City. In 1951, the University of Kentucky basket-

BILL GARRETT: Outstanding Player and Virtually Unknown Pioneer	
Bill Garrett, who had attended a segregated elementary school, starred for his integrated high school team, Shelbyville, leading it to the Indiana State High School Championship in 1947. He was also named "Mr. Basketball," recognizing the best high school player in the state of Indiana. Garrett, like Johnny Wilson who preceded him in earning this honor, was not recruited by Coach Branch McCracken to Indiana University. Through the efforts of several individuals, however, Garrett was allowed to walk-on to the freshman team. His outstanding play earned him a starting spot on the varsity the next three years.	Throughout his collegiate career, as he had experienced in high school, Garrett was subjected to racial taunts, refused service in restaurants and hotels, and relegated to second-class status on and off campus. As a consummate sportsman and gentleman, though, Garrett let his outstanding performances on the court prove his worth as he earned the respect of his coach, teammates, opponents, and fans. As the leading scorer and rebounder for Indiana as a senior in 1950–1951, he was named an All-American (Graham & Cody, 2006).

ball team played a home game in Lexington against a St. John's University team that had an African American player (Martin, 1993).

Still, basketball coaches in the Big Ten Conference adhered staunchly to a "gentleman's agreement" to not recruit African Americans, even though African Americans had occasionally played football on teams in this conference as early as the first decade of the twentieth century. Even though Dick Culberson played basketball sparingly at the University of Iowa during the 1944–1945 season, this was an exception and more related to the lack of availability of other players. Bill Garrett, as discussed in the corresponding sidebar, was the pioneer who broke through this prejudice and forever opened the door for African American basketball players in the Big Ten and other conferences.

While other institutions in the Big Ten Conference and nationally began to give African American athletes opportunities, in the former Confederate states in the South, laws and segregationist attitudes continued to prevail. To prevent a mixing of the races, men's basketball players in the South were often denied the right to compete in the NCAA men's basketball championship to prevent them from being matched against a team that included African American players. In 1963, the Mississippi State University's men's basketball team won the Southeastern Conference title to earn a berth in the NCAA tournament. Despite the governor's efforts and a judge's ruling that barred them from leaving the state, the team was able to play in the tournament after the state supreme court dissolved the judge's ruling (Martin, 1993).

While public institutions in the South continued to maintain segregated teams in the 1950s and 1960s, coaches at independent and small colleges were opportunistic in integrating their teams to help win games and advance the reputations of their institutions. In 1956, Charles Brown and Cecil Brown became the first African Americans to play basketball for the University of Texas at El Paso. In 1957, St. Mary's University in San Antonio recruited African American basketball player Maurice Harris. At the University of North Texas, football was integrated in 1958 and basketball in 1960. The University of Texas–Pan American began recruiting African Americans in 1959. In 1963, the University of Texas–Pan American men's basketball team won the NAIA championship led by African American Lucius Jackson (Martin, 1993).

The point-shaving scandals of the 1950s and 1960s involved several African Americans, even though most teams only included a few. Of the teams implicated in the scan-

---

CONNIE HAWKINS:
Wrongfully Denied the Opportunity to Play College Basketball

Connie Hawkins was recruited to the University of Iowa in 1960. He had been promised money, an active social life, preferential treatment, and an education by the coaches. That is, Hawkins was promised he would be taken care of if he would help the basketball team win games. Ill-prepared for college-level work, Hawkins ended up on academic probation at the end of his first semester. Since Iowa had few African Americans, he lacked individuals to date or others like him with whom to socialize. In May of 1961, he was falsely accused of acting as an intermediary for New York City gamblers in fixing college basketball games. Hawkins also was pressured by individuals from the athletics department at Iowa to not return as well as to recant his statements that he had been paid to play basketball at Iowa. Wiggins (1991) concluded that Hawkins was coerced into lying to the NCAA so Iowa could escape sanctions from the NCAA. Hawkins then lost his collegiate eligibility because he was falsely accused on being an intermediary for gamblers and the point shaving scandals.

dals, Fitzpatrick (1999) reported that 74% of the African American athletes were involved, while only 11% of the Caucasians were. Two factors may have contributed to these skewed numbers. First, most of the African American athletes were from low socioeconomic backgrounds and may have been lured by the attraction of easy money from the gamblers. Second, most of these African Americans were the leading players on their teams, and potentially the most likely targets for the gamblers when seeking players to shave points. An innocent victim of the point shaving scandals and persistent racism was Connie Hawkins, a high school and playground basketball legend from New York City (see sidebar).

Female Athletes in Track and Field

Since most competitive opportunities were closed to them, it was more difficult for African American females to challenge themselves and excel in sports. However, African Americans were allowed to compete in the AAU National Championships. In the 1948 Olympic Games, four female athletes from Tuskegee University and two from Tennessee State University represented the United States in track and field. The four included Alice Coachman in the high jump, Mabel Walker in the 100-meters, Nell Jackson in the 200 meters, and Theresa Manuel in the hurdles and javelin. The two were Audrey Patterson, who won a bronze medal in the 200 meters and Emma Reed, who competed in the long jump and high jump.

ALICE COACHMAN:
First Female African American Olympic Champion

Despite growing up in the segregated South, Alice Coachman took advantage of attending Tuskegee University, where she ran on the national champion 4 × 100-meter relay team in 1941 and 1942, won the 50-yard dash in 1943, and played basketball. She won 10 consecutive AAU high jump titles between 1939 and 1948. In 1945 and 1946, she also captured the 50-meter dash, 100-meter dash, and high jump AAU national titles. Overall, she won 26 individual national championships and 10 team titles. Of the 12-member US women's track and field team in the 1948 London Olympic Games, nine were African Americans. She qualified for the 50-meter dash in London but chose to focus on winning the high jump. Coachman was the first African American woman and only American woman to win an Olympic gold medal in the high jump in the 1948 London Olympic Games. Coachman became one of the first African American sport celebrities to endorse Coca-Cola (Gissendanner, 1996; Lansbury, 2006).

WILMA RUDOLPH: Three-Time Olympic Gold Medalist

Wilma Rudolph won gold medals in the 100-meters, 200-meters, and 4 × 100-meter relay in the 1960 Olympic Games. She was the highly publicized star of these Olympics not only because she won three gold medals, but also because of her physically striking beauty and life story of overcoming childhood scarlet fever, double pneumonia, and polio. After attending a summer camp run by Coach Ed Temple at Tennessee State University, at the age of 16 Rudolph qualified for the 200 meters and as a member of the 4 × 100-meter relay in the 1956 Olympic Games. Rudolph and three Tennessee State athletes, Mae Faggs, Margaret Mathews, and Isabelle Daniels, won a bronze medal in the 4 × 100-meter relay. In 1959 while a freshman at Tennessee State, Rudolph won three national sprint titles (Wilson, 2006).

Two outstanding female athletes in this era of time overcame economic barriers and racial discrimination to achieve at the highest levels athletically. Alice Coachman (see corresponding sidebar) and Wilma Rudolph (see corresponding sidebar) have provided remarkable examples of how, if given opportunities and treated more equitably, African American female athletes could excel.

Analysis of this Time Period

African American athletes who earned All-American recognition in NCAA football or basketball, or who won track and field championships and gold medals in the Olympic Games between 1946 and 1965, were analyzed to determine trends or significant changes from earlier decades. Of the All-American football players, slightly over half played running back, halfback, or fullback; none played quarterback. In 1946 through 1950, there were no African Americans named to All-American teams. Between 1951 and 1959, there were no more than two African Americans named All-Americans in any year and in two years there were none. Beginning in 1960 through 1965, there were three or four African Americans honored as All-Americans. Between 1935 and 1960, no African American won the Heisman Trophy, annually awarded to the outstanding college football player. The first African American to win the Heisman Trophy was Syracuse University's Ernie Davis in 1961; Mike Garrett, who played for the University of California at Los Angeles, won this award in 1965. Both were running backs. A critical event occurred in 1958, when University of Oklahoma football coach Bud Wilkinson signed Prentiss Gault, the first African American football player at a major predominantly Caucasian institution in the South (Martin, 1993).

The first African American basketball player to be named an All-American was Don Barksdale of the University of California at Los Angeles in 1947. With the exceptions of 1946, 1952, and 1962, at least one African American basketball player was named an All-American between 1946 and 1965. In 1958, the Associated Press, for the first time, named five African Americans to its All-American basketball team: Don Hennon of the University of Pittsburgh, Oscar Robertson of the University of Cincinnati, Guy Rodgers of Temple University, Elgin Baylor of Seattle University, and Wilt Chamberlain of the University of Kansas. In 1960 and 1964, four African American players were selected as All-Americans. Bill Russell of the University of San Francisco in 1956, Oscar Robertson at the University of Cincinnati in 1958 through 1960, and Walt Hazzard of University of California at Los Angeles in 1964 were also recognized as Player of the Year.

An African American first played on a United States Olympic basketball team when Don Barksdale helped the 1948 team win a gold medal. None played for the United States' team in 1952. Bill Russell and K.C. Jones, teammates at University of San Francisco, played on the gold medal winning team in 1956. In 1960, Walt Bellamy (Indiana University), Bob Boozer (Kansas State University), and Oscar Robertson (University of Cincinnati) helped the United States win the gold medal in basketball. In 1964, Walt Hazzard (University of California at Los Angeles) was joined by African Americans Jim Barnes (University of Texas at El Paso), Joe Caldwell (Arizona State University), Lucius Jackson (University of Texas–Pan American), and George Wilson (University of Cincinnati) on the gold medal winning team in 1964. The increasing recognition of the outstanding performances of African American players reflected a dramatic transition in Olympians in men's basketball.

Fifteen African American track and field athletes won Olympic medals between 1948 and 1964 excelling in the sprints, hurdles, high and long jumps, and decathlon. Gold medalists in 1948 included Harrison Dillard of Baldwin-Wallace College in the 100-

meters, Norwell Ewell of Pennsylvania State University and Dillard in the 4 × 100-meter relay, and Mal Whitfield of Ohio State University in the 800 meters and 4 × 400-meter relay. In 1952, African American gold medalists included Dillard in the 110-meter hurdles and 4 × 100-meter relay, a repeat for Whitfield in the 800-meters, and Andy Stanfield of Seton Hall University in the 200-meters and 4 × 100-meter relay. Gold medalists in 1956 included Milt Campbell of Indiana University in the decathlon, Charles Dumas of the University of Southern California in the high jump, Charlie Jenkins of Villanova University in the 400-meters and 4 × 400-meter relay, Greg Bell of Indiana University in the long jump, and Lee Calhoun of North Carolina Central University in the 110-meter hurdles. In 1960, African American gold medalists included Lee Calhoun again in the 110-meter hurdles, Ralph Boston of Tennessee State University in the long jump, Otis Davis of the University of Oregon in the 400-meters and 4 × 400-meter relay, and Rafer Johnson of the University of California at Los Angeles in the decathlon. It was especially noteworthy in 1960 that Johnson became the first African American athlete selected to carry the flag of the United States as the athletes entered the stadium in the opening ceremonies of the Rome Olympic Games. Gold medalists in 1964 included Hayes Jones of Eastern Michigan University in the 110-meter hurdles, Henry Carr of Arizona State University in the 200 meters and 4 × 400-meter relay, and Bob Hayes in the 100-meters and 4 × 100-meter relay. These African American track and field stars also won numerous NCAA and AAU titles between 1946 and 1965.

1966 THROUGH 1970s

And the Walls Came Tumbling Down

Fitzpatrick (1999) used these words in the title of his book that told the story of the watershed event in this time period. In the NCAA men's basketball championship in 1966, the unthinkable occurred when the University of Texas at El Paso defeated the University of Kentucky by a score of 72-65. The winning team in this game, which had five African Americans starters (and the only substitutes who played were also African Americans) defeated an all-Caucasian team. The monumental significance of this critical event was that the outcome influenced numerous African American athletes to believe that they could compete on an equal basis with Caucasians in basketball, including at traditionally Caucasian institutions.

This game drew attention to the resistance of most Caucasian coaches to giving African American basketball players a chance to play on their teams. While in the late 1940s Coach Adolph Rupp and his University of Kentucky team had played integrated teams, he had never recruited an African American to play on one of his teams. The discriminatory actions of Rupp and others to discount the abilities of African American were forever exposed when his Caucasian players were defeated. By way of contrast, when Coach Don Haskins went to the University of Texas at El Paso in 1961, he knew he had to recruit African Americans to have a chance to win.

Former NCAA championship teams at the University of Cincinnati in 1961 and 1962, Loyola University of Chicago in 1963, and the University of California at Los Angeles in 1964 and 1965 had started two to four African Americans, but no major college team had broken through the invisible barrier of starting an All-African American line-up until the 1966 NCAA championship game (Fitzpatrick, 1999). The University of San Francisco, which won NCAA championships in 1955 and 1956 led by African Americans' Bill Russell and K.C. Jones, had once played five African Americans in a NCAA tournament game. But, according to Fitzpatrick (1999), pressure from alumni prevented this from occurring again. Thus, the quota system of limiting the number of African American basketball players on the court at one time persisted for another decade.

Some Caucasians disparaged African American athletes by claiming that they were incapable of leading a team, such as by playing point guard. Many adhered to a racist view that African Americans could only play a run-and-gun offense, were incapable of playing disciplined games, and were unwilling to play defense. The victory by the University of Texas at El Paso team disproved these myths. The African Americans on this team walked the ball up the court and played a controlled, poised offense. Their ball-hawking defense held their opponents to fewer points per game that did the illustrious Kentucky team (Fitzpatrick, 1999).

Other illustrations of persistent racism were the myths perpetuated about the African Americans on the University of Texas at El Paso team. Some writers claimed that, unlike the players from Kentucky, the African American players had been recruited just to play basketball, did not have the academic credentials to succeed, and never graduated. Many people wanted to believe these myths because it soothed their distressed feelings that a no-name group of African Americans had won a national championship against an all-Caucasian team representing an institution with a winning tradition in basketball.

The upset of favored Kentucky in 1966 foreshadowed a dramatic change in college basketball as more African American athletes attended predominantly Caucasian institutions. Gradually, institutions moved away from the quota system as coaches sought out African American high school stars, instead of pretending they were invisible. Even in the South, this game signaled the beginning of the end of segregation. By the following season, there were African American freshmen on teams in the Southeastern, Southwest, and Atlantic Coast Conferences, even though Kentucky's Adolph Rupp maintained his all-Caucasian team (Fitzpatrick, 1999). By 1983, Fitzpatrick reported, 42 of the 50 starters on teams in the Southeastern Conference were African Americans, and all the starters on that year's Final Four teams, the Universities of Houston, Louisville, Georgia, and North Carolina, were African Americans. The gentleman's agreement of excluding African Americans and the quota system were ending.

An example of keeping African Americans from dominating sports occurred when dunking was made illegal in college basketball after the 1966–1967 season. It was possibly in response to the University of Texas at El Paso championship in 1966. Or maybe it was because of the dominating play of Lew Alcindor (Kareem Abdul-Jabbar), University of California at Los Angeles center for the 1967 NCAA champion. Hoose (1989) argued persuasively that this rule change occurred because of the association of dunking with African Americans and what was labeled as their street ball approach to the game. He stressed that this rule was enacted because African American athletes were embarrassing Caucasian players by dunking over them.

The residual racism of the 1960s discouraged the media of the time from reporting on the societal implications of the victory by the University of Texas at El Paso team on behalf of equal opportunity for African Americans. During a decade when African Americans protested, were imprisoned, and died, the African Americans on this team demonstrated that they were intelligent and skillful and capable of successfully competing with the best basketball players, regardless of race.

Athletes Fighting for Their Rights

The decade of the 1960s in the United States was a time of turmoil in the fight for civil rights. In the midst of the conflict and resistance associated with overt and subtle discrimination in accommodations, restaurants, transportation, education, and job opportunities, Harry Edwards initiated the Olympic Project for Human Rights and tried to foment a boycott of the 1968 Olympic Games. He encouraged African American male athletes to boycott in protest of the residual prejudice and discriminatory treatment they experienced on predominantly Caucasian campuses where they competed. Maybe because female athletes were provided few competitive opportunities in colleges at the time, Gissendanner (1996) stated that Edwards ignored female athletes in his organizing efforts.

Edwards's initiative demanded that the United States Olympic Committee ban South Africa due to its apartheid, asked for the resignation of Avery Brundage, President of the International Olympic Committee, and threatened an Olympic boycott if their demands were not met. Brundage sent a letter to African American athletes who were Olympians telling them they would be sent home if they did not perform honorably (Moore, 1991). Another illustration of disparate treatment toward African Americans occurred when Elvin Hayes (University of Houston), Bob Lanier (St. Bonaventure University), Wes Unseld (University of Louisville), and Lucius Allen, Lew Alcindor, and Mike Warren (University of California at Los Angeles) were labeled by Coach Hank Iba as bad citizens when they made themselves unavailable for the men's basketball team in the 1968 Olympic Games (Ashe, 1988).

Since many African American athletes did not support the proposed 1968 Olympic boycott, it was abandoned. Tommie Smith and John Carlos, however, chose to protest on the victory stand during the medal ceremony for the 200-meters. Smith wore a right-handed glove and Carlos wore a left-handed glove when they faced the flags for the national anthem. Both bowed their heads and lifted their fists to represent African American unity and power. Their stocking (unshod) feet represented poverty; Smith's black scarf and Carlos' beads represented the lynching of African Americans. Because of their visible protest against racism, Smith and Carlos were suspended from the United States' Olympic team and expelled from the Olympic village (Moore, 1991).

African American male athletes on college campuses began an athletic revolution as they directly confronted racial discrimination. For example, protests and associated racial tensions led to the cancellation of the San Jose State University football game against the University of Texas at El Paso in 1967 (Wiggins, 1991). An increase in African American athletes' social consciousness also occurred at San Francisco State University, the University of California, Berkeley University of Iowa, University of Kansas, and the University of Wisconsin, as they identified problems like stacking, racial stereotyping, restrictions against interracial dating, and quotas in recruiting and playing. They demanded changes (Spivey, 1983). In 1968, African American athletes accused the University of Washington football coach Jim Owens of discriminating against them. They demanded the hiring of an African American assistant coach. In 1970, African American athletes at the University of Pittsburgh accused the athletics department of discriminatory treatment. In 1972, the only African American basketball player at Oregon State University accused his coach of racial discrimination (Wiggins, 1988).

Boycotts of sporting events occurred at Michigan State University, Oklahoma City University, Oregon State University, San Francisco State University, Syracuse University, and the Universities of Arizona, California, Kansas, Texas at El Paso, Washington, and Wyoming. African American male athletes were protesting unfairness relative to issues like job opportunities for their wives and themselves, housing restrictions, prohibitions against inter-racial dating, disparate treatment by coaches, limited opportunities for a social life due the dearth of other African Americans on campus, and the lack of African American assistant coaches. Many of the African American athletes also stated that they were set up to fail academically because they were recruited to perform, not to take advantage of educational opportunities to prepare themselves for a better life after sports (Spivey, 1983).

In 1967, African American athletes on the University of Texas at El Paso football team staged a sit-in in the athletic dormitory to protest the lack of African American females on campus, jobs for their wives, and the racist comments to which they were subjected. Coach Bobby Dobbs was able to keep this incident quiet by promising to address these issues, although Olsen (1968) reported that nothing was actually done to address their complaints. These athletes had no recourse but to follow their coach's directives or lose their financial aid, leave the team, and drop out of college.

Even though African American militants tried to get African American track and field athletes to boycott a competition at the New York Athletic Club in 1968 because it refused membership to African Americans, University of Texas at El Paso long jumper Bob Beamon and quarter-miler Dave Morgan competed (Olsen, 1968). Shortly afterwards, though, eight African American track athletes from the University of Texas at El Paso, including Beamon and Morgan, boycotted a meet against Brigham Young University, because of that institution's affiliation with the Mormon religion that viewed African Americans as an inferior race. Coach Wayne Vandenburg suspended these African Americans from the track and field team, and the athletes lost their scholarships (Olsen, 1968). In 1969, University of Wyoming football coach Lloyd Eaton dropped 14 players from the team when they appealed to the coach not to play against Brigham Young University to draw attention to the Mormon Church's racist policies (Wiggins, 1988).

In the 1960s and 1970s, Caucasian coaches in the North and gradually in the South viewed African American athletes as necessary for achieving national prominence and winning games. Some coaches claimed they were supportive of improving race relations through sport, while simultaneously imposing quota systems and stacking African Americans into the more reactive and peripheral positions.

African Americans who were potential All-Americans were much more likely to be recruited and supported financially than were those less talented. Most Caucasian coaches used the NCAA's term of student-athlete freely, while they demanded a unilateral dedication to practice and competition to the detriment of learning and earning degrees. These Caucasian coaches may have failed to understand the social isolation felt by most African American athletes on their teams. Also, when the eligibility of African American athletes was completed, seldom were they offered coaching positions (Wiggins, 1991).

HBCUs

In the middle of the twentieth century on HBCU campuses, athletics and social opportunities for African American athletes thrived. The national championships among African American colleges won by several football teams attests to their excellence as coaches built successful programs that allowed African American athletes to display their talents. For example, Jake Gaither won six titles at Florida A&M University between 1945 and 1969; John Merritt at Jackson State University and Tennessee State University won seven titles between 1953 and 1983; and Eddie Robinson at Grambling State University won nine titles between 1941 and 1997. Clarence Gaines's teams at Winston Salem State University won 828 basketball games between 1946 and 1993. Leroy Walker in men's track and field and Ed Temple in women's track and field coached several collegiate and Olympic champions.

As more African American athletes, especially in basketball, football, and track and field, attended predominantly Caucasian institutions, however, there was a concomitant negative affect on the HBCUs where they would have competed and excelled. Ashe (1988) reported that these HBCUs tried to retain the status of their athletic programs by realigning conferences and weeding out weaker teams. These institutions began to specialize in a limited number of sports, enhanced their recruiting strategies, increased their coaching staffs, improved the athletic facilities, and tried to maximize their public relations efforts. But coaches at the HBCUs realized that African American football and basketball players were lured to Caucasian colleges because they believed it improved their chances of playing professionally.

Breaking Through Barriers

The 1960s and 1970s included a number of breakthroughs for African American athletes. In 1963, Darryl Hill became the first African American athlete to compete in football in the Atlantic Coast Conference playing for the University of Maryland. In 1964, the first basketball player (Billy Jones) was recruited to the University of Maryland, and the University of Louisville played Wade Houston, Stan Smith, and Eddie Whitehead on its basketball team. Also in 1964, Coach Guy Lewis at the University of Houston recruited basketball players Elvin Hayes and Don Chaney (they played 1965–1968) and put the Cougars on the national map in basketball.

Two private institutions led the integration of the Southwest Conference in 1965. Texas Christian University signed basketball player James Cash, and Southern Methodist University signed Jerry LeVias to a football scholarship (both played in 1966). Other integrated teams in the South in 1966 included Loyola University of New Orleans, Florida State University, and the University of Memphis; Baylor University and Miami University each had an integrated team in 1967 as did Tulane University and the University of Southern Mississippi in 1969. As these examples illustrate, the acceptance of African American athletes was gradual (Martin, 1993).

The Southeastern Conference, established in 1932, was the last major college athletics conference to integrate its teams as the vestiges of Southern bigotry died slowly. The year was 1967 when football players Nat Northington and Greg Page for the University of Kentucky became the first African American athletes recruited to play on teams in the Southeastern Conference. Neither of these men actually played for Kentucky, however. Northington quit the team after one year, and Page suffered a career-ending neck injury (Fitzpatrick, 1999). Later that year, Perry Wallace of Vanderbilt University became the first African American to play basketball in the Southeastern Conference, while James Craig and Audrey Hardy at the University of Tennessee and Harry Sims and James Hurley at the University of Georgia were the first African Americans on the track and field teams at these institutions. In 1970, Paul, McGhee, and Fant (1984) found that there were 41 African Americans receiving athletics scholarships in the Southeastern Conference, with 30 of them at the Universities of Florida, Kentucky, and Tennessee. Typically, only one or two African Americans were on any team.

In analyzing the integration of the Southeastern Conference, Paul, McGhee, and Fant (1984) found that about 90% of the 56 pioneer African American athletes lettered; 14% were All-Americans; 20% were All-Southeastern Conference honorees; and 9% were selected as captains or co-captains in their senior years. That is, a high percentage of these African Americans were outstanding athletes. However, 20% of these African American athletes dropped off their teams during or after their initial seasons. Possible reasons could have included racist or discriminatory treatment and social isolation. As a sign of the changing face of basketball and types of African Americans who were recruited, by the 1979–1980 season, there were more African American basketball players on the All-Southeastern Conference teams than there were Caucasians (Paul, McGhee, & Fant, 1984).

The University of Mississippi was the last Southeastern Conference institution to integrate any of its athletics teams beginning in 1971. In 1972, the University of Georgia and University of Mississippi were the last SEC institutions to integrate their football teams, and Mississippi State University was the last Southeastern Conference institution to integrate its basketball team, which occurred in 1972 (Martin, 1993).

Perry Wallace of Vanderbilt University, the first African American to play basketball in the Southeastern Conference, was subjected to racial epithets and had objects hurled at him (Fitzpatrick, 1999). When the first African American basketball players competed on teams in the Atlantic Coast Conference, they, too, had to endure disparaging words and discriminatory treatment. Charlie Scott excelled despite such mistreatment (see sidebar).

Persistent Discrimination

Racial turmoil persisted on many predominantly Caucasian campuses during the 1960s and 1970s. Wiggins (1988) described specific incidents at the University of California, Berkeley, Syracuse University, and Oregon State University to illustrate conflicts between coaches, athletes, and their respective perceptions of fair treatment and authority. In 1968, Coach Rene Herrerias of the University of California dismissed the star center and only African American player, Bob Presley, from the basketball team for missing a practice. After Presley's reinstatement two days later, the 11 Caucasian players on the team claimed that the coach had been pressured to reinstate Presley. Immediately, 25 out of the 35 African American athletes at the university claimed that Herrerias, two football coaches, and the athletic department business manager should be dismissed because of their unwillingness to relate to African American athletes. Despite the racial conflicts,

---

CHARLIE SCOTT: Outstanding Player Despite the Snub

In 1966, Charlie Scott was the first African American to sign a scholarship offer in basketball at any of the Atlantic Coast Conference institutions located in the ex-Confederate states. While the state of North Carolina had a reputation as being progressive in race relations, in reality the University of North Carolina had not led in integrating its campus or athletic teams. Faced with the possibility of integrating its athletic teams, some pro-segregationist alumni expressed displeasure; the state media were not supportive either. To illustrate this, Scott was often subjected to racist comments as well as other indignities from Caucasian fans while playing in games outside of Chapel Hill.

In 1969, despite leading his team to a 27-5 record, the ACC Championship, and the NCAA semi-final game, five sportswriters failed to include Scott on their ballots for conference Player of the Year. Most writers in main- stream newspapers failed to address this snub or use stories written by them to address the significance of Scott's breaking the color barrier or his outstanding play.

While the African American press heaped praise on him and took issue with the abuses experienced by Scott and other African American athletes playing on predominantly Caucasian campuses, Caucasian sportswriters seemed to ignore the social significance of Scott's breakthrough. Scott, however, was deeply aware of the significance of his role as a racial pioneer. Throughout his college years, he had to deal with colliding pressures between winning basketball games with the best players regardless of color and retaining segregated teams, dealing with racist prejudices and treatment while maintaining an expected public image, and facilitating the acceptance of African Americans as societal equals (Kaliss, 2008).

and especially among players on the basketball team, the season was completed. Later that year, athletic director Pete Newell resigned as did Coach Herrerias.

In 1970, Syracuse University football coach Floyd (Ben) Schwartzwalder dismissed seven African American football players who boycotted spring practice because an African American assistant coach had not been hired. These athletes also alleged that African Americans were subjected to a double standard in discipline, Caucasian athletes were preferentially treated, African American athletes were not given adequate academic support, and coaches used racist language. Nothing was done to address these issues.

In February of 1969, Oregon State University football coach Dee Andros told African American Fred Milton to shave off his mustache. When he did not, the coach kicked him off the team and told him that his football scholarship would be honored only for the remainder of the academic year. Andros, like almost all college coaches at the time, opposed long hair and facial hair and resisted any challenges to their authority. The Black Student Union at Oregon State supported Milton. The other African American athletes were in a difficult position of having to turn their back on other African American students or risk losing playing time, their scholarships, and possible opportunities in professional sports. It was a quandary because most of these athletes had learned to be obedient to their coaches and respectful of their authority. Coach Andros came out of the situation unscathed and retained his popularity. Athletes were allowed in the future to wear facial hair during the off-season. Also, the first African American assistant football coach, Gene Hilliard, was hired to join the Oregon State staff.

Continued Covert Discrimination and Possibly Addressing It

Davis (1995) stated that racism exists whenever Caucasians believe and act as if they are superior to people of color. He emphasized that some Caucasians, including members of the electronic and print media, have stereotypically and prejudicially attributed the successes of African American athletes to innate physical skills, rather than to intellect and hard work. The latter two attributes have been most often reserved for Caucasian athletes.

Illustrations of the disparate treatment experienced by African Americans attending predominantly Caucasian institutions have included poor academic support, academic marginalization, harsh discipline, positional stacking based on speed, quickness, and jumping ability, quotas, and social segregation. Davis (1995) and others have stressed that African American athletes seldom sat on the bench, because they either played or were not on the team.

Some African American athletes attending predominantly Caucasian campuses have been exploited for his athletic abilities and then cast aside when they could no longer help win games. Academically they were shortchanged whenever coaches kept them eligible by getting them enrolled in courses that did not lead to degrees and did not provide them with needed academic support services. Many African American athletes failed to earn their degrees, felt isolated socially, and endured race-based indignities and discriminatory treatment.

Davis (1995) questioned whether African American athletes were objectified or viewed as commodities to serve the financial interests of primarily Caucasian institutions without a reciprocal commitment to their educational advancement. That is, African American athletes had kept their part of the contractual agreement through their performances; many institutions and athletics departments did not put the same resources into helping these athletes benefit from their educational opportunities. Davis also questioned whether African American athletes lacked a support structure to help them to deal with the challenges of an oftentimes hostile or racist social climate on and off campus.

A glimmer of hope that discriminatory treatment might be addressed and eliminated occurred in one conference. In 1972, the Big Ten Conference appointed an advisory committee to investigate the complaints of African American athletes and associated racial disturbances on several campuses. The report, entitled "The Status of Blacks in the Big Ten Athletic Conference: Issues and Concerns," made several recommendations that were immediately implemented. According to Wiggins (1991), counseling programs were set up at all member institutions to help athletes make progress toward their degrees. All athletes were given a fifth year of financial aid, if needed, to complete their degrees. Educational seminars were conducted to improve communication between Caucasian coaches and African American athletes. Lists were developed of qualified African American candidates for coaching, athletic training, officiating, and administrative positions. The first African American assistant commissioner was hired in 1974. These actions foreshadowed increased sensitivity toward African American athletes as administrators and coaches began to address the disparate treatment that pioneer African American athletes had endured on the campuses of predominantly Caucasian institutions.

Analysis of This Time Period

In an analysis of the time period between 1966 and 1979, African American athletes gained greater access to the top competitive levels in football, basketball, and track and field. Those who achieved All-American status in the first two sports and those who were victorious in collegiate competition or the Olympics were examined to illustrate how, despite having to deal with racial indignities, many African American athletes excelled.

Between 1966 and 1979, there were almost 50 African Americans selected as All-Americans at the highest competitive level in college football. Of this number, seven won the Heisman Trophy: O. J. Simpson of the University of Southern California (1968); Johnny Rodgers of the University of Nebraska (1972); Archie Griffin of Ohio State University (1974–1975); Tony Dorsett of the University of Pittsburgh (1976); Earl Campbell of the University of Texas (1977); Billy Sims of the University of Oklahoma (1978); and Charles White of the University of Southern California (1979). Two items seem noteworthy about these years and players. First, a major breakthrough occurred in the decade of the 1970s as seven out of 10 of the recipients were African Americans. Second, in what could be classified as a continuation of stacking, each of these honorees played running back.

During these 14 years, an African American male was selected as Player of the Year in basketball in all but three years. These outstanding players included Cazzie Russell of the University of Michigan (1966), Lew Alcindor of the University of California at Los Angeles (1967 and 1969), Elvin Hayes of the University of Houston (1968), Austin Carr of the University of Notre Dame (1971), David Thompson of North Carolina State University (1974–1975), Scott May of Indiana University (1976), Marques Johnson of the University of California at Los Angeles (1977) and (co-recipients) Phil Ford of the University of North Carolina and Butch Lee of Marquette University (1978). Numerous African Americans earned All-American honors in basketball at traditionally Caucasian institutions during these years. Examples of these included Dave Bing of Syracuse University, Wes Unseld of the University of Louisville, Jo Jo White of the University of Kansas, Sidney Wicks of the University of California at Los Angeles, Robert McAdoo of the University of North Carolina, and Earvin Johnson of Michigan State University.

During these years, African American males were well represented on the United States' Olympic basketball teams. In 1968, there were five on the gold-medal winning team; in 1972, there were six; in 1976, there were eight on the gold-medal winning team. In the first appearance of women's basketball in the Olympic Games in 1976, Lusia Harris of Delta State University and Charlotte Lewis of Illinois State University helped the team win a silver medal.

Most of the African Americans who competed in the Olympic Games also won collegiate titles in track and field while attending the institutions listed. The 1968 gold medalists in track and field included: Jimmy Hines of Texas Southern University in the 100-meters; Tommie Smith of San Jose State University in the 200-meters; Hines, Melvin Pender, Jr., and Charles Greene of the University of Nebraska in the 4 × 100-meter relay; Bob Beamon of the University of Texas at El Paso in the long jump; Lee Evans of San Jose State University in the 400-meters; Larry James of Villanova University and Vincent Matthews in the 4 × 400-meter relay; and Willie Davenport of Southern University in the 110-meter hurdles. Rod Milburn of Southern University in the 110-meter hurdles, Vincent Matthews in the 200-meters, and Larry Black of North Carolina Central University in the 4 × 100-meter relay were the only African American males in track and field to win Olympic gold medals in 1972. Arnie Robinson of San Diego State University in the long jump, Edwin Moses of Morehouse College in the 400-meter hurdles, and Herman Frazier in the 4 × 400-meter relay were the only African American males to win Olympic gold medals in track and field in 1976.

There were only a small number of African American female gold medalists in track and field during this time due to limited opportunities for college women to compete in sports. Wyomia Tyus of Tennessee State University won the 100-meters in 1968, as she had in 1964. Also in 1968, Tyus and Barbara Ferrell of California State University at Los Angeles helped win a gold medal in the 4 × 100-meter relay, and Madeline Manning of Tennessee State University won the 800-meters. No African American females won gold medals in track and field in 1972 or 1976.

1980s TO PRESENT

Academic Exploitation

In the most recent decades, African American athletes have expressed less concern about discrimination in housing, social isolation, or racist treatment by teammates, opponents, and coaches. While overt bigotry was almost eliminated by the beginning of the 21st century, covert discrimination has continued to plague sports and society. A persistent issue has been academic exploitation. This problem occurred whenever African American athletes were encouraged to focus primarily on developing their athletic skills and playing their sports to the detriment of their academic work.

The NCAA has been criticized for what many have classified as lax academic standards for athletes, which allowed them to do the minimum to maintain eligibility, rather than being serious students seeking to learn and earn degrees. In response, with an implementation date in 1986, the NCAA passed a regulation that based the eligibility of a prospective athlete for receiving an athletic scholarship on having achieved a high school grade point average of at least 2.0 in a college-preparatory core curriculum and attained a minimum score on a standardized admissions test. Some African Americans believed that this rule, which came to be known as Proposition 48, discriminated against minorities because standardized tests were culturally biased. Possibly to diffuse this outcry, the NCAA changed this rule in 1983 (i.e., prior to this rule becoming effective in 1986) to allow an athlete to receive an athletic scholarship while attending an institution, but he or she was not permitted to play or practice during the first year. This partial qualifier, assuming the required grades in the first year of college courses were earned, had three years of varsity eligibility remaining.

Effective in August of 1990, Proposition 42 eliminated the partial qualifier loophole. That is, incoming freshmen had to meet all the requirements of Proposition 48. If a prospective athlete failed to meet this standard, he or she was not eligible for an athletic scholarship at a NCAA institution. Another firestorm erupted as African American coaches like John Thompson of Georgetown University and John Chaney of Temple University claimed this rule discriminated against African Americans who had attended inadequately funded urban schools or had been disadvantaged educationally. In 2003, the NCAA in an attempt to eliminate the perceived prejudice implemented a sliding scale that allowed a higher grade point average to offset a lower score on a standardized test, or vice versa.

The NCAA also has been criticized for its failure to enact rules to emphasize academics over athletics, because it was perceived that some athletes were being exploited to help win games and earn revenues for institutions. These accusations were especially directed at football and basketball, two sports with a high African American presence. The NCAA enacted several requirements associated with athletes making progress toward earning their degrees. For example, after the first year in college, athletes had to have completed 24 credit hours and achieved at least 90% of the grade point average required for graduation. These credit hours and minimum grades increased incrementally each successive year.

Because many athletes, and a disproportionally higher number of African Americans, had failed to graduate, in 2004 the NCAA initiated the Academic Progress Rate (APR) at the highest competitive level. This new rule has resulted in institutions facing sanctions if athletes on these teams failed academically. The APR and other data have revealed a wide gap between the graduation rates of African American and Caucasian athletes who play football and basketball (Lapchick, 2006; Lapchick, 2008a). So, despite numerous academic reforms, some African American athletes continue to feel that they are being exploited. This occurs when their eligibility to compete in their sports has been exhausted, their dreams of playing professionally have been dashed, and they remain dozens of credit hours away from earning a degree.

The Recognition of African American Athletes in Football, Basketball, and Track & Field

The Heisman Trophy honors the outstanding college football player annually. Of the 74 recipients since 1935, 27 have been African Americans (Archie Griffin was counted twice). By decades, there were three African Americans in the 1960s, seven in the 1970s, eight in the 1980s, seven in the 1990s, and two between 2000 and 2008. Twenty-one of the African American Heisman Trophy winners (78%) excelled as running backs. Out of the 47 Caucasians, 24 were quarterbacks; two of the African Americans played this position. An analysis of the recipients of the Heisman Trophy suggests these conclusions: (1) African American football players were denied opportunities to compete at the highest competitive level between 1935 and 1960 or were deemed undeserving of this recognition; (2) an African American who plays running back has a much greater chance of being selected for this honor; and (3) during the 1970s through 1990s, the best college football player was most likely an African American.

Since 1942, the *Sporting News* has selected a college football Player of the Year. Since 1967, the Walter Camp Award has honored the outstanding college football player, as has the Maxwell Award since 1937. The Associated Press began selecting its Player of the

Year in 1988. Of the recipients of this recognition by one of these four, there have been 32 African Americans honored; plus, O.J. Simpson of the University of Southern California and Archie Griffin of Ohio State University were each named in consecutive years. Over 62% of the African American recipients of at least one of the Player of the Year recognitions played running back. In analyzing the number of African American recipients by decade, in the 1970s, eight were honored; in the 1980s, nine were honored, including two different African Americans in one year; in the 1990s, eight were honored; between 2000 and 2008, six have been honored, including two each in two years. However, it should be noted that between 2000 and 2008, two African American quarterbacks have been honored, signaling a significant change from past practices of stacking.

In 1951, an inaugural class of 54 legends, including the first African American inductee, Fred (Duke) Slater of the University of Iowa, was inducted into the College Football Hall of Fame. Through 2008, there have been 959 players and coaches from all divisions of the NCAA and the NAIA enshrined in the College Football Hall of Fame. This number has included 130 African American players and 10 African American coaches.

Since 1966, the Associated Press has selected a male college basketball Player of the Year. Since 1969, the Naismith College Player of the Year has been named for males and since 1983 for females. The Wooden Award has been given since 1977 for men and 2004 for women to the outstanding college basketball player. African American males have been selected for one or more of these awards over 81% of the years during these 43 years. For females, in addition to the Naismith and Wooden award, the Wade Trophy since 1981 has recognized the best women's basketball player in college. In analyzing who has received these three awards, African American females have received at least one in all but five years through 2008. African American male and female basketball players dominate this game at the highest level of play as illustrated by these recognitions.

Since 1930, the AAU has presented the Sullivan Award to the outstanding amateur athlete in the United States who has demonstrated leadership, character, sportsmanship, and the ideals of amateurism. Of the 87 recipients through 2008, 12 (or less than 14%) have been African American athletes. It is noteworthy that 10 of these recipients competed in track and field (83%). These recipients have included the following: Mal Whitfield of Ohio State University (1954); Harrison Dillard of Baldwin-Wallace College (1955); Rafer Johnson of the University of California at Los Angeles (1960); Wilma Rudolph of Tennessee State University (1961); Carl Lewis of the University of Houston (1981); Edwin Moses of Morehouse College (1983); Jackie Joyner-Kersee of the University of California at Los Angeles (1986); Florence Griffin-Joyner of California State University at Northridge (1988); Mike Powell of the University of California at Los Angeles (1991); and Michael Johnson of Baylor University (1996). The other two honorees excelled in basketball and football (Charlie Ward of Florida State University in 1993) and basketball (Chamique Holdsclaw of the University of Tennessee in 1998). No African American athlete other than in these three sports has received this award. By comparison, Caucasian recipients of this award have excelled in 13 different sports. This seems to suggest that African Americans may have self-selected into these sports, possibly because of opportunities and role models; or, it may indicate limited opportunities to excel in other sports due to socio-economic factors.

At the NCAA Division I level in 2005–2006, 25% of the male athletes were African Americans, while 45% of the football players and 59% of the basketball players were African Americans. Of the females athletes at the NCAA Division I level in 2005–2006, 15% were African Americans, while 45% of the basketball players and 23% of the track and field/cross country athletes were African Americans. These data seem to reinforce that a disproportionate number (compared to their percentage of the population in the United States) of African American males and females choose to compete on football, basketball, and track and field teams. These data affirm that a relatively small number of African American athletes compete on college teams in other sports. This may be due to the lack of role models, socio-economic factors limiting their access to coaching and facilities, or racial discrimination. Most African American athletes choose sports without these barriers, and especially those publically funded in schools. Also, many African American athletes continue to chase an unrealistic dream of playing professional football and basketball and capitalizing on their talents financially in track and field.

In 2005–2006, 6% of the head football coaches and 25% of the head basketball coaches for male athletes were African Americans. For female athletes, 12% of the head basketball coaches and 15% of the track and field/cross country head coaches were African Americans (Lapchick, 2008b). Some members of the Black Coaches & Administrators (BCA) have claimed that inequities and subordination have persisted because few African Americans have been hired as coaches in these sports.

College sports in the 21st century continue to be governed and coached primarily by Caucasian males. Historically and prejudicially, African Americans were perceived as incapable of effectively leading athletics departments and coaching football, basketball, and track and field teams. This resulted in the exclusion, or token representation, of African Americans in administrative offices and the coaching ranks. For example, while the majority of football and basketball players are African Americans, the number of African American head coaches, assistant coaches, and other members of coaching staffs lag far behind. Athletics directors and their associate and assistant directors, academic support staff members, athletic trainers, and other personnel in athletics departments on college campuses remain primarily Caucasian and male. That only a comparative few minorities have been hired further verifies that color and ethnicity remain barriers for hiring the best qualified candidates and continuation of an old (white) boys' network when dealing with job openings and career advancement.

Many African Americans excel in football, basketball, and track and field because they have dedicated significant time and effort to developing their skills. One reason may be that sports provide the quickest path to prestige, wealth, and upward mobility. Also, there are role models of highly successful African Americans in professional sports. Because segregation has ended, most prejudices have been eliminated, and opportunities have been opened to all, African American athletes have demonstrated their athletic prowess. Still, sport, like society, must continue to be vigilant to ensure that equality of opportunity rewards merit and achievement. African Americans athletes deserve to be treated with the dignity and honor that racism in college sports too long denied them.

STUDY QUESTIONS

1. Why were some African Americans allowed to play football, basketball, and track and field at predominantly Caucasian institutions when most were not?

2. What are five specific examples of the racial indignities that African American athletes had to ensure?

3. For each individual described in a sidebar, identify two types of racial discrimination they had to endure and how each individual was able to overcome disparate and excel in their sports.

4. How have or have not African American athletes been academically exploited?

SUGGESTED READINGS

Baker, W. J. (1986). *Jesse Owens: An American life*. New York, NY: Free Press.

Cahn, S. K. (1994). *Coming on strong: Gender and sexuality in twentieth-century women's sport*. New York, NY: Free Press.

Carroll, J. M. (1992). *Fritz Pollard: Pioneer in racial advancement*. Urbana, IL: University of Illinois Press.

Chalk, O. (1976). *Black college sport*. New York, NY: Dodd, Mead.

Edwards, H. (1969). *The revolt of the Black athlete*. New York, NY: Free Press.

George, N. (1992). *Elevating the game: The history and aesthetics of Black men in basketball*. New York, NY: Simon and Schuster.

Gilliam, D. B. (1976). *Paul Robeson: All-American*. Washington, DC: New Republic Book Company.

Pennington, R. (1987). *Breaking the ice: The racial integration of Southwest Conference football*. Jefferson, NC: McFarland.

Roberts, R., & Olson, J. S. (1989). *Winning is the only thing: Sports in America since 1945*. Baltimore, MD: Johns Hopkins University Press.

Robinson, J., & Duckett, A. (1972). *I never had it made*. New York, NY: Putnam.

Rudolph, W. (1977). *Wilma*. New York, NY: New American Library.

Shropshire, K. L. (1996). *In black and white: Race and sports in America*. New York, NY: New York University Press.

Wiggins, D. K. (1997). *Glory bound: Black athletes in a white America*. Syracuse, NY: Syracuse University Press.

Wiggins, D. K., & Miller, P. B. (Eds.). (2003). *The unlevel playing field: A documentary history of the African American experience in sport*. Urbana, IL: University of Illinois Press.

Young, A. S. (1963). *Negro firsts in sports*. Chicago, IL: Johnson Publishing Company.

REFERENCES

Ashe, A. R. Jr. (1988). *A hard road to glory: A history of the African-American athlete*. New York, NY: Warner Books.

Ashe, A. R. Jr. (1993). *A hard road to glory: A history of the African-American athlete, 1919–1945 Vol.2.*, New York, NY: Warner Books.

Ashe, A. R. Jr. (1993). *A hard road to glory: A history of the African-American athlete since 1946*. New York, NY: Warner Books.

Bond, G. (2006). The strange career of William Henry Lewis. In D. K. Wiggins (Ed.), *Out of the shadows: A biographical history of African American athletes* (pp. 38–57). Fayetteville, AR: University of Arkansas Press.

Captain, G. (1991). Enter ladies and gentlemen of color: Gender, sport, and the ideal of African American manhood and womanhood during the late nineteenth and early twentieth centuries. *Journal of Sport History, 18*, 81–102.

Davis, T. (1995). The myth of the superspade: The persistence of racism in college athletics. *Fordham Urban Law Journal, 22*, 615–698.

Dyreson, M. (2006). Jesse Owens: The leading man in modern American tales of racial progress and limits. In D. K. Wiggins (Ed.), *Out of the shadows: A biographical history of African American athletes* (pp. 110–131). Fayetteville, AR: University of Arkansas Press.

Fitzpatrick, F. (1999). *And the walls came tumbling down: Kentucky, Texas Western, and the game that changed American sports*. New York, NY: Simon and Schuster.

Gissendanner, C. H. (1996). African American women Olympians: The impact of race, gender, and class ideologies, 1932–1968. *Research Quarterly for Exercise and Sport, 67*, 172–182.

Graham, T., & Cody, R. (2006). *Getting open: The unknown story of Bill Garrett and the integration of college basketball*. New York, NY: Atria Books.

Hoose, P. M. (1989). *Necessities: Racial barriers in American sports*. New York, NY: Random House.

Katz, M. S. (2007). *Breaking through: John B. McLendon,*

basketball legend and civil rights pioneer. Fayetteville, AR: University of Arkansas Press.

Kaliss, G. J. (2008). Un-civil discourse: Charlie Scott, the integration of college of basketball, and the "progressive mystique." *Journal of Sport History, 35*, 98–117.

Kish, F. B. (1998). *The role of the university president in the governance of intercollegiate athletics: A comparative case study of chancellors Strong and Budig at the University of Kansas*. Unpublished doctoral dissertation. University of Kansas, Lawrence, KS.

Lansbury, J. H. (2006). Alice Coachman: Quiet champion of the 1940s. In D. K. Wiggins (Ed.), *Out of the shadows: A biographical history of African American athletes* (pp.146–161). Fayetteville, AR: University of Arkansas Press.

Lapchick, R. (2006). Keeping score when it counts: Assessing the 2007–08 bowl-bound college football teams-academic performance improves but race still matters. Retrieved from http://www.tidesport.org/Grad%20Rates/2007-08%20Bowl_APR_GSR_Study.pdf

Lapchick, R. (2008a). Keeping score when it counts: Graduation rates for 2008 NCAA men's division I basketball tournament teams. Retrieved from http://www.bus.ucf.edu/sport/public/downloads/2008_Mens_Basketball_Tournament_PR.pdf

Lapchick, R. (2008b). The 2006–07 racial and gender report card: College sport. Retrieved from http://www.bus.ucf.edu/sport/public/downloads/2006-07_CollegeSportRGRC_PR.pdf

Martin, C. H. (1993). Jim Crow in the gymnasium: The integration of college basketball in the American south. *The International Journal of the History of Sport, 10*, 68–86.

Miller, P. B. (1995). To "bring the race along rapidly":

Sport, student culture, and educational mission at historically Black colleges during the interwar years. *History of Education Quarterly, 35*, 111–133.

Moore, K. (1991). A courageous stand. *Sports Illustrated, 75*(6), 60–66; 68–70; 72; 75.

National Track and Field Hall of Fame (2009). Retrieved from http://www.usatf.org/HallOfFame/TF/

Olsen, J. (1968). In an alien world. *Sports Illustrated, 29*(3), 28–36; 41–43.

Paul, J., McGhee, R. V., & Fant, H. (1984). The arrival and ascendence of Black athletes in the Southeastern Conference, 1966–1980. *Phylon, 45*, 284–297.

Sailes, G. (1991). The myth of Black sports supremacy. *Journal of Black Studies, 21*, 480–487.

Spivey, D. (1983). The Black athlete in big-time college sports, 1941–1968. *Phylon, 44*, 116–125.

Spivey, D. (1988). 'End Jim Crow in sports': The protest at New York University, 1940–1941. *Journal of Sport History, 15*, 282–303.

Wiggins, D. K. (1988). "The future of college athletics is at stake": Black athletes and racial turmoil on three predominantly white university campuses, 1968–1972. *Journal of Sport History, 15*, 304–333.

Wiggins, D. K. (1991). Prized performers, but frequently overlooked students: The involvement of Black athletes in college sports on predominantly white university campuses, 1890–1972. *Research Quarterly for Exercise and Sport, 62*, 164–177.

Wiggins, D. K. (Ed.). (2004). *African Americans in sports. Vols. 1 and 2*. Armonk, NY: Sharpe Reference.

Wilson, W. (2006). Wilma Rudolph: The making of an Olympic icon. In D. K. Wiggins (Ed.), *Out of the shadows: A biographical history of African American athletes* (pp. 206–221). Fayetteville, AR: University of Arkansas Press.

CHAPTER 2

Historically Black Colleges and Universities' Athletes and Sport Programs: Historical Overview, Evaluations, and Affiliations

SAMUEL R. HODGE, ROBERT A. BENNETT III, and FRANKIE G. COLLINS

Abstract

Historically Black colleges and universities (HBCUs) have long provided hallowed grounds for academic, social, and athletic expression of Black and other students and athletes. In the 2008–09 academic year, nearly 15,000 student-athletes participated in intercollegiate athletics for HBCUs (US Department of Education, 2010). But the extant literature is sparse on athletic programs and the sporting experiences of student-athletes at these historic institutions. In this chapter, our primary focus is on sports at America's HBCUs owing to historical and current events. First, we discuss the rise of athletics at Black colleges and universities. Second, the authors of this chapter discuss the participation of student-athletes and current status of athletics at HBCUs.

Key Terms	
• colored intercollegiate athletic association (CIAA)	• National Collegiate Athletic Association (NCAA)
• historically Black colleges and universities (HBCUs)	• predominantly White institutions of higher education (PW-IHE)
• intercollegiate athletics	• Southern Intercollegiate Athletic Conference
• Mid-Eastern Athletic Conference (MEAC)	• Southwestern Athletic Conference (SWAC)
• National Association of Intercollegiate Athletics (NAIA)	• student-athlete

INTRODUCTION

The National Center for Education Statistics (NCES) reported that in fall 2007 there were 18,248,128 students enrolled in the United States; 4,339 public and private two- and four-year degree-granting[1] colleges and universities. Of these, 64% were White, 13% Black[2], 11% Hispanic, 7% Asian/Pacific Islander, 1% Native American[3], and 3% international[4] students (Planty et al., 2009). Further some 52% of White students attended predominantly White colleges and universities where more than 75% of the enrollment was White. In comparison, about 13% of Black students attended colleges and universities where they constituted 75% or more of the enrollment. Many of these institutions were historically Black colleges and universities (HBCU). In fall 2006, about 11% of Black students in the US attended an HBCU (Planty et al., 2009; Snyder, Dillow, & Hoffman, 2009).

The Higher Education Act of 1965 defines HBCUs as institutions of higher education established before 1964 whose principal mission was then, and remains today, the education of Black Americans (Wilson, 2008). It is estimated that in fall 2006, there were 310,446 students enrolled at HBCUs across 21 states, the District of Columbia, and the US Virgin Islands. Of those students, 255,782 (82.4%) were Black. Of which, 159,377 were Black women (62%) and 96,405 were Black men (38%). Of the 103 accredited[5] HBCUs identified, there were 49 (47.6%) four-year private institutions, 41 (39.8%) four-year public institutions, 11 two-year public (10.7%), and only 2 (1.9%) two-year private HBCUs. Of these HBCUs, 93 had athletic programs. The enrollment at those HBCUs was 296,242 total students; Most of those students (N = 251,290, 84.8%) were identified as Black. Annually, thousands of these students participate in sports. In fact, a reported 14,928 student-athletes were members of intercollegiate athletic teams at HBCUs in 2008–2009 (U.S. Department of Education, 2010).

HBCUs have long provided hallowed grounds for academic, social, and athletic expression of Black and other students and athletes. But, the extant literature is sparse on athletic programs and the sporting experiences of student-athletes at these institutions. In this chapter, our primary focus is on sports at America's HBCUs owing to historical and current events. First, we discuss the rise of athletics at Black colleges and universities. Second, we discuss the participation of student-athletes at these institutions. Then, we discuss the current status of athletics at HBCUs.

HBCUS AND THE RISE OF ATHLETICS

In the 19th century, HBCUs were founded as institutions of higher education for Black citizens to combat the legal segregation that permeated much of the American society (Ayers, 1992; Shaw, 1996). Numerous Christian denominations including Baptist, Colored Methodist Episcopal (now Christian Methodist Episcopal, better known as CME), and the African Methodist Episcopal created private schools to instruct newly emancipated (from slavery) Blacks in industrial and traditional classical training consisting of reading, writing, philosophy, history, and Greek and Latin languages. The former, supported by many White citizens as a means of keeping Black Americans in a position of subordination, equipped Black students in the areas of agriculture, industry, technical skills, and religious and teacher training. The latter mirrored the curriculum of many predominantly White institutions of higher education (PW-IHE).

Although most HBCUs were founded after the Civil War, there were three established before the 1860s, these were the Institute for Colored Youth in 1830 (now Cheyney University of Pennsylvania), Ashmun Institute in 1854 (now Lincoln University; PA), and

Wilberforce University (OH) in 1856. On August 30, 1890, Congress passed the second Morrill Act and it required states with segregated systems of higher education (all-White and *colored*) to provide land-grant institutions for both systems (Provasnik & Shafer, 2004). This act led to the establishment of land-grant HBCUs for the teaching of the agricultural and mechanical arts to Black citizens (Craig, 1992; Wallenstein, 1992). Today, HBCUs are mostly four-year private and public liberal arts colleges and universities as well as two- and four-year community colleges, and various business, law, medical, theological, and technical institutions. There are more than 100 HBCUs with some 90% of them located in the southern region of the US (Bauchum, 2001; Jackson, 2001). In examining the history of these institutions, it is clear that they not only served as places of educational fulfillment, but also HBCUs were the most accepting places whereby Black students could participate in athletics at the collegiate level.

Progressively since 1912, most HBCUs with athletic programs competed as members within one of the major athletic conferences originally created specifically for them. Founded in 1912, the Colored Intercollegiate Athletic Association (CIAA) is often credited as the first historically Black athletic association established. However, it is believed that the Georgia-Carolina Athletic Association was established in 1910 with the following member institutions: Allen University, Haines Institute[6], Morris College, Paine College, Savannah State University (then Georgia State Industrial), and Walker Baptist Institute[7], and a couple preparatory schools ("Pinson re-elected head," 1926; Saylor, 2000). During this era, mostly all HBCUs maintained both a preparatory school and a college department and some had elementary schools as well (Chalk, 1976). It was not until two years later in 1912 that the CIAA was established.

In 1913, the Southeastern Intercollegiate Athletic Conference (now Southern Intercollegiate Athletic Conference) was established. In 1920, the Southwestern Athletic Conference (SWAC) was founded by leaders from six HBCUs in Texas. The SWAC represents another major Black athletic conference. Now the conference has member institutions in Alabama, Arkansas, Louisiana, Mississippi, and Texas. Founded in 1970, the Mid-Eastern Athletic Conference (MEAC) began athletic play in 1971 and marks the establishment of a fourth major historically Black conference. True to their mission of serving Black citizens, HBCUs have long provided a medium for academic and athletic expression. A brief chronology of historic events associated with sports and Black colleges and universities are presented in Appendix A.

Early Formation of Sports

Athletic programs at HBCUs were originally organized late into the 19th century and fielded teams in a variety of popular sports such as baseball, basketball, football, and track and field (Miller, 1995). Baseball and football were the prominent sports amongst HBCUs during the early years of their formation. In 1890, the first recorded baseball game between two HBCUs occurred between Morehouse College and the Atlanta University (Appendix A). In 1896, Morehouse College and Atlanta University, along with neighboring colleges, Clark College and Morris Brown College, officially formed the first Black college baseball league. Despite the bleak racial climate typifying the US in the latter part of the 19th century, there were rare instances where White schools played their Black counterparts. In 1898, Howard University (an HBCU) played the Yale Law School (White) baseball team. The first intercollegiate track meet amongst HBCUs was organized in the Atlanta University Center in 1907.

In 1891, James Naismith invented the game of basketball at the YMCA Training School (now Springfield College) in Springfield, Massachusetts. In 1904, Edwin B. Henderson

Members of the Morris Brown College baseball team pose for a photo in the early 20th century. Courtesy of Library of Congress Prints and Photographs Division

was exposed to basketball techniques at the Harvard Summer School of Physical Education, and he taught the game to students at Howard University later that fall. He also introduced the game to the Black community in Washington, DC, where it quickly gained in popularity (Wiggins, 1999). By 1910, basketball had emerged at Black colleges with Howard University and Hampton Institute fielding teams (Hine, Hine, & Harold, 2008). Its popularity remains strong still today at HBCUs.

For some 70 years between 1892–1964, "there were football playing colleges which had only Black students and which, with very rare exceptions, played only teams comprised of Black players" (Saylor, 2000, p. 4). On December 27, 1892, the first intercollegiate football game between HBCUs took place with Biddle College (now Johnson C. Smith University) beating Livingstone College. A year later in 1893, Howard University played football against the Washington, D.C. YMCA. The next year, Atlanta University defeated Tuskegee Institute and Lincoln (PA) was triumph over Howard in these early football contests (Saylor, 2000).

Organizational structure was first brought to Black college sports in 1910 with the formation of the Georgia-Carolina Athletic Association and soon after with the founding of the Colored Intercollegiate Athletic Association in 1912; as these were the first Black collegiate sport associations (Saylor, 2000; Wiggins, 2007). Later the Great Migration of the 1920s was typified by many Blacks leaving the South and moving to Northern and Western states and this did much to expand Black college sports across these regions. For example, witnessed by an estimated 10,000 spectators, Hampton Institute played football against Lincoln University (PA) in 1929 at the Polo Grounds, which was the home of the NY Giants and the NY Metropolitans (Hurd, 1993; Jeffries, 2001; Hine et al., 2008). During this time, HBCUs would regularly schedule games in northern cities playing before

thousands. There were a number of annual football rivalries developed between HBCUs throughout the 1920s, for example, Lincoln (PA) played Howard University in annual Thanksgiving Day football games (Wiggins & Miller, 2003).

From 1890 to 1940, many Black citizens experienced racism perpetrated by Whites through harsh or even unlawful imprisonment, threats and acts of lynching (mostly Black men), and other forms of intimidation and brutality. Despite, or as relief from, the terrorism of racism and White hegemony in the US, athletics thrived at HBCUs. By the 1920s, mostly all HBCUs sponsored athletic teams in baseball, bas-

Howard University is one of the most famous HBCUs. Courtesy of Carol M. Highsmith, Library of Congress Prints and Photographs Division

ketball, football, and track and field (Miller, 1995). In the 1940s segregation continued to prevent interracial athletic events in the South. But in 1944, a debate ensued between students about whether Duke University (a PW-IHE) or a local HBCU, the North Carolina College for Negroes (now North Carolina Central University) had the best college basketball team. A challenge was made by both squads to play. This event became known as the "Secret Game" and played in a clandestine manner as no one was allowed to view the game for fear of repercussion from local authorities and the public. In the end, the North Carolina

In 1936, the West Virginia State College football team was the national Negro collegiate champions. Courtesy of West Virginia State University Archives

HBCU led by Coach John B. McLendon was victorious, and a special relationship was created amongst the two teams (McLendon & Bryant, 2000). It was not until 1953 that a predominantly White collegiate athletic association, the National Association of Intercollegiate Athletics, voted to admit HBCUs as members (Saylor, 2000).

The US Supreme Court's ruling in the *Brown v. Board of Education* case in 1954 (hereafter called *Brown*) opened the doors to desegregating public schools. However, it was more than 10 years later in 1965 that the National Collegiate Athletic Association (NCAA) accepted HBCUs as member institutions into the association. Slowly, PW-IHE began to allow Black student-athletes onto their sport teams in the late 1960s, and more so in the 1970s, mostly due to a desire to create winning teams and increase revenue as opposed to moral or altruistic motives (Hodge, Harrison, Burden, & Dixson, 2008b). Hunt (1996) argued that in the mid-1970s when some of the major PW-IHE began recruiting Black student-athletes, HBCUs were "stripped of the best talent" (p. XII). For example, the University of Alabama's Coach Paul "Bear" Bryant and the University of Kentucky's Adolph Rupp, both legendary coaches, reluctantly recruited Black athletes to their respective football and basketball teams in the early 1970s. This exemplified many White coaches' hesitancy to integrate their teams, particularly in the South, and has been called the "Bear Bryant/Adolph Rupp epiphany" (Ladson-Billings, 2004, p. 10). In 1966, the University of Texas–El Paso started five Black basketball players against Adolph Rupp's all-White University of Kentucky team in the NCAA's championship game, which Texas–El Paso won. On September 17, 1970, Sam "Bam" Cunningham, a Black player on the University of Southern California's football team, scored three touchdowns against Bear Bryant's all-White University of Alabama defense in winning the game. Black collegiate athletes excelling on the playing field arguably lead to more White coaches experiencing an awakening that constructing winning teams meant the integration of Black players.

In that context as Black athletes were allowed and eventually recruited to participate in sports at majority White institutions, the underfunded HBCUs were disadvantaged and unable to recruit many of the top athletes to their athletic programs. One consequence of this drain of elite athletes is that fewer athletes have been drafted into professional sports in the last three decades from HBCUs. For example, between 1967 and 1976 National Football League teams drafted 443 players from HBCUs. During the next 20 years 291 were drafted (34% fewer) from HBCUs as more and more elite Black athletes elected to play for PW-IHE while in contrast hundreds of Black athletes were taken from majority White schools (Jones, 2007). Both the beneficial and controversial effects of integration can be seen today in the number of Black student-athletes on teams for majority White colleges and universities that have not always welcomed them.

Student-Athletes and Coaches at Historically Black Institutions

Since the early 1900s, student-athletes at HBCUs have demonstrated courage and skilled athletic performances while at these institutions and beyond. Between 1916 and 1947, for example, Tuskegee University (then Institute) men's teams won four Southern Intercollegiate Athletic Conference track and field championships. The first African American to win the singles title in tennis at the Wimbledon Championships was Althea Gibson whom achieved the feat in 1957. Gibson was a graduate of Florida A&M University. In fact, a number of Black student-athletes who participate in sports at HBCUs have gone on to successful professional careers (Hunt, 1996; Wiggins & Miller, 2003). Many Black men who were student-athletes at HBCUs have excelled in professional sports. For example, Doug Williams played quarterback at Grambling State University from 1973 to 1977 under Coach Eddie Robinson. In 1978, he was drafted by the Tampa Bay Buccaneers of the National Football League (NFL). He later had a stint in the United States Football League (USFL), which gained him attention from the NFL's Washington Redskins in 1986. In 1988, Williams would lead the team to a win in Super Bowl XXII, was named the game's MVP, and became the first Black quarterback to accomplish both of these feats. Walter Payton, considered one of the greatest running backs in the history of the NFL, was a graduate of Jackson State University, and Jerry Rice, considered by many the greatest receiver to play in the NFL, was a graduate of Mississippi Valley State University. Michael Strahan, the NFL's record-holder for the most quarterback sacks in a single season, was a graduate of Texas Southern University, and Grady Jackson, an alumnus of Knoxville College, played defensive tackle in the NFL, just to name a few examples.

Although Black men from PW-IHE participated in international athletic events, early on Black men who participated in sports at HBCUs were rarely included on the world stage of the Olympic Games. Chalk (1976) wrote that in 1935 the authorities of the Amateur Athletic Union (AAU), "under whose auspices the Olympic trials were conducted, were told that Negroes could not compete in the annual meet that was scheduled for New Orleans" (p. 319). Further, Chalk explained that throughout the 1920s, Black track athletes who had national recognition were those at PW-IHE but not so for those at HBCUs. In contrast, Black women who participated in the Olympic Games typically came from HBCUs rather than PW-IHE (Wiggins, 2007). Wiggins (2007) spoke to this paradoxical phenomenon:

> Ironically, African American female athletes who participated in the Olympic Games often came from Black colleges rather than predominantly White universities. The first wave of African American women Olympians, including high jumper Alice Coachman, the first African American woman to capture an Olympic gold medal, had been members at various times of Cleveland Abbott's great track teams at Tuskegee institute. The next outstanding group of African American women Olympians, including such great athletes as Wilma Rudolph, Barbara Jones, Martha Hudson, and Lucinda Williams, were products of Edward Temple's famous Tigerbelles track teams from Tennessee State University. (p. 30)

It has been argued that the dominant presence of Black women Olympians was due mostly to their training regimens and because they were accepted as *athletes* in Black communities more so than White women who were not as well accepted as athletes in their communities (Cahn, 1994; Fields, 2008; Wiggins, 2007). In the last four decades, the Olympics have seen the impact of male student-athletes from HBCUs as well. For example, Edwin Moses, a graduate of Morehouse College, was a two-time gold medal winner in the 400m hurdles in 1976 and 1984.

The late legendary Coach Eddie Robinson once led all football coaches in the NCAA in wins when he retired in 1997 with a record of 408 wins, 165 losses, and 15 ties all with Grambling State University where he coached for more than 50 seasons. While there he won eight Black college football championships, and 17 SWAC championships. From Coach Robinson's tutelage, over 200 men went on to play in the NFL. Paul Younger, a graduate of Grambling State University, became the first player from a HBCU to play for an NFL team in 1949, when he signed with the Los Angeles Rams. In 2003, Coach Robinson's record for all-time wins was surpassed by John Gagliardi, the head coach of Division III St. John's in Minnesota (Dufresne, 2007).

An alumnus of Knoxville College (TN), Alonzo "Jake" Gaither became a legendary football coach at Florida A&M University. Over a 25 year period (1945–1969), Coach Gaither won some 85% of his games and coached such NFL talents as Bob Hayes and Willie Galimore (Knoxville College, 2008).

Two prominent HBCU basketball coaches were Clarence "Big House" Gaines, Sr., and Ben Jobe. Coach Gaines, a graduate of Morgan State University, got his coaching experience at Winston Salem Teachers College (now Winston-Salem State University) where he started in 1946 serving as the head basketball and football coach, and athletic director for the first four years. After hiring a full-time coach for the university's football program, Coach Gaines remained as the head basketball coach and athletic director. Coach Gaines held these positions for 47 years. Two of his most prominent players were Cleo Hill, who was the first pick in the NBA draft in 1961, selected by the St. Louis Hawks, and Earl Monroe, known as "The Pearl," who was a perennial all-star in the NBA with the NY Knicks. Coach Gaines retired in 1993 second in NCAA all-time wins with a record of 828 victories to 447 defeats (Hunt, 1996).

Ben Jobe, a graduate of Fisk University, coached several teams on numerous levels, but is known mostly for being the head coach of the Southern University Men's Basketball Team from 1986–1996, and 2001–2003. His most notable win at the school came in 1993 in the first round of the NCAA tournament where they beat heavily favored Georgia Tech University (a PW-IHE). The most famous alum whom Jobe coached was Avery Johnson, who played in the NBA from 1988 to 2004, and later coached the Dallas Mavericks from 2004 until 2008. Afterward, Johnson became a sport analyst for the Entertainment and Sports Programming Network (best known as ESPN).

The aforementioned individuals are just some of the many accomplished athletes and coaches of sport teams at HBCUs. There are far too many coaches and student-athletes who competed for HBCUs to discuss them all in this chapter. For additional information on Black college athletics, including Black coaches and student-athletes, the reader should consult the following works: *Black College Sport* (Chalk, 1976); *Fields of Play: The Mediums through which Black Athletes Engaged in Sports in Jim Crow Georgia* (Jeffries, 2001); *Great Names in Black College Sports* (Hunt, 1996); and *The Unlevel Playing Field: A Documentary History of the African American Experience in Sport* (Wiggins & Miller, 2003). In this edition of the book, *Racism in College Athletics*, Angela Lumpkin's chapter offers a historical overview of ethnic *minority* student-athletes in college sports. In addition, Wardell Johnson, Delano Tucker, and Chevelle Hall speak to the transformation and rise of the African American college coach.

CURRENT STATUS OF ATHLETICS AT
THE HISTORIC BLACK INSTITUTIONS

Over 100 HBCUs have been designated as Title IV institutions[8] by the NCES (Snyder et al., 2009). These institutions include public and private 2- and 4-year colleges and universities including community, medical, law, liberal arts, technical, and theological institutions. Most are 4-year public and private liberal arts institutions located in the South and Southeastern regions of the US in Alabama, Arkansas, Florida, Georgia, Kentucky, Louisiana, Mississippi, North Carolina, South Carolina, Tennessee, and Virginia.

Of the 103 accredited HBCUs, 93 sponsored athletic programs with a reported 14,928 student-athletes on their respective campuses in academic year 2008–09 (see Table 2.1). Of these student-athletes, 9,507 were males (63.7%) and 5,421 were females (36.3%) on team rosters of the 93 accredited HBCUs fielding athletic teams (U.S. Department of Education, 2010).

Table 2.1.	Number of Men and Women Student-Athletes at HBCUs (Reporting Year 2008–09)					
				Student-Athletes		
HBCU	City	State	Men	Women	Total
Alabama A&M University	Normal	AL	189	92	281
Alabama State University	Montgomery	AL	189	89	278
Bishop State Community College	Mobile	AL	30	33	63
Concordia College, Selma	Selma	AL	132	52	184
Gadsden State Community	Gadsden	AL	49	52	101
Lawson State Community	Birmingham	AL	40	26	66
Miles College	Fairfield	AL	75	16	91
Oakwood University	Huntsville	AL	15	12	27
Selma University	Selma	AL	15	0	15
Shelton State Community	Tuscaloosa	AL	47	48	95
Stillman College	Tuscaloosa	AL	123	54	177
Talladega College	Talladega	AL	61	24	85
Tuskegee University	Tuskegee	AL	192	64	256
Arkansas Baptist College	Little Rock	AR	158	10	168
Philander Smith College	Little Rock	AR	13	25	38
University of Arkansas, Pine Bluff	Pine Bluff	AR	168	83	251
Delaware State University	Dover	DE	193	130	323
Howard University	Washington	DC	199	133	332
University of the District of Columbia	Washington	DC	41	40	81
Bethune-Cookman University	Daytona Beach	FL	151	92	243
Edwards Waters College	Jacksonville	FL	115	51	166
Florida A&M University	Tallahassee	FL	152	74	226
Florida Memorial University	Miami Gardens	FL	53	34	87
Albany State University	Albany	GA	156	83	239

Table 2.1.	Number of Men and Women Student-Athletes at HBCUs (Reporting Year 2008–09) [continued]				

HBCU	City	State	Men	Women	Total
Clark Atlanta University	Atlanta	GA	122	62	184
Fort Valley State University	Fort Valley	GA	130	66	196
Morehouse College	Atlanta	GA	185	0	185
Paine College.	Augusta	GA	73	63	136
Savannah State University	Savannah	GA	114	86	200
Spelman College	Atlanta	GA	0	72	72
Kentucky State University.	Frankfort	KY	152	53	205
Dillard University.	New Orleans	LA	14	23	37
Grambling State University.	Grambling	LA	148	101	249
Southern University and A&M College	Baton Rouge	LA	179	96	275
Southern University at New Orleans	New Orleans	LA	22	15	37
Southern University at Shreveport.	Shreveport	LA	17	15	32
Xavier University of Louisiana	New Orleans	LA	28	28	56
Bowie State University.	Bowie	MD	135	74	209
Coppin State University	Baltimore	MD	96	115	211
Morgan State University.	Baltimore	MD	138	90	228
University of Maryland, Eastern Shore	Princess Anne	MD	62	82	144
Alcorn State University	Alcorn State	MS	149	83	232
Coahoma Community College	Clarksdale	MS	90	31	121
Hinds Community College, Utica	Raymond	MS	161	63	224
Jackson State University	Jackson	MS	217	137	354
Mississippi Valley State University	Itta Bena	MS	140	92	232
Rust College.	Holly Springs	MS	64	50	114
Tougaloo College	Tougaloo	MS	35	22	57
Harris-Stowe State College	Saint Louis	MO	61	52	113
Lincoln University (MO).	Jefferson City	MO	119	65	184
Bennett College for Women	Greensboro	NC	0	15	15
Elizabeth City State University	Elizabeth City	NC	161	82	243
Fayetteville State University	Fayetteville	NC	101	66	167
Johnson C. Smith University.	Charlotte	NC	109	64	173
Livingstone College	Salisbury	NC	93	62	155
North Carolina A&T State University	Greensboro	NC	166	97	263
North Carolina Central University.	Durham	NC	168	83	251
Saint Augustine's College	Raleigh	NC	183	75	258
Shaw University	Raleigh	NC	118	58	176
Winston-Salem State University	Winton-Salem	NC	167	95	262
Central State University	Wilberforce	OH	105	41	146

Table 2.1.	Number of Men and Women Student-Athletes at HBCUs (Reporting Year 2008–09) [*continued*]					
				Student-Athletes		
HBCU	City	State	Men	Women	Total
Wilberforce University . . . . Wilberforce	OH	27	23	50
Langston University . . . . Langston	OK	97	44	141
Cheyney University of Pennsylvania. . . . . Cheyney	PA	90	58	148
Lincoln University of Pennsylvania . . . . Lincoln University	PA	136	61	197
Allen University . . . . Columbia	SC	20	17	37
Benedict College . . . . Columbia	SC	139	61	200
Claflin University . . . . Orangeburg	SC	70	56	126
Clinton Junior College. . . . . Rock Hill	SC	15	13	28
Denmark Technical College . . . . Denmark	SC	15	15	30
Morris College . . . . Sumter	SC	33	38	71
South Carolina State University . . . . Orangeburg	SC	159	96	255
Voorhees College . . . . Denmark	SC	38	43	81
Fisk University . . . . Nashville	TN	25	22	47
Lane College . . . . Jackson	TN	112	44	156
Le Moyne-Owen College . . . . Memphis	TN	31	30	61
Tennessee State University . . . . Nashville	TN	144	73	217
Huston-Tillotson College . . . . Austin	TX	153	96	249
Jarvis Christian College. . . . . Hawkins	TX	35	27	62
Paul Quinn College . . . . Dallas	TX	21	17	38
Prairie View A&M University. . . . . Prairie View	TX	234	143	377
Southwestern Christian College . . . . Terrell	TX	45	43	88
Texas College . . . . Tyler	TX	119	45	164
Texas Southern University . . . . Houston	TX	152	96	248
Wiley College. . . . . Marshall	TX	40	23	63
Hampton University . . . . Hampton	VA	156	115	271
Norfolk State University . . . . Norfolk	VA	169	95	264
Saint Paul's College . . . . Lawrenceville	VA	74	44	118
Virginia State University. Petersburg	VA	165	83	248
Virginia Union University . . . . Richmond	VA	128	55	183
Bluefield State College . . . . Bluefield	WV	75	45	120
West Virginia State University. . . . . Institute	WV	164	61	225
University of the US Virgin Islands . . . . Charlotte Amalie	VI	48	48	96
		Total	9,507	5,421	14,928

Note. Data on the number of men and women student-athletes were gleaned mostly from the Office of Postsecondary Education (USDE, 2010), but there were some exceptions: Selma University, Morehouse College, Spelman College, and Bennett College for Women, whereby the data were extracted from team rosters found at the web sites of these HBCUs.

In 2008–09, more so than any other sport, football team rosters accounted for a large proportion (46.6%) of all male student-athletes and the disparity between the number of men and women student-athletes on HBCU campuses (see Table 2.2). There were 4,430 football student-athletes at HBCUs in fall 2008. Fifty-five (59%) of the 93 HBCUs with athletic programs sponsored football teams, and their football team rosters ranged from 50 to 125 players. These teams comprised 81 football players on average with a median of 83. The next largest group of student-athletes were 1,904 men and 1,546 women track athletes followed by 1,537 baseball players (men only), and then 1,372 men and 1,287 women basketball players, and 1,044 women softball athletes and 841 women volleyball players (USDE, 2010). There were also 403, 348, and 268 women on tennis, soccer, and bowling teams, respectively. Further, there were 333 and 210 men on tennis and soccer teams. In golf, there were 266 men and 119 women student-athletes. Two hundred and eleven men and 175 women participated in cross country at these HBCUs.

Much less populated were swim teams with a total of 33 women and 24 men at Florida A&M University, Howard University, NC A&T State University, and the University of the Virgin Islands. Interestingly, Delaware State University had the only athletic program to sponsor equestrian (with 20 women) and wrestling (with 18 men) teams. Likewise,

Table 2.2.	Number of Student-Athletes by Gender and Sport Type					
	Men's		**Women's**		**Combined**	
Sport	Total	Percent	Total	Percent	Total	Percent
Football	4,430	46.6%	0	0.0%	4,430	29.7%
Track (indoor/outdoor)	1,904	20.0%	1,546	28.5%	3,450	23.1%
Basketball	1,372	14.4%	1287	23.7%	2,659	17.8%
Baseball	1,537	16.2%	0	0.0%	1,537	10.3%
Softball	0	0.0%	1044	19.3%	1044	7.0%
Volleyball	10	0.1%	841	15.5%	851	5.7%
Tennis	333	3.5%	403	7.4%	736	4.9%
Soccer	210	2.2%	348	6.4%	558	3.7%
Cross country	211	2.2%	175	3.2%	386	2.6%
Golf	266	2.8%	119	2.2%	385	2.6%
Bowling	6	0.1%	268	4.9%	274	1.8%
Swimming	24	0.3%	33	0.6%	57	0.4%
Equestrian	0	0.0%	20	0.4%	20	0.1%
Wrestling	18	0.2%	0	0.0%	18	0.1%
Lacrosse	0	0.0%	17	0.3%	17	0.1%
Table tennis	6	0.1%	8	0.1%	14	0.1%
Co-ed sailing	8	0.1%	5	0.1%	13	0.1%

Note. Percentages based on unduplicated count of male and female student-athletes, respectively.

Hampton University had the only athletic program to sponsor co-educational sailing, with eight men and five women student-athletes. The least populated teams were women's lacrosse (17 athletes); table tennis, with eight female and six male players; and the 10 athletes composing the men's volleyball team for the University of the Virgin Islands (USDE, 2010).

The 93 HBCUs with athletic programs fielded some 939 athletic teams, competed across 20 different conferences, and were affiliated with five intercollegiate athletic associations in 19 states, the District of Columbia, and US Virgin Islands (see Table 2.3). And of the 93 HBCUs, 15 sponsored independent athletic programs.

Table 2.3.	Number of Athletic Teams at HBCUs by Gender and Athletic Affiliations					
	Sport Teams			Athletic Affiliation		
HBCU	Men	Women	Total	Association	D	Conference
Total	441	498	939	+	+	+
Alabama A&M University	7	8	14	· NCAA	I	SWAC
Alabama State University	7	9	16	NCAA	I	SWAC
Bishop State Community	2	2	4	NJCAA	I	ACCC
Concordia College, Selma	5	4	9	USCAA	II	Independent
Gadsden State Community	3	4	7	NJCAA	I	ACCC
Lawson State Community	3	2	4	NJCAA	I	ACCC
Miles College	5	5	10	NCAA	II	SIAC
Oakwood University	1	1	2	USCAA	I	Independent
Selma University	1	0	1	USCAA	+	Independent
Shelton State Community	2	2	4	NJCAA	I	ACCC
Stillman College	6	6	12	NCAA	II	SIAC
Talladega College	3	2	5	NAIA	I	Independent
Tuskegee University	6	6	12	NCAA	II	SIAC
Arkansas Baptist College	3	1	4	NJCAA	I	Independent
Philander Smith College	1	2	3	NAIA	I	Independent
U. of Arkansas, Pine Bluff	7	8	15	NCAA	I	SWAC
Delaware State University	7	9	16	NCAA	I	MEAC
Howard University	7	10	17	NCAA	I	MEAC
U. District of Columbia	4	5	9	NCAA	II	Independent
Bethune-Cookman College	7	8	15	NCAA	I	MEAC
Edwards Waters College	6	6	12	NAIA	I	The Sun Conference
Florida A&M University	8	8	16	NCAA	I	MEAC
Florida Memorial University	4	4	8	NAIA	I	The Sun Conference
Albany State University	5	6	11	NCAA	II	SIAC
Clark Atlanta University	5	6	11	NCAA	II	SIAC
Fort Valley State University	5	6	11	NCAA	II	SIAC
Morehouse College	7	0	7	NCAA	II	SIAC
Paine College	4	3	7	NCAA	II	SIAC

Table 2.3.	Number of Athletic Teams at HBCUs by Gender and Athletic Affiliations (*Continued*)					
	Sport Teams			**Athletic Affiliation**		
HBCU	Men	Women	Total	Association	D	Conference
Total	441	498	939	+	+	+
Savannah State University	7	7	14	NCAA	I	Independent
Spelman College	0	6	6	NCAA	III	Great South Athletic
Kentucky State University	6	5	11	NCAA	II	SIAC
Dillard University	1	2	3	NAIA	I	Gulf Coast Athletic
Grambling State University	7	9	16	NCAA	I	SWAC
Southern U./A&M College	7	9	16	NCAA	I	SWAC
Southern U. at New Orleans	3	3	6	NAIA	I	Gulf Coast Athletic
Southern U. at Shreveport	1	1	2	NJCAA	I	MLJCC
Xavier University (LA)	3	3	6	NAIA	I	Gulf Coast Athletic
Bowie State University	4	7	11	NCAA	II	CIAA
Coppin State University	5	7	12	NCAA	I	MEAC
Morgan State University	5	7	12	NCAA	I	MEAC
U. of Maryland, Eastern Shore	5	7	12	NCAA	I	MEAC
Alcorn State University	7	8	15	NCAA	I	SWAC
Coahoma Community College	3	2	5	NJCAA	I	MACJC
Hinds Community College	7	4	11	NJCAA	I	MACJC
Jackson State University	7	9	16	NCAA	I	SWAC
Mississippi Valley State U.	7	9	16	NCAA	I	SWAC
Rust College	6	6	12	NCAA	III	Independent
Tougaloo College	6	4	8	NAIA	I	Gulf Coast Athletic
Harris-Stowe State College	3	4	7	NAIA	I	American Midwest
Lincoln University (MO)	5	4	9	NCAA	II	Heartland/GLFC
Bennett College for Women	0	1	1	USCAA	+	Independent
Elizabeth City State U.	6	7	13	NCAA	II	CIAA
Fayetteville State University	4	6	10	NCAA	II	CIAA
Johnson C. Smith University	6	7	13	NCAA	II	CIAA
Livingstone College	4	7	11	NCAA	II	CIAA
NC A&T State University	5	8	13	NCAA	I	MEAC
NC Central University	6	6	12	NCAA	II	MEAC
Saint Augustine's College	7	7	14	NCAA	II	CIAA
Shaw University	6	7	13	NCAA	II	CIAA
Winston-Salem State U.	6	7	13	NCAA	II	MEAC
Central State University	6	6	12	NCAA	II	Independent
Wilberforce University	3	3	6	NAIA	II	American Mideast
Langston University	4	4	8	NAIA	I	Red River Athletic
Cheyney University (PA)	4	6	10	NCAA	II	PSAC
Lincoln University (PA)	7	8	15	NCAA	II	CIAA

	Sport Teams			Athletic Affiliation		
HBCU	Men	Women	Total	Association	D	Conference
Total	441	498	939	+	+	+
Allen University	5	7	12	NAIA	I	Independent
Benedict College	7	8	15	NCAA	II	SIAC
Claflin University	4	6	10	NCAA	II	SIAC
Clinton Junior College	1	1	2	NJCAA	I	CJCC
Denmark Technical College	1	2	3	NJCAA	I	CJCC
Morris College	4	5	9	NAIA	I	Independent
South Carolina State U.	6	9	15	NCAA	I	MEAC
Voorhees College	4	5	9	NAIA	I	Independent
Fisk University	1	2	3	NAIA	III	Independent
Lane College	6	6	12	NCAA	II	SIAC
Le Moyne-Owen College	5	5	10	NCAA	II	SIAC
Tennessee State University	6	7	13	NCAA	I	Ohio Valley
Huston-Tillotson University	6	6	12	NAIA	I	Red River Athletic
Jarvis Christian College	2	2	4	NAIA	I	Red River Athletic
Paul Quinn College	2	2	4	NAIA	I	Red River Athletic
Prairie View A&M University	7	9	16	NCAA	I	SWAC
Southwestern Christian	2	2	4	NJCAA	I	WJCAC
Texas College	4	4	8	NAIA	I	Red River Athletic
Texas Southern University	6	8	14	NCAA	I	SWAC
Wiley College	3	3	6	NAIA	I	Red River Athletic
Hampton University	6	8	14	NCAA	I	MEAC
Norfolk State University	6	7	13	NCAA	I	MEAC
Saint Paul's College	7	7	14	NCAA	II	CIAA
Virginia State University	6	7	13	NCAA	II	CIAA
Virginia Union University	6	7	13	NCAA	II	CIAA
Bluefield State University	5	5	10	NCAA	II	WVIA
West Virginia State College	6	6	12	NCAA	II	WVIA
U. of the US Virgin Islands	7	5	12	CUSA	II	LAI

Table 2.3. Number of Athletic Teams at HBCUs by Gender and Athletic Affiliations (*Continued*)

+Not applicable.

Note. Data on athletic teams and their affiliations were gleaned from multiple sources including the Office of Postsecondary Education (US Department of Education, 2010) and the individual websites of the HBCUs with athletic programs, national associations, and athletic conferences.

Note. ACCC = Alabama Community College Conference; CIAA = Central Intercollegiate Athletic Conference; CJCC = Carolinas Junior College Conference; CUSA = Caribbean University Sports Association; GLFC = Great Lakes Football Conference; LAI = Liga Atlética Interuniversitaria Conference; MACJC = Mississippi Association of Community and Junior Colleges; MEAC = Mid-Eastern Athletic Conference; MLJCC = MISS-LOU Junior College Conference; PSAC = Pennsylvania State Athletic Conference; SIAC = Southern Intercollegiate Athletic Conference; SWAC = Southwestern Athletic Conference; WJCAC = Western Junior College Athletic Conference; and WVIA = West Virginia Intercollegiate Athletic Conference.

In the 2008–09 academic year, there were 498 (53%) women's teams and 441 (47%) men's teams representing intercollegiate athletics at HBCUs competing in 17 different sports (see Table 2.4). The most prevalent sports for men's intercollegiate athletics were basketball, track and field, baseball, cross country, football, and tennis. The most prevalent sports for women's intercollegiate competitions were basketball, volleyball, softball (fast-pitch), track, cross country, tennis, and bowling. By far the most popular men's and women's sport was basketball, which was offered at 97% of the HBCUs with athletic programs, followed by women's and men's track at 72% of the HBCUs with athletic programs (see Table 2.4). Nearly half (44%) of the HBCUs with athletic teams fielded men's golf teams; less so, 22.6% of them, fielded women's golf teams. Most of the HBCUs with athletic programs sponsored men's football (59%) and baseball (65%) teams. Not surprisingly, there were no women's football or baseball teams at the HBCUs. In contrast, women's volleyball, softball, and bowling teams were constituted at 72%, 67%, and 35% of the HBCUs with athletic programs, respectively, compared to only one men's volleyball and one men's bowling team plus no men's lacrosse or softball. What's more, about 23% of the HBCUs with athletic teams fielded women's soccer teams, but only 10.8% of such HBCUs fielded men's soccer teams. The least prevalent sports were swimming, table tennis, lacrosse, equestrian, and wrestling at 4% or less of the HBCUs. No HBCU reported intercollegiate participation in men's fencing, gymnastics, ice hockey,

Table 2.4.	Prevalence of Athletic Teams at HBCUs by Gender and Sport Type					
	Men's		Women's		Combined	
Sports Prevalence	Total	Percent	Total	Percent	Total	Percent
Basketball	90	96.7%	91	97.8%	182	97.3%
Track (indoor/outdoor)	68	73.1%	66	70.1%	134	72.0%
Cross Country	61	65.6%	64	68.8%	125	67.2%
Tennis	48	51.6%	54	58.1%	102	54.8%
Volleyball	1	1.1%	72	77.4%	73	39.2%
Softball	0	0.0%	67	72.0%	67	36.0%
Golf	41	44.1%	21	22.5%	62	33.3%
Baseball	61	65.6%	0	0.0%	60	32.8%
Football	55	59.1%	0	0.0%	55	29.6%
Bowling	1	1.1%	35	37.6%	36	19.4%
Soccer	10	10.8%	21	22.6%	31	16.7%
Swimming	3	3.2%	5	5.4%	8	4.3%
Table tennis	1	1.1%	1	1.1%	2	1.1%
Equestrian	0	0.0%	1	1.1%	1	0.5%
Lacrosse	0	0.0%	1	1.1%	1	0.5%
Wrestling	1	1.1%	0	0.0%	1	0.5%
Total	441		498		939	

Note. Percentages based on data from the 93 HBCUs identified in Table 3 and ranked by prevalence from combined frequencies of men and women teams.

lacrosse, skiing, water polo; or women's fencing, field hockey, gymnastics, ice hockey, rowing, skiing, water polo, or co-educational rifle competitions.

It is argued that there are social, cultural, and financial barriers that deter many Black athletes from playing soccer (Bennefield, 1999; Smith, 2007) or competing in equestrian, fencing, ice hockey, gymnastics, skiing, swimming, and so on. Hodge and colleagues argue that differences in sport participation tendencies of diverse ethnic groups are a result of complex and interrelated factors most notably access and opportunity, racial inequalities, resources (financial, structural), and cultural and social norms (Burden, Hodge, & Harrison, 2004; Hodge, Burden, Robinson, & Bennett, 2008a; Hodge et al., 2008b).

Common to the HBCUs with athletic programs, with some exceptions (e.g., Morehouse College for men only), there were equal numbers of or more women's than men's athletic teams (Tables 2.3 and 2.4). This suggests that Title IX of the Education Amendments of 1972 has had an influence on athletic programs at HBCUs. Yet, challenges exist in complying with Title IX's controversial proportionality standards. In Chapter 3 of this book, we speak to these issues in more detail (Hodge, Collins, & Bennett III, 2012).

ATHLETIC ASSOCIATIONS AND HBCUs

Most HBCUs with athletic programs are members of intercollegiate athletic associations and conferences. Fifteen (16%) of the HBCUs with athletic programs compete as independent entities and do so against athletic programs that have their affiliations with intercollegiate athletic associations. These associations are the Caribbean University Sports Association (CUSA); the National Association of Intercollegiate Athletics (NAIA), the National Collegiate Athletic Association (NCAA), the National Junior College Athletic Association (NJCAA), and the United States Collegiate Athletic Association (USCAA).

The Caribbean University Sports Association (CUSA) was established in 1993 as a voluntary nonprofit organization to govern Division II and III intercollegiate athletic programs in the Caribbean. The CUSA field men's and women's collegiate team sports in basketball, cross country, swimming, table tennis, tennis, track and field, and volleyball.

Table 2.5.	HBCUs' Athletic Programs Affiliations by Association and Division							
	Division I		Division II		Division III		Combined	
	Total	%	Total	%	Total	%	Total	%
CUSA	0	0.0%	1	1.1%	0	0.0%	1	1.1%
NAIA	16	17.2%	4	4.3%	0	0.0%	20	21.5%
NCAA	25	26.8%	30	32.3%	2	2.2%	57	61.3%
NJCAA	11	11.8%	0	0.0%	0	0.0%	11	11.8%
USCAA	1	1.1%	1	1.1%	2	2.2%	4	4.3%
Total	53	56.9%	36	38.7%	4	4.3%	93	100%

Note. CUSA = Caribbean University Sports Association; NAIA = National Association of Intercollegiate Athletics; NCAA = National Collegiate Athletic Association; NJCAA = National Junior College Athletic Association; USCAA = United States Collegiate Athletic Association.

There is but one HBCU affiliated with the CUSA (see Table 2.5). The University of the Virgin Islands is a member of the CUSA and a corresponding member of the NCAA. The university is also a member of the Liga Atlética Interuniversitaria (LAI) conference, which comprises universities in the Caribbean, with most of these universities located in Puerto Rico (see Table 2.6).

The National Association of Intercollegiate Athletics (NAIA) is an association that organizes intercollegiate athletic programs. The NAIA is comprised of nearly 300 relatively small colleges and universities across the US and several member institutions in Canada. Founded in 1937, the predecessor to the NAIA was the National Association of Intercollegiate Basketball (NAIB). In 1948, the NAIB became the first national organization to open its intercollegiate postseason to Black student-athletes. In that year, Indiana State University men's basketball team, led by Coach John Wooden, had the first Black student-athlete to participate in the national tournament. In 1952, the NAIB was expanded to include such sports as golf, tennis, and track and field, and was renamed the National Association of Intercollegiate Athletics (2009). Important also, the NAIA was the first majority White collegiate athletic association in 1953 to accept a historically Black institution as member. As a result in 1957, Tennessee State University became the first HBCU to win a mainstream collegiate basketball national championship. Currently, the NAIA sponsors 23 national championships and there are 20 HBCUs with athletic programs affiliated with the association (see tables 2.5 and 2.6). CBS College Sports is the national media for the conference.

In 1906, the Intercollegiate Athletic Association of the United States was established to set rules for amateur sports and is the predecessor to the National Collegiate Athletic Association (NCAA). Today, the NCAA has 1,045 member institutions who participate in intercollegiate athletics across 27 different sports in the US and Canada (U.S. Government Accountability Office, 2007). In 1973, the current three-tier divisional structure (Division I, II, and III) was instituted. Under NCAA rules, Division I and II schools can offer scholarships to student-athletes for sport participation. But no athletic scholarships are offered at the Division III level. In 1978, football programs were further subdivided into Divisions I-A and I-AA, and later the marker Division I-AAA was used to delineate Division I colleges with no football programs. In 2006, Divisions I-A and I-AA were renamed the NCAA's Football Bowl Subdivision and Football Championship Subdivision, respectively. Today, 57 HBCUs with athletic programs (61%) are affiliated with the NCAA and compete at the Division I, II, and III levels (revisit Table 2.3).

Founded in 1938, the National Junior College Athletic Association (NJCAA) is an athletic association and serves as a governing body of intercollegiate athletics for two-year community and junior colleges throughout the US. The association is also organized by divisional levels (i.e., Division I, II, and III). It has 24 regional conferences and some 525 member institutions affiliated. The NJCAA hosts most accredited historically Black community and junior colleges with athletic programs. Today, there are 11 HBCUs affiliated with the NJCAA: Bishop State, Gadsden State, Lawson State, and Shelton State community colleges in Alabama; Arkansas Baptist College in Arkansas; Southern University at Shreveport in Louisiana; Coahoma and Hinds community colleges in Mississippi; Clinton Junior College and Denmark Technical College in South Carolina; and Southwestern Christian College in Texas (see tables 2.5 and 2.6). The NJCAA has history of nearly 20% presence of student-athletes of color (Brown, 1988).

The United States Collegiate Athletic Association (USCAA) is an intercollegiate athletic association comprising small colleges and universities across the US. The USCAA's history dates back to 1966 with the establishment of the National Little College Athletic

Table 2.6.	HBCUs' Athletic Program Affiliations by Conference and Association		
Conference	**Association**	**Total**	**Percent**
Alabama Community College Conference	NJCAA	4	4.3%
American Mideast Conference	NAIA	1	1.1%
American Midwest Conference	NAIA	1	1.1%
Central Intercollegiate Athletic Association	NCAA	11	11.8%
Carolinas Junior College Conference	NJCAA	2	2.2%
Great South Athletic Conference	NCAA	1	1.1%
Gulf Coast Athletic Conference	NAIA	4	4.3%
Heartland Conference/Great Lakes Football	NCAA	1	1.1%
Independent	+	15	16.1%
Liga Atlética Interuniversitaria Conference	CUSA	1	1.1%
Mississippi Association of Community & Junior Coll.	NJCAA	2	2.2%
Mid-Eastern Athletic Conference	NCAA	13	13.9%
MISS-LOU Junior College Conference	NJCAA	1	1.1%
Ohio Valley Conference	NCAA	1	1.1%
Pennsylvania State Athletic Conference	NCAA	1	1.1%
Red River Athletic Conference	NAIA	6	6.5%
Southern Intercollegiate Athletic Conference	NCAA	13	14.0%
Southwestern Athletic Conference	NCAA	10	10.8%
The Sun Conference	NAIA	2	2.2%
Western Junior College Athletic Conference	NJCAA	1	1.1%
West Virginia Intercollegiate Athletic Conference	NCAA	2	2.2%
	Total	**93**	**100.0%**

+ Independent athletic programs not affiliated members of a particular conference or association, but compete against teams among the four major associations: NAIA, NCAA, NJCAA, USCAA.
Note. CUSA = Caribbean University Sports Association; NAIA = National Association of Intercollegiate Athletics; NCAA = National Collegiate Athletic Association; NJCAA = National Junior College Athletic Association; USCAA = United States Collegiate Athletic Association.

Association (NLCAA), which was formed and devoted to athletic competition for small colleges. In 1989, the association changed its name to the National *Small* College Athletic Association and later in 2001 to the United States Collegiate Athletic Association. The association's goal is to offer small colleges opportunities to compete against one another on a level playing field. To that goal, the USCAA hosts national championships, names All-Americans and scholar-athletes, and promotes its member institutions (USCAA, n.d.). Four HBCUs; Concordia College, Oakwood University, and Selma University in Alabama; and Bennett College for Women in North Carolina, compete as independents against colleges in the USCAA (see Table 2.5).

ATHLETIC CONFERENCES AND HBCUs

In the early years most HBCUs with athletic programs were affiliated with the four major historically Black athletic conferences: CIAA, MEAC, SIAC, and SWAC. Now, only half of the HBCUs are affiliated with these conferences and compete in the NCAA's Division I (Football Championship Subdivision) or Division II classifications. Specifically, today 47 of the 93 HBCUs with athletic programs (51%) are members of the major historically Black athletic conferences. Over the years, there have been membership changes in these conferences typified by various HBCUs withdrawing from the individual conferences, new members joining at different points in time, and in some cases past members rejoining the conferences (see Table 2.7). Now, we will explore some of the pertinent changes. We start with a brief description of the four major historically Black athletic conferences and the HBCUs with affiliation therein. Next, we offer a brief summary of several traditionally White conferences whereby HBCUs compete.

Historically Black Athletic Conferences

In 1912, the Colored Intercollegiate Athletic Association was founded and is often credited as the oldest major historically Black conference in the US (Wiggins, 2007). The association was founded by Allen Washington and C. H. Williams of Hampton Institute (now Hampton University); Ernest J. Marshall of Howard University; George Johnson of Lincoln University (PA); W. E. Atkins, Charles Frasher, and H. P. Hargrave of Shaw University; and J. W. Barco and J. W. Pierce of Virginia Union University (CIAA, 2009). The association changed its name to the Central Intercollegiate Athletic Association (CIAA) in 1950. The name change[9] from *Colored* to *Central* was voted on during an annual conference meeting held December 8th and 9th, 1950 in Washington, DC.

The CIAA teams participate in the NCAA's Division II system. The CIAA now has 13 member institutions with a 13th member institute, Winston-Salem State University, to rejoining the conference in 2010 (see Table 2.7). The 11 current HBCUs members are Bowie State University, Elizabeth City State University, Fayetteville State University, Johnson C. Smith University, Lincoln University, Livingstone College, St. Augustine's College, St. Paul's College, Shaw University, Virginia State University, and Virginia Union University (CIAA, 1997–2009).

The most recent additions to the CIAA are Lincoln University (PA), Chowan University, and Winston-Salem State University rejoined in 2010. In 2008–2009, Lincoln University (PA) added varsity football to its athletic program and transitioned from NCAA Division III to Division II status (Lincoln University, 2009). Lincoln competed in football dating back to 1894, but had not participated in intercollegiate football since 1960. A founding member of the CIAA back in 1912, the university's Board of Trustees voted to revive the football program in 2006 and sought full membership in the CIAA, where it was a charter member. On August 30, 2008, Lincoln University's football team played its first game in 48 years when the Lions hosted George Mason University at a local high school in West Grove, PA (Lincoln University, 2008).

Of its member institutions, all but one is an HBCU. In fall 2009, Chowan University began competition as a full member of the CIAA and is the first traditionally White institution with membership in the conference (NCAA News, 2009). Of note, Chowan University's student body is ethnically diverse with nearly 50% African American and 50% White, but also includes students from Japan, India, West Africa, Northern Ireland, and Palestine, among many others (Chowan University, 1997–2006).

Table 2.7.	Membership (Dates) of HBCUs in the Major Historically Black Athletic Conferences

Central Intercollegiate Athletic Conference (NCAA Division II)

Founding Members	Current	
Hampton Institute (1912)	Bowie State (1979)	J. C. Smith University (1926)
Howard University (1912)	Elizabeth City State (1957)	Lincoln (PA) (1912, 2008)
Lincoln University (PA) (1912)	Fayetteville State (1954)	Livingstone College (1931)
Shaw University (1912)	St. Augustine's (1933)	Winston-Salem State University (1945–2006, 2010)
Virginia Union (1912)	St. Paul's College (1923)	
	Shaw University	
	Virginia State (1920)	
	Virginia Union University	

Southern Intercollegiate Athletic Conference (NCAA Division II)

Founding Members	Current	
Alabama State University (1913)	Albany State (1969)	Le Moyne-Owen (1932)
Atlanta University (1913)	Benedict College (1932)	Miles College (1927)
Clark Atlanta University (1913)	Claflin University (2008)	Paine College (1985)
Fisk University (1913)	Clark Atlanta (1913)	Stillman College (1978)
Jackson College (1913)	Fort Valley State (1941)	
Morehouse College (1913)	Morehouse (1913)	
Morris Brown College (1913)	Kentucky State (1997)	
Talladega College (1913)	Lane College (1929)	
Tuskegee Institute (1913)	Tuskegee (1913)	

Southwestern Athletic Conference (NCAA Division I and FCS)

Founding Members	Current	
Bishop College (1920–1956)	Alabama A&M (1999)	Mississippi Valley St. (1968)
Paul Quinn College (1920–1929)	Alabama State (1982)	Prairie View A&M (1920)
Prairie View A&M (1920)	Alcorn State (1962)	Southern University (1934)
Sam Huston College (1920–59)	Arkansas, PB (1997)	Texas Southern (1954)
Texas College (1920–1968)	Grambling State (1958)	
Wiley College (1920–1968)	Jackson State (1958)	

Mid-Eastern Athletic Conference (NCAA Division I and FCS)

Founding Members	Current	
Delaware State (1970)	Delaware State University	Bethune-Cookman (1979)
Howard University (1970)	Howard University	Florida A&M (1979)
Maryland, Eastern Shore (1970)	Maryland, Eastern Shore	Coppin State (1985)
Morgan State University (1970)	Morgan State University	Hampton (1995)
NC A&T State University (1970)	NC A&T State University	Norfolk State (1997)
NC Central University (1970)	NC Central University	Winston-Salem State University (2007–09)
SC State University (1970)	SC State University	

Note. FCS = NCAA's Football Championship Subdivision (formerly known as Division 1-AA).
Note. Arkansas, PB = University of Arkansas, Pine Bluff.

Once more, Winston-Salem State University (WSSU) re-entered the conference, effective 2010–2011. In brief, WSSU joined the CIAA Division II from 1945 to 2006, then joined the MEAC and competed at the NCAA Division I level from 2007 to 2009, and now rejoins the CIAA Division II to start play in 2010–2011 (WSSU, 2009). On October 2, 2009, the CIAA's Board of Directors voted to reinstate WSSU as a member of the conference. This reclassifies the university's athletic program at the Division II level and also renews the longstanding history shared between the CIAA and WSSU for more than 60 years (WSSU, 2009). For several years, WSSU examined the possibility of transitioning to NCAA Division I classification. However, the university decided to rejoin the CIAA and compete at the NCAA Division II level subsequent to official certification from the NCAA (WSSU, 2009).

In 2005, the CIAA collaborated with ESPN, the "nation's sports leader," to create the largest HBCUs conference television package in history. Now with its headquarters located in Charlotte, NC, for consecutive years of 2007, 2008, and 2009, the CIAA has set tournament economic impact and attendance records (CIAA, 2009).

On December 30, 1913, pioneers from nine HBCUs assembled at Morehouse College and formed the Southeastern Intercollegiate Association. On January 21, 1928, the Southeastern Intercollegiate Association was renamed the Southeastern Intercollegiate Athletic Conference (SIAC). A year later in 1929, the SIAC changed its name again to *Southern* Intercollegiate Athletic Conference. In 1913, Atlanta University and Clark College (now Clark Atlanta University) were among the original nine HBCU members to establish the SIAC. In 1988, Atlanta University and Clark College merged to become Clark Atlanta University. Also among the original members were Alabama State Normal School (now Alabama State University), Fisk University, Jackson College (now Jackson State University), Morehouse College, Morris Brown College, Talladega College, and Tuskegee Institute (now Tuskegee University). In 1920, Florida A&M College (now Florida A&M University) and Knoxville College became chartered members in the conference. The SIAC is a collegiate athletic conference comprised of HBCUs in the southern region of the US. Moreover, the SIAC is an affiliated member of the NCAA at the Division II level. The conference is comprised of 13 member institutions across the states of Alabama, Georgia, Kentucky, South Carolina, and Tennessee. The members are Albany State University, Benedict College, Claflin University (provisional member), Clark Atlanta University, Fort Valley State University, Kentucky State University, Lane College, LeMoyne-Owen College, Miles College, Morehouse College, Paine College, Stillman College, and Tuskegee University (SIAC, 2007–2009). In 2004, Stillman College joined the SIAC Division II after it had withdrawn from the Great South Athletic Conference (GSAC); a NCAA Division III conference. The SIAC has had numerous shifts in memberships over the years (see Table 2.7). Only two of the original members have held continuous membership since 1913, and they are Clark College (now Clark Atlanta University) and Tuskegee University.

During various periods of time (dates in parentheses), the following HBCUs were members of the SIAC (SIAC, 2007):

- Alabama A&M University (1947–1998) joined the SWAC Division I.
- Alabama State University (1913–1976) joined the SWAC Division I.
- Allen University's (1947–1969) athletic program is now independent and affiliated with the NAIA Division I.
- Benedict College joined the SIAC in 1932 and is a current member of the conference.
- Bethune-Cookman University (1950–1979) joined the MEAC Division I.

- Edward Waters College (1930–1935) renewed its athletic program with the return of football in 2001 after a 34-year absence (EWC, 2009). Edward Waters College joined the South East Atlantic Conference (SEAC) in 2004 and was named the SEAC Champions that same year, but the SEAC dissolved after the 2008 season. EWC joined The Sun Conference (originally The Florida Sun Conference) and is affiliated with the NAIA.

- Fisk University (1920–1983), became a member of the Great South Athletic Conference in 1999, but withdrew from the GSAC after the 2005–06 season, and its athletic program is now independent and affiliated with the NAIA Division III.

- Florida A&M University (1920–1979) joined the MEAC.

- Jackson State University (1913–1914) joined the SWAC in 1958.

- Knoxville College (1924–1990) had accreditation difficulties and eliminated its athletic program.

- Morris Brown College's (1913–2000) athletic program was dissolved after an unsuccessful move to NCAA Division I and financial problems attributed to the lost of their accreditation.

- Rust College (1978–1988) is now independent and affiliated with the NCAA Division III.

- Savannah State University (1968–2000) is now independent and not affiliated with any conference, but competes against teams in the NCAA Division I and Football Championship Subdivision.

- South Carolina State University (1931–1971) joined the MEAC.

- Talladega College's (1913–1941) athletic program is independent and affiliated with the NAIA Division I.

- Tennessee State University (1924–1930) joined the Ohio Valley Conference in 1986.

- Xavier University of Louisiana (1936–1960) joined the Gulf Coast Athletic Conference.

The Southwestern Athletic Conference (SWAC) is an intercollegiate athletic conference comprised of HBCUs in the southern region of the US and is affiliated by the NCAA Division I. In 1920, the SWAC was created by leaders from six HBCUs in Texas, who met in Houston to discuss establishing an athletic conference in the state. These visionaries were C. H. Fuller of Bishop College; Red Randolph and C. H. Patterson of Paul Quinn College; E. G. Evans, H. J. Evans, and H. J. Starns of Prairie View A&M University; D. C. Fuller of Texas College; and G. Whitte Jordan of Wiley College (SWAC, 2009). Although, Sam Huston College (now Huston-Tillotson University) was one of the founding member institutions of the conference, it is unclear who (if anyone) represented the college at the aforementioned meeting. In 1952, Sam Huston College and Tillotson College merged to form Huston-Tillotson College and in 2005, the college became Huston-Tillotson University.

Only one of the original six member institutions has held continuous membership in the SWAC since 1920: Prairie View A&M University. The SWAC is now composed of 10 HBCUs in the states of Texas, Louisiana, Mississippi, Arkansas, and Alabama (see Table 2.7). The members are Alabama A&M University; Alabama State University; Alcorn State University; University of Arkansas, Pine Bluff; Grambling State University; Jackson State University; Mississippi Valley State University; Prairie View A&M University; Southern University and A&M College; and Texas Southern University (SWAC, 2009).

The SWAC member institutions participate in NCAA Division I athletics. Football programs in the SWAC participate in the NCAA's Football Championship Subdivision (FCS), which is the lower of two levels of Division I football (formerly known as Division I-AA). However, the SWAC members do not participate in the annual FCS tournament. Alternatively, the SWAC is subdivided into the Eastern and Western divisions and hosts its own conference championship game. In that regard, the *Bayou Classic*, which is an annual match-up of Southern University's Jaguars versus Grambling State University's Tigers and the *Turkey Day Classic* between Alabama State University's Hornets and its non-conference revival Tuskegee University's Golden Tigers from the SIAC are both important and historic athletic events within the SWAC. Some have criticized the SWAC's decision not to participate in the NCAA's FCS tournament, particularly leaders from the Mid-Eastern Athletic Conference (MEAC), which is the only other historically Black NCAA affiliated Division I conference.

In 1969, initial planning began with an ad hoc group of pioneers for what would later become the Mid-Eastern Athletic Conference (MEAC), which is devoted to intercollegiate athletics for HBCUs. The original member institutions were Delaware State College, Howard University, University of Maryland Eastern Shore, Morgan State University, North Carolina A&T State University, North Carolina Central University, and South Carolina State College (see Table 2.7). The MEAC was confirmed in 1970 and started football competitions in 1971 (MEAC, 2009a).

Morgan State University, North Carolina Central University and the University of Maryland Eastern Shore all withdrew from the MEAC at the end of fiscal year 1979. In 1981, however, the University of Maryland Eastern Shore rejoined the conference. Likewise in 1984, Morgan State University rejoined the MEAC. North Carolina Central University is currently seeking to rejoin the MEAC (MEAC, 2009b).

The MEAC is comprised of 12 HBCUs and these are Bethune-Cookman University, Coppin State University, Delaware State University, Florida A&M University, Hampton University, Howard University, University of Maryland Eastern Shore, Morgan State University, Norfolk State University, North Carolina A&T State University, South Carolina State University, and Winston-Salem State University (MEAC, 2009a). But again, North Carolina Central University (NCCU) has applied for reinstatement into the MEAC. This would be a case of returning home for NCCU, as it was one of the founding member institutions but withdrew from the MEAC in 1979 and held its Division II status when the conference moved to Division I play. Then from 1979–2007, NCCU competed in the CIAA. In a transitional era, NCCU sponsors an independent athletic program. But we've identified it as a MEAC conditional member because it competes at the NCAA Division I level and in 2011–2012 is eligible for full membership in the conference pending final approvals from the MEAC and NCAA (MEAC, 2009b). To the contrary, Winston-Salem State University leaves the MEAC to rejoin the CIAA and to participate at the Division II level, effective 2010–2011 (WSSU, 2009).

The MEAC members participate in Division I sports including the NCAA's Football Championship Subdivision. The MEAC has automatic qualifying bids for NCAA postseason play in baseball, basketball, football, softball, tennis, and volleyball. In 1999, bowling was sanctioned as a MEAC governed sport. It was the first conference to secure NCAA sanctioning for women's bowling by adopting the club sport prior to the 1996–97 school year (MEAC, 2009a). Bowling is quickly becoming a popular sport, particularly for women's intercollegiate competitions, and today is sponsored at 36 (38.7%) of the HBCUs with athletic programs. There were 268 female but only six male bowling team members at HBCUs in the 2008–2009 academic year (USDE, 2010).

Traditionally White Conferences where HBCUs Compete

In 1949, the Mid-Ohio League was established and changed its name to the American Mideast (AME) Conference in 1998. The AME Conference is affiliated with the NAIA to support intercollegiate athletic competition for eligible student-athletes (AME Conference, 2009). Today, the AME Conference is comprised of 14 member institutions with Wilberforce University as the only HBCU among its members. Wilberforce University joined the AME Conference in 1999. The next year in fall 2000, Central State University began regular season play in the conference, but withdrew in 2002 (AME Conference, 2009). Central State University's athletic program is now independent in all sports (i.e., basketball, cross-country, golf, tennis, track and field, volleyball) except football. Temporarily, Central State's football program was halted, but has been revived and entered the Great Lakes Football Conference in 2006 to compete at the NCAA Division II level.

Founded in 1986, the Show-Me Collegiate Conference changed its name to the American Midwest (AMW) Conference in 1994. The AMW Conference is a member of the NAIA in support of intercollegiate athletic competition for qualified student-athletes (AMW Conference, 2009). Currently, the AMW Conference is comprised of nine member institutions with Harris-Stowe State University as the only HBCU among its members. Harris-Stowe State University is one of the original five charter members of the conference.

The Association of Independent Institutions is an athletic association sponsoring institutions with independent programs and is affiliated with the NAIA. The association is comprised of some 33 members including six HBCUs, which are Allen University, Fisk University, Morris College, Philander Smith College, Talladega College, and Voorhees College (Association of Independent Institutions, 2009). In 2008, Fisk University and Philander Smith College were granted membership in the NAIA.

The Great South Athletic Conference (GSAC) was established in 1999 with five charter members affiliated with the NCAA at the Division III level from the Southeast (GSAC, 2008). The charter members were LaGrange College, Maryville College, Piedmont College, and two HBCUs: Fisk University and Stillman College. In 2002, Huntingdon College, Agnes Scott College, and Wesleyan College entered the conference. In 2003, Spelman College (an HBCU) entered the conference on a provisional basis and was granted full membership status in 2005. In 2009, Salem College (NC) entered the conference. These member institutions are located in Alabama, Georgia, North Carolina, and Tennessee.

Stillman College withdrew from the GSAC and in 2004 joined the SIAC to compete at the NCAA Division II level. Similarly, Fisk University withdrew from the GSAC after the 2005–06 season ended. On October 13, 2008, Fisk announced that it had joined the NAIA and began regular and postseason competitive play in the fall of 2009 as an independent.

The Gulf Coast Athletic Conference (GCAC) was organized in 1981 and is affiliated with the NAIA at the Division I level. GCAC member institutions are located in Alabama, Louisiana, and Mississippi. The 10 member institutions are Belhaven College, Dillard University, Louisiana State University at Shreveport, Loyola University of New Orleans, Southern University at New Orleans, Spring Hill College, Tougaloo College, University of Mobile, William Carey University, and Xavier University of Louisiana (GCAC, 2009). Of these member institutions, four are HBCUs: Dillard University, Southern University at New Orleans, Tougaloo College, and Xavier University of Louisiana.

The Alabama Community College Conference (ACCC) is an athletic conference comprised of community colleges in the state of Alabama. Member institutions fielding athletic teams constitute Region XXII of the National Junior College Athletic Association (NJCAA). The ACCC is comprised of 22 state supported institutions including three HBCUs: Bishop State Community College, Gadsden State Community College, and Lawson State Community College (ACCC, n.d). The member institutions field some 107 teams in baseball, basketball, softball (fast-pitch), volleyball, golf, tennis, cross country, track and field, and soccer.

Founded in 1970, the Bi-State Conference constitutes Region II of the NJCAA with some 16 member institutions. This conference is comprised of many technical and community colleges in the states of Arkansas and Oklahoma. Arkansas Baptist College, a historically Black liberal arts college is independent and competes in Region II.

The Carolinas Junior College Conference (CJCC) was established in 1978 and constitutes Region X of the NJCAA. Institutional members represent various junior, technical, and community colleges in the states of North Carolina, South Carolina, Virginia, and West Virginia. CJCC has some 30 member institutions. including two HBCUs, which are Clinton Junior College and Denmark Technical College in South Carolina.

Established in 1983, the Eastern Intercollegiate Athletic Conference (EIAC) was a Black intercollegiate athletic conference that participated in the NAIA's Division I. The members were all HBCUs: Allen University, Barber-Scotia College, Benedict College, Claflin University, Edward Waters College, Morris College, and Voorhees College in the states of Florida, North Carolina, and South Carolina. Following the 2005 season, the EIAC was dissolved. In 2004, Barber-Scotia College lost its accreditation and could no longer field athletics teams. Former members Benedict and Claflin joined the SIAC and are affiliated with NCAA Division II. Allen University, Morris College, and Voorhees College now compete as independents against teams in the NAIA. Edward Waters College joined The Sun Conference (originally The Florida Sun Conference) and is affiliated with the NAIA.

The Great Lakes Football Conference was established 2006 as an intercollegiate football conference and has six member institutions across four states: Indiana, Kentucky, Missouri, and Ohio competing at the NCAA Division II level. The conference members entering the 2009–2010 season were Central State University, Kentucky Wesleyan College, Lincoln University (MO), Missouri University of Science and Technology, and Saint Joseph's College (IN). A former member of the NAIA, Central State University's football program was revived in 2005 after a nine-year absence and entered the GLFC in 2006 to compete at the NCAA Division II level.

Founded in 1999, the Heartland Conference is an intercollegiate athletic conference made up of nine members located in the states of Kansas, Missouri, Oklahoma, and Texas. Only one HBCU, Lincoln University (Jefferson City, Missouri) competes in the Heartland Conference, which is a NCAA Division II conference. Lincoln also competes in the Great Lakes Football Conference (NCAA Division II). In 2009–2010, however, Lincoln University entered its final year in the Heartland Conference and rejoined the Mid-America Intercollegiate Athletics Association (MIAA) NCAA Division II in 2010–2011.

The Mid-America Intercollegiate Athletics Association (MIAA) is an athletic conference comprised of member institutions in Kansas, Missouri, and Nebraska and is affiliated with the NCAA Division II. The MIAA was first organized in 1912 as the Missouri Intercollegiate Athletic Association but changed its name in 1992 to Mid-America Intercollegiate Athletics Association to better represent member institutions both in and outside the state of Missouri. Lincoln University (Missouri) held membership in the MIAA from 1970 until 1999. But again, Lincoln University discontinued competing in the HCAC at the end of the 2009–10 season and rejoined the MIAA NCAA Division II effective academic year 2010–2011.

The Mississippi Association of Community and Junior Colleges (MACJC) began competitive league play with the sport of football in 1927. Together two intercollegiate athletic conferences, the MACJC and MISS-LOU Junior College Conference (MLJCC), make up Region XXIII of the NJCAA. MACJC is comprised of 14 member institutions equally divided into the Northern and Southern divisions of the conference. Two HBCUs are members of the MACJC, and they are Coahoma Community College in the Northern Division and Hinds Community College in the Southern Division.

Founded in 1971, the MISS-LOU Junior College Conference (MLJCC) is an intercollegiate athletic conference and combined with the MACJC constitute Region XXIII of the NJCAA. The MLJCC has five member institutions including Southern University at Shreveport (a HBCU). Southern University at Shreveport offers intercollegiate men's and women's basketball through the MLJCC, which is sanctioned by the NJCAA (Southern University at Shreveport, 2008).

Region V of the NJCAA is the Western Junior College Athletic Conference (WJCAC), which was established in 1972 as an intercollegiate athletic conference. The WJCAC has some 29 member institutions that are mostly technical and community colleges in the states of New Mexico and Texas. This includes the four-year private HBCU, Southwestern Christian College located in Terrell, Texas. In the WJCAC, the Southwestern Christian College men's and women's teams, known as the Rams and Lady Rams, compete in basketball and track.

The Ohio Valley Conference was established in 1948 and is an intercollegiate athletic conference affiliated with the NCAA Division I. The conference football programs compete in the Football Championship Subdivision (formerly known as Division I-AA). The conference's members are located in the Midwest and South regions (Alabama, Illinois, Kentucky, Missouri, and Tennessee) of the US. The Ohio Valley Conference, a predominantly White conference, is the only such conference competing in the NCAA Division I with at least one HBCU member. The conference has 11 member institutes with Tennessee State University as the only HBCU among its members. Tennessee State University joined the conference in 1986. However, most HBCUs with membership affiliation at the NCAA's Division I level are members of the MEAC or SWAC. For some time, North Carolina Central University (NCCU) and Savannah State University were not affiliated with any conference and competed at the NCAA Division I level as independents. However NCCU, a founding member, has applied to rejoin the MEAC. A former member of the SIAC (1968 to 2000), Savannah State University is now independent but also seeks to join the MEAC.

The Pennsylvania State Athletic Conference (PSAC) is a collegiate athletic conference that participates in the NCAA at the Division II level. In 1951, the Pennsylvania State System of Higher Education established the conference to promote competition in men's intercollegiate athletics. In 1977, the conference expanded to include women's sports. In 1980, the PSAC was reclassified with Division II status within the NCAA. The PSAC has 16 full-time members in the state of Pennsylvania and one associate member in New York. The conference members also include Cheyney University of Pennsylvania, a four-year public HBCU. A member since 1951, Cheyney University is one of the original 14 member institutions of the conference.

The Red River Athletic Conference (RRAC) is a collegiate athletic conference and an affiliate of the NAIA Division I and currently has 13 member institutions located in the states of New Mexico, Oklahoma, and Texas. If accepted, the University of St. Thomas will become the 14th member institution. Six of the current RRAC members are HBCUs. They are Huston-Tillotson University, Jarvis Christian College, Langston University, Paul Quinn College, Texas College, and Wiley College (RRAC, 2009). The conference had

North and South divisional champions from the 1998–1999 until the 2000–2001 season when it begin to identify the conference champions based on the regular season.

Established in 2004, the South East Atlantic Conference (SEAC) was an NAIA football conference. The SEAC commissioner was Henry Smith, assistant athletic director at Edward Waters College, a historically Black college. The conference was comprised of only three member institutions: Concordia College in Alabama, and Edward Waters College and Webber International University in Florida. Both Concordia College and Edward Waters College are private historically Black colleges. Webber International University is a predominantly White private business university. In the conference's inaugural year, the Tigers of Edward Waters College won the SEAC title. In 2005, the Hornets of Concordia College won the title, and the Warriors of Webber International were the 2006 champions. In 2007, the SEAC Championship was shared between Edward Waters and Concordia College. Following the 2008 season, the SEAC dissolved in part because Concordia College was unable to gain membership into the NAIA, and even more costly the SEAC was unable to expand its membership. Today, Webber International and Edward Waters College have affiliation with the NAIA and The Sun Conference. Concordia College is independent and competes in track and field, and soccer against colleges in the USCAA. Recently, Concordia College won the 2009 USCAA Men's Soccer National Championship against Saint Briarcliffe College. In football, Concordia College competes against HBCUs in the SIAC. For example, Concordia and Benedict colleges played in the 2009 Miami Dade Football Classic held at the Traz Powell Stadium in Miami, Florida.

The Sun Conference, formerly known as the Florida Sun Conference, is an intercollegiate athletic conference for small independent colleges and universities affiliated with the NAIA. In 1990, the conference was originally formed as the Florida Intercollegiate Athletic Conference and was comprised of eight member institutions: Embry-Riddle, Flagler, Florida Memorial, Nova (now Nova Southeastern), Palm Beach Atlantic, St. Thomas, Webber International, and Warner Southern. Today the conference has 12 member institutions, two of which are HBCUs: Edward Waters College and Florida Memorial University. Member institutions are located in Florida, Georgia, and South Carolina; one associate member is located outside the U.S. in the Bahamas (The Sun Conference, 2008).

Established in 1924, the West Virginia Intercollegiate Athletic Conference (WVIAC) is a intercollegiate athletic conference affiliated with the NCAA at the Division II level and has 16 institutional members, mostly in West Virginia. In 2006, the conference expanded to include two universities in Pennsylvania, which were the University of Pittsburgh at Johnstown and Seton Hill University. Plus, Bluefield State University and West Virginia State University (two four-year public HBCUs) are members of the WVIAC. The conference is one of the oldest and largest of any NCAA Division II level conference affiliates (WVIAC, 2007).

The College of the Virgin Islands was established in 1962 and is a four-year public institution of higher education located in the US Virgin Islands. In 1986, the institution changed its name to the University of the Virgin Islands, St. Thomas, and was federally designated an HBCU by the US Department of Education. The university sponsors basketball, tennis, volleyball, track and field, cross country, swimming, and table tennis at the Division II and/or III levels and is a member institution of the Liga Atlética Interuniversitaria conference. Established in 1929, the conference is comprised of 20 American universities in the Caribbean; that is, the University of the Virgin Islands plus 19 more institutions in Puerto Rico. Mostly, student-athletes at the University of the Virgin Islands compete against opponents from universities in Puerto Rico and some athletic teams from the US mainland (University of Virgin Island, 2008–09).

HBCUs Sponsoring Independent Athletic Programs

There are 15 HBCUs sponsoring independent athletic programs (see Table 2.3). Some of these athletic programs are in various stages of transition and most were discussed previously. There are a few additional independent athletic programs at HBCUs not mentioned thus far, including three 4-year private historically Black institutions: Oakwood University and Selma University in Alabama, and Bennett College for Women located in North Carolina.

Oakwood University is a historically black Seventh-day Adventists located in Huntsville, Alabama. Since its founding in 1896, the institution has undergone several names changes: Oakwood Industrial School, Oakwood Manual Training School, Oakwood Junior College, and Oakwood College. In 2008, the school's name was changed again to Oakwood University. The university emphasizes academic excellence: the congruent development of the mind, body, and spirit; and leadership through service to God and society. The university is regionally accredited by the Southern Accrediting Association of Colleges and Schools and the General Conference of Seventh-day Adventists Department of Education (Oakwood University, 1996–2009).

Selma University is a four-year, private historically Black, coed, liberal arts institution affiliated with the Alabama State Missionary Baptist Convention. It was founded in 1878 as the Alabama Baptist Normal and Theological School to prepare Black citizens to become ministers and teachers. The university served as a Christian liberal arts college for most of its history. In 2009, Selma University finalized its transition from a liberal arts college to a Bible college in receiving full accreditation from the Commission on Accreditation of the Association for Biblical Higher Education in Canada and the US (Selma University, 2007). The university's president, Dr. Alvin A. Cleveland, Sr., stated that the athletic program is independent, affiliated with the USCAA, and competes only in baseball (personal communication, November 5, 2009).

Bennett College for Women (NC) was established in 1878 as a co-educational Black college, but re-chartered in 1926 as a four-year private college for women. Ms. Wanda Mobley, Public Relations Director of Bennett College for Women, asserts that the college's athletic program is independent and participates in basketball and is not an affiliated member of any conference (personal communication, November 5, 2009). Nonetheless, the college competes in basketball against other institutions affiliated by the USCAA.

Unique Institutions

Often business, law, medical, theological, and technical institutions do not participate in intercollegiate athletics. The following HBCUs do not field intercollegiate athletic teams: H. Council Trenholm State Technical College; J. F. Drake State Technical College; Charles R. Drew U. Medicine and Science; University of the District of Columbia David A. Clark School of Law; Interdenominational Theological Center; Morehouse School of Medicine; Lewis College of Business; Meharry Medical College; and Virginia University of Lynchburg. Consequently, these HBCUs were not included in our discourse on athletic programs at HBCUs. It should be noted, however, that the David A. Clark School of Law is an arm of the University of the District of Columbia, which sponsors an independent athletic program and competes in both men's and women's sports affiliated by the NCAA Division II. Likewise, Morehouse School of Medicine is an arm of Morehouse College, which sponsors men's athletics as a member of the SIAC, an affiliated member of the NCAA Division II. There are other unique cases as well, such as Chicago State University and St. Philip's College.

Chicago State University (CSU) is an accredited four-year public urban institution (CSU, 2007). In fall 2007, CSU campus enrollment was mostly (80%) Black and less so White (8%), Hispanic (7%), and others (5%) combined (CSU, 2009). The university is located in Chicago, Illinois, and was founded in 1867 as a teacher training school (renamed several times: Cook County Normal School, Chicago Normal School, Chicago Normal College, and Chicago Teachers College), became a state college in 1967, and received university status in 1971 and given its current name. CSU now awards bachelors, master's, and certificate degrees and retains its emphasis on teaching and general education in the humanities (CSU, 2009). Although it has a high enrollment of Black students, CSU is not designated as an HBCU by educational or governmental authorities (Appiah & Gates, 2003; US Department of Education, 2008). Thus, CSU was not included in our analysis and discourse on athletic programs at HBCUs.

Founded in 1898, St. Philip's College is designed as a historically Black college and Hispanic serving institution. It is the only college in the US with this federal designation. St. Philip's College does not offer intercollegiate sports and therefore was not included in our analysis and discourse on athletic programs at HBCUs. However, intramurals are offered at St. Philip's College in the following men and women sports: basketball, swimming, table tennis, tennis, volleyball, and weightlifting (St. Philip's College, 2009).

In 2007, Virginia University of Lynchburg (Virginia), a four-year private HBCU, was approved by the Transnational Association of Christian Colleges and Schools (TACS) Accreditation Commission to offer a Certificate in Church Leadership (online), a Bachelor of Arts in Business Administration (online), and a Master of Divinity (online) (TACS, 2007). The university does not offer intercollegiate athletics and therefore was also not included in our analysis and discourse on athletic programs at HBCUs.

SUMMARY AND CONCLUSIONS

In the *Brown* case, the US Supreme Court decided that racial segregation in public schools violated the Equal Protection clause of the Fourteenth Amendment. Stated differently, the Court ruled in 1954 that state-sanctioned segregation of public schools was unconstitutional (Jacobs, 1998). Despite the legal decree of the ruling in *Brown*, many Whites resisted the integration of interscholastic and intercollegiate sports (Hodge et al., 2008b). Most predominantly White colleges and universities, especially in the southern states, denied Black students access to their academic programs and athletic teams. In response, most Black college students attended HBCUs. Many of the early HBCUs were established in the late 19th Century as land-grant, state-supported institutions (Evans, Evans, & Evans, 2002). Most of these institutions were established through the Second Morrill Act of 1890, which "provided for the establishment of segregated land grant colleges within the 16 southern and border states practicing both *de jure* and *de facto* racial discrimination" (Harris & Worthen, 2004, p. 447). The mission of HBCUs was to educate Black students as there were no other institutions of higher education that would do so. This mission was, and still remains, critical particularly in light of overt racism that existed in the US during times of legalized segregation (Evans et al., 2002). Thus from their very inception, HBCUs were and continue to be an educational and cultural safe haven for Black students and the important legacy of HBCUs should not be understated. There are an estimated 296,242 students enrolled at these HBCUs and nearly 85% of them are Black.

Important also to the ongoing legacy are athletics at HBCUs. Now, there are 93 HBCUs with athletic programs fielding 939 athletic teams comprising nearly 15,000 student-athletes who compete across 20 different conferences and five athletic associations, and

15 HBCUs that sponsor independent athletic programs. Since their inception, HBCUs have long provided hallowed grounds for academic, social, and athletic expression of students and athletes. It was around 1910 that organizational structure was first brought to Black college sports with the formation of the Georgia-Carolina Athletic Association and soon thereafter the founding of the CIAA in 1912 (Saylor, 2000; Wiggins, 2007). Since those early days, student-athletes have demonstrated courage and skilled athletic performances at HBCUs and beyond.

Today, most HBCUs have sport programs and compete in intercollegiate athletics affiliated with the Caribbean University Sports Association, the National Association of Intercollegiate Athletics (NAIA), the National Collegiate Athletic Association (NCAA), the National Junior College Athletic Association (NJCAA), or the United States Collegiate Athletic Association (USCAA). In the early years, most HBCUs with athletic programs were affiliated with the four major historically Black athletic conferences: CIAA, MEAC, SIAC, and SWAC. Today, only half of the HBCUs are affiliated with these conferences and compete in the NCAA's Division I (Football Championship Subdivision) or Division II systems. The NCAA is the most prominent intercollegiate athletic association with more than a thousand member institutions throughout the US and Canada. Importantly, all four of the major historically Black intercollegiate athletic conferences are affiliated with either NCAA Division I (FCS) or Division II play. In 2006–07, there were 62,165 Black student-athletes who participated in NCAA across the divisional levels. Over the past 10 years, the number and proportion of Black student-athletes has increased at all divisional levels for intercollegiate athletics at NCAA member institutions. In academic year 2007–08, the highest proportion of Black male student-athletes competed in basketball, football, outdoor track and field, and indoor track and field across NCAA divisions. The highest proportion of Black female student-athletes competed in bowling, basketball, outdoor track and field, and indoor track and field across the divisions. All other sports had much lower percentages of Black student-athletes (NCAA, 2009). The highest percentage of male and female basketball players in NCAA Division I were Black student-athletes. Noteworthy and even controversial, football teams make up nearly half of the total number of male student-athletes and the discrepancy between the number of men and women athletes at HBCUs. Popular for both men and women student-athletes are basketball and track competitions.

For the 14,928 student-athletes at HBCUs, there were 498 (53%) women's teams and 441 (47%) men's teams representing intercollegiate athletics at HBCUs competing in 17 different sports in 2008–09. For these student-athletes, the most prevalent sports for men were basketball, outdoor and indoor track, baseball, cross country, football, and tennis. For women, the most prevalent sports were basketball, volleyball, softball (fast-pitch), followed by outdoor and indoor track, cross country, tennis, and bowling. In contrast, the least prevalent sports were swimming, table tennis, lacrosse, and wrestling sponsored by 5% or less of the HBCUs. The low prevalence of these sports (i.e., swimming, table tennis, lacrosse, and wrestling) at HBCUs compares to the low participation rates of Black student-athletes for the same sports across the NCAA divisions.

STUDY QUESTIONS

1. Why were historically Black colleges and universities founded originally?

2. What influence did various religious denominations have in the formation of many HBCUs?

3. Organizational structure was first established in Black college sports in what year?

4. What are your impressions of the four major historically Black intercollegiate athletic conferences?

5. What does the absence of HBCUs from the NCAA's Football Bowl Subdivision mean for athletics at these colleges and universities?

6. How did the racial climate in the early 20th century help shape athletics at HBCUs?

7. What events and realizations led to major college sport programs at predominantly White institutions allowing Black student-athletes to participate in sports at these institutions?

8. How has racial integration affected both Black and White institutions of higher education?

9. Why are basketball, track and field, and football such prevalent sports at HBCUs?

10. Why do so few student-athletes at HBCUs compete in fencing, gymnastics, hockey, swimming, table tennis, and so on?

SUGGESTED READINGS

Chalk, O. (1976). *Black college sport*. New York, NY: Dodd, Mead & Company.

Hodge, S. R., Burden, J. Jr., Robinson, L., & Bennett, R. A., III. (2008a). Theorizing on the stereotyping of Black male student-athletes: Issues and implications. *Journal for the Study of Sports and Athletics in Education*, *2*(2), 203–226.

Hodge, S. R., Harrison, L., Jr., Burden, J., Jr., & Dixson, A. D. (2008b). Brown in Black and White—Then and now: A question of educating or sporting African American males in America. *American Behavioral Scientists*, *51*(7), 928–952.

Hunt, D. (1996). *Great names in black college sports*. Indianapolis, IN: Masters Press.

Hurd, M. (1993). *Black college football, 1892–1992: One hundred years of history, education, and pride*. Virginia Beach, VA: The Donning Company/Publishers.

Jeffries, H. K. (2001). Fields of play: The mediums through which Black athletes engaged in sports in Jim Crow Georgia. *Journal of Negro History*, *86*(3), 264–275.

Wiggins, D. K. (1999). Edwin Bancroft Henderson: Physical educator, civil rights activist, and chronicler of African American athletes. *Research Quarterly for Exercise and Sport*, *70*(2), 91–112.

Wiggins, D. K., & Miller, P. B. (2005). *The unlevel playing field: A documentary history of the African American experience in sport*. Urbana, IL: University of Illinois Press.

ENDNOTES

1. Degree-granting institutions are "defined as post-secondary institutions that grant associates or higher degrees and participate in Title IV federal financial aid programs" (Snyder et al., 2009, p. 3).

2. *Black* is used as an ethnic identifier for mostly African Americans native to the US.

3. *Native American* refers to American Indian and Alaska Native (U.S. Census Bureau, 2005).

4. *International* refers to a person who is not a citizen of the US and who is in the US on a temporary basis and has not been granted the right to stay permanently (Snyder et al., 2009).

5. The 103 HBCUs identified were accredited Title IV degree-granting institutions, or on probation pending full re-accreditation.

6. Found in 1883, Haines Institute was chartered in

1886 by the state of Georgia and renamed Haines Normal and Industrial Institute. By 1912, the school had 34 teachers, enrolled some 900 Black students, and offered a 5th year of college preparatory high school (Leslie, 2005). The institute expanded to include a kindergarten-to-junior college curriculum, the Lamar School of Nursing, and a teacher training program (Georgia Historical Society, 2009).

7. Founded by Dr. Charles T. Walker in 1888, the Walker Baptist Institute was moved from Waynesboro (GA) to Augusta (GA) in 1894. The school had both elementary and secondary levels and offered college preparatory courses for Black students.

8. Title IV institutions participate in any of the federal student financial assistance programs with the exceptions of the State Student Incentive Grant and the National Early Intervention Scholarship and Partnership programs (Planty et al., 2009).

9. Information about the CIAA name change was provided by Jim S. Junot, Sport Information Director, Virginia State University (personal communication, November 24, 2009).

REFERENCES

Alabama Community College Conference. (n.d). *ACCC home*. Retrieved from http://www.acccsports.org/

American Mideast Conference. (2009). *About the American Mideast Conference*. Retrieved from http://www.amcsports.org/

American Midwest Conference. (2009). *Constitution and bylaws 2009–2010*. Retrieved from http://www.amcsportsonline.com/

Appiah, K. A., & Gates, H. L. (2003). *Africana: The encyclopedia of the African and African-American experience. The concise desk reference*. Philadelphia, PA: Running Press.

Association of Independent Institutions. (2009). *Members*. Retrieved from http://www.aiisports.com/

Ayers, E. (1992). *The promise of the new south: Life after reconstruction*. New York, NY: Oxford University Press.

Bauchum, R. G. (2001). *African American organizations: 1794–1999. A selected bibliography sourcebook*. Lanham, MD: University Press of America, Inc.

Bennefield, R. M. (1999). Black women diving into the soccer spotlight. *Black Issues in Higher Education*, *16*(11), 18–19.

Brown, R. G. (1988). Current status of two-year college athletic programs in nongender specific and nonfootball playing schools of the NJCAA. Ed.D. dissertation, Oklahoma State University, United States—Oklahoma. Retrieved from Dissertations & Theses: A&I. (Publication No. AAT 8914987).

Burden, J. W., Jr., Hodge, S. R., & Harrison, L., Jr. (2004). African American and White American students' beliefs about ethnic groups' aspirations: A paradoxical dilemma of academic versus athletic pursuits. *E-Journal of Teaching and Learning in Diverse Settings*, *2*(1), 54–77.

Cahn, S. K. (1994). *Coming on strong: Gender and sexuality in twentieth-century women's sport*. Cambridge, MA: Harvard University Press.

Central Intercollegiate Athletic Association. (1997–2009). *About the CIAA*. Retrieved from http://www.theciaa.com/landing/index.html

Central Intercollegiate Athletic Association. (2009). *CIAA history*. Retrieved from http://www.ciaatournament.org/page/ciaa-history

Chalk, O. (1976). *Black college sport*. New York, NY: Dodd, Mead & Company.

Chicago State University. (2007). *Welcome President Wayne D. Watson, Ph.D.* Retrieved from http://www.csu.edu/president/history.htm

Chicago State University. (2009). *Twenty-first century strategic planning document 2009–2010*. Retrieved from http://www.csu.edu/pdf/strategicplan09.pdf

Chowan University. (1997–2006). *About Chowan: An overview*. Retrieved from http://www.chowan.edu/.

Craig, L. A. (1992). "Raising among themselves": Black educational advancement and the Morrill Act of 1890. *Agriculture and Human Values*, *1*(1), 31–37.

Dufresne, C. (2007, April 5). Record-setting Grambling coach made civil rights part of game plan. *Los Angeles Times*, A-1. Retrieved from http://articles.latimes.com/

Edward Waters College. (2009). *History of Edward Waters College*. Retrieved from http://www.ewc.edu/ewc-history

Evans, A. L., Evans, V., & Evans, A. M. (2002). Historically Black colleges and universities (HBCUS). *Education*, *123*(1), 3–16, 180.

Fields, S. (2008). Title IX and African American female athletes. In M. E. Lomax (Ed.), *Sports and the racial divide: African American and Latino experience in an era of change* (pp. 126–145). Jackson, MS: University Press of Mississippi.

Georgia Historical Society. (2009). *Augusta's historic Haines Institute recognized in new historical marker*. Retrieved from http://www.georgiahistory.com/stories/110

Great South Athletic Conference. (2008). *About GSAC*. Retrieved from http://www.greatsouth.org/

Gulf Coast Athletic Conference. (2009). *GCAC members*. Retrieved from http://www.gcaconf.com/

Harris, R. P., & Worthen, H. D. (2004). Working through the challenges: Struggle and resilience within the historically Black land grant institutions. *Education*, *124*, 447–455.

Hine, D. C., Hine, W. C., & Harrold, S. (2008). *The African-American odyssey: Combined volume* (4th ed.). Upper Saddle River, NJ: Prentice Hall.

Hodge, S. R., Burden, J. Jr., Robinson, L., & Bennett, R. A., III. (2008a). Theorizing on the stereotyping of Black male student-athletes: Issues and implications. *Journal for the Study of Sports and Athletics in Education*, *2*(2), 203–226.

Hodge, S. R., Collins, F. G., & Bennett III, R. A. (2013). The journey of the Black athlete on the HBCU playing field. In D. Brooks & R. Althouse (Eds.), *Racism in college athletics* (3rd ed., pp. 105-133). Morgantown, WV: Fitness Information Technology.

Hodge, S. R., Harrison, L., Jr., Burden, J., Jr., & Dixson, A. D. (2008b). Brown in Black and White—Then and now: A question of educating or sporting African American males in America. *American Behavioral Scientists*, *51*(7), 928–952.

Hunt, D. (1996). *Great names in black college sports*. Indianapolis, IN: Masters Press.

Hurd, M. (1993). *Black college football, 1892–1992: One hundred years of history, education, and pride.* Virginia Beach, VA: The Donning Company/Publishers.

Jackson, C. L. (2001). *African American education: A reference handbook.* Santa Barbara, CA: ABC-CLIO.

Jacobs, G. S. (1998). *Getting around Brown: Desegregation, development, and the Columbus Public Schools.* Columbus, OH: Ohio State University Press.

Jeffries, H. K. (2001). Fields of play: The mediums through which Black athletes engaged in sports in Jim Crow Georgia. *Journal of Negro History, 86*(3), 264–275.

Jones, B. (2007). *Progress, yes; but HBCUs paid a price for it.* Retrieved from ESPN.com

Knoxville College. (2008). *Knoxville College: Reclaiming the legacy.* Retrieved from http://www.kcalumni.org/PDF/KC%20Reclaiming%20the%20Legacy.pdf

Ladson-Billings, G. (2004). Landing on the wrong note: The price we paid for *Brown. Educational Researcher, 33,* 3–13.

Leslie, K. A. (2005). Lucy Craft Laney (1854–1933). *The New Georgia Encyclopedia.* Retrieved from http://www.georgiaencyclopedia.org/nge/

Lincoln University. (2008). *Lincoln University hosts its first football game in 48 years.* Retrieved from http://www.lulions.com/

Lincoln University. (2009). *Lincoln University: Student-athlete handbook 2009–2010.* Retrieved from http://www.lulions.com/

Lumpkin, A. (2012). Critical events: Historical overview of minorities (men and women) in college sports. In D. D. Brooks & R. C. Althouse (Eds.), *Racism in college athletics* (3rd ed.) (pp. 31–61). Morgantown, WV: Fitness Information Technology.

McLendon, J. B., & Bryant, J. I. (2000 May). "Basketball Coach John B. McLendon: The noble revolutionary of U.S. Sport—April 5, 1915—October 8, 1999." *Journal of Black Studies, 30*(5), 720–734.

Mid-Eastern Athletic Conference. (2009a). *About the MEAC.* Retrieved from http://www.meacsports.com/

Mid-Eastern Athletic Conference. (2009b). *North Carolina Central University joins MEAC.* Retrieved from http://www.meacsports.com/

Miller, P. B. (1995). To "Bring the race along rapidly": Sport, student culture, and educational mission at historically Black colleges during the interwar years. *History of Education Quarterly, 35*(2), 111–133.

National Collegiate Athletic Association. (2009). *1999–2000—2007–08 NCAA student-athlete ethnicity report.* Retrieved from http://www.ncaa.org

National Association of Intercollegiate Athletics. (2009). *History of the NAIA.* Retrieved from http://naia.cstv.com/

NCAA News. (2009, July 2). *Chowan first non-HBCU to join the CIAA.* Retrieved from www.ncaa.org.

Oakwood University. (1996–2009). *Oakwood University.* Retrieved from http://www.oakwood.edu/

Pinson re-elected head of GA.-Carolina Athletic Assn. (1926, February 13). *Chicago Defender, 21*(41), 11.

Planty, M., Hussar, W., Snyder, T., Kena, G., KewalRamani, A., Kemp, J., Bianco, K., & Dinkes, R. (2009). *The condition of education 2009* (NCES 2009–081). National Center for Education Statistics, Institute of Education Sciences, US Department of Education. Washington, DC. Retrieved from http://nces.ed.gov/pubs2009/2009081.pdf

Provasnik, S., & Shafer, L. L. (2004). *Historically Black colleges and universities, 1976 to 2001* (NCES 2004 –062). US Department of Education, National Center for Education Statistics. Retrieved from http://nces.ed.gov

Red River Athletic Conference. (2009). *Members.* Retrieved from http://www.redriverconference.com/

Saylor, R. B. (2000, May). Black college football. *College Football Historical Society Newsletter, 13*(3), 4–7.

Selma University. (2007). *President's welcome.* Retrieved from http://www.selmauniversity.org/

Shaw, S. J. (1996). *What a woman ought to be and to do: Black professional women workers during the Jim Crow era.* Chicago, IL: The University of Chicago Press.

Smith, L. (2007). Black female participation languishes outside basketball and track. *Chronicle of Higher Education, 53*(43), A34.

Snyder, T. D., Dillow, S. A., & Hoffman, C. M. (2009). *Digest of education statistics 2008* (NCES 2009–020). National Center for Education Statistics, US Department of Education. Washington, DC. Retrieved from http://nces.ed.gov/pubsearch

Southern Intercollegiate Athletic Conference. (2007). *SIAC history.* Retrieved from http://thesiac.com/

Southern University at Shreveport. (2008). *Athletics.* Retrieved from http://www1.susla.edu/

Southwestern Athletic Conference. (2009). *SWAC history.* Retrieved from http://www.swac.org/

St. Philip's College. (2009). *About St. Philip's College.* Retrieved from http://www.accd.edu/spc/main/about.aspx

Title IX of the Education Amendments of 1972, 20 U.S.C. §§ 1681 (1972). Retrieved from http://www.justice.gov/crt/cor/coord/titleixstat.php

The Sun Conference. (2008). *The Sun Conference members.* Retrieved from http://www.thesunconference.com/

Transnational Association of Christian Colleges and Schools. (2007). *Accreditation Commission action.* Retrieved from http://www.tracs.org/files/DOE_Nov07.pdf

Tucker, D., Hall, C., & Johnson, W., (2012). The transformation and rise of the African American college coach: A look at power and influence. In D. Brooks & R. C. Althouse (Eds.), *Racism in college athletics* (3rd ed., pp. 135–152). Morgantown, WV: Fitness Information Technology.

United States Collegiate Athletic Association. (n.d.). *USCAA: United States Collegiate Athletic Association . . . Leveling the playing field for America's small colleges.* Retrieved from http://www.theuscaa.com/

University of the Virgin Islands. (2008–09). *Athletics—About us.* Retrieved from http://www.uvi.edu/sites/uvi/

U.S. Census Bureau. (2005). *Race and origin in 2005.* Retrieved from http://www.census.gov/population/www/pop-profile/profiledynamic.html

U.S. Department of Education. (2008). *List of HBCUs—White House initiative on historically Black colleges and universities.* Retrieved from http://www.ed.gov/about/inits/list/whhbcu/edlite-list.html

U.S. Department of Education. (2010). *The equity in athletics data analysis cutting tool.* Office of Postsecondary Education. Retrieved from http://ope.ed.gov/athletics/Index.aspx

U.S. Government Accountability Office. (2007). *Intercollegiate athletics: Recent trends in teams and participants in National Collegiate Athletic Association sports.* GAO-07-535. Washington, DC.

Wallenstein, P. (1992). Morrill Act. In C. D. Lowery & J. F. Marszalek (Eds.), *Encyclopedia of African-American civil rights* (p. 369). Westpoint, CT: Greenwood Press.

West Virginia Intercollegiate Athletic Conference. (2007). *About the WVIAC*. Retrieved from http://www.wviac.org/

Wilson, V. R. (2008). The effect of attending an HBCU on persistence and graduation outcomes of African-American college students. In C. L. Betsey (Ed.), *historically Black colleges and universities* (pp. 5–47). New Burnswick, NJ: Transaction Publishers.

Wiggins, D. K. (1999). Edwin Bancroft Henderson: Physical educator, civil rights activist, and chronicler of African American athletes. *Research Quarterly for Exercise and Sport, 70*(2), 91–112.

Wiggins, D. K. (2007). Climbing the racial mountain: A history of the African American experience in sport. In D. D. Brooks & R. C. Althouse (Eds.), *Diversity and social justice in college sports: Sport management and the student athlete* (pp. 21–47). Morgantown, WV: Fitness Information Technology.

Wiggins, D. K., & Miller, P. B. (2005). *The unlevel playing field: A documentary history of the African American experience in sport*. Urbana, IL: University of Illinois Press.

Winston-Salem State University. (2009). *CIAA Board of Directors vote to re-admit WSSU: Rams and Lady Rams will renew their historic relationship with the CIAA*. Retrieved from http://www.wssurams.com/

Appendix A

CHRONOLOGY OF HISTORIC EVENTS AND PEOPLE ASSOCIATED WITH SPORTS AND HBCUs

TIME FRAME	HISTORIC EVENT
1854, 1865	Founded in 1854, the Ashmun Institute (Lower Oxford Township, Chester County, Pennsylvania) was the first Black college established. The institute's name was changed to Lincoln University (PA) in 1865.
1865	End of the Civil War, the Thirteenth Amendment to the US Constitution was ratified; in effect ending slavery in the US.
1890	Congress passed the 2nd Morrill Act, leading to the establishment of land-grant HBCUs.
1890	The first intercollegiate baseball game played between two historically Black institutions was Augusta Baptist College and Seminary (Morehouse College) against nearby opponent Atlanta University.
1890–1895	A period typified by a lack of organizational structure or institutional control over athletics.
1891	Basketball was invented by James Naismith, an instructor at the YMCA Training School (now Springfield College, MA).
1892	On December 27, 1892, the first intercollegiate football game between two Black colleges was held, and Biddle College (now Johnson C. Smith University) defeated Livingstone College on Livingstone's campus (Salisbury, NC).
1894	Howard University and Lincoln University (PA) competed in their first intercollegiate football game. The Thanksgiving Day game played on November 29, 1894, between Howard and Lincoln marked the start of an annual football classic rivalry.
1894	On January 1, 1894, Tuskegee Institute (now Tuskegee University) and Atlanta University (now Clark Atlanta University) played in their first intercollegiate football game.
1896	Morehouse College (then Augusta Baptist College and Seminary), the Atlanta University, along with neighboring colleges, Clark College and Morris Brown College, formed the first city (Atlanta) baseball league.
1896–1898	Augusta Baptist College and Seminary (now Morehouse College) won the city championship for three years consecutively.
1900	Football was formally organized at the Atlanta Baptist College (now Morehouse College).
1900	Virginia Normal and Collegiate Institute (now Virginia State University) defeated Virginia Union University in a football game, where some 400 spectators witnessed Virginia Union leave the football field before the game was over while losing 11-0.
1902	There were four Black institutions in Nashville (TN) that fielded collegiate football teams in the early 1900s. These institutions were Fisk Uni-

versity, Roger Williams University, Walden University, and Meharry Medical College (professional school).

1904   Edwin B. Henderson introduced basketball to students and athletes at Howard University. Moreover, he introduced the game to the Washington, D.C., Black community where it quickly gained in popularity.

1906   The Smart Set Athletic Club of Brooklyn (a Black YMCA in New York) was the first organized Black basketball team.

1907   The first intercollegiate track meet amongst HBCUs was organized in the Atlanta University Center.

1909   An intercollegiate baseball league was formed in Nashville (TN) and included Fisk University, an HBCU.

1909   Edwin B. Henderson was hired as athletic director for the Washington, DC, Public Schools System, and the Washington Interscholastic Athletic Association was formed.

1909–1911   Atlanta Baptist College (now Morehouse College) hosted the first intercollegiate track meet between HBCUs. Atlanta Baptist College won the meet in 1909 and again in 1910. In 1911, Atlanta University (now Clark Atlanta University) won the meet.

1910   Formation of the Georgia-Carolina Athletic Association, which was the first Black collegiate sport association.

1910–1911   Howard University fielded the first *strictly* collegiate varsity basketball team.

1910–1920s   An era when basketball competitions were prominent among Black Club teams, YMCA teams, and collegiate teams.

1912   Dean George W. Hubbard and the Board of Directors of Meharry Medical College decided to end the football program at the college. This ended the annual Thanksgiving Day football contests between Fisk University and Meharry Medical College.

1912   On February 2, 1912, a meeting was held at Hampton Institute that led to the establishment of the Colored (now *Central*) Intercollegiate Athletic Association (CIAA). The CIAA is often called the first major Black athletic conference founded.

1913   In December, 1913, a meeting was held at Morehouse College that led to formation of the Southeastern Intercollegiate Association. The association was renamed the Southeastern Intercollegiate Athletic Conference (SIAC) in 1928 (now *Southern* Intercollegiate Athletic Conference). The SIAC is considered the second major Black athletic conference established.

1913   Arkansas Baptist College had a perfect 17-0 baseball season.

1915–1916   Hampton Institute (now Hampton University) won the CIAA Basketball Championship.

1915, 1916   Morris Brown College won the SIAC Baseball Championship.

1920   Howard University track and field team participated in the Penn Relays and marks the beginning of HBCUs participating in this nation's most famous integrated track meets.

1920–1934   An era when baseball played by Black collegiate teams was most prominent (mid-1920s) to its demise (1934).

1920   In December, a meeting was held among leaders from six HBCUs in Texas, and it led to the establishment of the Southwestern Intercollegiate Athletic Conference (SWAC). It is considered the third major Black athletic conference established.

1920s   Black track athletes who had national recognition in the 1920s were those at PW-IHE, but not so for those at HBCUs. However, many HBCUs had begun to establish track and field programs.

1921   On May 14, 1921, one of the first major CIAA track meets was held at Howard University in Washington, D.C., and some 3,000 spectators witnessed Howard University's track team defeat track teams from Hampton Institute (Hampton University), Lincoln University (PA), and Virginia Normal and Industrial Institute (now Virginia State University).

1921, 1926   Virginia Normal and Industrial Institute (now Virginia State University) won the CIAA Baseball Championship.

1922   Hampton Institute (now Hampton University) won the CIAA Football Championship.

1923, 1925   Virginia Union University won the CIAA Baseball Championship.

1923–1933   A dynasty period for Morgan College of Baltimore (now Morgan State University) basketball teams, winning consecutive CIAA Basketball Championships in the 1931–1932 and 1932–1933 seasons.

1925–1926   Hampton Institute (now Hampton University) won the CIAA Basketball Championship.

1925–1926   Morehouse College won the SIAC Basketball Championship.

1926   Benedict College won the Georgia-South Carolina Athletic Association's Baseball Championship.

1927   On May 21, 1927, the CIAA hosted a major track meet at Hampton Institute (now Hampton University), and the spectators witnessed Hampton Institute's track team defeat track teams from Lincoln University (PA), St. Paul Normal College (now Saint Paul's College), Shaw University, and Virginia Union College (now Virginia Union University).

1926–1927   Clark College (now Clark Atlanta University) won the SIAC Basketball Championship.

1926–1927   Hampton Institute (now Hampton University) won the CIAA Basketball Championship.

1928   The CIAA banned professional school athletes from varsity competitions and enacted a four-year varsity eligibility rule.

1928   Women were first admitted to Olympic track and field competition.

1929   November 2, Hampton Institute and Lincoln University (PA) played the first football game between two HBCUs in New York City at the Polo Grounds, and some ten thousand spectators witnessed Lincoln defeat Hampton Institute, by a score of 13-7.

1929   On May 4, 1929, more than two hundred track and field athletes from some 25 HBCUs participated in the Third Annual Tuskegee Relays in Tuskegee, Alabama. Tuskegee Institute (now Tuskegee University) won the meet.

1929–1930   Howard University won the CIAA Basketball Championship.

1930   Morgan College (now Morgan State University) joined the CIAA.

1931–1933	Virginia State College (now Virginia State University) won the CIAA Baseball Championship for three years consecutively.
1931	Hampton Institute won the CIAA Football Championship.
1932	George Williams was the first athlete from a HBCU to try out for the Olympics, but he failed to qualify.
1932	Despite posting qualifying times in sprinting events, Tydia Pickett and Louise Stokes, both Black women, were left off the US Olympic team and replaced by two White athletes.
1933–1935	Howard University won the CIAA Basketball Championship two consecutive seasons.
1934–1935	Alabama State Teachers College (now Alabama State University) won the SIAC Basketball Championship.
1935–1937	Tougaloo College (MS) won the South-Central Conference Football Championship for three years consecutively.
1936	Virginia State College (now Virginia State University) won the CIAA Football Championship.
1936	Tuskegee Institute (now Tuskegee University) won the SIAC Football Championship.
1936–1937	Wiley College (TX) won the SIAC Basketball Championship.
1936–1937	Greensboro A&T College (now North Carolina A&T State University) won its first CIAA Basketball Championship.
1937	Texas College won the SWAC Football Championship.
1937	Florida A & M College (now Florida A & M University, or FAMU) won the SIAC Football Championship.
1937–1950	During this period, Tuskegee women's track team won 14 National Amateur Athletic Union (AAU) outdoor team championship titles, including eight consecutively. Tuskegee's track and field student-athletes won 65 indoor and outdoor individual titles.
1938–1939	Virginia Union College (now Virginia Union University) won its first CIAA Basketball Championship.
1939–1940	Clark College (now Clark Atlanta University) won the SIAC Basketball Championship.
1939–1940	Alcorn College (now Alcorn State University) won the South-Central Athletic Conference Basketball Championship.
1940	Ralph Oves, a White male, played center for the Lincoln University's (PA) football team. He was the only White player on a HBCU football varsity team at that time.
1940	Morris Brown College won the SIAC Football Championship.
1941	North Carolina College at Durham (now North Carolina Central University, or NCCU) won the SIAC Football Championship.
1942	Florida A & M College (now FAMU) won the SIAC Football Championship.
1942–1945	This was the World War II era, and nearly half of the HBCUs canceled their football competitions for one or more seasons, and other HBCUs played football but had limited schedules.
1943	Eight HBCUs in the CIAA canceled their football seasons due to World War II. These HBCUs were Bluefield Institute (now Bluefield State Uni-

versity), Howard University, Lincoln University (PA), North Carolina College at Durham (now NCCU), St. Augustine's College, St. Paul Polytechnic Institute (now Saint Paul's College), Shaw University, and Virginia Union University.

1945   On September 2, 1945, World War II ends.

1948   Alice Coachman, a student-athlete (track and field) at Tuskegee Institute (now Tuskegee University), was the first Black woman to win an Olympic gold medal. She won gold in the women's high jump while establishing a new Olympic record.

1949   September 23, 1949: Paul Younger beçomes the first athlete from an HBCU, Grambling, to play in the NFL.

1950   January 22, 1950: Robert Jackson of North Carolina A&T State University is the first player from an HBCU drafted by an NFL team (NY Giants) in the eleventh round.

1956   Wilma Rudolph, a member of Tennessee State University's Tiger Belles, won a bronze medal in the 400m relay at the 1956 Olympic Games and won three gold medals (100m dash, 200m dash, and 400m relay) in the 1960 Olympic Games.

1956–1958   Althea Gibson, a student-athlete (tennis) at Florida A & M University, won the French Open Tennis Championship in 1956, and was the first Black woman to win a singles title at Wimbledon. Gibson also won multiple titles, including two consecutive U.S. Open women's titles and two consecutive Wimbledon titles. She was named the 1957–58 Woman Athlete of the Year.

1957–1988   Sam Jones, a student-athlete (basketball) at North Carolina College (now NCCU) was drafted by the Boston Celtics of the NBA in 1957, played for 12 seasons, and was elected to the NBA Hall of Fame in 1988.

1962   December 1, 1962: "Buck" Buchannan, a football defensive linesman from Grambling State University, becomes the first No. 1 overall pick in the NFL draft from an HBCU.

1967   Earl "The Pearl" Monroe, a former student-athlete (basketball) at Winston-Salem State University, was drafted by the Baltimore Bullets (now Washington Wizards) and became Rookie of the Year. Monroe was a four-time NBA All-Star and elected to the Basketball Hall of Fame in 1990.

1968   January 30, 1968: Tennessee State University's Eldridge Dickey is the first quarterback drafted in the first round of the NFL by the Oakland Raiders.

1968, 1989   Art Shell, a former student-athlete (football) at the University of Maryland, Eastern Shore, was drafted in the third round of the combined AFL-NFL by the Oakland Raiders. Shell played on two Super Bowl Championship teams. He became the first Black head coach of a NFL team, the Los Angeles Raiders, in 1989.

1970   Fourth major Black athletic conference confirmed, Mid-Eastern Athletic Conference (MEAC).

1970   Willis Reed, a former student-athlete (basketball) at Grambling State University, became the first player to receive MVP honors in the NBA All-Star Game, regular season, and NBA playoffs in the same season.

1971   September 11, 1971: Morgan State University beat Grambling State University by a score of 9-7 in the first nationally televised college division game held at Yankee Stadium.

1972   Educational Amendments of Title IX became law and forbids discrimination based on gender. The intent of Title IX is to ensure equitable participation opportunities are afforded men and women.

1974   December 3, 1974: Walter Payton of Jackson State University finished fourteenth in the Heisman Trophy voting, becoming the first football player from an HBCU to gain votes.

1975   Andre Dawson, a former student-athlete (baseball) at Florida A & M University, was drafted by the Montreal Expos in 1975. He became the National League Rookie of the Year. Dawson played professional baseball for some 20 years.

1975–1987   Walter Payton, a former student-athlete (football) at Jackson State University, was the Chicago Bears of the NFL first draft choice in 1975 and during his career set numerous records. He was a Super Bowl Champion in 1985.

1976   September 25, 1976: The first collegiate football game outside of the United States between two HBCUs was held in Tokyo, Japan, as Grambling State University defeated Morgan State University by a score of 42-16.

1976, 1984   Edwin Moses, a graduate of Morehouse College, was a two-time gold medal winner in the 400m hurdles in 1976 and 1984. In 1976, Moses set a world record of 47.64 seconds in winning the 400m hurdles. By 1984, he had won 107 consecutive races.

1977   On November 29, 1977, Doug Williams, then quarterback of Grambling State University's football team, became the first HBCU player named to the Associated Press All-American First Team.

1978   December 9, 1978: Florida A&M University won the first NCAA Division I-AA Football National Championship defeating the University of Massachusetts by a score of 35–28.

1980–2009   Rick Mahorn, a former student-athlete (basketball) at Hampton University, was drafted in 1980 by the Washington Bullets (now Washington Wizards) of the NBA. He was traded to the NBA's Detroit Pistons in 1985 and won an NBA Championship in 1989. He played for several other teams during his career. During the 2009 season, Mahorn took over the head coaching position for the Detroit Shock of the WNBA after Coach Bill Laimbeer resigned. At the end of the 2009 WNBA season, the team announced the transfer of ownership of the Detroit Shock to the newest WNBA franchise in Tulsa, Oklahoma.

1982   Vivian Stringer, former coach of Cheyney State University's Women's Basketball Team, led the Lady Wolves to the National Championship game in the inaugural NCAA Tournament. Stringer has also coached successfully at the University of Iowa and now Rutgers University. Stringer has received numerous awards for her coaching genius, including National Coach of the Year in 1982, 1988, and 1993.

1985–1994   Charles Oakley, a basketball player at Virginia Union University, was the NCAA Division II Player of the Year. In 1985, Oakley was named to the NBA's All-Rookie Team as a member of the Chicago Bulls. In 1987 and again 1988, he led the NBA in total rebounds. In 1994, Oakley was selected to the NBA's All-Star Game and the NBA All-Defensive Team.

1985   Jerry Rice, a football player (wide receiver) at Mississippi Valley State University, was drafted by the San Francisco 49ers of the NFL. Rice is considered by some the best receiver to ever play professional football.

1986   John Taylor, a football player (wide receiver) at Delaware State University, was drafted by the San Francisco 49ers of the NFL.

1987–1988   Doug Williams, a former student-athlete (football) at Grambling State University, led the Washington Redskins Football Team to a win in Super Bowl XXII in the NFL, was named the game's MVP, and became the first Black quarterback to accomplish both of these feats.

1988–1995   Marquis Grissom, a former student-athlete (baseball) at Florida A & M University, was drafted by the Montreal Expos of Major League Baseball (MLB) in 1988. He won two Gold Gloves as a center fielder (1993, 1995) and twice led MLB in stolen bases (1991, 1992). Grissom was selected to MLB's All-Star Game twice (1993, 1994) and won a World Series Championship as a member of the Atlanta Braves in 1995.

1991   December 21, 1991: Alabama State University defeated North Carolina A&T State University in the first NCAA approved postseason football game between HBCUs, by a score of 36–13.

1991   Erik Williams, a football player (offensive lineman) at Central State University, was the first lineman drafted by the NFL from Central State University. He was drafted by the Dallas Cowboys, who picked him in the third round.

1992   Women's softball became a MEAC sanctioned sport.

1993   Southern University's Jaguars beat Georgia Tech's Yellow Jackets, the Atlantic Coast Conference Champions, in the first round of the NCAA Division I Basketball Championship.

1994   Anthony Mason, a former student-athlete (basketball) at Tennessee State University, was named the National Basketball Association's (NBA) Sixth Man of the Year.

1995   Steve McNair, a former student-athlete (football) at Alcorn State University, was drafted by the Houston Oilers (now Tennessee Titans) in 1995 and excelled in the quarterback position throughout his NFL career.

1996   Howard University was the only HBCU to offer women's soccer although numerous PW-IHE competed in women's soccer.

2000–2001   Prior to the passage of Title IX in 1972, the NCAA did not sponsor any sports for female student-athletes; however, by academic year 2000–2001, 43 percent of the association's athletics were for female student-athletes.

2003   Florida A & M University became the first MEAC member to win a women's volleyball match in the NCAA Championship.

2005   CIAA collaborated with ESPN to create the largest historically Black athletic conference television package in history.

2005   Bethune-Cookman University became the first MEAC member institution to earn an at-large bid to the NCAA Softball Championship. The Lady Wildcats became the first MEAC member to win a NCAA Division I Softball Regional.

2007	Eddie Robinson died at age 88. Robinson had coached Grambling State University's football team for 57 seasons from 1941 to his retirement in 1997. His career record was 408 wins, 165 defeats, and 15 ties, which included winning multiple college football championships.
2007–2009	For three consecutive years, the CIAA tournament for women's and men's basketball set new economic impact and attendance records for the Tournament, now annually held in Charlotte, NC.
2008	South Carolina State University football team named the MEAC Football Champions.
2008	South Carolina State University men's and women's teams won the MEAC Tennis Champions
2009	Grambling State University won the 36th Annual Bayou Classic Football Game versus Southern University and A&M College, Baton Rouge.
2009	Terrell Whitehead, a student-athlete (football) at Norfolk State University, was awarded the 2009 Defensive Player of the Year in the MEAC Division I. A defensive back, Whitehead had five interceptions and 37 solo tackles this season.
2009	Will Ford, a student-athlete (football) at South Carolina State University, was awarded the 2009 Offensive Player of the Year in the MEAC Division I. He became the all-time leading rusher in the conference with a total of 4,649 rushing yards for his career, surpassing Hampton University's Alonzo Coleman (2003–2006), who held the record with 4,648.
2009	Ulysses Banks, a student-athlete (football) at Alabama A & M University, was named Offensive Player of the Year in the SWAC Division I. A running back, Banks carried the football 194 times for 1,014 yards and seven touchdowns this season.
2009	Jeremy Maddox, a student-athlete (football) at Alabama A & M University, was named Defensive Player of the Year in the SWAC Division I. A defensive end, Maddox was the conference leader in sacks and tackles for loss.
2009	On Saturday, December 12, 2009, Prairie View (season record 8-1) competed against Alabama A & M University (7-4) for the SWAC Football Championship in Birmingham, Alabama. This is Prairie View's first appearance in the SWAC championship game seeking its first conference title since 1964.
2009	The 64th CIAA Tournament for men's and women's basketball was held and drew over 175,000 spectators at the games.
2010	The 65th CIAA Tournament for men's and women's basketball was held February 23–27, 2010, in Charlotte, NC.

Note. Information about historic events secured from multiple sources (e.g., Chalk, 1976; Hunt, 1996; Hurd, 1993) and various websites associated with athletic associations, conferences, and HBCUs.

CHAPTER 3

The Journey of the Black Athlete on the HBCU Playing Field

SAMUEL R. HODGE, FRANKIE G. COLLINS, and ROBERT A. BENNETT III

Abstract

Our nation's historically Black colleges and universities (HBCUs) are located in 20 states, the District of Columbia, and the US Virgin Islands. In the 2006–2007 academic year, these institutions served nearly 312,000 undergraduate and graduate students (Snyder, Dillow, & Hoffman, 2009). HBCUs have long been hallowed grounds for academic, social, and athletic expression of Black and other students and athletes. But the extant literature is undeveloped on the experiences of student-athletes at HBCUs. In this chapter, our primary focus is the participation and experiences of Black student-athletes in intercollegiate athletics at HBCUs. Then, the authors discuss current and future challenges and opportunities for HBCUs and their athletic programs and student-athletes.

Key Terms	
academic performance program	intercollegiate athletics
academic progress rate (APR)	National Collegiate Athletic Association (NCAA)
academic success rate (ASR)	predominantly White colleges and universities
accreditation, critical race theory (CRT)	proportionality conditions of Title IX
Educational Amendments of Title IX	psychological critical race theory
graduate success rate (GSR)	student-athlete
historically Black colleges and universities (HBCUs)	

INTRODUCTION

Participation of Black Student-Athletes

Prior to and for some time after the Civil Rights era of the 1960s, resistance to full integration existed in intercollegiate athletics as many predominantly White colleges and universities denied Black[1] students admission and excluded them from their sport teams (Hodge, Harrison, Burden, & Dixson, 2008b). Consequently, most Black collegians attended historically Black colleges and universities[2] (HBCUs). In that historical context, it comes as no surprise that the HBCUs were campuses where there was an elevated level of athletic participation before desegregation. To this point, Evans, Evans, and Evans (2002) stated that many HBCUs fielded highly competitive sport teams that comprised elite athletes, a number of whom eventually participated in professional sports.

There are many elite student-athletes who played at HBCUs, such as Darrell Armstrong (Fayetteville State University), Reggie Barlow (Alabama State University), Harry Carson (South Carolina State University), Wes Chamberlain (Jackson State University), Alice Coachmen (Tuskegee Institute), Ben Coates (Livingstone College), Anthony Cook (South Carolina State University), Charles Evans (Clark Atlanta University), Marvin Freeman (Jackson State University), Althea Gibson (Florida A &M University), Marquis Grissom (Florida A &M University), James Harris (Grambling State University), Bob Hayes (Florida A &M University), Thomas "Hollywood" Henderson (Langston University), Lester Holmes (Jackson State University), Lindsey Hunter (Jackson State University), Avery Johnson (Southern University), Yolanda Laney (Cheyney University of Pennsylvania), Priest Lauderdale (Central State University), Rick Mahorn (Hampton University), Anthony Mason (Tennessee State University), Marcus Mann (Mississippi Valley State University), Steve McNair (Alcorn State University), Earl Monroe (Winston Salem State University), Nate Newton (Florida A & M University), Charles Oakley (Virginia Union University), Walter Payton (Jackson State University), Bobby R. Phills II (Southern University, Baton Rouge), Willis Reed (Grambling State University), Jerry Rice (Mississippi Valley State University), Eddie Robinson (Alabama State University), Shannon Sharpe (Savannah State University), Jimmy Smith (Jackson State University), Michael Strahan (Texas Southern), Otis Taylor (Prairie View A & M University), Leroy T. Walker (Benedict College), Ben Wallace (Virginia Union University), Rickie Weeks (Southern University and A&M College), and Doug Williams (Grambling State University) (Hunt, 1996). These are some of the many student-athletes who participated in intercollegiate athletics at HBCUs and went on to successful careers in professional sports. But HBCUs have had a decrease in the number of elite student-athletes choosing to participate in athletics on their campuses (Evans et al., 2002). Today, most Black collegians matriculate at predominantly White colleges and universities (Anderson & South, 2007). The exodus of elite Black student-athletes from HBCUs campuses can be attributed largely to them opting to play for major college sport programs at Division I majority White institutions, often with hopes of becoming a professional athlete (Donnor, 2005), and albeit less so, to those who are able to enter into professional sport leagues directly from high school.

The National Collegiate Athletic Association (NCAA) is today's most prominent collegiate athletic association with more than 1,045 member institutions throughout the United States and Canada (US Government Accountability Office, 2007). Moreover, each of the four major historically Black intercollegiate athletic conferences[3] is affiliated with either NCAA Division I (Football Championship Subdivision[4]) or Division II play. For those reasons, our discourse on athletics at HBCUs concerns participation in sports at NCAA affiliated colleges and universities.

In 2006–07, there were 402,793 student-athletes who participated in intercollegiate sports for which the NCAA conducts championships (NCAA, 2008b). Of that total, 62,165 were Black student-athletes (42,685 men and 19,480 women) who participated in NCAA Division I, II, and III sports (NCAA, 2008a). For NCAA member institutions, most Black student-athletes (21,835 men, 11,371 women) competed at the Division I level, followed by 17,099 at the Division II and 11,860 at the Division III level (NCAA, 2008a). In the past decade, the number and proportion of Black student-athletes has increased at all divisional levels for intercollegiate athletics at NCAA member institutions.

In 2007–08, the highest percentage of male (72.2%) and female (78.9%) student-athletes in NCAA sports were White, followed by Black male (18.5%) and Black female (11.3%) student-athletes. Over the past decade, the percentage of Black male student-athletes has increased from 16.3 to 18.5%, and Black female student-athletes have increased from 9.4 to 11.3% for NCAA member institutions (NCAA, 2009c). In 2007–08, the highest proportion of Black male student-athletes competed in basketball (44.3%), football (34.4%), outdoor track and field (21.7%), and indoor track and field (21.4%) across the three divisional levels. The highest proportion of Black female student-athletes competed in bowling (47.8%), basketball (31.4%), outdoor track and field (21.7%), and indoor track and field (21.3%) across the NCAA divisional levels. All other sports had much lower percentages of Black student-athletes (NCAA, 2009c). However, the highest percentage of male (60.4%) and female (50.1%) basketball players in NCAA Division I were Black student-athletes. The next highest percentage of male (32.6%) and female (42.6%) basketball players in the NCAA were White student-athletes. Though the highest percentage of football student-athletes in NCAA Division I competition were White (46.6%), Black men were 46.4% of the football players in 2007–2008. Interestingly, the highest percentages of football players in the NCAA's Division I Football Bowl Subdivision (FBS) were Black (47.5%) men followed closely by White (45.1%) men. The proportion of Black football student-athletes in the NCAA Division I FBS has increased by more than 7% since 1999–2000 from 40.3% to the current 47.5% (NCAA, 2009c). For Division I, II, and III competitions, indoor and outdoor track and field events were among the sports with the highest percentage of Black male and female student-athletes in 2007–08.

Although Black student-athletes are well represented in basketball, football, and track, they are much less represented in other NCAA sports. In volleyball and softball, Black women represented 8.3% and 6.0% of the players, compared to White females, who represented 79.4% and 84% of the players, respectively. The proportions of Black student-athletes are similarly low in other sports such as archery, badminton, baseball, bowling, fencing, golf, gymnastics, ice hockey, lacrosse, and so on (NCAA, 2008a). In NCAA baseball, 85.2% of the players in 2006–07 were White, compared to 4.6% Black baseball student-athletes.

Specific to athletics at historically Black institutions of higher education, the most prevalent sports for men were basketball, outdoor and indoor track, baseball, cross country, football, and tennis. For women, the most prevalent sports were basketball, volleyball, softball (fast-pitch), followed by outdoor and indoor track, cross country, tennis, and bowling. Bowling is rapidly becoming a popular sport for women's competitions and is sponsored at 37% of the HBCUs with athletic programs. In contrast, the least prevalent sports were swimming, table tennis, lacrosse, and wrestling sponsored by 5%

or less of the HBCUs. The low prevalence of these sports (i.e., swimming, table tennis, lacrosse, and wrestling) at HBCUs compares to the low participation rates of Black student-athletes for the same sports across the NCAA's divisional levels. What's more, no HBCU reported fielding teams for men's fencing, gymnastics, ice hockey, lacrosse, skiing, water polo or women's fencing, field hockey, gymnastics, ice hockey, rowing, skiing, water polo or men and women rifle competitions. But there are clear differences in the sporting experiences of student-athletes at the intersection of race/ethnicity and gender. Scholars assert that the differences in sport participation tendencies of Black and White student-athletes are attributable to a number of complex and interrelated factors including access and opportunity, racial disparities, financial resources, and cultural and social norms (Burden, Hodge, & Harrison, 2004; Hodge, Burden, Robinson, & Bennett, 2008a; Hodge et al., 2008b).

Sporting Experiences

It is argued that differences in the sporting experiences of many Black and White Americans are a function of racial disparities in America's history, coupled with a higher proportion of White citizens with greater fiscal resources and access to sport facilities in their communities giving them participation advantages in certain sports (for example, golf, swimming, and tennis). Historically, such factors influenced Black citizens' choices for engaging in more economically accessible sports such as basketball, boxing, football, and track, as opposed to more costly sports as golf and tennis (Burden et al., 2004; Hodge et al., 2008a; Hodge et al., 2008b). Reflective of these cultural, economical, and social conditions are the types of sports on HBCU campuses.

The sport experiences of Black student-athletes on HBCU campuses have received limited attention in the literature. Importantly, however, the American Institutes for Research (AIR) released a 1989 report on the experiences of Black intercollegiate athletes at NCAA Division I institutions. The report was based on data collected from 42 NCAA Division I colleges and universities including three predominantly Black institutions[5] about their men's football and women's and men's basketball student-athletes. Descriptive survey data were collected from 4,083 student-athletes and comparison students (i.e., students who participated in extracurricular activities such as performing arts, drama, student newspaper, and so on, and students were not involved in athletics or extracurricular activities). Descriptive data were reported on (a) the students' background and the campus environment, (b) influences and sources of support, (c) academic and athletic requirements, and (d) progress towards personal goals (AIR, 1989). In the following paragraphs selected key findings, particularly for Black student-athletes, are presented for each of these areas as reported by the AIR (1989).

The first section of the report, *Background of Students and the Campus Environment*, detailed students' demographic data and selected campus environmental variables (AIR, 1989). In sum, the results indicated the following:

- Black student-athletes were overrepresented in football (37% Black men) and basketball (56% Black men and 33% Black women) at predominantly White Division I colleges and universities given their proportions in the general undergraduate student body (4%) at Division I majority White campuses and within the US population (about 12%). Only a few Black student-athletes (8%) participated in sports other than football or basketball.

- Black students, including Black student-athletes, were less well prepared academically for higher education matriculation compared to their White peers. This conclusion was based on high school grade-point averages and standardized tests (ACT, SAT) scores.

- More than half (58%) of the Black football and basketball student-athletes scored in the lowest quartile on the SAT (752 or below), and most (61%) had high school grade-point averages in the lowest quartile (B– or below).

- Black football and basketball student-athletes were actively recruited to participate in NCAA Division I athletics similar to student-athletes of other ethnic groups and were equally likely to receive full athletic scholarships.

- Nearly half (49%) of the Black football and basketball student-athletes were in the lowest quartile in socioeconomic status, and most (61%) reported having less than $25 per month for personal expenses.

- Black football and basketball student-athletes at majority White campuses were much more likely to have felt different from other students on campus, felt they lacked control over their lives, and experienced racial isolation and discrimination than Black students at majority Black institutions.

- Black football and basketball student-athletes, on majority White campuses with less than 4% Black undergraduate enrollments, experienced greater anxiety and depression than their peers at majority White campuses with more than 4% Black student enrollments.

The *Significant Influences and Sources of Support* section of the 1989 AIR report focused on who in the lives of Black student-athletes influenced them most concerning their educational and career aspirations. Most Black student-athletes (80%) rated their families as having the greatest influence in their educational and career aspirations. In addition, more than 29% of the Black basketball and football student-athletes rated their coaches as having a strong influence in their educational and career aspirations. Most Black student-athletes desired for their coaches to encourage them in their academic work and to listen to their personal concerns beyond athletics.

In the area of *Academic and Athletic Requirements* key results show that Black basketball and football student-athletes spend more time in their sports than in either preparing for or attending classes, and they missed an average of two class sessions per week during their in-season time and one class session per week missed in their off season periods (AIR, 1989). Moreover, the student-athletes felt that time demands associated with their sports had an

After a successful basketball career at West Virginia State College, an HBCU, Earl Francis Lloyd became the first African American to play in the National Basketball Association when he did so in 1950.
Courtesy of Earl Francis Lloyd

adverse affect on their class attendance and their study habits and preparation for classes, which negatively affected their ability to perform as well academically as they felt they were capable of doing. The cumulative grade-point average of the Black student-athletes (GPA 2.16) attending majority White institutions was lower than the grade-point averages of basketball and football student-athletes representing other ethnic groups (GPA 2.48), as well as Black students (2.30) who participated in extracurricular activities and Black students (GPA 2.28) in the general student body. For Black basketball and football student-athletes attending majority Black institutions, the GPA was 2.21. Forty-five percent of Black basketball and football student-athletes at majority White institutions were on academic probation at some point during their matriculation.

In the 1989 AIR report students' *Progress Towards Personal Goals* was also examined. Some key findings were that many Black basketball and football student-athletes set demanding goals for themselves such as earning a college degree, eventually attending a graduate or professional school, and expecting to get a high paying job by the age of 40. In addition, 44% of the Black basketball and football student-athletes at majority White colleges and universities and 36% of those at predominantly Black institutions expected to become professional athletes, compared to 20% of basketball and football players from other ethnic groups (mostly White student-athletes).

The overall results of the AIR (1989) study indicate that NCAA Division I Black basketball and football student-athletes were overrepresented in those sports at majority White campuses and were susceptible to feelings of isolation and racial discrimination, found it difficult to speak with others (coaches, teachers, peers) about their personal issues, experienced anxiety and depression, and struggled academically more so than Black student-athletes (basketball and football) attending predominantly Black institutions. More recent studies expose similar negative experiences for Black student-athletes on majority White campuses (Melendez, 2008). In a study of Black football players on a majority White college campus, Melendez (2008) found those student-athletes felt isolated, rejected, unfairly judged by coaches and the campus community, and they developed mistrust of their peers. These findings are troubling. But again, the literature on Black student-athletes at HBCUs is undeveloped. Most studies involving student-athletes at HBCUs focused on such psychosocial variables as aspirations, identity, nurturing, self-concept and self-efficacy (Hale, 1989; Hall, 1997; Hendricks, 2004; Martin, 2009; Steinfeldt, 2007).

Steinfeldt (2007) found Black football players at three HBCUs were socially well adjusted to college life and that the culture of the HBCUs was nurturing to their racial identities. But in a survey study, Martin (2009) found no statistical differences in nurturing by staff personnel of Black student-athletes at HBCUs versus those attending majority White institutions. In broader cultural and social contexts, Black students on majority White campuses have expressed feeling estranged (Lewis, Ginsberg, Davis, & Smith, 2004). The extant body of research suggest that many Black students experience adjustment difficulties, are marginalized and socially isolated, and have limited positive interracial contacts on majority White campuses (Bennett & Okinaka, 1990; Smedley, Myers, & Harrell, 1993; Strayhorn, 2008). For too many Black student-athletes low expectations of their academic capabilities, wrapped in negative stereotypic beliefs about their intellectual aptitude (Harrison & Boyd, 2007; Hodge et al., 2008a), coupled with poor academic preparation in high school position them at a disadvantage in college (Benson, 2000; Donnor, 2005). Stated in a different way, the historical and lingering vestiges of racism in the US are often manifested in the stereotyping of Black collegiate student-athletes who frequently come from underachieving high schools (Hodge et al., 2008a;

Sailes, 1991, 1993; Singer, 2005); in emphasizing Black student-athletes' athletic prowess over their academic promise, educational institutions are responsible for perpetuating social inequalities (Beamon, 2008).

Critical Perspectives on Sport, Education and Race

From a critical race perspective, we argue that our nation's troubled past and the present day vestiges of racism and stereotypic beliefs in collegiate sports warrant further explanation and study (Harrison & Lawrence, 2004). In education, *critical race theory* (CRT) is used to analyze and move against vestiges of racism and discrimination (Jay, 2003). It is "a framework or set of basic perspectives, methods, and pedagogy that seeks to identify, analyze, and transform those structural, cultural, and interpersonal aspects of education that maintain the marginal position and subordination of African American and Latino students" (Solórzano & Yosso, 2000, p. 42). Critical race theorists assert that racism continues to be a seemingly immovable structure in the landscape of the US society as constructed in the hegemony[6] of White male domination within a Euro-American paradigm (Gordon, 1995; Harper, Patton, & Wooden, 2009; Ladson-Billings, 2000). "The hegemony of the dominant paradigm makes it more than just another way to view the world—it claims to be the only legitimate way to view the world" (Ladson-Billings, 2000, p. 258). To challenge the dominant orthodoxy[7], more and more scholars are positioning their work in this critical framework (Dixson & Rousseau, 2005; Ladson-Billings, 2000). In recent years, critical race perspectives have shaped discourse on race and racism in intercollegiate athletics (Burden et al., 2004; Donnor, 2005; Hodge et al., 2008a; Singer, 2009).

Theorizing on the stereotyping of Black male student-athletes, Hodge et al. (2008a) used *psychological critical race theory* (PCRT), an extension of CRT, as an analytical tool to discuss social, economical, cultural, psychological, and racial factors that affect their academic and athletic experiences. PCRT declares that *race* is socially and psychologically constructed from accessible social information (Jones, 1998). Race, as a social construct, has defining properties that amplify racial group differences and contributes to perceptual and behavioral biases. Such biases, in turn, create inconsistent experiences for individuals across different racial groups. And inconsistencies in experiences can lead to conflicting understandings of social realities. Jones (1998) postulates PCRT's major tenets as, (a) spontaneous and persistent influences of race, (b) fairness derived from divergent racial experiences, (c) asymmetrical consequences of racial politics, (d) paradoxes of racial diversity, and (e) salience of racial identity.

In the tenet *spontaneous and persistent influences of race* there are three factors common to the social and psychological construction of *race*, which is spontaneously triggered in cognition. First, individuals naturally tend to categorize things, including themselves and other people; this sustains racial categories. Second, knowledge of race-based stereotypes is pervasive and firmly embedded in cognition. Third, knowledge of stereotypes can and often has automatic influences on beliefs, social judgments, and behaviors. For example, the University of Notre Dame's former football player and alumnus Paul Hornung's comment that "the school needs to lower academic standards to 'get the black athlete' (i.e., football players) . . . if we're going to compete" was considered by some as racist (Whiteside, 2004) and exemplifies race-sport stereotypic beliefs (Hodge et al., 2008a). Commonly held stereotypic beliefs that Blacks are athletically superior but intellectually inferior to Whites and vice versa, coupled with other historical and present-day issues (racism, economic disparities) continue to influence sport activity choices across racial groups (Burden et al., 2004; Harrison et al., 2004). Unwittingly stereotypic beliefs exacerbate perceived similarities and differences between racial groups (Jones, 1998).

The second tenet, *fairness and divergent racial experiences*, insists that owing to incongruent social histories and the construction of race, different racial groups inevitably perceive fairness differently. Perceptions about fairness are not consistent across racial lines and the psychological experience of fairness has not kept pace with the measurable indices of social progress in the US (Jones, 1998). In intercollegiate athletics, for example, a consistent history of marginalized and discriminatory experiences of Black student-athletes on majority White campuses are cause for concern (Benson, 2000; Brooks & Althouse, 2000; Donnor, 2005; Lawrence, 2005; Singer, 2005). Deeply troubling, Black student-athletes have voiced concern that racism is manifested in Blacks being (a) denied access to leadership positions on and off the playing field in sports, and (b) treated differently compared to White student-athletes (Singer, 2005).

In the third tenet, *asymmetrical consequences of racial policies*, for those who are targets of racism and discrimination "acting as if race doesn't matter, when in fact it does," places them susceptible to missed opportunities and acceptance of conditions "whose very enunciation puts one in a 'one-down' position" (Jones, 1998, p. 653). The commonness of missed opportunities in sport is sustained by a legacy of race-based stereotypic beliefs and good old boy practices at the collegiate level, as today there are few Black coaches in Division I-A basketball and even fewer represented in football. Of the 117 Division I-A football programs in the US, almost 50% of the players were Black, while only about 6% of the head coaches were Black (Walker, 2005).

Policies of race neutrality (such as so called "colorblind" admission polices) have negative asymmetrical consequences for targets of racial discrimination. For Black high school students including athletes who hope to one day attend a predominantly White Division I university, policies of race neutrality can have far-reaching consequences. Today, inconsistencies exist at colleges and universities as they grapple with the question of whether to consider race in their admission decisions. For example, the University of Texas adopted race-neutral admissions policies, while in contrast, the University of Georgia had policies that permitted consideration of race in admission decisions (Lum, 2005). Both race-neutral and race-conscious admission policies can be in compliance with the US Supreme Court rulings in light of the University of Michigan cases[8] allowing race to be used as an admissions factor. Still today, colleges and universities have yet to reach a consensus on this issue (Hodge et al., 2008b).

The fourth tenet, *paradoxes of racial diversity*, claims race is "both less and more than it seems" (Jones, 1998, p. 653). Common in sports, race is both more and less than what it seems. It seems more than what it actually is in the stereotypic belief that Black athletes dominate sports largely due to their strong presence and successes in the National Basketball Association (NBA) and National Football League (NFL). In contrast, it seems less salient with White athletes who are members of the dominant race in the US and *actually* dominate most sports in the country. This paradox is explainable in that "homogeneity supports the social significance of race, yet psychological and behavioral facts attest to significant heterogeneity within racial groups" (Jones, 1998, pp. 653–654). By suppressing racial influences in our judgments, we tend to make race even more salient cognitively, leading to a rebound effect, which heightens racial salience on those occasions where suppression becomes no longer compulsory. And because "we all belong to multiple groups, we can create groups whose members have multiple things in common and as a result, racial dimensions recede in importance" (Jones, 1998, p. 654).

In the last tenet, *salience of racial identity*, Jones espoused that racial identity is frequently a source of in-group pride and out-group hostility. In sport, Appiah (2000) exclaimed that for many Black Americans basketball is a source of racial pride and identity.

Likewise, Ogden and Hilt (2003) suggest that Black Americans *consume* basketball and use it as a part of their culture and collective identity. They assert that a *consumption* of basketball is influenced by social and cultural variables such as (a) societal expectations of Blacks to pursue basketball participation (b) presence of Black role models in basketball at the collegiate and professional levels and (c) a belief by many in Black communities that basketball is a viable means of upward mobility. Some empirical data suggest that Black athletes on college campuses have a stronger sense of ethnic identity and perceive it more integrally to their self-concept than White athletes (Hall, 1997).

Consistently, studies have shown that Black youth tend to identify with basketball, football, and track more so than White peers, (Harrison, Lee, & Belcher, 1999) and that basketball is a highly valued sport for Black youth (Harris, 1994; Phillip, 1998). Burden et al. (2004) reported that almost half the Black collegians they interviewed believed that sociocultural variables (e.g., cultural norms, group identity, media images) were influential in their ethnic groups' high preference for basketball and football. Contrasting this, most White collegians believed that their ethnic groups' preferences for golf, tennis, and swimming were resultant of cultural, economical, and social influences. In theory, stereotypic beliefs and in-group pride situated in the cultural normalcy of basketball in the Black community is manifested in years of practice and play, and helps account for Black athletes' large presence in collegiate and professional basketball (Hodge et al., 2008a). As Hartmann (2000) points out, some scholars assert that sports such as basketball and football are essential spaces for "social interaction and community building among African Americans as well as an important symbol of racial accomplishment and a source of pride and collective identification" (p. 233). Basketball is commonly thought of as a means of upward mobility. In speaking of such a mindset, the academic and athletic journey of a Black student-athlete at a historically Black university was highlighted in a recent *USA Today* cover story (Miller, 2010). The student-athlete, a basketball player at Prairie View A&M University, "still dreams of playing in the NBA" despite a history of family struggles, a season-ending leg injury, and averaging less than five points per game as a backup forward in the 2009–2010 season (p. 1C). This story is all too familiar where a Black youth or young adult dreams of becoming a professional athlete, and such dreams, whether they are realistic or not, are reinforced as Black men and women are highly visible in the NBA and WNBA, respectively.

Empirical data suggests that Black student-athletes entering college from disadvantaged circumstances typified with family hardships hold even stronger aspirations of becoming professional athletes than those from more stable families and higher socioeconomic status (Beamon, 2008). From a critical race perspective, we submit that America's legacy of racial inequities and economical disparities coupled with sociocultural norms influence racial identity and, in-turn, play an influential role in the common participation of Black men and women in basketball (Hodge et al., 2008a, 2008b). Evidence of this cultural phenomenon is obvious in that the most prevalent women's and men's teams at today's HBCUs are basketball teams. In other words, competitive basketball games are sponsored at most HBCUs with social and cultural ramifications.

Today, most HBCUs are members of intercollegiate athletic associations and conferences. There are also 15 HBCUs with independent athletic programs. The 93 HBCUs with athletic programs compete in athletics sponsored by the Caribbean University Sports Association, the National Association of Intercollegiate Athletics (NAIA), the National Collegiate Athletic Association (NCAA), the National Junior College Athletic Association (NJCAA), or the United States Collegiate Athletic Association (USCAA). In the early years, most HBCUs with athletic programs were affiliated with the four major historically

Black athletic conferences: Colored (now Central) Intercollegiate Athletic Association (CIAA), Mid-Eastern Athletic Conference (MEAC), Southern Intercollegiate Athletic Conference (SIAC), and Southwestern Athletic Conference (SWAC). Yet today, only half of the HBCUs are affiliated with these conferences and compete in the NCAA's Division I Football Championship Subdivision (FCS) or Division II systems. Importantly, all four of the major historically Black intercollegiate athletic conferences are affiliated with either NCAA Division I (FCS) or Division II play. In 2008–09, there were 498 (53%) women's and 441 (47%) men's intercollegiate athletic teams at HBCUs competing in 17 different sports. For these student-athletes, the most prevalent sports for men were basketball, outdoor and indoor track, baseball, cross country, football, and tennis. For women, the most prevalent sports were basketball, volleyball, softball (fast-pitch), followed by outdoor and indoor track, cross country, tennis, and bowling. In contrast, the least prevalent sports were swimming, table tennis, lacrosse, and wrestling, sponsored by 5% or less of the HBCUs. The low prevalence of these sports (i.e., swimming, table tennis, lacrosse, and wrestling) at HBCUs compares to the low participation rates of Black student-athletes for the same sports across the NCAA divisions. In this book, we speak to these issues in more detail (Hodge, Bennett III, & Collins, 2013).

CURRENT AND FUTURE CHALLENGES AND OPPORTUNITIES

Student-athletes and athletic programs at historically Black institutions of higher education are faced with a host of current and future challenges and opportunities. Now, we will discuss some of the challenges and opportunities, in particular student-athletes' academic performance and women's athletics and Title IX compliance. Further, we discuss the alarming number of HBCUs faced with accreditation difficulties and economical woes that negatively affect their athletic programs and student-athletes, and ultimately, put into jeopardy the very existence of these historic institutions.

Academics and Athletics

In regards to students seeking a bachelor's degree or its equivalent and attending a four-year college or university in 2000–01, Asian/Pacific Islander (67%) students had the highest six-year graduation rate, followed by White (60%), Hispanic (49%), Black (42%), and Native American (40%) students (Planty et al., 2009). Although college graduation rates for Black students have increased markedly since 1970 to today, Black collegians still graduate at a much lower rate than their Asian and White peers (Wilson, 2007). Some assert, however, that Black students fare much better academically at HBCUs than their Black peers on majority White campuses. Generally, they contend that this is due to nurturing and supportive landscapes at HBCUs, whereby Black students' self-identities and cultural pride are enhanced (Cokley, 2000, 2001; Sellers, Chavous, & Cooke, 1998). Expectantly, HBCUs are places where Black students will do well socially and academically for these institutions offer guidance and support (Cohen & Nee, 2000), and this is crucial, particularly for those students not well-prepared academically (Palmer & Gasman, 2008).

Wilson (2007) examined whether there are unique benefits to Black students who attend HBCUs by comparing four-year persistence rates, and six-year graduation rates of Black students at HBCUs and predominantly White colleges and universities. In regards to persistence, Wilson's analyses indicate that Black collegians "who attend HBCUs are statistically no more likely to experience an interruption in their college enrollment" than Black students at majority White institutions (p. 49). The strongest predictors of persistence were academic performance (e.g., high school GPA) and family background (e.g., parents educational level). Similarly, she found that high school GPAs were significant determinants of a six-year degree attainment. Wilson concluded that "a student's performance in the higher education arena is intricately linked to his or her ability to develop the skills necessary to compete and meet the demands of college before they arrive" (p. 49). Stated differently, institutional type (historically Black or majority White) was found to be less salient a predictor of Black students' persistence and graduation rates than pre-college academic preparation and family background. Likewise, results from studies on Black student-athletes show that pre-college academic preparation (which is often inferred from high school cumulative GPAs and standardized tests) is a strong predictor of academic achievement for those at majority White institutions (Comeaux, 2008; Comeaux & Harrison, 2007). But many Black student-athletes attend high schools where they receive poor academic preparation, which hinders future college success (Comeaux & Harrison, 2007).

For the past three decades, scholars have analyzed variables linked to student-athletes' academic performance and achievement (Purdy, Eitzen, & Hufnagel, 1982). Some of the early studies indicated that student-athletes were less well prepared for college and achieved less academically than the general student body. In particular, scholarship athletes, Black student-athletes, and those who participated in the revenue-producing sports of football and basketball had the poorest academic potential and performance (Purdy et al., 1982). But more recent NCAA graduation data leads to the conclusion that Black student-athletes tend to perform comparable to or even better than Black peers in the general student body (NCAA, 2007). The recent 2007 US federal graduation data (cohorts who entered as freshmen in 2000–2001) reveal that student-athletes (63%) graduated at a rate slightly higher (62%) than cohorts in the general student populace (NCAA, 2007). Of note, the NCAA (2007) reported that federal data on race and gender "show that virtually every subgroup of student-athletes is exceeding the graduation success of their counterparts in the student-body" (p. 1). In fact, the data illustrates that Black student-athletes (53%) graduated at a rate higher compared to their Black cohorts (46%) in the general student body (NCAA, 2007).

Importantly, however, the methodology used to determine federal graduation rates has been "criticized for not making adjustments for variables that would result in higher institutional graduation rates" (Davis, 2007, p. 282). The NCAA responded to such criticism by developing an alternative methodology, the *graduation success rate* (GSR), which measures graduation rates at NCAA Division I affiliated institutions and includes student-athletes who transfer into the institution. Moreover, the GSR permits colleges and universities to subtract student-athletes who leave their institutions prior to graduation but would have been academically eligible to compete had they remained (Davis, 2007; NCAA, 2009b). The pertinent details of the NCAA's academic reform program and GSR will be discussed more fully later in this chapter. Suffice to mention here that the NCAA's GSR for Black men's basketball players was 58% in 2008, up 12 percentage points over the past seven years (NCAA News Release, 2008). Similarly the GSR for Black women's basketball players was 78%, up eight percentage points over the past seven years. In the NCAA Football Bowl Subdivision, the GSR was 80% for White and 58% for Black football players, which were up four and five percentage points, respectively, over the past seven years (NCAA News Release, 2008).

It is estimated that in fall 2006, there were 310,446 students enrolled at HBCUs across 21 states, the District of Columbia, and the US Virgin Islands. Of those, 255,782 (82.4%) were Black. Specifically, 159,377 were Black female (62%) and 96,405 were Black male

(38%) students at HBCUs. Of the 103 accredited[9] HBCUs identified, there were 49 (47.6%) four-year private, 41 (39.8%) four-year public, 11 two-year public (10.7%), and only 2 (1.9%) two-year private institutions. Of these degree-granting[10] HBCUs, 93 had athletic programs with an enrollment of 296,242 students. Most of those students (N = 251,290, 84.8%) were Black. Each year, thousands of these students participate in intercollegiate athletics. In 2008–09, a reported 14,928 student-athletes were on athletic teams at HBCUs (US Department of Education, 2010). For sure, student-athletes face pressure to meet academic and athletic demands while attending US colleges and universities including

Table 3.1.	Graduation Data (2002–2003) on Students at HBCUs with NCAA Division I Affiliation		
HBCU	**All Students**	**Student-Athletes**	**GSR**
Alabama A&M University	33%	52%	61%
Alabama State University	21%	44%	55%
University of Arkansas, Pine Bluff	28%	53%	57%
Delaware State University	35%	56%	45%
Howard University	66%	55%	66%
Bethune-Cookman University	41%	57%	67%
Florida A&M University	41%	44%	41%
Savannah State University	33%	45%	46%
Grambling State University	35%	53%	68%
Southern University, Baton Rouge	29%	57%	48%
Coppin State University 16%	16%	47%	58%
Morgan State University	32%	35%	56%
University of Maryland, Eastern Shore	38%	75%	77%
Alcorn State University	40%	19%	80%
Jackson State University	43%	58%	43%
Mississippi Valley State University	29%	36%	57%
North Carolina A&T State University	38%	46%	42%
South Carolina State University	45%	64%	75%
Tennessee State University	35%	62%	79%
Prairie View A&M University	37%	50%	69%
Texas Southern University	13%	38%	47%
Hampton University	52%	56%	72%
Norfolk State University	32%	42%	60%
Mean	35.3%	49.7%	59.5%

Note. GSR = student-athlete graduate success rate.
Note. Data on 2002–2003 graduation rates gleaned from the NCAA (2009b) web site.

those at HBCUs. Increasingly, colleges and universities are faced with academic challenges in regards to student-athletes' retention and graduation rates.

Our analysis of federal graduation data (cohorts who entered as freshmen in 1984–85) reveals significant variation in rates for the general student body and student-athletes who compete in NCAA Division I sports at HBCUs (NCAA, 2009b). A test of significance using Kruskal-Wallis analysis of variance (ANOVA), confirms that a higher percentage of student-athletes (49.7%) graduated in a six-year period than students (35.3%) in the general body at HBCUs with NCAA Division I affiliation. Moreover, GSR data shows a nearly 60% graduation rate for student-athletes at these HBCUs. It appears that many in the student body fail even more than student-athletes to complete their educational journey at a number of these institutions (see Table 3.1).

Likened to those at NCAA Division I institutions, federal data (cohorts who entered as freshmen in 1984–85) reveal significant variation in graduation rates for those in the general student body and student-athletes who compete in NCAA Division II athletics at HBCUs (NCAA, 2009b). A Kruskal-Wallis ANOVA test confirms that a significantly higher percentage of student-athletes graduated in a six-year period than their peers in the general student body at HBCUs with NCAA Division II affiliation (see Table 3.2). What's more NCAA Division II institutions report *academic success rates* (ASR). Recent ASR data indicates a nearly 50% graduation rate for student-athletes at HBCUs with NCAA Division II affiliation. ASR measures graduation rates of student-athletes with athletic financial aid as well as those freshmen who were recruited to the institution but did not receive athletic financial aid (NCAA, 2009b).

Fewer than half of the student-athletes and only about one-third of all students in the general student body graduated in a six year period (1984 to 2002–03) from HBCUs with either NCAA Division I or II affiliation. Students in the general body (35.5%) at HBCUs with NCAA Division I affiliation did not differ appreciably in graduation rates from those (31.8%) in the general body at HBCUs with NCAA Division II affiliation. Likewise, student-athletes (49.7%) at HBCUs with NCAA Division I affiliation were not statistically different in graduation rates from student-athletes (45.6%) at HBCUs with NCAA Division II affiliation. But a Kruskal-Wallis ANOVA test confirms that student-athletes had significantly higher graduation rates than their peers in the general population at NCAA Division I and II affiliated HBCUs. Nonetheless, both student-athletes and students in the general body had less than ideal rates of success at completing their academic journey at most HBCUs. There is continued need for analysis of factors contributing to low graduation rates of student-athletes and their peers in the general student body at these institutions (Wilson, 2007). Why are so many students failing to complete their educational journey at many HBCUs? *USA Today's* editors asserted,

> Too many schools seem obsessed with bringing students in, then seem to lose interest in what happens after they are admitted. With so much money being wasted in futile pursuits of degrees, colleges need to work harder to improve their graduation rates, especially for minority, male and low-income students who are particularly at risk. The graduation rate for Black male college students, for example, has dipped to 31%, down from 38% in the 1990s. ("Too many colleges," 2009, p. 8A)

Once more it is important to mention that empirical evidence indicates that among the most salient predictors of Black students' persistence and degree attainment are pre-college academic preparation and family stability (Wilson, 2007). Likewise in intercollegiate sports, it has been reported that precollege academic preparation (high school GPA) is a strong predictor of college grades for Black male basketball and football student-

Table 3.2.	Graduation Data (2002–2003) on Students at HBCUs with NCAA Division II Affiliation		
HBCU	**All Students**	**Student-Athletes**	**ASR**
Miles College	18%	9%	33%
Stillman College	19%	0%	0%
Tuskegee University	46%	41%	61%
University of the District of Columbia	8%	11%	31%
Albany State University	50%	53%	66%
Clark Atlanta University	45%	40%	39%
Fort Valley State University	47%	58%	71%
Morehouse College	67%	59%	75%
Paine College	25%	68%	44%
Kentucky State University	23%	38%	30%
Bowie State University	5%	38%	59%
Lincoln University (MO)	26%	33%	38%
Elizabeth City State University	43%	86%	80%
Fayetteville State University	38%	75%	73%
Johnson C. Smith University	39%	38%	75%
Livingstone College	27%	6%	41%
North Carolina Central University	48%	71%	74%
Saint Augustine's College	24%	45%	65%
Shaw University	27%	50%	65%
Winston-Salem State University	39%	36%	25%
Central State University	28%	67%	43%
Cheyney University of Pennsylvania	21%	40%	35%
Benedict College	28%	60%	71%
Claflin University	51%	74%	0%
Lane College	32%	25%	53%
Le Moyne-Owen College	26%	86%	40%
Saint Paul's College	20%	23%	48%
Virginia State University	39%	61%	55%
Virginia Union University	31%	22%	41%
Bluefield State College	18%	50%	53%
West Virginia State University	29%	49%	47%
Mean	**31.8%**	**45.5%**	**49.4%**

Note. ASR = student-athlete academic success rate.
Note. Data on 2002–2003 graduation rates gleaned from the NCAA (2009b) web site.
Note. These analyses do not include NCAA Division III Spelman College, Rust College, or Lincoln University (Pennsylvania) as no graduation data for student-athletes were reported.
Note. Federal Graduation data not reported for the University of the US Virgin Islands.

athletes on majority White campuses (Comeaux, 2008; Comeaux & Harrison, 2007; Sellers, 1992). Numerous studies, reports and commentaries have identified a host of variables that plausibly hinder Black student-athletes' academic success:

- Overemphasis on athletics coupled with a minimized emphasis on academics, where student-athletes receive greater reinforcement for athletic than for academic behaviors.

- Stereotype threat and race-based stereotyping of athletic prowess and notions of intellectual inferiority.

- The commercialization of sports in general and the exploitation of Black student-athletes (particularly basketball and football players) in major college sports on majority White college and university campuses.

- Difficulties in managing time constraints while trying to balance athletic demands (e.g., training, practices, travel) with academic expectations (e.g., attending classes regularly, studying) and social roles.

- Difficulties in overcoming psychological and physical fatigue from sport participation as well as from studentship responsibilities.

- Entering college academically underprepared and socially immature.

- Entering college from disadvantaged circumstances and family hardships.

- Experiences of discrimination, racism, social isolation, marginalization, and depression on majority White college and university campuses.

- Lack of social capital or institutional support (e.g., indifferent or limited support from faculty, coaches, and peers) on majority White college and university campuses.

- Institutional neglect (e.g., failure to make available ample academic resources and support).

Most studies regarding the aforementioned variables and the academic plight of Black student-athletes has focused specifically on Black male student-athletes who participate in the revenue-producing sports of basketball and football usually for major college sport programs at predominantly White colleges and universities. The weight of empirical evidence suggests that many Black male student-athletes face academic and social struggles in those athletic programs. Largely absent from the existing research base are studies of persistence, academic and social experiences, and graduation variables with respect to Black student-athletes (men and women) at historically Black institutions of higher education. There is a need for additional research in this area (Hale, 1989; Martin, 2009; Steinfeldt, 2007). Of the many important questions that need further inquiry and explanation here are two related questions to consider: Why are NCAA Division I and II student-athletes graduating at significantly higher rates than are their peers in the general student body at HBCUs? Does the current trend in graduation success rates of student-athletes provide evidence that recent academic reforms by the NCAA are working?

On April 29, 2004, the NCAA Board of Directors announced academic reform intended to promote student-athletes' academic success. The academic reform program is known as the *Academic Performance Program* (APP) and has two main components, which are the graduation success rate (GSR) and the academic progress rate (APR) for athletic programs with NCAA Division I affiliation (Blackman, 2008). As mentioned previously, the GSR is a formulaic tool used to measure student-athletes' graduation rates while accounting for transfer students who either enter or leave the institution as well as those student-athletes who enroll during an academic term. NCAA Division II member institutions report on *academic success rates* (ASR), which has the same basic function as GSR for NCAA Division I institutions except that ASR accounts for student-athletes that were recruited but did not receive an athletic scholarship (Blackman, 2008).

In pressing for academic reform, the NCAA's APR formula is used to assess team's academic progress (as opposed to individual athletes per se). The APR awards two points each academic term (quarter/semester) to student-athletes who meet academic eligibility standards set forth by the NCAA and its member institutions, and who remain with the institution. A team's APR is the total points earned by the team at a given point in time divided by the total points possible, which is 1,000 points (NCAA, 2009a). Using this formula, teams that fall below the cut off score of 925 out of 1000 face immediate (contemporaneous) penalties and may lose athletic scholarships (grant-in-aid). More specifically, a contemporaneous penalty "is assessed if a student-athlete fails to earn both APR points in the same academic term than his or her team scores below the 925 cut score" (Blackman, 2008, p. 239). A team that falls below a 900 APR may be assessed a historical penalty and face significant sanctions that increase in severity with each subsequent offense. The institution's athletic program receives a public warning on the first occasion that a team falls below the 900 cut off score. But after an initial public warning, the institution or team is subject to three years of academic performance analyses and potentially more severe penalties such as practice times reduced, or disqualification from postseason competitions (Blackman, 2008; NCAA, 2009a). The 925 APR score translates to an approximate 60% GSR, and a 900 APR score translates to an approximate 45% GSR (NCAA, 2009a). Blackman (2008) asserts that the NCAA's academic reform program must be critically examined because there seemingly is an uneven level of punishment being imposed against historically Black institutions in general and Black male student-athletes in particular.

Blackman (2008) points out historically *underfunded* and economically disadvantaged Black institutions receive a disparate number of penalties under the NCAA's reform system compared to major college sport programs at predominantly White colleges and universities. In that vein, Blackman argues that socioeconomic status can act as proxy for race. In this case, a lack of financial resources is a proxy for race in the context of higher education and college athletics contributing to "the discriminatory impact of the APP" (p. 243). There are additional reasons for HBCUs encountering a disproportionate level of punishment.

> HBCUs traditionally have been more willing to accept academically at-risk student-athletes in hopes of providing them a positive and structured formal educational experience. Others claim the problem lies in the school administrators' lack of understanding about how the APR works. A full and developed understanding of the APR could be sacrificed if there is a limited staff to oversee the athletic department. Finally, the effects of Hurricane Katrina [on HBCUs in Louisiana] could have contributed to the disproportionate impact. (Blackman, 2008, p. 243)

These factors likely contribute to the struggles of student-athletes in terms of academic performance, retention, and graduation at HBCUs. Most salient to these issues are the institutions' financial woes, limited resources, and limited capacities to provide adequate academic support and resources to its student-athletes, claims Blackman. Also of concern, given that the NCAA can penalize Division I colleges and universities for student-athletes not meeting its APP provisions, institutions are now more likely than ever to deny admission to student-athletes most at academic risk. Blackman's position is that this disproportionally results in denying admission and athletic scholarships to Black male student-athletes who may not otherwise be able to attend college. Arguably, the NCAA's APP penalties are counterproductive to the educational mission of HBCUs as they in effect (*even if not in intent*) discriminate against these typically underfunded and economically disadvantaged colleges and universities.

In recent years, some historically Black universities have been penalized as they struggle to meet the educational standards set forth by the NCAA. For example, Florida A&M University was placed on a four year probation starting in 2006, had to forfeit eleven championship titles, had a reduction in athletic scholarships (grants-in-aid), and had additional penalties due to numerous NCAA violations (Davis, 2006). In 2008–09, there were 14 HBCUs with athletic teams subject to immediate and/or historical penalties. These NCAA Division I member institutions were Alcorn State University; Bethune-Cookman University; Delaware State University; Grambling State University; Hampton University;

Black athletes wishing to play collegiate sports, such as these members of the 1943 Bethune Cookman College football team, were able to turn to HBCUs. Courtesy of Gordon Parks, Library of Congress Prints and Photographs Division

Howard University; Jackson State University; Morgan State University; Norfolk State University; NC A&T State University; Prairie View A&M University; Southern University, Baton Rouge; Texas Southern University; and University of Maryland, Eastern Shore (NCAA, 2009d). Expectantly, HBCUs must do more to ensure student-athletes experience a high quality education, perform well academically, and graduate in a timely period. To that end, for example, Hampton University's Department of Intercollegiate Athletics uses various programs and strategies to support student-athletes. These academic programs and strategies include academic advising; free tutoring services; open access to technology (computer lab); success skills workshops (e.g., workshops on improving study skills and time management); required weekly study hall sessions; assistance for students with special academic needs; and a *Student-Athletes Involved in Learning, Leadership and Service* (SAILLS) program (Hampton University, 2009). In such contexts, Black female student-athletes generally perform better academically than their male peers. For example, the NCAA's GSR for Black men's basketball players was 58% in 2008 compared to the GSR for Black women's basketball players, which was 78%, a 20% difference (NCAA News Release, 2008). But female student-athletes have historically not enjoyed the same sporting opportunities as male student-athletes at the nation's colleges and universities.

Women's Athletics and Title IX Compliance

Women's sports on HBCU campuses have had a unique history from the early days of women's basketball and the glory days of the dominant women's track teams at Tuskegee institute (now Tuskegee University), and later the well-known Tigerbelles track teams from Tennessee State University, to the longstanding issues of equity and recent progress in women's athletics and controversies associated with maintaining compliance with the proportionality requirements of Title IX.

Black women at HBCUs have a long history of participating in a variety of sports (Fields, 2008; Liberti, 1999). For example, at its annual meeting on January 29, 1926, members of the Georgia-Carolina Athletic Association[11] decided to offer conference championships for women's basketball ("Pinson re-elected head," 1926). Members of the association at that time included Allen University, Haines Institute[12], Morris College, Paine College, Savannah State University (then Georgia State Industrial), Walker Baptist Institute,[13] and a couple preparatory schools. In track and field, Black women have a long history of excellence. Between 1937 and 1950, Tuskegee Institute women's track team won 14 National AAU outdoor championships, including eight in a row (Tuskegee University, 2003). In the 1950s, the Tiger belles of Tennessee State University joined Tuskegee as one of the nation's most dominant track and field teams to ever compete regionally, nationally, and internationally (Fields, 2008; Wiggins, 2007). Today, the four most prevalent women's sports at HBCUs are basketball, volleyball, softball, and track and field. But their athletic programs are generally underfunded (Fields, 2008; Suggs, 2001). In comparison to predominantly White institutions, Suggs (2001) argued that many HBCUs may not give women student-athletes the best chance to compete. Suggs explained,

> Colleges in the Mid-Eastern and in the Southwestern Athletic Conferences—which together include all but one of the historically Black colleges in Division I—tend to allocate less money for women's sports than other comparably sized predominantly white institutions in their regions. They also offer fewer playing opportunities for women, especially given that there are far more women than men at those colleges. (p. A36)

Further, Suggs points out that most HBCUs sponsor football teams and that these teams require many male student-athletes (on average over 80 players per team) and significant fiscal support, but rarely do these teams make profits that athletics departments might choose to use for women's athletics.

For years, advocates of women's sports have used legal remedies such as the Educational Amendments of Title IX of 1972 in seeking equitable representation of sport opportunities and financial support for their athletic programs. Title IX reads, "No person in the United States shall, on the basis of sex, be excluded from participation in, be denied the benefits of, or be subjected to discrimination under any education program or activity receiving Federal financial assistance" (Sec. 1681). Specific to collegiate athletics this has been interpreted to mean the number of female and male student-athletes must be to a large extent *proportionate* to the number of female and male students at a particular institution. Some argue that due to the high enrollments of female students at many colleges and universities, particularly HBCUs may struggle to comply with the proportionality condition of Title IX (McErlain, 2008; Naughton, 1998).

Tellingly, HBCUs have experienced difficulty in making progress toward gender equity in athletics as mandated under Title IX. According to advocates of men's sports such as the College Sports Council, this is due to the typically high percentage of female students at most historically Black institutions and this makes it difficult for these institutions to meet the proportionality standard of Title IX (McErlain, 2008; Naughton, 1998; Sander, 2008). On that point, women accounted for 62% of the student body in the fall of 2006 at HBCUs (Snyder et al., 2009). In 2008, the College Sports Council reported that athletic departments at most HBCUs were out of compliance with Title IX and claimed that the law's *proportionality* requirement hinders these institutions in sponsoring more men's sports (Sander, 2008). The Council analyzed data from 74 co-educational HBCUs with athletic programs affiliated by the NCAA Division I and reported that 72 (97%) of these institutions were out of compliance with the standard. It is argued that the law's proportionality condition has had a negative impact on men's athletic programs, especially the nonrevenue producing sports such as baseball and wrestling. For instance, although Howard University disbanded its baseball and wrestling teams in 2002 and added women's bowling, the university has struggled to stay in compliance. Its wrestling coach, Wade Hughes, stated that the proportionality condition hinders HBCUs from adding more men's athletic teams that could, in turn, attract more male students (Sander, 2008). Numerous HBCUs have cut various men's sports and added women's sports, only to later be out of compliance with the ruling (Naughton, 1998).

Norma V. Cantu, the US Department of Education's Assistant Secretary of the Office for Civil Rights, challenges the claim that Title IX adversely affects men's sports. Cantu asserts that an institution can still be in compliance with Title IX even if men receive significantly more athletic opportunities than women do as long as women athletes are not denied opportunities. The intent of Title IX is to ensure equitable participation opportunities are afforded men and women and this can be accomplished whenever institutions have substantial proportionality between men's and women's enrollment rates and their athletic participation rates (Cantu, 2000).

In September 2008, the Women's Sports Foundation released a report indicating that both men's and women's participation in collegiate sports have increased over the past 25 years. The report showed that men's and women's participation on NCAA collegiate sport teams increased by some 6% and 20%, respectively, between the academic years of 1995–96 and 2004–05. And the study reveals that colleges and universities have mostly responded to the proportionality standard of Title IX by increasing women's participation in athletics rather than by decreasing men's. On another key point, the study shows that the initial increase in women's athletic participation was in sports with the highest levels of racial and ethnic diversity (i.e., sports where more women of color participated). But recent increases in NCAA participation rates favor women's sports where there is less ethnic diversity. Marj Snyder, an executive at the Women's Sports Foundation, said the trend affects Black women most as they are largely segregated by sport. Overall, regarding NCAA affiliated athletic programs, almost 68% of Black female student-athletes participate in either track and field or basketball (Moltz, 2008).

Today's athletic programs are often marred in financial struggle, have inadequate resources and facilities, or have witnessed an exodus of elite Black athletes who opt to play for major college sport programs at predominantly White colleges and universities. In that context, some argue that the glory days of sports at HBCUs are forever gone. Too often HBCUs are faced with financial woes that adversely affect their athletic programs and this is exacerbated by issues associated with compliance to Title IX's proportionality standard. In some cases, these types of struggles have created tensions between women's and men's athletic programs (Fields, 2008). Under financial stress, some HBCUs have also eliminated various nonrevenue-producing sports (e.g., baseball, wrestling) in favor of more popular revenue-producing sports such as football.

Accreditation and Athletics

In recent years, there have been far too many HBCUs troubled by difficulties associated with accreditation and financial struggle including spending irregularities, significant reductions in student enrollments, and suspended athletic programs. Examples of those with such difficulties include Knoxville College (TN), Barber-Scotia College (NC), Bishop State Community College (AL), Florida A&M University, Mary Homes College (MS), Morris Brown College (GA), Paul Quinn College (TX), Shorter College (AR), and Texas Southern University (American Association of University Professors [AAUP], 2007). The regional accreditation governing body for most of these institutions is (or was in some cases) the Commission on Colleges (COC) of the Southern Association of Colleges and Schools (SACS). This commission is responsible for accrediting degree-granting Title IV institutions in Alabama, Florida, Georgia, Kentucky, Louisiana, Mississippi, North Carolina, South Carolina, Tennessee, Texas, Virginia, and some institutions in Latin America (COC SACS, 2009a).

In 1997, Knoxville College (TN) accreditation was revoked by SACS due to the college's failure to comply with the association's standards on adequate financial resources, administrative processes, and financial aid. Under the new leadership of Dr. Robert Harvey (acting president), the college declared it is striding toward recovery (Knoxville College, 2008). Subsequent to losing its accreditation in SACS, the college reorganized and joined the Work College Consortium, which is comprised of small predominantly White colleges. Knoxville College is the first HBCU to join the Work College Consortium (AAUP, 2007).

On October 18, 2009, it was reported that Barber-Scotia College's total enrollment was down to only 12 students. The college lost its accreditation in 2004, and total enrollment has fallen ever since (Kelderman, 2009). In 2002, Morris Brown College accreditation was revoked, and it has overwhelming financial debts and is at risk of closing permanently. More troubling, Shorter College (AR) accreditation was revoked in 1998 and the college has since closed. Troubling as well, Mary Homes College, a historically Black Presbyterian-affiliated college, closed in the fall of 2003 due to losing its accreditation and overwhelming financial struggles (Silverstein, 2005).

Of concern, Florida A&M University and Texas Southern University have encountered fiscal difficulties and controversies, and both of these historic institutions were placed on accreditation probation in recent years by SACS (Walker, 2008). Confidently, administrative leaders at both universities asserted that they would successfully comply with SACS requirements to gain full reaccreditation (Walker, 2008).

On June 25, 2009, the SACS COC Board of Trustees took a number of actions regarding the accreditation status of applicant, candidate, and member institutions in its region. Among the Board's actions was lifting sanctions from several colleges and universities including removing Dillard University (LA) and Texas Southern University from probation (SACS COC, 2009a). On the other hand, the commission continued on warning Florida Memorial University due to a failure to comply with financial standards. The Board also denied reaffirmation, continued accreditation, and placed Tougaloo College (MS) on warning for failure to comply with financial standards. In addition, the association denied reaffirmation, continued accreditation, and placed Concordia College (AL) on probation for 12 months due to failure to comply with multiple accreditation standards. Lastly, the commission revoked Paul Quinn College's (TX) membership in the association for failure to comply with several accreditation standards. Paul Quinn College immediately appealed the commission's decision in July 2009. On August 27, 2009, a US District Court in Georgia issued a preliminary injunction that reinstated the accreditation of Paul Quinn College as a member on Probation with the commission and the two parties agreed to abide by the court's order (COC SACS, 2009b).

Additional HBCUs have encountered accreditation difficulties for various reasons in recent years, with most recovering to varying degrees, such as Bennett College for Women (NC), Edward Waters College (FL), Grambling State University (LA), LeMoyne-Owen

College (TN), Lewis College of Business (MI), and Selma University (AL). On June 25, 2009, the SACS COC (2009a) reaffirmed the accreditation of a number of colleges and universities including Bennett College for Women, Morehouse College, Shelton State Community College, and Talladega College. Similarly in 2009, Selma University received full accreditation from the Commission on Accreditation of the Association for Biblical Higher Education in Canada and the US (Selma University, 2007). The bottom line is that some HBCUs are thriving, some are failing, but most are caught somewhere in between (AAUP, 2007). Likewise, the athletic programs at these and other HBCUs are thriving, failing, or merely surviving.

Economics and Athletics

The current US economic crisis has had far-reaching implications for HBCUs, but this is not a new phenomenon for these historic institutions. From the inception of the early athletic programs at HBCUs in the late 19th Century and still today, these programs have lacked the financial resources needed to hire large well paid coaching staffs, purchase ample equipment, and build state-of-the-art athletic facilities (Wiggins, 2007). This places many student-athletes at a disadvantage on and off the playing fields (Evans et al., 2002). In that light, HBCUs have come to rely on two major sources of funding for their athletic programs (a) participating in annual historically Black football classics and basketball tournaments, and (b) playing major college sport teams at predominantly White institutions (Armstrong, 2001; Seymour, 2006).

In the 1920s, it was commonplace for Lincoln University (PA) to take on Howard University in the annual Thanksgiving Day football games. Currently, there are some 25 annual historically Black collegiate football classics. Perhaps the most widely recognized game is held every November on Thanksgiving weekend when Southern University takes on Grambling State University in the Bayou Classic. The game has been nationally televised by the National Broadcasting Company (NBC) for many years. In 1974, the inaugural Bayou Classic was held at Tulane Stadium in New Orleans, Louisiana. The first game was witnessed by more than 76,000 spectators as Grambling State's Tigers beat Southern University's Jaguars, 21-0. The game is now held at the Louisiana Superdome (New Orleans) and named the State Farm Bayou Classic, drawing some 200,000 spectators who add more than $30 million into the New Orleans economy, annually (State Farm Bayou Classic, 2009). In 2009, Grambling defeated Southern University in the 36th Annual State Farm Bayou Classic. Clearly, participating in historically Black athletic conferences' annual tournaments can prove profitable. Moreover, the CIAA women's and men's basketball championships set new economic impact and attendance records for the tournament for three consecutive years (2007–2009) in Charlotte, NC.

For many schools these events are profitable and important to the financial empowerment of their athletic programs. In addition, HBCUs are scheduling basketball and football games with major college Division I teams to supplement their athletic budgets. For example, in 2007, South Carolina State University and Norfolk State University (two HBCUs) played the University of South Carolina and Rutgers University, respectively (two major PW-IHE). Both HBCUs received over $200,000 for participating in these games (Matthews, 2007).

Funds from sport classics, conference tournaments, and *guaranteed games* (HBCUs versus Division I PW-IHE) are vital as the monies from these contests are used to increase budgets, develop and maintain scholarship funds, aid in travel expenses, and upgrade facilities (Seymour, 2006). To further supplement their budgets, HBCUs could focus more on marketing (Armstrong, 2001; Jackson, Lyons, & Gooden, 2001). Sport marketing is a process in which athletic departments plan and implement activities in order to promote and distribute sport products to satisfy public demands while simultaneously meeting the needs of the organization (Pitts & Stotler, 1996). Many HBCUs do not reach their full potential due to their lack of commitment to marketing, and most have limited funds, staff, and expertise in the area of marketing (Jackson et al., 2001). To start, athletic programs at HBCUs should identify corporate prospects, offer ticket packages to various events, seek ways in which marketing can be beneficial to the school by determining the needs of the program as well as the desired outcomes, and identify target markets (Diboll, 1997; Jackson et al., 2001).

SUMMARY AND CONCLUSIONS

From their very inception, historically Black institutions of higher learning were and continue to be educational and cultural safe havens for Black and other students, and the important legacy of these historic institutions should not be understated. Recently, Arne Duncan, the United States Secretary of Education, stated that the historical and present-day importance of HBCUs cannot be overemphasized (The White House Initiative, 2010). Fortunately, America's legacy of racial disparities did not prevent Black athletes from competing in such relatively inexpensive sports such as basketball, baseball, boxing, and track and field. Even though organized football can be rather expensive, it has been a staple of competitive play at HBCUs since 1892, when the first intercollegiate football game was played between Biddle College (now Johnson C. Smith University) and Livingstone College (now Livingstone University). Of note, baseball and football were the prominent sports amongst HBCUs during the early years of their formation (Chalk, 1976). Since the early days, competitive sport experiences have and continue to play an important role in the cultural and social experiences of students on HBCU campuses.

As of fall 2010, there were 93 HBCUs with athletic programs fielding 939 athletic teams to compete across 20 different conferences and five athletic associations. This also includes 15 HBCUs that sponsor independent athletic programs. There are an estimated 296,242 students enrolled at these HBCUs and nearly 85% of them are Black. Many of them participate in college sports. In fact, some 14,928 student-athletes at HBCUs participated in intercollegiate athletics in 2008–09 (US Department of Education, 2010). Since their inception, HBCUs have long been hallowed grounds for academic, cultural, social, and athletic expression. It was 1910 that organizational structure was first brought to Black college sports with the formation of the Georgia-Carolina Athletic Association and soon thereafter the founding of the CIAA in 1912 (Saylor, 2000; Wiggins, 2007). Since those early days, student-athletes have demonstrated courage and skilled athletic performances at HBCUs and beyond.

But there are marked differences in the athletic experiences of student-athletes at the intersection of race/ethnicity and gender. Arguably, the differences in sporting experiences of Black and White student-athletes are likely due to several complex and interrelated variables such as access and opportunity, racial disparities, financial resources, and cultural and social norms (Hodge et al., 2008b). These factors influence Black citizens' choices about participating in various sports such as basketball and track; as opposed to more costly sports such as golf and tennis. In that context, competitive sport experiences have historically and continue to play an important role in the cultural and social experiences of students on HBCU campuses.

Nonetheless, student-athletes and athletic programs at HBCUs face a host of challenges and opportunities. These include student-athletes striding for academic success and seeking fair opportunities to compete in men's and women's athletics. Most troubling, there have been an alarming number of HBCUs faced with accreditation difficulties and economical woes that negatively affect their athletic programs and student-athletes, and jeopardize these institutions.

Still today, Black female student-athletes mostly participate in the traditional sports of basketball, and track and field. However, the expansion of women's athletics, since passage of Title IX, has largely involved sports that Black women have not participated in at high rates such as fencing, gymnastics, swimming, lacrosse, and soccer. Greenlee (1997) implied that Black female student-athletes should expand their sporting experiences beyond such traditional sports as basketball and track and field in order to take advantage of the increased scholarship opportunities in the rising sports for women owing to the proportionality conditions of Title IX.

It is commonly held that attending and participating in intercollegiate athletics at a HBCU is a unique opportunity for student-athletes. Students at HBCUs benefit academically, athletically, and socially (Betsey, 2008; Laird, Williams, Bridges, Holmes, & Morelon-Quainnoo, 2007). Some empirical data indicate that Black students perform better and are more satisfied with their college experiences at HBCUs compared to those at majority White colleges and universities (Outcalt & Skewes-Cox, 2002). Wilson (2007), however, found institutional type (HBCUs versus majority White campuses) less salient a predictor of Black students' persistence and degree attainment than precollege academic preparation and family stability. It is therefore important that academic programs in high school focus on "developing the academic talents of Black student-athlete for competitive college readiness and also formulating critical strategies to overcome or circumvent any impediments" (Comeaux, 2008, p. 9).

All colleges and universities that participate in NCAA Division I athletics must report their teams' academic progress as required by the association's comprehensive academic reform plan. Each NCAA Division I athletic team must calculate its APR scores each academic year, based on the eligibility, retention, and graduation of each scholarship student-athlete, and report the team's APR (NCAA, 2009a; NCAA News Release, 2009). NCAA Division I colleges and universities also report GSR of student-athletes. Similarly, NCAA Division II institutions report ASR of its student-athletes. For each NCAA divisional level, including Division III, federal graduation rates are reported on student-athletes (NCAA, 2009a; NCAA News, 2009).

A number of historically Black institutions of higher education have not been able to meet the educational standards, particularly the minimum APR score of 925, set forth by the NCAA, which is troubling. These institutions are subject to immediate or historic penalties and jeopardize losing student-athletes' scholarships (grants-in-aid), practice reductions, and exclusion from postseason play (Davis, 2006). Some HBCUs have failed to meet the NCAA academic standards and have been given contemporaneous (occuring at the same time) or historic penalties. Teams that score below 925 on their four-year APR and have a student-athlete leave the college or university academically ineligible can lose up to 10% of their scholarships through immediate penalties. Historic penalties can be imposed on teams for poor academic performance over time, defined as scoring below 900 APR on their four-year rate and failing to show significant, sustained improvement or meet other factors. Academic year 2009–2010 marks the fourth year of immediate penalties and the third for historically based penalties. In addition to scholarship losses and restricted practice time, athletic programs with teams facing a third year of historically based penalties can be disqualified from postseason competitions (NCAA News Release, 2009).

Surely, Black students including athletes are able to develop and strengthen their identities, which must include an intellectual dimension (Anderson & South, 2007) and a sense of pride while attending HBCUs (Hall & Closson, 2005). Epitomizing their experiences, students and athletes typically feel supported and nurtured on Black college and university campuses, all of which are rich in history and culture, and higher learning. Recently, President Obama reaffirmed the importance of HBCUs by renewing the White House Initiative on HBCUs in his executive order on February 26, 2010. The order, *Promoting Excellence, Innovation, and Sustainability at historically Black colleges and universities*, reads in part:

> By the authority vested in me as President by the Constitution and the laws of the United States of America, in order to advance the development of the Nation's full human potential and to advance equal opportunity in higher education, strengthen the capacity of historically Black colleges and universities to provide the highest quality education, increase opportunities for these institutions to participate in and benefit from Federal programs, and ensure that our Nation has the highest proportion of college graduates in the world by the year 2020, it is hereby ordered. (Office of the Press Secretary, 2010)

Much is yet to be done to reach these important goals; but surely, Black students are capable of achieving academically, socially, and athletically while matriculating at our nation's historically Black colleges and universities. Our challenge is to better equip them to do so.

STUDY QUESTIONS

1. Why did most Black student-athletes attend HBCUs prior to and for some years after the Civil Rights era in the United States?

2. What type of colleges and universities do most Black college students attend today and why?

3. The exodus of elite Black student-athletes from HBCUs campuses can be attributed largely to what phenomena?

4. What is today's most prominent intercollegiate athletic association in the United States?

5. How many male and female student-athletes participated in sports affiliated by the NCAA?

6. What are the four major historically Black intercollegiate athletic conferences in the United States? Why were these conferences founded?

7. Specific to athletics at HBCUs, what are the most prevalent sport teams?

8. What factors contribute to the differences in the sporting experiences of many Black and White student-athletes?

9. What is critical race theory? What is psychological critical race theory? Are these theoretical frameworks useful in explaining the sporting experiences of different racial or ethnic groups?

10. Student-athletes and athletic programs at HBCUs are faced with a host of current and future challenges and opportunities. What are the most salient challenges and opportunities?

11. What is your understanding of the NCAA's academic performance program; APR, ASR, and GSR? What affect has the NCAA's academic reforms had on student-athletes' academic performance? Are the NCAA's reforms racially or economically discriminatory?

12. What role has Title IX played in gender equality regarding athletic competition at HBCUs?

SUGGESTED READINGS

Chalk, O. (1976). *Black college sport*. New York, NY: Dodd, Mead & Company.

Hartmann, D. (2000). Rethinking the relationship between sport and race in American culture: Golden ghettos and contested terrain. *Sociology of Sport Journal, 17*, 229–253.

Hodge, S. R., Burden, J. Jr., Robinson, L., & Bennett, R. A., III. (2008a). Theorizing on the stereotyping of Black male student-athletes: Issues and implications. *Journal for the Study of Sports and Athletics in Education, 2*(2), 203–226.

Hodge, S. R., Harrison, L., Jr., Burden, J., Jr., & Dixson, A. D. (2008b). Brown in Black and White—Then and now: A question of educating or sporting African American males in America. *American Behavioral Scientists, 51*(7), 928–952.

Hunt, D. (1996). *Great names in black college sports*. Indianapolis, IN: Masters Press.

Wiggins, D. K. (1999). Edwin Bancroft Henderson: Physical educator, civil rights activist, and chronicler of African American athletes. *Research Quarterly for Exercise and Sport, 70*(2), 91–112.

Wiggins, D. K., & Miller, P. B. (2005). *The unlevel playing field: A documentary history of the African American experience in sport*. Urbana, IL: University of Illinois Press.

ENDNOTES

1. Black is used as an ethnic identifier for mostly African Americans native to the US.

2. The Higher Education Act of 1965 defines HBCUs as institutions of higher education established before 1964 whose principal mission was then, and remains today, the education of Black Americans (Wilson, 2007).

3. The major historically Black intercollegiate athletic conferences are the Central Intercollegiate Athletic Association, the Mid-Eastern Athletic Conference, the Southern Intercollegiate Athletic Conference, and the Southwestern Athletic Conference.

4. The NCAA's Football Championship Subdivision (FCS) was formerly called Division 1-AA.

5. Majority Black institutions refer to HBCUs as well as colleges and universities with a majority Black student body enrollment (American Institutes for Research, 1989).

6. *Hegemony* refers to domination, control, power structures, and authority.

7. *Orthodoxy* refers to the holding of correct or generally accepted views or beliefs.

8. The US Supreme Court, on June 23, 2003, ruled in two cases (i.e., *Gratz v. Bollinger* and *Grutter v. Bollinger*) on admission policies at the University of Michigan. The Court ruled that race and ethnicity, among other factors, can be taken into account in the admission process, but racial quotas are prohibited (American Council on Education, 2003).

9. The 103 HBCUs identified were accredited Title IV degree-granting institutions or on probation pending full re-accreditation.

10. Degree-granting institutions are "defined as postsecondary institutions that grant associate's or higher degrees and participate in Title IV federal financial aid programs"

(Snyder et al., 2009, p. 3). Title IV institutions participate in any of the federal student financial assistance programs with the exceptions of the State Student Incentive Grant and the National Early Intervention Scholarship and Partnership programs (Planty et al., 2009).

11. Georgia-Carolina Athletic Association was established in 1910 with the following member institutions: Allen University, Haines Institute, Morris College, Paine College, Savannah State University (then Georgia State Industrial), Walker Baptist Institute,[7] and a couple preparatory schools ("Pinson re-elected head," 1926; Saylor, 2000).

12. Founded in 1883, Haines Institute was chartered in 1886 by the state of Georgia and renamed Haines Normal and Industrial Institute. By 1912, the school had 34 teachers, enrolled some 900 Black students, and offered a 5th year of college preparatory high school (Leslie, 2005). The institute expanded to include a kindergarten-to-junior college curriculum, the Lamar School of Nursing, and a teacher-training program (Georgia Historical Society, 2009).

13. Founded by Dr. Charles T. Walker in 1888, the Walker Baptist Institute was moved from Waynesboro (GA) to Augusta (GA) in 1894. The school had both elementary and secondary levels and offered college preparatory courses for Black students.

REFERENCES

American Association of University Professors. (2007). *Historically Black colleges and universities: Recent trends*. Retrieved from http://www.aaup.org/

American Council on Education. (2003, September). *Affirmative action in higher education after* Grutter v. Bollinger *and* Gratz v. Bollinger. Retrieved from http://www.acenet.edu

American Institutes for Research, Center for the Study of Athletics. (1989). *The experiences of Black intercollegiate athletes at NCAA Division I institutions* (Report No. 3). Studies of Intercollegiate Athletics. Palo Alto, CA.

Anderson, A., & South, D. (2007). The academic experiences of African American collegiate athletes: Implications for policy and practice. In D. D. Brooks & R. C. Althouse (Eds.), *Diversity and social justice in college sports: Sport management and the student athlete* (pp. 77–114). Morgantown, WV: Fitness Information Technology.

Appiah, K. A. (2000). Race identity and racial identification. In L. Back & J. Solomos (Eds.), *Theories of race and racism* (pp. 607–615). London: Routledge.

Armstrong, K. L. (2001). Black consumers' spending and historically Black college sport events: The marketing implications. *Sport Marketing Quarterly, 10*, 102–111.

Beamon, K. K. (2008). "Used goods": Former African American college student-athletes' perception of exploitation by Division I universities. *The Journal of Negro Education, 77*(4), 352–364.

Bennett, C., & Okinaka, A. M. (1990). Factors related to persistence among Asian, Black, Hispanic, and White undergraduates at a predominantly White university: Comparison between first and fourth year cohorts. *Urban Review, 22*(1), 33–60.

Benson, K. F. (2000). Constructing academic inadequacy: African American athletes' stories of schooling. *Journal of Higher Education, 71*(2), 223–246.

Betsey, C. (Ed.). (2008). *Historically Black colleges and universities*. New Brunswick, NJ: Transaction Publishers.

Blackman, P. C. (2008). The NCAA's academic performance program: Academic reform or academic racism? *UCLA Entertainment Law Review, 15*(2), 225–289.

Brief History of the Inter-University Athletic League of Puerto Rico. (2009). *Encyclopedia of Puerto Rico*. Retrieved from http://www.enciclopediapr1.org/

Brooks, D., & Althouse, R. (Eds.). (2000). *Racism in college athletics: The African-American athlete's experi-*

ence (2nd ed.). Morgantown, WV: Fitness Information Technology.

Burden, J. W., Jr., Hodge, S. R., & Harrison, L., Jr. (2004). African American and White American students' beliefs about ethnic groups' aspirations: A paradoxical dilemma of academic versus athletic pursuits. *E-Journal of Teaching and Learning in Diverse Settings, 2*(1), 54–77.

Cantu, N. V. (2000, May 12). Enforcing Title IX. *The Chronicle of Higher Education*. Retrieved from http://chronicle.com

Chalk, O. (1976). *Black college sport*. New York, NY: Dodd, Mead & Company.

Cohen, C., & Nee, C. (2000). Sex differentials in African American communities. *American Behavioral Scientist, 43*, 1159–1206.

Cokley, K. (2000). An investigation of academic self-concept and its relationship to academic achievement in African American college students. *Journal of Black Psychology, 26*, 148–164.

Cokley, K. (2001). Gender differences among African American students in the impact of racial identity on academic psychosocial development. *Journal of College Student Development, 42*, 480–487.

Comeaux, E. (2008). Black males in the college classroom: A quantitative analysis of student athlete-faculty interactions. *A Journal of Research on African American Men, 14*(1), 1–13.

Comeaux, E., & Harrison, C. K. (2007). Faculty and male student athletes: Racial differences in the environmental predictors of academic achievement. *Race, Ethnicity and Education, 10*(2), 199–214.

Commission on Colleges, Southern Association of Colleges and Schools. (2009a). *Actions taken by the SACS COC Board of Trustees: June 25, 2009*. Retrieved from http://www.sacscoc.org/

Commission on Colleges, Southern Association of Colleges and Schools. (2009b). *Disclosure statement regarding the status of Paul Quinn College, Dallas, Texas*. Retrieved from http://www.sacscoc.org/

Davis, K. (2006). In the penalty box. *Diverse Issues in Higher Education, 23*(4), 24–26.

Davis, T. (2007). Academic inequity and the impact of NCAA rules. In D. D. Brooks & R. C. Althouse (Eds.), *Diversity and social justice in college sports: Sport management and the student athlete* (pp. 281–294). Morgantown, WV: Fitness Information Technology.

Diboll, D. (1997). Sports marketing: A key element in our financial future. *Athletics Administration, 32*, 9–12.

Dixson, A. D., & Rousseau, C. K. (2005). And we are still not saved: Critical race theory in education ten years later. *Race, Ethnicity and Education, 8*, 7–27.

Donnor, J. K. (2005). Towards an interest-convergence in the education of African-American football student athletes in major college sports. *Race, Ethnicity and Education, 8*(1), 45–67.

Evans, A. L., Evans, V., & Evans, A. M. (2002). Historically Black colleges and universities (HBCUS). *Education, 123*(1), 3–16, 180.

Fields, S. (2008). Title IX and African American female athletes. In M. E. Lomax (Ed.), *Sports and the racial divide: African American and Latino experience in an era of change* (pp. 126–145). Jackson, MS: University Press of Mississippi.

Georgia Historical Society. (2009). *Augusta's historic Haines Institute recognized in new historical marker.* Retrieved from http://www.georgiahistory.com/stories/110

Gordon, B. M. (1995). Knowledge construction, competing critical theories, and education. In J. A. Banks and C. A. McGee Banks (Eds.), *Handbook of research on multicultural education* (pp. 184–199). New York: MacMillan.

Gratz v. Bollinger, 80 Fed. Appx.417, 2003 US App. LEXIS 22468 (6th Cir. Mich., Oct. 29, 2003).

Greenlee, C. T. (1997). Slow motion penalty. *Black Issues in Higher Education, 14*, 12–14.

Grutter v. Bollinger, 539 U.S. 982, 156 L. Ed. 2d 694, 124 S. Ct. 35, 2003 U.S. LEXIS 5357 (U.S. 2003).

Hale, J. A. (1989). *The effects of personal background and psychosocial variables on student athletes' academic performance and retention at Black private colleges.* Dissertation Abstracts International. (UMI No. 9920418).

Hall, B., & Closson, R. B. (2005). When the majority is the minority: White graduate students' social adjustment at a historically black university. *Journal of College Student Development, 46*(1), 28–42.

Hall, R. L. (1997). *Ethnic identity and cross racial experiences of college athletes.* (Unpublished master's thesis). Temple University, Philadelphia, PA.

Hampton University. (2009). *Academic support.* Retrieved from http://www.hamptonpirates.com/

Harper, S. R., Patton, L. D., & Wooden, O. S. (2009). Access and equity for African American students in higher education: A critical race historical analysis of policy efforts. *The Journal of Higher Education, 80*(4), 389–414.

Harris, O. (1994). Race, sport, and social support. *Sociology of Sport Journal, 11*, 40–50.

Harris, R. P., & Worthen, H. D. (2004). Working through the challenges: Struggle and resilience within the historically Black land grant institutions. *Education, 124*, 447–455.

Harrison, C. K., & Boyd, J. (2007). Mainstreaming and integrating the spectacle and substance of scholar-baller: A new blueprint for higher education, the NCAA, and society. In D. D. Brooks & R. C. Althouse (Eds.), *Diversity and social justice in college sports: Sport management and the student athlete* (pp. 201–231). Morgantown, WV: Fitness Information Technology.

Harrison, C. K., & Lawrence, S. M. (2004). College students' perceptions, myths, and stereotypes about African American athleticism: A qualitative investigation. *Sport, Education and Society, 9*(1), 33–52.

Harrison, L., Jr., Lee, A., & Belcher, D. (1999). Self-schemata for specific sports and physical activities: The influence of race and gender. *Journal of Sport and Social Issues, 23*, 287–307.

Hartmann, D. (2000). Rethinking the relationship between sport and race in American culture: Golden ghettos and contested terrain. *Sociology of Sport Journal, 17*, 229–253.

Hendricks, D. L. (2004). *The relationship of hope and self-efficacy to health promoting behaviors among student-athletes attending historically Black colleges and universities.* Ed.D. dissertation, Auburn University, Alabama. Retrieved from Dissertations & Theses: A&I. (Publication No. AAT 3135997).

Hodge, S. R., Burden, J. Jr., Robinson, L., & Bennett, R. A., III. (2008a). Theorizing on the stereotyping of Black male student-athletes: Issues and implications. *Journal for the Study of Sports and Athletics in Education, 2*(2), 203–226.

Hodge, S. R., Harrison, L., Jr., Burden, J., Jr., & Dixson, A. D. (2008b). Brown in Black and White—Then and now: A question of educating or sporting African American males in America. *American Behavioral Scientists, 51*(7), 928–952.

Hunt, D. (1996). *Great names in black college sports.* Indianapolis, IN: Masters Press.

Jacobs, G. S. (1998). *Getting around Brown: Desegregation, development, and the Columbus Public Schools.* Columbus, OH: Ohio State University Press.

Jackson, E. N., Lyons, R., & Gooden, S. C. (2001). The marketing of Black-college sports. *Sports Marketing Quarterly, 10*, 138–146.

Jay, M. (2003). Critical race theory, multicultural education, and the hidden curriculum of hegemony. *Multicultural Perspectives, 5*, 3–9.

Jones, J. M. (1998). Psychological knowledge and the new American dilemma of race. *Journal of Social Issues, 54*(4), 641–663.

Kelderman, E. (2009, October 18). Troubled Barber-Scotia College seeks revival. *The Chronicle of Higher Education, 56*(9), A1–A22. Retrieved from http://chronicle.com/

Knoxville College. (2008). *Knoxville College: Reclaiming the legacy.* Retrieved from http://www.kcalumni.org/PDF/KC%20Reclaiming%20the%20Legacy.pdf

Ladson-Billings, G. (2000). Racialized discourses and ethnic epistemologies. In N. K. Denzin & Y. S. Lincoln (Eds.), *Handbook of qualitative research* (2nd ed.) (pp. 257–277). Thousand Oaks, CA: Sage.

Lawrence, S. M. (2005). African American athletes' experiences of race in sport. *International Review for the Sociology of Sport, 40*(1), 99–110.

Leslie, K. A. (2005). Lucy Craft Laney (1854–1933). *The New Georgia Encyclopedia.* Retrieved from http://www.georgiaencyclopedia.org/nge/

Lewis, C., Ginsberg, R., Davis, T., & Smith, K. (2004). The experiences of African American Ph.D students at a predominantly White Carnegie I-research institution. *College Student Journal, 38*(2), 231–245.

Liberti, R. (1999). "We were ladies; We just played basketball like boys": African American womanhood and competitive college basketball at Bennett College,

1928–1942. *Journal of Sport History, 26,* 568.

Matthews, F. J. (2007, October 18). HBCU football teams get a shot at big paydays: National exposure. *Diverse Issues in Higher Education, 24*(18), 19–20.

McErlain, E. (2008). *College Sports Council study shows historically Black colleges struggle to meet Title IX proportionality.* Retrieved from http://www.themat.com

Miller, J. (2010, March 10). Basketball travels and travails: After 12 school stops amid family woes, Green's journey remains a bumpy ride. *USA Today,* 1C–2C.

Melendez, M. C. (2008). Black football players on a predominantly White college campus: Psychosocial and emotional realities of the Black college athlete experience. *Journal of Black Psychology, 34*(4), 423–451.

Moltz, D. (2008, September 24). Title IX tantrum. *Inside Higher Ed.* Retrieved from http://www.insidehighered.com/

Martin, G. (2009). A comparison of African-American athletes' nurturing experiences at historically Black and historically White colleges/universities. Ed.D. dissertation, The University of North Carolina at Greensboro, North Carolina. Retrieved from Dissertations & Theses: A&I. (Publication No. AAT 3355955).

National Collegiate Athletic Association. (2007). *2007 NCAA Division I federal graduation rates—Key findings.* Retrieved from http://www.ncaa.org

National Collegiate Athletic Association. (2008a). *1999–00—2006–07 NCAA student-athlete race and ethnicity report.* Retrieved from http://www.ncaa.org

National Collegiate Athletic Association. (2008b). *Participation 1981–82—2006–07 NCAA sports sponsorship and participation rates report.* Retrieved from http://www.ncaa.org

National Collegiate Athletic Association. (2009a). *Defining academic reform.* Retrieved from http://www.ncaa.org/

National Collegiate Athletic Association. (2009b). *Division I graduation success rate/Division II academic success rate.* Retrieved from http://www.ncaa.org

National Collegiate Athletic Association. (2009c). *1999–2000—2007–08 NCAA student-athlete ethnicity report.* Retrieved from http://www.ncaa.org

National Collegiate Athletic Association. (2009d). *Teams subject to penalties 2008–09 by institution.* Retrieved from http://www.ncaa.org

Naughton, J. (1998, February). Title IX poses a particular challenge at predominantly Black institutions. *The Chronicle of Higher Education, 44,* A55–A56.

NCAA News. (2009, November 18). *Division I graduation rates reach all-time highs.* Retrieved from http://www.ncaa.org

NCAA News Release. (2008, October 14). *NCAA student-athletes graduating at highest rates ever.* Retrieved from http://www.ncaa.org

NCAA News Release. (2009, June). *Postseason ban upheld for Jacksonville State.* Retrieved from http://www.ncaa.org

Nelson Laird, T. F., Williams, J. M., Bridges, B. K., Holmes, M. S., & Morelon–Quainoo, C. L. (2007). African American and Hispanic student engagement at minority serving and predominantly White institutions. *Journal of College Student Development, 48*(1), 39–56.

Office of the Press Secretary. The White House. (2010, February 26). *Promoting excellence, innovation, and sustainability at historically Black colleges and universities.* Retrieved from http://www.ed.gov/

Ogden, D. C., & Hilt, M. (2003). Collective identity and basketball: An explanation for the decreasing number of African-Americans on America's baseball diamonds. *Journal of Leisure Research, 35,* 213–227.

Outcalt, C. L., & Skewes-Cox, T. E. (2002). Involvement, interaction, and satisfaction: The human environment at HBCUs. *The Review of Higher Education, 25*(3), 331–347.

Palmer, R., & Gasman, M. (2008). "It takes a village to raise a child": The role of social capital in promoting academic success for African American men at a Black college. *Journal of College Student Development, 49*(1), 52–70.

Phillip, S. F. (1998). African-Americans' perceptions of leisure, racial discrimination, and life satisfaction. *Perceptual and Motor Skills, 87,* 14–18.

Pinson re-elected head of GA.—Carolina Athletic Assn. (1926, February 13). *Chicago Defender, 21*(41), 11.

Pitts, B. G., & Stotler, D. K. (1996). *Fundamentals of sport marketing.* Morgantown, WV: Fitness Information Technology.

Planty, M., Hussar, W., Snyder, T., Kena, G., KewalRamani, A., Kemp, J., Bianco, K., & Dinkes, R. (2009). *The condition of education 2009* (NCES 2009-081). National Center for Education Statistics, Institute of Education Sciences, US Department of Education. Washington, DC. Retrieved from http://nces.ed.gov/pubs2009/2009081.pdf

Purdy, D. A., Eitzen, D. S., & Hufnagel, R. (1982). Are athletes also students? The educational attainment of college athletes. *Social Problems, 29*(4), 439–448.

Sailes, G. A. (1991). The myth of Black sports supremacy. *Journal of Black Studies, 21*(4), 480–487.

Sailes, G. A. (1993). An investigation of campus stereotypes: The myth of Black athletic superiority and the dumb jock stereotype. *Sociology of Sport Journal, 10,* 88–97.

Sander, L. (2008, February 27). Historically Black colleges are not in compliance with Title IX, study finds. *The Chronicle of Higher Education.* Retrieved from http://chronicle.com

Saylor, R. B. (2000, May). Black college football. *College Football Historical Society Newsletter, 13*(3), 4–7.

Sellers, R. M. (1992). Racial differences in the predictors for academic achievement of student-athletes in Division I revenue producing sports. *Sociology of Sport Journal, 9,* 48–59.

Sellers, R. M., Chavous, T. M., & Cooke, D. Y. (1998). Racial ideology and racial centrality as predictors of African American college students' academic performance. *Journal of Black Psychology, 24,* 8–27.

Selma University. (2007). *President's welcome.* Retrieved from http://www.selmauniversity.org/

Seymour, A., Jr. (2006). Pigskin payday. *Diverse Issues in Higher Education, 23,* 37–39.

Silverstein, E. (2005, March 7). It's official: Mary Holmes is closed. *Presbyterian News Service.* Retrieved from http://www.pcusa.org/pcnews/2005/05127.htm

Singer, J. N. (2005). Understanding racism through the eyes of African American male student-athletes. *Race, Ethnicity and Education, 8,* 365–386.

Singer, J. N. (2009). African American football athletes'

perspectives on institutional integrity in college sport. *Research Quarterly for Exercise and Sport*, *80*(1), 102–116.

Smedley, B. D., Myers, H. F., & Harell, S. P. (1993). Minority status stress and college adjustment of ethnic minority freshmen. *Journal of Higher Education*, *64*(4), 434–452.

Snyder, T. D., Dillow, S. A., & Hoffman, C. M. (2009). *Digest of education statistics 2008* (NCES 2009-020). National Center for Education Statistics, U.S. Department of Education. Washington, DC. Retrieved from http:// nces.ed.gov/pubsearch

Solórzano, D., & Yosso, T. (2000). Towards a critical race theory of Chicano and Chicana education. In C. Tejada, C. Martinez, & Z. Leonardo (Eds.), *Charting new terrains in Chicana(o)/Latina(o) education* (pp. 35–66). Cresskill, NJ: Hampton Press.

State Farm Bayou Classic. (2009). Retrieved from http:// www.travelnola.com/novemberneworleans/Bayou-Clas sic-Battle-of-the-bands/

Steinfeldt, J. A. (2007). *The role of racial and athletic identity in the college adjustment of African American student-athletes at historically Black colleges and universities (HBCU)*. Dissertation Abstracts International. (UMI No. 3262942)

Strayhorn, T. L. (2008). Fittin' in: Do diverse interactions with peers affect sense of belonging for Black men at predominantly White institutions? *NASPA Journal*, *45*(4), 501–527.

Suggs, W. (2001, November 30). Left behind. *Chronicle of Higher Education*, *48*(14), A35–A37.

Title IX of the Education Amendments of 1972, 20 U.S.C. §§ 1681 (1972). Retrieved from http://www.justice.gov /crt/cor/coord/titleixstat.php

The White House Initiative on historically Black colleges and universities. (2010). *Strengthening our nation's historically Black colleges and universities*. Retrieved from http://www2.ed.gov/about/inits/list/whhbcu /strengthening-hbcus.pdf

Too many colleges fail to graduate students. Our view: But performance varies widely—with many lessons to learn. (2009, June 24). *USA Today*, p. 8A.

Tuskegee University. (2003). *Tuskegee track and field milestones*. Retrieved from http://www.tuskegee.edu/

US Department of Education. (2010). *Equity in athletics data analysis cutting tool*. Office of Postsecondary Education. Retrieved from http://ope.ed.gov/athletics/In dex.aspx

US Government Accountability Office. (2007). *Intercollegiate athletics: Recent trends in teams and participants in National Collegiate Athletic Association sports*. GAO-07-535. Washington, DC.

Walker, M. A. (2005). Black coaches are ready, willing— and still waiting. *Black Issues in Higher Education*, *22*(6), 26–29.

Walker, M. A. (2008). Accreditation probation for country's two largest HBCUs. *Diverse Issues in Higher Education*, *24*(25), 10.

Whiteside, K. (2004, April 1). Hornung's 'black athlete' comment irks Notre Dame. *USA Today*, 1C.

Wilson, V. R. (2007). The effect of attending an HBCU on persistence and graduation outcomes of African-American college students. *The Review of Black Political Economy*, *34*(1–2), 11–52.

Wiggins, D. K. (2007). Climbing the racial mountain: A history of the African American experience in sport. In D. D. Brooks & R. C. Althouse (Eds.), *Diversity and social justice in college sports: Sport management and the student athlete* (pp. 21–47). Morgantown, WV: Fitness Information Technology.

CHAPTER 4

The Transformation and Rise of the African American College Coach: A Look at Power and Influence

DELANO TUCKER, CHEVELLE HALL, and WARDELL JOHNSON

Abstract

Black coaches (men and women) were presented with numerous barriers as they attempted to integrate the playing, coaching and administrative ranks on predominately White college campus. Analysis of current employment data suggests the struggle for social justice and inclusion in the market place is still a dream deferred for many coaches of color. The transformation and rise of the Black coach begins on the campus of historical Black colleges and universities. Legendary coaches such as Eddie Robinson, Arnett Mumford, Clarence "Big House" Gaines and Jake Gaither gained notoriety and fame for their coaching prowess and leadership. Similarly, Black coaches located on predominately White college campuses developed outstanding careers and coaching legacies.

The chapter will trace the historical and social contributions of Black coaches. Looking towards the future, the authors will offer suggestions to enhance coaching opportunities for minority coaches in the college athletic market place.

Key Terms		
● BCA hiring report card		● informational roles
● decisional roles		● interpersonal roles
● dynasty		● legacy
● historical Black colleges and universities (HBCUs)		

INTRODUCTION

It is a hot and humid day down in the deep bayous of New Orleans, Louisiana. It is the Saturday after Thanksgiving and the sun is scorching. The people are fanning feverishly and praying for a wind to offer solace, but none blows. As the sweat pours down their faces, they wait patiently to get inside the stadium. It is inside that one can hear jazz music playing and people laughing. On one side of the stadium people are wearing black and gold, while on the other side there is a sea of blue and gold. The band walks onto the field and plays with such enthusiasm that the crowd jumps to their feet and begin to dance as if they were following the pied piper. Suddenly, there is a boom and a group of young men run across the field and an elderly man jumps up and yells, "The G Men are coming!" Out on the field the great Eddie Robinson stares at the G-Men (an endearing term given to his Grambling State University players) running on the field with intensity. Arnett "Ace" Mumford stares at the Jaguars with the same intensity, both men demanding a victory and the bragging rights for the year. No, this is not an ordinary football game; this is the Bayou Classic!

The Bayou Classic is one of more than 30 classics offered by historically Black colleges and universities (HBCUs) that not only showcase the talent of athletes, but also demonstrate the determination and skills of Black college coaches. Black college coaches over the years have endured criticism, fought for opportunities in the mist of the color barrier, been ignored by most Americans, and yet have procured countless achievements often with grace and a stylish flare unique to every one of them. This chapter will elucidate the rise and struggles of Black college coaches both at HBCUs and majority institutions in America and the future of this unique group.

Coaching During Segregation

Only a man who knows what it is like to be defeated can reach down to the bottom of his soul and come up with the extra ounce of power it takes to win when the match is even.

—Muhammad Ali

Many early Black college coaches were graduates of majority institutions and sought to pursue coaching as a career. However, due to a lack of opportunities to coach at those institutions, they went on to coach at HBCUs. Under *Plessy v. Ferguson* in 1896 (separate but equal), HBCUs were the only institutions in which Black college coaches could work. They were able to utilize the skills they obtained at the majority institutions to build Black college sports programs. Many HBCUs had very few resources to produce good sport programs, yet this did not hinder their determination to excel and produce outstanding athletes. Entertainment and Sports Programming Network (ESPN) produced a television series highlighting the achievements and struggles of these coaches and athletes called "Black Magic," which aired in March 2008. In addition, Mannie Jackson, the chairman of the board of directors of the college Basketball Hall of Fame, organized a committee that researched the credentials of Black college coaches from HBCUs for proper recognition by the Hall.

> There has been a push for the Hall of Fame to do something since ESPN aired a documentary in March, "Black Magic," that focused on basketball at historically Black schools. The producers of "Black Magic" and groups such as the Black Coaches and Administrators, and the NBA Retired Players Association, began writing letters to Jackson urging him to help get more of these coaches and players enshrined. (CBSSports.com, 2008)

Although segregation officially ended in 1954 in the *Brown v. Board of Education* case; Jim Crow laws lingered until the passing of both the Civil Rights Act (1964) and the Voting Right Act (1965) (Danielson, 2009, Kirk, 2007; Civil Rights Act of 1964; 2009). Even with the passing of all of the aforementioned laws, Blacks were still not granted fair opportunities regarding education and jobs. Lack of opportunities in coaching will be discussed in the latter part of this chapter.

COACHING ROLES

According to Mintzberg (1973) there are three categorical roles of an effective sport administrator (and coaches, athletic directors, etc.): informational, interpersonal, and decisional. Although each category is distinctive, they do however interact with one another in order to provide effectiveness. For Black coaches at HBCUs the roles do not change, however, finances may dictate how each task gets carried out. These roles are essentially expectations for a person in a leadership position. Having clear set roles are paramount to both student-athletes and university administrators.

Interpersonal roles include the figurehead, leader and liaison. The figurehead is the representative. He/she makes official visits, hosts alumni outings and raises funds. The leader is responsible for human resource matters such as hiring, firing, etc., in addition to serving as a mentor and motivator. The liaison corresponds with the media and any other source within the university (Krotee & Bucher, 2007).

Informational roles include serving as the monitor, the disseminator, and the spokesperson. As the monitor, the sport administrator oversees budgets, performance, and the overall facilities. The disseminator promulgates information from the university to external sources and from external sources to internal sources. The spokesperson speaks on behalf the university to the general public (Krotee & Bucher, 2007).

The decisional roles are comprised of entrepreneurial, disturbance-handler, resource allocator, and negotiator. As an entrepreneur, a coach must initiate projects and search for opportunities to build the athletic program. The disturbance-handler or problem solver seeks to resolve all issues within the program; this includes risk management and compliance. The resource allocator is responsible for overseeing the budget and ensuring that money is allocated appropriately. Finally, the negotiator oversees negotiations within the program (Krotee & Bucher, 2007).

In addition to complying with the standard coaching roles, Black coaches historically have also added father figure to the list, especially to those athletes who come from homes without a father present. Further, they act as a mental and spiritual guides. Many Black coaches today pray with their team before a game. Although this is not mandatory, many athletes come from homes in which spirituality played a major role. Finally, Black coaches serve as role models, and Black athletes are then better able to visualize what type of individual they should be in their future careers as a minority.

COACHING MOBILITY

Don't look back. Something might be gaining on you.

—Satchel Paige

The process of ascending to a head coaching position in higher education is perceived by some as a formidable task that differs among institutions. According to Coakley (2004) when we consider mobility in coaching we must keep in mind that career opportunities overall are limited and although opportunities for women and minorities have increased over the years, they are still truncated. Typically in coaching mobility, an individual would serve as a graduate assistant coach, then move to assistant coach and finally to head coach. The hiring process should proceed as follows:

> After looking at all the objectively measurable qualifications, such as years of experience and win-loss records, the search committee members try to subjectively assess such things as a candidate's abilities to recruit and motivate players, raise money, command respect on the team and the surrounding community, build toughness and character among players, maintain team discipline and interact effectively with others in the athletic department or sport organization. (Coakley, 2004, p. 256)

In the past, some coaches at HBCUs would go through this process within the same institution. They would wait for the current head coach to retire and then ascend to the role. Some Black coaches would move to another HBCU to take a head coaching position there. This process is still very common today. Opportunities to advance to a majority institution aren't as prevalent as some would like. The Black Coaches and Administrators (BCA) seek to minimize the disparities. The BCA was founded to address ethnic-minority advancement in sport and primarily in intercollegiate athletics, through employment as well as participation. The BCA was founded in 1988 and continues to thrive promoting its mission through program development and community interaction (bcasports .cstv.com/bcahistory).

The National Collegiate Athletic Association (NCAA) elucidates the hiring practices of minorities through its intercollegiate athletic certification process in which all universities that have athletic programs must apply to in order to continue to provide scholarships. This process demands that universities list the ethnicity of the coaches as well as the student-athletes. It allows for universities to reflect on their hiring practices involving minority groups.

Coaching mobility largely depends upon networking. Aspiring coaches should promote themselves and their abilities for key positions. The glass-ceiling effect, however, may impede this process. The term *glass ceiling* refers to an "invisible (unofficial and informal) barrier to career advancement resulting from unfair discrimination based on gender, race, ethnicity or other non job-related characteristics" (McGee, Bucklin, Dickinson, & McSweeney, 2003, p. 5). White males in top administration may seek to employ their friends to assume the head coaching or other coaching positions. This would imply that a White male hegemony exists, causing the glass-ceiling effect.

> Many Whites hired as coaches had mediocre or unimpressive playing careers, and some have unimpressive past coaching records as well. Meanwhile, minority candidates with similar or better playing careers are routinely passed over as coaching candidates in a range of sports. It seems that because coaching and administrative abilities cannot be measured as objectively as playing abilities, the subjective feelings of those doing the hiring come into play when coaching and top management candidates are assessed. (Coakley, 2004, p. 320)

BLACK WOMEN IN COACHING

My mother taught me very early to believe I could achieve any accomplishment I wanted to. The first was to walk without braces.

> —Wilma Rudolph

Even with the enactment of Title IX, which sought to decrease the barriers for women participating in sport, the opportunities for women coaching still remain meager. The percentages of women in head coaching positions have faltered within recent years (Acosta & Carpenter, 2004; Sagas, Cunningham, & Pastore, 2006). Research has also indicated that women assistant head coaches are less likely to apply for head coaching positions (Cunningham & Sagas, 2002; Cunningham, Sagas, & Ashley, 2003; Sagas, Cunningham, & Ashley, 2000). The numbers are even lower for Black women in coaching. This section will feature the coaching history of four Black female coaches both at majority institutions and HBCUs who have accomplished many goals and yet struggled through racism and sexism.

Vivian Stringer

Vivian Stringer, head basketball coach at Rutgers University, has broken many barriers and stood tall during a national scandal in which a radio talk show host, Don Imus referred to her female players as "nappy headed hoes." In her book entitled *Standing Tall*, Vivian reported feeling baffled about the statement made:

Why would a media personality go after student-athletes-young people who give everything of themselves to represent their university, and without getting paid a dime? These weren't politicians or professionals with multi-million dollar contracts. Why would he go out of his way to demoralize young women to be: disciplines role models working to get an education and to get an education and to make a difference in the world? And why attack this group after an extraordinary season and all we'd been through? (Stringer, 2008, p. 266)

Dealing with the scandal at Rutgers wasn't the only issue Stringer had to contend with in her career. Stringer details of another story that happened after she and her husband both interviewed for jobs at SUNY Cortland. She reported that both interviews went well and both she and her husband were both looking forward to working at the institution. However, at the time, several Black students were protesting on campus. When asked did she know of the students' protests she replied that she did and did not see how disclosing that information would hinder her getting the job. The dean responded that it is imperative to always be on the side of the administration. Nonetheless, neither Stringer nor her husband received the opportunity to work at SUNY. She was later offered a teaching position at Cheney State College (HBCU). Stringer soared at Cheney and later went on to coach at Rutgers University.

Dana "Pokey" Chatman

Pokey Chatman, the former head basketball coach at Louisiana State University (LSU) both coached and played at the university for 18 years. Chatman led her team to three consecutive Final Fours. As a coach, Chatman received many awards and titles including the SEC, BCA, and Louisiana Coach of the Year. She is also an inductee in the LSU Hall of Fame. In 2005, Pokey had a four-year contract worth $400,000 with signing bonuses, including $70,000 for a national title (ESPN News, 2007). In the height of her career Chatman fell amidst a scandal in which she was accused of having a sexual relationship with one of her players. After many years at the university Pokey was perturbed at how the university officials handled the situation and she later resigned. In a statement, Chatman proclaimed:

I had a 20-year career at LSU and that didn't warrant a 20-minute conversation. Would I do things different? That's difficult to say because I didn't get to do anything. And I'll just leave it at that. I don't want to wrestle in the mud with the pigs. (Winchester, 2007, p. 22)

Chatman later signed to an international basketball team as an assistant coach.

Patricia Bibbs

Patricia Bibbs, a graduate of Grambling State University, made history when she garnered 400 wins, becoming the 38th head women's basketball coach to do so. Bibbs' coaching career victories span in both the MEAC and the SWAC. Bibbs coached at Grambling State University for 13 years and amassed 244 victories. She was also the first head women's basketball coach in the SWAC to have an undefeated season. Bibbs' overall record as a coach is 422-246. She was coach of the year nine times and had seven SWAC championships and two MEAC awards.

Bibbs filed a civil action suit against the Lubbock Police department after being falsely arrested in 1989, in which a shopper at local store reported that a woman asked her about a lost purse. Another woman approached her about the purse as well. The shopper told the police, and the police claimed that the two were con artists. The police later saw Bibbs, her assistant coach, and her husband outside the store and accused them of being the con artists and arrested them. Bibbs claimed it was racial profiling and sued for $30 million. The Supreme Court rejected their arguments and stated the officers had the right to make the arrests (BI News Briefs, 2000).

Barbara Lewis

Barbara Lewis has served as both a track and field coach and bowling coach for over 12 years at Grambling State University. During her tenure as coach, she received awards and accolades including Louisiana Women's State Team Bowling Champions (1989), SWAC Men's Cross Country Champions, SWAC Cross Country Champions for the following years: 1995, 1996, 1997, 1998, 1999, 2002, 2003, and 2004. Regarding bowling, Lewis' team was the SWAC Champions for 1998 and she was the 1998 SWAC Coach of the Year in addition to serving on several committees such as the NCAA National Bowling Championship Tournament Committee and the USA Junior Olympic Gold National Bowling Championship Tournament Official.

Lewis believes that the respect for the sport of bowling is contingent upon the sport and administration's support of the sport (personal communication, 2009). Bowling is viewed by minorities as a social sport as opposed to a competitive sport; this is caused by a lack of knowledge and a lack of respect of the sport. Other issues regarding bowling involve lack of funding and scheduling. As an African American female, Lewis contends that women have to work harder in order to gain recognition as coaches (personal communication, 2009). Bowling as with many other sports requires math skills, endurance, agility, and coordination. Currently, there are 34 HBCUs and 17 majority institutions that have bowling teams.

HBCU DYNASTIES

There were many Black coaches who made an impact on college sports. However, there were a few that turned their sport programs into dynasties. These institutions have amassed not only national attention, but worldwide attention as well. These coaches worked for many years under the same institution, garnered a multitude of achievements, and enhanced the lives of their players. Due to today's climate, in which Black coaches have opportunities to coach at major institutions and with offers of higher salaries, it is a rarity that a coach will stay at the same institution for a long period of time. A *dynasty* in sport is defined as an era in which a coach has coached for many years for the same institution, created a strong network of support systems, received exceptional support for administration and alumni, established a successful athletic program, and has demonstrated success of the alumni of the program. This section includes a selection of coaches who have ruled for at least 25 years: Eddie Robinson, Jake Gaither, Arnett "Ace" Mumford, and Clarence "Big House" Gaines. These coaches persevered in the era of segregation. Many of their accomplishments are not known to the American public, yet they have a special place in history.

Eddie Robinson and the G-Men Dynasty

One does not talk about successful football programs without mentioning the legendary Eddie Robinson (born Edward Gay Robinson). Robinson had a coaching career that spanned over 57 years. Robinson put Grambling State University on the map for college football. He acquired 408 wins and nine Black college titles. Under his tutelage, 200 players went on to play in the NFL. One of those players was Doug Williams, who was the first Black quarterback to win a Super Bowl.

> *Joe Paterno of Penn State claimed, "Nobody has ever done or ever will do what he has done for this game." (Hurd, 1998, p. 104)*

Robinson started his dynasty in 1941 at the age of 22 at the Louisiana Negro Normal and Industrial Institute in Grambling, Louisiana (later named Grambling State University).

Robinson, who was a first-rate student-athlete, was eager to get a job at the Louisiana college. He met Dr. Ralph Waldo Emerson Jones, who was the president at the time. The two bragged about their baseball skills; Dr. Jones (affectionately called "Prez") was an outstanding pitcher. Robinson doted about his batting skills. After the practice, Robinson landed himself a job as the football coach. The two, along with Collie Nicholson (sports information director) created the "Grambling dynasty."

In Robinson's first year as coach, the team had a record of 3-5; however, the following year, the team went 8-0 and was unscored on. Robinson went on to 408 wins, the best in collegiate history; in addition to having served as president of the American Football Coaches Association. Robinson believed in the American dream; with hard work and persistence, anything can be accomplished. "I've always believed in the American system. I felt if I worked hard enough within the system, if I paid my dues, I could get the most out of life in America" (Hurd, 1998, p. 107). He endured the racism in the South, yet Robinson wanted his life story to not be about race, but an American story. Robinson died April 3, 2007. He was admired and respected by many. He has indeed left a legacy of hard work and dedication

Legendary coach Eddie Robinson turned Grambling State University into a football power while amassing more than 400 career victories. Courtesy of the National Consortium for Academics and Sports

to college football. Grambling State University's football team continues to carry out the legacy of Eddie Robinson as an outstanding program dedicated to hard work with a winning attitude whose success is known around the world. This was continued with the coaching leadership of Doug Williams, Melvin Spears, and Rod Broadway and will continue to maintain power for several generations, continuing the G-Men dynasty.

Jake Gaither and the Rattler Dynasty

Alonzo Smith "Jake" Gaither was born in 1903 in Dayton, Tennessee. Gaither began his legacy in 1938 at the Florida A&M College for Negroes in Tallahassee, Florida, as an assistant football coach. He was later named head football coach in 1945 after the former head coach left for the military. Gaither was noted for stating that he wanted his players "mo-bile, a-gile, and hos-tile," a quote that football players at Florida A&M University repeat today. Football played a big part in Jake's upbringing.

He was the son of a preacher and an avid football fan. It was without a doubt that after completing a bachelor's degree (Knoxville College) and a master's degree (Ohio State University) that he would coach football. Gaither initially coached high school football before joining the collegiate rank. Gaither created the split-line T, which was an offensive formation, later characterized as "genius." This formation has since been utilized by other colleges and universities.

Gaither was a devoted Christian who was noted for having a sense of humor. He treated his players with dignity and garnered absolute respect. He went on to 203 wins, six Black national championships, and was the first Black to serve on the Orange Bowl committee. Adding to his many athletic talents, Gaither also coached basketball and track. One of Gaither's most notable football players was Bob Hayes, who won two gold medals in the 1964 Olympics in Tokyo. Hayes was then known as the fastest human.

After his retirement, Gaither was called a great American "who broke racial barriers before it was fashionable" (Hurd, 1998, p. 45). He was heavily involved in civil rights issues through nonviolent means. Regarding the racial issues in the South, he stated "It's hell to be a Black man in the deep South. We tried to avoid hostility and things that were depressing and humiliating" (Hurd, 1998, p. 45).

Arnett Mumford and the Southern Jaguars

When they talk about football, they talk about "The Legend" and they refer to Grambling's Eddie Robinson. They however, err in number. They should really discuss "The Legends." One is Robinson, the other is Mumford, who elevated Southern football to a plateau where it became the envy of other Southwestern Athletic Conference Schools. (Hurd, 1998, p. 54)

Arnett "Ace" Mumford coaching career spans 36 years, 25 of which were at Southern University in Baton Rouge, Louisiana. Mumford was born in Buckhannon, West Virginia. He completed a bachelor's degree from Wilberforce University and a master's degree from the University of Southern California. Mumford began his dynasty at Southern in 1936 after coaching at Jarvis Christian College, Bishop College, and Texas College. Mumford loved football, and he absolutely adored Southern University. He was categorized as a perfectionist and would work the players late at night until they got it just right.

Mumford was respected by many as he was a straightforward man who was serious about the game of football and serious about beating Eddie Robinson. This was a rivalry that lasted many years. Mumford had a coaching style that was certainly before his time. When he first started with the Jaguars, the team was 2-5-2. When he left, the team was an impressive 169-57-14. He also gained the distinction of having four consecutive undefeated seasons, six Black national titles, and 11 SWAC titles. In addition to having 30 student-athletes obtain the All-American status.

When you mention the name of Mumford to Southern graduates, their eyes will close and immediately a smile will appear on their faces. Legends will garner that kind of reaction from individuals and indeed Mumford is a legend (Coach and Athlete Director, 2007).

Clarence "Big House" Gaines

Clarence Edward "Big House" Gaines had a basketball coaching career at Winston-Salem State University that spanned an impressive 47 years. Gaines was born in Paducah, Kentucky, and attended Morgan State College on a football scholarship, yet, he also participated in basketball and track. He later graduated from Morgan State College with a degree in chemistry and obtained a master's degree from Columbia University.

Gaines began his dynasty at Winston-Salem State in 1946 and coached until 1993. His coaching record at the university was 828-447. Under Gaines's reign, the university was able to boast 18 20-win seasons, a Division II championship—which distinguished them as the first HBCU to receive such a distinction—and eight CIAA titles. His win-loss record propelled him to be fifth in NCAA history. He is also the only Black coach to be inducted into the Basketball Hall of Fame. Gaines was declared CIAA coach of the year (six times), CIAA Basketball Tournament Outstanding Coach Award (eight times), inducted into the CIAA Hall of Fame and the NC Sports Hall of Fame, and was a member of the United States Olympic Committee, in addition to receiving several other awards and distinctions (Black Issues in Higher Education, 2005).

A LEGACY AMASSED

Just as a piece of coal gradually shapes into a diamond, so does the legacy of a Black college coach. There is relentless pressure and heat that must be endured. There are racial barriers that must be overcome. Black coaches must prove to be better than the rest to even be considered for a top position. Only given time and the ability to withstand such pressure does a diamond appear; thus a legacy is created. Being a legacy isn't just about wins, but about the affect you have on student-athletes and society as a whole. This section will highlight two individuals who have created legacies through their athletic and civil achievements.

John McClendon

John McClendon was an outstanding athlete participating in multiple sports. He however, loved basketball more. He did in fact learn the game from James Naismith, who was the founder of basketball. Due to segregation, McClendon did not ever play the game at Kansas University. But that did not sway his interest. He decided to coach at Hampton Institute and later coached at Tennessee A&T University, North Carolina College, and Cleveland State University (first Black to hold this distinction). He won the coveted title of NAIA Coach of the Year three times. McClendon also coached the Cleveland Pipers in the American Basketball League, becoming the first Black professional head coach. Affectionately called "Coach Mac," John was one of the founders of the Central Intercollegiate Athletic Association tournament. Deemed a hero by the CIAA commissioner Leon Kerry, he was initially inducted into the Basketball Hall of Fame as only a contributor to the sport. In 2007, he was inducted as a coach. "His presence at courtside was a constant reminder that the Naismith Basketball Hall of Famer, class of 1978, was one of the most beloved individuals in the history of Black college sports" (Evans, 2000, p. 54).

Edwin Bancroft Henderson

Dr. Edwin Bancroft Henderson, the Father of Black Basketball, was not only a physical educator, but also a civil rights activist. He fought to alleviate the segregation that existed within recreational sports programs and introduced basketball to Black children in our nation's capital. Henderson, widely known as E. B., was the leading figure in equal rights among athletics. Henderson wrote *The Negro in Sports* a request made by Carter G. Woodson, which outlines the historical achievement of Blacks in sports. He championed for interracial athletic competition as well as organized an athletic league for Blacks in public schools (Public Schools Athletic League). Henderson was not only known for athletics for being a civil rights activist. Henderson was forced to leave his seat on a train bound for Washington, DC, by a White segregationist. Henderson sought legal representation and won the case. He helped to form a rural NAACP branch in northern Virginia. Henderson was noted for utilizing sport as a means to bring about racial unity (Wiggins, 1999).

RECRUITING

Coakley (2004) suggests that colleges and universities must be aggressive in recruiting Black coaches and athletes. The author further suggests that it is in the best interest of the Black student athlete to have support on the campus for which they are recruited. That is, there needs to be Black administrators, coaches, faculty, etc. The issues pertaining to the recruiting and hiring process of Blacks at majority institutions will be discussed further in the BCH Hiring Report section. This section will focus on recruiting challenges that Black coaches face at HBCUs.

Recruiting at HBCUs

Recruiting Black athletes during segregation was never an issue for Black coaches at HBCUs. Blacks that were athletic went to college and participated in sports. Coaches at HBCUs not only trained the athletes, they were also seen as father figures. Black coaches prioritized discipline; while conveying the hardships the athletes would endure as a minority once they graduated. Therefore, academics were paramount and so was hard work. These athletes were given life lessons on how to cope in a segregated society.

Many Black athletes at HBCUs had opportunities to play professional and become successful at that level. Coaches would recruit players by going to their homes, talking with parents, assuring them that their child will be taken care of. These parents were comforted and more than willing to allow their child to go. Games at HBCUs were not televised, but games brought a wealth of fans. However, with integration Blacks were given education options that did not exist before. Coaches from majority institutions recruited Black players promising television exposure which would then increase their chances to go professional. Given this option, many Black athletes opted for attending majority institutions leaving HBCUs at a clear disadvantage. Although more games at HBCUs are now televised, they are certainly not as televised as majority institutions. They cannot guarantee the amount of exposure as their counterparts. Recruiting suffers and some HBCUs are limited to where they can go to get athletes due to financial constraints, whereas majority institutions are not as limited.

> The past 40 years of the NFL draft makes clear the change in the football landscape. Between 1967 and 1976, as segregation began to fall, NFL teams selected 443 players from historically Black schools. During the next 20 years, 291 players from Black colleges were drafted. Only 55 players from Black schools have been selected in the

past 10 drafts. In states like Louisiana, Mississippi and Texas, where talent was great, the drop off was most staggering. Between 1967 and 1976, Southern University, Grambling, Jackson State, Alcorn State, Mississippi Valley State, Texas Southern and Prairie View produced more than 35 NFL draft picks per school. In the past 10 years, those schools had a total of 15 players drafted. (Jones, 2007, p. 2)

The most important difference in Black college recruiting and recruiting at a majority institution is recruiting budgets. However, in today's technologically advanced society some schools are getting around the limited budgets as well as the current rules of the NCAA through text messaging, Facebook, Twitter, MySpace, and other means of the internet. Does the ability to communicate with players using these methods ease the pockets of HBCUs and Division II institutions? Will it help to level the playing field between both groups? Is it possible to police the communication taking place between coaches and recruits? Maher (2007) questions whose responsibility is it to regulate the use of the modern methods in recruiting. Can the NCAA keep up with growing technology? Only time will indicate whether these new communication methods will assist universities dealing with budgetary constraints.

CONFERENCES

Black athletic conferences consist of historically Black institutions separated by regions. They were conceived as a means to offer competition among HBCUs. Currently, there are four Black conferences: Mid-Eastern Athletic Conference, Central Intercollegiate Athletic Association, Southern Intercollegiate Athletic Conference, and the South Western Athletic Conference.

The Central Intercollegiate Athletic Association (CIAA) is the oldest of the Black athletic conferences, established in 1912. It is made up of ten historical Black institutions and is divided into two divisions: Eastern and Western. The CIAA is part of the NCAA Division II membership. The institutions that comprise the CIAA include Bowie State University, Elizabeth City State University, Fayetteville State University, Johnson C. Smith University, Livingstone College, St. Augustine's College, St. Paul's College, Shaw University, Virginia State University, and Virginia Union University.

The South Western Athletic Conference began in 1920 and was initially made up of six colleges: Bishop College, Paul Quinn, Prairie View A&M, Texas College, Sam Houston, and Wiley College. Today the SWAC has 10 member institutions: Alabama A&M University, Alabama State University, Alcorn State University, University of Arkansas at Pine Bluff, Grambling State University, Jackson State University, Mississippi Valley State University, Prairie View A&M University, Southern University and A&M College, and Texas Southern University. Many SWAC athletes have made it to the professional ranks and boast several Hall of Fame inductees.

The Mid-Eastern Athletic Conference was formed in 1969 by a group of individuals who met in Durham, North Carolina, in order to create a new conference. Initially, the seven institutions that joined the MEAC were: Delaware State College, Howard University, University of Maryland Eastern Shore, Morgan State University, North Carolina A&T State University, North Carolina Central University, and South Carolina State University. Since its inception, the MEAC has adopted six additional institutions: Bethune-Cookman University, Coppin State University, Florida A&M University, Hampton University, Norfolk State University and Savannah State University. Winton Salem withdrew bringing the membership total to 13.

The Southern Intercollegiate Athletic Conference (SIAC) began in 1913 with 11 Black institutions represented. Five institutions later left the conference to form the Collegiate Athletic Conference. However, in 1929, the two conferences merged and retained the SIAC name. Currently, the SIAC membership institutions comprise 13 institutions in five states: Alabama, Georgia, Kentucky, South Carolina and Tennessee: Albany State University, Benedict College, Claflin University, Clark Atlanta University, Fort Valley State University, Kentucky State University, Lane College, LeMoyne-Owen College, Miles College, Morehouse College, Paine College, Stillman College, and Tuskegee University.

HISTORICAL ROLES OF COLLEGE COACHES

Early Black coaches were not only former student-athletes, but they attended top tier majority institutions and were more than willing to take what they learned to help build Black college athletics. Subsequently, they were able to build outstanding Black athletes. Early Black college coaches would stress getting a degree more so than becoming an outstanding athlete. Jake Gaither of Florida A&M University would say to all incoming freshmen, "If you came to Florida A&M for anything other than a degree, get the hell out of here" (Hurd, 1998, p. 46). Obtaining a degree was and still is believed to be the best way to succeed in America. Marino Casem, who coached football at Alcorn State for 20 years, believed that there must be an intense desire to coach and appreciated the ability to transform lives.

> Coaching is one of the last areas where you can touch kids and it means something. But the fire has to burn every day. When it burns only when you stoke it, you've got to look somewhere else. The fire has to burn in your innards, when you're sleeping. My fire is burning now to do something to build this program, to make facilities better than anyone in the SWAC or state and graduate kids at a level no one else is doing. (Hurd, 1998, p. 39)

Black coaches at historical Black institutions also had similar backgrounds to their players, hence making it easier to relate. With limited budgets for their teams, coaches had to make something out of nothing. Many learned this skill from their own upbringing. Blacks were able to survive with very little resources. No one complained; it was what they had to do. Unfortunately, this survival technique remains true today at HBCUs. Many still do not have adequate resources for their coaches to recruit or to build their athletic programs.

Black coaches were seen as parental figures. They had the same expectations and rules as the parents and the players respected that. A Black athlete sees a Black coach as someone who not only physically reminds them of a parent, but as a person who exhibits the same attitude and demeanor as well. Black coaches at HBCUs are aware of this interaction and take on the parental role even today. Stephen A. Smith, an ESPN analyst and a 1991 graduate of Winston-Salem State, said this of Clarence "Big House" Gaines; "Coach Gaines is like a father figure to me. He's an icon. He hasn't just done things for Winston-Salem State. He's done a lot for the sport of basketball" (Hill, 2005, p. 44). Therefore, Black coaches at historically Black institutions are parents, teachers and coaches.

COACHING STYLES

Coaching is more than a skill to be mastered, but more of an artistic form unique to all coaches. It is a style that should not be duplicated and requires an individualistic that is to be admired and respected by players and fans alike. Coach Mike Krzyzewski, currently the head basketball coach of Duke University, and Bob Knight notably have different coaching styles. Just as Vivian Stringer, head women's basketball coach at Rutgers differs from Pat Bibbs, head women's basketball coach at North Carolina A&T University. As with all coaches, Black coaches were motivators, wanting to create an environment of high performance and building leadership skills. During segregation, coaching styles also reflected a changing society, one that did not honor diversity. Black coaches taught their players how to survive in this environment. Many strides have been made since segregation among people of color. Barack Obama was the first Black president elected to office in 2008; yet there are other areas that Blacks have yet to overcome. There are still too very few Black head coaches coaching at majority institutions. This scarcity is mimicked is professional sports as well.

Black coaches historically were not only known for being father and mother figures and teachers, they were also known for their *swagger*. They were known for their attire: their hats, their shoes and on occa-

Georgetown men's basketball coach John Thompson was a masterful motivator and an intimidating presence on the sideline. Courtesy of John Thompson

sion maybe even a cigar would adorn the mouth of a few. For the women, their hair neatly coiffed, make-up perfectly placed on their faces and the quintessence of femininity that grabbed the attention of all those in the room. Coaching was not just a job, but a career and a lifestyle. Eddie Robinson was known for always wearing a suit and in his early years, he even wore a hat. He never argued with the officials, yet he always had an intense look on his face. He was suave, debonair, and always walked with confidence. That is the soul of a Black coach.

BLACK COACHES AT MAJORITY INSTITUTIONS

There are several Blacks who have made their mark in sports at majority institutions. This section will highlight a few of those coaches and some of the issues they may have faced in their quest to fill these top-rated collegiate vacancies. An analysis of Richard Lapchick's *Race and Gender Report Card*, shows the percentages of Blacks transcending the glass-ceiling effect is small and their ability to sustain success is slight.

The primary problem, regarding racial hiring practices is that Whites still dominate key positions. They hold between 88–97% of all positions in the following categories in Divisions I, II and III: university presidents, athletics directors, head coaches, associate athletic directors, faculty athletics reps, and sports information directors. They hold 100% of the conference commissioner positions in Division I excluding the historically Black colleges and universities. (Lapchick, 2009, p. 1)

Tyrone Willingham

Tyrone Willingham signed as the head football coach at Notre Dame, becoming the first African-American male football coach to do so in 2002. During his first year, Willingham won 10 games, becoming the first coach ever to do so at Notre Dame to achieve this remarkable feat. However after a dismal season in 2004 with a 6-5 record, Willingham was terminated as head coach. Many African-Americans were disturbed by the decision to fire Willingham and wondered would he ever receive another chance to coach another Division I school. However, Willingham bounced back and took the helms at Washington State. Willingham is one of six Blacks to become head coach of a majority (major) institution football team (Moore, n.d.). Unfortunately in 2008, after his worst season at Washington State, he was winless and his job was terminated.

Nolan Richardson

Nolan Richardson spent 17 years as head basketball coach at the University of Arkansas. He led his team to three Final Fours and a National Championship in 1994. During the same year Richardson received National Coach of the Year, in addition to two NCAA title games (Harris, 2005). He was terminated at Arkansas in 2001, for which the university had to pay him $3 million, buying out six of the seven-year contract. Richardson filed a lawsuit against the university on the grounds of racism and freedom of speech. Richardson sought $8.7 million in the suit, but the case was dismissed by a Federal District Court Judge. He later made the following statement regarding hiring practices in intercollegiate athletics: "We never had the good jobs, we had to take jobs and make them better. I feel that we're behind in the race" (Harris, 2005, p. 38).

> Many Black athletes and coaches will attest to the facts of what Richardson said that Black coaches are treated differently, that they are expected to win all of the time and held up to more criticism than others, fired more quickly when they don't meet those higher expectations, given fewer opportunities to come back if fired, and watched more closely in every word and action in between. (Banks, Nunley, Rambsy, Gilyard, Stringer, Hurt, et al., 2002)

BCA HIRING REPORT CARD: ISSUES FACING COLLEGE COACHES TODAY

History has not been favorable to the Black male student-athlete as Blacks were absent from intercollegiate sport until the early 1900s. A few Ivy League and other eastern schools had Black athletes at an earlier time, but they were exceptions. For the most part, prior to World War II, Black athletes played at all-Black colleges, in Black leagues. Although the system was segregated, it did provide many Blacks with the opportunity to engage in organized sport. The University of Alabama perhaps best illustrates the transition from segregated programs to integrated ones. In 1968, there were no Blacks on any of its athletic teams. In 1975, its basketball team had an all-Black starting lineup (Johnson, 2003).

As more predominantly White schools searched for talented blacks to bolster their athletic programs, historically Black schools lost their monopoly on Black athletic talent.

The best Black athletes found it advantageous to play at predominantly White schools because of greater visibility, especially on television. This visibility meant, for the best athletes, a better chance to become professional athletes. The result of this trend was a depleted athletic program at historically Black schools, forcing some to drop their athletic programs and some previously Black leagues to disband (Johnson, 2003). Naturally, this impacted the opportunities for Black players, move in the professional ranks of football as head coaches, offensive and defensive coordinators, and other administrative positions within the athletic arena.

As a result of the slow progression of Black into the administrative arena, the Black Coaches & Administrators (formerly the Black Coaches Association) financed a hiring report for NCAA Division IA and IAA football head coaching positions (Harrison, 2007b). The primary purpose of this "Hiring Report Card" was to shed light on this slow progression with the hope of improving administrative opportunities for talented Black coaches. The principal investigator was Dr. C. Keith Harrison, Director of the Paul Robeson Research Center for Leadership, Academic and Athletic Prowess (Roberson Center and BCA). The reason behind such an investigation is clearly stated in an email to Harrison. The email to Harrison, author of the Hiring Report Card dated October 23, 2003, illustrates this point:

> Students cannot understand why 50% of football players are African American and less than five college coaches are, Harrison said. Maybe the students should also be trying to understand why only 13% of the population is African American yet 50% of football players are. Do you think it's about time we applied affirmative action, or better yet, a five-part system to evaluate the discrepancies in these numbers? Maybe 87% of all new athletes should be other than African American starting next year. Heck, I'll settle for 51%. (Harrison, 2004, p. 1)

The report continues by stating since 1996, there have been 142 openings for head coaching positions in Division IA football (Hill, 2004). From 1996 to 2004, only one African American head football coach has been hired each year. Clearly, there is a pattern. The 2004 Hiring Report Card conducted by the Roberson Center, and supported and produced for the Black Coaches Association (BCA), seeks to theoretically and empirically assesses this pattern and why it continues to persist. This pattern and social formula that equals the *overrepresentation of* African-American players at the same time as the *under representation* of African-American and other coaches of color clearly reveal a challenge (Harrison, 2004).

As of the latest 2011 hiring report card, there were 19 coaches of color at the 120 FBS schools and nine coaches of color at FCS schools (Lapchick, 2011). There were 29 head coaching positions open during this period and of those openings, 10 were filled by minority coaches and two schools received a letter grade of F. This compares to one F during the inaugural year (2004) of the report (Harrison, 2004).

Opportunities for women and women of color have pretty much remained the same as well. Of the 11 athletic conferences, all are headed by white males. Regarding women's teams, the percentages of Whites in head coaching positions were 87.7, 88.9, and 91.9 for Division I, Division II, and Division III, respectively. Conversely, the percentages for African Americans coaching women's teams were 7.0, 5.1 and 4.4 in Division I, Division II, and Division III, respectively (Lapchick, 2009). The picture is not better when the presidents of these colleges and universities are viewed, athletic directors and their assistants. The sport writers/columnists and editors have similar issues as the overwhelmingly majority (84–95%) of Associated Press Sports Editors (APSC) are White men.

Richard Lapchick, chairman of the DeVos Sport Business Management Graduate Program and director of Institute for Diversity and Ethics in Sport at the University of Central Florida stated that former NCAA president Myles Brand worked hard for racial equality. However, current NCAA president Mark Emmert, who succeeded the deceased Brand, needs some new tools to bring real change. In nearly every major position in college sports, no matter what division, nearly 85%, and often more, are held by Whites. Lapchick continues by saying the system is broken when it is so exclusive. We need to fix it now (Lapchick, 2008). "As is previous sports, the 2008 College Racial and Gender Report Card data shows that college athletics departments' hiring practices do not nearly reflect the number of student-athletes of color competing on their teams" (p. 25).

In order for these and similar issues to changed, we must look at a better way of getting quality coaches and athletic administrators into the mix. To have something in place similar to the Rooney Rule (teams were required to interview at least one minority candidate when filling a head coaching position, or be fined) is a start but by no means the only way to change many of these numbers. We as coaches, teachers and athletic administrators must be serious about inclusion. Our future depends on it.

FUTURE OF BLACK COACHES

My motto was always to keep swinging. Whether I was in a slump or feeling badly or having trouble off the field, the only thing to do was keep swinging.
—Hank Aaron

Analysis of the numbers of minorities in top coaching positions reveals how dismal the future of Black coaches looks. Less than five percent of head college football coaches are minority. On the NCAA's list of minority coaches in all sports, the numbers do not look much better. However, there is hope that this current trend will change. History has shown that Black coaches have survived adversity, and there is no reason to think they will not survive now. As society starts to change in views and there is a genuine need to disband the good old boy network, more opportunities will be given to minorities and women in college athletics. Sagas and Cunningham (2005) suggests promoting the value of diversity in the workplace as an effective way of combating discrimination in intercollegiate athletics. It is also important for universities to continue to monitor and uphold policies that enforce equal opportunity regarding the hiring process. Black coaches are not asking for leniency or a hand out, they are simply asking to be evaluated based upon merit.

As for the future opportunities for Black coaches, this goal can best be summed up by the words of the late great Eddie Robinson: "A man's only limitation is his imagination" (Nance, 2007, p. 11).

STUDY QUESTIONS

1. How does coaching for Blacks during segregation differ from today?
2. What are some of the recruiting issues facing Black coaches today?
3. Review the historical roles (characteristics) of Black college coaches. List three coaches today with similar characteristics.
4. Do you think Black coaches at majority institutions experience fewer issues (e.g., recruiting, compensation) than Black coaches at HBCUs?
5. Since there are so few Black head coaches at majority institutions, what policy would you put in place to ensure equity?

SUGGESTED READINGS

Cunningham, G. B., Sagas, M., & Ashley, F. B. (2003). Coaching self efficacy, desire to head coach, and occupational turnover intent: Gender differences between NCAA assistant coaches of women's teams. *International Journal of Sport Psychology*, *34*, 125–137.

Hurd, M. (1998). *Black college football*. Virginia Beach, VA: Donning Company.

Jones, B. (2007). *Progress, yes; but HBCUs paid a price for it.* Retrieved from http://sports.espn.go/espn/blackhistory2007/news/story?id = 2780876

Stringer, V. (2008). *Standing tall*. New York, NY: Random House.

REFERENCES

Acosta, R. V., & Carpenter, L. J. (2004). *Women in intercollegiate sport. A longitudinal study—twenty-five year update—1977–2004*. Unpublished manuscript, Brooklyn College.

2006 AFCA Trailblazer and award winner. (2007, January). *Coach & Athletic Director*. Retrieved from Academic Search Complete database.

Banks, A., Nunley, V., Rambsy, H., Gilyard, K., Stringer, R., Hurt, T., et al. (2002, April 11). Just another angry Black man? *Black Issues in Higher Education*, *19*(4), 68. Retrieved from Academic Search Complete database.

Black Coaches & Administrators history (n.d.). Retrieved from http://www.bcasports.org/index.php?option = com_content&view = article&id = 49&Itemid = 172

BI News Briefs. (2000, January 6). *Black Issues in Higher Education*, Retrieved from Academic Search Complete database.

Coakley, J. (2004). *Sports in society: Issues and controversies* (8th ed.). Boston, MA: McGraw-Hill.

Central Intercollegiate Athletic Association history (n.d.). Retrieved from http://www.theciaa.com/

Civil Rights Act of 1964. (2009, January 3). *Civil Rights Act of 1964*, Retrieved from Academic Search Complete database.

Clarence 'Big House' Gaines, 1923–2005. (2005, June 2). *Black Issues in Higher Education*, Retrieved from Academic Search Complete database.

Cunningham, G. B., & Sagas, M. (2002). The differential effects of human capital for male and female division I basketball coaches. *Research Quarterly for Exercise and Sport*, *73*, 489–495.

Cunningham, G., & Sagas, M. (2005, May). Access discrimination in intercollegiate athletics. *Journal of Sport & Social Issues*, *29*(2), 148–163. doi:10.1177/0193723504271706

Cunningham, G. B., Sagas, M., & Ashley, F. B. (2003). Coaching self efficacy, desire to head coach, and occupational turnover intent: Gender differences between NCAA assistant coaches of women's teams. *International Journal of Sport Psychology*, *34*, 125–137.

Danielson, C. (2009, February). Lily White and hard right: The Mississippi republican party and Black voting, 1965–1980. *Journal of Southern History*, *75*(1), 83–118. Retrieved from Academic Search Complete database.

Eddie Robinson. (2007, December 27). *Diverse: Issues in Higher Education*. Retrieved from Academic Search Complete database.

ESPN News (2007, March 9). Sources: Chatman quit amid sexual misconduct claims. Retrieved from http://sports.espn.go.com/ncw/news/story?id = 2791950

Evans, H. (2000, February 17). CIAA settles into new home for legendary hoops tournament. *New York Amsterdam News*, *91*(7), 54. Retrieved from Academic Search Complete database.

Hampton considers legal action over wrongful arrest. (1998, December 10). *Black Issues in Higher Education*. Retrieved from Academic Search Complete database.

Harris, P. (2005, April 7). Catching up with Nolan Richardson. *Black Issues in Higher Education*, *22*(4), 38. Retrieved from Academic Search Complete database.

Harrison, C. K. (2004). The score: Hiring practices of Division IA and IAA head football coaches. BCA HRC #1, 2003–2004.

Harrison, C. K. (2007a). The score: Hiring practices of Division IA and IAA head football coaches. BCA HRC #1, 2003–2004.

Harrison, C. K. (2007b). The big game in sport management and higher education: The Hiring Practices of Division IA and IAA head football coaches. BCA HRC #5, 2007–2008.

Hill, A. (2005). Winston-Salem with Coach Clarence "Big House" Gaines. *New York Amsterdam News*, *96*(18), 44.

Hill, F. (2004, March). Shattering the glass ceiling: Blacks in coaching. *Black Issues in Higher Education*, *21*(4), 36–37.

Hurd, M. (1998). *Black college football*. Virginia Beach, VA: Donning Company.

Johnson, W. (2003). *A comparative study of the perceived experiences of Black male student-athletes attending historically Black university compared to those attending a predominantly White university* (Unpublished doctoral dissertation). University of Kentucky.

Jones, B. (2007). Progress, yes; but HBCUs paid a price for it. Retrieved from http://sports.espn.go/espn/blackhistory2007/news/story?id = 2780876

Kirk, J. (2007, Summer). The 1957 Little Rock crisis: A fiftieth anniversary retrospective. *Arkansas Historical Quarterly*, *66*(2), 91–111. Retrieved from Academic Search Complete database.

Krotee, M., & Bucher, C. (2007). *Management of physical education and sport (13th ed.)*. Boston, MA: McGraw Hill.

Lapchick, R. (2009). Sense of urgency needed to address college's lack of diversity. *Street & Smith's Sports Business Journal*, *11*(34). Retrieved from http://www

.sportsbusinessdaily.com/Journal/Issues/2008/12/2008
1222/Opinion/Sense-Of-Urgency-Needed-To-Address-
Colleges-Lack-Of-Diversity.aspx

Lapchick, R. (2011). Building positive change: The Black
Coaches and Administrators (BCA) hiring report card
for NCAA FBS and FCS football head coaching positions (2010–11). Retrieved from http://www.bcasports
.org/images/pdf/bca_fb_hiring_final_11.20.2011.pdf

Lapchick, R., Little, E., Lerner, C., & Mathew, R. (2009).
The 2008 racial and gender report card: College sport.
Retrieved from: http://www.tidesport.org/RGRC/2008
/2008CollegRGRC.pdf

Maher, M. (2007, Spring). You've got messages: Modern
technology recruiting through text-messaging and the
intrusiveness of Facebook. *Texas Review of Entertainment & Sports Law, 8*(1), 125–151. Retrieved from Academic Search Complete database.

McGee, H., Bucklin, B., Dickinson, A., & McSweeney, F.
(2003, January). Participation of women in the Journal of Organizational Behavior Management. *Journal
of Organizational Behavior Management, 23*(1), 3–31.
Retrieved from Academic Search Complete database.

Mid-Eastern Atlantic Conference History (n.d.). Retrieved
from http://www.meacsports.com/

Mintzberg, H. (1973). *The nature of managerial work*.
New York, NY: Harper & Row.

Moore, D. (n.d.). Washington teams in sad state. *USA
Today*. Retrieved from Academic Search Complete
database.

Nance, R. (2007, May). Eddie Robinson: King of the Gridiron. *Crisis (15591573), 114*(3), 11–11. Retrieved from
Academic Search Complete database.

NCAA 2009 Bowling Championship (2009). 2008 Championship recap. National Collegiate, Canton, MI.

Sagas, M., Cunningham, G., & Pastore, D. (2006, May).
Predicting head coaching intentions of male and female assistant coaches: An application of the theory
of planned behavior. *Sex Roles, 54*(9/10), 695–705.
doi:10.1007/s11199-006-9035-x

Southern Intercollegiate Athletic Conference History
(n.d.). Retrieved from http://thesiac.com/

Southwestern Athletic Conference History (n.d.). Retrieved from http://www.swac.org/

Stringer, V. (2008). *Standing tall*. New York, NY: Random
House.

Supreme Court Refuses to Hear Coach's Racial-Profiling
Complaint. (2001, June 21). *Black Issues in Higher Education*, Retrieved from Academic Search Complete
database.

Wiggins, D. (1999, June). Edwin Bancroft Henderson:
Physical educator, civil rights activist, and chronicler
of African. *Research Quarterly for Exercise & Sport,
70*(2), 91. Retrieved from Academic Search Complete
database.

Winchester, A. (2007, September). Tis the season for basketball. *Lesbian News, 33*(2), 22–22. Retrieved from
Academic Search Complete database.

Section II: Recruitment, Retention, and NCAA Rules and Regulations

The three original pieces in this section focus on student-athlete academic policies, concerns about academic integrity, and remediation and eligibility policies and practices at two-year junior/community colleges.

Almost without question, any examination of NCAA regulations of student-athlete academic policies such as Proposition 48 or Proposition 16 will bring into play an array of concerns about the disparate impact of such policies on minority student-athletes. In Chapter 5, Martin, Gregg, and Kramer II write that the "numerical facts" clearly show a negative effect on the eligibility of prospective African American student-athletes during the post-Proposition 48 era, thus limiting their opportunities to participate and to attend and graduate from college. Ever cautious of various benchmarks calculated to handle the relationship between education and athletics, and weighing the extent to which exploitation appears behind a mask of academic eligibility, the authors bring a critical appraisal to the NCAA policies that are intended to foster academic achievement and institutional accountability.

Corbett tells readers in Chapter 6 that it is somehow considered virtuous to ignore academic concerns related specifically to the African American student who is an athlete because of a fear of the accusation of "playing the race card." In a five-part essay, she reviews how the academic progress rate (APR) is used to determine the overall academic performance of student-athletes, the colossal overemphasis on winning and financial gains, and the egregious corruption in sport (e.g., lenient admissions, grade fabrication, recruiting scandals). Reclaiming academic integrity in higher education demands that the stakeholders in college sports (i.e., college presidents, faculty, alumni, booster clubs) undertake academic reform.

In Chapter 7, Althouse and Brooks focus on intercollegiate athletics and the effect of race at community and junior colleges. These two-year schools are typically open door institutions, providing a wide range of students with access to attend colleges. There are benefits of these institutions for student-athletes (e.g., personal development, access to college) as well as benefits for the colleges (e.g., school spirit, enrollment growth, and opportunity for funding). A key benefit for students, and particularly for the student-athlete, is an opportunity to transfer to four-year institutions. However, one major issue relating to student-athletes' transition from two-year to four-year colleges has been graduation rates with references to Proposition 48 (i.e., remediation and recruitment), while another is the effect of the National Collegiate Athletic Association (NCAA) guidelines for eligibility compliance.

CHAPTER 5

NCAA Academic Regulations: Impact on Participation Rates for African American Males

BRANDON E. MARTIN, DERRICK L. GRAGG, and DENNIS A. KRAMER II

Abstract

For more than a century, the marriage between academia and intercollegiate athletics has been a conundrum. Intercollegiate athletics has faced immense scrutiny and criticism since its introduction into the mainstream of American higher education. Colleges and universities are faced with a paradox of maintaining academic integrity while exploiting the athletic entertainment value of youth who are often academically ill-prepared for the rigors of college life (Anderson & South, 2000; Smith, 2011). Critics of college athletics often contend that intercollegiate sport participation has severe negative consequences on the academic performance, campus integration, and nonathletic career aspirations of student-athletes. (Eitzen, 1987; Knight Commission on Intercollegiate Athletics, 1993; 2001; Sperber 2000). Additionally, several scholars have concluded that collegiate athletes are underprepared and uninterested in academic excellence—contending their motivation for college entrance is related to their athletic aspirations rather than academic achievement (Adler & Adler, 1985; Bowen & Levin, 2003; Miller & Kerr, 2002; Shulman & Bowen, 2001).

To exacerbate the negative commentary associated with student-athlete academic underachievement, academic improprieties and scandals have continually embarrassed institutions. In response, the NCAA has routinely established policies to foster academic achievement and institutional accountability. The historical initial eligibility policy, Proposition 48, as well as other contemporary academic standards, has resulted in much needed accountability metrics. However, what needs further examination is whether such policies have a negative and disparaging impact on minority student-athlete participation in intercollegiate athletics. This chapter examines NCAA academic polices within the scope of academic, athletic, and social experiences of African American male student-athletes in a post-Proposition 48 era. Special consideration is given to the barriers minority student-athletes face as a product of initial and continuing NCAA academic eligibility standards.

Key Terms		
● 1.6 Rule and 2.0 Rule	●	Jim Crow
● Academic Performance Report (APR)	●	Proposition 16
	●	Proposition 48
● dumb jock image	●	Sanity Code
● graduation success rate (GSR)	●	Title VI of the Civil Rights Act of 1964

INTRODUCTION

The Genesis of African American Athletes as Scholars

During the days of Jim Crow, most African American athletes attended historically Black colleges and universities (HBCUs). They first appeared on predominantly White university campuses during the latter half of the 19th century when intercollegiate sport was evolving from an unorganized to a highly structured activity. Throughout this period, numerous African American male college athletes accomplished great feats both on and off the athletic fields. Despite rampant discrimination and hardship, some of the best athletes between 1870 and the new century were African Americans who were frequently better educated than their White counterparts (Entine, 2000). These men, by whatever standards employed, were an elite group of individuals who approached sport with the utmost seriousness, but unlike many college athletes of the future, always considered sports less important than academic success and educational achievements.

William Henry Lewis was one of the first true Black scholar-athletes to grace a college campus at the end of the nineteenth century. After enrolling at Amherst College, he became class orator, college senator, president of the Hitchcock Society of Inquiry, star of the football team, and captain his senior season (Wiggins, 1991). Lewis, who was the first Black All-American football player, successfully graduated from the Harvard School of Law and was appointed the first African American to earn the position of US assistant attorney general. Other impressive Black scholar-athletes of the period include Lewis's teammate William Tecumseh Sherman Jackson, who became an instructor in Greek and Latin after graduation, and George Flippin, a star running back at the University of Nebraska, who later became a physician.

Comparable with other African American student-athletes of this era, the legendary Paul Robeson, a scholar-athlete who attended Rutgers University, entered the university as the exemplification of athleticism and scholarship. Robeson is widely considered a model African American student-athlete due to the volume of his accomplishes both athletically and academically. While attending the university from 1915 to 1918, Robeson was twice named an All-American football player and won 15 varsity letters in four sports. While demonstrating athletic prowess, Robeson's academic and extracurricular achievements reveal an even more impressive story. Robeson's high grade point average cemented him as one of four undergraduates (in a class of 80) along with admittance to Phi Beta Kappa his junior year. Robeson graduated Rutgers as the class valedictorian, a revered athlete, and a member of the Cap and Skull Honor Society. Subsequently, Robeson earned a law degree at Columbia University and became a famed actor and civil rights champion. Along with several other noteworthy African American scholar-athletes of this period, Paul Robeson seemed to have debunked the myth of African American athletic and academic inferiority.

African American Athletes of the Modern Era

During Jim Crow era, a select few African American scholar-athletes grew to prominence. However, the transition and socialization during the integration period proved to be difficult as the vast majority of African American athletes faced social and intrapersonal barriers attending predominantly white institutions. Despite enjoying increase of access to educational opportunities, many view the integration process for African American student-athletes as the beginning of the end—where athletic prowess (or the capacity to athletic success) began to overshadow the emphasis on academic achievement. Brooks and Althouse (1993) contend:

> The integration of American colleges, the massive commercialism of collegiate sports, and the desire by white colleges and universities to benefit from talented African American athletes in building commercialized athletic programs resulted in more and more schools searching for talented African Americans to bolster their teams; consequently, African American colleges lost their monopoly on African American athletic talent. The best African American athletes found it advantageous to play at predominantly white schools because of their greater visibility, especially on television. This visibility meant a better chance to sign a professional contract at the conclusion of their eligibility. (p. 9)

Lack of focus on academic achievement created student-athletes that were less prepared for and oftentimes ill-equipped to handle the rigors of higher education. Nowhere was this more pronounced than within the African American community. Scholars, such Jomills Broddack (1981), Harry Edwards (1984), Richard Lapchick (2000), and Edward Taylor (1999) concluded that today's African American children are seemingly "programmed" by society from an early age to pursue professional athletics. In a recent study, The Center for Study and Sport at Northeastern University (2004) found that African American families are seven times more likely to socialize their children into participating in sports and to believe in the obtainment of a professional contract, compared to the White families. This mentality is contrary to the previous generations of African American athletes, who viewed sport as a vehicle to gain access to higher education for social mobility.

The cultural exclusion of African Americans from professional basketball and football during the late 19th and early 20th centuries forced African American student-athletes to place a concerted effort on academic achievement instead of professional athletic pursuits. Since the inception of professional sport integration, the notion of academic substance within the African American community has deteriorated. In addition to finding increased family pressure to participate in sports, the Center for Study and Sport (2004) also found 66% of all African American males between the ages of 13 and 18 believe they can earn a living playing professional sports . These professional athletic ambitions are carried into the collegiate setting, whereby regulatory force (by the professional leagues), student-athletes enroll in college for the minimum required time before abandoning college for the benefits professional stardom.

In addition to an overemphasis on professional athletic opportunities, some educators fear that contemporary African American youth devalue education within society (Adler

& Adler, 1985; Edwards, 1984; Fleming, 1984; Sailes, 1998). African Americans are significantly more likely drop out of school or underachieve academically in order to save face with their peers and gain acceptance with the perceived hegemonic culture (Sailes, 1998). A number of African American student-athletes embrace and exude the same anti-intellectualism attitudes. Some modern-day African American athletes are better compared to primordial Roman gladiators who were admired solely for their physical strength and abilities than to their African American forefathers who epitomized the well-rounded scholar-athlete. Thus, many contemporary African American student-athletes uphold the dumb jock image (Adler & Adler, 1985; Edwards, 1984; Sailes, 1998) that the general public, members of the media, faculty members, and a number of their nonathletic peers associate with being African American and an athlete on a college campus. Stereotypes, for traditional students and student-athletes, can have negative impacts on academic performance when the student begins to identity with the stereotype (Steele & Aronson, 1995).

In their qualitative longitudinal study of student-athletes who attended a major university, Adler and Adler (1985) found that one of the most prevalent influences of student-athlete peer subculture was the pervasive and persistent anti-intellectual and anti-academic culture. This anti-intellectualism was reinforced in the athletic dormitory where conversations rarely centered on academic endeavors. Student-athletes who did show an interest in academic achievement experienced ridicule from their teammates. Others simply did not try to do well academically because they were embarrassed by frequent academic failures. Therefore, many of them abandoned any notions of achieving success academically. Such attitudes have led to abysmal academic and success rates for contemporary African American student-athletes.

BRIEF HISTORY OF FRESHMAN ELIGIBILITY STANDARDS

College and university officials, for some time, have acknowledged the dismal scholastic performance of student-athletes compared to that of student non-athletes; thus, the NCAA's freshman initial eligibility Propositions 48 and 16 were developed to address student-athletes' academic performance in colleges (Harris, 2000). Originally, individual colleges and universities bore responsibility for enforcing academic eligibility requirements (Waller, 2003); however, without any governing authority, schools in the early years often courted athletes who had no interest in academic success or matriculating toward graduation (Shropshire, 1997). In response to the growing concerns over student-athletes academic exploitation, the NCAA implemented a series of measures to help improve student-athlete academic quality.

The NCAA's first attempt at academic reform came in 1947, with the establishment of the Sanity Code, which banned the distribution of athletic scholarships in an attempt to curb rampant recruiting and financial aid abuse. However, colleges and universities circumvented the new measure by either providing athletes with secret scholarships or discreetly paying them for their services. Additionally, ahtletic donors eluded the Sanity Code by awarding student-athletes menial jobs with extraordinary wages (Grant, Leadley & Zygmont, 2008). Due to the inability of the Sanity Code to provide substantive change, the policy was disbanded three years later (Waller, 2003).

The NCAA's next major attempt at academic reform came in 1965 with the establishment of the 1.6 Rule. This rule required universities to limit athletics eligibility to students whose predicted grade-point-average (GPA) was a 1.60 or greater—on a 4.0 scale—

during their initial year in college. This rule was predicated on a complex formula that weighed a prospective student-athlete's high school class rank, high school GPA, and standardized college entrance test scores. The success of the 1.6 rule led to increased demand for academic success and in 1973 the 1.6 Rule was subsequently replaced by the 2.0 Rule—requiring a 2.0 GPA. Critics of the 2.0 Rule cited not only the lack of uniformity in the precollege socialization and grading process, but also feared issues of grade inflation by high school faculty to ensure the ineligible of perspective student-athletes (Hunt, 2000). The NCAA's response to critics was the development of Proposition 48, which aimed at improving graduation rates for student-athletes and bolstering the integrity of college sports (Waller, 2003).

THE EMERGENCE OF PROPOSITION 48 AND RACIAL MAGNITUDES

Since its establishment, Proposition 48 has been the source of controversy, consternation, and division among high and college educators, coaches, prospective college student-athletes, and other stakeholders connected to the intercollegiate athletics enterprise. Perhaps no other athletic policy has been both widely praised and criticized during the past 25 years. NCAA executives and the representatives of member schools justified the inception of Proposition 48 as a mechanism to promote the academic life both on the secondary and postsecondary environments. Critics questioned this policy on the basis of disproportionate impact of eligibility loss despite a demonstrated ability to pass college course work (Fleischer, Goff, & Tollison, 1992).

Originally introduced by the American Council on Education's (ACE) Ad Hoc subcommittee on Problems of Major Intercollegiate Athletics in 1982, the core of Proposition 48 called for uniform standardization of entrance standards, emphasizing grade-point average (GPA) and Scholastic Aptitude Test (SAT) scores to project future postsecondary academic success. Comprised of university presidents and chaired by then President of Harvard University Derek Bok, the ACE subcommittee ultimately determined a cumulative high school grade point average (GPA) of 2.0, combined SAT score of at least 700, or a composite score of 15 on the American College Testing (ACT), along with satisfactory completion of 11 high school core courses, provided an accurate predictor of college-level academic aptitude. Prospective student-athletes who met the requirements were deemed "qualifiers" and were eligible for athletic competition during their first year of college; however, those who did not meet the requirements were either deemed "partial qualifiers," those who met at least some of the requirements, or "nonqualifiers," those who did not meet any of the requirements. Neither partial nor nonqualifiers were allowed to compete athletically during their first year of college. In contrast to nonqualifiers, partial qualifiers were allowed to receive athletic financial aid to attend college during their first year of enrollment.

Despite its positive intentions, the major fallout of Proposition 48 resulted from its racial consequences (Anderson & South, 2000). Due to the fact that minority students have historically obtained lower scores on standardized tests and attended high schools that underprepared them for the rigors of college level work (Brooks & Alhouse, 1993; Ferrante, Etzel, & Lantz, 1996; Sedlacek & Gaston, 1992), some opponents of the proposition accused the NCAA of blatant racial discrimination. For example, during the 77th Annual Convention of the NCAA (the convention in which Proposition 48 was adopted) Clark, Horton, and Alford (1986) observed the overwhelming disdain for the new legislation, writing that most African American convention participants called the new proposition "a racist, overtly exclusionary, and arrogant act" (p. 8). Other adversarial opponents argued that the policy was devised and implemented without any African American input or participation whatsoever.

One major accusation critics asserted dealt with the intentionality of the policy to reduce the number of African American student-athletes. Particularly, critics focused on the application of standardized test scores, since it is well-established that minority students score significantly lower on standardized tests compared to Caucasian students. According to Edwards (1983), the most outspoken of Proposition 48 critic was Dr. Jesse N. Stone, Jr., the president of the Southern University system of Louisiana, who reported,

> The end result of this is the Black athlete has been too good. If it [Proposition 48] is followed to its logical conclusion, we say to our youngsters, "Let the White boy win once in a while." This has set the Black athlete back 25 or 30 years. The message is that White schools no longer want Black athletes. (p. 33)

Critics of Proposition 48 initially predicted that African-American athletes would be forced out of college sport participation altogether. Although not a reality, there is no denying that the number of African American student-athletes decreased in the Proposition 48 era. Proposition 48 disqualified a large number of potential African American student-athletes from college sport participation. Early reports regarding the effectiveness of Proposition 48 showed that 85% of those losing eligibility under Proposition 48 have been African American (Cross & Koball, 1991; Johnson, 1988). An NCAA study conducted only one year after the implementation of Proposition 48 found that of 424 potential student-athletes meeting the core curriculum and GPA requirements but not standardized test requirements, 299 were African American and 104 were White (NCAA, 1987). Summarized, more than 70% of those negatively affected by the newly implemented rules were African American. A subsequent NCAA survey showed that 97.8% of White freshmen were deemed qualifiers in 1988 while only 85.5% of African American freshmen qualified under the new provisions (NCAA, 1989). Even more startling is the aforementioned 1987 NCAA study found that applying Proposition 48 to the 16,000 Division I freshmen receiving scholarships between 1977 and 1982, 69% of African Americans who went on to graduate would have not received admission based on the NCAA criteria.

Although many Division I African American athletes were disqualified from participation because of Proposition 48, the negative effects of the guidelines were even more pronounced at HBCUs, which have a long tradition of remediating the academic shortcomings of African American students (Anderson & South, 2000). The main negative impact felt by HBCUs, institutions that operate on the margins financially, was economic in nature, as these institutions could not afford to fund athletic scholarships for partial qualifiers who did not meet all the necessary requirements of Proposition 48. Becker and Weinberg (1986) state that 34% of all Mid-Eastern Athletic Conference (MEAC) and 27% of all Southwestern Athletic Conference (SWAC)—two conferences where a majority of HBCUs participate—entering freshmen student-athletes were ineligible during the initial year Proposition 48 was implemented. Thus, there was no way for the institutions to fund the initial year of education for such a high number of ineligible student-athletes. Additionally, many predominantly White institutions (PWI) simply refused to admit partial qualifiers under Prop 48 altogether, regardless if they could afford to fund their athletic scholarships.

Despite being handed evidence that African Americans routinely do not score as high as Whites on standardized tests, and even conducting their own research regarding the disproportionate impact of Proposition 48 on African American student-athletes, the

NCAA stayed the course on not only utilizing, but also further strengthening the application of standardized test on initial eligible standards.

PROPOSITION 16 AND COURTROOM BACKLASH

In another attempt to strengthen initial eligibility regulations for prospective Division IA student-athletes, the NCAA established Proposition 16. Essentially, Proposition 16 modified previous propositions by providing a sliding scale of eligibility requirements. Specifically, the sliding scale used standardized test scores and grade point averages to classify student-athletes as qualifiers, partial qualifiers, or nonqualifiers (Howard-Hamilton & Watt, 2001). The new legislation provided provisions where student-athletes could offset either a low standardized test score or grade point average with higher scores in other areas. For example, a student-athlete with a GPA as low as 2.0 in core courses needed to obtain a combined score of 1010 on the SAT or a composite of 86 on the ACT to be considered an NCAA qualifier. Conversely, a student with a GPA of 2.5 or better only needed to score 820 on the SAT or 68 on the ACT to become a qualifier. The new legislation also provided increases to secondary course requirements, from 11 to 13.

Similar to Proposition 48, the new legislation had an immediate and negative impact on African American high school student-athletes. Preliminary enrollment data for 1994–1996 revealed a drop in the proportion of African Americans among first-year scholarship athletes in Division I from 23.6% to 20.3%—accompanied by a 2% increase in White student-athletes and a 1.3% increase in student-athletes from all other ethnic groups combined. While only 3.1% of White student-athletes were ineligible under Proposition 16, an enormous 19.4% of African American student-athletes did not qualify (NCAA, 1998). In 1996, under the new academic standards, 26.9% of all African American prospective student-athletes failed to qualify for athletic competition in comparison to only 3.5% of all White prospective student-athletes. This percentage decrease amounted to more than 667 fewer student-athletes ruled eligible for athletic participation in 1996 than in 1995 (CH II Publishers, Inc., 1998). Additionally, of those African American student-athletes appearing on a Division I Institution Request List submitted to the NCAA Initial-Eligibility Clearinghouse, 26.6% did not meet Proposition 16 standards in 1996 and 21.4% failed to qualify in 1997 (compared to 6.4% of White student-athletes in 1996 and 4.2%, respectively, in 1997). This disproportionate impact also was seen to a lesser degree in other ethnic-minority groups (NCAA, 1998).

The consequence of the new academic legislation was not only seen by race or ethnicity. Low-income student-athletes (many of whom are African American or other ethnic minorities) also have been affected to a greater degree than other student-athletes by Proposition 16 standards. For example, in 1997, 18% of all student-athletes with a self-reported family income below $30,000 failed to qualify, whereas only 2.5% of student-athletes with a family income of greater than $80,000 failed to qualify. For both African American and low-income student-athletes, the single largest reason for not meeting Proposition 16 standards was failure to meet the minimum standardized test score (NCAA, 1998).

CURETON v. NCAA and *PRYOR v. NCAA*

The public outcry regarding Proposition 16 was as robust as the reaction to Proposition 48. Coupled with the usual rhetoric that accompanied the rules changes, a group of African American students decided to combat the regulations through the legal system. In

1999, Proposition 16 first came under scrutiny in the case of *Cureton v. NCAA* (Waller, 2003). After being declared ineligible to compete during their first years of collegiate eligibility as track & field student-athletes, Tai Kwan Cureton and Leatrice Shaw, both 1996 graduates of a Philadelphia high school, filed a class-action suit against the NCAA for discrimination based on the application of biased standardized tests. Both students had earned academic honors at their former high school, yet failed to meet the necessary SAT scores for NCAA eligibility. In their complaint, Cureton and Shaw (who were later joined by Andrea Gardner and Alex Wesby, African American students who also failed to meet the minimum test scores) claimed that the use of standardized test scores, as a mechanism for eligibility, was in violation of the Title VI of the 1964 Civil Rights Act and that the use of Proposition 16 was an intentional instrument of discrimination against African American student-athletes. The complainants also asserted that Proposition 16's minimum SAT component created an unjustified disparate impact on African American student-athletes (Waller, 2003) and that African American and low-income student-athletes have been disproportionately affected by Proposition 16 standards.

A federal judge initially ruled in the students' favor, agreeing that the NCAA's policies regarding initial eligibility did indeed discriminate against African American student-athletes; however, the decision was overturned two years later by the U.S. Court of Appeals for the Third Circuit. Although their legal claim was ultimately denied, the evidence supporting their claim shed new light on issues of equity within college sports, which ultimately led to an even stronger lawsuit against the NCAA.

Not long after the *Cureton* case was decided, Kelly Pryor and Warren Spivey, both African American student-athletes who, similar to the student-athletes in *Cureton*, failed to meet the requirements of Proposition 16, jointly filed a suit against the NCAA claiming that by adopting Proposition 16, the NCAA intentionally discriminated against them in violation of Title VI of the Civil Rights Act of 1964 (Waller, 2003). Although the district court dismissed all the claims against the NCAA, the U.S. Court of Appeals for the Third Circuit agreed with the plaintiffs and held that based on the various studies (some generated by the NCAA itself) and other information that had proven that African Americans would undoubtedly be declared ineligible under Proposition 16, the NCAA at least partially intended to reduce the number of African American athletes who could attend college on an athletic scholarship by adopting the heightened academic requirements of Proposition 16 (*Pryor*, 288, F.3d at 564). Due to this decision and the increased pressures regarding Proposition 16, the NCAA made significant changes to the legislation by extending the range of the initial eligibility index sliding scale, thus, giving more credence to high school GPAs and lessening the chance that prospective student-athletes would be ineligible due to unsatisfactory standardized test scores. Thus, the baseline minimum GPA/standardized test score remains 2.0 with a 1010 SAT or 86 ACT sum score; however, a prospective student-athlete with a core course GPA of 3.0 can score as low as 620 on the SAT and 52 on the ACT. A student with a 3.5 or better GPA can score as low as a 420 on the SAT or 39 on the ACT (NCAA, 2009).

INCREASE IN HIGH SCHOOL CORE COURSE REQUIREMENTS

In recent years, as the arguments for and against stronger academic policies for student-athletes volleyed back and forth, one thing remained consistent—the steady increase in the number of core courses necessary for NCAA Division IA eligibility. Newly appointed NCAA president Mark Emmert, reported "Academics are vitally important and demand just as much attention as athletics, especially in college." Emmert stresses that NCAA student-athletes need to be prepared for the rigors of college work in order that they might be academically successful (NCAA, 2012b).

Initially when Proposition 48 was created, student-athletes were required to satisfactorily complete 11 core courses. The number of necessary core courses was increased to 13 when Proposition 16 was established. In August of 2008, the necessary number of core courses was increased to 16. Beginning in August 2013, the core course requirements for Division II eligibility will be increased from 14 to 16, the same requirement currently for Division I. By continuing to increase the number of necessary high school core courses, the NCAA continues to emphasize the importance of high school academic achievement and preparation for success in college.

CONTINUING ELIGIBILITY RULE FOR CURRENT STUDENT-ATHLETES

Although initial eligibility rules have been made somewhat lenient by the addition of the sliding scale, the rules regarding continuing eligibility for Division I student-athletes have been enhanced during the past few years. Thus, while it has become somewhat easier for student-athletes to gain admittance into college, the more stringent continuing eligibility rules appear to make it more difficult for student-athletes to maintain eligibility while in college.

One of the strongest proponents of academic reform for college athletics was Myles Brand, the first sitting university president to be named CEO/President of the NCAA. Along with increasing university/college presidential involvement in college athletics and championing diversity and inclusion in college athletics, Brand's other objective was to fortify the academic rules and regulations for student-athletes. Several new initial and continuing eligibility academic rules and regulations were instilled during his tenure as NCAA President, the most notable of which are the 40/60/80 rule and the establishment of the academic pProgress rate (APR) regulations.

Student-athletes have experienced evolving academic regulations by the NCAA.
Courtesy of UT Lady Vols Media Relations

40/60/80 RULE

The dispiriting treatment of African American male student-athletes does not end at the admission process. Mechanisms to illustrate progress to a degree also disenfranchise these student-athletes. As a precursor to the NCAA graduation success rate (GSR) or the "real-time" academic progress rate (APR), the NCAA implemented the rule known as 40/60/80 in October 2002—modifying the previous 25/50/75 rule that required student-athletes to complete 25% of the degree requirements prior to the beginning on the third year, 50% by the fourth, and 75% by the fifth year (Pickle, 1992). The new 40/60/80 provision stated that in addition to maintaining six credit hours per semester, a student-athlete must complete 40% of his/her degree prior to the start of the third year in college, 60% by the fourth, and 80% by the fifth to ensure eligibility the following year. The true impact of the 40/60/80 rule can be explained by the work of Edwards (2000), who found, while examining Division I athletic programs, that this provision "targeted African Americans evident by the fact that over 50% of African American male student-athletes who actually graduated did so with either a degree in physical education or other less rigorous majors specifically designed to maintain student-athletes' eligibility during college" (p. 9). The number of those funneled to "easy majors" who did not graduate is even more alarming and often unquantifiable.

Major clustering is a well-documented phenomenon in college sport (Shulman & Bowen, 2011; Bowen & Levin, 2003; NCAA, 2011). The Associated Press analyzed media guides, reporting that at 22 instituions, over 50% of football players were majoring in one of three disciplines. At Georgia Tech, 70% of the football team in 2011 majored in management. At Vanderbilt University, approximately 60% were part of the human and organizational development major and at UCLA 57% of football players were history majors (NCAA, 2011). Approximately 20% of student-athletes believe that athletic participation prevented them from majoring in their desired major. In addition, five percent of NCAA student-athlete respondents felt regret for not being able to participate in their desired major. Lastly, 40 percent of student-athletes surveyed by the NCAA believed athletic participation prevented them from enrolling in classes they were interested in (Wolverton, 2007).

ACADEMIC PERFORMANCE REPORT (APR)

In response to the low graduation rates for men's basketball, former NCAA Presidents Myles Brand asserted, "There must be a base below which academic performance is acceptable. Under no circumstances can it be acceptable not to graduate any men's basketball player in five years, which has recently occurred at 36 Division I schools;" (NCAA, 2004) and it was time for a "real-time" metric to assess the academic matriculation of student-athletes (NCAA, 2009). With recommendation from a reform committee such as the Knight Commission on Intercollegiate Athletics, the NCAA implemented the academic progress report (APR) program to assess overall classroom performance and provide disincentives for poor academic performance and recognition for high performers (NCAA, 2009).

The APR metric provides an individual score to each Division I team based on eligibility, retention rates, and graduation rates of its scholarship athletes only. The benchmark APR score of 925 out of 1,000 is roughly equated to a 60% graduation rate (NCAA, 2008). Teams with academic progress rates below 925 can lose scholarships, and scores below 900 trigger even more severe sanctions. Institutions that continue to fail to comply with the academic regulations face even more stringent penalties such as ineligibility for postseason championship competition, including bowl games and NCAA basketball and other sport championship participation. In 2012, the NCAA banned 15 teams from post-season play, including 10 men's basketball teams, three football teams, one men's soccer team and one wrestling team (Scandoval, 2012). Institutions can also be stripped of their NCAA membership status.

The original intent of the APR was to continue to incentivize a refocus of academic priority; unfortunately, similar to Propositions 48 and 16, the APR system has produced results that both marginalize academic success and disproportionally affect African American males. Since 2004, African American student-athletes have seen an increase in ineligibility (e.g., "0–2" students who do not return to their original institution for the subsequent academic year and would be academically ineligible to participate in athletics even had the student-athlete returned to the institution) from 44% to 61%. This is in contrast to the decrease experienced by White student-athletes, whose ineligibility rate decreased from 50% to 33% in 2008 (Green, 2008). Additionally, male student-athletes become ineligible at a significantly higher rate than that of their females peers (81% and 19%), with much disparity coming from the revenue-generating sports that have the highest rates of ineligibility (10% to 40%).

In August 2011, the NCAA Board of Directors enacted legislation that requires a team to have a 900 average over four years or a 930 over two years to qualify for postseason participation. This legislation was in response to advocates' call for increased accountability for student athlete academic success and the failures of men's basketball program programs to monitor the success of African American athletes in particular. For the 2013 season, institutions such as the University of Connecticut will be banned from participating in both the annual NCAA tournament and their conference postseason tournament. The key remaining question is the reach of this legislation into men's football. Since men's football postseason is governed by the independent Bowl Championship Series (BCS) there is uncertainty as to how the new standards relate to the BCS selection of institutions for postseason play.

During the 2011–12 football season, the average APR school of teams who participated in bowl games was 951.9 and had a average graduation rate of 68.2%. The University of Louisville had the APR score 908, which was the lowest of all teams participating. In contrast, Northwestern achieved an APR score of 993, the highest of all the teams participating in the 2011 bowl season. Twelve other teams had APRs scores above 970, including Rutgers (988), Northern Illinois (987), Ohio State (985), Clemson (977), Stanford (977), Vanderbilt (977), Florida (976), Georgia (976), Penn State (972), Wake Forest (971), Wake Forest (971), and Notre Dame (971) (Lapchick, 2011a).

Of the teams participating in the 2011 NCAA men's basketball tournament, 10 teams had an APR below the 925 benchmark. This showed an improvement from the previous year where 19 teams scored below 925. Twenty-six teams participating in the 2011 tournament had an APR score at or above 970 (Lapchick, 2011b). Given that 62 percent of men's basketball student-athletes are African American, this data is revealing (Lapchick, 2011b).

Improved Graduation Rates

Amidst the constant negativity surrounding NCAA regulations and their effect on minority student-athletes, one cannot ignore the positive benefits of the academic regulations and standards. One of the more noteworthy benefits of the stringent rules is the improved graduation rates for student-athletes. Student-athlete graduation rates have increased steadily over the years since the passage of Propositions 48 and 16.

Division I student-athletes who entered their respective institutions in 1996–97 set an all-time record for graduation rates (NCAA, 2003). In 2008, overall, the graduation rate for athletes, as calculated by the U.S. Education Department, was 64%, compared with 62% for the general student body. This is the highest overall student-athlete graduation rate in the history of the NCAA. Also, African American male student-athlete graduation rates rose an amazing 15% from 1984 to 2001. Additionally, male African American student-athletes graduated at a rate of 48%, 10 percentage points higher than the rate for male African American students overall. For female African American athletes, the rate was 63%, 13 percentage points higher than the rate for their counterparts in the student body at large (NCAA, 2008). Finally, African American men's basketball and football student-athletes increased their graduation rates 15 percentage points over that same pe-riod of time. While in the sports of men's basketball and football the overall graduation rates lag behind the rates of males in the student body, the rates for the African Ameri-cans in those sports are higher than African American males in the student body (by six percentage points in basketball and five percentage points in football).

Between 2006 and 2009, the graduation success rate of male African American student-athletes increased three percentage points, from 54% to 57%. Likewise, the rates for female, African American student-athletes increased three percent. Both men's bas-ketball and football saw increases in graduation success rates as well, increasing 5% and 4% respectively. This represented "dramatic progress" (Lapchick, 2009, p.1) in gradua-tion rates for African American student-athletes.

Analysis of the 2011–12 football bowl-bound teams again showed an improvement for African American student-athletes, but also highlighted disparity between African Ameri-can and Caucasians. Of the 70 schools that participated in the 2011–12 bowl season, 52 schools graduated 50% or more of their African American players. In contrast, 100% of those 70 teams graduated over 50% of their white football players. Moreover, two schools graduated less than 40% of their African American football players. Thirty-nine schools were found to have a 20% graduation success rate gap between African Ameri-can football players and white football players. Additionally, 16 schools had a GSR gap of 30%. Only one team, Notre Dame, had a higher GSR for African American football players than white players. Two football teams, Rutgers and Louisiana Tech, had Gradua-tion success rates that were higher than the overall student-athlete population. Boise State's football team had a GSR that was equivalent to all other student-athletes (Lapchick, 2011a).

Of the teams participating in the 2011 NCAA men's basketball tournament, 51 teams graduated at least 50% of their players. In contrast, only seven teams graduated fewer than 40% of their players (Lapchick, 2011b). Only seven teams graduated 100% of their players. While men's basketball has seen an increase in graduate rates, racial disparities still exist. Thirty-six teams in the tournament had a gradation gap at or above 20% be-tween African American and white players. In addition, 30 teams had a graduation gap at or above 30 percent (Lapchick, 2011b).

CONCLUSION

Throughout history, the leadership of the NCAA along with other higher education asso-ciations have made attempts to regulate academic priorities; however, these attempts have often created barriers for the success of African American student-athletes. The es-sential question is whether initial-eligibility rules such as Propositions 48 and 16 have had a disparate or negative effect on the opportunity for African American prospective student-athletes to pursue college athletics. An extensive perusal of the literature verifies that there is an overwhelming amount of data underscoring both Proposition 48 and Proposition 16 having a distinct impact on African American student-athletes. Based on existing literature, one cannot deny that percentage-wise many more African American prospective student-athletes have been declared ineligible under NCAA initial eligibility legislation during the post-Proposition 48 period; therefore, limiting their opportunities to participate in sport and attend and graduate from college.

Despite the more stringent initial and continuing eligibility rules that have limited some of the opportunities for African American student-athletes, there is no denying that graduation rates for student-athletes have improved steadily since the passage of Proposition 48. In recent years, graduation success rates for African American student-athletes have risen 3% for both men and women. Additionally, 74% of who participated in the 2011–12 bowl season graduated 50% or more of their African American student-athletes. Likewise, approximately 79% of schools that participated in the 2011 NCAA men's basketball tournament graduated at least 50% of their African American players (Lapchick, 2011a). Such improved rates are undoubtedly commendable. However, there is a possibility that the increased graduation rates do not outweigh the number of African Americans who may have been excluded from participating in athletics and attending college collectively. For instance, if 1,000 African Americans receive athletic scholarships and 33% graduate, this equates to 330 student-athletes receiving degrees. However, if the number of African American student-athletes were reduced to 700 because of higher eligibility standards but 41% graduate, only 287 student-athletes would receive degrees. Thus, increased graduation percentage rates for African American student-athletes may be deceptive at first glance. Until we receive more comprehensive data regarding participation rates, we should exhibit caution while celebrating the academic success of African American student-athletes.

STUDY QUESTIONS

1. Provide a description of the genesis of African American male athletic participation in higher education.
2. Discuss the impact the following NCAA Legislation had on African American student-athlete college experiences: 1.6 Rule, 2.0 Rule, Proposition 48, and Proposition 16.
3. Discuss current NCAA academic reform initiatives such as graduation success rate (GSR) and academic performance rate (APR), and newly implemented initial eligibility standards.
4. How did *Cureton v. NCAA* and *Pryor v. NACC* influence NCAA academic legislation and governance?
6. Given the history of NCAA initial eligibility regulations, how will African American male student-athletes be able to meet future academic benchmarks proposed by the NCAA?

SUGGESTED READINGS

Amato, L., Gandar, J. M., Tucker, I.B., & Zuber, R.A. (2001). The impact of Proposition 48 on the relationship between football success and football player graduation rate. *Journal of Sports Economics*, 2(2), 101–112.

Brand, M. (1 April 2001). Academic first: Reforming intercollegiate athletics. *Vital Speeches of the Day*, 67(12), 367.

Christy, K., & Seifred C. (2008). Intercollegiate athletics: A preliminary study examining the opinions of the impact of the academic performance rate (APR). *Journal of Issues in Intercollegiate Athletics*, 1, 1–10.

Dawkins, M. P., Braddock, J.H,II, & Celaya, A. (2008). Academic engagement among African American males who hold aspirations for athletic careers in professional sports. *Challenge: A Journal of Research on African American Men*, 14(2), 51–65.

Ferris, E., Finster, M., & McDonald, D. (2004). Academic fit of student-athletes: An analysis of NCAA division1-A graduation rates. *Research in Higher Education*, *45*(6), 555–575.

Gaston-Gayles, J. (2003). Advising student athletes: An examination of academic support programs with high graduation rates. *National Academic Advising Association Journal*, *23*(1&2), 50–57.

Hollis, L. P. (2002). Service ace? Which academic services and resources truly benefit student athletes? *Journal of College Students Retention*, *3*(3), 26–283.

Hyatt, R. (2003). Barriers to persistence among African American intercollegiate athletes: A literature review of non-cognitive variables. *College Student Development*, *37*(2), 260–276.

Knight Foundation Commission on Intercollegiate Athletics. (2001). *A call to action: Reconnecting college sports and higher education*. Charlotte, NC: The Knight Foundation.

Simons, H. D., Bosworth, C., Fujita, S., & Jensen, M. (2007). The athlete stigma in higher education. *College Student Journal*, *41*(2), 251–273.

REFERENCES

Bowen, W., & Levin, S. (2003). *Reclaiming the game: College sports and educational values*. Princeton: Princeton University Press.

Braddock, J. H. (1981). Race, athletics, and educational achievement. *Youth and Society*, *12*, 335–350.

Brooks, D., & Althouse, R. (1993). *Racism in college athletics*. Morgantown, WV: Fitness Information Technology.

Coakley, J. J. (1998). *Sport in society: Issues and controversies* (6th ed.). Boston, MA: McGraw-Hill.

Chubb, M. (1989, January 17). Thompson protests 'racist' proposition. *The Hoya*. Retrieved from http:www.thehoya.com/node/8163

Clow, C.T. (2001). Student-athletes' perceived value of education: Effects of career exploration intervention. *Dissertation Abstracts International*, *61*.

Cureton et. al v. NCAA. 37 F. Supp. 2D 687. 1999 U.S. Dist. LEXIS 2359.

DeFrancesco, C., & Gropper, R. (1996). Support services for African American student athletes: A case study analysis. *College Student Journal*, *30*, 2–8.

Edwards, H. (1984, Spring). The Black "dumb jock": An American sports tragedy. *The College Board Review*, *131*, 8–13.

Edwards, H. (2000). Crisis of black athletes on the eve of the 21st century. *Society*, *37*, 913.

Engstrom, C., & Sedlacek, W. (1991). A study of prejudice towards college student-athletes. *Journal of Counseling and Development*, *70*, 189–193.

Engstrom, C., Sedlacek, W., & McEwen, M. (1995). Faculty attitudes towards male revenue-generating and non-revenue student-athletes. *Journal of College Student Development*, *36*, 217–227.

Ferrante, A., Etzel, E., & Lantz, C. (1996). Counseling college student athletes: The problem, the need. In E. F. Etzel, A. P. Ferrante, & J. W. Pinkney (Eds.), *Counseling college student athletes: Issues and interventions* (2nd ed.) (pp. 3–26). Morgantown, WV: Fitness Information Technology.

Francisco, R. (2001). *The effects of proposition 48 and 16 on African American male student-athletes': Graduate rates*. Unpublished manuscript, San Jose State University.

Gaston-Gayles, J. (2003). Advising student athletes: An examination of academic support programs with high graduation rates. *National Academic Advising Association Journal*, *23*(1&2), 50–57.

Gerdy, J. R. (1997). *The successful college athletic program: The new standard*. Phoenix, AZ: The Oryx Press.

Grant, R. R., Leadley, J., & Zygmont, Z. (2008). *The economics of intercollegiate sports*. Singapore: World Scientific Publishing Company.

Green, S. J. (2008). *A profile of the ineligible and not-retained (0/2) student-athletes of the Atlantic Coast Conference*. Doctoral dissertation, University of North Carolina.

Harris, O. (1994). Race, sport, and social support. *Sociology of Sport Journal*, *11*, 40–50.

Hollis, L. P. (2002). Service Ace? Which academic services and resources truly benefit student athletes? *Journal of College Students Retention*, *3*(3), 26–283.

Howard-Hamilton, M. F., & Watts, S. K. (2001, Spring). Student services for athletes. *New Directions for Student Services*, *93*, 1–6.

Hyatt, R. (2003). Barriers to persistence among African American intercollegiate athletes: A literature review of non-cognitive variables. *College Student Development*, *37*(2), 260–276.

Knight Foundation Commission on Intercollegiate Athletics. (1993). *Keeping faith with the student-athlete: A solid start and a new beginning for a new century*. Charlotte, NC: The Knight Foundation.

Knight Foundation Commission on Intercollegiate Athletics. (2001). *A call to action: Reconnecting college sports and higher education*. Charlotte, NC: The Knight Foundation.

Kulics, J. M. (2007). An analysis of the academic behaviors and beliefs of Division I student athletes and academic administrators: The impact of the increased percentage toward degree requirements. Doctoral dissertation, Kent State University.

Lapchick, R. (2000). Crime and athletes: New radical stereotypes. *Society, 37,* 14–20.

Lapchick, R. (2003). *2003 racial and gender report card.* Orlando, FL: University of Central Florida, Institute for Diversity and Ethics in Sport.

Lapchick, R. (2009). *New study reveals marked improvements for the graduation rates for African-American student-athletes.* Orlando, FL: University of Central Florida, Institute for Diversity and Ethics in Sport.

Lapchick, R., (2011a). *Keeping score when it counts: Assessing the 2011–12 bowl-bound college football teams.* Orlando, FL: University of Central Florida, Institute for Diversity and Ethics in Sport.

Lapchick, R. (2011b). *Keeping score when it counts: Graduation success and academic progress rates for the 2011 NCAA division I men's basketball tournament teams.* Orlando, FL: University of Central Florida, Institute for Diversity and Ethics in Sport.

Martin, B. E., & Kramer II, D. A. (2007, May). *"State of emergency:" Enacting a multi-pronged approach towards improving the academic achievement of African American male high school student-athletes.* Conference presentation presented at the meeting of the College Board: Dream Deferred Conference, Los Angeles.

Miller, P. S., & Kerr, G. (2002). The athletic, academic and social experiences of intercollegiate student-athletes. *Journal of Sport Behavior, 25*(4), 346–367.

National Center for Fair and Open Testing. (2007). *What's wrong with the NCAA's test score requirements.* Retrieved from http://www.fairtest.org/whats-wrong-proposition-48-and-16

National Collegiate Athletic Association. (2001). *NCAA Division I graduation rate report.* Overland Park, KS: NCAA.

National Collegiate Athletic Association. (2003). *NCAA Division I graduation rate report.* Overland Park, KS: NCAA.

National Collegiate Athletic Association. (2004). *The NCAA Manual,* Indianapolis, IN: NCAA.

National Collegiate Athletic Association. (2011). Athletes sticking together in classes. Retrieved from http://www.ncaa.com/news/football/article/2011-09-05/athletes-sticking-together-classes

National Collegiate Athletic Association, (2012). National and sport-group APR averages, trends, and penalties. Retrieved from http://www.ncaa.org/wps/wcm/connect/public/ncaa/pdfs/2012/apr + 2012 + trends

National Collegiate Athletic Association, (2012b). Emmert stresses academics to open Final Four weekend.

Retrieved from http://www.ncaa.org/wps/wcm/connect/public/ncaa/resources/latest + news/2012/march/emmert + stresses + academics + to + open + final + four + weekend

Pickle, P. D. (1992, January 15). Reform agenda passes easily at convention. *The NCAA News, 29,* 1, 22. Retrieved from http://web1.ncaa.org/web_video/NCAA NewsArchive/1992/19920115.pdf

Perlmutter, D. (2003). Black athletes and White professor: A twilight zone of uncertainty. *The Chronicle of Higher Education,* B7–B9.

Person, D. R., & LeNoir, K. M. (1997). Retention issues and models for African American male athletes. *New Directions or Student Service, 80,* 79–91.

Richards, S., & Aries, E. (1999). The Division III student-athlete: Academic performance, campus involvement, and growth. *Journal of College Student Development, 40*(3), 211–218.

Sack, A. L. (1987). College sport and the student athlete. *Journal of Sport and Social Issues, 11,* 31–48.

Sack, A., & Stuarowsky, E. (1998). *College athletes for hire: The evolution and legacy of the NCAA's amateur myth.* Westport, CT: Praeger.

Sailes, G. A. (1984). Sport socialization comparisons among Black and White adult male athletes and non-athletes. *Dissertation Abstracts International.*

Sandoval, T. (2012). For poor academic progress, NCAA bans 15 teams from postseason games. Retrieved from http://chronicle.com/article/For-Poor-Academic-Progress/132423/

Sedlacek, W. E. (2004). *Beyond the big test: Noncognitive assessment in higher education.* San Francisco, CA: John Wiley & Sons.

Shulman, J., Bowen, W. (2001). *The game of life: College sports and educational values.* Princeton, NJ: Princeton University Press.

Smith, R. (2011). *Pay for play: A history of big-time college athletic reform.* Chicago, IL: University of Illinois Press.

Steele, C.M., & Aronson, J. (1995). Stereotype threat and the intellectual test performance of African Americans. *Journal of Personality and Social Psychology, 69,* 797–811.

Taylor, E. (1999). Bring in "da noise": Race, sports, and the role of sports. *Educational Leadership, 56*(7), 75–78.

Underwood, C. (1984). *The student athlete: Eligibility and academic integrity.* Lansing, MI: Michigan State University Press.

Wolverton, B. (2007). Athletes question effectiveness of NCAA rule. *Chronicle of Higher Education, 53*(18), A33.

Zimbalist, A. (1999). *Unpaid professionals: Commercialism and conflict in big-time college sports.* Princeton, NJ: Princeton University Press.

CHAPTER 6

Academic Integrity and the Plight of the African American Student-Athlete

DORIS R. CORBETT

Abstract

The primary goal of this chapter is to give the reader an understanding of the current academic state of affairs for African American students who are athletes in higher education. Throughout this chapter, the term African American will be used interchangeably with Black. The chapter is divided into five parts. Much of the literature has suggested that African American athletes have been academically and economically exploited in the world of sport in higher education.

The first section reviews some of the well-known notions presented in the literature on the academic exploitation of the African American athlete in the academy. Although the annual report card for scholarship athletes continues to improve, there is much work to be done. The academic progress rate (APR), which measures eligibility, retention rates, and graduation rates, is the key academic tool athletic departments and university administrators use to determine the overall academic performance of their students who are athletes.

The second section of the chapter provides an overview of empirical data on the academic status of African American student-athletes at HBCUs and PWIs (predominantly White institutions). The NCAA Academic Progress Report (APR) is used to measure college athletes' performance in the classroom; historically Black colleges and universities (HBCUs) struggle to meet the NCAA's standards for academic progress.

The end of exclusionary practices and most other overt forms of discrimination in collegiate sport have increased the opportunities for African Americans to participate in sport at majority White institutions. But, although obvious forms of discrimination have lessened considerably in intercollegiate sport, racism continues to persist. The third section of the chapter will identify related academic issues impacting African American student-athletes. The reclaiming of academic integrity in higher education, particularly in sport, is in itself an overwhelming contest. Because college presidents, faculty, alumni and booster clubs are all stakeholders in the college sports academic reform movement, it behooves them to address the salient negative stereotypes surrounding academic performance for African American athletes.

In the fourth section of the chapter, best practices and recommendations for academic reform in sport is presented. Special attention is given to prevention practices and strategies proposed by selected advocacy groups concerned with the exploitation of African American athletes in the university setting.

The fifth section on proposed research provides the reader and researcher with some direction for future research engagement that will have the potential to advance the academic performance of African American athletes. In closing, the chapter provides a brief overview designed to emphasize the importance of understanding the attitudes, assumptions, and stereotypes about African American athletes, thereby enhancing their effectiveness academically.

Key Terms	
• academic integrity	• exploitation
• academic reform	• stereotyping
• clustering	• student-athlete

INTRODUCTION

One of the many justifications for intercollegiate sport is the perspective that athletes will have an opportunity to secure an education (Singer, 2008) and improve their opportunities for career advancement (Smith, 2007; Rudman, 1986). There are many student-athletes for whom this would be true. For African American athletes in particular, securing an education and reaping the benefits of an enhanced career opportunity is less plausible.

Over the past two decades, the research literature has shown that African American athletes are not a part of the academic and social mainstream on many of the predominately White college campuses (Davis, 1995; Davis, 1994; Adler & Adler, 1991; Bissinger, 1990; Sellers, 1992). Lower graduation rates reflect a devaluation of the African American athlete's educational pursuit (Harris, 1993).

We are at a place in our society in which race is not a comfortable topic of discussion, and this is part of the problem. It is somehow considered virtuous to ignore academic concerns related specifically to the African American student who is an athlete because some fear the accusation of playing the race card. The implication is that it is not acceptable to discuss race or racial consequences as it pertains to sport. Discussions concerning the academic experiences of African American athletes are largely ignored in the Academy. Black athletes are not taken seriously as students. The expectation is that African American students who are athletes should just perform their sporting jobs. Davis (1994–1995) writes that the "presumed role of the African American student athlete is as a valued sports commodity" (p. 679). Davis argues that the role of student-athletes for African Americans "results in the failure of many colleges and universities to improve support services and take measures necessary to reduce the social isolation of black athletes." And, as a result, "isolation ultimately negatively impacts the black student-athletes' academic performance" (p. 679).

Generally, African American student-athletes are in a state of academic crisis. They are exploited for economic gain (Singer, 2008; Alder & Alder, 1991; American Institute for Research, 1989; Benson, 2000; Daniels, 1987; Hawkins, 1999). The value of the African American athlete as a student is of little academic importance. I would argue that any serious discourse about the academic plight of the African American in sport is about integrity, dignity, human rights, justice and honor in the academy. Icon Charles Barkley publicly condemned the overemphasis on sport mindset that is present in so many African American families, some institutions of higher learning, and some members of the Black community. Barkley declared that

> Sports are a detriment to Blacks, not a positive. You have a society now where every Black kid in the country thinks the only way he can be successful is through athletics. People look at athletes and entertainers as the sum total of Black America. This is a terrible, terrible thing, because that ain't even one tenth of what we are. (McCallum, 2002, p. 33)

Intercollegiate sports should be practiced in a manner that supports the personal and academic development of students who are athletes. The academic values attributed to college sports cannot be appreciated if the principles connecting athletics, personal development and academic achievement are discarded. The overemphasis on winning in major intercollegiate athletic programs undercuts academic integrity and conveys a disposition that academic achievement is ancillary to the ideals of higher education (Stern, 2000).

Academic Exploitation of the African American Student-Athlete in the Academy

The culture of sport has changed significantly since the integration of African Americans into predominately White institutions. A number of sport sociologists, educators, and other scholars have investigated the interrelationship of race and educational experiences (Adler & Adler, 1991; Bissinger, 1990; Comeaux & Harrison, 2007; Edwards, 1983; Hawkins et al., 2007; Hyatt, 2003; Parham, 1993; Purdy et al., 1982; Sellers, 1992; Siegel, 1994; Upthegrove et al., 1999). A close examination of the literature suggests that the level of dishonesty and duplicity in collegiate athletics is pervasive. The exploitation of college athletes who are students first is a prevailing concern and African American students are particularly affected. Exploitation in sport is a multifaceted intercollegiate experience. It has fiscal, educational, racial, social, and moral overtones. African American students who are athletes have been taken advantage of and are especially susceptible to academic abuses. Figler (1981) argued that an athlete is exploited when

> . . . impeded or counseled against taking courses that would lead to responsible and direct progress toward a degree. And, that exploitation occurs when the athlete is recruited into the college or university without possessing the necessary abilities or background to have a reasonable chance of succeeding academically (p. 128).

Reggie Dymally, an African American who chose to attend The University of Hawaii, was a responsible student and interscholastic athlete who sought to achieve a quality education in 1980. Dymally registered for courses in English, business, and computer science. Upon receiving his final course schedule, it had been changed to reflect courses in swimming, courses on how to coach football and soccer, and a course in military science. In response to his predicament, Dymally said,

> I didn't leave L.A. to learn how to shoot guns . . . It was a terrible insult. I was like, "No, you want me to play baseball for you, you give me something that's not baseball." People don't see that. They wonder why Black athletes don't have an education, but it's not always because they don't want one. (Sokolove, 2004, pp. 155–156)

Sack (1979) posits that because of the demands on an athletes' time, the temptation is great for the African American athlete to take shortcuts by seeking academic favors, cut

COLLEGE
FOOTBALL VS. ACADEMICS

Corbett Academics

classes, miss exams, cheat, and enroll in nondemanding courses. Sack (1979) argues that African American athletes are more likely than the average athlete and student to be denied the opportunity to advance intellectually. For example, some coaches have circumvented the 20-hour practice rule, which stipulates that athletes may spend no more than 20 hours per week in their sports during the season. Some coaches have evaded this rule by implementing "voluntary practices" that do not count toward the 20-hour NCAA policy. There is little doubt these practices are considered mandatory and athletes fear the consequences of noncompliance. Without question, the obedience to "voluntary practice" participation can negatively impact the academic performance of the athlete.

The literature is rampant with reports about transcript irregularities, the admission of students who are academically underprepared because of lenient admission standards, grade fabrication and forgery, and plummeting graduation rates (Michener, 1976; Edwards, 1983; Figler, 1981; Sack, 1979). Former Penn State football coach Joe Paterno touted that

> We have raped a generation and a half of Black athletes. We have taken kids and sold them on bouncing a ball or running with a football and that being able to do certain things athletically was going to be an end itself. We cannot afford to do this to another generation. (Edwards, 1983, p. 29)

The research literature suggests that African American athletes have been exploited academically, and that the framework, purpose, and activities of intercollegiate sporting programs have compromised the African American student athlete's ability to take advantage of the educational benefits associated with sport participation (Adler & Adler, 1991; American Institute for Research, 1989; Benson, 2000; Daniels, 1987; Hawkins, 1999). In Olsen's well-known book, *The Black Athlete: A Shameful Story*, sport sociologist Harry Edwards wrote that

> African American students aren't given athletic scholarships for the purpose of education. African Americans are brought in to perform. Any education they get is incidental to their main job, which is playing sports. In most cases, their college lives are educational blanks. (Olsen, 1968, p. 10)

Purdy et al.'s (1986) research confirms that big-time intercollegiate sporting programs more often recruit African American athletes who are academically marginal. Some specific cases and anecdotal examples have been reported that demonstrate academic exploitation:

- Situations like those of Dexter Manley at Oklahoma and James Brooks at Auburn got the attention of the national media and resulted in embarrassments for their institutions. Manley informed a Congressional subcommittee that after spending five years at the University of Oklahoma, he could not read.

- Kevin Ross was highlighted in a Chicago newspaper photograph sitting in a grade school classroom learning to read after his basketball career was over (Smith, 2007). While on a full scholarship, Kevin Ross attended Creighton University for three years without the ability to read or write beyond a second grade level (Ross, 1983). Just as countless other athletes, Ross fell subject to the *rebounding over reading* idea, at the hands of victory-minded college coaches, professors and school administrators. Shortly after his stint as a nationally known basketball player, Ross opted to enroll in Chicago's Westside Prep, with students nearly half his age, to get an education without the dual demand of athletics.

- *The Sporting News* in 1985 reported on the academic risks taken with exceptional athletes. For example, at North Carolina State, 40–60% of both basketball and football African American athletes were admitted with grade point averages below the 1.7 (D+) that was required for admission (Kirshenbaum, 1985).

- At the University of California-Berkeley between 1971 and 1981, 72 athletes were granted special exemptions in order to be admitted, and only two graduated (Edwards, 1985).

- Chris Washburn in 1984 was recruited by more than 100 schools to play basketball. He enrolled at North Carolina State University. On the Scholastic Aptitude Test, Washburn earned a score of 470, which was 70 points higher than the lowest possible score one could earn (Kirshenbaum, 1985).

- A lawsuit was brought by eight African American athletes at California State University, Los Angeles. They alleged that one athlete scored 450 on the SAT, but was credited with a score of 900 because a substitute retook the exam using his name; another athlete majored in criminology for four years, but never completed a criminology course. The student was instead advised to take courses in badminton, rugby, and backpacking (Ofari, 1979).

Many have supported the NCAA's efforts to address the issue of graduation rate. The Black Coaches & Administrators (BCA) has criticized the NCAA's approach to raise admission standards (Siegel, 1994). From the viewpoint of some BCA members, scholarship reductions eliminate opportunities for Black student-athletes to receive an education and to advance their careers. Members of the BCA argued that Proposition 16, and Proposition 48 revealed a lack of compassion and understanding for the African American community (Davis, 1994–1995). The BCA's strongest criticism addresses the NCAA's eligibility requirements that allegedly adversely impact African American student-athletes. Proponents have disputed this assertion, arguing that the advanced standards would place the "student" back into the term "student-athlete." Proponents suggest that the heightened standards are a way whereby student-athletes have a chance to obtain a meaningful degree (Davis, 1994–1995). The opposition to Proposition 48 centered on the allegation that it is blatantly racist. Critics took the view that the standards served as a way to undermine the domination of Blacks in the revenue-producing sports. A number of Black educators and civil rights supporters insisted that the new standards would reduce college access to Black student-athletes who scored below 700 on the SAT in greater numbers than whites. Consequently, Proposition 48 was believed to be racist because of the contrasting impact of eligibility standards on African American student-athletes (Davis, 1994–1995).

The ethical and academic problems associated with sport in higher education persecute and discriminate against both the African American and White athletes. The current and recent efforts to reform sport via Proposition 48 (1986) and Proposition 16 (1995) have created minimum requirements such as a high school GPA in core courses and SAT or ACT scores for students who are athletes planning to go to college. Under Proposition 16 students would have a minimum GPA in 13 core courses and a minimum SAT or ACT. There is a sliding scale that allows for some flexibility; the higher the SAT, the lower the required GPA, and vice versa.

The reform movement in sport has been described by sociologist Earl Smith (2007) as "merely window dressing," in that what the measures actually accomplish is the opening of new and different avenues for academic fraud (Smith, 2007, p. 105). With the release of the Carnegie Foundation Report in 1929, efforts to create substantive reform in sport has continued to be part of the higher education landscape, but have yielded few results (Gerdy, 2006).

Students who are athletes and the average college student are very similar in the sense that both are enrolled in a college or university and are faced with similar experiences related to intellectual and personal growth, career exploration, and mental, social, and emotional adjustments (Watt & Moore, 2001). The most obvious difference between the athletes and nonathletes is that one group participates in athletic competition and the other group function as traditional college students. All students must regularly attend classes, stay on top of assignments, and choose whether or not to attend social university events. On top of maintaining college life, the student who is an athlete has an added layer of student life. Students who are athletes double the work as they are forced to manage dual demands. They are required to focus on academics, practice each day, travel to and from away games, and focus on learning team plays and strategies (Watt & Moore, 2001).

Experiences of collegiate level students, specifically African American athletes, have sparked considerable interest among researchers to question and examine the educational and academic challenges these athletes face in their effort to compete at an elite level. Reviewing existing research sheds light on the complex relationships between engagement in athletic competition and academics among minorities. Most notably, a significant portion of student-athletes at the collegiate level sacrifice the advancement of their education to pursue a sporting career in their respective sport. Blind faith has set the African American student-athlete up for academic, intercollegiate and professional athletic exploitation.

The most recent reform initiative by the NCAA, the academic performance rating (APR), dictates that schools must have a combined score for all sports of 925. The APR score consists of graduation, grade point average, and progress towards graduation.

Empirical Data on the Academic Status of African American Students Who Are Athletes

Now in its sixth year, the annual analysis of the academic performance of Division I athletes report some improvements in the performance of students who are athletes. The report also underscores the many challenges that continue to plague institutions whose resources are strained (2010 NCAA Academic Progress Report Penalty Impact Analysis for historically Black colleges and universities). The academic-progress rate measures eligibility, retention rates, and graduation rates for each of the 6,400 plus teams that are apart of Division I (Sander, 2010; Sander, 2008).

The NCAA Academic Progress Report (APR) is used to measure college athletes' performance in the classroom. The data the NCAA utilizes to determine APR scores for athletic teams at all Division I schools are collected from a rolling, four-year period. The 2010–2011 averages reflect performances from the academic years of 2006–2007 through 2009–2010. Teams that fail to earn scores at or above 925 can receive penalties that may include scholarship reductions.

Out of a total score of 1,000, a score of 925 roughly correlates to a 50% success rate in graduating players within six years. Teams with academic progress rates below 925 may lose scholarships, and scores below 900 can prompt more severe penalties that may lead to restrictions on practice time and post season play. A team may post low scores and not be penalized. In 2010, only 137 of 428 teams with scores lower than 925 received some type of injunction or sanction. NCAA officials postulate that the academic-progress analysis has improved the academic discourse among university presidents, athletic directors, coaches, and athletes. Some universities now require coaches to include minimum requirements for academic progress rates (Sander, 2010). What is clear from the report is that financially constrained institutions rank in the bottom 10% of Division I universities in terms of spending per student and tend to have greater difficulty in advancing the academic performance of their students.

The graduation gap between NCAA Black and White student-athletes has increased. According to a recent study conducted by the University of Central Florida's Institute for Diversity and Ethics in Sport, there is "a staggering gap between the graduation rates of African American and White student-athletes" (Lapchick, 2011, p. 1). The gap between White and Black basketball players is at 32% overall. For example, at Kentucky, only 31% of the African American basketball players' graduate compared to 100% of the White players. The University of Connecticut's graduation rate of 25% for Black players is abysmal, while 100% of their White basketball players graduate. Butler University does the best in terms of the gap, with half of its Black basketball student-athletes graduating versus all of their White student-athletes graduating. On the other hand, Virginia Commonwealth University has a 64% graduation rate for Black basketball players and no White players. See Table 6.1 (graduation rates for 2011 men's teams in the NCAA Division I Basketball Tournament), Table 6.2 (Academic rates for teams in the 2010–2011 NCAA Division Bowl Games), and Table 6.3 (shows the 2009 degree of improvement in graduation rates for African American athletes) for a closer inspection of the academic performance of student-athletes.

For reasons that I believe are largely associated with economics, historically Black colleges and universities (HBCUs) struggle to meet the NCAA's standards for academic progress. In the academic year 2010–2011, several HBCUs had at least one team scoring below the cutoff. Some HBCUs had as many as eight or 10 teams that did not measure up. Usually, the NCAA will give institutions a public warning rather than impose stronger sanctions (Sander, 2010). HBCU Conference schools have taken a big hit in the latest (2010–2011) NCAA Academic Progress Report. Michael Marot, AP sports writer, in a May 25, 2011, article in *Diverse Issues in Higher Education* reported that the NCAA has denied Jackson State and Southern of the Southwestern Athletic Conference from postseason play in football for the 2011–2012 academic seasons. Similarly, Southern and Grambling

Table 6.1.	Graduation Rates for 2011 Men's Teams in the NCAA Division I Basketball Tournament				
School	APR	Overall Student-Athlete	African-American Basketball Student-Athlete	White Basketball Student-Athlete	Overall Basketball Student-Athlete
Akron	951	77	0	100	38
Alabama State	907	54	71	–	63
Arizona	944	65	14	100	20
Arkansas-Little Rock	962	76	92	100	92
Belmont	995	90	100	100	100
Boston	964	94	100	80	90
Bucknell	994	95	80	100	91
Butler	1000	84	50	100	83
BYU	995	78	100	100	100
Cincinnati	945	77	5	–	53
Clemson	946	83	80	–	71
Connecticut	930	83	25	50	31
Duke	980	97	80	100	83
Florida	956	82	33	100	44
Florida State	944	79	63	100	73
George Mason	995	77	55	100	67
Georgetown	937	94	75	–	78
Georgia	944	77	30	100	36
Gonzaga	976	92	50	86	73
Hampton	948	70	71	–	67
Illinois	979	86	100	100	100
Indiana State	935	80	40	100	67
Kansas	1000	77	67	100	80
Kansas State	924	81	14	100	40
Kentucky	954	74	31	100	44
Long Island	940	82	71	–	78
Louisville	951	80	50	100	50
Marquette	975	92	83	100	91
Memphis	974	76	50	–	58
Michigan	956	79	33	100	36
Michigan State	1000	80	38	100	50
Missouri	979	80	38	–	44
Morehead State	906	64	33	50	43
North Carolina	995	87	83	100	88
Northern Colorado	969	82	100	78	77

			African-American Basketball Student-Athlete	White Basketball Student-Athlete	Overall Basketball Student-Athlete
School	APR	Overall Student-Athlete			
Notre Dame	983	99	100	100	100
Oakland	962	85	71	75	75
Ohio State	929	79	55	100	64
Old Dominion	947	69	50	33	63
Penn State	995	90	80	100	86
Pittsburgh	962	81	60	50	64
Princeton	996				
Purdue	919	78	50	83	67
Richmond	967	93	50	100	83
San Diego State	921	67	71	100	58
St. John's	961	89	67	–	70
St. Peter's College	928	74	67	100	70
Syracuse	912	83	44	75	54
Temple	934	76	30	–	33
Tennessee	935	74	33	50	40
Texas	1000	70	17	60	42
Texas A&M	986	72	63	100	64
UAB	825	67	18	100	25
UC Santa Barbara	902	84	33	100	77
UCLA	968	79	63	100	70
UNC Ashville	960	64	57	50	50
UNLV	947	72	33	100	67
USC	924	78	38	100	42
UT San Antonio	885	60	50	100	50
Utah State	946	83	100	100	100
Vanderbilt	980	93	100	100	93
VCU	975	75	64	–	56
Villanova	980	94	100	100	100
Washington	990	87	17	100	44
West Virginia	990	76	57	80	71
Wisconsin	966	81	50	100	70
Wofford	972	95	100	100	100
Xavier	985	94	89	100	92

Table 6.1. Graduation Rates for 2011 Men's Teams in the NCAA Division I Basketball Tournament (*Continued*)

Table 6.2.	Academic Rates for Teams in the 2010–2011 NCAA Bowl Games					
			Graduation Success Rates (GSR)			
Bowl Name	Participants	APR	Overall Football Student-Athlete	African-American Football Student-Athlete	White Football Student-Athlete	Overall Football Student-Athlete
BCS National	Oregon	942	54	41	76	76
Championship	Auburn	935	63	49	100	77
Allstate Sugar	Arkansas	930	55	45	79	72
	Ohio State	975	63	54	77	79
Discover Orange	Virginia Tech	940	79	79	76	89
	Stanford	976	86	71	97	94
Tostitos Fiesta	Oklahoma	962	44	43	45	69
	Connecticut	949	77	74	87	83
Rose Bowl Game	Wisconsin	968	65	51	79	81
Presented by Vizio	TCU	968	71	63	85	81
Kraft	Boston College	967	90	86	94	96
Fight Hunger	Nevada	946	66	54	81	75
BBVA Compass	Pittsburgh	950	69	63	79	81
	Kentucky	951	63	58	71	74
AT&T Cotton	Texas A&M	934	57	45	82	72
	LSU	965	67	62	76	74
GoDaddy.com	Miami (OH)	970	79	71	83	86
	Middle Tennessee	967	55	56	56	76
Gator	Michigan	936	72	70	77	79
	Mississippi State	939	64	58	78	80
Capital One	Michigan State	941	55	45	74	80
	Alabama	957	67	60	89	81
Outack	Penn State	974	84	86	86	90
	Florida	971	67	64	81	82
TicketCity	Northwestern	986	95	95	94	97
	Texas Tech	944	69	60	82	67
Chick-fil-a	Florida State	927	64	56	92	79
	South Carolina	938	57	48	88	74
Autozone	UCF	972	70	64	86	80
Liberty	Georgia	973	68	65	72	77
Hyundai Sun	Miami	978	81	71	100	86
	Notre Dame	978	96	97	93	99
Meineke	Clemson	967	60	55	89	83
Car Care	South Florida	930	46	37	67	71
Bridgepoint	Nebraska	950	68	62	77	73
Education Holiday	Washington	948	82	77	83	87
Franklin American	North Carolina	957	75	69	89	87
Mortgage Music City	Tennessee	944	53	54	60	74
New Era	Syracuse	947	76	69	91	83
Pinstripe	Kansas State	934	69	59	80	81
Bell Hellicopter	SMU	947	76	72	81	86
Armed Forces	Army	964	85	77	88	90
Valero Alamo	Oklahoma State	945	59	49	74	76
	Arizona	940	48	38	62	65

Table 6.2.	Academic Rates for Teams in the 2010–2011 NCAA Bowl Games (*Continued*)						
			Graduation Success Rates (GSR)				
Bowl Name	Participants	APR	Overall Football Student-Athlete	African-American Football Student-Athlete	White Football Student-Athlete	Overall Football Student-Athlete
Texas	Baylor	945	64	63	68	78
	Illinois	951	76	67	83	86
Military Bowl Presented by Northrop Grumman	Maryland	929	64	62	70	80
	East Carolina	941	63	50	91	74
Insight	Iowa	945	79	68	94	84
	Missouri	958	71	66	84	80
Champs Sports	NC State	937	56	45	89	72
	West Virginia	952	72	65	78	76
AdvoCare V100 Independence	Georgia Tech	967	49	43	75	75
	Air Force	988	86	81	87	90
Little Caesars	Toledo	934	65	57	71	79
	Florida International	906	46	30	59	57
Sheraton Hawaii	Tulsa	939	66	52	80	80
	Hawaii	950	46	29	63	69
S.D. County Credit Union Poinsettia	San Diego State	931	55	58	73	67
	Navy	973	92	78	97	96
Maaco Las Vegas	Utah	949	62	43	81	79
	Boise State	974	65	60	64	71
Beef o' Brady's St. Petersburg	Louisville	926	63	61	76	80
	Southern Miss	938	84	84	81	85
R + L Carriers New Orleans	Ohio	953	71	57	90	83
	Troy	940	75	78	68	75
uDrove Humanitarian	Northern Illinois	975	67	70	75	81
	Fresno State	946	52	36	75	64
New Mexico	BYU	940	62	53	70	78
	UTEP	928	57	46	71	69
2010–11 Averages		951.4	67.4	60.3	79.6	79.3

Courtesy of Richard Lapchick, The Institute for Diversity and Ethics in Sport

Table 6.3.	2009 Study Reveals Marked Improvement for Graduation Rates for African American Athletes		
	Student Body Federal Grad. Rate	Student-Athlete Federal Grad. Rate	NCAA Graduation Success Rate
All African Americans	45%	53%	62%
Male African Americans	38%	48%	57%
Female African Americans	50%	66%	76%

Courtesy of Richard Lapchick, The Institute for Diversity and Ethics in Sport

are banned from postseason play in men's basketball. A number of other HBCUs in the SWAC and Mid-Eastern Athletic conferences also received penalties (Marot, 2007). The important message inherent in the results is that the academic success of student-athletes must be encouraged and promoted.

Southern is the first school to be banned from postseason competition in two sports in the same year (football and men's basketball) because of academic performance (Marot, 2011). Both SWAC and MEAC are composed of HBCUs. As a result, the nature of the penalties could alter the balance of power in the SWAC and MEAC Conferences. The fact that both conferences receive automatic bids to the NCAA basketball championship further complicates the situation.

The academic condition of African American athletes who are students first are striking: The NCAA evaluated more than 340 schools for the APR report but only 24 of them, about 7% of the total, are considered historically Black colleges or universities. Of the 58 harshest penalties received by institutions in 2010–2011, half of the sanctions were directed at teams in SWAC and the MEAC conferences (Marot, 2011).

How have the HBCUs been affected by the NCAA's APR and resulting sanctions?

- Texas Southern, which played for last year's SWAC football title, must give up nearly 15 football scholarships, while Jackson State lost half a dozen. Both of these schools will also have their practice time reduced.

- The 13-member MEAC is similarly affected, but did not receive the bans.

- Delaware State will lose nine football scholarships, and North Carolina A&T will lose three football scholarships. Both universities are faced with revised practice limitations.

- In basketball, Coppin State will lose four scholarships, while Norfolk State will lose two. Coppin State, Norfolk State, and Morgan State University will each receive practice reductions.

- Mississippi Valley State and Southern will each lose two scholarships in basketball, and Grambling will have one scholarship taken away.

- Eight Howard University athletic teams were subject to NCAA penalties for poor classroom performance after falling below the cut line in the APR. However, only two Howard teams (football and women's lacrosse were assessed penalties in the form of scholarship reductions).

A birds-eye view of the 2010 NCAA Academic Progress Report provides a fuller understanding of the academic status of African American students who are athletes at HBCUs. Three hundred thirty-one colleges make up the 6,411 teams given an APR score by the NCAA. There are 24 HBCUs among these schools, totaling 393 teams; 24% (80) of all schools received penalties. Among HBCUs, 54% (13) were penalized. HBCU teams comprised 6.1% of all teams accounting for 18.2% of the punishments. In each sport, the top 10% of scores are recognized by the NCAA. Of the 841 teams that earned this award, just 1.2% was from HBCUs. Tables 4, 5, and 6 provide data on the penalty impact analysis for HBCUs.

The impact of the penalties on the conferences will be significant. But, without question, the academic condition of the African American athletes at HBCUs is in need of repair (Marot, 2011). To improve the situation, there are a number of strategies that could be utilized:

- The African American family and the African American community must be advo-cates for change and take responsibility for ensuring that the athletes receive an education for their commitment to sport (Smith, 2007).

- Black athletes must take an active role in galvanizing support to prioritize their role in the academy as students-first.

- In far greater numbers, African American students who are athletes should con-sider HBCU institutions of higher learning for their educational and athletic pur-suits. An alignment with and commitment to HBCUs provides the student-athlete

Table 6.4.	2011 NCAA Academic Progress Report Penalty Impact Analysis for HBCUs	
Average APRs by Sport for Men's Teams		
Sport	**Four-Year Average**	**HBCU Average**
Baseball	954	897
Basketball	940	901
Cross Country	967	939
Fencing	967	
Football (FBS)	947	
Football (FCS)	940	909
Golf	969	938
Gymnastics	979	
Ice Hockey	975	
Lacrosse	971	
Rifle	971	
Skiing	974	
Soccer	962	943 (2 teams)
Swimming	970	931 (2 teams)
Tennis	966	953
Track (Indoor)	957	935
Track (Outdoor)	959	937
Volleyball	975	
Water Polo	966	
Wrestling	954	902 (1 team)

Courtesy of Robert Clayton, Chair
2010 NCAA Academic Progress Report,
Jackson/Lewis Sports Compliance Group

Table 6.5.	2011 NCAA Academic Progress Report Penalty Impact Analysis for HBCUs	
Average APRs by Sport for Women's Teams		
Sport	**Four-Year Average**	**HBCU Average**
Basketball	966	941
Bowling	952	942
Crew	985	
Cross Country	974	956
Fencing	978	
Field Hockey	987	
Golf	981	975
Gymnastics	985	
Ice Hockey	982	
Lacrosse	986	943 (1 team)
Skiing	978	
Soccer	976	944
Softball	972	
Swimming	981	950 (3 teams)
Tennis	978	966
Track (indoor)	967	951
Track (Outdoor)	969	955
Volleyball	976	951
Water Polo	973	

Courtesy of Robert Clayton, Chair
2010 NCAA Academic Progress Report,
Jackson/Lewis Sports Compliance Group

with a culturally rich and competitive higher education experience. It would allow HBCUs to become more competitive athletically and academically, and would provide the African American student-athlete with a strong nurturing and supportive learning environment.

- On the face of it, the suggestion that African American student-athletes should matriculate at HBCUs might seem like a radical and unreasonable proposal. However, unlike many majority institutions, most HBCUs do not have deep pockets. And, thus, the talented and elite performing Black student-athlete can make a significant difference and contribution by giving back their talent to a community they represent.

- Departments and offices of student affairs might create programs and services designed to support and affirm cultural differences, and thereby encourage participation in the fullness of college life.

Table 6.6. 2009–2010 Penalties for HBCUs

Institution	Sport	APR	Immediate Penalty School Reduction	Historical Penalty Public Notice	School Reduction	Practice Reduction
Alabama State University	Baseball	851		Yes		
Coppin State University	Baseball	789		Yes	1.17	
	M—Basketball	887		Yes		
Delaware State University	M—Basketball	880		Yes		
	Football	894		Yes		
	Wrestling	936	0.35	No		
	W—Soccer	922	1.25	No		
Grambling State University	M—Basketball	884		Yes	2	Yes
Hampton University	Football	922	3	No		
	M—Track (I)	901	0.5	No		
Howard University	M—Basketball	874	0.71	Yes		
	M—Cross Country	885		Yes		
	M—Track (I)	895		Yes		
	M—Track (O)	894		Yes		
Jackson State University	M—Basketball	881		Yes		
	Football	872		Yes	6.3	Yes
Miss. Valley St. University	M—Basketball	895		Yes		
North Carolina A&T	Football	843		Yes	6.3	Yes
Prairie View A&M	Baseball	831		Yes	1.17	Yes
Southern University	M—Basketball	847		Yes	2	Yes
	W—Track (I)	888		Yes		
	W—Track (O)	896		Yes		
Texas Southern University	M—Basketball	878		Yes	2	Yes
	Football	863		Yes		
U. Maryland—Eastern Shore	Baseball	899		Yes	0.58	Yes

Courtesy of Robert Clayton, Chair
2010 NCAA Academic Progress Report, Jackson/Lewis Sports Compliance Group

- African American athletes must integrate in a meaningful way into their university communities (Davis, 1994–1995, p. 638).

- The practice of including the development of culturally relevant curricula is essential to the promotion of an inclusive academic environment (Ladson-Billings, 1995).

Related Academic Issues—Stereotypes Are an Academic Issue

The sporting reform movement has heightened awareness, identified major issues that impact sport in higher education, and drawn special attention to concerns affecting the sporting experience of African American athletes. Athletes who are students first are affected by more than what takes place on a college or university campus. The fact that we live in a global marketplace influences contemporary modern culture and influences the social and moral issues of today. In a consumer-driven society, sport plays a significant role (Zimbalist, 1999). Because athletic competition at the collegiate level is a popular form of entertainment, it is an attractive catharsis. The catharsis effect is represented by a release of pent-up frustration that makes one feel better (Cox, 2002). Given the high energy and stressful life college students typically experience on a daily basis, sport entertainment on college and university campuses may serve as a viable catharsis.

The dominant images or issues cited below that are tied to sport are all related to academic performance for African American athletes and are topics that have become an important academic concern (Martinet et al., 2010; Blum, 1994; Brown, 1996; Zimbalist, 1999).

- Overcommercialization—the total revenue received by the NCAA for fiscal year ending in 2011 was $757 million. The result of commercialization and the investment in athletics has led to a greater emphasis on producing winning seasons to attract corporate sponsors at the sacrifice of student-athletes' academic achievement (Comeaux & Harrison, 2011).

- Underprepared students—Precollege educational experiences and preparation relate to college academic achievement. A student's interscholastic GPA is a greater predictor of academic performance than the SAT (Astin, 1993; Comeaux, 2005; Sellers, 1992). Structural inequalities such as access to qualified teachers, culturally relevant curricula, clean and safe facilities, advanced placement classes, honors courses, and other college preparatory services can affect a students' high school GPA (Ladson-Billings, 1995; Oakes, Rogers, Siler, Horng, & Goode, 2004; Solórzano & Ornelas, 2004). The variations in resources provide an uneven playing field for the African American student athlete when one compares the kinds of available learning opportunities for students in high- and low-income communities (Kozol, 1991, 2005).

- Falsification of grades—Falsification of standardized college admission test score, transcripts, and course grades at the hands of college and university administrators pose a conflict between athletic and academic excellence. Relaxed admission standards of high profile high school athletes entering college negatively impact academic integrity (LaForge & Hodge, 2011). As a direct result, these athletes typically do not fare well during their college academic careers.

- Falling graduation rates—Motivation for college athletes to excel in academia and successfully graduate appears to fall second to winning.

- Recruiting scandals—Questionable tactics of administrators and recruiting scandals continue to plague athletic teams at the college level and have drastically affected Division I athletic programs (Pogge, 2010). In spite of the recent scrutiny surrounding recruitment scandals and the resulting tarnished reputations of a number of college programs (Binghamton University, University of Minnesota, the University of Georgia, Louisiana State University, the University of Tennessee, Florida State University, Auburn University, the University Michigan, the University of Memphis, the University of Southern California, and the University of Colorado), scandals of corruption in sport continue to occur. The vastness of the problem illustrates the underlying ethical concerns related to current recruitment practices (Splitt, 2010).

- Overzealous booster clubs and alumni—While universities strive for student retention and academic success, they also face pressure both internally and externally to maintain successful athletic programs (Zimbalist, 1999).

- Fiscal improprieties—on many campuses, intercollegiate athletics are supposed to be a self-supporting program and a bread-winner for the university. Instead, funds to support the athletic programs are often taken from central campus funds and student registration fees. In addition, the sport programs amass enormous debt without a pragmatic plan to recover expenditures. There is a myth that intercollegiate athletics is a revenue-producer for college campuses. Although this might be true on some campuses, in-depth analyses indicate otherwise for most campuses (NCAA CAPRA—Committee on Academic Planning and Resources Allocation).

- Relaxed admission standards—The new NCAA rules established in 2003 give minority athletes greater access to higher education by creating a sliding scale for grade-point averages and standardized-test scores, while abandoning a minimum requirement of a composite 17 on the ACT or 820 on the SAT. Since the change, which occurred in 2003, only a modest increase has been attained in African American participation in the Division I basketball and football (Wolverton, 2011). The 2003 changes have not made a substantial difference in the achievement of the NCAA's stated goals of increasing the number of minority athletes who graduate from college. Gurney (2011) suggest that, "the lower test-score standards, combined with high-school grade inflation, have led to greater numbers of athletes who qualify with very low test scores. Those students possess inadequate skills to manage college academics, creating a greater need for academic-support services at institutions already struggling with strained budgets, staffs, and faculties" (Gurney, 2011).

- The exploitation of student-athletes—The time demands on student-athletes exceed the 20-hour rule. African American athletes tend to spend more time during their sport season in sport-related hours per week than academic time (Singer, 2008).

- Salient negative stereotypes have led to the presence of very few African American head football and head basketball college coaches and athletic directors.

The problem with stereotypes is that untrue stereotypes trigger diplomatic, judicious, tactless, subtle, unnoticeable, unobtrusive, and restrained types and styles of racism in intercollegiate sport. As a result, a discussion on the academic issues related to stereotypes is warranted. African American athletes are particularly vulnerable to the surreptitious and racist character of sport (Davis, 1995). Stereotypes of African American student-athletes as dumb jocks, who are overprivileged, coddled, indolent, and out of control, and whose primary incentive to attend college is to participate in sport is not representative of all African American athletes. Many African American athletes take their academic performance seriously (Ferrante et al., 1996). In contrast to the dumb-jock image, Smith (2007) writes that, "long before Jackie Robinson became a Brooklyn

Dodger, the image of the strong, confident, capable African American athlete replaced the lazy, lethargic, indolent stereotype" (p. 22). There is the other extreme whereby faculty may give preferential treatment to athletes, and by doing so perpetuate negative academic stereotypes that suggest that athletes are held to different academic standards and expectations. African American athletes in such situations become frustrated and confused about their dual student-athlete roles, and thus receive mixed messages pertaining to their expected performance in the classroom.

Martin et al. (2010) report that the academic performance problems associated with stereotypes about African American athletes are not well documented and that few cultural processes or methodologies have been organized and developed to enhance the performance of student-athletes in the classroom setting. It is essential for researchers to ascertain and document student-athlete's experiences of coping with negative stereotypes to provide useful tools that will enable investigators to gain insight on important sources of bias in American higher education as it relates to athletics and the African American athlete.

According to Martin and Harris (2006), researchers have not systematically examined what contributes to African American success in sport. Harrison et al. (2009) report that "stereotype threat" processes of minority groups exist, are salient negative stereotypes effecting the academic performance of African American athletes. Researchers (Benson, 2000; Donnor, 2005; Godley, 1999; Harrison, 1998) have investigated African American male student-athletes' academic achievement utilizing qualitative approaches. What is needed, however, are comprehensive ethnographies with high-achieving African American student-athletes. Administrators, educators, and coaches need to have a balance focus and understanding of the sporting experience for both the underachiever and the high-achieving African-American student-athlete (Martin et al., 2010).

There is much disagreement regarding what measures are needed to remedy the academic ills associated with intercollegiate sport. Although the solutions are not simple, it is clear that if reform is to occur, the issues must be addressed, including the issues related to the stereotyping of African American athletes. Responsible leaders who are university presidents, faculty governing boards, athletic directors and coaches in the academic community must find appropriate techniques to assist the African American student-athletes achieve academically.

Best Practices, Strategies and Recommendations for Academic Reform

Candice Millard (2005) in her book, *The River of Doubt: Theodore Roosevelt's Darkest Journey*, provides a useful guide for reformers trying to revolutionize the status quo whether in the environment, education, or college sports:

> Rarely in the rain forest do animals or insects allow themselves to be seen, and any that do generally do so with ulterior motives. In a world of endless, life-or-death competition, the need to hide from potential predators and deceive sophisticated prey is a fundamental requirement of longevity, and it has produced a staggering range of specialized attributes and behavior aimed at manipulating—or erasing entirely—any visible for that an enemy or victim might see. So refined is the specialization of life in the rain forest that every inch of the jungle, and each part of the cycle of day and night, have plant, animal, and insect specialists that have adapted to exploit the unique appearance-altering potential it offers. (p. 176)

It is customary for faculty to be gate keepers representing the socially responsible conscience of the university. Higher education's best hope is to align itself with a "Faculty-

Student-Athlete Awakening." That is, faculty must become involved, wake up, and serve as an advocate for student-athletes by taking an active role in the prioritization of academic achievement for African Americans in sport as a function of their role and responsibility as faculty. In order for academic reform in sport to be realized, faculty leadership must be cultivated and employed to build up a support against the intimidating efforts to maintain the status quo. The research literature has reported on the practices and strategies that could bring about academic integrity to collegiate sport (Fletcher et al., 2003; Smith, 2007). This section of the chapter discusses academic integrity best practices and strategies in sport and provides recommendations for academic reform. Special attention is given to prevention practices and strategies proposed by selected advocacy groups concerned with the exploitation of African American athletes in the university setting.

Best Practices and Strategies

- Discontinue the use of the concept *student-athlete*. The phrase student-athlete is an unacceptable label, is an inappropriate and incorrect description of who athletes are, particularly given the huge amount of time athletes are expected to devote to their sport. The term student-athlete functions as a deterrent to achieving overall educational development (Stavrowsky & Sack, 2005). Athletes should be considered a central part of the student body. We do not define debate team students as student-debate team members. Nor do we refer to the university choir student as student-choir members, or members of the marching band as student-band members. Similarly, there is not a need to define athletes as student-athletes. Whether athletes, members of a debate team or university choir, they are simply STUDENTS.

- The control/oversight of academic counseling and support programs for athletes should be the same for all students. The purpose of academic counseling is to focus on gaining an education, not ensuring athletic eligibility. Problems evolve when the desire to win is allowed to compromise academic success.

- Transparency and academic disclosure of student's academic major, academic advisor, courses listed by academic major, general education requirements, electives, course GPA and instructors will facilitate and result in accountability, establish a public social conscious by board of trustee members, faculty senates, and university administrators. This strategy would not involve revealing individual student grades. Academic abuses such as clustering can be significantly diminished when information on how students are educated is available. Clustering is a phenomenon that occurs when athletes in certain sports are overrepresented in specific courses and majors. The clustering of courses and majors typically occurs when athletes face rigid and demanding team expectations (Coakley, 2009).

Information about institutional behavior will enable universities to more effectively monitor grade inflation, educational practices, and strategies, and the quality of the degree.

- The Coalition on Intercollegiate Athletics (COIA), a faculty-based governance coalition have developed a set of athletic reform guidelines with regard to the impact of academic integrity in sport. Highlighted for the reader are just a few of the best practice guidelines proposed (Coalition on Intercollegiate Athletics, 2005):
  - ○ Campuses should develop a means to track and share with faculty senates or faculty governance bodies the academic performance of scholarship athletes who enroll through special admission, but in accordance with the Family educational Rights and Privacy Act (FERPA).

○ The basis for athletic scholarship is merit in athletics, but the essential function of the award is to provide entrée to higher education.

- The New England Small College Athletic Conference's decision to limit post-season play (Suggs, 1999) exemplifies an approach to establish a proper role for athletic competition within the context of academic institutions. The decision was based on an eight year study of the impact of including post-season play in NCAA conferences (Suggs, 2000).

- The Drake Group (TDG) have put forth seven reform proposals (Benford, 2007) worthy of acknowledgment:

    1. Athletes must maintain a cumulative 2.0 grade point average each semester.
    2. Institute a one-year residency requirement (i.e., no freshman eligibility) in order to participate in intercollegiate athletics.
    3. Replace one-year renewable scholarships with need-based financial aid (or) with multiyear athletic scholarships that extend to graduation (five years maximum).
    4. Establish university policies that emphasize the importance of class attendance for all students and ensure that the scheduling of athletic contests does not conflict with class attendance.
    5. Retire the term student-athlete.
    6. Make the location and control of academic counseling and support services for athletes the same as for all students.
    7. Ensure that universities provide accountability of trustees, administrators, and faculty by disclosure of such things as a student's academic major, academic adviser, courses listed by academic major, general education requirements, electives, course GPA, and instructors.

Several examples follow on how colleges and universities and their athletic departments and coaches might benefit by working together to improve academic performance of the African American students who are athletes.

Recommendations

- Athletic departments must work in concert with administrators to insure that African American athletes clearly understand their responsibility to adhere to academic standards, and must provide ample resources to provide a balance in their roles as student and athlete.

- Athletic directors need to be attentive to the academic side of African American students who are athletes.

- Recruitment and retention of African American athletic administrators, coaches and academic staff is essential to the improvement of the academic performance of African American athletes.

- Athletic directors must hold head coaches accountable for the academic performance and success of African American athletes. Although the NCAA allows each college/university to develop and adopt its own policies, procedures, and philosophies for student-athletes, institutions must put in place policies to protect students who are athletes from being penalized for missing classes since their sport participation in athletics dictates their absence. The absence of college/university policies can cause athletes to become frustrated and confused about their dual roles as a student-athlete (Fletcher, Benshoff, & Richburg, 2003; Smith, 2007).

- The type of students who are athletes recruited by coaches must be carefully monitored by the athletic director. Based in large measure on interscholastic GPA, athletes who have a reasonable chance of successful academic performance should be recruited.

- Institutional self-studies can bring together a wide spectrum of stakeholders to provide information that gives direction for needed action to improve the academic performance of African American athletes.

- Governmental intervention from Congress is essential at this stage of the game if academic reform is to have any teeth. Congress could follow up on previous reviews with hearings that would address the scandals (cheating in college athletics) supported by tax-free dollars generated by the NCAA's participation in the business of college sport entertainment (Splitt, 2008).

In an effort to create an environment that enhances the promotion of academic integrity, necessary and tough reform measures are essential to improve the academic performance of our students who are athletes. Although the resistance to real change will continue to be difficult, the proposed practices and recommendations offer realistic and viable solutions.

PROPOSED RESEARCH AREAS RELATING TO ACADEMIC PERFORMANCE INVOLVING AFRICAN AMERICAN INTERCOLLEGIATE ATHLETES

Research has turned its attention to the effect of collegiate athletics' impact on the educational aspirations, social interactions, and overall fulfillment of student-athletes. Spivey (1983) notes that the "failure of the scholarly community to examine seriously the history of Blacks in intercollegiate sport is a 'missed opportunity' to understand an important dimension of African American intellectual history, the nature and development of the modern civil rights struggle, and the Black protest movement." This section provides a few examples of some of the critical topics for research pertaining to the African American athlete:

- There is a need for additional research on the attitudes, perceptions, and academic expectations of African American athletes (Harrison et al., 2009). Research on this topic would provide the academic community with essential information to develop informed strategies to improve academic performance of athletes who are students first, but the results should also shed light on measures to combat the promotion of stereotypes.

- Researchers should investigate academically driven high-achieving students who are athletes and academically low-achieving students who are athletes. Failure to fully understand the impact of distinct experiences of college student-athletes can have an impact on the extent to which college and university support programs that can affect university policy (Comeaux & Harrison, 2011; Davis, 1994, 1995).

- More information is needed concerning the academic experiences of African American athletes and the kinds of activities that foster learning (e.g., athletic compensation, impact of athlete academic support programs, and services, athlete activism and recruitment of athletes who are underprivileged, career transition and white privilege in athletic departments, (Singer, 2008; Comeaux & Harrison, 2011).

- A comprehensive review of the research literature on the African American students who are athletes would provide an over-review, and a more complete understanding of what information currently exists on the African American athlete (Winbush, 1987).

- A longitudinal study on the academic performance of African American male and female intercollegiate students who are athletes from freshman to senior year should reflect interviews, information about academic support programs, and the notion of social isolation (Winbush, 1987).

- Determine the institutional impact of highly competitive sport programs in higher education to ascertain their value to the mission of higher education (Gerdy, 2002).

Given all of the above, it would seem that these suggestions formulate an appropriate strategy for a coalition of researchers to build on the current body of literature to expand and expound on the knowledge and understanding of the plight of the African American intercollegiate athlete as it relates to the promotion of academic integrity in higher education.

CONCLUSION

The chapter has examined an area of study often overlooked, academic integrity, and the plight of the African American student-athlete. Present research findings suggest that there is more than the deficit perspective to African American academic performance (Benson, 2000).

Over the past decade, academic communities have become increasingly concerned about the educational experience of African American students who are athletes. Recent and past occurrences of low graduation rates, academic scandals, and the frequency with which African American athletes leave higher education institutions in mediocre, if not poor academic standing have annihilated the public's faith regarding the educational benefits of sports participation at the collegiate level. Faculty-driven reform has been spearheaded by advocacy bodies such as the Drake Group and the Coalition on Intercollegiate Athletics (COIA). The Drake Group works to support faculty whose job security is threatened for defending academic standards, disseminates information on current issues and controversies in sports. As previously cited, COIA is a faculty group advocating for reform in intercollegiate athletics (Splitt, 2003). Finding the appropriate balance between intercollegiate athletics and the academic goals of higher education is not an easy task, but it is one that must be achieved so that African American students can experience gains in student learning and academic performance.

In conclusion, lessons learned are that

- HBCUs struggle to meet the NCAA's standards for academic progress.

- African American athletes are more likely than the average athlete and student to be denied the opportunity to advance intellectually.

- The research literature is rampant with evidence of transcript irregularities, the admission of students who are academically underprepared due to lenient admission standards, grade fabrication and forgery, and low graduation rates.

- African American students are not given athletic scholarships for the purpose of gaining an education, but are brought to the university to perform athletically.

- The role and definition of a successful coach should be tied to student-athletes academic success and graduation performance.

- A reduction in course credit loads during an athlete's sport season is warranted, and student-athletes should be allowed at least five years to graduate.

- Some faculty must be on the front lines addressing the challenge to promote academic integrity.

In summary, Black athletes who are students first must have a realistic opportunity to achieve an education and to graduate. Given the large sums of money athletes generate for their institutions, one would expect the institution to provide the resources for athletes to make the grade for academic success.

STUDY QUESTIONS

1. How have the HBCUs been affected by the NCAA's APR and resulting sanctions?

2. Identify the problems associated with academic integrity in higher education?

3. What is meant by APR and what does it measure?

SUGGESTED READINGS

Adler, P., & Adler, P. (1991). *Backboards and blackboards: College athletics and role engulfment*. New York, NY: Columbia University Press.

Bowen, W. G., & Shulman, J. L. (2001). *The game of life: College sports and educational value*. Princeton, NJ: Princeton Press.

Rhoden, W. C. (2006). *Forty million dollar slaves*. New York, NY: Crown Publisher.

Sailes, G. A. (2010). *Modern sports and the African American experience*. San Diego, CA: Cognella Press.

Siegel, D. (1994). Higher education and the plight of the black male athlete. *Journal of Sport and Social Issues, 18*(3), 207–223.

Smith, E. (2007). *Race, sport, and the American dream*. Durham, NC: Carolina Academic Press.

Smith, E. (2010). *Sociology of sport and society theory*. Winston-Salem, NC: Human Kinetics.

REFERENCES

Academic integrity in intercollegiate athletes: Principles, rules, and best practices. (2005). *Coalition on Intercollegiate Athletics*. Retrieved from http://coia.comm.psu.edu/AID.pdf

Adler, P. A., & Adler, P. (1991). *Backboards and blackboards: College athletes and role engulfment*. New York, NY: Columbia University Press.

Astin, A. W. (1993a). *Assessment for excellence*. Phoenix, AZ: American Council on Education and Oryx Press.

Astin, A. (1993b). *What matters in college?* San Francisco, CA: Jossey-Bass.

American Institutes for Research (1989). Report No. 3: *The experiences of Black intercollegiate athletes at NCAA division I institutions*. Palo Alto, CA: Center for the Study of Athletics.

Benford, R. D. (2007). The college sports reform movement: Reframing the "edutainment" industry. *The Sociological Quarterly, 48*, 1–28.

Benson, K. F. (2000). Constructing academic inadequacy: African American athletes' stories of schooling. *Journal of Higher Education, 71*(2), 223–246.

Bissinger, H. G. (1990). *Friday night lights: A town, a team and a dream*. New York, NY: Harper Collins.

Blum, D. E. (1994, April 13). Top players produce up to $1 million in revenue for their universities. *Chronicle of Higher Education*, A33–A34.

Bowen, W. G., & Levin, S. A. (2003). *Reclaiming the game: College sports and educational values*. Princeton, NJ: Princeton University Press.

Brown, R. W. (1996). The revenues associated with relaxing admission standards at division I-A colleges. *Applied Economics, 28*(7), 807–814.

Coakley, J. (2009). *Sports in society issues and controversies*. Boston: McGraw-Hill Companies.

Comeaux, E. (2005). Environmental predictors of academic achievement among student-athletes in the revenue-producing sports of men's basketball and football. *The Sport Journal, 8*(3). Retrieved from http://www.thesportjournal.org/article/predictors-academic-achievement-among-student-athletes-revenue-producing-sports-men-basketb

Comeaux, E. (2007). Student(less) athlete: Identifying the unidentified college student. *Journal for the Study of Sports and Athletes in Education, 1*, 37–43.

Comeaux, E., & Harrison, C.K. (2007). Faculty and male student athletes in American higher education: Racial differences in the environmental predictors of academic achievement. *Race, Ethnicity, and Education, 10*(2), 199–214.

Comeaux, E., & Harrison, C. K. (June/July, 2011). A Conceptual model of academic success for student-athletes. *Educational Researcher, 40*(5), 235–245.

Cox, R. H. (2002). *Sport psychology concepts and applications*. Boston, MA: McGraw Hill Publishers.

Daniels, O. C. B. (1987). Perceiving and nurturing the intellectual development of Black student-athletes: A case for institutional integrity. *Western Journal of Black Studies, 11*, 155–163.

Davis, T. (1995). A model of institutional governance for intercollegiate athletics. *Wisconsin Law Review*, 599–645.

Davis, T. (1995). Racism in athletics: Subtle yet persistent. *University of Arkansas at Little Rock Review, 21*, 881–900.

Davis, T. (1994–1995). The myth of the superspade: The persistence of racism in college athletics. *Fordham Urban Law Journal. 22*, 638.

Donnor, J. (2005). Towards an interest-convergence in the education of African-American football student athletes in major college sports. *Race, Ethnicity & Education, 8*, 45–67.

Duderstadt, J. (2000). *Intercollegiate athletics and the American university: A university president's perspective*. Ann Arbor: University of Michigan Press.

Edwards, H. (1973). *Sociology of sport*. Homewood, IL: Dorsey Press.

Edwards, H. (1983). Educating Black athletes. *The Atlantic Monthly, 252*, 31–38.

Edwards, H. (1985, February 21). The education of Black athletes. *Speech delivered at Colorado State University*, Fort Collins.

Eitzen, D. (2009). *Fair and foul: Beyond the myths and paradoxes of sport*. New York, NY: Rowman & Littlefield.

Ferrante, A. P., Etzel, E., & Lantz, C. (1996). Counseling college student-athletes: The problem, the need. In E. F. Etzel, A. P. Ferrante, & J. W. Pinkney (Eds.), *Counseling college student-athletes: Issues and interventions* (2nd ed.) (pp. 3–26). Morgantown, WV: Fitness Information Technology.

Figler, S. K. (1981). *Sport and play in American life*. Philadelphia, PA: Saunders College Publishing.

Fletcher, T. B., Benshoff, J. M., & Richburg, M. J. (Spring, 2003). A systems approach to understanding and counseling college student-athletes. *Journal of College Counseling, 6*, 35–45.

Gerdy, J. (2006). *Air ball: American education's failed experiment with elite athletics*. Oxford, MS: University of Mississippi Press.

Gerdy, J.(2002). Athletic victories, educational defeats. *Academe Online*. Retrieved from http://aaup.org/AAUP/pubsres/academe/2002/JF/Feat/gerd.htm

Godley, A. (1999, November). *The creation of the student-athlete dichotomy in urban high school culture*. Paper presented at the annual conference of the North America Society for the Sociology of Sport, Cleveland, OH.

Gurney, G. S. (2011, April 10). Stop Lowering the Bar. *The Chronicle of Higher Education*. Retrieved from http://chronicle.com/article/Stop-Lowering-the-Bar-for/127058/

Harris, O. (1993). African American predominance in collegiate sport. In D. Brooks & R. Althouse (Eds.), *Racism in college athletics: The African American athlete's experience* (pp. 51–74) Morgantown, WV: Fitness Information Technology.

Harrison, C. K., Lawrence, S. M., Plecha, M., Scott, J. B., & Janson, N. K. (2009). Stereotypes and stigmas of college athletes in Tank McNamara's cartoon strip: Fact or fiction? *Journal of Issues in Intercollegiate Athletics*, 2009 Special Issue, 1–18.

Harrison, C. K. (1998). Themes that thread society: Racism and athletic manifestation of sport in the African American community. *Race, Ethnicity & Education, 1*, 63–74.

Harrison, C. K., Stone, J., Shapiro, J., Yee, S., Boyd, J., & Rullan, V. (2009). The role of gender identities and stereotypes salience with the academic performance of male and female college athletes. *Journal of Sport & Social Issues, 33*(1), 78–96.

Hawkins, B. (1999). Black student athletes at predominately white national collegiate athletic association (NCAA) division I institutions and the pattern of oscillating migrant laborers. *Western Journal of Black Studies, 23*(1), 1–9.

Hawkins, B., Milan-Williams, B., & Carter, A. (2007). From glory to glory: The transition of African American athletes from college into athletic retirement. In R. Althouse & D. Brooks (Eds.), *Diversity and social justice in college sports: Sport management and the college athletes* (pp. 95–114). Morgantown, WV: Fitness Information Technology.

Hyatt, R. (2003). Barriers to persistence among African American intercollegiate athletes: A literature review of non-cognitive variables. *College Student Journal, 37*(2), 260–275.

Kirshenbaum, J. (1985, February 18). Scorecard. *Sports Illustrated, 62*, 9.

Knight Commission on Intercollegiate Athletics. (2010). *Restoring the balance: Dollars, values, and the future of college sports*. Miami, FL: Author.

Kozol, J. (1991). *Savage inequalities: Children in America's schools*. New York, NY: Crown.

Kozol, J. (2005). *The same of the nation: The restoration of apartheid schooling in America*. New York, NY: Crown.

Ladson-Billings, G. (1995). Toward a theory of culturally relevant pedagogy. *American Educational Research Journal, 32*, 465–491.

Lapchick, R. (2011). *Keeping score when it counts: Graduation success and academic progress rates for the 2011 NCAA Division I men's basketball tournament teams*. The Institute for Diversity and Ethics in Sports. Retrieved from http://www.tidesport.org/grad%20rates/2011_mens_bball_final.pdf

Martin, B. E., & Harris, F. (2006). Examining productive conceptions of masculinities: Lessons learned from academically driven African American male student-athletes. *Journal of Men's Studies, 14*, 359–378.

Martin, B. E., Harrison, C. K., Stone, J., & Lawrence, S. M. (2010). Athletic voices and academic male student-athlete experiences in the Pac-10. *Journal of Sport and Social Issues, 34*(2), 131–153.

Marot, M. (2007, May 2). NCAA's academic report hits Black colleges, Louisiana schools hardest. Retrieved from http://www.floydcountytimes.com/view/full_story/1427005/article-NCAA-s-academic-report-hits-black-colleges—Louisiana-schools-hardest

Marot, M. (2011, May 25). HBCU conference schools take big hits on latest NCAA academic progress report. *Diverse Issues in Higher Education*. Retrieved from http://diverseeducation.com/article/15687/

McCallum, J. (2002). Citizen Barkley. *Sports Illustrated*. 32–38.

Meyer, S. K. (2005). NCAA academic reforms: Maintaining the balance between academics and athletics. *Phi Kappa Phi Forum, 85*(3), 15–18.

Michener, J. (1976): *Sports in America*. New York, NY: Random House.

Oakes, J., Rogers, J., Siler, D., Horng, E., & Goode, J. (2004). *Separate and unequal 50 years after Brown: California's racial "opportunity gap."* Los Angeles, CA: Institute for Democracy, Education, and Access.

Ofari, E. (1979). Basketball's biggest losers. *The Progressive, 43*, 48–49.

Olsen, J. (1968). *The Black athlete*. New York, NY: Time-Life Books.

Parham, W. D. (1993). The intercollegiate athlete: A 1990s profile. *The Counseling Psychologist. 21*(3), 411–429.

Purdy, D. A., Eitzen, D. S., & Hufnagel, R. (1982). Are athletes also students? The educational attainment of college athletes. *Social Problems, 29*(4), 439–448.

Ross, K., & Hall, S. (1983, February 21). Late in the game, a college athlete learns to read. *People Magazine, 19*(7).

Rudman, W. J. (1986). The sport mystique in Black culture. *Sociology of Sport Journal, 3*(4), 305–319.

Sack, A. L. (1979). Big time college football: Whose free ride? In A. Yiannakis et al. (Eds.), *Sport sociology: Contemporary themes*. (pp. 96–100). Dubuque, IA: Kendall/ Hunt Publishing Company.

Sack, A. (2001). Big-time athletics vs. academic values: It's a rout. *Chronicle of Higher Education, 59*(1), 2–21.

Sander, L. (2008). Athletes' graduation rates are highest ever: NCAA Data show. *The Chronicle of Higher Education, 55*(9), 16.

Sander, L. (2010, June). *Athletes' academic performance improves, but work is not finished, NCAA says*. Retrieved from http://chronicle.com/article/Athletes-Academic-Performance/65846

Sellers, R. (1992). Racial differences in the predictors for academic achievement of student-athletes in division revenue producing sports. *Sociology of Sport Journal, 1*, 46–59.

Siegel, D. (1994). Higher education and the plight of the Black male athlete. *Journal of Sport & Social Issues, 18*(3), 207–223.

Singer, J. (2008). Benefits and detriments of African American male athletes' participation in a big-time college football program. *International Review for the Sociology of Sport, 43*(4), 399–408.

Smith, E. (2007). *Race, sport and the American dream*. Durham, NC: Carolina Academic Press.

Sokolove, M. (2004). The ticket out: Darryl Strawberry and the Boys of Crenshaw. New York, NY: Simon & Schuster.

Solórzano, D., & Ornelas, A. (2004). A critical race analysis of advanced placement classes and selective admissions. *High School Journal, 87*, 15–26.

Spivey, D. 1983. The Black athlete in big-time intercollegiate sports 1941–1968. *Phylan, 44*, 116–125.

Splitt, F. G. (2010). *Ending academic corruption in collegiate athletics won't be easy*. Sponsored by the College Sport Research Institute: The University of North Carolina, Chapel Hill, NC.

Splitt, F. G. (2003). *Reclaiming academic primacy in higher education: A brief*. IEC Publications. Retrieved from http://thedrakegroup.org/Splitt_Reclaiming_Academic_Primacy

Splitt, F. G. (2008, February 23). *Cheating in college athletics: Presidential oversight notwithstanding*. Retrieved from http://thedrakegroup.org/Splitt_Cheating.pdf

Staurowsky, E. J., & Sack, A. L. (2005). Reconsidering the use of the term student-athlete in academic research. *Journal of Sport Management, 19*, 103–116.

Stern, C. S., et al. (2002, October). *The faculty role in the reform of intercollegiate athletics*, AAUP. Retrieved from http://www.aaup.org/statements/REPORTS/03athlet.htm

Suggs, W. (1999, June 18). Should teams lose when athletes fail? *Chronicle of Higher Education*, A46.

Suggs, W. (2000). Postseason play creates tensions for an unusual athletics conference: A group of liberal arts colleges says that academics will take precedence over championships. *Chronicle of Higher Education*, A45–A46.

Thelin, J. R. (1994). *Games colleges play: Scandal and reform in intercollegiate athletics*. Baltimore, MD: Johns Hopkins University Press.

Upthegrove, T. R., Roscigno, V. J., & Charles, C. Z (1999). Big money collegiate sports: Racial concentration, contradictory pressures, and academic performance. *Social Science Quarterly, 80*(4), 718–737.

Watts, S., & Moore, J. (2001). Who are student athletes? *New Directions for Student Services, 93*, 7–18.

Winbush, R. A (1987). The furious passage of the African American intercollegiate athlete. *Journal of Sports and Social Issues, 11*(1–2) 97–103.

Wolverton, B. (2011, April 28). Have relaxed admission standards helped minority athletes? The Chronicle of Higher Education. Retrieved from http://chronicle.com/blogs/players/have-relaxed-admissions-standards-helped-minority-athletes/28525

Zimbalist, A. (1999). *Unpaid professionals: Commercialism and conflicts in big-time college sports*. Princeton, NJ: Princeton University Press.

CHAPTER 7

Community and Junior College Athletic Programs: New Models for Success—Transition from Junior/Community College to Four-Year Institution

RONALD ALTHOUSE and DANA BROOKS

Abstract

Community and junior colleges in America have long been recognized as *pilots* for ethnic minorities to gain access to higher education. On a national scale, as open-door policy educational institutions where many entering students may require academic remediation, the community and two-year colleges were established to meet the needs of the local communities and to enhance the technical skills of a diverse work force. Likewise, these colleges also provided ethnic minorities the opportunity to play sports and, in some cases, to transfer to four-year institutions to complete their education and improve playing skills. Some observers, however, have suggested the nation's junior/community colleges act as feeders to Division I colleges, thus raising questions about academic accountability as well as doubting the qualifications and transfer of student-athletes into four-year colleges. Those who don't favor sports programs apt to see junior college sports as a farm system, yielding quick fixes for coaches afflicted with winning at all costs.

Intercollegiate programs at two-year colleges seldom attain any media attention, and are expected to function with low operating costs. Coaching is not particularly lucrative, often below the average community college faculty salary. Furthermore, most reports on minorities—men and women—show that those who earned major posts or coaching positions in community/junior college sports are seriously underrepresented.

The chapter about two-year junior/community colleges reflects how intercollegiate *juco* sports were shaped as they adapted to "big-time" collegiate athletics in the context of NCAA polices and its rules.

Key Terms	
• community colleges	• junior colleges
• cooling out	• NJCAA
• farm teams	• open-door policy

INTRODUCTION

Junior and community colleges have a long and distinguished history of providing quality and affordable higher education opportunities for Americans, especially for ethnic minorities. US community colleges have long been regarded as beacons of access and educational opportunity for the masses and at no time has this function been more critical than at the present. Fusch (1996) and Bryant (2008) recognized the unique mission of community colleges in providing access to higher education, especially for ethnic minorities and the economically disadvantaged.

Cohen and Brawer (1996) analyzed the growth of two-year public and private colleges between 1915 and 1999. These data revealed the number of two-year colleges (public and private) grew from 74 (1915–16) to some 1,200 (1998–99). The American Association of Community Colleges (2008) reported 1,195 two-year colleges (987 public; 177 independent; 31 tribal). Demographic data noted 85% of students enrolled in community colleges were between 21 and 39 years of age

In the fall of 2005, community colleges provided access to higher education to nearly half of the undergraduate students in America. According to Doyle (2006), "40% of all first-time freshmen begin their post-secondary careers at community colleges" (p. 56). During the academic year 2006–2007, there were 1,045 community colleges in America, enrolling over six million students.

THE TWO-YEAR COMMUNITY COLLEGE MOVEMENT

The historical development of junior/community colleges in America was impacted by social and economic factors such as expanding industrialization, need to hire highly skilled workers, and expansive access to higher education in America (Cohen & Brawer, 1996). They concluded the most significant factor leading to the growth of two-year junior colleges was the general belief that "whatever the social or personal problem, schools were supposed to solve it" (p. 2).

By the middle of the 20th century the Truman Commission on Higher Education was to have a profound impact on the future growth of community and junior colleges in this country. The commission realized the need for affordable access to higher education for all Americans. During the decades of the 1950s and 1960s, junior and community colleges in this country began to expand. The terms *junior college* and *community college*, during this time frame, took on two different meanings: junior college referred to a lower division of private colleges and two-year colleges; while the term community college referred to comprehensive and publicly supported organizations (Cohen & Brawer, 1996).

The Open-Door Policy

Bailey, Calcagno, Jenkins, Leinbach, and Kienzle (2006) remind us, "community colleges have long been recognized as open-door institutions, with an emphasis on providing a wide range of students with access to college" (p. 492). In democratic societies both effort and reward are hierarchical in the sense that training (education) is needed to allow selective achievements—fewer succeed at hierarchical higher levels. But situations of opportunity are also situations of denial and failure. Individuals are encouraged to consume mobility, as if it is universally possible—status is won through individual effort and rewards go to those who try, so they say. Hence, democratic societies need not only to motivate achievement, but also to mollify those denied in order to sustain motivation in the face of disappointment and to deflect resentment. In modern mass democracies, which are laced with large scale organizations and are serviced through elaborate ideologies of equal access and participation, the task becomes critical.

The perceived dissociation between culturally instilled goals and institutionally provided means of realization (a discrepancy between means and ends) was employed to account for the responses of junior college student-athletes to means-ends disparities, but most specifically focusing on the ameliorative processes which lessen strains of dissociation. The notion of the *open-door college* provided the institutionalized mooring for such apparent structural strain, while the junior college reduces the stress of disparity and individual denial.

According to Clark (1960) the two-year junior and community college provided a means that was labeled the *cooling out function*, describing how disappointing expectations are handled by the disappointed person and especially by those responsible for the disappointments. In Goffman's (1952) earlier rendition the individual's failure was a consequence of those who acted in good faith (college recruitment, selection, and counseling personnel) because of their obligation to operate and perform under the open-door admissions policy. Such policy implies that deserving youth should be guaranteed equal educational opportunities.

Accordingly, the trend toward a tighter connection of higher education and higher occupation, of greater professionalization and increased specialization, was seen to imply that those students, quite often the student-athletes, lacking the qualification for entry into four-year institutions, regardless of their record, would seek to enter some college or gain post-secondary education. It seemed that the junior college provided the means by which entry into the four-year institution would be possible.

TWO-YEAR COLLEGES: MISSION AND FUNCTION

Students attend community colleges for a variety of reasons: to upgrade skills, to enhance professional skills, to earn a degree or certificate, or to transfer to a four-year institution (Bryant, 2008; Cohen & Brawer, 1996; Voorhees & Zhon, 2000). These colleges serve a variety of educational and social needs ranging from enhancing technical skill development to providing access to college for first-generation college students. They also tend to be tied more directly to local marketplaces. Students from diverse backgrounds often combine work and academics with a sense of life-long learning. The 2002–03 Minorities in Higher Education Report found a 142% increase between 1980 and 2000 in the number of associate degrees awarded to minority students.

Reitano (1998) found that four fundamental missions are reflected through two-year colleges: "compensatory, career, community, plus the collegiate or transfer function" (p. 125). Cohen and Brawer (1996) added general education as a fifth mission. But notice, in particular, that the place of intercollegiate athletics was hardly mentioned, and when it was, it was placed as follows: "Unless athletics sponsored by the college are truly a part of the college education process and support and promote the goals of the institution, then the entire mission of the institution is in jeopardy and the athletic program has no basis for existence" (Raepple, Peery, & Hohman, 1982, p. 162).

Paterson, Redrick, Alsop, and Brooks (1980) examined three traditional ways in which ethnic minorities utilized higher education as a means to rise above their disadvantaged status: (1) athletics, (2) the community college, and (3) professional education. The authors noted, "the community college model by contrast (to athletics) focuses on the structural nature of this alternative type of institution which offers parallel but not necessarily comparable instruction, more geared to local than national markets" (p. 4).

THE EVOLUTION OF THE TWO-YEAR INTERCOLLEGIATE ATHLETIC ASSOCIATION: AN OVERVIEW

While sports are sponsored differently today than they were two or three decades ago, there still remains the view that athletics must be aligned with the educational mission. Even today in the state of California, which has had the greatest number of community and junior colleges, awarding of athletic scholarships was not permitted because the emphasis must be on "creating a team consisting of students who had athletic skills."

According to Raepple et al. (1982) the National Junior College Athletic Association (NJCAA) was established in California. The newly formed organization sponsored the first junior college track and field event in 1939. Following World War II, the junior college movement began to spread throughout the United States. The number of national junior college tournaments began to expand. Records suggest that in 1949 the first National Junior College Basketball Tournament was held in Hutchinson, Kansas. During this same time period, the NJCAA divided the nation into 16 geographic regions (Raepple et al., 1982, p. 159).

In 1957, the NJCAA became affiliated with the National State High School Association and the National Association of Intercollegiate Athletics (NAIA). By 1959, the NJCAA added the National Baseball Championship Tournament. During the decade of the 1960s, the NJCAA continued to forge partnerships with the United States Track and Field Association, US Gymnastics Federation, President's Council on Physical Fitness, US Olympic Committee, US Wrestling Federation, and the US Baseball Federation. As the NJCAA grew in complexity and scope, the need was established for a full-time executive director to head the organization. Thus, in 1969, George Killian was hired to fulfill this role.

The decade of the 1970s witnessed the inclusion of more sports which included fencing, decathlon, indoor track, and championships in volleyball, basketball, and tennis for women. In 1973, the NJCAA was once again reorganized into 21 regions. It is important to note: In 1973 a women's division was added to the NJCAA. Records indicated by 1976 there were 296 NJCAA women's divisions and 586 men's divisions. By 1980–81, there were 490 women's division members. Expanded growth once again led to reorganization from 22 to 24 regions. In 1985–86, the National NJCAA Headquarters was moved from Hutchinson, Kansas, to Colorado Springs, Colorado. After much debate, in 1988–89, the NJCAA adopted the National Letter of Intent and Scholarship Agreement Policies and Procedures. The decades of the 1980s and 1990s saw the addition of Division III for men's basketball, expanded publications, debated about eligibility standards, debated about gender equality and Title IX, sportsmanship debate, Division III volleyball for women, and renewed the women's golf championship.

Fully engaged, by 1990 junior/community college athletic programs were actively involved in recruiting student-athletes, athletic grants-in-aid were offered to student-athletes, and most athletic programs received the majority of financial support from the

Table 7.1.	Study of Benefits of Intercollegiate Athletics at the Community College Locus Level	
	Internal	**External**
Student	Supporting Activities Personal Development Access to College	Athletic Transfer Scholarships
College	School Spirit Enrollment Growth State Reimbursement	Community Linkages Publicity/Marketing
Adopted from Castaneda, 2004, p. 7		

general college budget and student activity fees. But there is broad agreement that the emphasis must be on creating a team consisting of students who had athletic skills, or essentially, that athletics must be aligned with the educational mission. Today, there are over 500 NJCAA schools and 50,000 student-athletes organized into 24 different regions and 3 divisions throughout the United States. There are 221 Division I teams, 117 Division II teams, and 98 Division III teams.

Castaneda depicted the ways in which intercollegiate athletics benefit the community college and its students (Castaneda, 2004). The more that leading universities and colleges broadcast through their actions how much they value athletic talent (e.g., recall the media frenzy generated by commercially driven agendas for conference realignments dealing with Big Ten and PAC-10 league expansion), the greater the emphasis that potential athletic recruits will place on these activities; sports is the road to opportunity. On the one hand, athletic scholarships and "tickets of admission" provide powerful incentives, and this has become particularly poignant among minorities and for women. For the athlete as well as her/his sponsors, the fancier the college, the more selective the program, or the more vivid the promise of visibility, the more that the players' admission calls for a clear indication that the prospective athletes skills can fit within the system, thus assuring the right mix of talent is assembled (Shulman & Bowen, 2001).

On the other hand, increases in expenditures on coaching and facilities at all levels of play has put tremendous pressure of the admissions process, so much so that there seems to be no limit for more and more information about precollege achievements of athletes and likewise, the mobility of coaches between colleges. Given that a number of the freshmen or of first-year athletes may not continue to be academically qualified, and to allow for such attrition, more athletes must be recruited initially. Consequently, coaches have a considerable role determining which athletically talented applicants gain admission.

GRADUATION RATES

Graduation rates have been used as benchmarkers to evaluate academic performance. Yet it is important to understand, as some professionals point out, that "graduation rates are misleading outcome measures for community colleges; many students at these institutions are seeking neither degrees nor transfers to a baccalaureate institution" (Bailey et al., 2006, p. 494). Arguably, numerous factors impact graduation rates (e.g., family income, job responsibilities, academic preparation). Unfortunately, community colleges still suffer from second-class academic status when compared to their four-year college institutions. One might argue that the second-class status is one of the factors that permit racial and ethnic minorities to gain access to these institutions of higher learning.

Nationally, when more than two-thirds of the entering population requires remediation in special programs, these schools face a remarkable challenge in bringing even a modicum of its students through to credentials (Crow, p. 11). Even when faced with the looming evidence of variation between states and schools in how readiness is defined and measured, absence of academic readiness often functions as a way to tell applicants they are unqualified, undesirable, or ill-fitted. It is not surprising, however, that the institution's admission officers and enrollment management staff strive to reduce attrition. In the case of minorities, among African Americans particularly, public school preparation pushes them to be "resigned to social norms of inequity and avoid developing the skills, habits, and content necessary for continued study at the college level."

PROPOSITION 48 AND THE STANDARD OF AMATEURISM

From its inception in 1986–87, Proposition 48 has been one of the most controversial proposals ever adopted by the NCAA. George Sage (1990) regards Proposition 48 as a classic example of "blaming the victim" by placing blame on the student-athlete for being academically ill-prepared for college-level work, while at the same time, university officials willingly admit academically ill-prepared students to gain advantage in intercollegiate sports. Sage claims that these standards direct attention away from the "commercialized structure of major college athletic programs and focused it on the athlete" (p. 169). A major fallout is its racial consequences because reports have shown that those whose eligibility is affected have largely been African American students.

Anderson and South (2000) noted that one of latent functions of these eligibility standards is that "it created a situation whereby the nation's junior colleges, which are not governed by the by-law, act as a kind of 'feeder' to Division I schools" (p. 161). As these researchers indicate, if the commercialization of sports—"the profit-making ideology of college athletic programs"—is to be remedied by the NCAA it must address not only the economic exploitation of collegiate athletes, but also "the racial nature of this exploitation" (p. 163). Underlying the evolution of big-time sports, the strategy for funding of the student-athlete is centered on the appropriateness of the label amateur applied to football and basketball players at universities which realize high profits from these sports.

While many researchers have reviewed the influence of profit-making on sports, "the most reprehensible feature . . . is that many universities engage in what amounts to professional football, but hold fast to the illusion that their athletes are amateurs" (Sack, 1988, p. 165). African American athletes at predominately White institutions continue to be faced with overcoming the stereotype of being intellectually inferior while possessing innate athletic superiority.

REMEDIATION AND RECRUITMENT

As open-door institutions their educational processes facilitate and express an ideological atmosphere based on varying themes toward guarantees for equal educational opportunities. Indeed, the two-year junior and community college is often regarded as an entitlement. In most states the junior or two-year college is part of the post-secondary, higher education system. No matter which path one chooses to trace the experiences of students in post-secondary or junior colleges, the issues of the student-athletes subsequently transferring from or to other four-year colleges and institutions has been a continuing concern for study about national standards and practices. Student-athletes' transfer is a key feature in any calls for reform and legislation dealing with academic eligibility and compliance that are used to position student athletes' likelihood of being academically successful in colleges at any level of NCAA sports.

Furthermore, it is not uncommon that as notable instances of violations are uncovered, the mass media surely report it as somehow surprising news within the sports world (we usually learn that the NCAA, or another sanctioning group, is investigating such-and-such an episode, and that an NCAA "task-force" has been established to study as well as to sanction the offending schools). In contrast, claims from all quarters about dire consequences accompany these "crackdowns," suggesting that any such assertions about which programs are legitimate will cost many dozens of athletes to be unable to get Division I scholarships (Wolfe, 1987).

As already noted, the two-year junior/community college presents a significant pathway to college entrance and to the conditions set out in relation to academic eligibility and compliance. While highly publicized incidents at big-time schools get all the press, athletics has become an increasingly serious business in terms of its direct impact on admissions and the composition and ethos of the student body across all divisions, large and small. Recruitment of athletes and, of course, transfers to or from other programs has implications for rationing of educational opportunity in competition for places in colleges and universities.

Over the past 50 years, new players from all socioeconomic classes, women, and minorities have been encouraged to seek places where previously they may not have been welcomed. Shulman and Bowen (2001) suggest that "academic underperformance is now found among women athletes as well as men, among those who play the lower profile sports, as well as those on football and basketball teams, and among athletes playing at the Division III level competition, as well as those playing in bowl games and competing for national championships" (p. 171).

Indeed, one of the ironies of the increasing intensification of college sports is that standards of performance have risen so dramatically. Athletic specialization has grown to be so important that intercollegiate programs demand more of those who can perform, that is, those who are already trained-up, placing heavy demands on student athletes.

Some observers have suggested that there is an even larger divide, if not polarization, between the demand for greater athletic intensity and the academic intensity for success expected of the rest of the campus community. In the case of those athletes playing high profile sports at universities with big-time programs, there may be separation and self-isolating tendencies for both women and men who are being recruited on the basis of talent that differentiates them from other students.

Undoubtedly, healthy competition requires considerable parity that makes the game worth playing, and sustaining such competition is anything but easy. Shulman and Bowen (2001) comment that "even winning is never enough, since there are always more levels to aspire to, more ways to excel, and if all else fails, future seasons to think about; athletics," they say, "can come to represent an arms race without end" (p. 170).

As important as competition is in shaping athletics, an equally powerful force is emulation. As a driver, *emulation* moves in the direction of "fairness," with other nonrevenue sports and "minor sports" deserving equal treatment such that more coaches are hired, facilities are improved, and scholarships are provided. "Fairness" mandates that they be given the same opportunity. At the present time, the application of the fairness doctrine has been exported to women's athletics with the passage of Title IX in 1972.

TRANSFER-ELIGIBILITY AND COMPLIANCE

Community colleges have been, and will remain, innovative institutions providing affordable access to higher education, especially for ethnic minorities (Romano & Wisniewski, 2005). A significant issue facing ethnic minorities is not lack of access to colleges, but rather the impact of social class status on student enrollment data and transfer rate data, especially at the community college level.

The following factors may have an impact on community college student transfer rates (Bailey et al., 2006):

(1) Type of community college (*Technical/Skill Development*)

(2) Geographic location of the community college (*Urban, Rural*)

(3) Articulation agreements between community colleges and universities

(4) Gender differences and ratio of male to female students enrolled

(5) Selected major—athletics/coaching v. *others*

(6) Double-edge-sword—Community colleges enroll students with lower entry skills, yet attempts to raise academic standards may be counterproductive to the mission of community colleges.

Bailey et al.'s (2006) analysis of community colleges found colleges with a high percentage of ethnic minorities, part-time students, and female students tend to have lower graduation rates. Moreover, Doyle's (2006) research found that only one-fifth of those students who entered two-year community colleges as full-time students actually completed their bachelor's degree within six years. It is also important to note about one-half of the students were able to transfer all of their credits.

Pflueger (1988) analyzed personal background and social psychological factors on the academic qualification and retention of community college athletes and non-athletes and found significant academic performance differences between White and Black athletes. For example, the average GPA for White athletes was 2.14 as compared to 1.61 GPA for Black athletes. It is also important to note, 73% of the Black athletes earned grades less than 2.0, as compared to 34% of the White athletes. Nonetheless, no differences were found in success and retention of athletes and nonathletes.

Pflueger attempted to explain his finding by referring to differences in the number of credit hours taken, time spent on course work outside of the class, enrollment in required English and math classes, and enrollment in remedial classes. Finally, 71% of the athletes in this study expressed a desire to pursue an athletic career at four-year institutions or in professional sports. This is a very interesting finding since Bennion (1992) wrote, "The vast majority of junior and senior college student-athletes will never play professionally" (p. 27). Nevertheless, Bennion (1992) insisted, "There is indeed a critical need to demonstrate academic accountability for student-athletes and their progress toward a degree" (p. 26).

NCAA STUDENT-ATHLETE TRANSFER AND QUALIFICATION GUIDES

Writing about academic transfer from two-year junior and community colleges, Gerdy (1997) noted that

Coaches and athletic administrators from both two-and four-year institutions view junior college transfers differently from student-athletes who enroll in an NCAA

Junior college student-athletes often find the transition to four-year institutions difficult both on and off the field. Courtesy of iStockPhoto

institution on directly from high school. Because most will be in the athletic program only two years, junior college transfers are viewed not as students or even student-athletes, but rather as "quick fixes." (p. 142)

As previously noted, the need for academic accountability, that is, regular progress toward completing an academic program, must be expected of all student athletes. While some view the junior college as a farm system for student-athletes into four-year college programs, this is only one of several outcomes for the students they serve. Proposition 48, the NCAA rule requiring an underperforming athlete to graduate from a two-year college before deserving eligibility to play at a four-year college, should solidify the expectation for adequate ongoing academic success. And, by and large, the promised outcomes have been effective.

There is a critical need to demonstrate academic accountability and progress toward it, so that if you do not perform academically, you do not participate athletically, nor can you realize opportunities for personal success. Nonetheless, for many more student-athletes, these schools foster the opportunities for participation as a worthwhile experience in and of itself. As a matter of fact, only a small minority of all junior college student athletes will pursue a career in athletics.

THE IMPACT OF NCAA RULES:
COMMUNITY COLLEGE ATTENDANCE AND TRANSFER RATES

The National Collegiate Athletic Association published specific guidelines regarding qualifiers and nonqualifiers to participate in NCAA sports. (For a comprehensive review of NCAA eligibility policies, see Covell & Barr, 2001.) Examples of these posted guidelines are as follows:

Title: 14.02.10.2—Non-qualifier.
A non-qualifier is a student who has not graduated from high school or who, at the time specified in the regulation (see Bylaw 14.3), has not successfully completed the required core-curriculum corresponding SAT/ACT score required for a qualifier.

Title: 14.3.2.1.1—Eligibility for Aid, Practice and Competition.

An entering freshman with no previous college attendance who was a non-qualifier at the time of enrollment in a Division I institution shall not be eligible for regular-season competition or practice during the first academic year in residence. However, such a student shall be eligible for non-athletics institutional financial aid that is not from an athletics source and is based on financial need only, consistent with institutional and conference regulations. (Revised: 1/10/95, effective 8/1/96.)

Title: 14.3.4—Residence Requirement—Non-qualifier.

A non-qualifier must fulfill an academic year of residence in order to be eligible for practice, competition and athletically related financial aid (see Bylaw 14.3.2.2.2). The requirements that must be met to fulfill an academic year of residence are set forth in Bylaw 14.5.1.1. A non-qualifier admitted after the 12th class day may not use that semester or quarter for the purpose of establishing residency. (Revised: 1/10/90, effective 8/1/90; revised: 1/10/95, effective 8/1/96.)

The Big East Athletic Conference provided a list of minimum qualifying standards. Accompanying minimum standards that the Conference listed, it is important to note the following statement:

In order for a non-qualifier out of high school to be eligible to transfer to a BIG EAST Conference institution from a two-year junior college, he or she must first graduate with an associate degree and meet all NCAA and member institution's minimal eligibility regulations. If these standards are met, the student-athlete shall then be eligible for financial aid, practice and athletic competition at a BIG EAST Conference member institution. (Cox, 2006)

Heck and Takahashi (2006) examined the impact of Proposition 48 on Division IA football programs. Specifically, the authors were interested in determining what consequences, if any, Proposition 48 had on the recruitment of freshman athletes and junior college athletes. One of the Proposition's initiatives suggested by the authors: After the implementation of Proposition 48, Division IA programs will recruit more junior college transfer student-athletes. The study found Proposition 48 did have an impact on recruiting of freshmen athletes. Yet, with a smaller freshman class, Division IA football programs witnessed higher levels of student-athletes transferring from junior colleges.

The report spurred a follow-up that focused on the NCAA's 1996 enactment of Proposition 16, which increased the admission standards for freshmen student-athletes at the Division I schools in an effort to improve graduation rates (Price, 2007). Price reports that Proposition 16 increased graduation rates significantly for Black student-athletes, but showed no significant effect for White student-athletes. However, the results also indicate that graduation rates declined for Black student-athletes at Division II schools. Price takes these finding to mean that as a result of the higher admission standard, the Division I schools changed recruiting patterns and came to rely less on freshmen student-athletes, particularly Black athletes, to fill their scholarships. Overall, he suggests while fewer Black freshmen athletes enrolled in Division I schools, the overall number of Black student-athletes did not change, *thus suggesting that a greater proportion of transfer students into Division I schools were Black* (Price, 2007).

In light of past abuses, "the NJCAA regulations capped at 25% the number of athletic scholarships that can be awarded to foreign students" (Brown, 1988, p.12). This suggested that scholarship awards were frequently made to students who were out-of-district, if not out-of-state or country, which is countered with concern for violating *the community-centered mission.* During the 1970s and '80s, for example, the University of Texas–El Paso track coach lured an array of long distance runners from Africa and won a number of titles. Some of these runners were already in their 30s. Currently, NJCAA caps at 25% the number of athletic scholarships that can be awarded to foreign students participating in Division I sports. Records showed out-of-state and international students represented 14.6% of all community college athletes in 1988.

The same study reported that 19.1% of all athletes at two-year colleges were people of color and that athletes of color accounted for 15.5% and 21% of all female and male athletes, respectively (Brown, 1988). Also, with regard to gender disparity, in a 2004 report the community colleges' greatest disparity in athletics was in the area of participation. In fact, only 8% of the 91 responding colleges were in compliance with Title IX based on proportionality—that is, had participation rates that were within five percentage points of the enrollment rates for each gender—and 84% were considerably outside the range of acceptability.

Wolff (1987), writing in *Sports Illustrated*, noted, "As a way around Proposition 48, Division I coaches would rather sign a junior college (JUCO) graduate for two seasons than take a chance on using up a scholarship on a high school senior who might not score the requisite 700 on his college boards, as the NCAA rule, properly known as By-law 5-1(J), requires" (p. 9). While sounding a rather alarming message, Wolff (1987) acknowledges Proposition 48 did have an impact on junior college student-athlete recruiting rates and transfers to four-year colleges. Wolff indicates that Rich Ball, who was a scout for junior colleges, claimed that as many as half of high school seniors in 1987 did not meet Proposition 48 guidelines (Wolff, 1987). During the 1980s and '90s major college and university academic programs tended to steer academically challenged recruits to two-year colleges to foster opportunity to earn grades up to standards. The list of two-year athletes who have had notable careers and gone on to professional sports is a long one.

Accessibility and eligibility are always burdened by violations and reform. Today, while talented athletes still flow through two-year colleges, the prep schools (i.e., private independent high schools, funded by tuition, donation) have proliferated during the past two decades. In order to curb academic abuses in prep basketball, the NCAA approved a rule that bars the controversial issue of players attending prep schools for the fifth year of high school in order to get their grades up (effective 2008). The rule states that upon entering the ninth grade, athletes will have four years to meet NCAA mandated core academic requirements. After four years, student-athletes can take only one additional course at an NCAA-recognized high school.

The rule is built to target so-called "diploma mills," particularly with regard to basketball. (See Lutheran Christian Academy in Philadelphia and the impact on the George Washington Colonials highly ranked basketball team: http://www.nytimes.com/2006.) A number of diploma mills exploited recruitment as academically deficit athletes turned to the prep school for remarkable quick fixes. In an effort to curb academic abuses, especially prep school basketball, the NCAA approved a rule to bar the controversial practice of players attending prep schools for a fifth year of high school in order to get grades up. Many prep schools have operated with little or no oversight, opening them to charges of greater interests in athletics than education (Ullman, 2009).

The rule is expected to push more top-tier athletes back into the community college pipeline. Some observers insisted that, in particular, community college basketball teams had been drained of talent as the number of prep schools grew. Simply put, a successful year at a prep school left players with four years of athletic eligibility at a university. After two years at a junior/community college, athletes had just two years left. Furthermore, there is competition from the NBAs nascent developmental league which serves as an option for players who don't meet NCAA requirements, thereby draining away from those who might have looked to the JUCO programs. Some observers, however, believe community colleges that send athletes to colleges, only to see them fail to obtain a degree, will be shunned by universities eager to avoid embarrassment of low graduation rates among athletes.

TWO-TEAR COLLEGE ATHLETICS: 'FARM TEAMS' OR 'ATHLETIC EXCELLENCE'

An answer to the question "who's playing?" has been incomplete because most estimates of participation rates that have been generated are drawn from only a few comprehensive reports which have themselves suffered shortcomings. To gain perspective regarding the location of most intercollegiate athletes, the vast majority of these athletes compete outside the limelight of national media. Cheslock (2007) reports that nearly half the schools that offer athletics (around 48%) are not in the NCAA. (We follow John Cheslock, who has cautiously based his results on a "complete $N = 1895$ institutions sample" of all two-year education institutions that reported for 2001–02 and 2004–05 and thus, arguably contains a complete roster of all postsecondary institutions with departments that offer athletic programs.) These schools are most affiliated with the National Association of Intercollegiate Athletics (NAIA) (about 13%) and the National Junior College Athletic Association (NJCAA) (nearly 22%), while the remaining 13% are smaller athletic association's (California AAC, Northwest AAC, and National Christian AAC) (p. 155).

According to Bennion (1992), the nature and extent of diversity among junior colleges drives certain kinds of issues reflected through the several divisions among them. While about half the colleges offering athletics are not in the NCAA, the smaller size of the athletic programs at non-NCAA schools cause them to contain only 27% of the total athletes engaged in intercollegiate sports. Some junior colleges maintain one or two sports that may be recruited on a highly competitive basis with full scholarship support, while others have sports activities barely distinguishable from intramurals and offer no scholarships. Among schools that have a broader selection of programs and attempt to be competitive in all sports programs, there may be a goal to provide activity benefits to as many student-athletes as possible, men as well as women (LeCrom et al., 2009). Consequently, NJCAA athletic programs are arranged into three divisions, with Division I offering full scholarships, Division II offers tuition and fees, and Division III provides no assistance (Castaneda, 2004).

Two-year junior or community college participation in intercollegiate sport is significant, on-going, but not evenly distributed across the 50 states. California continues as the citadel of NJCAA action and has 94% participation, with only 6 of 107 that do not sponsor intercollegiate athletics. Reiterating, intercollegiate athletics are found at 57% of all public community colleges. In 2002, 567 colleges sponsored competition in 30 different sports, resulting in 4,277 teams and 73,926 athletes. The *highest* percentage of sponsorship is at large rural colleges, higher than at urban or suburban campuses, the *lowest* percentage at small rural campuses, usually fewer than 2,000 total enrollments (Castaneda, 2004).

In some measure, athletics requires a critical mass of full-time students, which also is reflected in the fact that sizeable urban colleges do not need to rely on athletics as much to provide the marginal growth benefits gained by rural counterparts. When the enrollment requirements are presented in compliance with the NJCAA, COA, and NWAACC requirements of degree-seeking, full-time students the number of athletes accounted for some 7.7% of full time undergraduates, with women comprising 5.3% of full-time females and men providing 10.9% of all full-time male students. But Castaneda (2004) cautiously adds, "this number only includes athletes on first or varsity teams," because "few teams reported athletes other than first teams" (pp. 4–5).

As top level/tier NCAA schools have gone out-of-state, national in the scope of their recruiting, pressures have mounted for coaches to offer scholarship aid to the best players in-state whether or not they qualify, and to run summer camps or tour All-Star/ Top 20 media-driven events in national talent-hunts (Farrell, 1992; Bradley, 2007; Moltz, 2009). The four-year school may not offer, or the student may fail to qualify. Among athletes attempting to qualify, the two-year college may be a promising alternative. Once engaged, options emerge. Every two-year junior or community college has its list of outstanding athletes and every conference ranks its team's win-loss records, along with top-rated athletes in the sports/positions they compete in, and advertise their All Star teams.

Intercollegiate athletics are important for public community colleges, especially with regard to achieving gender equity. First, athletes accounted for a higher percentage of full-time students at rural than at suburban or urban campuses. Overall, 10.9% of full-time degree/certificate seeking women and men were athletes. Next, the total number of opportunities for women and men to compete on athletic teams showed some balance (Castaneda, 2004, p. 24), with 51.3% men's teams compared to 48.7% of women's teams accounting for all teams. It is shown, however, that women accounted for 55% of all full-time enrollments, but only 37% of all athletes were women. On the other hand, 56% of total aid went to men, and 44% went to women (Mumford, 2006)

With regard to data reflecting diversity, past studies of athletic scholarships suggested that awards were frequently made to students who were *out-of-district, if not out-of-country*. Among two-year colleges, football and basketball (particularly basketball, with more than 320 scholarship-offering teams competing), along with baseball, produced the critical core of dominate sports teams that are committed to recruitment among men. These sports also are more likely to have scholarships awarded to out-of-state athletes. Notably, athletic scholarships in track, baseball, swimming, volleyball, cut across gender, and at times have gilded a discernable international texture to local team successes. During the 1990s international recruiting came to be a strategy for a number of coaches— in soccer, track, tennis, skiing, even golf—who established pipelines with athletes badgering for scholarships. The chance to play sports and thereby get a college education is attractive to international students, and coaches soon found international students who regarded the scholarship as an opportunity (Teets, 2011).

Overall, 63.1% of all colleges that sponsored intercollegiate athletics in 2002–03 had at least one sport in which they could have chosen to award athletically-related student aid. Two-year public community colleges spent more money recruiting male athletes than female athletes. For women, the greatest potential scholarship availability was basketball at 295 teams. Women might have found athletic aid more easily available for softball at 263 schools and volleyball at 226. Male basketball players had more opportunities to compete for athletic scholarships/aid than in any other sport. There were 184 Division I and 133 Division II teams, equaling 317 teams in two-year colleges at which aid was available. Baseball ranked second in the number of teams where aid might have been available with 294. Golf and soccer were next most popular, with 129 and 101 teams, respectively. More broadly, rural colleges in all three categories (Div. I, II, & III) were more likely to sponsor aid with scholarship assistance at a rate of 71%, 81%, and 76%. (see Castaneda, 2004, p. 30 ff.)

NJCAA COACHES

There is indication that the ability to wall-off the impact of the athlete culture is likely to be more successful in large, big-time universities than at many other colleges and universities. Even so, across all levels of participation, the trend to be competitive in fielding intercollegiate sports drives a good deal of the funding outlays for these extracurricular pursuits that subsidize athletic recruiting and enable a level of near-professional elites to arise among coaches and their staffs. In *The Game of Life*, Shulman and Bowen (2001) note that expenditure on athletics has increasingly moved toward attracting revenues from commercial sponsors, but winning large financial incentives brings the obvious danger that the academic integrity of the institution will be corrupted. No revenues come without costs, and the risk is what has been called *mission drift*. In essence, the increasing commercialization of athletics carries within it the requirement to act like a business.

Observers seem to agree that as the growing number of 18- through 24-year-olds going to two-year colleges because of the rising tuition and academic standards at many four-year colleges, there is more expectation of a full-college experience. Colleges are recognizing that a full program of student activities is likely to bear fruit. For one reason, the number of women's programs is skyrocketing. Additionally, sports can command local media attention, while searching for known "name" coaches, and facilitating commercially hot sports (e.g., X-treme sports) can also mean money, allowing colleges to tap alumni and supporters for fund-raising purposes.

The colleges that are participating in fewer sports tend to have less emphasis on the role of spectators in their athletic experiences. Guided by good coaching and training staff, these colleges produce athletes ready and capable of high performance in their sports. These schools sometimes can provide high competition in a less stressful environment. They often can allow access to a level of competition that is open to all divisions and colleges (e.g., track and field). Accordingly, NJCAA-based colleges have generated new scholarship-aid availability as well as provided opportunities for competition not otherwise possible (e.g., track, baseball, and volleyball), particularly affecting African American women, who can compete along aside D-I athletes. Among the claims stressed to prospective student-athletes are

- seasonal play and championship opportunities,
- flexibility to transfer without missing a season of eligibility,
- fewer recruiting restrictions,
- focus on character and educational opportunities,
- opportunity for regional and national recognition, and
- smaller classes and closer student-faculty interactions (Dye, 2010).

A recent survey showed that not all college presidents or observers agree or think that a two-year college sport is a good idea (Bradley, 2007). Reporting about a study involving 88 college presidents in a six-state region showed agreement that sports teams can foster school pride, promote diversity, and bolster enrollment, but disagreed on whether sports teams support the core mission of colleges. Not surprisingly, presidents whose colleges fielded sports teams said sports supports the college mission; presidents without teams disagreed. Proponents noted that athletic programs benefit from a more intensive support system—coaches make students attend classes and tutors monitor academic progress. But those who don't favor sports programs complain that sports strain college resources, and too often coaches are afflicted with *win at all costs* (Williams & Pennington, 2006).

Bennion (1992) argues coaches have a considerable role in providing indices of accountability, which could demonstrate that student-athletes are deserving students as well as athletes. Coaches need to work with faculty to ensure academic progress. "When performance is measured, performance improves. When performance is measured and reported back, the rate of improvement accelerates" (Washington & Karen, 2010, p 174). Coaches are aware of the academic threshold that they must meet and are apt to push as far as they can. But they have little or no interest in wasting their own time putting forth candidates who will not be admissible under any circumstances. If you tell them "this is what you can have, they accept and do it" (Washington & Karen, 2010, p. 175). If you let them have any grey area, they just can't stop testing to see how much they can get—how iffy a candidate, how many players. But within the boundaries, coaches are likely to feel they own the admission slots set aside for their team.

Castaneda (2004) estimates that over 30% of athletes at public community colleges received athletically related aid in 2002–03. There also is evidence that colleges try to comply with Title IX. Women accounted for 42% of all athletes receiving aid and received/earned a higher average scholarship by nearly $300. The proportion receiving aid was higher than their representation of 37% in the population of athletes.

College athletic success is often tied to the coach's ability to identify, recruit, and retain athletes with a high level of athletic prowess. As early as 1969 and 1974, Rooney attempted to model collegiate recruiting practices from college, high school, and junior colleges. Brooks, Weimer, and Blakemore (1989) investigated the role of the coach in the junior college recruitment process. The researchers found that basketball coaches initially observed basketball talent on a high school team or trying out for the varsity. It was also found that a majority of the junior college basketball players were recruited within the state in which the junior college was located. It is not surprising that states such as Texas, Florida, and California have a large, complex and successful JUCO athletic program. Yet the authors were unable to identify the number of ethnic minorities coaching the various NJCAA sports teams.

Fielding any team requires both student participants and appropriate coaching staff. Castaneda (2004) reports that the number of full-time and part-time coaches employed by these colleges showed low variability; most teams had only the head coach who worked at least half-time. For men, the teams with the highest average number of full-time coaches were football and cross-country. Each college, on average, has one full-time coach. For women, only track (combined) rated one full-time coach. She noted that men, on average, both head and assistant coaches, had a higher FTE salary than did coaches on women's teams. Further, men's and women's salaries were significantly higher at larger rural colleges and lowest on urban campuses.

A recent report about women's teams in Maryland's two-year colleges concluded that women are left behind in a dramatic fashion because even with a notable increase in women's participation, women remain significantly underrepresented to the degree that the two-year colleges are out of compliance with Title IX (Mumford, 2006). The document shows that athletic directors and coaches at the colleges are mostly White and predominately male, and most coaches are part-time (81%) and paid a stipend or given release time. Women comprised 23% of coaches in Maryland's JUCO.

Additionally, coaching at two-year colleges is not particularly lucrative. During 2002–03, the college average FTE was about $25,000 for a head coach and slightly over $12,000 for an assistant coach on men's teams. Few sports *averaged* even one full-time head or assistant coach. Also, coaching salaries were well below the *average* community college faculty salary for 2002–03 which was $51,000, and even instructors, the lowest faculty group, average around $38,000 (Castaneda, 2004, pp. 38–39). It is not uncommon for coaches to have their primary professions outside of the community college and have a coaching contract that mirrors the way of other adjunct instructions.

CONCLUSIONS

Susan Estler (2005) believes that oftentimes intercollegiate athletic programs at junior and community colleges are growing and have grown to levels that challenge the finances, facilities, reputations, and ethics of the schools. As external forces, such as commercialization, laws and regulations, and the public obsession with sports escalate, the incentives to relax ethical and educational considerations also intensify. Even when these institutions and their presidents are intellectually committed to a strong academic mission, they are still constrained. The external forces, almost like an invisible hand, inform and empower stakeholders, from trustees to alumni, to gain a share in governance at these colleges. And, says Estler, "the stakes are very high when things go wrong in athletics" (p. 3).

There is no single organization that governs community college athletics, although there are nearly 600 campuses with intercollegiate athletics, the greatest proportion of which are member schools of the National Junior College Athletic Association (NJCAA). A total of $47,442,588 of aid was awarded to 24,863 student-athletes by two-year junior and community colleges in 2002–03, of which 42% was awarded to women and 58% went to men.

Intercollegiate programs at two-year colleges usually do not generate as much criticism as those at four-year colleges, not only because of less media attention but also because they do not cost as much to operate. And many two-year schools have no intercollegiate athletics at all. Nonetheless, with little or no economic recovery in sight since 2008, community college administrators wonder what they can reasonably cut on campuses while fulfilling their educational mission. For some, the answer is athletics.

Recently, two-year community colleges have supported passage of the federally-sponsored Student Aid and Fiscal Responsibility Act of 2009, urging support for the technical training partnerships which is perceived as a way to secure a substantial boost to add to the number of two-year graduates, ensuring different outcomes for different college-type campus locales: rural, suburban, and urban. We know that intercollegiate sports are very important on many of these campuses, and for rural-serving community colleges specifically. While athletics was found at 58% of all two year-colleges, participation was skewed to rural campuses that accounted for almost half of all athletes at two-year public community colleges (Castaneda, 2004).

In effect, smaller, often rural, colleges show a higher percentage of athletes among full-time students. The use of student-athlete financial-aid as a device to increase enrollment by rural-serving Division I and II college teams is available to use not only to assist recruiting athletes but also to ensure an enrollment/entertainment attraction for the fans/student body—these rates of aid-sponsorship vary from 77% of rural-serving colleges compared to 43% for suburban-serving and 50% for urban-serving schools. Castaneda (2004) observes that intercollegiate athletics positively impacts full-time male enrollment on college campuses, especially if a college sponsors football, a sport usually requiring rosters of 60 or more players. Alternatively, handling the "missing male" problem on these campuses can affect how Title IX requirements are met and may exacerbate gender inequality.

The implication of student-aid sponsorship is also reflected is the notion of critical mass needed to build athletic programs. Generally, the sports that are able to take advantage of shared facilities are more popular and can offer greater dollar return amounts from the athletic aid invested. For example, volleyball and basketball can be played in the same gym, whether men or women participate. Football and soccer require fields for practice and for games, while golf requires no on-campus space. Furthermore, gender equality is impacted through the teams' roster-size as well as by out-of-state or international recruitment, commonly involving a diverse student body, and specifically African American student-athletes who are focusing on transfer into "big-time" programs.

Since colleges and universities at all levels attempt to make a name for themselves through sports, athletic programs can serve as important tools to recruit students, playing a role in building institutional identity even among smaller colleges. Our review shows that campus leaders must be realistic about the increasing commercialization of sports and come to terms with the fact that forces supporting the current state of intercollegiate athletics are considerably more powerful than a college president, athletic director, or even a whole campus. Issues of diversity and equity continue to plague higher education as a whole. As we noted, meek as they may be seen, proactive programs and various affirmative action policies were established to enhance the pool of minority applicants for athletic leadership positions. These protocols often aligned with the perception that African Americans and women lacked the skills to be viable candidates for coaching and other leadership positions.

Hartman's (2003) work directed our attention to how, during the 1980s and '90s, the American sports enterprise was especially instrumental in reconstructing America's perception of racial inequality and injustice, inside and outside of sports. Hartman (2003) showed how issues of race were buried beneath labels of "community relations" or "human resources," while African American and other minority athletes appear and are represented *without* specific textual reference to race, as if it is only their individual effort and identity that matter. For the NCAA and collegiate facilitators, this crossover involved them in learning how to avoid social resistance and unrest by incorporating moderate but symbolically powerful racial actors (Jackie Robinson, Michael Jordan, and Walter Peyton) into its practice and official policy. Big-time collegiate sport also gained an enormous sponsorship from media moguls and market executives engaged in marketing their products (Brooks & Althouse, 2007).

Thus, the continual confrontation between profit-making commercialization and athletic amateurism within big-time intercollegiate athletics is reflected in the conflict between economic interests of schools and academic pursuits of student-athletes. Clearly, coaches, their athletic directors, college presidents, as well as other professional athletic staff are the essential ingredients in the drive for diversity and equity in college sports, and the push manifests in ways that negatively affects student-athletes and minority coaches, and is shown by the lack of minority coaches. Although recent NCAA reforms may stymie the worst of the abuses, and in some measure, mitigate the persistent underevaluation of academic collegiate experiences by and for African American athletes, the impact of and spin-offs from these reforms affect intercollegiate athletics at junior and community two-year colleges (e.g., NJCAA, COA, NWAAC) in acute, sometimes negatively focused ways. It remains correct that in an age when minorities are gaining positions of prominence throughout American culture, racial disparities remain a serious feature of intercollegiate sports.

As most chapters in this book report, the number of minorities—women and men— who earn a place among top positions in any major intercollegiate sport appears to be seriously underrepresented and notably, college football coaches looking the most dismal. There is no expectation for handouts, rather simply a quest to be evaluated on merit. But public exposure alone does not change the outcome. As Floyd Keith suggests, "not much seems to be happening to increase the diversity amongst coaches when left in the hands of the individual institutions" (Keith, 2013).

Tactically, the energy poured into correcting social injustices for hiring of women and of minorities—including the proposed uses of the Rooney Rule or employing Title VII lawsuits—has focused principally on outcomes aimed toward NCAA college's athletic programs, and mainly at the prime-time, big-time NCAA colleges and their conferences. There may be some overflow to press for greater outcomes into the two-year junior and community college athletic programs, but there is no equivalent to the BCA *Hiring Report Card* pertaining to Black coaches and administrators among these colleges. Among these schools, accounting procedures are relatively invisible, with indications that not much seems to be happening to increase diversity when left in the hands of an individual school.

As already noted, the wide array of state policies and the multiplicity of regional conference rules, as well as the local status quo bearing on two-year junior and community college budgets have a bearing on which sports, if any, are offered, and thus significantly affect the nature of diversity employment and tenure/longevity of their athletic programs and coaches. Furthermore, two-year junior and community college coaches may mount their own campaigns for recognition or achievement, and gain job mobility. With increased stakes placed on winning, coaching may become more focused on reloading, rather than rebuilding, a strategy that certainly is recognizable in basketball and practiced in football. For example, during his first three seasons as head coach at Kansas State, Ron Prince's recruiting classes included 37 JUCOs, signing 19 of a total 32 opening in the 2008 class, and facilitating a pipeline for 12 football players alone from southern California two-year colleges (Dodd, 2008). Although the NCAA imposed stricter standards in 2008 NJCAA leadership has regarded the issue, by and large, as one about academic integrity and accreditation. Furthermore, NJCAA members argue that the two-year schools have neither the resources nor oversight to write rules that would be fair to all involved in athletics. Realistically, if any student-athlete transfers outside of her/his two-year colleges' state, every university has different criteria for deciding what classes are accepted for transfer.

With regard to hiring coaches at two-year colleges, short of Title IX obligations not much seems to be happening to increase diversity when left in the hands of individual institutions. Assembling information about coaches at two-year junior and community colleges suggests that you can find good coaches who are keen on educationally based athletics; that is, giving expression to teaching life's lessons such as sportsmanship, integrity, teamwork, and leadership which coincides with a coach's concern for student-athletes' getting their academic work in order and moving on to the next level (Martin & Christy, 2010).

There is a considerably body of information about the role and impact of the two-year junior and community colleges in the United States, and a significant assessment, ongoing as well as reflective, of the nature and developments in intercollegiate JUCO sports programs, particularly as collegiate athletics was shaped and reflected in the context of NCAA polices and its rules. Adapting and coping with the spin-offs and direct effects of the rules have been represented and reviewed throughout the chapter, noting that community colleges were regarded as a primary pipeline for athletes who wanted to go on to big-time Division I programs.

Perhaps the change that needs to be made is incubating now, and a new civil rights movement is developing. Richard Lapchick thinks so and insists that "we need to change the hiring practices for coaches and to revitalize the system of education so that student-athletes and parents can let athletic departments know they care about what's going on at colleges and universities" (Lapchick, 2008, p. 1). On the level of hiring practices, an *Eddie Robinson Rule* is imperative: a system needs to be set up that would cost the school scholarships if it fails to interview a candidate of color when it has a coaching opening. There also must be sanctions.

The NCAA leadership, as well as voices from other assorted athletic association, says its membership will not agree to the Eddie Robinson Rule. Without consequences, schools would not comply. In the 1980s, the NCAA said the same thing—that its membership could not publish graduation rates because members would not make the information public, but legislation was fashioned by the government requiring annually reported college graduation rates, broken down by race and sport, along with the breakdown by race of each team's coaching staff. Similarly, after years of stalling, Title IX lawsuits changed funding for women's sports. Without teeth, the current process is a failure (Lapchick, 2008).

An Eddie Robinson Rule, accompanied with lawsuits, might promote serious forward movement. As it is now, schools with vacancies rush to fill them, on average, in 14 days. And support for minority coaches has a tendency to evaporate because if key alumni are not enthusiastic about hiring a minority, they won't donate—a few big-dollar alumni who withhold their support can make a crucial difference. Out of the limelight, at America's two-year colleges, similar forces will be at work, only on a smaller scale.

STUDY QUESTIONS

1. Discuss the various economic and political factors impacting the historical development of junior/community colleges in America.

2. Discuss the junior/community college open-door policy.

3. What factors contributed to increased student-athlete participation in junior/community college athletic programs?

4. Discuss the historical evaluation of the two-year intercollegiate athletic association.

5. Discuss the impact of NCAA academic reform on junior/community college student-athlete recruitment at retention.

6. What is the nature of the coaching experiences at two-year colleges?

SUGGESTED READINGS

Heck, R., & Takahashi, R. (2006). Examining the impact of Proposition 48 on graduation rates in Division IA football recruiting behavior: Testing a policy change model. *Educational Policy*, 20(4), 587–614.

Wolff, A. (1987). The JUCO express. *Sports Illustrated*, 67(24), 6–8.

Wolff, A. (1991). Junior colleges. *Sports Illustrated*, 75(23), 119.

REFERENCES

Alnes, M. M., & Humm, L. (1993). A closer look at community/junior colleges. *Journal of National Intramural-Recreation Sports, 17*(3), 27–32.

Anderson, A., & South, D. (2000). Racial differences in collegiate recruitment, retention and graduation rates. In D. Brooks & R. Althouse (Eds.), *Racism in college athletics* (2nd ed., pp. 155–169). Morgantown, WV: Fitness Information Technology.

Bailey, T., Calcagno, J. C., Jenkins, D., Leinbach, T., & Kienzle, G. (2006). Is student-right-to-know all you should know? An analysis of community college graduation rates. *Research in Higher Education, 47*(5), 491–519.

Bennion, S. D. (1992). Junior college athletics: Participation opportunities and academic accountability. *New Directions for Institutional Research, 74*, 23–27.

Bradley, P. (2007). Priming the pipeline. *Community College Week*. Retrieved from http://www.ccweek.com/news/teplates/template.aspx?articleid = 124&zoneif = 7

Brooks, D. D., & Althouse, R. (Eds.). (2007). *Diversity and social justice in college sports*. Morgantown, WV: Fitness Information Technology.

Brooks, D., Weimer, T., & Blakemore, K. (1989, October). The coaches' role in the junior college recruitment network process. *JUCO Review, 4–6*, 17.

Brown, R. G. (1988). Current status of two-year college athletic programs in non-gender specific and non-football playing schools of the NJCAA. *Dissertation Abstracts International: 1189A*, (UMI No. 8914987)

Bryant, A. N. (2008). ERIC review: Community college students: Recent findings and trends. *Community College Review, 29*(3), 77–93.a

Castaneda, C. (2004). *A national overview of intercollegiate athletics at public community colleges*. Meridan, MS: MidSouth Partnership for Rural Community Colleges. Retrieved from: http://www.msgovt.org/files/castaneda.pdf

Cheslock, J. (2007). Who's playing college sports? *Women's Sports Foundation*.

Clark, B. R. (1960). *The open door college*. New York, McGraw-Hill.

Cohen, A. M., & Brawer, F. (1996). *The American community college*. San Francisco: Jossey-Bass Publishers.

Cox, B. (June, 2006). Changes in the Big East. *West Virginia University Compliance Monthly, 2*(5), 1–10.

Crow, M. G. (2006). Stayers and leavers among newbies: Influences on the early departure of HBCU freshmen. *University of Michigan*. Retrieved from http://gradwork.umi.com/3253252.html

Covell, D., & Barr, C.A. (2001). The ties that bind. *Journal of Higher Education, 72*(4), 414–452.

Doyle, W. R. (2006, May/June). *Community college transfers and college graduation. change, 38*(3), 56–58.

Dodd, D. (Feb, 2008). *Junior achievement: K-State counting on transfers for revival*. Retrieved from http://www.cbssports.com/print/collegefootball/story/10674645

Dye, D. (2010). Beyond division I: Other great options for high-school athletes. *College Choices. ESPN RISE*. Retrieved from www.dyestat.com/?pg = usCollege-Choices-Articles-Beyond-Division-I

Estler, S. E., &Nelson, L. (Eds.). (2005) Who calls the shots? Sports and university leadership, culture, and decision making. *ASHE Higher Education Report, 30*(5), 1–125.

Farrell, C. S. (1992). Junior colleges refute, address charges of athletic dumping ground. *Community College Week, 5*(7). Retrieved from www.ccweek.com/news/teplates/default.aspx?a = print.html

Fusch, G. E. (1996). *The community college of the 21st century*. British Columbia: Canada. CERIC Reproductive Service Document No. ED 417771.

Flowers, L. A. (2006). Effects of attending a 2-year institution on African American males' academic and social integration in the first year of college. *Teachers College Record, 108*(2), 267–286.

Gerdy, J. R. (1997). *The successful college athletic program: The new standard*. Phoenix, AZ: American Council on Education/Oryx Press.

Hartman, D. (2003). *Race, culture, and the revolt of the Black athlete: The 1968 Olympic protests and their aftermath*. Chicago, IL: University of Chicago Press.

Heck, R. H., & Takahashi, R. (2006). Examining the impact of Proposition 48 on graduation rates in Division 1A football and program recruiting behavior. *Educational Policy, 20*(4), 587–614.

Goffman, E. (1952). On cooling the mark out: Some aspects of adaption to failure. *Psychiatry: Journal of the Study of Interpersonal Relations, 15*(4), 451–463.

Keith, F. (2013). Minorities are separate and unequal: A look at minority hiring practices in collegiate and professional athletics. In D. Brooks & R. Althouse (Eds.), *Racism in college athletics* (3rd ed., pp. ix–xii). Morgantown, WV: Fitness Information Technology.

Lapchick, R. (2008). *A call to civil rights action in college football*. Retrieved from http://sports.espn.go.com/espn/print?id = 3755312

LeCrom, C., Warren, B., Cleark, H., Marolla, J., & Gerber, P. (2009). Factors contributing to student-athlete retention. *Journal of Issues in Intercollegiate Athletic*, 14–24. Reprinted from http://csri-jiia.org

Martin, K. L., & Christy, K. (2010). The rise and impact of high profile spectator sports on American higher education. *Journal of issues in Intercollegiate Athletics, 3*, 1–15. Reprinted from http://csri-jiia.org

Moltz, D. (2009). Hoop dream or recruiting nightmare? *Inside Higher Ed*. Retrieved from http://www.insidehighered.com/layout/set/print/2009/01/16/ncaa

Mumford, V. E. (2006). A look at women's participation in sports in Maryland two-year colleges. *The Sport Journal*. Retrieved from http://www.thesportjournal.org/article/look-womens-participation-sports-maryland-two-year-colleges

NCAA Student-Athlete Ethnicity Report. (1999–2009). Student-athlete ethnicity. Indianapolis, IN: NCAA.

Oakley, J. R. (1979). *The origins and development of the public junior college movement, 1850–1921* (Unpublished thesis). The University of North Carolina at Greensboro.

Paterson, A., Redrick, R., Alsop, W., & Brooks, D. (1980). Access to higher education for minorities: Lessons from the past. *Third Annual Conference of the World Future Society—Education Section, the Future Studies Program of Education*. University of Massachusetts at Amherst.

Pflueger, H. G. (1988). *The academic success and retention of community college athletes and non-athletes* (Doctoral dissertation). University of Maryland.

Price, J. (2007). The effects of higher admission standards on NCAA student-athletes: An analysis of Proposition 16. *Cornell University, Department of Policy Analysis and Management*. Ithaca, NY. Retrieved from http://Digitalcommons.ilr.cornell.edu/working papers

Raepple, R., Peery, D., & Hohman, H. (1982) Athletics in junior and community colleges. In J. Frey (Ed.), *The governance of intercollegiate athletics* (pp. 155–167). West Point, NY: Leisure Press.

Reitano, J. R. (1998). The community college mission: Access or anarchy? *Community Review, 16*, 119–126.

Romano, R. M., & Wisniewski, M. (2005). Tracking community college transfers using national student clearinghouse data. *AIR Professional File, 94*, 1–13.

Rooney, J. F. (1969). Up from the mines and out from the prairies: Some geographical implications of football in the United States. *Geographical Review, 49*(4), 471–492.

Rooney, J. F. (1974). *A geography of American sport from cabin creek to Anaheim*. Reading, MA: Addison Wesley Publishing Company.

Sack, A. L. (1988). College sport and the student-athlete. *Journal of Sport and Social Issues, 11*(1), 165–166.

Sage, G. (1990). *Power and ideology in American sport: A critical perspective*. Champaign, IL: Human Kinetics.

Shulman, J. L., & Bowen, W. G. (2001). *The game of life: College sports and educational values*. Princeton, NJ: Princeton University Press.

Student Aid and Fiscal Responsibility Act of 2009 (H.R. 3221). Retrieved from http://www.govtrack.us/congress/bills/111/hr3221

Teets, K. (2013). Migration of the international student athlete into the NCAA. In D. Brooks & R. Althouse (Eds.), *Racism in college athletics* (3rd ed.) (pp. 379–392). Morgantown, WV: Fitness Information Technology

Voorhees, R. A., & Zhan, J. (2000). Intentions and goals at the community college: Associating student perceptions and demographics. *Community College Journal of Research and Practice, 24*(3), 219–232.

Washington, R. E., & Karen, D. (2010). *Sport, power and society: Institutions and practices: A reader*. Boulder, CO: Westview Press.

Williams, M., & Pennington, K. (2006). Community college president's perception of intercollegiate athletics. *Community College Enterprise, 12*(2), 91–104.

Wolff, A. (1987). The JUCO express. *Sports llustrated, 67*(24), 6–8.

Wolff, A. (1991). Junior colleges. *Sports Illustrated, 75*(23), 119.

Ullmann, J. (2010). *Guilty by association*. Retrieved from http://www.sportsullmannac.clippings/guiltybyassociation.php

Section III:
Gender and Race Intersections

Forty years after the passing of the Educational Amendment Act of 1972, also known as Title IX, gender equity continues to be a serious issue confronting the National Collegiate Athletic Association (NCAA). Jackson provides a discussion of the origin of Title IX legislation, offers enforcement cases, and describes the three-prong test to measure compliance in Chapter 8. Schools can comply by using any one of a three-prong test: 1) proportionality, 2) continuing history and expansion, and 3) interests and abilities. Most colleges and universities comply using proportionality. The enrollment for males at historically Black colleges and universities (HBCUs) is decreasing and enrollment for females is increasing. Consequently, if this trend is not reversed (i.e., increased enrollment of African American males) HBCUs will not be able to meet the proportionality prong under Title IX.

Since 1972 participation of women in college sports has continued to increase, while at the same time the number of African American women in NCAA leadership positions continues to lag far behind. With passage of federal legislation (i.e., Title IX, Civil Rights Act of 1991) one might have anticipated an increase in the number of women holding leadership positions within collegiate athletics, but data does not support this expectation. In Chapter 9, Abney examines the glass-ceiling effect on the ability of African American females to gain access to NCAA head coaching and administrative positions within sports. Abney's recommendation to change the employment process and workplace culture depends upon the NCAA to establish a rule to ensure that institutions interview at least one minority candidate for coaching and athletic administrative positions.

CHAPTER 8

The Impact of Title IX on HBCU Campuses

CRYSHANNA A. JACKSON

Abstract

Thirty six years after the passing of the Educational Amendment Act of 1972, also known as Title IX, gender equity continues to emerge as a serious issue for the National Collegiate Athletic Association (NCAA). Colleges and universities can comply with Title IX by using the three-prong test: prong one (proportionality), prong two (continuing history and expansion), and prong three (interests and abilities). The majority of colleges and universities comply with Title IX by using prong one (proportionality). This prong requires the college or university to spend the same percentage on their athletic programs as the undergraduate population of the institution. historically Black colleges and universities (HBCUs) are put at a disadvantage when trying to comply with Title IX requirements because the average undergraduate population for females is 69% as compared to 31% males. It is impossible for HBCUs to spend almost 70% of their athletic budget on female athletics. Another pressing issue that HBCUs face is that the enrollment for men in higher education overall has decreased and currently there is almost a 2-1 female-male ratio. This chapter explains the historical impact of Title IX on women's athletics over time, examines unintended consequences of Title IX, researches recent trends in the enrollment of African American males, and offers suggestions for future Title IX legislation.

Key Terms		
• emerging sports	•	Office of Civil Rights
• gender discrimination	•	racial discrimination
• gender equity	•	social equity
• HBCUs	•	three-prong test
• nonrevenue sports	•	Title IX

TITLE IX: THE EDUCATION AMENDMENT ACT OF 1972

Introduction

History. After the civil rights and women's rights movement of the 1960s and 70s, there was still a lingering concern about social equity in regards to women. *Social equity* is the notion that all men and women are created equal and therefore should be provided with equal opportunities in every area of society (Rice, 2004). However, when it came to education women were found to be at a significant disadvantage when compared to men due to gender discrimination. For example in the early part of the 1900s only 4% of students that attended medical schools were women (Cole, 1986). Cole (1986) attributes this to the socialization of the time that women were the weaker sex and their main responsibility to society was to stay home and bear children. Title IX is part of the Educational Amendment Act of 1972 and was passed in an attempt to prohibit gender discrimination in any educational setting that receives federal funding. Title IX states,

> No person in the United States shall, on the basis of sex, be excluded from participation in, be denied the benefits of, or be subjected to discrimination under any educational program or activity receiving federal financial assistance. (Title 20 U.S.C.)

Title IX was legislation passed by Congress on June 8, 1972 (Valentin, 1997). Title IX covers every area of an educational institution and makes it illegal for any educational institution, from pre kindergarten all the way to post secondary, to discriminate based on gender in admission of students, recruitment of students, courses offered, counseling, financial aid, housing, scholarships, or any other service that is provided to students by that particular institution, including athletics (Gavora, 2002). Title IX can be applied to every school that receives federal funds through grants, scholarships, or any other type of support given to students for extracurricular programs, research, and/or academics, directly or indirectly. If an institution, public or private, does not comply with Title IX and is found by the Office of Civil Rights (OCR) to participate in gender-based discrimination, federal funds can be withdrawn from that institution (Coakley, 2004). Although Title IX covers every area of an educational setting, over the past 36 years it has become synonymous with college athletics.

Coakley (2004) argued that the notoriety between Title IX and college athletics emerged when it was realized that Title IX would also be applied to interscholastic sports. In the world of sports, where everything had been highly male dominated and organized around the interests of males for over 100 years, the idea of gender equity was thought to be extremely radical and politically motivated.

Problems with Title IX Compliance

Once Title IX was officially signed into legislation it could and would be enforced. It seemed clear to colleges and institutions how to combat gender discrimination when it came to recruitment, admission, housing, and other areas in the classroom setting but providing gender equity in college athletics under Title IX proved to be a confusing and difficult task. In 1979, seven years after Title IX was passed, the assistant secretary of the OCR sent out a letter to clarify Title IX compliance questions for intercollegiate athletics. The letter stated that institutions sponsoring any athletic program were required by law to provide equal athletic opportunities for males and females. This letter also informed the institutions of their obligation to effectively accommodate the athletic interests and abilities of both genders using whatever means necessary in order to provide equal athletic opportunities (U.S. Department of Civil Rights the Assistant Secretary, 1979). The OCR is responsible for the enforcement of the regulations specified by Title IX, including the specific context pertaining to college athletics.

Once Title IX was enacted the OCR received numerous complaints alleging noncompliance with Title IX (Valentin, 1997). These complaints could not always be resolved amicably and the parties were forced into court to make their claims. There were numerous cases in regards to Title IX but three particular cases impacted the way Title IX is currently enforced. One of the most talked about and influential court cases where students sought to have Title IX enforced was *Grove City v. Bell* (1984). The ruling of this case affected what type of universities, private, public, or both, were found under Title IX's jurisdiction (Agthe & Billings, 2000). Grove City College (Pennsylvania) claimed that since they were a private college and their athletic program did not receive federal funds directly, they were not under the jurisdiction of Title IX in regards to athletics. In 1984 the Supreme Court ruled in favor of Grove City College, citing that the government did not provide

The introduction of Title IX has had both positive and negative effects on female athletes at HBCUs. Courtesy of iStockPhoto

direct funding. The ruling by the Supreme Court in this case made it so that the tenets of Title IX applied only to programs that received federal funds directly. Most athletic departments do not receive direct federal funds, and therefore did not have to comply with Title IX legislation under this ruling.

Title IX supporters felt that the *Grove City v. Bell* ruling was unjust and that gender discrimination should not be tolerated in any college or university's athletic program. After a review of the previous case the court agreed and in 1987 the Civil Rights Restoration Act was passed. This Act was passed as an attempt to encourage institutions to comply with Title IX by stating that if any part of the institution was receiving any federal funds, directly or indirectly, that institution must then comply with Title IX (Agthe & Billings, 2000). Therefore, an educational institution as a whole must comply with Title IX as long as any part of the institution received federal funds. If a public or private institution enrolled students who receive federal funds for any educational purposes, that institution is prohibited from gender discrimination under Title IX. The majority of colleges and universities enroll students that receive Pell grants, making Title IX applicable to them.

Another case pertaining to the interpretation of Title IX dealt with measuring the interests of the underrepresented gender (prong three). In the case *Cohen v. Brown* (1992), female students brought suit against Brown University to maintain varsity status for women's gymnastics and volleyball programs. Brown University claimed that it needed to drop four sport programs for financial reasons, men's water polo and golf along with the women's gymnastics and volleyball teams (Shaw, 1995). Members of the university's women's volleyball and gymnastic teams sued under Title IX claiming that by dropping the two women sports the university was not meeting the interests or abilities of the female students. The district court ordered Brown University to submit a plan to demonstrate how they would be in compliance with Title IX if they eliminated the women's programs. The court reviewed the plan that Brown University submitted and rejected it, claiming it did not meet the requirements of Title IX. Brown University was ordered by the court to maintain the women's programs at varsity status. In the court's opinion, "an institution violates Title IX if it ineffectively accommodates its students' interests and abilities in athletics" (Pieronek, 2000).

Franklin v. Gwinnett (1992) was very instrumental in the enforcement of Title IX because this case was the first time that any monetary damages were awarded to a plaintiff. However, *Franklin v. Gwinnett* was not a Title IX case pertaining to athletics, but it involved sexual harassment. The plaintiffs in this case fought all the way to the Supreme Court in an effort to find out the availability of monetary damages. Franklin, a high school sophomore in 1986, alleged that she was sexually harassed by one of her teachers. Franklin filed a lawsuit with OCR and it was found that the school district was in violation of Title IX. Franklin filed for damages in a trial court, but her case was dismissed (Russo, 2001).

The court dismissed Franklin's complaint on the basis that monetary awards were not available under Title IX (Cullers, 1995). When taken to the Supreme Court the ruling was reversed, and it was found that Title IX does support the right for damages to be awarded. Carpenter and Acosta (2004) suggested that the 1992 *Franklin v. Gwinnett* decision was an important victory for Title IX supporters, because before this case plaintiffs could not receive punitive and compensatory damages. Colleges and universities now had an even larger incentive to enforce Title IX because if they were found noncompliant and sued they would have to pay the plaintiffs monetary damages.

In an effort to eliminate gender discrimination from schools several bills were passed, including the Improving America's Schools Act (H.R.6). President Clinton signed this bill into law on October 4, 1994. This bill authorized the awarding of grants in an effort to conduct activities at all educational levels in order to help those institutions become compliant with Title IX (US Department of Education, 1994). The counterpart to this bill was the Equity in Interscholastic Athletics Disclosure Act (EIADA); the passing of this Act was seen as a much needed change for Title IX supporters. The EADA requires all colleges with male and female students enrolled, that participate in federal student aid programs, and sponsor intercollegiate athletic programs to make available an annual report available to the general public. The report must include for each varsity team the number of participants, total operating expenses, gender of the head coach of each team, number of assistant coaches and gender, amount of money spent on athletic aid, total recruiting expenses, total revenues produced by all male and female teams, and the annual salaries of all head coaches. This information is to be collected and reported yearly and disclosed to students and the public on an annual basis (U.S. Department of Education, 1994).

Additional research found that lawsuits brought under Title IX provided more knowledge and ways to effectively become in compliance with Title IX by focusing more on enforcement and not just jurisdiction (Carpenter & Acosta, 2004).

The Three-Prong Test

Even though Title IX was passed more than 35 years ago, compliance issues still remain. Public pressures along with the rulings in *Grove City v. Bell*, *Cohen v. Brown*, and *Franklin v. Gwinnett* have supported the enforcement of Title IX. One of the problems with compliance is that university athletic departments along with the NCAA did not start their efforts to comply with Title IX when it was first passed in 1972. Thelin (2000) suggested that the reason institutions did not move quicker to promote gender equity was they disagreed with the law and were silently protesting. Another reason for the delay in enforcement was due to federal agencies trying to agree on a criterion to hold colleges and universities accountable and the NCAA did not incorporate women's sports into their jurisdiction until 1981.

Eitzen and Sage (2003) suggested that delay in enforcement has been a major obstacle when dealing with Title IX. Some of these obstacles included legal challenges staged by various groups along with the NCAA being resistant when it comes to compliance. The NCAA did not form the gender equity task force until 1992 to examine problems of compliance at colleges and universities (NCAA, 1993). The lack of compliance over the past 35 years has resulted in many of the current issues such as budgetary constraints, the elimination of men's sports, and a negative impact on historically Black colleges and universities (HBCUs).

Title IX does not require schools and universities to treat men and women's sports as equal, but it does mandate that benefits should be comparable for both (Greenlee, 1997). There are three main criteria a university must meet in order to be in compliance with Title IX, which is commonly referred to as the three-prong test. The Office of Civil Rights uses the three prong test in stages, because if a school is unable to comply under the first section it may do so under the second part, and if they still do not comply they have one final opportunity to comply under the third section (Gavora, 2002).

The first prong is *proportionality*, which means that the number of women competing on sports teams must be in proportion with the institution's undergraduate population. The Academic Performance Index says that in order for a school to be in compliance with part one, they must provide reasonable participation opportunities and provide comparable award opportunities for the members of each sex. For example, if a school has an undergraduate population that is 48% male and 52% female then approximately 52% of the athletic budget should be allocated to female athletics (Suggs, 2003). Along with the first part the OCR stressed that the equitable assignment of a colleges athletic scholarship should be made available for men's and women's programs in a way that is substantially proportionate to participation rates of male and female athletes (O'Shea & Cantu, 1998).

The second prong of the three-prong test is a *continuing history* of providing opportunities by the athletic department being evaluated. Colleges and universities must show a continuing practice of program expansion for the underrepresented gender, which in the majority of cases are women. However, no set standards of continuing expansion exist (Suggs, 2003a). The third prong of the test is the *interests and abilities* section. The school must show a good faith effort that they are fully and effectively accommodating the interests and abilities of the underrepresented gender attending the university (Suggs, 2003a). If an institution does not have women's sports, then, in theory, the institution must show that none of the women enrolled in that institution are interested in participating in athletics. An institution can also use this part if they offer a few women's sports and the institution believes that there are no other varsity sports in which women want to participate in. However, if there are club sports in existence requesting varsity status, this part cannot be used. If an institution has a club sport with enough members to promote it to a varsity sport, that institution is unable to use the interests and abilities part (Suggs, 2003b).

Gavora (2002) believes that the three-prong test is regressive and is not the best way to measure compliance with Title IX. If noncompliance is found under prong one then the second prong is measured as a way to support the first. The problem with using prong two, which requires colleges and universities to show proof of a continuing history of program expansion, is that it does not specify how long institutions must demonstrate program expansion. The third prong of interest and abilities has been found by some to be unreliable. Gavora (2002) argued that this is because the OCR has provided limited guidance for institutions and many critics of the law argue that the three-prong test is really a one-part test of proportionality.

Unintended Consequences of Title IX

Once Title IX enforcement is underway, colleges and universities must decide how they will comply. Title IX specialist and administrators are placed in difficult situations when trying meet compliance. The intent of Title IX was to alleviate gender discrimination but many administrators are forced with the decision of considering the student athlete's best interest (providing sport opportunities) versus what is financially affordable for the institution (eliminating sport teams). In order to meet proportionality many universities have eliminated men's nonrevenue sports teams. Nonrevenue sports teams are those sports other than football and men's basketball that do not bring in a profit to the university. The elimination of men's sport programs is one of the unintended consequences of Title IX. The frequent assertion opponents of Title IX argue is that the progress that women have made under Title IX has required nonrevenue male sports to be eliminated, therefore taking away opportunities for men in order to provide opportunities for women (Sabo,1998).

Table 8.1 shows that between 1981 and 1999 the number of participants in college athletics varied by the sports programs offered. However women participants increased 81% while male participants only increased by 5%. The number of male participants is significantly greater than the number of female participants. There are 72,683 male student athletes as compared to 11, 688 for females. There are 330 more women's athletic teams but men's teams require larger rosters, giving men more opportunities to participate but in fewer sports.

Table 8.2 shows the number of male and female sports teams added between 1981 and 1999. As shown in Table 8.2 over half of men's sports experienced a decrease in the number of teams. For women, soccer had the largest increase of teams with 135. About 80% of colleges and universities added one or more women's sport teams and two-thirds of these institutions were able to complete this without discontinuing any teams. The results show that overall between 1982 and 1999 women's sport teams increased by 66% while men's teams increased by less than one percent.

Most colleges and universities use prong one (proportionality) to meet Title IX compliance (Gavora, 2002). The reason for using the proportionality prong of Title IX is lack of information on what constitutes compliance under prong two (continuing history of expansion) and prong three (interests and abilities). It is unclear under prong two how much expansion is enough to meet compliance. Also, due to budgetary constraints and space, an institution can only feasibly add a certain number of sport programs. Prong three also provides challenges to colleges and universities. The NCAA has developed a survey that schools can send out to incoming freshmen to measure interests and abilities, but responses to the survey are not mandatory, the surveys are sent out electronically using email, schools have a low response rate, and the institutions are responsible for analyzing the data and submitting the report, which is very time consuming (Jackson, 2006). These restrictions make it almost impossible for colleges and universities to meet Title IX compliance using any prong but prong one.

One way in which schools are held accountable is the Equity in Disclosure Act. The Equity in Disclosure Act requires that institutions of higher education publish their par-

Table 8.1.	Change in Number of Participants for NAIA and NCAA Schools 1981–1999			
	Women		**Men**	
Sport	Participants	% of change	Participants	% of change
Soccer	18,132	977	1,932	10
Indoor Track	9,901	164	2,037	13
Outdoor Track	7,678	64	−1,706	−7
Cross Country	7,488	135	−151	−1
Softball	6,504	60	−1,706	−7
Rowing	4,441	374	391	19
Basketball	4,419	35	1,552	9
Volleyball	3,841	33	246	28
Swimming	3,516	54	943	11
Golf	2,080	196	42	>1
Lacrosse	2,101	79	2,000	48
Tennis	1,470	19	−1,405	−14
Waterpolo	727	3,826	−95	−9
Ice Hockey	564	168	−129	−3
Equestrian	532	527	351	−1,755
Skiing	176	49	−282	33
Squash	127	53	1	>1
Rifle	94	104	−436	−56
Synchronized Swimming	90	184	n/a	n/a
Archery	31	41	3	5
Badminton	−47	−33	−12	−32
Bowling	68	−77	39	38
Fencing	−171	−22	−773	−54
Field Hockey	−229	−4	n/a	n/a
Gymnastics	−683	−31	−1,022	−73
Football	n/a	n/a	7,199	14
Baseball	n/a	n/a	5,452	22
Sailing	n/a	n/a	45	19
Wrestling	n/a	n/a	−2,648	−29
TOTAL	**72,683**	**81**	**11,688**	**5**

Source: US General Accounting Office Report to Congressional Requesters. Intercollegiate Athletics Four-Year Colleges' Experiences Adding and Discontinuing Teams. March, 2001

Table 8.2.	Change in Number of Teams for NAIA and NCAA Schools 1981–1999			
	Women		**Men**	
Sport	Number added	% of change	Number added	% of change
Soccer	846	1,058	135	18
Indoor Track	304	106	25	5
Outdoor Track	243	46	−27	−4
Cross Country	516	104	31	3
Softball	432	78	n/a	n/a
Rowing	79	184	22	46
Basketball	302	33	82	7
Volleyball	350	43	16	25
Swimming	101	28	−25	−6
Golf	277	222	62	8
Lacrosse	108	103	59	43
Tennis	248	34	−84	−9
Waterpolo	36	3,600	−6	−12
Ice Hockey	23	135	−10	−7
Equestrian	34	486	31	1,550
Skiing	11	33	−15	−27
Squash	11	69	0	0
Rifle	28	175	−42	−51
Synchronized Swimming	4	133	n/a	n/a
Archery	−3	−33	n/a	n/a
Badminton	−1	−9	0	0
Bowling	−6	−55	−3	−23
Fencing	−31	−41	−42	−53
Field Hockey	−28	−10	n/a	n/a
Gymnastics	−100	−53	−56	−68
Football	n/a	n/a	−37	−5
Baseball	n/a	n/a	85	9
Sailing	n/a	n/a	7	47
Wrestling	n/a	n/a	−171	−40
TOTAL	**3,784**	**66**	**36**	**0.4**

Source: US General Accounting Office Report to Congressional Requesters. Intercollegiate Athletics Four-Year Colleges' Experiences Adding and Discontinuing Teams. March, 2001

ticipation rates for male and female athletes, operating expenses, coaches' salaries, scholarship budgets and more. This information is provided by the U.S. Department of Education to help give prospective students and their families a way to gain valuable information on schools of interest to prospective applicants. The Secretary of Education collects financial and statistical information on men's and women's college sports (http://ope.ed.gov/athletics/index.asp). Suggs (1999) found that the U.S. Department of Education require colleges and universities to provide additional information about the money spent on men and women's sport teams to help alleviate any argument about discrepancies in spending on athletics but also furthers the argument that prong one is the only viable option for Title IX compliance.

Even with the elimination of men's sports, the threat of losing federal funding, and possibly being required to pay monetary damages, Title IX compliance is still lacking. In 2000 women at Division I universities made up approximately 53% of the undergraduate population, around 42% of the student-athlete population but only received 30% of the total operating expenses at the universities. It has been argued that schools with football programs are less likely to be in compliance (Jackson, 2006). Football programs typically command a larger portion of the athletic budget and have a large number of players on the roster. When compared with the number of women participating in sports program, some argue that compliance and equity is very difficult to achieve for institutions with football programs due to their large rosters and its expense.

Suggs (2002a) suggests that many times athletic directors spend the majority of the athletic budget on the larger sports of football and men's basketball in an attempt to bring in money to the college or university. Athletic directors also have an incentive to support women's sports so that they will not be sued under Title IX; this leads to the smaller men's sports receiving whatever money is left over, often leading to men's sport teams being eliminated due to a lack of resources.

The dilemma when it pertains to college athletics is that college sports programs are suppose to be an educational venture, making them covered under Title IX. However, most college athletic departments are operated as a "big business." This puts pressure on colleges and universities to overlook the law of Title IX and follow the money. Almost all of the other departments at colleges and universities were able to adapt to Title IX without any major debate proving that if college sports were truly an educational venture, the idea that equitable opportunities should not be afforded to males and females would be considered absurd, but since schools are making a profit from college sports, equity is disregarded as the mitigating factor and opportunities are provided to whatever sports are bringing in the most money (Suggs, 2002b).

Pressure for Enforcement

In 1992, a gender equity task force was formed, which consisted of a 16-member panel that completed a gender equity survey and submitted the final report to the NCAA council in August 1993. Recommendations included that the NCAA should take an affirmative stance in an effort to ensure equality for women in intercollegiate athletics and develop a firm definition of gender equity (Shaw, 1995).

The NCAA gender task force defined gender equity as follows:

- The Association asserts the values of equitable participation and treatment of men and women in intercollegiate athletics through its structure, programs, legislation and policies. It is the responsibility of the Association to act affirmatively to ensure equity in the quantity and quality of participation in women's athletics.

- At an institutional level, gender equity in intercollegiate athletics describes an environment in which fair and equitable distribution of overall athletics opportunities benefits and resources are available to women and men and in which student-athletes, coaches, and athletic administrators are not subject to gender-based discrimination.

- An athletic program can be considered gender equitable when the participants in both the men's and women's sports programs would accept as fair and equitable the overall program of the other gender. No individual should be discriminated against on the basis of gender, institutionally or nationally, in intercollegiate athletics. (NCAA Gender-Equity Task Force Report, 1993, p. 2)

Table 8.3.	2009 NCAA Emerging Sports for Female Athletes	
Emerging Sports	**Former Emerging Sports***
Archery	Rowing
Badminton	Water Polo
Equestrian	Ice Hockey
Rugby	Bowling
Squash	
Synchronized Swimming	
Team Handball	

*Currently, part of the NCAA championships and are no longer considered emerging.
Source: http://www.ncaa.org/wps/ncaa?ContentID=40539.

The NCAA task force encouraged NCAA member institutions to support emerging sports for women and endorsed the three-prong test as an appropriate measure of equitable participation. Emerging sports are sports recognized by the NCAA that are intended to provide additional athletic opportunities to female student-athletes. Colleges and universities are allowed to use emerging sports to help meet the NCAA minimum sports-sponsorship requirements and also to meet the NCAA's minimum financial aid awards.

These recommendations added even more pressure to colleges and universities to meet Title IX compliance and did nothing to address the major concerns over prongs two and three of the prong test. It reasserted a commitment to use the three-prong test as a way to measure Title IX compliance without addressing ways to better accommodate an institution using prongs two and three, making compliance under prong one the major focus of institutions of higher education.

AFRICAN AMERICANS AND HIGHER EDUCATION

Historically Black Colleges and Universities

Historically Black colleges and universities (HBCUs) were established to provide quality opportunities for African American students in higher education. African Americans faced racial discrimination at predominately White institutions and had restricted access. An HBCU is defined as any historically Black college or university established prior to 1964, with a mission focused on the education of Black Americans, and nationally accredited by a nationally recognized accrediting agency or association (U.S. Department of Education, 2009).

The establishment of HBCUs came about with the assistance of numerous institutions such as Black churches, missionaries, private philanthropists, and some government initiatives (Palmer & Gasman, 2008). Research has shown that HBCUs offer more inclusive learning environments and support programs for African American students and positively affect student outcomes (Harper et al., 2004). HBCUs were created during a time that education for African Americans was not supported by society as a whole. African Americans were discouraged from learning and often education was nearly impossible to obtain (HBCUs models for success, 2006). *Brown v. Board of Education* was a landmark case in history when the United States Supreme Court ruled that separate facilities were always inherently unequal and that students were no longer legally allowed to be sent to race based schools. Even with the Supreme Court ruling society was unreceptive to the notion of allowing African American students to integrate White schools.

According to Harper et al. (2004), when comparing African American students attending HBCUs and those attending predominately White institutions, HBCUs offered a larger assortment of culturally appealing venues, students felt a greater sense of connection and power, and students were found to have to have a significantly higher sense of self (psychological, cognitive, and intellectual). However, while these studies show the positive impact of HBCUs, when comparing African American women to African American men in the 1960s (pre Title IX), women were found to have significant disadvantages to their male counterparts. Female students had lower educational and career goals than men, men were three times as likely to show an interest in enrolling in graduate and professional school upon graduation, and male students reported higher levels of satisfaction with their experiences in the classroom (Harper et al., 2004). These finding suggest that African American women suffered a double disadvantage in society facing racial and gender discrimination. The passing of Title IX in 1972 provided African American women opportunities to receive the same benefits from their education as their male counterparts.

Recent research suggests that HBCUs provide a nurturing family-like environment with faculty members supporting the progress of the students allowing for more community involvement and student satisfaction. Studies have also found that African American students perform well academically regardless of their socioeconomic backgrounds (Palmer & Gasman, 2008). This success can be attributed to the HBCUs willingness to admit students who would be considered not ready for college level work and providing them with the skills necessary to not only graduate, but to also make a positive contribution to society.

HBCUs were established during a time when racial discrimination in the United States made it impossible for African American students to receive a quality education. Therefore students relied on these institutions to make sure that they were able to receive a proper education and contribute to society. However, legislation, integration, and programming initiatives have made enrollment in predominately White institutions more accessible for African American students. Certain government programs were designed to help eliminate de jure segregation all together by encouraging integration. *De jure segregation* refers to segregation not based on law but on choices that individuals make that put them in homogeneous environments such as Black churches, schools or associations. This has caused enrollment at HBCUs to rapidly decrease. Whereas there was a time when most African Americans attending colleges and universities attended an HBCU, HBCUs currently enroll only about 16% of African American undergraduates (Palmer & Gasman, 2008). Low enrollment and the problems HBCUs face in regards to Title IX compliance in athletics have caused concern over the future of HBCUs. Currently, HBCUs only make up 3% of the total US institutions of higher education and about 2% of the total college enrollment. As a group HBCUs have undergone a decline in enrollment because federal desegregation policies have not increased the number of non-Black students attending these institutions (Sissisko & Shiau, 2005).

HBCUs and Title IX Compliance

HBCUs are held to the same standards as other colleges and universities when it comes to Title IX compliance in athletics. Title IX has provided numerous opportunities for women athletes in regards to admission, recruitment, counseling, facilities, and athletics. However, when it comes to athletics the majority of schools use prong one (proportionality) to prove compliance. Although universities are allowed to choose to use prong two or three as a way to meet compliance, very few institutions view continuing history of expansion or interests and abilities as viable options.

The difficulty colleges and universities face in using prongs two or three to meet compliance requirements force institutions of higher education to use prong one. This holds true for HBCUs as well. The problem facing HBCUs as compared to other colleges and universities is that enrollment for males at HBCUs is decreasing and enrollment for females is increasing. The average enrollment for men at HBCUs is 39% and for women it is 61% ("Study shows," 2008). In order to meet Title IX compliance 39% of HBCUs athletic budget should go to male athletes and 61% to female athletes. A 2008 report released by the college sports council found that 73% of HBCUs are in noncompliance with prong one. It was also found that the gender ratio for male and females is reaching 2-1 (study shows, 2008).

Table 8.4 shows the enrollment data for 75 HBCUs in 2007. The data was collected by the U.S. Department of Education Database. The table shows that on average women make up 61% of the undergraduate population. In order to be in compliance with prong one, on average 61% of the athletic budget should be spent on female athletics. If schools have large male sport programs such as football, it makes it difficult to meet compliance under prong one.

Increasing male enrollment at HBCUs is viewed by some as a daunting task. There are numerous factors that can be attributed to the high disparities of enrollment when comparing male and female students at HBCUs. According to Smith and Fleming (2006) there is a disparity between African American female students and male students, in which women by far outnumber men enrolled in college. Studies have shown that only 41% of African American young men graduate with their high school class (HBCUs model for success, 2006). If African American males are unable to obtain a high school diploma they will be unable to attend college. HBCUs historically attract African American students to enroll; The fewer students graduating from high school, the smaller the pool of eligible students to choose from.

This makes compliance under Title IX's prong one very difficult for HBCUs. HBCUs are unable to meet the proportionality standards of Title IX due to disproportionate gender enrollment at the institutions. The decrease of enrollment at HBCUs can also be attributed to the increased opportunities African Americans have to attend predominately White institutions. Predominately White institutions have programs and funding de-

Table 8.4.	Historically Black Colleges and Universities Enrollment Rates	
	Male	**Female**
Number of Students	82,736	129,140
Undergraduate Percentage	39%	61%

Source: http://www.savingsports.org. Study shows historically Black colleges and universities Struggle to meet Title IX's proportionality test.

signed in order to recruit and maintain minority students. An example of such programs is affirmative action. This policy was designed to take an applicant's race, ethnicity, and gender into consideration when selecting future students for enrollment and has substantially increased the number of women and African American enrollment at colleges and universities (Moses, 2002). Allen et al. (2005) released a study that showed African American women enroll in four-year institutions at higher rates than their male counterparts. About 59% of all first time African American students are women and women constitute about 56% of all undergraduates. One way schools attract students is by offering sport programs. However under Title IX regulations' many HBCUs cannot offer anymore male sport programs to recruit more male students (Allen et al., 2005). HBCUs also have not been able to recruit a significant amount of non-Black students to enroll. The desegregation and affirmative action program have allowed African Americans access to predominately White colleges and universities, but non-Black students have not used these programs in the same way to enroll in HBCUs.

Prong two has also caused problems with enrollment at HBCUs. Under prong two institutions can prove compliance with Title IX if they show an effort of continuing history of expansion. HBCUs were not as quick to add sport programs as some of the predominately White colleges and universities (Lomax, 2008). From 1981–1999, 846 colleges and universities added soccer programs (Table 8.2); however, only one HBCU added soccer. HBCUs have added bowling as a varsity level women's sport. HBCUs chose bowling as a sport program to add for women because it was inexpensive and did not require the institutions to build any new facilities (Lomax, 2008).

This leaves prong three (interests and abilities). HBCUs can prove compliance with Title IX if they can fully and effectively accommodate the interests and abilities of the underrepresented gender. The use of surveys as a way to measure Title IX compliance has been debated over the years. The Office of Civil Rights released a report saying the survey approach alone is inadequate when measuring Title IX compliance and the methodology in which the surveys are sent out can provide unreliable results (Sabo & Grant, 2005). HBCUs must find a way to comply with Title IX so that they are not penalized.

CONCLUSION

Title IX has changed the way colleges and universities view college athletics. This legislation has had a significant impact on the way in which women athletes are viewed in society. Women's basketball is becoming more popular and teams like the University of Tennessee are putting women athletes in the spotlight. However, the progress of Title IX has come at the expense of some. Male athletes that participate in wrestling, swimming, and other nonrevenue sports have seen their sports being eliminated while women's teams have been added in the name of Title IX compliance. This is one of the many unintended consequences of Title IX. HBCUs are also on the losing end of Title IX compliance. Societal factors that have provided African American's opportunities to end practices of racial discrimination have inadvertently taken away students that would have otherwise only been allowed to attend HBCUs. Over the years HBCUs have watched their enrollment drop. Now with the current trend of more women enrolled in college than men, and even more disproportionate enrollment of African American females in college than African American males, the majority of HBCUs cannot meet compliance under Title IX, Colleges and universities that have a football program are especially at a disadvantage.

These factors lead researchers to question what can be done to ensure women still are treated fairly, but not at the expense of men. The OCR has a duty to make sure that prongs two and three are viable prongs to use in order to measure Title IX compliance. HBCUs should be in a position in which they can prove compliance of Title IX by using prong one, two, or three. It is recommended that all colleges and universities are required to identify which part of the three-part test they use to meet Title IX compliance and why. This would help HBCUs to identify other institutions that are in compliance and develop methods to benefit their institutions. This would also allow schools to be held accountable for noncompliance immediately and not have a long OCR investigation. Race should also be a factor with looking at Title IX compliance. Women of color are less likely to participate in the emerging sports offered by the NCAA, putting HBCUs at another disadvantage. If schools choose to use prong three to measure Title IX compliance, the surveys should be mandatory and must be completed online before students can register for classes. This would increase the response rates and ensure that all the students' interests and abilities were measured. It is also recommended that a more efficient measure of compliance is developed by the OCR. Currently, only prong one can accurately be measured, and over 90% of Division I schools are not in compliance with Title IX using prong one (Jackson, 2006).

Providing efficient ways to measure prongs two and three would give colleges and universities who are not close to meeting prong one other ways to prove gender equity. Until the recent trends are reversed and more African American males are entering into colleges and universities, Title IX compliance will remain an issue for HBCUs. The OCR needs to provide all colleges and universities ways to accurately measure Title IX and provide gender equity to all students.

STUDY QUESTIONS

1. Why was *Franklin v. Gwinnett* significant to Title IX even though it dealt with sexual harassment?

2. Why do the majority of colleges and universities tend to use prong one for Title IX compliance as opposed to prongs two and three?

3. What factor makes it nearly impossible for HBCUs to meet Title IX compliance?

4. What are some societal factors that make it less likely for African American males to enroll in colleges and universities?

5. What might HBCUs do in an effort to meet Title IX compliance?

SUGGESTED READINGS

Lomax, M. (2008) *Sports and the racial divide African American and Latino experience in an era of change*. Jackson, MS: University Press of Mississippi.

Smith, E. (2007). *Race, sport, and the American dream*. Durham, NC: Carolina Academic Press.

REFERENCES

Agthe, D., & Billings, R. (2000). The role of football profits in meeting Title IX gender equity regulations and policy. *Journal of Sport Management, 14*, 28–40.

Allen, W., Jayakuma, U., Griffin, K., Korn, W., & Hurtado, S. (2005). *Black undergraduates from Bakke to Grutter: Freshmen status trends and prospects, 1971–2004*. Los Angeles, CA: Higher Education Research Institute, UCLA.

Carpenter, L., & Acosta, V. (2004). *Women in intercollegiate sport: A longitudinal study twenty-seven year update*. Brooklyn College, NY: City University of New York.

Coakley, J. (2004). *Sports in society*. Colorado Springs, CO: University of Colorado.

Cole, S. (1986) Sex discrimination and admission to medical school, 1929–1984. *The American Journal of Sociology*, *92*(3), 549–567.

Cullers, M. (1995, Sum). The availability of Title IX damages for employees after Franklin v. Gwinnett county public schools. *Case Western Reserve Law Review, 45,* 1325–1341.

Eitzen, D., & Sage, G. (2003). *Sociology of North American sport* (7th ed.). Boston, MA: McGraw Hill.

Gavora, J. (2002). *Tilting the playing field*. San Francisco, CA: Encounter Books.

Greenlee, C. (1997). Title IX: Does help for women come at the expense of African-American? *Black Issues in Higher Education, 14,* 24–27.

Harper, S., Carini, R., Bridges, B., & Hayek, J. (2004). Gender differences in student engagement among African American undergraduates at historically Black colleges and universities. *Journal of College Student Development, 45*(3), 271–284.

HBCUs models for success supporting achievement and retention of Black males. (2006). *A publication of the Thurgood Marshall Scholarship Fund Inc.* Brooklyn, NY: Word for Word.

Jackson, C. (2006) *Measuring the impact of Title IX on women of color* (Doctoral dissertation). Retrieved from http://www.ohiolink.edu

Lomax, M. (2008) *Sports and the racial divide African American and Latino experience in an era of change*. Jackson, MS: University Press of Mississippi.

McErlain, E. (2008, February 27). *Study shows historically Black colleges and universities struggle to meet Title IX's proportionality test*. Retrieved from http://saving sports.org/2008/02/27/study-shows-historically-black -colleges-and-universities-struggle-to-meet-title-ixs-pro portionality-test/

Moses, M. (2002). *Embracing race: Why we need race-conscious education policy*. New York, NY: Teachers College Press.

NCAA. (1993). *Final report of the NCAA gender-equity task force*. Overland Park, KS: NCAA.

O'Shea, M., & Cantu, N. (1998). *Regarding the application of Title IX of the educational amendments of 1972 as it relates to the funding of athletic scholarships for men's and women's intercollegiate athletics programs* (Report NO. HE-031–532). Office of Civil Rights. Washington, DC (ERIC document reproductive service NO. ED462022)

Palmer, M., & Gasman, R. (2004). It takes a village to raise a child: The role of social capital in promoting academic success for African American men at a Black college. *Journal of College Student Development, 49*(1), 52–70.

Pieronek, C. (2000). Title IX and intercollegiate athletics in the federal appeals court: Myth vs. reality. *Journal of College and University Law, 27,* 447–518.

Rice, M. (2004) Organizational culture, social equity, and diversity: Teaching public administration education. *Journal of Public Affairs Education, 2,* 143–154.

Shaw, P. (1995, February). Achieving Title IX gender equity in college athletics in an era of fiscal austerity. *Journal of Sport and Social Issues, 19,* 6–27.

Sissoko, M., & Shiau, L. (2005). Minority enrollment demand for higher education at historically Black colleges and universities from 1976 to 1998: An empirical analysis. *The Journal of Higher Education, 76*(2) 181–208.

Sabo, D., & Grant, C. H. B. (June, 2005). *Limitations of the department of education's online survey method for measuring athletic interest and ability on USA campuses*. Buffalo, NY: Center for Research on Physical Activity, Sport & Health, D'Youville College.

Suggs, W. (1999, May 21). Education department may ask colleges for more date in athletic equity reports. *Chronicle of Higher Education, 45*(37), A49.

Suggs, W. (2002a, June 21). Budgets grow as colleges seek to comply with gender equity rules. *Chronicle of Higher Education, 48,* A41–A42.

Suggs, W. (2002b, June 21). Title IX at 30 in the arena of women's college sports, the 1972 law created a legacy of debate. *Chronicle of Higher Education, 48,* A38–A41.

Suggs, W. (2003a, Feb). Smoke obscures fire in Title IX debate as federal panel adjourns. *Chronicle of Higher Education, 49*(22), A31–A32.

Suggs, W. (2003b, March). Cheers and condemnation greet report on gender equity. *Chronicle of Higher Education, 49*(26), A40–A41.

Thelin, J. (2000, Jul/Aug.). Good sports? Historical perspective on the political economy of intercollegiate athletics in the era of Title IX, 1972–1997. *The Journal of Higher Education, 71,* 391–410.

U.S. Department of Education, Office for Civil Rights. (1994). Improving America's schools act. *Public Law,* 103–382,

U.S. Department of Education. *White House initiative on historically Black colleges and universities*. Retrieved from http://www.ed.gov/about/inits/list/whhbcu /edlite-index.html

Valentin, I. (1997). *Title IX a brief history*. Newton, MA: Women's Educational Equity Act (WEEA) Resource Center at EDC; Washington, DC: U.S. Dept. of Education, Office of Educational Research and Improvement, Educational Resources Information Center.

ENDNOTES

1. Jackson, C. (2006) *Measuring the impact of Title IX on women of color*. Dissertation. Retrieved from http:// www.ohio link.edu

2. U.S. Department of Education, Office for Civil Rights. (2005). *Additional clarification of intercollegiate athletics policy: Three-part test—Part three*. Washington, DC.

3. Study shows historically Black colleges and universities struggle to meet Title IX's proportionality test. (2008). *CSC calls on NCAA to support HBCUs use of surveys in order to improve enrollment gender disparity*. Retrieved from http://sav ingsports.org/newsroom/display_releases.cfm?ID=22

4. Retrieved from http://www.dll.org/HBCUs/gateway _files/FAQs.asp#Of ficialList

CASE STUDY: Should NCAA Allow the Use of Surveys for HBCU to Meet Title IX Compliance?

In order to meet Title IX compliance, colleges and universities are required to show that their athletic programs comply with at least one part of the three-prong test:

1. Proportionality—The proportion of women competing on sports teams must be in proportion with the institution's undergraduate population. If an institution has an undergraduate population of 52% females, then about 52% of the athletic budget should be spend on female athletics.
2. Continuing history of expansion—Colleges and universities must show a continuing practice of program expansion for the underrepresented gender. This prong requires universities to prove that they have added sport programs for the underrepresented gender, which in most cases is female.
3. Interests and abilities—requires the institution to show a good faith effort that they are fully and effectively accommodating the interests and abilities of the underrepresented gender.[1]

In 2005 the NCAA developed a survey instrument to measure the interests and abilities of undergraduate students. Additional clarifications in regards to Title IX were sent out to colleges and universities by the Office for Civil Rights. This document aimed to clarify the use of part three of Title IX compliance by providing the institutions with a survey and user's guide, in which Title IX compliance could be measured.[2] Proponents of the use of this survey instrument argue that it is a great way for colleges and universities to show compliance with Title IX. Others argue that the survey is an invalid measure to accurately predict the interests and abilities of female students.

According to the National Women's Law Center (http://www.nwlc.org) there are numerous problems with the new policy:

- The new policy allows schools to use surveys alone to demonstrate Title IX compliance.
- The surveys only provide a measure of the discrimination that has limited sport opportunities for women but does nothing to address them.
- The new policy allows schools to restrict their surveys to enrolled and admitted students only, therefore not accurately measuring interests.

With the ongoing debate about the validity and reliability of the NCAA survey to measure prong three colleges and universities are still relying heavily on proportionality as a way to prove Title IX compliance. The College Sports Council released a study in February 2008 that showed nearly all of the nation's historically Black colleges and universities (HBCUs) failed to meet Title IX compliance under prong one (proportionality).[3]

Nationally known athletic programs such as Florida A&M University, Howard University, and Jackson State University have failed to meet prong one (proportionality). There are 104 documented HBCUs and women enrollment is about 61% of the undergraduate population at these institutions. However, many of these students are older, nontraditional students that are not interested in the responsibility of playing sports on the collegiate level.[4] It is apparent that HBCUs are at a disadvantage when it comes to Title IX compliance. They fail to meet prong one, and prong two (continuing history of expansion) is hard to meet as well due to budgetary constraints. This calls in the question of the intent of Title IX. The goal of the Education Amendment Act is to prohibit gender discrimination in any educational setting. HBCUs are at a double disadvantage because their enrollment has been decreasing over the years. African Americans have more opportunities to attend other universities due to integration and equal opportunity policies. In order to fully measure whether or not HBCUs are meeting the intended goal of Title IX, prong three seems to be most feasible. The largest HBCU only has an enrollment rate of 3,000 students. The small size of HBCUs would allow the surveys to be sent out and collected in an accurate way.

Due to the dynamics of HBCUs as smaller institutions with a disproportionate amount of female students enrolled, should HBCUs be forced to meet Title IX compliance by using prongs one (proportionality) and two (continuing history of expansion) or should the NCAA allow HBCUs the ability to use the surveys to measure compliance? What are the implications of this? What are some of the challenges HBCUs face in meeting Title IX Compliance?

CHAPTER 9

The Glass Ceiling Effect for African American Women Coaches and Athletic Administrators

ROBERTHA ABNEY

Abstract

With the passage of Affirmative Action, the Civil Rights Act of 1991, Title IX, and gender equity laws, one would anticipate an increase in the status of African American women as administrators and coaches in intercollegiate athletics. The 33-year update by Acosta and Carpenter (2010) revealed four interesting facts:

1. The number of women's teams per school is nearly the highest it has ever been.

2. Women hold 57.6% of paid assistant coaches' positions of women's teams.

3. Of the head coaches of women's teams, 42.6% are females.

4. More women hold positions within the administrative ranks at all levels than any time since the mid-1970s. However, it is unclear what percentage of these figures represents African American women and/or women of color. Research pertaining to the status of African American women as administrators is extremely limited and, perhaps, an unexplored area.

This chapter will provide overview of the impact of the glass-ceiling effect on the status of African American women as athletic administrators and coaches in intercollegiate athletics. The author presents a historical review of the roles and duties of African American women since the 1970s. The literature suggests a noticeable increase of women's participation in college sport. However, women, especially African American women, are still underutilized in NCAA coaching and administrative positions at all levels. Suggestions for change are discussed, and strategies and recommendations for recruiting and retaining African American women are provided.

Key Terms			
●	affirmative action	●	glass ceiling effect
●	athletic administrator	●	inclusion
●	Civil Rights Act of 1991	●	senior woman administrator
●	diversity	●	Title IX
●	gender equity		

INTRODUCTION

Morrison et al. (1987) described the *glass ceiling effect* as the organizational, attitudinal, and social barriers that effectively keep women and minorities from advancing up the career ladder. The glass ceiling is a more subtle form of workplace discrimination. With the increase of African American sport participants in intercollegiate athletics, the use of affirmative action guidelines, and the adoption of The Civil Rights Act of 1991, an increase in the number of African Americans as athletic administrators, head coaches, assistant coaches, and sports information directors could be anticipated. Unfortunately, that has not occurred. The affirmative action guidelines, the Civil Rights Act of 1991, and Title IX have served to only slightly overcome some of the glass ceiling phenomenon.

Since the passage of Title IX, the opportunity for female athletes to participate in intercollegiate athletics has increased in the past 33 years (Acosta & Carpenter, 2010). In 1978, the academic year just before the Title IX mandatory compliance date, the number of sports offered for women was 5.61 per school. In 1988, the number was 7.31; a decade later it grew to 7.71; and by 2008 the number had grown to 8.65 (an all-time high). Currently, it is at 8.64 (Acosta & Carpenter, 2010). However, the increase in the number of women, more specifically African American women, in athletic administrative and coaching positions is not reflective of the increased number of participants.

According to the Women's Sports Foundation (WSF), "while there has been an obvious increase for women of color in athletics since the inception of Title IX, there is still work to be done in order to gain equal representation and opportunities in collegiate athletics" (WSF, 2008). Lapchick (2010) reported the percentage of White female student-athletes at the Division I, II, and III combined were 78.9%, while 11.3% were African American females. He also suggested that race remains an ongoing academic issue given the continued graduation disparity between White and African American student-athletes. Although the gap has narrowed slightly there is still a disparity. African American women are underrepresented in administrative and coaching positions in intercollegiate athletic departments.

Purpose of Chapter

The purpose of this chapter is to examine the existence of the glass ceiling effect during the career progression of African American women within intercollegiate athletics. Women have made strides in intercollegiate athletics, and the number of women in coaching and administrative positions within intercollegiate athletic departments has increased; however, there are very few African American women in the top- and middle-level administrative positions. Most African American women are concentrated in lower-level positions such as academic advisor/counselor (9.9%), life skills coordinator (11.5%), administrative assistant (8.4%), intern (5.1%), compliance coordinator /officer (5.6%), business manager (5.6%), graduate assistant and other (3.9% and 3.2%), or assistant coach (19.0%) (NCAA, 2011). They are stacked or clustered into positions that keep them from attaining power and prestige (Sage, 1993). With the exception of the Senior Woman Administrator (SWA) position, it is clear that there are a higher percentage of African American women found in assistant or lower level positions. Given the inflated number in the SWA position, one may wonder if it is simply the token position given to a female in a male-dominated athletic department. Filling the SWA position with a female is an easy way to show that an athletic department is willing to have female leaders (Borland, 2008). A lack of representation of African American women has been apparent at all levels of intercollegiate athletics, for example in officiating, coaching, administration, sports information, and athletic training (Houzer, 1974).

In Houzer's (1974) article, "Black Women in Athletics," the situation is stated well:

Black women have been irrespectably quiescent with respect to their status in athletics . . . participation in athletics by women has increased both in number of participants and variations of activity. This broad expansion of participation in sports and athletics by women has not been proportionately represented by Black women. (p. 209)

Alexander (1978) examined the status of minority women in all active member institutions of the Association of Intercollegiate Athletics for Women (AIAW). Her study revealed the following facts: 1) There is a great underrepresentation of minority women athletes, minority women administrative personnel, and minority women coaches; 2) sports where participation by minority athletes was greater than 10% were badminton, basketball, and track and field; and 3) administrative personnel positions where minority involvement was greater than 5% were assistant directors, sport information directors, and team managers. Only 5% of the athletic directors in women's athletic departments in the 213 member institutions of the AIAW participating in the study were African American women. Also, only 2% of the assistant athletic director positions and 5% of the coaching positions were held by African American women. Instead of improving, the relative position of African American women remained virtually static during the 1970s. Murphy (1980) examined the participation of minority women as athletes and coaches within the AIAW structure. According to Murphy (1980), in 1974 there were 556 head coaches in women's athletic departments, of whom 16 (3%) were African American women, 443 (80%) were White women, four (1%) were African American males, and 93 (17%) were White males. Among assistant coaches, one (2%) was an African American woman, four (6%) were White women, 13 (19%) were African American males, and 48 (73%) were White males. During 1978–79, the number of head coaches increased to 1,009 (an increase of 79%). The number of African American women increased by only 23; that is, only 5% of the new head coaches were African American women. During the same period, 184 more White women head coaches were added, comprising 41% of the additional head coaches. The greatest change was recorded in the addition of assistant coaches. There were 296 (an increase of 48%) more individuals in that group in 1979 than in 1974. Of those new ones, three (1%) were African American women, 189 (64%) were White women, 3 (1%) were African American males, and 89 (30%) were White males. Murphy (1980) reported that the number of African American women occupying administrative positions in women's athletic departments, in all active member institutions of the AIAW, was 15 (5%) in assistant coaching positions, 39 (5%) in head coaching positions, and five (2%) in athletic director positions. She further found that the percentage of African Americans, both male and female, occupying athletic administrative positions (5% head coaches, 8% assistant coaches, 5% other support staff) was close to the percentage (5%) of historically Black colleges and universities (HBCU's) that participated in the study. She argued that it seems likely then that African American women held a very limited number of athletic positions in traditionally White institutions.

LIMITED ACCESS TO LEADERSHIP POSITIONS

African Americans have restricted access to certain roles in college sport. African Americans at White institutions tend to be underrepresented in roles associated with leadership and decision making. They are "assistants to," that is, they serve as coordinators or assistants to a major decision maker. As long as racist and sexist practices influence hiring practices, the numbers of African American women in high authority sport positions will not increase.

Efforts to assess the effects of the glass ceiling on coaches and athletic administrators can be difficult because hiring and promotion decisions can be subjective, and universities use different criteria in making decisions to hire and promote. However, the experiences of individuals during their career, development, and statistics indicating the number of African American women employed in coaching and athletic administrative positions can be used to determine the glass ceiling effect phenomenon. The hiring problem has been blamed on the position held by African American women during their career development.

Abney (1988) investigated the career development of African American women coaches and athletic administrators in intercollegiate athletics at HBCUs and predominately White institutions. The women were asked to complete a survey questionnaire, and interviews were conducted with 10 women from the HBCUs and 10 women at predominately White institutions. From a list of obstacles or problems that were listed in the survey questionnaire, the women were asked to identify whether or not the problems or obstacles were major, minor, no problem, or not applicable in their careers. Abney (1988) reported the 10 highest ranking obstacles for African American women coaches and athletic administrators at African American institutions were inadequate salary, lack of support groups, being a woman, employer discrimination (sexism), low expectations by administrators and others, male coworker resentment (sexism), being too young, sense of tokenism, lack of cultural and social outlets in the community, and burden of being the official minority spokesperson. The African American women at White institutions indicated inadequate salary, lack of support groups, being African American, being a woman, lack of cultural and social outlets in community, sense of tokenism, employer discrimination (sexism), employer discrimination (racism), burden of being the official minority spokesperson, and male coworker resentment (sexism). The African American women at White institutions differed from the African American women at historically Black institutions in that they selected being African American and employer discrimination (racism) as significant factors. The women were very similar in that they both selected inadequate salary, lack of support groups, being a woman, employer discrimination (sexism), male coworker resentment (sexism), sense of tokenism, lack of cultural and social outlets in the community, and burden of being the official minority spokesperson as obstacles or problems during their career development.

The interviews with the women revealed additional details about the obstacles encountered in developing their careers. Problems encountered as a result of being a woman consisted of constantly questioning of their abilities; people who resented women being in key positions; dead-end positions or lack of upward mobility; lack of respect from the administration; and lack of support from bosses, co-workers, and the administration. Several women stated that women in athletics have a problem that people do not perceive them as being competent. These women also dealt with the problem of people who felt the women should not have had the position or did not promote women. One woman stated her experience as such: "He [co-worker] felt that some of the other schools that he had dealt with did not have a women's Athletic Director, and he didn't see the need for [this institution] to have a women's Athletic Director" (quoted in Abney, 1988, p. 91). Some women recalled discriminatory practices during career interviews.

I interviewed for a major job last year which I did get, but I subsequently decided not to take it. Their questions to me were different than their questions to the

White candidates, and I happen to know that because I happen to know other people who were interviewing. Their concerns were about what I could do, were more based on my color rather than my record. (quoted in Abney, 1988, p. 93)

The majority of the women believed their biggest obstacles or problems related to sex and/or race. Several African American women vividly recalled being excluded from participating in events, from leadership positions, and from membership on key committees. Both sexual and racial discrimination are burdens that African American women bear in the university setting and in American society. This *double jeopardy* adds to the difficulty of African American women who are seeking career advancement. Research suggested that double jeopardy prevented African American women gain acceptance from formal and informal social networks, as a result, these women may not be offered the opportunity to move into administrative position (Clayton, 2010).

Abney (1988) provided reasons why very few African American women were in coaching and athletic administration. Their responses were attitude of society toward minorities and women, sexism, racism, lack of qualifications, inadequate salaries, lack of interest, lack of role models, lack of mentors, family responsibilities, time consuming, dead-end positions, politics, stereotypes, lack of opportunity, and lack of networks.

Schneider et al. (2010) reported perceptions regarding discrimination factors preventing the advancement of women in the National Collegiate Athletic Association (NCAA) athletic departments. A five-point Likert scale (agree/disagree) survey containing 20 discrimination factors was electronically mailed to all NCAA senior woman administrators (SWAs) throughout the United States. Overall, the top five discrimination factors were: the domination of the "old boys' club," inequitable salaries (wage discrimination), lack of women mentors, family commitments conflicting with job, and job burnout. More than two decades later, sexism, salaries, lack of mentors, and family responsibilities/commitments continue to be strong factors preventing the advancement of women and minorities in intercollegiate athletic departments.

Many African American women have a common value of high achievement and the desire to pursue a coaching and/or administrative position in institutions of higher education. However, there are societal and institutional barriers that are hindrances, and thus, many Black women are denied the opportunity of achieving such positions. "The perpetuation of fatalistic stereotypes, coupled with contradictions in the literature concerning the images of African American women, have had a profound effect on personal relationships and professional opportunities for African American women in a society . . ." (Stratta, 1995, p. 50).

BARRIERS TO SUCCESS

Several explanations have been advanced to explain the small number of African American women as coaches and administrators in sport. Houzer (1974) stated that fewer African American women prepared for professional occupations in sport. Perhaps the lack of role models and mentors has been a deterrent. According to Smith (1991), planned interventions with adult role models and mentors do appear to have a positive effect on the career behavior and aspirations of African American youth. The majority of the African American women occupying positions as administrators or coaches in sport are former athletes. In most traditionally White institutions, the African American woman athlete lacks African American women administrators and coaches with whom she can identify. In most traditionally Black institutions, African American males occupy a large percentage of the positions in sport. As a result, professional occupations in sport are not perceived as a "visible" goal for the African American woman; therefore she may not desire to pursue the area.

Career mentors are of special value to African American women during their career development process. Unfortunately, a small number of women are in positions in athletic departments to provide the type of mentoring desired. African American women are rarely hired in high-level coaching and/or athletic administrative positions in college and universities. African American women continue to be underrepresented as administrators and coaches. Consequently, there are fewer African American women role models and mentors available to African American student athletes.

Evidence of the glass ceiling effect can be traced back to the experience of and team position held by African American women as student-athletes. Many educators will attest that the sports experience prepares the student-athlete for career and life experiences. According to Malveaux (1993), "the teamwork needed to participate in sports teaches students life lessons about cooperation, human relations, dignity and poise" (p. 54). The role that the student-athlete plays on a team can serve as the basis for career preparation. Sport sociologist have presented the theory that African American athletes are stacked in positions that do not require them to become leaders of their teams and are scarce in positions that are more central to the teams' operations. Fuller stated, "Even in sports in which African American women are represented in significant numbers, basketball and track, they are often not in decision making, or what she called 'control' positions" (quoted in Blum, 1993, p. 40). She further stated "Look at the point guards on many of the teams. The African American women are out there in the scoring positions and making big contributions, but they are not directing traffic" (quoted in Blum, 1993, p. 40).

If African Americans student-athletes have a quality intercollegiate athletic experience, an experience where they believe that they are being provided a legitimate opportunity to succeed and prosper, they will be more inclined to invest in a career in intercollegiate athletics. If more African American student-athletes graduate, the pool of those individuals able to consider a career in college athletics will expand (Vance, 1984). A better sporting experience means more interested and qualified candidate for positions as coaches and athletic administrators.

African American student-athletes must be provided leadership and graduate school opportunities after their playing days are over. Although progress has been made in creating new internships and postgraduate scholarship opportunities at the institutional, conference, and national levels, these opportunities must be expanded (Gerdy, 1994). Our current African American student-athletes should be our future coaches, athletic administrators and conference commissioners. Unfortunately, very few African American women student-athletes are being hired into intercollegiate athletic departments.

LEADERSHIP OPPORTUNITIES: A LOOK AT THE DATA

Acosta and Carpenter (1986–1987) reported the total number of African Americans holding athletic administrative positions was .156 per school, for a total of about 123 in NCAA schools. Thus, it was concluded that there is a minority group member in only one out of five of the athletic administrative structures found in NCAA member colleges and universities. The total number of head coaches was .494 per school, for a total of about 387 in NCAA schools. There is no minority group member serving as head coach in either the men's or women's programs in one out of three colleges and universities. Assistant coaches were 1.35 per school for a total of about 1,065 in NCAA schools (Acosta

& Carpenter, 1987). It was concluded that the number of representatives of minority groups who hold a position as administrator, coach, or assistant coach in all of NCAA sports is about 1979, or in other words, about 2.5 per school.

In 1990, it was reported that minority women comprised fewer than 5% of all women coaches (Grant & Curtiss, 1993). In 1996, Acosta and Carpenter reported that 6,580 head coaching jobs existed in 1996 for coaches of women's NCAA teams, an increase of 209 jobs from 1994. Women held 3,138, nine less than in 1994 in spite of the growth in number of teams by 209. Women held 61.1% of the 5,902 paid assistant coaching positions for women's teams. Women held 35.9% of all administrative jobs in women's programs. Today, there are fewer programs totally lacking women than in any of the last years. It was concluded that on an average, there is almost one female involved in athletic administration per school; this is up from 0.96 in 1994 and up from 0.83 in 1992 (Acosta & Carpenter, 1986–87).

In 1993, the Black Coaches Association (BCA) threatened a boycott unless its concerns about equity in intercollegiate athletics were addressed. The congressional Black Caucus intervened, getting the United States Department of Justice to mediate an agreement between the two parties to make significant steps toward the expansion of educational, employment and governance participation opportunities for African Americans and other ethnic minorities. Cedric Dempsey, NCAA executive director, conceded at the BCA annual convention that there was "a moral obligation for women and minorities to have better opportunities to become coaches and administrators" (quoted in Farrell, 1994, p. 22). An agreement was developed. Dempsey agreed that the state of minority hiring in the NCAA was "simply indefensible," but vowed that an upper management position in the association will soon go to an African American.

The NCAA Minority Opportunities and Interests Committee conducted a four-year study by race demographics of NCAA member institutions. Data were collected from annual certification reports that provided a breakdown of the number of administrators by race from 1990–1991, 1993–1994, and 1995–1996. Administrators were defined as those in the following positions: administrative assistant, associate athletic director, assistant coach, academic advisor, athletics director, assistant athletic director, auxiliary services, business manager, compliance coordinator, equipment manager, eligibility officer, faculty athletic representative, graduate assistant, head coach, promotions/marketing director, strength coach, sports information director, ticket manager, and trainer (The NCAA Minority Opportunities and Interests Committee's Four-Year Study of Race Demographics of Member Institutions, 1994).

The report presented several significant findings:

1. From 1990–91 to 1993–94, there were 5,889 additional athletics administrator positions. Of those positions, African Americans represented 597, or 10.1% of the new administrators. With historically Black colleges and universities excluded, these were 5,843 additional athletics administrators. The increase in the overall percentage age of African American administrators was 0.8%, from 5.4% to 6.2%; however, this increase was still well below the percentage of African American student-athletes in the Division I student-athlete population.

2. There were 124 additional athletics directors. African Americans represented 19, or 15.3% of the new athletics directors; however, when historically Black institutions are excluded, there are 15, or 12.3% in the additional positions and 3.6% of the 897 total athletics directors in 1993–94. There were 29 more African American associate athletic directors, an increase from 4.2% to 5.6%, from 1990–91 to 1993–94.

When historically Black schools were excluded, African Americans represent 11 of 127 new associate athletic directors, 8.7%.

3. Assistant athletic directors' percentages are bleaker. There was an increase of 333 assistant athletic directors from 1990–91 to 1993–94. African Americans represented only 20 or 6.0% of the additional assistant athletic directors, since the percentage of these individuals has not grown since 1990. The data suggest that future African American athletics directors will not come from the current ranks of associate and assistant athletic directors because the percentage of these individuals has not grown since 1990. The data suggest that there has been an increase in representation, though not dramatically, among the numbers of head coaches.

4. There were 1,109 additional head coaches, excluding historically Black schools. African Americans represented 143 or 12.9%, of the additional coaches but only 3.9% of the total number of head coaches (10,176). For revenue-producing sports, excluding historically Black schools, African Americans represent 86 of 417 or 20.6% of additional head coaches. In nonrevenue sports, African Americans represent 57 of 692 or 8.2% of the additional head coaches.

Table 9.1.	Percentage of Black Administrators at NCAA member Institutions					
	All Institutions			Historically Black Institutions Excluded		
Position	1995–1996	2009–2010	Change	1995–1996	2009–2010	Change
Overall Percentages						
Director of Athletics	7.6	8.9	1.3	2.7	3.9	1.2
Associate Director of Athletics	8.2	9.6	1.4	5.9	7.6	1.7
Assistant Director of Athletics	8.4	9.6	1.2	6.7	7.3	0.6
Senior Women Administrator	9.1	10.4	1.3	3.3	5.8	2.5
Academic Advisor	21	20.1	−0.9	18	17.2	−0.8
Overall	8.3	9.7	1.4	5.1	7.3	2.2
Division 1						
Director of Athletics	10.1	13.2	3.1	3.8	6.6	2.8
Associate Director of Athletics	9.1	10.1	1.0	7.0	8.5	1.5
Assistant Director of Athletics	9.5	10.8	1.3	8.0	8.9	0.9
Senior Women Administrator	8.4	15.8	7.4	2.4	9.6	7.2
Academic Advisor	22.9	22.1	−0.8	20.3	20	−0.3
Overall	9.0	10.9	1.9	6.3	9.0	2.7
Division 2						
Director of Athletics	10.6	12.4	1.8	2.5	3.4	0.9
Associate Director of Athletics	9.6	13.2	3.6	4.0	6.7	2.7
Assistant Director of Athletics	7.0	11.5	4.5	3.1	6.0	2.9
Senior Women Administrator	16.7	14.0	−2.7	5.7	6.2	0.5
Academic Advisor	15.1	19.7	4.6	6.3	9.1	2.8
Overall	11.2	11.6	0.4	3.8	5.6	1.8
Division 3						
Director of Athletics	3.6	3.3	−0.3	2.1	2.3	0.2
Associate Director of Athletics	3.0	3.2	0.2	2.9	3.2	0.3
Assistant Director of Athletics	6.6	5.6	−1.0	5.6	4.9	−0.7
Senior Women Administrator	2.9	3.5	0.6	2.3	2.6	0.3
Academic Advisor	10.3	9.3	−1.0	10.5	7.8	−2.7
Overall	4.3	4.4	0.1	3.3	3.7	0.4

5. The number of assistant coaches increased by 2,394 but African Americans represents only 213, or 8.9% of these additional assistant coaches. Over the last four years, there has been no percentage increase in the total number of assistant coaches ("The NCAA Minority Opportunities,"1994).

More recent studies suggested that there is still no significant increase of hiring of African Americans. NCAA Gender and Race Demographics 2009–2010 (2011) summarized the change of hiring of African Americans from 1995–96 and 2009–10 (see Table 1 and 2).

The previous reports provide data regarding the status of African Americans in intercollegiate athletics; however, specific data pertaining to the status of African American women as athletic administrators and coaches in intercollegiate athletics remains unclear. In 1998, the NCAA Minority Opportunities and Interests Committee released the findings of a two-year study on race demographics of NCAA member institutions' athletics personnel. In general, the data revealed that there has been no improvement in Black representation in the athletic departments at NCAA member institutions, with the exception of the following areas:

- Academic advisors show the greatest percentage increase of all administrative positions both overall and in Division I groups.
- The Division I assistant coaches show marked increases in both men's and women's teams, as well as in men's and women's teams, as well as in men's and women's revenue sports.

Table 9.2.	Percentage of Black Head Coaches at NCAA Member Institutions					
	All Institutions			**Historically Black Institutions Excluded**		
Team/Sports	1995–1996	2009–2010	Change	1995–1996	2009–2010	Change
Overall Percentages						
Men's teams	7.6	9.1	1.5	4.2	5.3	1.1
Women's teams	7.5	8.9	1.4	4.2	5.2	1
Men's revenue sports	12.7	14.7	2.0	8.0	9.4	1.4
Women's revenue sports	12.2	14.5	2.3	7.7	9.7	2.0
Division 1						
Men's teams	9.3	12.0	2.7	4.9	7.1	2.2
Women's teams	9.7	12.1	2.4	5.3	7.3	2.0
Men's revenue sports	17.9	21.1	3.2	12.1	15	2.9
FBS	5.6	7.1	1.5	5.6	7.8	2.2
FCS	19.6	10.8	−8.8	5.3	8.1	2.8
Women's revenue sports	15.5	19.7	4.2	10.1	13.5	3.4
Division 2						
Men's teams	11.6	12.9	1.3	5.2	5.1	−0.1
Women's teams	10.9	11.6	0.7	4.5	5	0.5
Men's revenue sports	15.7	19.2	3.5	6.8	8.4	1.6
Women's revenue sports	15.4	18.6	3.2	7.0	10.0	3.0
Division 3						
Men's teams	3.6	4.7	1.1	3.1	4	0.9
Women's teams	3.9	4.7	0.8	3.3	3.9	0.6
Men's revenue sports	5.6	6.1	0.5	5.1	5.4	0.3
Women's revenue sports	7.2	7.8	0.6	6.5	6.7	0.2

- Division I shows an increase in overall administrative positions held by African Americans.

- Division II shows the greatest percentage decrease in African American administrators and head coaches of both men's and women's sports teams.

- There has been relatively no change in Division III in any of the categories.

Although the number of women and minorities within intercollegiate athletics departments has increased, the number of African American women as athletic directors, associate athletic directors, and head coaches has not increased significantly and continues to be disappointing.

Abney (1997) investigated the positions held by African American women in intercollegiate athletic departments of member institutions within the NCAA, the National Association for Intercollegiate Athletics (NAIA), and the National Junior College Athletic Association (NJCAA). A total of 1,300 survey questionnaires were mailed. Six hundred and ninety-three (52%) were returned. The results were that a total of 1,912 African American men and women names were identified as holding athletic administrative and coaching positions, with 475 (25%) identified as African American women athletic administrators and coaches (see Table 3).

Of the 475, 304 (64%) were coaches. Of the 304 coaches, 12 were identified as graduate assistants, interns, or volunteers and 26 of the women held another position, that is coached another sport or were administrators. One hundred seventy-one, (36%) were athletic administrators. Of the 171, six were identified as interns or graduate assistants and seven held another position. These percentages are much smaller when compared to the overall number of positions, male and female, within intercollegiate athletic departments. The top five administrative positions held by African-American women in intercollegiate athletic departments were secretary/receptionist, academic counselor/student services, athletic trainer, administrative assistant, business/account executive (see Table 4).

According to Fuller, "there are seven African American males who are athletic directors at White schools and there is one African American woman: me" (quoted in Blum, 1995, p. A39). Abney (1997) identified 0.44%, or three, African American women as athletic directors. All three women were employed at NCAA member institutions. One was employed at a Division I White institution, whereas the other two were employed at Division II, historically Black institutions.

The top five head coaching positions held by African American women in intercollegiate athletics departments were basketball, volleyball, track and field, cheerleading, and softball. The top five assistant coaching positions were basketball, track and field, volleyball, cheerleading, and softball.

Table 9.3.	Overall Percentage of African Americans			
	NCAA	**NAIA**	**NJCAA**	**Total**
Total number of African American names submitted	0.90% (1736)	0.01% (12)	0.09% (164)	100% (1912)
Total number of African American Women	0.94% (449)	0.01% (4)	0.05% (22)	100% (475)
Total number of African American Men	0.89% (1287)	0.01% (8)	10% (142)	100% (1437)

Table 9.4.	Top Five Administrator Positions			
POSITION	**NCAA**	**NAIA**	**NJCAA**	**Total**
Secretary/Receptionist	7.8% (42)	0.0% (0)	0.0% (0)	6.2% (42)
Academic Counselor/ Student Services				
Director	2.4% (13)	0.0% (0)	0.0% (0)	1.9% (13)
Assistant	0.93 (5)	0.0% (0)	0.0% (0)	0.73% (5)
Athletic Trainer				
Head	0.75% (4)	0.0% (0)	0.0% (0)	0.59% (4)
*Assistant	2.2% (12)	0.0% (0)	0.0% (0)	1.7% (12)
Administrative Assistant	2.8% (15)	0.0% (0)	0.0% (0)	2.2% (15)
Business Manager/ Account Executive				
Director	1.5% (8)	0.0% (0)	0.78% (1)	1.3% (9)
Assistant	0.56% (3)	0.0% (0)	0.0% (0)	0.44% (3)

* Six (6) of the assistant trainers were employed at one institution.

The void of African Americans as coaches and athletic administrators has been attributed to a number of factors: "not enough jobs available in collegiate coaching or athletic departments" and "difficulty in identifying qualified African American coaches" and the "reluctance to hire African American coaches for fear of booster backlash" (Farrell, 1992, p. 36). The data do not support these justifications. It was reported that there are 800 NCAA members in all divisions, with an average of 15.5 teams per school, or 12,400 teams. NCAA teams have an average of two assistants per team. The National Association for Intercollegiate Athletic (NAIA) has 503 members, with an average of 7.66 teams per school and 1.5 assistants per team. There are approximately 68,888 college sports related jobs (Lapchick, 1989).

A commitment to promote job opportunities for women and minorities at the collegiate level was apparent under the leadership of the late NCAA President Myles Brand. Brand hired Charlotte Westerhaus in 2005 to be the NCAA Vice-President for Diversity and Inclusion Office that is currently called the NCAA Diversity and Inclusion Department. The role of the Department is to develop and implement strategies, policies, and programs that promote diversity and inclusion throughout intercollegiate athletics (NCAA, 2008). Although the opportunities for women and minorities have expanded in college sport, there is still room for significant improvements.

During 2005–06, the number of African American women athletic directors was approximately 1.2% (of 1,017). When excluding HBCUs from the data, African American

Table 9.5.	NCAA All Divisions Head Coach Data (2010–2011)							
	Men's Team				Women's Team			
	White		Black		White		Black	
	Male	Female	Male	Female	Male	Female	Male	Female
Baseball	838	7	36	0	389	510	62	92
Basketball	857	4	177	0	21	10	20	11
Cross Country	721	77	96	14	707	141	92	38
Fencing	25	2	0	0	28	6	0	1
Football	561	1	74	0	24	222	2	1
Golf	734	12	32	1	317	226	13	1
Gymnastics	15	0	1	0	38	42	3	0
Ice Hockey	130	0	0	0	59	24	0	0
Lacrosse	269	3	6	0	57	291	1	4
Rifle	25	1	1	0	28	5	1	0
Rowing	57	2	0	0	85	51	1	0
Skiing	35	4	0	0	37	6	0	0
Soccer	666	1	41	0	588	284	29	5
Swimming	346	55	2	1	334	542	24	27
Tennis	602	43	49	2	386	123	1	2
Track Indoor	472	24	100	11	544	227	49	15
Track Outdoor	534	33	116	18	483	66	94	38
Volleyball	70	7	6	0	527	73	107	46
Water Polo	37	0	0	0	390	481	30	53
Wrestling	207	1	9	0	44	12	0	0
Other	67	21	3	1	70	73	1	6

Table 9.6.	NCAA All Divisions Assistant Coach (2010–2011)							
	Men's Team				Women's Team			
	White		Black		White		Black	
	Male	Female	Male	Female	Male	Female	Male	Female
Baseball	2147	79	67	0	586	1104	238	433
Basketball	1773	47	848	4	10	5	12	4
Cross Country	677	263	142	47	627	349	135	59
Fencing	51	12	1	0	48	17	2	2
Football	4498	39	1371	1	46	349	3	3
Golf	421	27	14	0	188	152	7	4
Gymnastics	28	0	0	0	56	80	7	2
Ice Hockey	279	3	0	0	68	76	1	0
Lacrosse	574	9	15	0	66	462	5	4
Rifle	13	3	0	0	15	4	0	0
Rowing	88	13	0	0	93	183	1	1
Skiing	37	11	2	0	36	15	0	0
Soccer	1172	28	64	0	669	802	43	24
Swimming	513	302	13	3	504	1137	26	47
Tennis	409	66	25	3	558	418	12	6
Track Indoor	1295	357	348	115	346	242	28	12
Track Outdoor	1420	404	386	122	1345	479	356	139
Volleyball	102	16	4	2	1418	509	382	151
Water Polo	37	4	0	0	546	823	32	69
Wrestling	456	13	32	0	26	29	1	0
Other	89	27	9	2	58	83	2	7

women occupied 0.3% of the athletic director positions at NCAA Division I, II, and III institutions (NCAA, 2007).

The *2007–2008 NCAA Race and Gender Demographics Report* revealed

- Of the head coaches at Division I institutions, 5.4% were African Americans. 3.7% of the head coaches at Division II, and 1.4% of the head coaches at Division III were African American women (NCAA, 2009)

- Overall, 1.8% of the athletic directors at Division I institutions, 2.7% of the athletic directors at Division II, and 0.5% of the athletic directors at Division III were African American women. (NCAA, 2009)

Richard E. Lapchick (2009) released *The 2008 Racial and Gender Report Card*, a report on the hiring practices by professional sports teams and college athletics. The Report Card for College Sport showed that NCAA member institutions and their conferences lost ground for both their record for gender hiring practices and hiring practices by race. In fact, college sport had the lowest grade for racial hiring practices in 2008. Although little progress has been made between 2008 and 2011, only 3.2% of African American women were Division I head coaches, and only 1.2% of African American women were Division I athletic directors (NCAA, 2012).

Table 9.7.	NCAA Athletics Administrative Staff (2010–2011)			
Position	White		Black	
	Male	Female	Male	Female
Director of Athletics	779	190	78	15
Associate Director of Athletics	1199	600	117	77
Assistant Director of Athletics	1189	588	133	78
Senior Woman Administrator	3	920	2	108
Administrative Assistant	141	2268	49	261
Academic Advisor/Counselor	488	825	192	189
Business Manager	297	452	36	50
Compliance Coordinator/Officer	539	623	82	82
Equipment Manager	818	122	115	6
Fund Raiser/Development Manager	758	362	51	23
Facility Manager	971	176	127	14
Faulty Athletics Representative	729	302	64	19
Life Skills Coordinator	122	362	52	75
Promotions/Marketing Manager	521	275	43	20
Sport Information Director	949	133	49	16
Assistant or Associate Director of Sports Information	883	288	24	15
Strength Coach	1105	187	189	18
Ticket Manager	376	329	34	49
Head Athletic Trainer	733	316	25	22
Assistant or Associate Athletic Trainer	1187	1301	64	57
Graduate Assistant (Excluding football)	1594	1443	189	137
Intern	836	547	117	84

More than three-and-a-half decades after the passage of Title IX, African American women are still underrepresented as coaches and athletic administrator in college sport. In 1975, the first female athletic director was hired. As director of athletics at Chicago State University, Dr. Dorothy Richey, an African American, became the first woman on record ever to hold such a position at a coed institution (Ebony, 1975). By fall 2009, only eight women held an athletic director position at NCAA Division I, II, and III institutions (personal communication, Jacqueline McDowell, 2010 NASSM Convention, Tampa, FL).

Change has to occur at the top of an organization in order to impact the entire organization. Until diversification occurs within the offices of national organizations and the administration and athletic departments on college campuses, the glass ceiling effect will remain for African American women. African American women who aspire to obtain and advance in positions within intercollegiate athletic departments are faced with a seemingly shatterproof ceiling. The positions are available, but significant numbers of African American

C. Vivian Stringer is among the few African American women who have been afforded the opportunity to coach at the highest level. She has guided three different schools to the NCAA Final Four, including two trips with Rutgers University. Courtesy of Rutgers Athletics/Nick Romanenko

women are not being hired in decision-making positions within intercollegiate athletics departments, and those that have been hired are in dead-end positions. If hired in the middle-or lower-level positions, they are not rapidly advancing up the career ladder.

African American women must develop strategies to reach and shatter the glass ceiling. Changes in the following areas would increase the number of African American women in athletics: society's attitude towards African American women; affirmative hiring procedures; more African American women interested in the area; elimination of sexism and racism; and more mentors, role models, networks, and opportunity for African American women. African American women should make themselves more visible and qualified, and design, develop, and promote programs to help prepare student-athletes for careers in athletics. The North American Society for Sport Management (NASSM) and the National Association for Sport and Physical Education (NASPE) maintain websites that list universities that offer undergraduate and graduate sport management programs.

RECOMMENDATION AND STRATEGIES: BREAKING DOWN THE GLASS CEILING

Academic programs designed to prepare student for a managerial or administrative career in the front office of various sport organizations have become very popular across the country.

The following are recommendations and strategies for shattering the glass ceiling:

- Efforts to achieve diversity within athletic departments should be an integral part of strategic plans, and the administration must be held accountable for progress toward breaking the glass ceiling.

- Organizations must expand their traditional recruitment networks and seek candidates with noncustomary backgrounds and experiences.
- Formal mentoring and career development programs can help stop minorities from being channeled into staff positions that provide little access that leads to the decision-making positions.
- The top leadership of colleges and universities must demonstrate its commitment to the recruitment and advancement of African Americans by removing obstacles embedded in personnel practices.
- African American women must receive challenging job assignments and the necessary training to advance.
- Organizations must establish ongoing training and educational programs on race relations for all organizational members. Such training can help to eliminate many of the barriers African American experience of racism and prejudice.

Abney and Richey (1991) provided the following strategies to African American women who aspire to pursue a career in intercollegiate athletics:

- Start support groups, organizations, and/or programs to exchange ideas and share experiences.
- Investigate initiating formal and informal mentoring programs within the athletic arena and the governing bodies of sport.
- Become qualified and compete for leadership roles at all levels in sport; become actively involved in sport associations, organizations, committees, and/or governing bodies.
- Be confident, competent, determined, and willing to persevere when unpleasant experiences arise.
- Develop and maintain a positive sense of self while remaining in sport; be inspired to meet sport challenges.
- After having secured career positions in athletic-related professions, help other African American women with career development.

African American women must utilize online sports job boards, professional websites, professional blogs, and social networking sites (e.g., LinkedIn, Facebook, and Twitter) to develop support networks and seek career opportunities in sport. There is a need to be more actively involved in sport organizations such as the Black Coaches Association (http://bcasports.cstv.com/), Black Women in Sport Foundation (http://www.black womeninsport.org/), Women's Basketball Coaches Association (http://www.wbca .org/), National Association of Collegiate Athletic Administrators (http://www.nac waa.org/), and National Collegiate Athletic Association (NCAA). The NCAA has implemented various strategies to enhance diversity in college athletics, such as providing postgraduate scholarships for racial minorities and women, developing internship programs aimed at racial minorities and women who want to work in university athletics administration, providing matching funds to Division II and III universities that hire full-time administrators to increase the department's sex and racial diversity, giving matching grants for minority women coaches, creating a leadership institute for racial minority males, and requiring diversity education. Apply for grants or financial assistance to attend developmental programs such as the BCA's Achieving Coaching Excellence (ACE) program, the "So You Want to Be a Coach?", and National Collegiate Athletic Association (NCAA)/National Association of Collegiate Athletic Administrators (NACWAA) Institutes. NACWAA partnered with the NCAA to offer three professional/leadership development programs (with two NCAA/NACWAA Institutes for Administrative Advancement held each year): The NCAA/NACWAA Leadership Enhancement Institute and the NCAA/NACWAA Institute for Athletics Executives alternate years. There is a program beneficial to every female athletic administrator—no matter where she is in her career. The primary objective for all of the NCAA/NACWAA programming is to provide opportunities for women working in intercollegiate athletics administration to increase their skills to enhance opportunities for growth in the field. NACWAA's Summer Institutes include: 1) NCAA/NACWAA Institute for Administrative Advancement; 2) NCAA/NACWAA: Leadership Enhancement Institute; and 3) NCAA/NACWAA Institute for Athletics Executives (NACWAA, 2010).

Although laws have opened the doors of opportunity for African Americans in intercollegiate athletics, stereotypes, ignorance, societal attitudes towards differences, and discriminatory institutional practices have limited employment in athletic leadership positions such as athletic administrators, coaches, officials, commentators, athletic trainers, and sports information directors. Political constraints in sport organizations also hinder the opportunities and/or advancement of African American women in intercollegiate athletics. Building the ranks of African American women in athletic department decision-making positions will require a change in the organizational mindset. Those individuals in positions to hire must be committed and sensitive to diversifying the ranks of college coaches and athletic administrators. The college athletics community, both collectively and individually, and institutions, must make a firm commitment to increase African Americans representation at all levels and positions. The NCAA and other national governing bodies of sport need to further show their commitment and emulate the National Football League (NFL) by establishing a rule similar to the Rooney Rule with strong sanctions if violated. The Rooney Rule, established in 2003 and expanded in 2009, requires NFL teams to interview minority candidates for head coaching positions, senior football operations opportunities, general manager jobs, and equivalent front-office positions (Maske, 2009). The NCAA has resisted taking the formal step of implementing the Rooney Rule. However, the NCAA Division I Athletic Director's Association has made a commitment by issuing guidelines that mirror the Rooney Rule (Wieberg, 2008). The NCAA claims that it is not in a position to affect whom its member programs interview and hire. Whenever member institutions of the NCAA decided that something was a problem, appropriate authority has been provided to the NCAA to fix the problem (Wieberg, 2008). Former NCAA executive director Cedric Dempsey, the late NCAA president Miles Brand, and the Division I-A Athletic Directors' Association have acknowledged that the lack of minority coaches and athletic administrators in college sport is a problem. The commitment by the NCAA to establish a rule to ensure that institutions interview at least one minority candidate for coaching and athletic administrative positions would not only constitute an acknowledgement that a problem or glass ceiling exists, but strategies are being implemented to provide opportunities for minorities to reach and shatter the ceiling.

STUDY QUESTIONS

1. Discuss the glass-ceiling effect as it relates to African American women coaches and intercollegiate athletic administrators.

2. List several strategies to assist African American women in overcoming the glass ceiling effect.

3. List several strategies that can be implemented by the NCAA member institutions to shatter the glass ceiling.

4. What is the role of the NCAA Diversity and Inclusion Department?

5. What is the role of the Black Coaches & Administrators?

6. What is the Rooney Rule?

7. Discuss impact of Title IX on the campuses of HBCUs.

8. What factors or conditions account for the lack of African American female head coaches and administrators?

9. List two (2) sports job boards, two (2) professional websites, two (2) professional blogs, and two (2) social networking sites that may be used by African American women to develop support networks and seek career opportunities in sport.

REFERENCES

Abney, R. (1988). The effects of role models and mentors on career patterns of African American women coaches and athletic administrators in historically African American and historically White institutions of higher education (Unpublished doctoral dissertation). The University of Iowa, Iowa City.

Abney, R. (1997, April). The impact of gender equity on the status of Black women as athletic administrators and coaches in sport. Paper presented at the American Alliance for Health, Physical Education, Recreation and Dance, St. Louis, MO.

Abney, R., & Richey, D. (1991). Barriers encountered by Black female athletic administrators and coaches. *Journal of Physical Education, Recreation, and Dance, 62*(6), 19–21.

Acosta, R. V., & Carpenter, L. J. (1987). Minority group members in athletic leadership. Unpublished manuscript. Department of Physical Education, Brooklyn College, Brooklyn, NY.

Acosta, R. V., & Carpenter, L. J. (Eds.). (1994). Women in intercollegiate sport: A longitudinal study—seventeen year update, 1977–1994. Unpublished manuscript. Department of Physical Education, Brooklyn College, Brooklyn, NY.

Acosta, R. V., & Carpenter, L. J. (Eds.). (1996). Women in intercollegiate sport: A longitudinal study—nineteen year update (1977–1996). Unpublished manuscript. Department of Physical Education, Brooklyn College, Brooklyn, NY.

Acosta, R. V., & Carpenter, L. J. (2010). *Women in intercollegiate sport: A longitudinal study thirty-three year update (1977–2010).* Retrieved from http://www.acostacarpenter.org

Alexander, A. (1978). *Status of minority women in the association of intercollegiate athletics for women.* Unpublished master's thesis. Temple University, Philadelphia, PA.

Blum, D. E. (1993, April 21). Forum examines discrimination against Black women in college sports. *The Chronicle of Higher Education,* A39–A40.

Borland, J. F. (2008). The under-representation of Black females in NCAA Division I women's basketball head coaching positions. Unpublished doctoral dissertation. University of Connecticut, Storrs, CT.

Clayton, T. B. (2010). The role of race and gender in the mentoring experiences and career success of African American female senior executive administrators in higher education. *Dissertation Abstracts International, 71,* 4-A.

Ebony Magazine. (1975, June). *Winning her point in a man's arena.* Chicago, IL: Author.

Farrell, C. S. (1992, December 3). NCAA minorities committee addresses absence of Black football head coaches. *Black Issues in Higher Education, 9,* 36–37.

Farrell, C. S. (1994a, June 16). Jump ball: Black coaches, NCAA have benign standoff. *Black Issues in Higher Education, 11,* 22–24.

Farrell, C. S. (1994b, September 22). NCAA: Blacks make the plays but call few of the shots. *Black Issues of Higher Education, 11,* 34–36.

Gerdy, J. R. (1994, August 11). You reap what you sow. *Black Issues in Higher Education, 11,* 30–31.

Grant, C., & Curtis, M. (1993, December 2). Women in sports. *The Chronicle of Higher Education, 11,* 25.

Houzer, S. (1974). Black women in athletics. *Physical Educator, 31,* 208–209.

Kinder, T. (1993). *Organizational management administration for athletic programs.* Dubuque, IA: Eddie Bowers Publishing.

Lapchick, R. (1989, Spring). Future of the Black student-athlete: Ethical issue of the 1990s. *Educational Record, 70,* 32–37.

Lapchick, R. (2010, March 11). 2008 racial and gender report card. Orlando, FL: University of Central Florida.

Malveaux, J. (1993). Sports scholars aren't the only outstanding students. *Black Issues in Higher Education, 10,* 54.

Maske, M. (2009). NFL expands Rooney rule to cover front-office hires. *The Washington Post.* Retrieved from http://www.washingtonpost.com/wp-dyn/content/article/2009/06/15/AR2009061502806.html

Morrison, S., White, R. P., Velsor E. V., & The Center for

Creative Leadership (1987). *Breaking the glass ceiling.* Reading, MA: Addison-Wesely Publishing Company.

Murphy, D. M. (1980). The involvement of Blacks in women's athletics in member institutions of the AIAW. Unpublished doctoral dissertation. Florida State University, Tallahassee, FL.

NACWAA (2010, July), *National Association of Collegiate Women Athletic Administrators.* Retrieved from http://www.nacwaa.org/?page_id = 61

National Collegiate Athletic Association. (2010). *2008–09 race and gender demographics of NCAA member institutions' personnel report.* Retrieved from http://www.ncaapublications.com/productdownloads/RGDMEMB10.pdf

National Collegiate Athletic Association. (2011). *2009–2010 race and gender demographics of NCAA member institutions' personnel report.* Retrieved from http://www.ncaapublications.com/productdownloads/2010RaceGenderMember. pdf

National Collegiate Athletic Association. (2007, February). *The NCAA minority opportunities and interests committee's biennial study on race and gender demographics of NCAA member institutions' personnel report.* Indianapolis, IN: Author.

National Collegiate Athletic Association. (2012). NCAA race and gender demographics. Retrieved from http://web1.ncaa.org/rgdSearch/exec/main

National Collegiate Athletic Association. (2008, December). *Diversity and inclusion: Enhancing diversity in intercollegiate athletics.* Retrieved from http://www.ncaa.org/wps/wcm/connect/8c3c29004e0d5ab7abc9fb1ad6fc8b25/diversity_and_inclusion.pdf?MOD = AJPERES&CACHEID = 8c3c29004e0d5ab7abc9fb1ad6fc8b25

National Collegiate Athletic Association. (1998, April). *The NCAA minority opportunities and interests committee's two-year study on race demographics of NCAA member institutions' athletic personnel.* Overland, KS: Author.

National Collegiate Athletic Association. (1996–1997). *Achieving gender equity, a basic guide to Title IX and gender equity in athletics for colleges and universities* (2nd ed.). Overland, KS: Author.

National Collegiate Athletic Association. (1994, August). *The NCAA minority opportunities and interests committee's four-year study on race demographics of member institutions.* Overland, KS: Author.

Naughton, J. (1998, March 6). New report decries dearth of Black coaches in football and basketball. *The Chronicle of Higher Education,* A45–A46.

Nelson, W. J. (1982). Society defining its members. In *Racial definition handbook.* Retrieved from http://www.webcom.com/intvoice/handbook.htm/

Sage, G. H. (1993). Introduction. In D. Brooks & R. Althouse (Eds.), *Racism in college athletics: The African American athlete's experience* (pp. 1–17). Morgantown, WV: Fitness Information Technology.

Schneider, R. C., Stier, W. F., Henry, T. J., & Wilding, G. E. (2010). Senior women administrators' perceptions of factors leading to discrimination of women in intercollegiate athletic departments. *Journal of Issues in Intercollegiate Athletics, 3,* 16–34.

Smith, Y. R. (1991). Issues and strategies for working with multicultural athletes. *Journal of Physical Education, Recreation, and Dance, 62*(3), 39–44.

Social Equity Office. (1997a). Social equity at Slippery Rock University [Poster]. Slippery Rock, PA: Author.

Social Equity Office. (1997b). Social equity office policies [Brochure]. Slippery Rock, PA: Author.

Stratta, T. M. (1995). *An ethnography of the sport experience of African American female athletes* Unpublished doctoral dissertation. Southern Illinois University, Carbondale, IL.

Vance, N. S. (1984, April 25). Football study links race, player positions: Reason aren't clear, 3 researchers caution. *The Chronicle of Higher Education, 21,* 24.

Wieberg, S. (2008, January 16) *Minority-hiring policy stiffens for major football programs.* Retrieved from http://www.usatoday.com/sports/college/football/2008-01-15-Minorityhiring_N.htm

Women's Sports Foundation (2008). *Race and sport: The women's sports foundation position.* Retrieved from http://www.womenssportsfoundation.org/Content/Articles/Issues/Title-IX/R/Race-and-Sport-A-Womens-Sports-Foundation-Position.aspx

Section IV:
The African American Student-Athlete and Popular Culture

These two chapters take readers into the tenuous relationship between pop culture and higher education. Chapter 10 examines the question, "Is it possible to create more balance between the player and her/his academic performance as a student in American higher education?" by implementing programs and strategies using pop culture to improve academic performance. In their examination of that question, Harrison and Sutton bring a fresh view of the intersection between pop culture, athletic participation, and academic success. The authors want to enable professors, students on campus, and university administrators to "crack the world" of today's student-athlete through the concept of *educationalism and academic swagger*. The Scholar-Baller initiative serves as the reference point and as an example of a cultural movement that blends education, sport, and entertainment into one lifestyle that embraces academic performance. In other words, pop culture can be utilized in an effective and self-affirming context to challenge and culturally motivate student-athletes in the 21st century.

Chapter 11 undertakes a remarkable exploration about the relationship between hip hop culture and collegiate athletics, suggesting that coaches who have players attached to the hip hop culture are often confronting double doses of hypermasculity. Smith claims "to demonstrate that strength is hip hop's highest normative principle and that personal integrity and group loyalty are its most obvious hallmarks." To follow up the claim, Smith argues that for coaches as well as others dealing with scholastic athletics "the best technique for influencing a hip hop athlete or any youth intensely committed to personal integrity and group loyalty is to help them 'expand' their game instead of 'changing' it." Dealing with hip hop athletes "can be more successful, not by feigning understanding and adoption of hip hop music and culture, and certainly not by treating hip hop as a lesser culture, but by respecting its normative order." In essence, the *hood way* is not subordinate to mainstream culture, but rather allows the hip hop athlete to opt for learning new things that help him expand his own *personhood* and use this knowledge to elevate group loyalty.

CHAPTER 10

Cracking Their World: Utilizing Pop Culture to Impact Academic Success of Today's Student-Athlete

C. KEITH HARRISON and BILL SUTTON

Abstract

The purpose of this chapter is to explain how pop culture can be utilized in an effective and self-affirming context to challenge and culturally motivate student-athletes in the 21st Century. While African American male student-athletes will be the target population in this chapter as opposed to other groups (i.e., women), the ultimate objective is for this chapter to have broader applications to *all* intercollegiate student-athletes. This chapter sets forth the concept of integrating education with pop culture by cultivating academic performance through the use of culturally relevant messages from the sport and entertainment industries in addition to higher education. Also, this includes an examination of the academic fusion of music, fashion, art, media, and the internet, as well as the food and beverage industry as *real-time* incentives that parallel human lifestyles. All of the above-mentioned cultural factors contribute to a student-athlete's ideas about, and consumption patterns relating to, academic achievement and athletic motivation, in which the student athlete's consumption choices are deemed either *cool* or *uncool*. This chapter hypothesizes that much like other urban pop culture trends set by African American males, society will also follow the academic production and educational preferences of this particular ethnic population in concert with all other ethnicities. This chapter also provides practical solutions for college professors, students, and other stakeholders on campus. The goal of these recommendations is to enable faculty, students on campus, and university administrators to "crack the world" of today's student-athlete through the concept of *educationalism and academic swagger*. Scholar-Baller will serve as the reference point and case example as a cultural movement that blends education, sport and entertainment into one lifestyle that embraces academic performance.

Harrison: "What if Jay-Z and Beyonce agreed to perform a concert for every student-athlete in the country with a GPA of 3.0 or higher?"

Jermaine Taylor/NBA Draft Pick: "Then everyone would get a B or better average. I know I would." (dialogue between a faculty member and student-athlete at UCF during the spring 2009)

Key Terms		
● academic performance	● early adoptees
● African American male student-athletes	● educationalism
● cool, pop culture	● innovation
● cultural motivation	● Scholar-Baller

INTRODUCTION

Each fall when college football season kicks off and signifies the beginning of the academic school year, the popular ESPN sports show *College GameDay* airs on Saturday mornings at 10 a.m. EST and takes place at select campuses throughout the United States. The *College GameDay* "Comin' To Your City Tour" and college football's bowl season are followed in the spring by the month of men's college basketball known as "March Madness," which has become a cultural phenomenon at schools and workplaces and in communities nationwide. Sports fans and members of the general public are culturally motivated to be a part of the college sports experience.

These cultural events in college football and basketball are consumed by millions of viewers. Thousands of loyal fans attend each game. Merchandise and apparel are sold in large quantities. Pictures are taken of star athletes, and movies are made about the successes of college teams. Websites are dedicated to player rosters and statistics on the physical (not mental or academic) performances of student-athletes. With these consumption patterns and the commercialization of intercollegiate athletics in mind, this chapter addresses and attempts to answer the following core questions: In terms of the popularity of college football and basketball (as well as other college sports), is it possible to create more balance and synergy between the player and his/her academic performance as a student in American higher education? If so, how can academic institutions and individual stakeholders proactively implement programs and strategies to utilize pop culture to improve academic performance?

SELF-AFFIRMATION, SUCCESS, AND AFRICAN AMERICAN MALES (I AM WHAT I SEE . . . AND DO NOT SEE)

In terms of the identity and academic success of African American males involved in high school and college athletics, there are some important existing research findings and trends regarding African American male student-athletes that should be considered before we further develop the central concepts of this chapter. Previous research indicates that African American male and/or African American male student-athletes

- graduate from college at a lower rate than White American male student-athletes (Lapchick, 2009);
- have success with retention, matriculation, and graduation when they have positive African American peers, mentors, and support systems on campus (Allen, 1988);
- perform relatively better academically when they have African American male role

models, regardless of the educational achievements of their role models (Harper, 2006);

- tend to see the world through a binary or dichotomous prism and adopt an either/ or (versus a win/win) perspective in terms of goals, desires, dreams and popularity (White & Cones, 1999);

- focus on athletic performance instead of on long-term goals in sport business management and other fields that require leadership beyond physical participation, and have limited access to activities and programs that focus on long-term career goals and planning (Harrison, Jr. , 2009);

- accentuate their athlete identity (as compared to their student identity) as a result of embracing what they perceive as a positive stereotype and in an effort to form a positive racial identity (Harrison, Jr. 2009);

- are often forced by their peers to choose between being popular and being smart (Kunjufu, 1988);

- face the challenge of discovering how to emphasize their male identity and invest in their education with the same enthusiasm and work ethic that they dedicate on the playing fields and to other social expressions such as fashion, music and art (Harrison, 2002); and

- were the only group that experienced serious and significant disidentification with academics in a large sample of high school students from the National Educational Longitudinal Study (NELS) data (Osborne, 1997).

These findings from the scholarship on African American males and African American male student-athletes are relevant when discussing the concept of being a "cool" male in society, as well as when discussing self-concept and identity issues (Martin & Harris, 2006). The next section examines what it means to be cool.

DEFINITION OF COOL

According to Kerner and Pressman (2007), authors of the book *Chasing Cool*, there is no objective definition for what makes something or someone cool. The concept of cool, and the attributes of being cool, are inherently subjective in nature and can vary dramatically depending on the perceptions of a target group or audience at a particular point in time. Pountain and Robins (2000) explain that the contemporary conceptualization of cool inevitably varies from culture to culture and interacts with, and is modified by, local attitudes in a very complex fashion. Ideas and attitudes related to the concept of cool have existed for centuries in numerous cultures throughout the world; the fundamental notion of cool has been "modified, added to and subtracted from in a million subtle ways" (p. 40).

The term *cool* has been used in a variety of contexts and has assumed the following meanings depending upon the context or situation in which the term is used:

- Fashionable, trendy, stylish, sophisticated and intriguing (without being overly flamboyant or ostentatious).
- In touch with popular opinion, and socially adept and desirable.
- Composed, self-controlled, relaxed and unemotional.
- Indication of agreement, approval or admiration.
- Expression of dislike, unresponsiveness or enthusiasm. (Kerner & Pressman, 2007)

Cool in Popular Culture

The word *cool* can be used to describe an individual who is composed, calm and collected, and can also refer to something that is aesthetically appealing. Historically speaking, cool may have originated as an attitude exuded by rebels and nonconformists such as prisoners, slaves and political dissidents—classes of persons for which direct rebellion would likely result in punishment. As a result, these individuals oftentimes masked their defiance behind a wall of ironic detachment, thereby distancing themselves from the source of authority rather than directly confronting it (Major & Billison, 1993).

Cool evolved into a form of passive resistance through personal style, and functioned as an effective defense mechanism to oppression and depression (Pountain & Robins, 2000).

Historically, Hollywood filmmakers capitalized on this notion of coolness with movies such as *Rebel Without a Cause* (1955) starring James Dean; *Five Easy Pieces* (1970) and *Carnal Knowledge* (1971) starring Jack Nicholson; and perhaps the ultimate portrayal of cool by Paul Newman in the acclaimed *Cool Hand Luke* (1967). In fact, in *Cool Hand Luke* the viewer is able to gain an understanding of the aspirational nature of cool, as Luke is envied by all of the other convicts because he acts in a way that they cannot behave—even though they would like to emulate Luke's conduct. This aspirational component of cool is the major cultural driving force of the concept. We all want to be cool, even if we are not perceived to be cool by those whom we have determined to be worthy judges. The success of the current CBS comedy *Big Bang Theory* is based upon watching four men who would widely be described as nerds or un-cool outside of their own social circle set their own standards for cool within their current peer group. The show chronicles the aspirational drive of these four men to be perceived as cool by a broader audience than their current social circle. Another example of nerd-like images represented as cool is Best Buy's computer assistance team known as the "Geek Squad;" the employees wear clothes that resemble the stereotypical white button up shirt and skinny black tie.

Cool is also an attitude widely adopted by artists, intellectuals and, in particular, musicians who have aided its infiltration and ultimate cultural dissemination throughout popular culture. Musicians have been extremely influential in portraying what is cool not only in terms of sound (blues, jazz, rock and roll, soul, punk rock, alternative rock, and hip hop just to mention a few), but also in terms of fashion (hair in particular, along with clothing and sunglasses), speech and political viewpoints. Elvis Presley, The Beatles, The Temptations, Madonna, Neil Young, Run DMC, Eminem, and Bono have all affected popular culture and influenced our perception of cool. In other words, they have all demonstrated the ability to "crack our world" in one way or another.

Cool and the African American Culture

African Americans have made major contributions to what is considered hip and cool nationally and internationally. According to Pountain and Robins (2000), "the roots of modern cool lie in African (and later African American) culture" (p. 52). Cool has been used to describe a general state of well-being, a transcendent, internal peace and serenity (Thompson, 1973). It can also refer to an absence of conflict, a state of harmony and balance as in "the land is cool" or as in a "cool (spiritual) heart." Such meanings according to Thompson (1973) are African in origin. This concept has evolved into slang and, later, accepted English terms. Expressions such as "don't let it blow your cool," which was eventually replaced with "chill out" and the use of *chill* as a verb all have their origins in African American Vernacular English (Lee, 1999).

Dr. Harrison (center) with many Scholar-Baller (SB) student-athletes from Toledo University in a game against another SB school, Akron University. Prior to the kick-off, the fans from both teams gave all the players recognition for competing in the classroom and making school cool as they stood at the 50-year line with the Thinkman logo on their helmets and/ or jerseys (circa 2008).

Marlene Connor (1995) connects cool and the post-war African American experience in her book *What is Cool? Understanding Black Manhood in America*. Connor writes that cool is the silent and knowing rejection of racial oppression, a self-dignified expression of masculinity developed by black men denied mainstream expressions of manhood. It is her opinion that the mainstream perception of cool is narrow and distorted, with cool often perceived merely as style or arrogance rather than a way to achieve respect.

Another viewpoint on this issue is the concept of *cool pose*, which may speak to the heart of the issue regarding African American perceptions of educational achievement evidenced by an academically based recognition program such as Scholar-Baller. Majors and Billson (1993) offer the concept of *cool pose* and argue that it is a strategy that helps African American men counter stress caused by social oppression, rejection and racism. Majors and Billson also contend that it furnishes the African American male with a sense of control, strength, confidence and stability, and helps African American men deal with the closed doors and negative messages of the "generalized other." Stated differently, it takes the classic definitions of cool and shows African American men to be indifferent to certain opportunities and possibilities because ultimately they may be unaccepted or rejected in their pursuits of these opportunities—therefore they are "cool" towards it.

The term *early adopters* is extremely applicable to the concept of cool as these men and women attempt to set trends for others to follow. Simply stated, they determine what could be cool and attempt to make their view dominant (Kerner & Pressman, 2007). Our next section examines how youth as early adopters are influenced and shaped by cultural messages that lead to specific consumption patterns.

MORE THINGS THAT ARE CONSIDERED COOL
(CONSUMPTION AND POP CULTURE)

A landmark study in 1992–93 known as the MEE Report, which was conducted in Philadelphia with urban youth, found that African American male and female youth ages 12 to 18 spend their disposable income on clothes, food, shoes, music, and jewelry, respectively. Further, "The Young Urban Consumer: How Hip-Hop Culture Affects the Lifestyle and Buying Decisions of 12- to 34-Year Olds" (2006) provides an in-depth view of how hip hop culture continues to influence the lifestyle and buying decisions of young urban consumers as young as 12 years old and as old as 34. The 37 million young urban consumers analyzed in this report live in all parts of the country and have an urban mindset, regardless of whether they live in a city, a suburb or a small town. Young urban consumers enjoy an aggregate income of $600 billion and they love to shop and spend. These trendsetters and influencers who affiliate themselves with hip hop culture exercise a powerful impact on the direction of the fashion, media, entertainment and other key consumer-focused industries. Examples of this impact include the popular songs by artists such as Jay-Z and Kanye West used often at NFL and NBA events ("Brothers in Paris"); Beats by Dr. Dre headphones that are used by millions of athletes and non-athletes across the globe; and the language of hip hop is embedded in mass media marketing campaigns, television shows, etc., with phrases such as "da bomb"—meaning the best that something can be—and "no she/he didn't," which is used to describe a top performance by elite athletes on ESPN highlights. All these cultural messages impact the perception of consumers in society.

WHY PERCEPTION IS REALITY:
ALTERING PERCEPTIONS IN SOCIETAL CULTURE

Perception is commonly defined as the way someone thinks about something they have seen, read, heard or experienced. Perception is highly subjective and people witnessing the same thing, seeing the same film, or reading the same book are apt to have different perceptions about what they have seen or read. Often these perceptions are based upon personal values and past experiences, while in other cases they can be influenced by a peer group or the perception may be simply an emotional response to something rather than a logical response (Harper, 2006).

Because perceptions are highly subjective, they can be correct or they can be incorrect in terms of the message being sent or the intent of the sender. From a marketing viewpoint, the perception of the target audience, regardless of whether or not that perception is correct, is the marketing reality that the marketer must face. In other words, the marketer cannot ignore a perception that is incorrect because he or she must then attempt to alter that perception. Bars, restaurants, movies, and other elements of pop culture can be perceived as cool, and then resultantly become successful. If they are not perceived to be cool, they are often ignored and finally close because of that perception of not being the cool place or the cool thing. This is a serious challenge for 21st century athletic departments that still operate with a traditional cultural model and that sometimes fail to understand the importance of using relevant concepts and constructs to challenge student-athletes to compete in the classroom and encourage student-athletes to take pride in their academic performance versus barely remaining eligible.

If we are to convince student-athletes (and African American male student-athletes in particular) that studying and being successful in the classroom is cool, we will have to create a perception of being cool (in school) to overcome the existing perception of un-cool (in school). The current notions that studying is not cool and you are selling out if you work to achieve high grades are the basis for the un-cool perception, and that is the perception reinforced by the thinking and behavior of student-athletes' peers. This perception in particular—because of the heavy reliance of peer opinion and values is much more difficult to alter—further illustrates the need to "crack this world."

On the Field (Athletics)	Off the Field (Academics)
Uniform/colors/attire	Jerseys, clothes
Slang/language	Communication/jargon
Food/beverage	Hanging out at the cool spot/establishment
Women watching them perform	"Hollering" at girls
Swagger and style	P. Diddy or Fonzworth Bentley
Cars	Transportation and parking
Sneakers	Kicks/shoes
Haircuts	Grooming
Athletic performance	Academic performance

Figure 10.1. Things to Consider that Are Cool When Creating Incentives for African American Male and Other Student-Athletes on Campus.

EXAMPLES OF SCHOOL IS COOL: SCHOLAR-BALLER SNAPSHOTS AND INNOVATION

The Scholar-Baller program has experienced significant impact in terms of student-athletes that embrace educational recognition through pop culture (see the photos that accompany this chapter). This impact has resulted from the program's focus on cultural motivation and the concept of *educationalism* (which is the convergence of education, sport, entertainment and commercialism). What follows is a summary of various benchmarks from taking an innovative and culturally relevant approach to academic performance and intellectual recognition through pop culture (see Figure 10.1). First, this section will summarize examples of this impact that are of a narrative and qualitative nature. Second, we will briefly summarize some of the descriptive data about the impact of this innovative program.

Myron Rolle: Passing Up a Guaranteed Spot in the NFL to Continue Hitting the Books

Myron Rolle graduated from high school with a 4.0 grade point average (GPA) and was the top-ranked high school football player by ESPN. Rolle went on to attend Florida State University, where he starred for the Seminoles' football team and developed into one of the top prospects for the 2009 NFL draft. In addition to making plays on the football field, Rolle also excelled in the classroom.

Rolle graduated Magna Cum Laude from Florida State's pre-med program in two and a half years (five semesters) with a 3.75 GPA, and he is in the process of earning his master's degree in public administration from Florida State. In an interview with Robert Siegel of National Public Radio (2008), Rolle stated that "my nickname is the doctor or the president in the locker room . . . academics and education is a priority for me." Rolle's dedication to academics was confirmed when he decided to miss part of a pivotal college football game against Maryland to partake in a final interview for the Rhodes Scholarship, which is considered the most prestigious honor in all of college academics.

In November 2008, Rolle became the first starting player on a major college football team to receive a Rhodes Scholarship since Stanford tight end Cory Booker in 1992 (Booker is currently the mayor of Newark, New Jersey) (Elish, 2009). Instead of entering the 2009 NFL draft and earning millions of dollars, Rolle decided to accept the Rhodes Scholarship and spend the following year studying medical anthropology at Oxford University in England. Rolle was later selected in the sixth round of the 2010 NFL Draft by the Tennessee Titans.

Jordan Farmar: Attending Class Moments after Declaring for the NBA Draft

Jordan Farmar is likely one of the few players in the NBA who transferred high schools primarily for academic purposes and whose decision on what college to attend was strongly based on the quality of the school's academic (not athletic) program (Springer, 2006). Farmar reiterated his focus on academic studies when he stated the following in an interview during his freshman year at UCLA: "I know that I won't be able to play forever, and I've got to plan for a career after basketball" (Bogen, 2005).

After excelling as a starting point guard for the UCLA Bruins basketball team for two seasons and also earning a nomination for the Anson Mount Scholar-Athlete Award, Farmar decided to forgo his final two seasons of collegiate eligibility and enter the 2006 NBA draft. Moments after his press conference announcing that he was declaring for the NBA draft—and in true scholar-baller style—Farmar walked up "the Hill" with his counselor Kenny Donaldson on UCLA's campus to attend a lecture by Drs. Keith Harrison and Eddie Comeaux on education, sport, and hip hop in the class "Sociological Perspectives of Sport in American Higher Education." Farmar's commitment to lifelong learning and to community service (Farmar established the Jordan Farmar Foundation in 2008 in order to make a positive impact in his local community, with an emphasis on youth programs in Southern California) should help current student-athletes better comprehend that it is cool to succeed in the classroom and make a difference in their local community.

Academic Momentum Award (AMA)

Each year Scholar-Baller, in conjunction with the National Consortium for Academics and Sports (NCAS), sponsors the Academic Momentum Award, which recognizes ap-

Larry English (graduate of Northern Illinois) is one of the most visible Scholar-Baller (SB) student-athletes ever as a former NFL draft pick of the San Diego Chargers and All-American defensive end/outside linebacker for the NIU Huskies (circa 2008). NIU has averaged more than 40 student-athletes with a 3.0 GPA or higher since 2006 as an official partner of the SB Group.

proximately 20 student-athletes every year for their academic performance. In 2008, 63 nominations were received from various colleges and universities across the country. In 2009, more than 79 student-athletes were nominated for this innovative and meaningful award and this trend has continued in 2010, 2011, and 2012, with approximately 90 nominations each year. One unintended positive outcome from the AMA is that some institutions and athletic departments have created an added recognition ceremony to the recipients of the award and compete with one another for the most winners and nominees the last five years.

Scholar-Baller Success on the Playing Field, in the Classroom, and in the Uniform

On September 2, 2004, Arizona State University, in partnership with Scholar-Baller, became the first NCAA team in any division to wear an academic performance patch on their game day uniform and jersey against UTEP (ASU would go on to wear it for every season since the inaugural year on home and away jerseys). This historically significant moment was followed with another important twist. During the 2008 season, three different ASU Scholar-Ballers scored three consecutive touchdowns on defense in a game against UCLA on national television.

Sewing Kits for Scholar-Baller Patches at Morgan State University (MSU)

While ASU was the first intercollegiate athletic team in the NCAA to wear the patch, two historically Black college universities (HBCUs) were the second and third respectively. The Scholar-Baller Group spoke to both teams prior to the New York Urban League Classic (NYULC) about the importance of academic performance and positioning themselves for long-term success. The day before the game, Hampton's equipment leader John "Buster" Jackson agreed to sew the patches on for the contest played at the New York Giants stadium. However, MSU did not have the same luxury, so the players took the ownership of displaying the patch on game day.

Examples of Student-Athletes Competing in the Classroom and on the Playing Field

- The average GPA for student-athletes on a Division I basketball team gradually increased from 2.3 to 2.8 and from 3.1 to 3.3 during a four-semester period based on the Scholar-Baller of the Month Recognition and Incentive Model. Student-athletes on this particular basketball team enthusiastically embrace the Scholar-Baller message, a message that is clearly evident based on the environment in the team's locker room and the players' approach to academic performance.

- A Football Championship Subdivision (FCS) football team has made historical progress and has established new standards for academic success, as this football team recently shifted from the lowest team sport GPA to the highest football team GPA in school history. This school also reported the highest athletic department GPA in school history, and currently has one of the highest graduation rates in the nation at the FCS level for African-American male student-athletes who play collegiate football.

- A community college in California experienced an increase from 36 to 85 student-athletes with Scholar-Baller status (GPA of 3.0 or better) over a two-year period.

- At another community college, the team GPA for a women's soccer team increased by an entire letter grade during a single semester.

These are just a few examples of how attention to culture can impact the world of student-athletes on campus. The next section examines how the Scholar-Baller concept and movement could potentially crack the world.

CRACKING THEIR WORLD (Making School Cool)

Everyone has a *worldview*. A worldview can be defined as the sum of one's experiences, relationships, education and values and how those factors interrelate to form one's view of the world as they see it. Once defined, this worldview also delineates what one is concerned with, what they feel is important, and what they believe to be fact or fiction. This element of what is real and what is not real is not scientifically defined but is more emotionally defined by the values and experiences that compose the worldview. For example, scientific evidence may lead one to believe that smoking is harmful to one's health. Conversely, one could have a worldview based upon a variety of factors (for example, they smoke themselves, know lots of other people who smoke and none of those people have health issues, and therefore they believe that smoking poses no health risk). You may argue that this particular worldview, given the overwhelming scientific data to the contrary, is inaccurate and you would be seen by most as correct. But to the person with the worldview that smoking is not a health risk, that is their perception and thus their worldview is the reality in which they operate. This is the key point: In order to crack their world and make a substantive change in what they believe or how they act, the person wanting to alter their worldview must find a way that is meaningful to the worldview holder in such a way as to gain entry and establish a foothold in their worldview.

To gain entry and in order to comprehend someone's worldview, the person or idea seeking entry must come from a source that the worldview holder has defined as relevant and important to them. If the source is not viewed as relevant or important, the likelihood of gaining entry and ultimately understanding and acceptance is highly unlikely. Let us undertake the task of making educational achievement and performance excellence an accepted view as a criterion for success in career and life. Let us assume that the world we wish to crack is the perception of an individual, or to be even more challenging, a group of individuals who either feel that they cannot compete in an educational environment or that they have seen numerous people who were not academically motivated or competitive yet have been successful in life. In this scenario you are attempting to crack multiple worlds that have a peer network for additional support of their worldview.

In a number of peer groups, particularly those with a documented history of poor academic performance, there are some things to consider. The realities of high dropout rates, lack of mentorship, and general disinterest may cultivate a focus on the success stories of people in either the sport or entertainment industries. The perception sometimes is that these people have been successful because of natural talent and abilities and not from an academic route or delayed gratification type of career experience. As these successful people compose their worldview, the only way to crack that worldview after first gaining an understanding of it is to introduce two other types of people into their worldview—unsuccessful people who tried to be successful without education and people who became successful in other industries because of their education and not because of their natural talents. In either case, these people have to be seen as relevant to that worldview and must be known, visible, or easily accepted as "that could be me." If the people introduced into the worldview are seen as exceptions or as "that isn't me," then the attempt to crack that worldview will fail. They need to look and act like the worldview holder.

For example, if the person I am trying to emulate is a musical artist who dropped out of high school but is recognized as successful, then I would need to introduce a number of people who tried to follow that path and failed as well as someone lacking the talent but because of their education was able to secure a management position in the entertainment industry and is also perceived as successful.

In the world of athletics, it is an athlete who not only has achieved success on the field but off and, most importantly, how that off-field success is related to educational achievement. Lebron James and Kobe Bryant must be seen as exceptions, while other successful athletes playing in sport or working in sport must be seen as the best chance for success. In our last section we sketch out some practical recommendations on how cracking the world of youth and young adults might become a huge tipping point in society through various cultural forces.

SUMMARY AND RECOMMENDATIONS: EDUCATIONALISM AND ACADEMIC SWAGGER

In this chapter we have addressed how to increase the *academic performance* and *cultural motivation* of today's student-athletes with a particular focus on African American male student-athletes. In the 21st century, educators, sport managers, spectators, students, and the student-athletes themselves must continue to push the boundaries of culture so that school becoming cool moves beyond the pages of this chapter. This concept from our perspective is educationalism, a way to marry education with commerce through sport and entertainment. Hence, these are our top ten items that may serve as powerful inertia with changing the existing paradigm of what is considered cool and un-cool in the academic and athletic domains across the country. This list is a sketch of how student-athletes (in general) might adopt and access these images/representations/identities can create messages of academic swagger (to walk with a lofty proud gait, often in an attempt to impress others). The key is that these associations and synergies will include an educational tie and academic connection to what is considered cool versus connected to what is un-cool:

1) Sneakers associated with cool people (Michael Eric Dyson, Cornel West, Benjamin Carson, and President Obama)
2) Associated with cool things (Scholar-Baller incentives such as hats, sneakers, and polos)
3) Wearing things that are cool (Brand Jordan, Nike)
4) Hanging (traveling) out at places that are cool (Professional Football Player Mothers' Association/PFPMA)
5) Being different is cool (Scholar-Baller Status)
6) Sayings and slang is cool (Are you ballin' or fallin'?)
7) Gestures and posturing is cool (ballin')
8) Being respected for who you are as an individual is cool (Do You)
9) Being an athlete is cool (Michael Jordan, Candace Parker, Kobe Bryant, Donovan McNabb)
10) Being an artist is cool (Jay-Z, LL Cool J, John Legend, Queen Latifah)

In the final analysis, "the developments at interface of race, sport, and society are dynamic. The struggle is therefore perpetual and there are no final victories; not Jackie

Robinson, not Tommy Smith and John Carlos, not Curt Flood who challenged the reserve rule. The question is who is going to stand up and analyze and project a vision of those challenges today" (Edwards, 2008).

Interestingly enough, urban Black male youth for decades, if not centuries, have set the standard of what is considered cool in terms of sport and entertainment and this same demographic continues to be the prize recruit for football and basketball teams from coast to coast. What irony it would be for this same ethnic gender whose focal representation by mainstream media has been on their bodies not their brains to shift the tide and create a sea change when it comes to the consumption patterns and revolutionary identities in the context of education, literacy, and ultimately freedom/liberation.

STUDY QUESTIONS

1. What is *cool*?

2. What does the research indicate about the identity of African American males in college and society?

3. What are some consumption patterns by youth and young adults in terms of lifestyle and disposable income?

4. What are some things that athletic department leaders and sport managers might consider when attempting to alter the perceptions of student-athletes?

5. What are some case examples of Scholar-Baller tapping into pop culture for educational outcomes and academic performance?

6. What are some things that student-athletes, especially African American males, might think are cool?

7. How might the concept of educationalism be a win/win for educational, athletic, and entertainment stakeholders in terms of cracking the world?

SUGGESTED READINGS

Cheville, J. (2001). *Minding the body: What student-athletes know about learning.* Portsmouth, NH. Heinemann.

Dyson, M. (2007). *Know what I mean?: Reflections on hip-hop [KNOW WHAT I MEAN].* New York, NY: Basic Civitas Books.

Dyson, M. E. (2009). *Can you hear me now?* New York, NY: Basic Civitas Books.

Gladwell, M. (2000). *The tipping point: How little things can make a big difference.* Boston, MA: Little, Brown and Company.

Gladwell, M. (2008). *Outliers.* London, UK: Little, Brown and Company.

Liles, K. (2006). *Make it happen: The hip-hop generation guide to success.* New York, NY: Atria.

Simmons, R., & Morrow, C. (2007). *Do you! 12 laws to access the power in you to achieve happiness and success.* New York, London, Sydney: Gotham Books.

SUGGESTED MOVIES

Finding Forester (2000)
Freedom Writers (2007)
The Express (2008)
Notorious (2009)

SUGGESTED MUSIC

KRS 1—"Why Is That?" (1989)
Young MC—"Principal's Office" (1989)
Jay-Z—"Guns N Roses" (2002)
NAS—"Carry on Tradition" (2006)
Talib Kweli—"More or Less" (2007)
Lupe Fiasco—"The Coolest" (2007)
Common—"Drivin' Me Wild" (2007)
Anthony Hamilton (featuring David Banner)—"Cool" (2008)

REFERENCES

Allen, W. (1988). Black students in U.S. higher education: Toward improved access, adjustment and achievement. *The Urban Review, 20*(3), 165–188.

Bogen, A. (2005). *UCLA's Jewish Jordan.* Retrieved from http://www.ynetnews.com/articles/0,7340,L-3177805,00.html

Connor, M. K. (1995). *What is cool? Understanding Black manhood in America.* New York, NY: Crown Publishers.

Edwards, H. (2008). Remarks at the American ethnic sports hall of fame. San Francisco, CA.

Elish, J. (February/March 2009), On a Rolle: Myron Rolle awarded Rhodes scholarship. *Florida State Times*, 1, 8.

Harper, S. (2006). Peer support for African American male college achievement: Beyond internalized racism and the burden of "acting White." *The Journal of Men's Studies, 14*(3), 336–358.

Harrison, C. K. (2002). Scholar or baller? A photo and visual elicitation with student athletes. *NASPAJ, 8*(1), 66–81.

Harrison Jr., L. (2009). *Race and athletic performance.* Paper presented at the CSRI conference in Chapel Hill, NC.

Kerner, N., & Pressman, G. (2007). *Chasing cool.* New York, NY: Atria Books.

Kunjufu, J. (1988). *To be popular or smart? The Black peer group.* Chicago, IL: African American images.

Lapchick, R. E. (2009). Graduation rates. The Institute for Diversity and Ethics in Sport. University of Central Florida (UCF), Orlando, Florida.

Lee, M. (1999). Out of the hood and into the news: Borrowed Black verbal expressions in a mainstream newspaper. *American Speech, 74*(4), 369–388.

Majors, R., & Bilson, J. M. (1993). *Cool pose: The dilemmas of Black men in America.* Austin, TX: Touchstone Publishers.

Martin, B. E., & Harris III, F. (2006). Examining productive conceptions of masculinities: Lessons learned from academically driven African American male student-athletes. *The Journal of Men's Studies, 14*(3), 359–378.

Osborne, J. W. (1997). Race and academic disidentification. *Journal of Educational Psychology, 89*(4), 728–735.

Pountain, D., & Robins, D. (2000). *Cool rules: Anatomy of an attitude.* London, UK: Reaktion Books Ltd.

Siegel, R. (2008). FSU football star wins rhodes scholarship. *National Public Radio.* Retrieved from http://www.npr.org/templates/story/story.php?storyId = 97418935

Springer, S. (2006, March 13). Preeminent domain: Farmar joined a long list of recruits from talent-rich Southland who stayed home to play for UCLA, but it was no slam-dunk. *Los Angeles Times.*

Thompson, R. F. (1973). An aesthetic of the cool. *African Arts, 7*(1), 40–43, 64–67, 89–91.

White, J. L., & Cones, J. H. (1999). *Black men emerging: Facing the past and seizing a future in America.* New York, NY: Routledge.

CHAPTER 11

Coaching Hip Hop Athletes, Confronting Double Doses of Hypermasculinity

ANDRE L. SMITH

Abstract

Why would an All-Star basketball player like Carmelo Anthony be caught in an underground video promoting a "stop snitching" campaign designed to discourage people from informing authorities about illegal activities? This chapter contends that it is because, as a member of the hip hop community, an alternative culture created by and for inner-city youths, he would have been perceived there as being weak for allowing his commercial success to prevent him from staying loyal to his friends, and the scorn from his peers would be worse if not participating would have been inconsistent with statements he might have previously made about snitching before he became a professional basketball player.

This chapter attempts to demonstrate that strength is hip hop's highest normative principle and that personal integrity and group loyalty are its most obvious hallmarks. In the author's estimation, the majority of discourse relating to sports follows the same normative order, strength over both wealth and justice. For scholastic athletics, this means coaches who have players attached to the hip hop community are often confronting double doses of hypermasculinity. But this chapter contends that since the two social systems are fairly symmetrical, the same techniques for dampening hypermasculinity in sports may be deployed by coaches and other educators who attempt to dampen the hypermasculinity of members of the hip hop community generally. Towards that end, this chapter ultimately suggests that the best technique for influencing a hip hop athlete or any youth intensely committed to personal integrity and group loyalty is to help them *expand* their game instead of *changing* it.

Key Terms		
• autopoiesis	•	marginalization
• epistemology	•	norms or normativity
• hip hop	•	relativity
• hypermasculinity	•	symmetry
• justice discourse	•	utility, efficiency

INTRODUCTION

"Every Black man that goes in the studio has always got two people in his head: him in terms of who he really is, and the thug that he feels he has to project."
—Byron Hurt, former college quarterback
(Northeastern University), and hip hop documentary film producer.[1]

The quote above applies to many student-athletes, some of whom are finding themselves at a time when they are being bombarded by peers, mentors and media with messages as to who they should be. These sometimes-inconsistent and confusing messages can cause deep personal conflict within a teenager whose missteps of any substantial consequence will likely be on display to the entire sports watching public. For an increasing many who operate within the sphere of hip hop, and for those outside of hip hop who must nevertheless relate to it, the conflicting messages are plenty and seemingly irreconcilable. This chapter, however, attempts to show that the worlds of sport and hip hop are closer than initially thought. The same approaches to dampening hypermasculinity in collegiate sports generally may be applied to properly contextualize strength as a normative principle embraced by hip hop athletes specifically. More specifically, coaches and mentors charged with molding and shaping the conduct of youths should not try to get student-athletes to disavow hip hop culture specifically or to diminish their affection for strength generally. Instead, they should encourage those youths to direct their strengths towards their own personal development and helping others.

The relationship between hip hop and collegiate athletics is not entirely obvious. While it is easy to observe the increasing presence of hip hop music and themes in collegiate arenas and stadiums, and in athletic department marketing and promotion material, it is often hard for those outside the hip hop community to understand how to deal constructively with an increasing number of collegiate athletes who adopt the dress and mannerisms of hip hop culture. Recruits from inner-city high schools and elsewhere are arriving on college campuses far removed from the streets where hip hop began and enjoys its greatest allegiance, and they are bringing the 'hood with them.' They tend not to fit in with the norms and ethos of the white majority they find themselves amongst, and seem damn proud of it. How should or can coaches, whose job is to develop both the body and mind of these teenagers, effectively guide them through an environment that relies heavily on athletic labor for its prestige and diversion but shuns and belittles the culture with which the same athletes they rely upon identify?

On one hand, hip hop athletes[2] are proud of their culture and will not disavow it for reasons related simply to fitting in with the majority.[3] In a hostile or foreign environment, like a college campus sometimes hundreds of miles from home, people cling in various degrees to their familiar culture as a source of refuge and sometimes protection.[4] But, on the other, loyalty to one's associates and culture and maintenance of one's own personal integrity can sometimes mask fear and is used as an excuse not to confront difficult challenges. Some hip hop athletes wilt in front of hard math and science or even a typical Eurocentric liberal arts class, yet mask their fear with false bravado.[5] They declare the subject's unimportance or irrelevance to their experience in the streets (which is their real world), and the experience of many in their communities. Why should they change just because White people, even obviously well-intentioned ones, seem desperately to want them to?

And they are right, to some extent. Most universities, to the extent their purpose is other than abstract higher learning, are neither organized nor operated towards the elevation of subordinated classes.[6] The knowledge to be gained in many sciences and Eurocentric liberal arts classes cannot usually be taken back to the 'hood and deployed successfully in the struggle for survival, and even greater knowledge of business dealings from taking commercial courses cannot be transported back *around the way* without also transporting back access to capital as well. But obviously this view is too cynical. While gaining these skills do not immediately transform the athletes into a potential community-saving superhero, in the long run education of almost any sort expands the mind of the athlete.[7] It supplies them with social capital such that they can further develop and take the aggregate of all the skills they've learned, combine them with others of like mind, and return to their community to make a difference. The question remains, how can coaches get their mentees to understand and adopt this mentality towards their education?

Coaches interested in better dealing with recruits who are hip hop might take traditional routes towards understanding them. They might connect with people who are knowledgeable of hip hop, hire them as assistant coaches or consultants, and rely on their advice. They might endeavor to independently research the history and culture of hip hop, or to incorporate hip hop studies into a traditional coaching curriculum. They, or an assistant, might even enroll in some training program, attend some conferences, secure and watch videos, obtain books on hip hop, or scour the internet. They might even do nothing and take the attitude that no athlete is fundamentally different from any other and that they are going to treat everyone on the team exactly the same. The latter option simply ignores the responsibility a coach has to the athletes he is relying on for his own success. Managing a football factory is different than coaching student-athletes on a football team. *Managing a factory* requires only that each item of production is treated the same, while *coaching* student-athletes includes attending to the needs of collegiate men and women and helping them overcome impediments to their off-the field and on-the-field successes. So the dutiful coach hopefully considers undertaking the former options, but they cost considerable time which a coach of a major sports program is unlikely to have in abundance.

This chapter suggests, however, that because hip hop and sports have a common ordering with respect to norms it is easier for college coaches to relate to hip hop than it first appears. While some privilege the accumulation of wealth and others privilege justice and fairness, both hip hop and sports, on the other hand, share the exaltation of strength as a normative principle over utility, efficiency and selfishness as well as morality, righteousness, and other abstract concepts of justice. This author does not suggest at all that hip hop has no place either for economic efficiency or for justice. This author does mean, however, that strength can be shorthanded here as an adherence to personal integrity and group loyalty, and its place as the premier normative principle of hip hop and sports means that both wealth and justice are good so long as attaining either is done consistently with the notion of strength.

UBIQUITOUS CONNECTIONS BETWEEN HIP HOP AND SPORTS

In order to talk about a social system like *sports* or *hip hop,* we should define what it is we are talking about. But this becomes problematic as many people define these systems differently. For example, whether cheerleading is a sport depends on how one defines sport. Similarly, whether Kid Rock or MC Hammer is hip hop depends on how one defines hip hop. I believe the most useful way to understand social systems is to accept that one cannot know the true essence of a thing. Instead, one is limited to examining all of what is said and done related to the thing, which will lead to observations of trends and consistencies. Here, I argue that an observation of sports and hip hop show a tendency to privilege strength over both justice and profit. Ultimately, the things that are said in, out, and about hip hop suggests that hip hop is dangerously hypermasculine. To the extent Black men are disproportionately involved in both sports and hip hop, this hypermasculinity contributes to the division between Black men and women and becomes a distraction from the joint task of confronting White supremacy.

Hip Hop as a Discursive Social System

Hip hop is composed of emceeing, deejaying, breakdancing, and graffiti.[8] It includes sampling and activism. Hip hop continues the development of Black music since precolonial Africa. Hip hop is as Latin as it is Black. Hip hop is as American as it is Black and Latin. Hip hop is a musical means for poor people to express and represent their social situation. It is something one does. It is something one is. Hip hop is universal. Hip hop is a way of life. Hip hop is life. Hip hop is rhythm and poetry. Hip hop is rap music. Hip hop is vulgar and profane. Hip hop distracts and poisons children. Hip hop is an affront to decent people. Hip hop is misogynistic and homophobic. Hip hop is gangster rap. Hip hop is some bullshit. Hip hop is dead.

All of these assertions regarding hip hop are true and not true, depending on your perspective. Just as with any one thing, there is no verifiable rightness or wrongness unto the thing, there is only whether it tends to be useful to someone in a particular situation, or to some people who are similarly situated.[9] This view of hip hop (and of things) is both pragmatic and relative. It rejects the conception of hip hop as something with an identifiable essence, determined by some authority, in relation to which all other things hip hop are judged or justified. Such is the nature of things generally, unless of course one can discern why God or Nature gave us hip hop specifically and decipher what its exact contours are.

No, humans cannot know the thing in and of itself.[10] It is not located anywhere, except in the collective.[11] It is the aggregate of all human relationships with the thing, all verbal and nonverbal expressions about the thing. The entirety of all those expressions concerning the thing cannot be known, so the thing cannot be known fully. One cannot even know all of what one does not know about the thing, and cannot know which is greater, what one knows or what one does not know! Thus, hip hop is not the creation of any one person, even Kool Herc, or its essence determined, governed and sanctified by any one group, including Afrikaa Bambaataa and the Zulu Nation or KRS-One's Temple of hip hop (even though the author wishes it were). Hip hop, like any other thing, is all that is said and done about hip hop, by hip hoppers and others, though what is said and done by others outside of hip hop may count for less. Put simply, hip hop is what it is.[12]

Hip Hop, the Rap Music Industry, and the Streetz

The common refrain is that hip hop begins in the South Bronx when Kool Herc takes over the streets with his Jamaican-styled sound-system, using power from the streetlights to energize his turntables, speakers, and the neighborhood.[13] Other innovations follow, looping the funky break in a record so that dancers could perform extensive and elaborate moves versus one another's crews; adding emcees who gave shout outs and recited toasting or comedic lyrics; transforming the turntable into a musical instrument by scratching and cutting the record in rhythmical patterns; encouraging a unique and discernible style of visual artistry in the form of graffiti tags and burners; and developing a language and styles of speech sometimes almost impenetrable to outsiders meanwhile almost perfectly understood by insiders. Some components were quite old and decidedly Black, emphasizing percussion and call and response techniques; even rapping could be found long before hip hop in the works of Cab Calloway, Bill Bojangles Robinson, Jocko Henderson, and many others.

What seems clear from all accounts is that hip hop begins as compensation for alienation from mainstream society and its music, including Black music of the time. In 1970s New York City, musical instruments and training are missing, access to studio and recording equipment is lacking, funds for art supplies and places for exhibition are unavailable; even the romanticism of Motown rhythm and blues is increasingly alien to the harshness of urban socioeconomic circumstances. A combination of old and new, poor Black and Latino kids in the South Bronx developed a form of expression that better relates to their similar situation (i.e., youthful expressions of fun, concern and hopefulness within the spectra 1970s New York City poverty and despair).[14] Thus, hip hop at its best, its most useful, to the extent it is emceeing, deejaying, dancing, and visual art in the service of poor people; the Streetz.

The rap music industry appears shortly thereafter, most notably with the Sugar Hill Gang[15] and their radio hit "Rappers Delight," which was taken (bitten) from Grandmaster Caz[16] It is telling that this song identifies for the first time hip hop emcees, or M.C.'s, as *rappers* as this begins the rap music industry's emphasis on rapping and the rapper and marginalization to near exclusion of the deejay, break dancer, and graffiti artist. The hip hop intelligentsia, on the other hand, are often middle class activists and academics with a significant detachment from most of the rest of hip hop. The hip hop intelligentsia point out that media consolidation with respect to radio, internet, record stores, music distribution, production, manufacturing, lead to greater influence of and definition by the rap music industry.[17] And since its prime objective is profit and its largest consumer base is suburban White males, the rap music industry injects overwhelming amounts of discourse caricaturing inner-city life. Invariably then, some who were once outsiders but were attracted to the messages emanating from the rap music industry's version of hip hop then claim hip hop and become insiders to it, expanding its scope, increasing the discourse comprising it, overwhelming the practices of those outside the rap music industry and beginning the process of marginalizing its originators and alienating its intended beneficiaries. Of course the marginalized respond by claiming for themselves true hip hop, real hip hop, old school hip hop, classic hip hop, conscious hip hop, progressive hip hop, righteous hip hop, etc.

The Streetz neither fully accepts nor rejects both the rap music industry or the hip hop intelligentsia. The Streetz are alienated and marginalized by both, since both attempt to make a claim to the essence of hip hop. Those in hip hop living in poverty tend to subordinate justice in favor of utility, while middle class or suburban hip hop tends to focus more on consciousness. The tension between Biggie Smalls[18] and the Fugees[19] perfectly illustrates this dynamic within hip hop, with Biggie representing poverty-stricken hip hop who appreciate a *playalistic* lifestyle versus the *playa-haters* represented best by Lauryn Hill[20] who prefer hip hop deal more often with issues of social equity. Both were hot in the Streetz, because they represented their social views from a position and manner of strength.[21]

Nexus between Hip Hop and Sports

Similar to the way hip hop praises strength over both justice and profit, sports fans and participants are torn between *winning at all costs* versus *playing the game the right way*, and use strength as the tiebreaker. On one hand, athletes are expected to do everything within their power to win and achieve greatness. On the other, athletes are expected to

There is an increasing presence of the hip hop culture among student-athletes. Courtesy of 4freephotos.com

sacrifice for their teammates, or their team owners, or the fans or the sport. Beyond this confusion, athletes are expected to remain strong in body and mind whichever ethos they adopt. The similarities between sports and hip hop suggest that the same techniques used to dampen hypermasculinity in sports may apply to dampening hypermasculinity relating to hip hop (i.e., expanding one's game rather than changing it and using one's strength to help others).

Hip hop and sports as distinct social systems are more symmetrical with each other than either of them is with mainstream culture. Part of the symmetry between hip hop and sports includes the way each system develops language, generates esteem, and orders social relations. College coaches may do well to appreciate this sort of kinship. According to John Wertheim's book *Transition game: How Hoosiers Have Gone Hip Hop*, perhaps scholastic athletics as a whole already do.[22]

The essence of a hip hop athlete's hypermasculinity is that they are often inculcated within a community (economically subordinate) and form of expression (hip hop) and primary personal activity (sport), all of which privilege behaviors and expressions exhibiting notions of strength over those exhibiting notions of utility and justice. There has always been something of a connection between sports, entertainment, and the economically subordinate; even more now that exorbitant wealth is available to those who make it to the premier level of their sport or art. Between capital-intensive enterprise on one hand and sports and entertainment on the other, poor peoples' comparative disadvantages, especially in terms of know-how and access, are lesser with respect to sports and entertainment. Thus, sports and entertainment routinely consumes and digests large helpings of discourse offered by the economically subordinate. Hip hop's entanglement with sports occurs almost as soon as the emcee and her lyrics becomes the most important aspect of hip hop.

Kurtis Blow's "Basketball," recorded in 1984, might be the earliest and certainly the most famous entwinement of hip hop and sport.[23] What's interesting here is that in 1984, NBA basketball and hip hop were at a crossroads, albeit different intersections. The NBA had been hampered by drug allegations relating to many of its stars, like Michael Ray Richardson. However, superstar talent like Magic Johnson, Larry Bird, Michael Jordan, and Isiah Thomas were beginning to be shown nationwide on cable television, and the sport took off; same with hip hop in the mid 1980s. At first, mainstream media shunned hip hop. That is, until it found ways to market hip hop stars. Cable television combined with the talent of Run-DMC, Rakim, KRS-One, and LL Cool J,[24] took hip hop from a niche activity to a global powerhouse.

Also, who can forget the 1985 Chicago Bears rapping the "Super Bowl Shuffle." A subtle influence of that song was its unprofessionalism, which contrasted dramatically and importantly from the concurrent hip hop of the day. Subconsciously, listeners must have appreciated more elaborate, syncopated rhymes of mid-80s artists like T La Rock, Just-Ice and Kool G Rap after hearing the off-beat, static, corny lyrics of the "Super Bowl Shuffle"! After Kurtis Blow and the Chicago Bears, sports references became standard in hip hop lyrics. In the 1980s, Chuck D. threatened to "Throw it down your throat like [Charles] Barkley!" and GangStarr invited everyone to "A friendly game of baseball," which included the short-lived dance "the baseball."

Also consider the 1990s when NBA players Shaquille O'Neal, Kobe Bryant, and Allen Iverson became or tried to become emcees. Shaq recorded and sold the most, over a million units. Kobe, from the outskirts of Philadelphia, grew up the closest to New York and the East Coast hip hop scene. Yet, Allen Iverson, from southern Virginia, is thought by many to represent the epitome of the hip hop athlete.[25] Strength, in terms of personal integrity and group loyalty, as the premier normative principle in hip hop explains why. Iverson is exceedingly original and exhibits an acute sense of personal integrity and loyalty to his roots. Philadelphia media types disparaged him and his family for keeping to their old (read "poor") ways, despite the amount of money he was being paid to represent his new bosses, the Sixers, and the NBA. Iverson did not hide his tattoos; he got more. He did not give up his braids and cornrows; he styled them even more elaborately.

Iverson recorded a song, entitled "40 Bars," where he named himself "Jewelz" and rhymed as an ordinary street emcee, complete with lyrics considered profane in polite company.[26] He seemed not to make any attempt to adopt the culture of his new employer and their sponsors. He would not change his game for Hall of Fame coaches, John Thompson in college and Larry Brown in the NBA, forcing them to change their style of play to suit him. And if that made him "ghetto" in the eyes of some fans and cost him valuable endorsements, it also made him hardcore in the eyes of hip hop. Shaq, on the other hand, has successfully maintained associations with both mainstream and hip hop culture. He is more hip hop than Kobe, but more mainstream than Iverson. He was original and unapologetic about his fun-loving style, as he recorded with a harmless group called the Fu-Schnickens.[27] But Shaq was also embraced by the mainstream because he did not "rep" exclusively for hip hop. Kobe is not received well by hip hop, mainly because his attempt at recording and his personality generally is perceived as accommodating to mainstream mores and to the wishes of corporate sponsors. It is interesting to watch Lebron James's relationship with the mainstream begin to resemble Shaq's, rather than Kobe Bryant's or Allen Iverson's. Like Shaq before him, Lebron will do well to adopt mainstream culture as a means of enhancing and expanding his game, rather than changing it. Freshman athletes from hip hop backgrounds will also do well to follow Shaq's lead, and expand both their physical and mental game rather than change it.

SYMMETRIES AND PARALLELS BETWEEN HIP HOP AND SPORTS

Both hip hop and sports are useful to youths for roughly the same reasons; they are competitive, hierarchical systems that provide opportunities to attain personal fulfillment and achievement while also fostering team loyalty. Both hip hop and sports express themselves in coded languages that, once understood, are often adopted by the mainstream as colorful expression, and, as previously suggested, both hip hop and sports share the same normative order, with strength at the top over both justice and profit. However, it might be argued that the functions, expressions, and norms associated with both hip hop and sports support a hypermasculinity that is dangerous to others, society and the athletes themselves.

Expressive and Functional Symmetry

Sports and hip hop are alike in many ways. The language of both hip hop and sports can be virtually impenetrable to the uninitiated.[28] The linguistics of a Brett Favre touchdown drive is as foreign to most English-speakers as the rhymes of the Ghost Face Killa.[29, 30] But once the mainstream understands hip hop and sport terminology, it co-opts it for its pizzazz and bastardizes it until it is passé and useless.

Hip hop and sports also serve similar functions, as an acceptable place for blatant competition and hierarchy. Participants in both hip hop and sports accept competition as a natural means of ordering relationships. Emceeing, deejaying, and break-dancing are displayed best as part of a "battle." In an emcee battle, the goal is to show "I am better than you, because I say that I am better than you, better than you." "Saying that I am better than you, better than you" requires superior style, breath control, vocabulary, story-telling, metaphors and similes, alliteration, etc.[31]

In both hip hop and sports there is an appreciation for individual accomplishment within a competition between groups.[32] LL Cool J may be the most successful and long lasting emcee to rap entirely independent of a musical "crew," yet after over 25 years of making music he still shouts out in interviews those who live and still live on Farmers. Blvd. (Queens, NY). All of the most popular graffiti writers performed within the group dynamic,[33] break dancers as well. Like an athlete in a team sport, the emcee exemplifies his personal integrity by portraying himself and the group well. This gives the emcee self esteem while elevating the quality of the group. Similarly, even a good player on a bad team can represent for himself and elevate the standing of his organization or school. Recognizing these dynamics may be critical to a scholastic coach's understanding of hip hop athletes.

When the hip hop athlete expresses himself individually and in a manner not consistent with the rest of the team, he is usually not intending to disavow or separate himself from his teammates. Instead, he is attempting to bring esteem upon himself and his team, as they are inseparable. Still, there may be something to the idea that this commitment to individualism is male-centered and exacerbates hypermasculinity in society.

Normative Symmetry

Sports and hip hop also have a symmetrical normative order. Hip hop and sports think utility and justice are attractive, important even, but that they yield to strength as the premier normative principle. Competition, assertiveness, leadership, loyalty, strategy, persistence, and perseverance are used as proxies for strength and often embraced over more egalitarian ideals of assistance and compassion. Even where assistance and compassion are displayed it is usually referred to as one person having so much strength they can afford to give some to another. Hardly ever is there room for sympathy.

In both sports and hip hop, there is also a tension between performing for the love of the game and performing for money.[34] The performer's duty to the collective is supposed to trump her desire for compensation. Love of the game could mean that the performer would perform even if no compensation were available. Or love of the game could mean that the performer is supposed to forego compensation or lucrative transactions that are against the principles of the game, she is to hold the game's utility function over her own. Ultimately, however, maintaining the integrity of the collective—adherence to the rules of the game, on the field and off, in the studio booth and in the streets—is supposed to be more important in both hip hop and sports than attempting to please critics or seek monetary riches. This represents in hip hop the exaltation of strength over profit.

Similarly, people otherwise committed to a free market in "the real world" criticize team owners and players especially for seeking to maximize their profits.[35] Athletes are expected to remain loyal to their teammates, organization, and to the fans that often unfairly criticize and harass them rather than sell their services to the highest bidder. Players are expected to be strong enough to play through injuries even if the injury may threaten their career or at least affect their future earning potential. And if a player is hurt either physically or emotionally he is discouraged from admitting it publicly. As Tom Hanks screamed in *A League of Their Own*, "There's no crying in baseball!" Athletes are trained not just to play hard, but to be hard. But again, as the *A League of Their Own* comment demonstrates, the way in which one exhibits strength is gendered.

Strength in Hip Hop Means What?

But strength in hip hop means what, exactly?[36] Again, like hip hop itself, it cannot be described, for it cannot be encapsulated here all that is and was said and done and thought from all those who have opined about strength in hip hop, being that any and all of it is deserving of some modicum of respect. But here is a useful account from the perspective of one who sees hip hop at its best as a vehicle for poor peoples' expression. This part aims to describe strength in hip hop towards assigning it hip hop's premier normative position, then compare it to symmetrical conceptions of strength within both sports as a distinct social system within general society and society as a first order social system. Hopefully, demonstrating that behavior considered under the dominant social gaze to be irrational or at least suboptimal is in the context of both hip hop and sports is useful and perhaps necessary towards a student athlete's sense of self.

In hip hop, as in Clint Eastwood western movies, the strong survive and the weak perish, or at least they are supposed to. Notice that most of hip hop, regardless whether concerned with utility or justice, hardly ever describes things as wrong or bad. Notice that being bad, wicked, sick, ill, wild, all things that seem inconsistent with either the accumulation of wealth or justice, are good things in hip hop.[37] Being weak or soft, on the other hand, is a bad thing. For example, in the realm of conscious hip hop, Public Enemy[38] and KRS-One are revered by all quarters of hip hop as they all are considered hardcore, whereas PM Dawn[39] and Digable Planets[40] are forgotten because they were considered soft or weak. Consider that some of the most commercially successful acts of all time are considered 'wack' by the Streetz. Vanilla Ice[41], Mc Hammer[42]—and to some people's minds, Will Smith, the Fresh Prince of Bel-Air,[43]—are not respected by much of hip hop, because their persona is considered soft. Making money off of rap is fine so long as you are considered hard.[44]

Notice the difficulty that successful acts have maintaining their so-called street credibility once they have softened and accepted mainstream values. Notice that female emcees are respected to the extent they rhyme from a position of strength, they do not ask for or need a man's help, and they are in control of their own sexuality, and within the competitive aspects of a romantic relationship they win, at least by word if not by deed. White rappers like Vanilla Ice are clowned because they are perceived as soft, whereas White rappers like House of Pain[45] and the Beastie Boys[46] are celebrated because they are hard.

Hip hop is self-referential. That is, it does not look outside of itself for justification. It is unapologetic. It is truly alternative and purposefully autonomous. When Run of Run-DMC said in 1985, "He's the 'Big Bad Wolf' in your neighborhood. . . . Not bad meaning bad but bad meaning good!" he declared the existence of a value system separate from the dominant gaze. Fleshing out the notion of strength is a function of identifying what it is and, as importantly, what it is not. Since it is good to be strong, it is bad to be weak. As much as strong and weak are used normatively within hip hop, as well as sports, hard and soft are also used indefatigably for evaluative purposes. To be hard is strong, while being soft is weak. "Hardness" connotes many things, most importantly among them are autonomous, independent, unapologetic, self-referential, perhaps even risk-taking. On the other hand, "softness" connotes submissive, compliant, impressionable, meek, naive, perhaps risk-averse.

Personal integrity and group loyalty. Personal integrity is hard. It represents strength. Hip hop abounds with phrases praising personal integrity, regardless whether one's routine behavior would likely be adjudged unfavorably by the dominant gaze. It includes consistency, originality, and an inner coherence. For instance, with respect to consistency, it is a disrespectful charge to be called "sometimey." Or, "don't talk about, be about it." To talk about it without being about it, is putting up a false front or "frontin'" or "perpetratin' a fraud." Consider that when one in hip hop offers a statement specifically for the truth of the matter she will often put it "on the strength of my word as my bond." Rappers are expected to perpetuate their artistic personas to a far greater degree than, say, rhythm and blues singers or actors. Hip hop expects coherence. It praises "Knowledge of Self." Regardless whether the dominant gaze is favorable or unfavorable, hip hop must "keep it real." This commitment to personal integrity, perhaps considerably greater than society at large, poses the biggest challenge to authority figures responsible for "molding" the minds of inner-city youth, like coaches.

Group loyalty is expected. Once one declares allegiance or belonging to a particular group, one "represents" for that group in the sense that each member takes the others wherever they go. In hip hop, friends claim one another, literally. "Representing" for one and one's group is an important dual responsibility. Group loyalty is expected, but so is originality, a classic conundrum within hip hop. The solution is to express one's originality in a way that reflects strength rather than weakness, as that reflects well on the individual and the group.

Group loyalty is treasured by hip hop because with respect to poor people loyalty is necessary to defense.[47] When poor people in inner city communities bend or break the law while trying to get by, they are at the mercy of those who might inform the authorities. In order to have any social relationships at all in that environment, a strong sense of loyalty must emerge. Here may be where sports and hip hop diverge most stridently from the dominant sphere. In society general, allowing one's group status to influence one's economic motivations is considered irrational. But in sports and hip hop it is beyond taboo to hold oneself out for economic favors when doing so would disadvantage the group or the team, (i.e., selling out) Carmelo Anthony's involvement in the Stop Snitching campaign is discussed later.

Consequently, submitting to the value system of an "other" is usually considered weak. However, incorporating it and intertwining it with one's personal value system, on the other hand, can enhance one's claim to originality, and thus strength. The difference is in maintaining the primary structure of one's personal value system and infusing elements of another in ways that "expand the game" rather than change it. This is perhaps the gift of an artist such as Jay-Z,[48] that, unlike emcees before him who rejected the value system of their upbringing in favor of adopting the dominant gaze once economic conditions for themselves improved, perspicuously maintains a value system established in the Marcy Housing Projects while simultaneously infusing and expanding it towards navigating the dominant social and commercial systems. Perhaps it is this balancing act that Lebron James is learning by associating himself with Jay-Z. And perhaps it is the way in which hip hop athletes on college campuses should balance their lifestyles.

Strength relating to hip hop women. Strength is a gendered term[49] and invoking it here may by itself reinforce hypermasculinity. Strength usually relates to maleness, though it ought not, especially in the context of personal integrity. Strength as integrity as masculinity suggests that femininity represents malleability, the idea that one can and should be open to personal change. This in turn suggests that understanding and accommodation are soft and weak. But in a strange way, hip hop is helping detach the relationship between these terms and gender assignment. Consider that while many outside of hip hop criticize hip hop for prevalence of the word *bitch*, its presence within hip hop refers most times to weakness, an individual's inability to resist outside influences, their malleability, and their willingness to change or disavow their practices at the behest of others, their weakness.[50] Hip hop has not yet severed the false relationship between strength and gender, but it helps in its own weird way.

Women in hip hop are also judged by the Streetz on their hardness. The common thread between the role of women in Lil' Kim's "Get Money"[51] and Eve's "My Bitches"[52] on one hand, and MC Lyte's "Paper Thin"[53] and Queen Latifah's "Ladies First"[54] is that in each the female emcees are not soft in any way. Each woman expresses control over her environment, and unapologetically so. Interestingly, male emcees in hip hop do not diss female emcees. One never hears a male emcee complain that women can't rap or that he hates feminist rappers like Bahamadia[55] or Eve.[56] Contrast these women with those who perform in videos as aesthetic accoutrements, and you'll find that within hip hop the "video chick" occupies a lower social rung because she privileges profit over representing for her family, her neighborhood, clique or crew, and most importantly, for herself as something other than submissive and useable.

Also consider the ideal mate for a woman in hip hop; according to hip hop women, his premier quality must be strength, even if that term means something different from male to female. After MC Lyte dissed her weak lover, Sam, by saying, "When you say you love me it doesn't matter, it goes into my head as just chit-chatter. It may be egotistical or just very free, but what you say I take none of it seriously," she sought out someone more suitable, "Gotta get a, what, gotta get a roughneck!" After Queen Latifah put Ladies First, she praises her man in *I Wanna Be Down* for being "the first one to tame me." Of course, it is possible that these statements and others like it are institutionally created and controlled by the rap music industry. However, that notion leaves absolutely no notion of agency or responsibility (a sense of absolute powerlessness) for hip hop generally or hip hop women in particular. This, I think, would be too much. The answer somewhere lies in the middle because, yes, men largely control the discourse of hip hop, but women determine what songs are hot in the club and what trends men follow so as to impress women. And even male domination over the production of hip hop is slightly exaggerated considering Kool Herc's sister is as responsible for the birth of hip hop as he is, Sylvia Robinson is the first to nationally distribute a rap record, and the president of MTV from 2005–2008 was a Black woman, Christina Norman.

Weakness. Left in hip hop normative wilderness are restraint, silence, compassion, caring, and fear, as these notions are strong or weak depending on the context in which the behavior occurs and the way it is expressed. When expressed by Tupac,[57] T.I.,[58] Dead Prez,[59] or Chuck D, these notions have solid currency, because the idea is that one in order to be strong must share their strength with others. One must be strong enough to be soft, as it were. Consider especially KRS-One, who for over 20 years has advocated for intelligence and justice within the hip hop community as a means of expanding the game, but who remains able to frame these issues in ways that are consistent with strength and being hardcore. "I don't mean to knock you Nelly, but ain't you the MTV house-nigga with a smile like jelly . . . I'm all about the unity of miss and misters, you all about money and dissin' our sisters. Take yo' ass back to TV land, and let this be a lesson, you can't see me, man!" Weakness, on the other hand, is expressed in the context of fear of loss—be it loss of standing, personal security or an intimate relationship—they evidence no commitment to strength.

Hyper-masculinity. Sport has long been accused of overemphasizing strength. College athletes across the country have for decades been accused of being above the system and of using their popularity to get away with what others cannot. The privilege of being an athlete has often extended to misogynist treatment of women. Similarly, hip hop stands accused of also mistreating women and portraying them as subordinate to men in most contexts. But while programs have been developed towards bringing athletes within the broader educational sphere, little has been done to develop programs towards assimilating students who identify with hip hop into the collegiate mainstream. This chapter contends that such a program for hip hop would mirror those which has been developed for sports. Specifically, mentors and coaches should not encourage hip hop students or athletes to disavow hip hop culture, but to accept and adopt other cultures as useful. Furthermore, coaches who expect athletes to use their strength positively to help the less fortunate generally, hip hop athletes should be encouraged to use their expanded game in ways that help the less fortunate in hip hop, of which there are many.

CONCLUSION: USING STRENGTH TO REHABILITATE EFFICIENCY AND JUSTICE WITHIN HIP HOP AND SPORTS

A scholastic coach in command of hip hop cultural norms can more effectively express these variable notions to hypermasculine student athletes. And since the cultural norms relating to hip hop are not much different if at all than those relating to sports, it is less difficult than most think. More directly, the college coach will do well to approach the hip hop student-athlete as one who is endowed with extraordinary talents that he must build upon so that he can share them with others, rather than as naturally talented in one distinct area and naturally deficient in others. The athlete must be convinced to expand his game, as he will never accept that his game needs to be changed (i.e., that the old game must be abandoned as inferior). Even if under some objective and universal standard, a particular athlete is indeed naturally deficient in a specific academic area, a coach's ability to encourage the athlete to address it with vigor increases when the coach frames the need for extra effort and less immediate leisure in terms of eventually providing for others for whom he cares a great deal, rather than as a means to make the athlete a "better person" in the eyes of the dominant gaze.

Perhaps all or most cultures do this: take something against most peoples' sense of justice and justify it not be its utility but by its consistency with personal strength and group loyalty (i.e., naked capitalism and greed being dressed up as meritocracy and democracy rather than justified on grounds of self-interest). But in hip hop such tactics may be even more effective. The rap music industry seems to have adopted this strategy, writ large, as they promote consumerism, violence, and waste as something the "hardcore" do.

The bottom line is that a scholastic athletic coach who wants to inspire hip hop athletes should approach the task in a manner not substantially different than what is necessary to inspire athletes generally. In both sports and hip hop, strength is the normative

CASE STUDY: Carmelo Anthony and the Stop Snitching Campaign

The foregoing was intended to demonstrate that both sports and hip hop have similar functions, types of expressions and norms, such that a coach of a hip hop athlete need not venture outside of the sports construct when attempting to counsel the youth towards what the mainstream considers success. What follows is an example of a professional athlete who because of his affiliation with the hip hop community would sacrifice his wealth and his moral standing for the purpose of staying loyal to his persona and circle of friends.

Hip hop expects but one persona! Consider the case of an emcee whose rise to the top of the music charts is accompanied by a loss of following in the streets.[60] Hip hop accepts that emcees are usually representing for actual notorious and violent drug dealers, gangsters and street toughs. By unapologetically relying on personal stories, he is both creative and displaying personal integrity. By portraying drug dealers and street thugs with who he associates in a strong light, he satisfies group loyalty. By casting the story in terms of violence, riches and fame, he attracts suburbanites and others interested in the street exotic. The truth of the matter, though, is that royalties and concert fees are greater with respect to suburban hip hop fans. So in order for the emcee to continue his success he might choose to give suburban fans more of what they want, fantasies dealing with urban sex and violence. At this point, the emcee stops reciting things he's heard or seen, but simply making up violent stories to please an uninitiated audience. He is no longer repping for his 'hood in any meaningful way.

When the Streetz no longer accepts the emcee as representing hip hop, as it eventually will, he loses popularity among suburban listeners because he is no longer authentically exotic. He is no longer accepted by mainstream culture as anything except a caricature for immorality and disutility. Nor is he accepted in hip hop since he violated personal integrity and group loyalty. He is not keeping it real about who he is or what he's seen or done, nor is he representing for those to which he belongs. He is forgotten. This concerns not just emcees, but all who claim hip hop, especially those who are or become public figures, such as in sports. Hip hop athletes, particularly 18 year olds who have been recruited from the streets onto faraway college campuses, face this same balancing act.

To illustrate how something disfavored by the dominant gaze can be something to praise in hip hop because of its strength, I call upon a not too distant controversy involving the Denver Nuggets' Carmelo Anthony, a Black and Latino hip hopper who spent many years as a youth in economically impoverished Baltimore, Maryland. Carmelo appeared on an independently made and distributed video, entitled "Stop Snitching," where he appeared to advocate against informing police of criminal activity. Snitching is not the simple act of informing authority of bad behavior. Instead, snitching in the inner-city involves participating in criminal activity, getting caught, then informing on one's former compatriots for the purpose of obtaining favor from the police and the justice system. Snitching, then, is consistent with the dominant sphere's view of justice, as it brings those that cause harm and the harm they cause to their proper end. It is consistent with profit-maximizing, as it provides material benefit to the individual and at the expense of criminals no less.

But in hip hop it is an affront to personal integrity and group loyalty. Snitching is fronting. It is talking about it and not being about it. It is selling out. And to the extent it is accepted in the inner city that some participation in criminal activity (from drug dealing to food stamp fraud) is unavoidable in order put food on the table in the inner-city, that everybody has to hustle, it violates one's duty to be loyal to the community as it struggles against the dominant society. For Carmelo not to condemn a practice so obviously against the hip hop ethos would strongly suggest to others that he has adopted a value system other than that with which was instilled in him by the 'hood. It would've been said that Carmelo "done sold us out." This illustrates almost perfectly the difficult choices hip hop athletes must make, and the difficult position in which it places their coaches. In the same way, Ron Artest HAD to run up in the stands and defend himself against the one he thought threw beer on him. To do otherwise, to wait for authorities to intervene on his behalf and to leave it to them his aggressor's punishment, would have been so un-hip hop.

principle exalted over all others. That utility and justice are subordinate to strength do not make them irrelevant. Instead, coaches' intent on indoctrinating athletes into mainstream society's ideas of utility and justice should frame those principles in terms of strength. Specifically, coaches dealing with hip hop athletes are likely to be more successful, not by feigning understanding and adoption of hip hop music and culture, and certainly not by treating hip hop as lesser culture, but by respecting its normative order.

Strength being at the pinnacle of the hip hop ethos, coaching hip hop athletes requires that coaches relate to the youth's sense of personal integrity and group loyalty. Coaches who recruit and guide hip hop athletes must understand that the young person is more likely to respect, listen to, and be guided by those who present opportunities to increase one's social capital. Hip hop athletes will be more inclined to master English, mathematics, and other liberal arts to the extent it expands their game, rather than in terms of it being the right thing to do or that it will gain them wealth in their post-collegiate life.

The idea that a hip hop athlete is expanding his game instead of changing it is important towards maintaining one's personal integrity, towards being hard. A colossal mistake coaches make in terms of trying to relate to hip hop athletes, especially those from the urban environments, is insisting that a player abandon the esteem system to which he is most accustomed because the 'hood way is somehow subordinate to mainstream culture. First of all, it is not. But second, and more importantly, to the extent an athlete is likely to graduate school and find himself within mainstream culture it is decidedly helpful to be able to maneuver within it, which does not necessitate abandoning one's own culture. Rather than asking the player to change, it is better to show how learning new things helps him expand his own personhood, helps him expand his knowledge of self. From there, the coach can refer to the hip hop athlete's heightened sense of loyalty to convince him that his new found knowledge is necessary and best deployed towards elevating his peers in terms of justice, profit, strength or combinations of the three.

STUDY QUESTIONS

1. When two or more people define a thing, how do you determine which one is the truth? What is hip hop? What is the difference between hip hop and rap music, if any?

2. What is culture? Language? Style? Is hip hop just a form of music, or does hip hop have a culture? Does the United States have a culture? What is it?

3. What is a normative principle? What are the normative principles of society? What are your normative principles? Which is your highest normative principle?

4. Must hip hop be justified on grounds important to the rest of society? Must sports? Does it matter normatively that short people are at a disadvantage as it comes to basketball? Does it matter if there are fewer Blacks in baseball than, say, in the 1960s?

5. Does strength connote masculinity? Are the terms masculinity and femininity inherently sexist?

SUGGESTED READINGS

Bernal, M. (1991). *Black Athena: The Afroasiatic roots of classical civilization.* Piscataway, NJ: Rutgers University Press.

Brown, T. (2006). Welcome to the Terrordome: Exploring the contradictions of a hip-hop black masculinity. In A. D. Matua (Ed.), *Progressive Black masculinities* (pp. 191–214). New York, NY: Routledge.

Dyson, M. E. (2005). *Is Bill Cosby right or has the black middle class lost its mind?* New York, NY: Basic Civitas Books.

Posner, R. A. (2003). *Law, pragmatism, and democracy.* Cambridge, MA: Harvard University Press.

Showalter, B. D. (2007). Technical foul: David Stern's excessive use of rule-making authority. *Marquette Sports Law Review, 18*(1), 205–223.

ENDNOTES

1. Hurt, B. (Producer) & Schmidt-Gordon, S. (Director). 2006. *HipHop: Beyond Beats & Rhymes*

2. KRS-One (2003). *Ruminations.* New York, NY: Welcome Rain Publishers. "Some people continue to regard HipHop as a form of music and dance, while others are only interested in using HipHop to further their individual careers. Still there are others (like myself) that live HipHop beyond its entertainment value." The author of this chapter considers himself 'hip hop,' but concedes that he has been in the process of selling out hip hop for the last 10 years, as I have abandoned or marginalized his personal adherence to aspects of hip hop culture that conflict with my employment.

3. Timothy Brown identifies Allen Iverson an athlete who represents Hip hop culture, both in terms of his embrace of Hip hop cultural products like dress and language as well as his refusal to abandon his identity as a member of the Hip hop community. See Brown, T. (2006). Welcome to the Terrordome: Exploring the contradictions of a hip-hop Black masculinity. In A. D.Matua (Ed.), *Progressive black masculinities* (p. 191). New York: Routledge.

Others like Shaquille O'Neal, Jermaine O'Neal, Ron Artest and Kobe Bryant have done things to represent hip hop culture, most notably produce hip hop music. However, the NBA dress code is the greatest testimony towards the notion that hip hop athletes are proud of their culture and are generally unwilling to relinquish it. Despite years of subtle disparagement by NBA officials and mainstream media types, NBA players would not disavow hip hop culture, particular its style of dress. The only way for the NBA to subordinate hip hop culture was to adopt a dress code prohibiting hip hop fashion and heavily penalizing players for violating it. See Brent D. Showalter, *Technical Foul: David Stern's Excessive Use of Rule-Making Authority*, p. 18. Marq. Sports L. Rev. 205, 210 (2007) ("Stern instituted the player dress code at the beginning of the 2005–2006 season to soften the NBA's hip-hop image and increase the league's appeal to its fans.").

Jon Wertheim makes the point that, after unsuccessfully trying to squelch hip hop, many athletic departments, businesses and institutions, have embraced it, or at least accepted its presence in the American cultural cosmos. Wertheim, L. J. (2005). *Transition game: How Hoosiers went hip hop.* New York: The Berkeley Publishing Group.

4. Tatum, B. D. (1997). *"Why are all the Black kids sitting together in the cafeteria?" A psychologist explains the development of racial identity.*

5. Jawanza Kunjufu has spent a lifetime trying to determine how to bridge the learning gap between White and Black youths. Part of the reason for this gap is that many educational institutions employ curricula designed to support White supremacy. Kunjufu, J. (1990) *Countering the Conspiracy to Destroy Black Boys.* African American Images. However, others point out that some Blacks use White supremacy as a reason not to take control over one's personal situation. For a microcosm of this debate, see Dyson, Michael Eric (2005). *Is Bill Cosby Right or Has the Black Middle Class Lost Its Mind?* (New York, NY: Basic Civitas Books). See also, KRS-One, Ruminations, p. 61 ("For many people, it is their education that prevents them from fulfilling their lives. Not that they are uneducated, but that they have been miseducated.").

6. In *Black Athena*, Martin Bernal explains how the modern university system is modeled after the University of Gottingen, which was founded for the purpose of promoting European supremacy or at least chauvinism. Bernal, Martin (1991). *Black Athena, the AfroAsiatic Roots of Classical Civilization (The Fabrication of Ancient Greece 1785–1985, Volume I).* Rutgers University Press.

7. Cf. KRS-One (2003). *Ruminations*, pp. 60–61. New York: Welcome Rain Publishers. "For many people, it is their education that prevents them from fulfilling their lives. Not that they are uneducated, but that they have been miseducated."

8. Jeff Chang refers to Afrika Bambaataa as the preacher of the gospel of the four elements. Chang, Jeff (2005). *Can't Stop, Won't Stop: A History of the HipHop Generation*, p. 90. New York: St. Martin's Press. However, in the same volume, DJ Kool Herc, acknowledged by most as the first hip hop deejay, includes several other aspects of hip hop culture. In *Ruminations*, KRS-One includes beatboxin', street fashion, street language, street knowledge, and street entrepreneurialism. KRS-One (2003). *Ruminations*, p. 179. New York: Welcome Rain Publishers.

9. Such is related to a philosophy called pragmatism. See, e.g., Posner, R. (2003). *Law, Pragmatism and Democracy*, p. 24. (Cambridge: Harvard University Press).

10. Immanuel Kant, in his *Critique of Pure Reason*, used the term *noumenon* to refer to the thing in and of itself, as opposed to what is known about the thing.

11. KRS-One (2003). *Ruminations*, p. 180. New York: Welcome Rain Publishers. "Hip hop is the collective behavior of a distinct group of people." For philosophical discussions of and about Hip hop, see *Hip hop and Philosophy: Rhyme 2 Reason* (2005) (ed. T. Shelby & D. Darby).

12. Tuebner, Gunther (1993), *Law as an Autopoietic System*. Oxford: Blackwell Publishers.

13. Chang, Jeff (2005). *Can't Stop, Won't Stop: A History of the HipHop Generation*. New York: St. Martin's Press.

14. Chang, Jeff (2005). *Can't Stop, Won't Stop: A History of the HipHop Generation*. New York: St. Martin's Press. Similarly, KRS-One places the beginnings of modern Hip hop at around 1970. KRS-One, *Ruminations*, p. 89. He also suggests that hip hop is borne from urban despair, and that the context of this despair is different than any other. For this reason, he introduces Urban Inspirational Metaphysics as a means of directing hip hop towards a higher purpose. *Ruminations*, p. 40. "HipHop is the true inner-city reality, constantly fighting against the made-up reality of today's society. This is why HipHop culture appears to always be at odds with the laws of society, as well as the basic education of society." *Ruminations*, p. 211.

15. George, Nelson (1998). *HipHop America*, p. 93. Viking.

16. Rose, Tricia (1994). *Black Noise: Rap Music and Black Culture in Contemporary America*, p. 56. Hanover: Wesley University Press.

17. Smith, Andre, Other People's Property: HipHop's Inherent Clashes with Property Laws and its Ascendance as Global Counter Culture, In *Virginia Sports and Entertainment Law Journal*, *59*, 94–96 (2007).

18. Price, Emmet George (2006). *HipHop Culture*, p. 173. ABC-CLIO.

19. Price, Emmet George (2006). *HipHop Culture*, p. 158. ABC-CLIO.

20. Price, Emmet George (2006). *HipHop Culture*, p. 158. ABC-CLIO.

21. Perry, Imani (2004). *Prophets of the Hood: Politics and Poetics in HipHop*, p. 117. Durham: Duke University Press. Professor Perry, like many other authors, describes hip hop in terms of its masculinity or hypermasculinity. Hence, the title of this chapter. However, this author believes hip hop is enamored by strength, which the rest of society genders as male.

22. Wertheim, L. J. (2005). *Transition game: How Hoosiers went HipHop*. New York: The Berkeley Publishing Group.

23. Price, Emmet George (2006). *HipHop Culture*, p. 167. ABC-CLIO.

24. Price, Emmet George (2006). *HipHop Culture*, p. 168. ABC-CLIO.

25. Brown, Timothy. (2006). Welcome to the Terrordome: Exploring the contradictions of a hip-hop Black masculinity. In A. D. Matua (Ed.), *Progressive Black masculinities*, (p. 191). New York: Routledge.

26. Brown, Timothy. (2006). Welcome to the Terrordome: Exploring the contradictions of a hip-hop Black masculinity. In A. D. Matua (Ed.), *Progressive Black masculinities*, (p. 191). New York: Routledge.

27. Fu-Shnickens, All Music Guide to HipHop

28. KRS-One (2003). *Ruminations*, p. 89. New York: Welcome Rain Publishers.

29. Price, Emmet George (2006). *HipHop Culture*, p. 190. ABC-CLIO.

30. Perry, Imani (2004). *Prophets of the Hood: Politics and Poetics in HipHop*, p. 50. Durham: Duke University Press.

31. KRS-One (2003). *Ruminations*, p. 211. New York: Welcome Rain Publishers.

32. The sport hip hop most resembles is gymnastics. When done right, both activities require and exquisitely combine intellectual creativity, and muscular dynamism and flexibility. When done wrong, both are clumsy and hilarious. Rather than scored, performances are judged, which under any system involves heaps of discretion. What makes gymnastics most like Hip hop is that one's performance scores towards individual and team competition, and a performer may specialize in one style, but it is better to master several.

33. Chang, Jeff. (2005). *Can't Stop, Won't Stop: A History of the HipHop Generation*. New York: St. Martin's Press.

34. KRS-One (2003). *Ruminations*, pp. 190–91. New York: Welcome Rain Publishers.

35. Michael McCann demonstrates the economic irrationality of high school phenoms choosing to play college basketball, rather than immediately becoming a professional. Michael McCann, *The Reckless Pursuit of Dominion: A Situational Analysis of the NBA and Diminishing Player Autonomy*, 8 U. Pa. J. Lab. & Emp. L. 819 (2006). Yet, plenty of otherwise intelligent black folks discourage the practice.

36. Collins, Patricia Hill. A Telling Difference: Dominance, Strength, and Black Masculinities. (2006). In Matua, Athena D. (Ed.) *Progressive Black Masculinities*, p. 75. New York: Routledge. "Arrayed along a continuum, virtually all of the representation of black masculinity pivot on questions of weakness."

37. KRS-One (2003). *Ruminations*, p. 89. New York: Welcome Rain Publishers.

38. Price, Emmet George (2006). *HipHop Culture*, p. 177. ABC-CLIO.

39. PM Dawn, All Music Guide to HipHop.

40. Digable Planets, All Music Guide to HipHop.

41. George, Nelson (1998). *HipHop America*, p. 62. Viking.

42. George, Nelson (1998). *HipHop America*, p. 54. Viking.

43. Price, Emmet George (2006). *HipHop Culture*, p. 163. ABC-CLIO.

44. KRS-One. (2003). *Ruminations*, pp. 217–219. New York: Welcome Rain Publishers. "The problem comes when you forget who you were in the past."

45. George, Nelson (1998). *HipHop America*, p. 63. Viking.

46. Price, Emmet George (2006). *HipHop Culture*, p. 143. ABC-CLIO.

47. KRS-One. (2003). *Ruminations*, p. 91. New York: Welcome Rain Publishers.

48. Price, Emmet George (2006). *HipHop Culture*, p. 162. ABC-CLIO.

49. Collins, Patricia Hill. A Telling Difference: Dominance, Strength, and Black Masculinities. (2006). In Matua, Athena D. (Ed.) *Progressive Black Masculinities*, p. 91. New York: Routledge. "Black men do immense damage to themselves, to women, and to children, all under the banner of protecting their manhood. The need to tell the difference between strength and dominance in defining progressive black masculinities raises several interrelated questions".

50. KRS-One (2003). *Ruminations*. New York: Welcome

Rain Publishers. "Bitch is more of an attitude than a female dog, spiteful woman, or an unpleasant or difficult thing."

51. Perry, Imani. (2004). *Prophets of the Hood: Politics and Poetics in HipHop*, p. 164. Durham: Duke University Press.

52. Perry, Imani. (2004). *Prophets of the Hood: Politics and Poetics in HipHop*, p. 173. Durham: Duke University Press.

53. Perry, Imani. (2004). *Prophets of the Hood: Politics and Poetics in HipHop*, p. 164. Durham: Duke University Press.

54. Price, Emmet George (2006). *HipHop Culture*, p. 178. ABC-CLIO.

55. Rivera, Raquel Z. (2003). *New York Ricans from the HipHop Zone*, p. 141. MacMillan.

56. Rivera, Raquel Z. (2003). *New York Ricans from the HipHop Zone*, p. 141. MacMillan.

57. Price, Emmet George (2006). *HipHop Culture*, p. 187. ABC-CLIO.

58. T.I., All Music Guide to HipHop

59. Price, Emmet George (2006). *HipHop Culture*, p. 64. ABC-CLIO

60. KRS-One (2003). *Ruminations*, p. 217. New York: Welcome Rain Publishers. "[W]henever a Rapper begins to live wealthy, that Rapper begins to lose his/her edge."

REFERENCES

Chang, J. (2005). *Can't stop, won't stop: A history of the hip-hop generation*. New York, NY: St. Martin's Press.

Collins, P. H. (2006). A telling difference: Dominance, strength, and black masculinities. In A. Matua (Ed.), *Progressive black masculinities* (pp. 75–97). New York, NY: Routledge.

George, N. (1998). *Hip hop America*. New York, NY: Viking.

Hal Leonard Corp. (2004). *All music guide to hip-hop: The definitive guide to rap and hip-hop*. Wisconsin, MN: Backbeat Books.

Hurt, B. (Producer/Director), & Schmidt-Gordon, S. (Producer). (2006). *Hip-hop: Beyond beats & rhymes* [Documentary]. United States: The Media Education Foundation.

KRS-One. (2003). *Ruminations*. New York, NY: Welcome Rain Publishers.

Kunjufu, J. (1990). *Countering the conspiracy to destroy black boys, vol. 3*. Sauk Village, IL: African American Images.

McCann, M. A. (2006). The reckless pursuit of dominion: A situational analysis of the NBA and diminishing player autonomy. *University of Pennsylvania Journal of Labor and Employment Law, 8*(4), 819–860.

Nelson, G. (1998). *Hip hop America*. New York, NY: Viking.

Perry, I. (2004). *Prophets of the hood: Politics and poetics in hip hop*. Durham, NC: Duke University Press Books.

Price, E. G. (2006). *Hip hop culture*. Santa Barbara, CA: ABC-CLIO, Inc.

Rivera, R. Z. (2003). *New York Ricans from the hip hop zone*. New York, NY: MacMillan.

Rose, T. (1994). *Black noise: Rap music and black culture in contemporary America*. Hanover, NH: Wesleyan University Press.

Smith, A. (2007). Other peoples' property: HipHop's inherent clashes with U.S. property laws and its rise as global counter culture. *Virginia Sports and Entertainment Law Journal, 59*(7), 94–96.

Tatum, B. D. (1997). *"Why are all the black kids sitting together in the cafeteria?" A psychologist explains the development of racial identity*. New York, NY: Basic Books.

Teubner, G. (1993). *Law as an autopoietic system*. Oxford, UK: Blackwell Publishers.

Wertheim, L. J. (2005). *Transition game: How Hoosiers went hip hop*. New York, NY: The Berkeley Publishing Group.

Section V:
Race, Gender, and Fan Support

College athletics are a multi-million dollar sport industry with big-time athletic departments constantly seeking new sources to help meet costs associated with coaches' salaries, scholarships, travel, new facilities, and other expenses. Empowered stakeholders, from trustees to deeply committed alumni, continue to up the ante for support for their schools. The extent to which stakeholder advocacy, usually opted for by former student-athletes, especially among ethnic minorities and women, lays claim to their sponsorship and contributes to their colleges is little understood.

Chapter 12 brings attention to the extent to which former student-athletes, especially ethnic minorities and women, contribute financially to their alma maters. As the cost of big-time athletic programs continues to escalate, colleges and universities are seeking additional revenue support from the fundraising and development officers associated with the athletic programs. Almost invariably, the issue is whether the intercollegiate sports system is financially sustainable. While most college athletic programs have turned to alumni and friends of the university to support the athletic department activities and programs, Althouse and colleagues note that antidotal evidence shows former student-athletes, now professional athletes, may give back occasionally, but are not typically significant contributors to their alma mater. Only a few studies even investigated the extent to which women and ethnic minorities make donations to the athletic programs at their alma maters.

Chapter 13 commemorates the 40th anniversary of Title IX legislation, which was enacted to protect against discrimination in education and athletics on the basis of sex. The passage of time evokes the need to critically assess how social justice advocacy can ensure that efforts are made to dismantle racial discrimination and how concerned groups can affect policy's capacity to deliver social justice for female athletes of color. Gill and Sloan-Green ask, ". . . if advocates are aware of the obvious racial disparities in women's sports participation, then why do they overlook this issue in organized conversation, national meetings, and international expert media commentary?" Looking ahead, the authors call for more engagement in Participatory Action Research (PAR), and issue a challenge to become more inclusive, be greater advocates for Hispanic women, and be more willing to create "public space" at conferences to articulate issues facing African American women and their experiences in college sports.

CHAPTER 12

Alumni Support, Ethnicity, and Fan Loyalty

RONALD ALTHOUSE, DANA BROOKS, ANDREA DEAN-CROWLEY, and LYN DOTSON

Abstract

College athletics are a multimillion dollar sport industry with big-time, athletic departments constantly seeking new revenue sources to help meet spending costs associated with coaches' salaries, scholarships, travel, new facilities, and other expenses. Empowered stakeholders, from trustees to deeply committed alumni, continue to up the ante for winning the top ratings and dollars for their schools. Donors provide funding to support athletic programs for a variety of reasons (i.e., loyalty, team success). Sports are associated with moral character and physical strength, and are associated with the physicality and aggression expressed in big-time commercialized games, like football and basketball. Yet the extent to which former student-athletes, and especially ethnic minorities and women, handle their sponsorship and contribute financially to their *alma mater* is little understood and open to question.

Key Terms			
●	annual giving	●	endowment
●	board of directors	●	foundation
●	cartel	●	fund development
●	commercialism	●	restricted giving
●	corporate athleticism	●	social exchange theory

INTRODUCTION

Historical records indicate college sport had its genesis as unorganized, yet enthusiastic, events and activities led by gatherings of male college students (Hardy & Berryman, 1982). The first recorded intercollegiate sporting event took place in 1852 between Harvard and Yale's crew teams. During the 1880s and '90s, male college students organized clubs in baseball, football, track and field, lacrosse, and tennis (Hardy & Berryman, 1982). The early college sport programs were governed and financed principally as student initiatives; however, by the 1890s football was being incorporated into college sport and gaining popularity on campuses.

The expanding enterprise of men's athletics was truly conceived with the rising stakes of intercollegiate football. Intercollegiate football was viewed as a vehicle to gain visibility for the institution to press for and generated alumni support among the newly emerging corporate and professional White collar classes spawned in America's colleges (Davenport, 1985). This was important because college presidents at this time were under tremendous pressure to generate revenues to support the academic mission of the institutions.

Between 1890 and 1930, collegiate sports witnessed a tremendous transition in America. The college sport industry moved from a student-organized model to one that visualized college sports as a vehicle to recruit students, to gain national visibility for the college, and to generate needed revenues for the college. During this time, college football grew in popularity and folk heroes such as Knute Rockne became legends. Schools like Notre Dame or national academies like Army and Navy, could count on national visibility and influence (e.g., the parish priest or a state's congressional representative) to recruit and confirm the quality of its athletes.

According to Davenport (1985), by the 1920s colleges/universities began to recognize college sports as a part of the institution, regardless of any relevance to the educational mission of the rest of the university. Reaffirming the amateur nature of college sports, Chu (1986) traced the historical development of college sports and found, "By the late 19th and early 20th centuries, it was often felt by college leadership that the exploits of the athletic teams attracted monies from state, alumni, and other donors" (p. 57).

From the 1930s into the '50s, intercollegiate sports continued to experience expansion, wrapping itself into league-like arrangements of sports programs. College sports became synonymous with commercialization. The highly acclaimed Carnegie Foundation Report (1929) outlined the following commercialized conditions:

1. College sport had become a commercial enterprise;
2. Growth of professionalism in college football; and
3. Athletes work under the direct supervision of a professional coach.

With limited successes, NCAA legislators during this time targeted grant-in-aid policies and regulated recruitment practices. Stakeholders laid claim to new benefits forthcoming from sport program revenues, showing how college football was used to build tennis courts as well as other athletic facilities on campus.

There was a public outcry for college presidents and faculty to take control over college athletics. Recruiting priorities and gambling also played a factor in the establishment of the Sanity Code drafted in 1946. This code was an attempt to reduce the perceived influence of economics and professionalism in college athletics. In 1948, the Sanity Code only permitted the extension of scholarships and jobs to student-athletes based solely on financial need. The thesis of the Sanity Code was to proclaim the principle of amateurism and define the term *student-athletes*. But college officials voiced concern over the implementation and enforcement of the Code. As a result, the Code was rescinded in 1951. During the 1952 NCAA Convention, the conferees developed a core of regulating and enforcing codes to appease some of the concerns not addressed in the Sanity Code (Depken & Wilson, 2006).

NCAA college athletics during the decades of the 1960s and '70s marked a shift with an influx of more African American student-athletes, expansion of televised college sports, passage of Title IX, and more opportunities for women to participate in sports.

The decades of the 1980s and 1990s continued a growth in the number of college sports and television revenue and a call for academic reform in college sports such as the passage of Proposition 48 (1983) and Proposition 16 (1992). The new academic guidelines required entering college student-athletes to have a minimum GPA in high school core classes and score on the SAT.

The period between 1990 and 2010 witnessed the NCAA addressing diversity and hiring practices, escalating cost of college athletics, gender equality issues, sponsorship, graduation rates of all athletes, especially ethnic minorities, and academic standards.

Today, it is a widely held belief by the lay public that NCAA Division I college athletic programs generate significant revenue for universities via bowl appearances, gate receipts, alumni support, and television revenue (Gerdy, 1997). However, Gerdy (1997) concluded when you removed institution support (i.e., tuition waivers, etc.) most Division I college athletic programs lose money. In fact, Rodney Fort, in a recent publication dealing with the sustainability of FBS (Football Bowl Subdivision) NCAA Division I athletic departments suggests that "those impacted by the current recession [2008 thru 2010] are primarily taking a hit in their portfolios, rather than their annual incomes"(Fort, 2010, p. 17). And the majority of observers are likely to agree with Andrew Zimbalist's judgment, "Actual FBS budgets . . . run in substantial deficit and the gap between expenses and revenues is growing at the vast majority of schools." Zimbalist notes that reasons for understating true athletic deficits is that the very magnitude of the programs are at stake, "these athletic departments are large, not-for-profit bureaucracies" that do not follow the usual imperatives to boost profits and prices, but rather follow a "bureaucratic imperative to grow at any cost and to do anything they can to win" (Zimbalist, 2010, pp. 112–113).

NCAA COLLEGE SPORT FUNDING: REVENUE SOURCES

NCAA intercollegiate athletic programs generate funds from gate receipts, state financial support, concerts, concessions, television and bowl receipts, sponsorships, summer camps, student fees, alumni support, investments and endowments, guarantees, NCAA and conference distributions (Grant, Leadley, & Zygmont, 2008).

According to Atwell, Grimes, and Lapiano (1980), gate receipts constituted 50% of all income. About 10–15% of college sport revenues during this time period (1980s) were generated from television and bowl receipts. The authors' analysis of gate receipt income data during the 1970s witnessed a decline in the percentage of revenue from this source; thus a need to generate additional resources from the alumni. During the early 1980s NCAA D1 football programs received private gifts between $250,000 and $1 million annually (Atwell, Grimes, & Lapiano, 1980).

Football produces the most significant amount of revenues for NCAA Division I athletic programs. For example, in 2006, Ohio State generated $60.8 million, Georgia generated $58.7 million, Oklahoma generated $33.8 million, and West Virginia University generated $22.1 million. However, it is also important to note the same football programs also spent a great deal of money: Ohio State ($32.3 million), Georgia ($14.6 million), West Virginia ($11.9 million), and Oklahoma ($8.1 million).

Recent reports suggest a relationship between athletic department fundraising and standing in the 2007 BCS Rankings. For example, the University of North Carolina at

Chapel Hill generated $51 million in athletic donations in 2006; the University of Virginia generated $45.2 million in 2006; Ohio State University received $39 million in athletic donations in 2006; and the University of Florida recorded $37.4 million in athletic donations in 2006 ("Fundraising for Athletics and the 2007 BCS Rankings," 2007).

COST TO THE ATHLETIC PROGRAM

During the last two decades there has been some significant progress in implementation of reforms for intercollegiate athletics—presidential control directed toward academic integrity, fiscal integrity, and independent certification of that integrity ("Knight Foundation Commission on Intercollegiate Athletics," 1999; Cowen, 2005; Sanders, 2004). But despite the progress claimed to have been made with academic and governance reforms, the escalating costs of competing in big-time intercollegiate sports, especially at FBS institutions, have remained a nearly intractable problem. Indeed, in January 2009 the NCAA reported evidence of a growing financial dilemma, particularly for the 120 FBS colleges: universities were accelerating spending on sport, with the rate of increase in athletics' expenditures in Division I exceeding the rate of increase in general university budgets by a factor of three to four (p. 3). Revenues for athletics increased faster than the general university budget, but have not kept pace with expenditures and since 2004, only six athletic programs in Division I have been in the black for each of the five past years.

To gain a better understanding of the costs associated with college athletics, it is also important to understand the magnitude of costs associated with operating this organization on a daily basis (Sander, 2009). Student-athlete grants-in-aid, coaches and staff salaries, meals, transportation, facility repairs and alterations, team travel, housing, insurance payments, recruiting, building new facilities, equipment, memberships, sports camps, medical expenses, promotion, and fundraising make up a bulk of the expenditures associated with college sports (Grant, Leadley, & Zygmond, 2008). It is also important to note, coaches' salaries and privileges as well as increasing costs of the expanding number of sports specific personnel appear to be increasing at an alarming rate. For example, University of Texas football coach Mack Brown was the highest-paid collegiate football coach in 2012, earning an annual salary of $5.2 million. The University of Oklahoma's Bob Stoops was set to earn $4.55 million in 2012 (Stevenson, 2012). Upton and Wieberg (2006) believe revenue from television and apparel contracts are two major factors driving the increase in coaching salaries.

Wieberg and Jodi (2007) reported in *USA Today* substantial pay raises for some notable college basketball coaches: George Mason, LSU, Memphis, Texas, and UCLA. The average pay increases (2006–2007) for these coaches was $332,000. The authors also found 58 of the 65 schools in the 2006 NCAA Basketball Tournament had average salaries of $800,000. In 2010, the highest reported NCAA basketball coaches' salaries included John Calipari (Kentucky—$4 million) and Billy Donovan (Florida—$3.5 million).

As early as 1986, Nand Hart-Nibbrig and Clement Cottingham had coined the term *corporate athleticism* to note the influence of business in college sports. The authors concluded, "at the college level, the amateur concept has steadily eroded in the face of relentless commercialization. College sports are increasingly associated with money, the salary of coaches . . ." (p. 2). Hart-Nibbrig and Cottingham (1986) believed the rise of television revenue led to the end of amateurism in college sports.

The costs associated with conducting big-time college sports programs continues to increase each year. By 1999, the athletic department at the University of Wisconsin at Madison predicted the department's budget would grow from $39.6 million (1999–2000)

Chasing the Big Dollars

The business of college sports is a big, sophisticated business wherein athletic directors oversee multi-million dollar licensing deals, integrated sponsorships, apparel contracts, preferred seating, seat licensing programs, and cable and TV contracts. Booster clubs and athletic funds become institutions unto themselves. Supporting college athletic programs is a favorite of alumni and donors and is almost seen as a civic virtue, as well as a good marketing investment for corporate America.

The term of Nick Saban's 32-page contract (2007) at Alabama is eight years, earning approximately 4.5 million dollars per season ("Saban Contract Largest in History," http://blog.al.com/live/2007/06/saban_contract_hist.html).

With regard to his June 2007 contract, Saban's compensation is: a) an annual base salary of $225,000 which remains the same throughout, from February, 2007 to January, 2015, and b) "personal service fees" which require participation in certain media programs, obligated events, and non-commercial activities. The "personal service fee" compensation is listed as $3,275,000 in 2007 increasing to $3,975,000 by 2012 and remains at his amount for 2013 and 2014. His activities include:

1) Weekly radio programs during the football season and post-season, spring practice period, national signing day, plus other special events (national championships, etc.);
2) Weekly television programs during the season, prior to any post-season and/or bowl game, plus other special events, as they arise;
3) Production of "reasonable content" for an internet web-site;
4) University authorized or produced publications (game programs, books and pieces relating to the school, its team, and athletic program), media guides, films, artwork, media and videos; and
5) Non-endorsement activities each year on behalf of the university, athletic department,

supporting foundations, or university-approved marketing contractor, before alumni, booster, or similar associations or affiliated groups, clubs, or clinics and gatherings related to the schools athletically-related marketing efforts and contracts.

Sabin's contract also allows, with written approval from the school, for additional compensation while employed at the university for personal promotions and endorsements, public speaking engagements, authoring or co-authoring books, and media programs and non-endorsement activities.

The document contains significant perks and perquisites including: an entire skybox in the Bryant-Denny Stadium, additional tickets per home game, golf/country club membership, moving expenses, a non-commercial airplane for personal non-business travel, and two full-size, all-expenses paid automobiles for business and personal use.

Saban's contract has a "Termination without Cause" clause which indicates the University has the right to terminate any time without cause and for its convenience. If the contract is terminated without cause, it is subject to a liquidated damage provision—the school pays Saban an amount equal to the sum of the annual base salary and personal service fees for each month yet remaining on the term of the contract calculated from the effective date of termination. There is an offset and reduction clause, but according to Martin Greenberg, Saban's contract does not obligate the coach to pay liquidated damage should he want to terminate early and take another job—Saban could leave any time without owing Alabama a penny.

Some observers of the spiraling arms race among programs in college athletic regard "buyouts" as a golden parachute for fired coaches and an expensive security blanket for successful coaches the schools want to keep. Buyout offer protection both ways.

Excerpt from Martin Greenberg, *College Athletics—Chasing the Big Bucks*

to $50.5 million in 2004–05 (Suggs, 1999). Escalating costs were associated with the addition of women sports teams, maintenance costs, lower levels of football game attendance, and costs associated with maintaining athletic facilities.

In 2008, the College of Charleston, South Carolina, made plans to move forward with the construction of a $44 million football arena. This decision was made during a time in which state support for higher education in the South Carolina was reduced (Budig, 2008). Yet it is important to realize that, with expanded college athletic revenues and expenditures, fewer than 10 departments of athletics in the county received no funds from state subsidies or taxes (White, 2009). In *Writing in College Sports: Bigger Isn't Better* (2003) it was reported of the 117 NCAA Division I-A programs, 40% reported an operating profit in 2001. However, without state support, only 6% of the programs generated a profit.

FUND DEVELOPMENT SUPPORT FOR THE ATHLETIC PROGRAM

By the early 1980s college athletic directors were going to need to generate additional revenue to support the growth of athletic departments on their campuses. To generate new revenue streams, they began to focus on developing alumni support systems, via private fundraising and athletic association programs. Siegelman and Carter (1979) initially analyzed the relationship between athletic program success and level of alumni giving. A critique of 138 NCAA college sport programs found no relationship between increasing percentages in football, basketball, and bowl appearances and increase in alumni giving. In contradiction, Brooker and Klastorin (1981) studied 58 major universities by athletic conference affiliation and type of institution (i.e., public/private). It was found that Ivy League football success was related to athletic success. The authors concluded, "colleges and universities would be well advised to develop well-rounded programs for solicitation and for creating alumni support and loyalty through other methods to prepare for the eventual losing year in athletics" (Brooker & Klastorin, 1981, p. 750). Richards (1983) analyzed the fundraising methods used by Temple, Villanova, St. Joseph's, Penn State, and LaSalle. The researcher found the major reason alumni contributed to the athletic programs was to improved facilities. Fundraising strategies employed by the universities cited above consisted of telephone solicitation, correspondence, and personal visits. In the early 1980s only one institution had engaged in a major formal capital campaign, allowing Richards to conclude that the universities located in the Philadelphia area were not heavily engaged in fundraising activities. Indeed, the "arms race" was on the horizon.

Hammersmith (1985) profiled athletic donors to West Virginia University and found that levels of contributions to the athletics was tied to income level, contributions to other campus activities, attendance/purchase of home and away football and basketball tickets, attendance at bowl games, priority seating, and number of years of contributions to WVU Athletics. Similar to other investigations of giving, results showed a plurality of significant donors lived regionally close-by the state flagship university campus, at least within a few hours. By and large, the increased cost associated with running college athletic programs forced many college administrators to seek donations from alumni and nonalumni. But the rumbling was becoming clearer and claims for support of athletic programs often seized on the notion that a successful football or basketball team increases student applications (i.e., "the Flutie effect") and that this, in turn, allows a school to be more selective and increase the quality of its student body.

The degree to which professional athletes such as the NFL's Larry Fitzgerald give back financially to their alma maters is an area in need of further examination. Courtesy of Senior Airman Larry Reid Jr./U.S. Air Force

Reports indicate that during 2007–08, 55 colleges including Boston College, Clemson, Florida State University, University of Virginia, Wake Forest, Notre Dame, West Virginia University, Indiana University, University of Southern California, University of Michigan, University of Florida, and the University of Alabama raised a·grand total of $1.1 billion in cash donations (Wolverton, 2009).

Budig (2008) commented that support for higher education institutions has lagged for years, while the cost to operate these institutions has escalated. Budig, who had been a president of West Virginia University, Illinois State University, University of Kansas, and is past-president of major league baseball's American League, claims that, "a growing number of faculty members resent the bigness of college athletics, but many of them acknowledge that options are few, given the dire need for income. Many colleges and universities, public and private, have either completed a major capital fund drive or are about to launch one" (Budig, 2008).

More recent work on the relationship between private giving to athletic programs and private giving to academic programs documented shifting donor patterns over the past decade (Stinson & Howard, 2008). With regard to NCAA Division I-A institutions, both alumni and nonalumni donors increasingly supported the intercollegiate athletics program, often at the apparent expense of support to academic programs. Stinson and Howard state that "donors were directing substantially larger percentages of their institutional support toward intercollegiate athletics." In extreme cases, "some institutions were even witnessing a decline in total dollars donated for academic purposes, while athletic programs continued to generate increases in both the number of donors making gifts and total dollars donated" (pp. 2–3). A cautious judgment showed that while wins and losses and post-season appearances did not have a direct influence on academic giving, athletic performance indirectly affected academic giving by significantly altering the allocation of a donor's gift between athletic and academic programs. Thus, even when donors increased their total giving, "athletic programs were the primary, if not the sole, beneficiaries of the increased total gift" (p. 3). A number of researchers have suggested, over all, that when the competition between fundraising for athletics and academics is examined, athletic fundraising often has a "crowding out" effect on academic programs (p. 4).

Less than a decade ago J. J. Duderstadt's (2000) critique of intercollegiate athletics and the university community concluded that retrospectively, college sports in America can be placed in three distinctive models/stages: first, the earliest, somewhat "heroic," and affirmed within the Sanity Code, was the student-organized Amateur Model; next was the Exhibition Model, accompanying the growth of intercollegiate sports, laying claim to an inherently *racialized manliness*; and lately, the Show Business model, tied to big-time intercollegiate/corporate athletics. Shortly after Duderstadt's critique, J. J. Rosenthal (2003) took the position that NCAA college sports currently compete in a global marketplace.

The Kellogg Commission on the Future of State and Land-Grant Universities (2000) concluded, "coaches in big-time programs are under tremendous pressure to produce winning teams, often victimized by the myth that big-time sports programs are huge profit centers. These pressures are intensified by growing campus dependence on the financial contributions of individuals and corporations, *a dependence that continues to erode the distinction between "collegiate and professional sports"* (pp. 15–16).

Throughout NCAA history, social, political, cultural, and economic issues such as professionalism, communication, exploitation, cartel behavior, and conflict over the role and purpose of intercollegiate athletics on the college campus have been a focus for spirited controversy, and significantly serious reform efforts. Whatever proponents may say, it is largely agreed that the ever-increasing need to generate funds to support college athletics, especially football and basketball, has led college administrators to seek additional funding sources. Alumni of the colleges soon become a target to solicit support. However, this support comes at a cost.

A recent discussion dealing with the current model of intercollegiate sports—particularly the Division I level—raises the issue of sustainability: Can it be sustained or not? (*Journal of Intercollegiate Sport*, 2010, v 3). Focusing on results of a study of the presidents of 119 FBS colleges, the issue seems not to be *whether*, but rather *how long* can the current model be sustained. Among them, collectively, key *accelerants of competing*:

- Increases in coaches' salaries and privileges, as well as the increasing costs of sport-specific personnel.
- Commercialization, including TV contracts and other corporate interests that have injected substantial revenue into intercollegiate sports.
- Costs of building more and better appointed facilities (p. 37).

A number of significant challenges accompany the increasing costs of participation such as:

- Insidious and growing cultural divide between academics and athletics in which athletics is in an increasingly privileged position . . . conflicts with institutional mission and values.
- Difficulties in balancing the athletic budget and keeping costs under control . . .
- Concerns about the proportion of institutional resources used to fund athletics.
- Growing imbalance between the haves and have-nots both within *equity conferences* and between equity and non-equity institutions . . . being unfairly exploited.

- Concern that competitive and financial pressures created by the "arms race" have a negative impact on student-athletes.

- Challenges to continue to be competitive or to maintain Division I status (p. 37).

During the 2009 NCAA Convention, President Brand noted commercialism may be the dominant issue facing NCAA member institutions now and in the foreseeable future. Clearly, the NCAA has come to embrace commercial activity as a way of life within the organization. A point in all of these discussion was that much greater *transparency* of athletics' department operating and capital costs is needed to buoyup consensus and maintain legitimating and trust, at the very least within the NCAA format of *financial dashboard indicators* for one's institutional and league/conference comparisons (Hesel & Perko, 2010).

DONORS AND NONDONORS TO THE ATHLETIC DEPARTMENT

The literature is uneven about athletics' success for promoting giving and donations to a college's general funds. There are some colleges, especially those that experience a spectacular rise to national prominence, where success leads booster, alumnae, and a state's politicians to open their checkbooks. Generally, the effect is modest and specific to the schools. As noted already, athletic success may lead to increased giving to an athletic department or its foundation and boosters, but giving to the general fund is more uncertain. If improved performance generates increased donations, then poorer performance may decrease donations. And besides, the quest for winning may push schools to violate NCAA rules, such that investigations and scandals can have negative impacts that last for years.

Previous studies attempted to analyze the characteristics of donors and nondonors to various agencies and programs. Investigators analyzed the following contribution factors: involvement in student activities, membership in social fraternities, athletic participation, game attendance, involvement in alumni activities, and length of attendance at the college (Hammersmith, 1985). However, few studies investigated the extent to which women and ethnic minorities (especially African Americans and student-athletes) make donations to the athletic program following graduation. This is an important question/concern given the fact African American college student-athletes comprise more than 50% of the NCAA Division I football and basketball teams.

During the next section of this chapter, the authors will explore the relationship between donor support, success of athletic programs, and other factors that may contribute to the desire for alumni to make gifts to their alma mater.

ATHLETIC DEPARTMENT FUNDING

Intercollegiate sports are often viewed as an enhancement to the student life experience. However, intercollegiate sports are much more than an activity to enrich a student's college experience; they are also a business—a business that operates by means of costs and revenues. Revenues, the income received within an athletic program, have certainly been growing through time. On the other hand, costs within an athletic program are growing as well. In fact, only 43.3% of all Division I programs are running a surplus, including state support (Lee, 2000).

The most notable costs for an athletic program are salaries, facilities, and scholarships. Athletic spending has been exponentially increasing due to the high salaries of athletic directors and coaches, which are nearly 20 times greater than the average college professor's salary (Smith, 2005). The costs of salaries, combined with facilities and student-athlete scholarships make fund-raising efforts increasingly important.

With state subsidies decreasing and athletic spending increasing, higher education athletic departments must now focus on private donations to cover costs. In fact, *The Chronicle of Higher Education's* survey found that 54 of the largest sports programs received $1.1 billion in private contributions during the year 2008 (Wolverton, 2009). The majority of these donations are used to fund the construction or renovation of athletic facilities, coaches' salaries, and student-athlete scholarships.

Some higher education athletic departments established their own foundation, also known as a booster club, to raise money from alumni of the program and other potential donors, such as corporations and other private foundations. The foundation raises the money, but then turns it over to the institution, including the athletic department, to spend. This type of foundation is valuable because while it helps to support student-athletes through school (by means of scholarships). It also encourages a philanthropic disposition, in hopes of future contributions to the athletic department. According to a survey issued by *The Chronicle of Higher Education*, the nation's largest athletic departments are involved in endowment campaigns, for a combined fundraising goal of $2.3 billion (Wolverton, 2009).

Endowment campaigns are becoming increasingly relevant in today's economy. Annual giving, typically smaller donations made over a period of years, has been declining, leaving higher education athletic departments with the alternative fundraising method of endowments. An endowment consists of a large sum of money, usually in the millions, which will perpetually exist in a bank account. The interest produced by the en-

---

All-American Society

Recognition in the ALPHA STATE Athletic Club's All-American Society is reserved exclusively for those who have gone the extra mile in support of the ALPHA's. All major gifts and pledges to the Intercollegiate Athletic Department at ALPHA STATE University above and beyond ticket priorities, that match or exceed $50,000 qualify for All-American Society status.

Major gifts benefit various aspects of intercollegiate athletics. Current major gift categories are available in facility campaigns, program enhancements, recruiting funds, scholarship endowments and mentorship programs. All major gifts must be pledged and paid in full over a maximum five-year period.

Private support at this significant level of philanthropy provides the lifeblood for ALPHA Intercollegiate Athletics and is essential to the overall success of our teams and programs. Similar to a private business, the athletic program at ALPHA STATE operates off of what revenue it generates. Rising scholarship costs, escalating team travel expenses, facility renovations and construction, hiring and retaining quality coaches and providing academic services to our student-athletes necessitates financial stability. These factors, coupled with shrinking state and federal support, make private financial support imperative if ALPHA is to complete for championships at the conference or national level.

All-American Society donors are invited to exclusive events with ALPHA's coaches and administrators throughout the year and recognized on the campus. In addition, Society donors are recognized at the highest levels in all ASAA game day and departmental publications and listings. All-America Society gifts do not offer season ticket priority, although they may have an impact on season ticket and parking locations should donors participate in the ALPHA Athletic Club's annual giving program.

dowment is used to fund nearly anything (depending on the donor's intent) from a coach's salary to a new video-editing system. However, endowment donations may take many years to cultivate; therefore, endowments cannot be relied upon for immediate funding needs.

A recent development in the athletic department fundraising world is planned giving. In fact, many institutions are hiring specialists for this very activity. A higher education foundation may ask a wealthy individual to consider leaving a portion of their estate to the athletic department in their will.

Endowed, annual, and planned giving are all important fundraising tactics to raise private funds for athletic departments. However, it is important to consider the incentive structure behind athletic department donations. Private donations may be given to an athletic department for many reasons, some more technical than others. For instance, many wealthy individuals donate money to receive a tax benefit from the Internal Revenue Service (IRS). These individuals would rather see their money go to a cause they personally support than directly to the federal government. Other individuals would like some type of personal recognition for their contribution. A wealthy individual may give a large sum of money to an athletic department to build a new training facility for the institution, but require that the new building be named in his or her honor. Other reasons for giving include, but are not limited to, in memory or honor of a certain individual, desire for social recognition, social responsibility, or passion about a cause. Lastly, some institutions require a minimum donation to the annual giving fund in order to purchase football or basketball tickets. According to *The Chronicle of Higher Education's* survey, a little more than 40% of private donations to athletic departments went to the purchase of seats or suites (Wolverton, 2009). On the other hand, sometimes tickets are used as a "thank you" for a private contribution. For instance, if a donation is over a certain threshold amount, the athletic department will thank that donor by providing him or her with season tickets. Athletic departments may also thank their private donors by hosting a dinner or reception in honor of the philanthropic activities. Some athletic departments provide additional incentives, such as access to closed-door practices and the opportunity to travel with the team (Wolverton, 2009).

THE ROLE OF A UNIVERSITY FOUNDATION

College and university foundations support the academic institution by means of fundraising and asset management. Over 1,500 public college and university foundations exist in the United States. However, not all foundations participate in both forms of support. Approximately 76% of academic foundations are responsible for both the fundraising efforts and asset management. Eleven percent of academic foundations are only responsible for the institution's fundraising efforts and 10% are only responsible for asset management. The remaining 3% of foundations are not only responsible for both the fundraising efforts and asset management, but also other responsibilities, such as sponsored research, funding entrepreneurial activities, and managing retail operations (Phelan, 1996).

In order to maintain checks and balances, all foundations have a Board of Directors, a voluntary body of elected or appointed people who oversee the activities of a foundation. The Board of Directors is responsible for several important functions, such as approving the foundation's mission and vision statement, promoting a strong relationship between the foundation and its host institution, and appointing and assessing the foundation's chief executive. The Board of Directors is also responsible for protecting donors' rights and honoring all gift restrictions.

It is important to note that not all academic foundations are incorporated within the academic institution. Forty percent of all institutionally related foundations are autonomous, otherwise known as *self-governed*. These foundations are not formally a member of the academic institution—they exist as their own private entity. In fact, only 17% of all academic foundations are dependent on their host institution. The remaining 43% of academic foundations are interdependently related with their host institution (Phelan, 1996).

ALUMNI GIVING PATTERNS TO THE INSTITUTION

Higher education athletic departments rely heavily on private donations. However, it is important to consider who donates. Bruggink and Siddiqui (1995) found that income, age, alumni activity, being single, graduating with an engineering degree, and affiliation with a fraternity/sorority were all significantly related to donating to one's alma mater. The authors also found that alumni who live further away from their alma mater are less likely to donate.

According to Monk (2003), academic institution's donations from alumni are most strongly correlated with the alumnus' undergraduate experience. The participation in extracurricular activities, including intercollegiate athletics, is also strongly related to one's propensity to donate to their alma mater. In fact, alumni who participated in intercollegiate sports gave 1.3 times more to their alma mater than the average student (Monk, 2003).

Coughlin and Erekson (1984) investigated private giving particular to athletic departments. The authors analyze which alumni characteristics are most likely to lead to a donation to the alma mater's athletic department. According to these authors, season football attendance, affiliation with the Atlantic Coast Conference, participation in a bowl, state population, basketball winning percentage, and professional competition are the main determinants of athletic department contributions (Coughlin & Erekson, 1984).

STUDENT-ATHLETE CONTRIBUTION

The previous section discussed characteristics of alumni that lead to private contributions. This section will focus on one particular type of alumnus: the student-athlete. Shulman and Bowen found that the general giving rates of athletes from what they called "high profile" teams actually dropped substantially within class cohorts. Whereas 64% of athletes entering college in 1951 in the high profile sports (football, men's basketball) gave back to their institutions, that figure dropped to 39% in the class cohort for 1989. In effect, even those individuals participating in the programs that receive the most emphasis and experience the most success are less inclined to give than they were 50 years ago.

O'Neil and Schenke (2007) studied the attitudes held by athletic alumni about donating to their alma maters. The authors based their research on the social exchange theory in an attempt to explain why student-athlete alumni may choose not to donate to their alma mater. The social exchange theory is based on a simple economic cost-benefit analysis. All people want to maximize their personal benefits and minimize their personal costs. Athlete-alumni feel as if they have already significantly contributed to their alma mater by playing a sport while they attended. These athletes feel as if they have already paid a substantial cost to the institution, such as being isolated from the general student body, traveling, and balancing rigorous practice schedules with class demands. These student-athletes may not feel as if they received enough benefits from the school to outweigh the costs, making any voluntary costs, such as a donation, incredibly unlikely. Student-athletes that reach the professional sports level tend to feel more loyalty to their employer, rather than their alma mater (O'Neil & Schenke, 2007). According to Shulman and Bowen (2000), male athletes from the 1950s and 1970s were just as likely to donate to their alma mater as the general alumni; high-profile athletes during the 1980s were less likely to contribute to their alma mater than the general alumni—supporting the social exchange theory.

According to Lapchick (2010) race remains contentious in college sports along two fronts, the first has to do with hiring practices and the second focuses on the graduation gap between African American athletes and White athletes. Funding cutbacks could hurt progress toward academic progress of student-athletes generally and student-athletes of color particularly, and affect the hiring of coaches and staff. With regard to issues of gender and race and the potential for giving and donation by student-athletes, the information has been uneven and inconsistent. The unevenness has been attributed to various factors, including how records are kept and how schools execute the task. Certainly, to some extent, successes have to do with how alumni are connected—the nature of departure and reconnection—and cultivation of participation over time. In general, the relationship between athletic participation and donating is weak.

Shifting to on-the-field impact, Billy Hawkins (2010) writes that one aspect that stands out as a feature of the economic downturn is "the increased need for the Black body as a necessary premium for athletic performance and for the economic sustainability of college sports" (p. 98). The need for NCAA Division I colleges to compete athletically at elite levels and to maintain "multimillion dollar athletic budgets will increase the pressure to recruit Black male athletes for sports and football" (p. 99). There is no secret that football and basketball generate the most revenue and that Black males play a dominant role as starters on FBS teams. In 2005–06 season Black males composed 47% of Football (FBS) teams and 59% of NCAA Division I basketball teams. The need for Black male athleticism creates contrasting experiences. It creates a burden because the need for their athletic abilities impact the academic performance of some male athletes, especially as preparation academically does not meet demands of academically rigorous institutions. Lack of preparation is often ignored when elite athletic talent is present—graduation rates linger below the average because of priorities, not intelligence. Hawkins questions the priorities being established when athletes witness coaches whose premiums are on winning, not academics, and also when coaches show little or no loyalty to their programs or to academic/educational process, moving higher up the big-time food chain elsewhere for a larger payday and personal acclaim. Not once, but through repeated episodes.

However, that is not always the case. There exists some antidotal evidence to suggest that former student-athletes, who emerge as professional athletes and maybe achieve notoriety within coaching ranks or join management's cadre in the sports enterprise, do sometimes plan to and give back to their alma mater. Former NBA player Steve Smith donated $2.5 million to Michigan State, his alma mater, in honor of his mother. The money was used to construct the Clara Bell Smith Student-Athlete Academic Center (O'Connor, 1997). Carmelo Anthony of the NBA's New York Knicks donated $3 million to Syracuse, where he attended college, for the construction of a basketball practice facility for both the men's and women's programs (Spears, 2006). And Richard Jefferson, currently with the Golden State Warriors, donated $3.5 million to the University of Arizona, his alma mater, to build a new multisport practice facility (AP, 2007). The caveat here has been that many professional athletes are financially ruined despite their large pro salaries. For athletes, often uninterested in securities, it is the "thrill of tangibility" that rules spending. According to *Sport Illustrated* (Torre, 2009), although salaries have risen over the past three decades, a host of sources (athletes, players' associations, agents, and financial advisors) indicate that by the time they have retired for two years, 78% of former NFL players have gone bankrupt or are under financial distress and that within five years of retirement, an estimated 60% of former NBA players are broke. These results once again reflect O'Neil and Schenke's (2007) social exchange account on the impact of *giving back*.

Sports are often at the center—and even create—a sense of identity and community, along with engendering feelings of local and national pride for one's team, university, and state. While sports' spending has put enormous pressure on the fiscal stability of colleges, intercollegiate sport programs have attracted millions of recurring dollars to those very colleges and universities. Nor should we underestimate the role of sport as a sociocultural force in maintaining and reinforcing ideologies and practices of male power and privilege. Sports such as football and basketball serve as a key site for the production of male supremacy and hypermasculinity, and thus play a significant role in maintaining the balance of (male) power in the post-Title IX era, where, in spite of significant inroads made by sportswomen, they remain second on the priority list when it comes to an institution's commitment to investing resources (Stemple, 2010). Big time sports are, by definition, male sports. "Attempts to curtail, limit, or downsize what is at the very core of big-time college athletics—money and power—may be seen as a direct threat not just to sports overall, but to the 'natural' order of male supremacy. Any serious challenge to the status quo—and structural financial reforms would qualify—could be interpreted as a change that may fundamentally alter the balance of power and would therefore be (and is) fiercely resisted" (Kane, 2010, p. 142).

The studies that have been done on athletic success and institutional fundraising fall pitifully short, if not failing altogether to include women in the analyses. Staurowsky (1996) observed that athletic fund raisers have a tendency to use trial-and-error methods of identifying potential donors, at time missing opportunities to diversify the potential donor base. Recently, developmental personnel have insisted on "getting to know your donor, or potential donor base," claiming that the present generation of women grew up participating in sport (McClure, 2008). Furthermore, women represent a viable portion of the donor population, yet female donors account for 25% or less of individual athletic donors at various institutions (Mahony, Gladden, & Funk, 2003; Tsiotsou, 2006).

The issue of involvement has become a central feature in consumer behavior literature. The notion of involvement in terms of the acquisition of knowledge, attitudes, emotions towards sports and athletic programs has helped athletic development officers to scope out the basis for giving behavior and contribution decisions (Verner, 1996). Results have shown that donor *involvement* may have an impact on donor *amount*. Women donors were not as motivated as men by material gain associated with giving and by the social interaction and approval related offered by the athletic support group. Verner suggested that women's giving included personal commitment, volunteer involvement, and strong feelings about cause or charitable organization. Family giving was also an influential factor. Women also expressed a sense of responsibility or desire to give back to causes that make a difference or bring change. It is crucial for women donors to be informed about the impact of their contributions and to cultivate a connection with the organization. Especially among women, personal preferences are the essence of involvement to pursue future intentions. Data results show that affective involvement distinguishes between male and female donors, such affective involvement is focused on emotional and self-image issues that influence attitude formation. Verner (1996) firmly holds to the uses of affect as a strategy to prop up efforts to build and make financial contributions—to meet and great coaches and players or to build more attachment via consistent and continuing communication (e.g., website, email, social media).

While most research has been focused on the revenue-producing sports (i.e., football and men's basketball), recent work addressing women and athletic fundraising reveals that women's sports have the capacity to generate interest and revenue and that institutional fund-raisers (whether located in the athletic department or advancement office) need to learn more about specific strategies for appealing to women graduates as legitimate donor constituencies, which means expanding the base of information about women and philanthropy that is growing in the fields of education, politics, female-owned and -operated businesses, and charitable community giving (Curtis, 2000; Staurowsky, 1996; Verner, 1996).

IMPACT OF TEAM SUCCESS AND ALUMNI GIVING TO THE ATHLETIC DEPARTMENT

The characteristics of potential donors are very important to study, but possible outside influences for private giving, such as team success, are also important. According to Meer and Rosen (2008), if a male student-athlete's team wins a conference championship during his senior year, he is likely to donate 8% more to the athletic department annually than he would have otherwise. Further, if a male student-athlete's team wins a conference championship at any point in his student career, donations for the athletic department will increase by seven percent. Women student-athlete alumni donations, on the other hand, are not influenced by her team's success.

Humphreys and Mondello (2005) found post season football bowl games and NCAA Division I men's basketball tournament appearances are strongly related to increases in restricted giving. Football bowl appearances increase private giving by 43% and post season basketball appearances increase private giving by thirty percent. The majority of these donations are restricted to the athletic department (Humphreys & Mondello, 2005). Frank (2004) also finds that post season appearances in football and men's basketball are the only measures of success that are positively correlated with an increase in donations.

On the other hand, Baade and Sundberg (1996) found that winning records do not necessarily translate into higher gifts; however, bowl game appearances do result in higher amounts of private giving. For instance, if Team A has a 6-6 record but proceeds to a bowl game and Team B has a 7-5 record but does not proceed to a bowl game, Team A will likely receive more private donations than Team B. NCAA basketball tournament appearances also result in larger donations to public universities. However, the effect in football is greater than in basketball. Baade and Sundberg (1996) explain the difference in football and basketball:

> Football bowl bids are announced in mid-November, though the games do not begin until mid-December, with the majority played in late December or on January 1st. Alumni whose alma mater will appear in a bowl game have at least a month to celebrate. On the other hand, NCAA basketball tournament bids are announced less than one week before the tournament begins. Even schools that have already automatically qualified do not know their opponent, the location of the game, or its exact date until the bids are announced. Three-quarters of the teams are eliminated one week after the pairings are announced. Television coverage is mostly regional. The small amount of publicity afforded to the 32 first-round and 16 second-round losers reduces the impact of a tournament appearance on many alumni. (p. 794)

There is a common fear that there is only a discrete amount of money that alumni and non-alumni are willing to donate to an academic institution. Many believe that if more money is donated to the athletic department then the academic side the institution must be receiving fewer donations. Let's attempt to further investigate this concept.

Donations to the nation's largest 119 athletic departments have risen significantly in recent years. However, overall giving to those institutions has stayed relatively steady (Masterson, 2009). Therefore, even as athletic department giving increases, the academic side of the institution does not hurt. As economists would say, "There is no fixed pie." In fact, Grimes and Chressanthis (1994) found that the athletic success of a school's sports program can positively influence the level of alumni donations to the academic side of the institution. Intercollegiate sports are found to produce a spillover benefit to all areas within the university.

Martinez, Stinson, Kang, and Jubenville (2010) conducted a comprehensive Meta analysis of existing studies completed between 1976 and 2008 and found gift targeted, alumni status, and football program status were significant moderators on levels of private giving to athletics.

CONCLUSION

America's intercollegiate sports are an enormous enterprise that includes not only 1,281 NCAA universities and thousands of student-athletes, but also some 300 NAIA schools as well as nearly 1,200 two-year junior/community colleges. Its driving force, however, is concentrated in NCAA Division I-A athletic departments and their programs, most especially the 120 FBS universities with "big time" football and basketball sports entertainment-commercial enterprises. The revenue to support college athletics is generated from the following sources: bowl games, ticket sales, institutional support, conference distributions, sports camps, and royalties and licensing. Yet the costs (e.g., student aid, coaching salaries, massive facilities, team travel, and medical expenses) associated with maintaining highly competitive programs continue to escalate. Almost invariably, the issue is whether the system is sustainable. Presumably joking, yet strikingly close to the heart of the matter, the wisdom of a recent past big-time university president was captured through his shopworn wisecrack: "We need to give the football team a school to be proud of" (Universities, 1967). Thus, the need for athletic administrators to garner additional external funding to support the athletic mission is simultaneously under siege, and conspicuously self-justifying. Most college athletic programs have turned to alumni (i.e., former student-athletes and alumni and friends of the university) to support the athletic department activities and programs.

The relative independence of athletic associations and other athletic fundraising groups on college campuses, separated as they often are from institutional advancement offices, provides some insight into this mistaken notion that there is a positive link between the athletic department and the institution when it comes to matters of fundraising (Zimbalist, 2010). Many big-time athletic programs are run as independent, profit-driven, auxiliary enterprises. The separation and mistrust that exist between academic and athletic communities means that virtually all athletic department fundraising efforts are directed at raising money specifically for sports, rather than for the institution generally. Athletic departments rarely donate money to their institutions because there usually is no excess revenue to donate (Gerdy, 2002).

Duderstatt (2000) explains how tenuous athletic budgets actually are:

The financing of intercollegiate athletics is complicated by the fact that while costs such as staff salaries, student-athlete financial aid, and facilities maintenance are usually fixed, revenues are highly variable. In fact, in a given year, only television revenue for regular events is predictable. All other revenue streams . . . are highly variable. While some revenues such as gate receipts can be accurately predicted . . . others such as licensing and private giving are quite volatile. Yet many athletic departments (including Michigan of late) build these speculative revenues into annual budgets that sometimes crash and burn in serious deficits when these revenues fail to materialize. (pp. 128–129)

He goes on to note that the perceived economic viability and profitability of men's revenue-generating athletic programs has been fed from a well-spring of myth that has little foundation in fact (Duderstadt, 2000).

If we come to terms with the fact that athletic programs clearly raise funds for their own needs, while winking at the overall fundraising goals of colleges and universities, we can begin to understand why the notion of a "spillover benefit" from athletics has been questioned repeatedly (Zimbalist, 2000). In other words, even if we were to concede that indirect benefits in the form of brand name recognition exist, spillover, should there be any, goes back to most athletic programs in the form of institutional subsidies. Without full disclosure of the entire institutional fundraising record with a complete breakdown of athletic and general fund donations, the assumed spillover benefit may in fact mask the undermining effect that occurs when athletic fundraising creates a clear competing interest with academic and other educational priorities where limited financial resources exist (Staurowsky, 2010).

The question of whether alumni support the current emphasis on sports in colleges and universities yields interesting, if uneven, results. Clearly, we need to learn more about specific strategies for appealing to women graduates as legitimate donor constituencies (Curtis, 2000; Staurowsky, 1996; Verner, 1996). Note also that during 2008–09, Black males constituted 24.8% and Black females constituted 16% of all NCAA Division I sport participants. Hispanic male and female participation rates consisted of 4% and 3.9%, respectively. During the same time period, White male participation rates were 63.8% and White female participate rate data were 71.3% (NCAA, 1999–2000—2008–09). To date, few researchers have investigated the extent to which ethnic minorities, particularly African American student-athletes, actively contribute financial assistance back to their athletic program upon graduation.

STUDY QUESTIONS

1. Explain the similarities and differences in annual giving, planned giving, and endowments.

2. List reasons why a wealthy individual or family would donate money to an athletic department.

3. What are the main determinants of athletic department contributions?

4. Contrary to the social exchange theory, name a few professional athletes that have given back to their alma mater? What characteristic do all of these professional athletes have in common?

5. Do winning records necessarily result in more donations? Explain.

SUGGESTED READINGS

Baade, R., & Sundberg , J. (1966). Fourth down and gold to go? Assessing the link between athletics and alumni giving. *Social Science Quarterly*, *77*(4), 789–803.

REFERENCES

Associated Press. (2007, August 17). Nets' Jefferson donates $3.5 M for new Arizona practice facility. *USA Today*. Retrieved from http://www.usatoday.com/sports/basketball/2007-08-17-jefferson-donation_N.htm

Atwell, R. H., Grimes, B., & Lapiano, D. A. (1980). *The money game: Financing collegiate athletics*. Washington, DC: The American Council on Education.

Baade, R., & Sundberg J. (1996). Fourth down and gold to go? Assessing the link between athletics and alumni giving. *Social Science Quarterly*, *77*(4), 789–803.

Brooker, G. W., & Klastorin, T. D. (1981). To the victors belong the sports? College athletics and alumni giving. *Sport Science Quarterly*, *62*(4), 743–750.

Broussard, C. (1999, October 29). Pro basketball: Williams makes donation, $2.1 Million, to St. Johns. *New York Times*. Sect. D, p. 7.

Bruggink, T. H., & Siddiqui, K. (1995). An econometric model of alumni giving: A case study for a liberal arts college. *The American Economist*, *39*(2), 53–60.

Budig, G. A. (2008, November 24). College's athletics essential. *Charleston Gazette*. Retrived from http://wild wonderfulwv.us/julian/#sb2008.

Chu, D., Seagrave, J., & Beckher, B. (Eds.). (1985). *Sport and higher education*. Champaign, IL: Human Kinetics.

Coughlin, C. C., & Erekson, O. H. (1984). An examination of contributions to support intercollegiate athletics. *Southern Economic Journal*, *51*(1), 180–195.

Covell, D. (2001). The role of corporate sponsorship in intercollegiate athletics. *Sports Marketing Quarterly*, *10*(2), 245–247.

Cowen, S. S. (2005). College presidents must take charge of college sports. *The Chronicle Review, Chronicle of Higher Education*. Retrieved from http://chronicle.com/article/College-Presidents

Davenport, J. (1985). From crew to commercialism—The paradox of sport in higher education. In D. Chu, J. Seagrave, & B. Beckher (Eds.), *Sport and higher education* (pp. 5–16). Champaign, IL: Human Kinetics.

Depken, C. A., & Wilson, D. (2006). NCAA enforcement and competitive balance in college football (National Collegiate Athletic Association). *Southern Economic Journal*, Southern Economic Association. Retrieved from http://www.highbeam.com

Duderstadt, J. J. (2000). *Intercollegiate athletics and the university: A university president's perspective*. Ann Arbor, MI: University of Michigan Press.

Estler, S. E., & Nelson, L. (2005). Who calls the shots? Sports and university leadership, culture, and decision making. *ASHE Higher Education Report*.

Frank, R. H. (2004). *Challenging the myth: A review of the links among college athletic success, student quality, and donations*. Paper prepared for the Knight Foundation in Intercollegiate Athletics.

Fort, R. (2010). An economic look at the sustainability of FBS athletic departments. *Journal of Intercollegiate Sport*, *3*(1), 3–21.

Fundraising for athletics and the 2007 BCS rankings. University of Hawaii, Manoa. *Office of the Chancellor, Institutional Research*.

Gerdy, J. R. (2007). *The successful college athletic program: The new standard. American council on education*. Phoenix, AZ: Onyx Press.

Grant, R. R., Leadley, J., & Zygmont, Z. (2008). *The economics of intercollegiate sports*. Hackensack, NJ: World Scientific.

Greenberg, M. (2008). College athletics—Chasing the big bucks. *Marquette Sports Law Review*, *19*(2), 6–10. Retrieved from http://blog.al.com/live/2007/06/saban contract hist.html

Grimes, P. W., & Chressanthis, G. A. (1994). Alumni contributions to academics: The role of intercollegiate sports and NCAA sanctions. *American Journal of Economics and Sociology*, *53*(1), 27–40.

Hammersmith, V. (1985). *The development of a survey instrument to profile donors* (Unpublished doctoral dissertation). West Virginia University, Morgantown, WV.

Hardy, S. H., & Berryman, J. W. (1986). A historical view of the governance issue. In J. Frey, *The governance of intercollegiate athletics* (pp. 15–28). West Point, NY: Leisure Press.

Hart-Nibbrig, N., & Cottingham, C. (1986). *The political economy of college sports*. Lexington, MA: Lexington Books, D.C. Heath and Company.

Hawkins, B. (2010). Economic recession, college athletics, and issues of diversity and inclusion: When White America sneezes, Black America catches pneumonia. *Journal of Intercollegiate Sport*, *3*, 96–100.

Hesel, R., & Perko, A. (2010). A sustainability model? University presidents assess the costs and financing of intercollegiate athletics. *Journal of Intercollegiate Sport*, *3*, 33–50.

Hogshead-Makar, N. (2010). Attitudes, platitudes, and the collegiate sports arms race: Unsustainable spending and its consequences for Olympic and women's sports. *Journal of Intercollegiate Sport*, *3*, 69–80.

Humphreys, B. R., & Mondello, M. (2005). *More evidence on intercollegiate athletic success and donations*. Unpublished paper. University of Illinois.

Kane, M. J. (2010). We have passed this way before: A response to 'dollar dilemmas during the downturn: A financial crossroads for college sports.' *Journal of Intercollegiate Sport*, *3*, 135–145.

Knight foundation commission on intercollegiate athletics. (1999). Retrieved from http://www.knightcom mission.org

Lapchick, R. (2010). The effect of economic downturn on college athletics and athletic departments on issues of diversity and inclusion. *Journal of Intercollegiate Sport*, *3*, 81–95.

Lee, J. (2000). Commerce comes to campus. *Street & Smith's SportsBusiness Journal*, 29–36.

Lee, C. (2004). The case for diversifying: Beyond the usual

suspects. *New Directions for Philanthropic Fundraising*, *44*, 57–72.

Mahony, D. F., Gladden, J. M., & Funk, D. C. (2003). Examining athletic donors at NCAA Division I institutions. *International Sports Journal*, *7*(1), 9–27.

Martin, K. L., & Christy, K. (2010). The rise and impact of high profile spectator sports on American higher education. *Journal of Issues in Intercollegiate Athletics*, *3*(1), 1–15. Retrieved from http://crsi-jiia.org

Martinez, J. M., Stinson, J. L., Kang, M., & Jubenville, B. (2010). Intercollegiate athletics and institutional fundraising: A meta analysis, *Sport Marketing Quarterly*, *19*(1), 36–47.

Masterson, K. (2009). Fundraisers predict that gifts to education will decline in 2009. *The Chronicle of Higher Education*, A1.

McClure, A. (2008). Advancement goes digital. *University Business*, *11*(7), 51–53.

Meer, J., & Rosen H. S. (2008). The impact of athletic performance on alumni giving: An analysis of micro data. *Economics of Education Review*, *28*(3), 287–294.

Monk, J. (2003). Patterns of giving to one's alma mater among young graduates from selective institutions. *Economics of Education Review*, *22*(2), 121–130.

NCAA Student-athlete ethnicity report (1999–2009). *Student-athlete ethnicity*. Indianapolis, IN: NCAA.

O'Connor, I. (1997, January 18). NBA guard shares wealth with alma mater—Hawks' Smith remembers mother with $2.5 million donation to Michigan State. *Seattle Times*. Retrieved from http://search.nwsource.com

O'Neil, J., & Schenke, M. (2007). An examination of factors impacting athlete alumni donations to their alma mater: A case study of a US university. *International Journal of Nonprofit and Voluntary Sector Marketing*, *12*(1), 59–74.

Phelan, J. F. & Associates. *College and university foundations: Serving America's public higher education*. Washington, DC: AGC, 1996.

Returning to our roots. (2000). Executive summaries of the reports of the Kellogg Commission on the future of state and land-grant universities. Retrieved from http://www.aplu.org/NetCommunity/Document.Doc?id = 187

Richards, M. E. (1983). *An analysis of the fundraising methods for intercollegiate athletics on the Philadelphia big five* (Unpublished doctoral dissertation) West Virginia University, Morgantown, WV.

Rosenthal, L. J. (2003). From regulating organizations to multi-billion dollar businesses: The NCAA is commercializing the amateur competition it has taken almost a century to create. *Seton Hall Journal of Sport Law*, *13*(2), 321–344.

Sanders, C. (2004). The administrative report structure of athletic directors in NCAA divisions I, II, and III intercollegiate athletics. Boseman, MT, Montana State University.

Sanders, L. (2009, May). Sports budgets outrace university spending over all. *The Chronicle of Higher Education*. Retrieved from http://chronicle.com/article/Sports-Budgets

Siegelman, L., & Carter, R. (1979). Win one for the giver? Alumni giving and Big-Ten college sports. *Sport Science Quarterly*, *60*(2), 284–294.

Smith, E., & Hattery, A. (2005). Commercialization of college sports. *Berkshire Encyclopedia of World Sport*, *1*, 347–352.

Shulman, J. L., & Bowen, W. G. (2000). Giving back. *The Game of Life*. Princeton, NJ: Princeton University.

Soloman, J., & Perrin, M. (2008, February 23). How the southeastern conference got rich. *The Birmingham News*, A1.

Spears, J. J. (2006, November 7). Melo to donate millions to 'Cuse. *Denver Post*. Retrived from http://www.forbes.com/home/feeds/ap/2006/11/07/ap3153372.html

Torre, P. S. (2009), March 23). How (and why) athletes go broke. *Sports Illustrated*. Retrieved from http://sports illustrated.cnn.com/vault/article/magazine/MAG1153 364/index.html

Staurowsky, E. (1996). Women and athletic fundraising: Exploring the relationship between gender and giving. *Journal of Sport Management*, *10*, 401–416.

Staurowsky, E. (2004). *The relationship between athletics and higher education fundraising: The myths far outweigh the facts*. A Report prepared for the United States Department of Education Commission on Opportunities in Athletics. Retrieved from http://www.bringback track.com/About Sport_Giving_Non-Correla tion .asp

Stemple, C. (2010). Televised sport, masculinist moral capital, and support for the invasion of Iraq. In R. E. Washington & D. Karen (Eds.), *Sport power and society: Institutions and practices* (pp. 237–262). Philadelphia, PA: Westview Press.

Stevenson, S. (2012, May 8). TCU's Patterson behind only Brown, Stoops, Gundy in Big 12 salary. *Fort Worth Star-Telegram*. Retrieved from http://www.star-telegram.com/2012/05/08/3946538/tcus-patterson-be hind-only-brown.html

Stinson, J. L., & Howard, D. R. (2008). Winning does matter: Patterns in private giving to athletic and academic programs at NCAA division I-AA and I-AAA institutions. *Sport Management Review*, *11*, 1–20.

Suggs, W. (1999). A look at the future bottom line of big-time sports. *The Chronicle of Higher Education*, *46*(15), A.57.

Suggs, W. (2005). *A place on the team: The triumph and tragedy of Title IX*. Princeton, NJ: Princeton University Press.

Torre, P. S. (2009, March 23). How (and why) athletes go broke. *Sports Illustrated*. Retrieved form http://sports illustrated.cnn.com/vault/article/magazine/MAG1153 364/index.htm

Tsiotsou, R. (2006). Investigating differences between female and male athletic donors: A comparative study. *International Journal of Nonprofit and Voluntary Sector Marketing*, *11*(3), 209–223.

Universities: The creation of quality. (1967, June 02). *Time Magazine*. Retrieved from http://www.time.com/time/magazine/article/0,9171,902065,00.html

Upton, J., & Wieberg, S. (2006). Contracts for college coaches cover more than salaries. *USA Today*. Retrieved from http://www.USAToday.com/sports/col lege/football/2006-11-16-Coaches-Salaries-Cover

Verner, M. E. (1996) Developing women as financial donors and philanthropists: A way to enhance intercollegiate athletics opportunities. *Women in Sport and Physical Activity Journal*, *5*(1), 29–49.

White, C. (2009, January). UT will explore generally more money for education from athletics. *Knoxville News Sentinel*. Retrieved from http://www.knoxnews.com/2009/jan/17

Wieberg, S., & Upton, J. (2007, March 8). Success on the

court translates to big money for coaches. *USA Today*. Retrived from http://www.usatoday.com/sports/college/mensbasketball/2007-03-08-coaches-salary-cover_N.htm

Wolverton, B. (2009, January 09). Endowment campaigns devoted solely to sports at some colleges offer rewards to donors. *The Chronicle of Higher Education, 55*(20), A1, A12, A16.

Wolverton, B. (2009, January 23). For athletics, a billion-dollar goal line. *The Chronicle of Higher Education*, A1.

Zimbalist, A. (2010). Be careful what you wish for revisited: A response to Jeff Orleans. *Journal of Intercollegiate Sport, 3*, 147–150.

Zimbalist, A. (2010). Dollar dilemmas during the downturn: A financial crossroads for college sports. *Journal of Intercollegiate Sport, 3*, 111–124.

Zimbalist, A. (2011). *Circling the bases: Essays in the challenge and prospects of the sports industry*. Philadelphia, PA: Temple University Press.

CHAPTER 13

Title IX and Black Female Student-Athletes: Increasing Sports Participation Through Shared Advocacy

EMMETT L. GILL, JR. and TINA SLOAN-GREEN

Abstract

On June 23, 1972, the United States enacted Title IX, the legislation that provides protection against discrimination in education and athletics on the basis of sex. After surpassing its 40th anniversary, we reflect that Title IX has positively impacted the issue of gender bias within collegiate athletics settings. Given what sporting circles have learned over three plus decades about the multifaceted dynamics of discrimination, we need to critically assess how advocacy supports efforts to dismantle racial discrimination and how concerned groups can effectively impact policy's capacity to deliver social justice for female athletes of color. We will frame our points around the current issues faced by Black female collegiate student athletes. Our objectives are three-fold—to take a peek at the state of Black female collegiate athletes, discuss the impact of the demography of Title IX on Black female athletes, and explore, through a social justice lens, the notion of social justice advocacy for Black women in sport.

Key Terms		
• advocacy	•	social justice
• college sports	•	Title IX
• female Black student-athletes		

INTRODUCTION

Title IX states that no person in the United States shall, on the basis of sex, be excluded from participation in, be denied the benefits of, or be subject to discrimination under any educational programs or activity receiving federal financial assistance (Department of Labor, 1988). In the case of Title IX, activities include athletics and equity pertains to the evenhanded distribution of interscholastic and collegiate sports opportunities for women when compared to men. In 1972, the year Title IX went into effect, only one in 27 high school girls played varsity sports (Women in Sports Foundation, 2008). Today, one in 2.5 high school girls compete in interscholastic athletics (WSF, 2008). Title IX has been enormously successful in terms of integrating women into athletics. In spite of this there is uncertainty whether females of all ethnicities have benefited from Title IX.

In particular, concern remains over the scarcity of Black females in collegiate athletics (Corbett & Johnson, 1993; Corbett, 2002; Sellers, Kuperminc, & Dumas, 1997; Greene & Sloan-Green, 2006; Suggs, 2001). Despite a 955% increase in Black female participation in sports (WSF, 2008), scholars still suggest that Black female athletes have been silenced (Smith, 1999), face double jeopardy (Lapchick, 2000), become invisible (Edwards, 1999) and are subsequently left behind (Corbett, 2002; Evans, 1998; Goff, 2002). Scranton (2001) writes that our failure to consider the impact of race and gender in sports leads to marginalization and oversimplification of Black female experiences in sports. An example of oversimplification occurs when racism and sexism converge and we recognize sexism, but ignore the uniqueness of its intersection with racism. Mathewson (1996) calls this the "Function at the Junction." Meanwhile, Black female student-athletes received only 2.7% of Division I athletic scholarships awarded for women's sports in 2000 and 5% in 2005 (Lattimer, 2005; Suggs, 2001). In particular, Black female student-athletes are not fully integrated into country club sports. Country club sports refer to Olympic sports that typically require substantial financial and time investments, but are not revenue-generating sports on the college level. Country club sports include equestrian, field hockey, golf, gymnastics, lacrosse, rowing, soccer, swimming and diving, tennis and volleyball. On the collegiate level Black females have gained equity in basketball and track and field, but in the country club sports their presence is virtually nonexistent. During the first two decades of Title IX comparisons between the proportion of male versus female athletes, and their resources, were appropriate. However, now racial equity within women's athletics should also become a measuring stick for the effectiveness of Title IX. Parents, coaches, scholars and activists cannot expect for racial equity in women's sports to come about without aggressive social justice advocacy.

The conception, adoption, improvement, and enforcement of Title IX are the work of higher education and athletics advocates. Advocacy is the act of pleading or arguing for something in pursuit of influencing outcomes, through public policy and resource allocation (Cohen, 2001). When we think of advocacy images of town hall meetings, distributing flyers and public rallies might come to mind, but advocacy is much more. Advocacy is also "the exclusive and mutual representation of a cause in a forum to attempt to systematically influence decision making in an unjust or unresponsive system(s)" (Schneider & Lester, 2001, p. 65). Although advocacy tends to be an ambiguous subject (Engelhardt, 1989) there are several guiding characteristics including—defining the problem, agenda setting, research and inclusion (Schneider & Lester, 2001, p. 65). Advocacy affords the opportunity for groups to have a voice which impacts policy. One of the most popular forms of advocacy is social justice advocacy.

Rawls (1999) refers to social justice as fairness. In *Defining Social Justice* Novak says *social justice* is applicable to various systems including athletics (2000). Like advocacy a great deal of ambiguity surrounds the term social justice (Novak, 2000). However, one characteristic scholar's agree upon is social justice should lead to the public alleviation of social inequities created by class, race, ethnicity, and gender. When we examine NCAA participation rates for female student-athletes we see the inequities between male and female student-athletes are disappearing, yet when comparing White females to Black females inequities reappear. Title IX has induced less social justice for Black females given that over 70% of women participating in collegiate sports are White (Greene & Sloan-Green, 2006).

This chapter will present a summary of the latest NCAA race and gender data, which supports the assertion Black female participation in collegiate prep sports is paltry compared to White female collegiate student-athletes. The chapter will continue by exploring two interrelated political explanations for why Black female student-athletes have not benefited to the degree of White female student-athletes. The first explanation revolves around the inattention of some White advocates to the unique circumstances of Black women and their lack of willingness to tackle issues existing Title IX enforcement approaches alone cannot resolve. This explanation manifests itself in the reality organizations that advocate for Title IX have few Blacks in leadership, issues germane to poor Black female participation in sports are rarely discussed in Title IX forums and experts who serve as the voice for Title IX advocacy are overwhelmingly White. The second explanation involves the failure of some Black feminists to aggressively insert themselves in the Title IX fight and include the issue of athletics on the agenda of Black females. The second explanation manifests itself in the actuality there are very few Black feminists who have written on the role of sports in the lives of Black adolescent females. The existing scholarship comes for the field of sport management or White scholars. Finally, the chapter will focus on five select social justice advocacy strategies that Black and White advocates can share responsibility in implementing that will increase the probability of Black female athletic participation. The recommendations include redefining the problem, targeting specific political systems, engaging in participatory action research (PAR), promoting engagement and creating additional space for public augmentation. While the focus of the discussion is collegiate sports, it is important to point out in order to increase participation on the collegiate level we must include and reference youth, junior high and high athletics.

STATE OF BLACK FEMALE DIVISION I STUDENT-ATHLETES

Black females composed approximately 12% of all undergraduates at predominately White institutions in 2004 (Digest of Education Statistics, 2007) and 14.9% of all Division I female athletes (Lapchick, 2005). In 2004–2005, 10,913 Black females competed in Division I athletics compared to 49,976 White females (NCAA, 2008). In 2007–2008, 11,371 Black females competed in Division I athletics compared to 52,237 White females (NCAA, 2008). If we examine the 10 female collegiate prep sports the numbers are more inequitable. In 2004–2005, 25,676 White female student-athletes competed in the 10 prep sports compared to only 1,447 Black female student athletes or 5%. In 2007–2008, 27,119 White female student-athletes competed in the 10 prep sports compared to only 1,618 Black female student athletes. In 2004–2005, in women's soccer, lacrosse, and rowing (the sports that have experienced the most growth because of Title IX) White females outnumber Black females 11,692 to 594. In 2007–2008, 12,859 White females competed in these 3 sports compared to 624 Black female student-athletes. During the same time period, only 16 Blacks competed in Division I collegiate field hockey, 37 in gymnastics and only 45 Black females competed in lacrosse (see Table 1).

Likelihood statistics and net gains also can be used to assess equity across race and ethnicity in women's Division I college sports. Likelihood, or the probability of a specified outcome, of a female student-athlete refers to the chance a Division I female student-athlete is White versus Black. In 2007–2008, when compared to Black female student-athletes, equestrian female student-athletes were 166 more times likely to be White, field

Table 13.1.	Division I Club Sports Race and Gender Frequencies and Net Gains					
	1999 Black Female Student-Athletes	1999 White Female Student-Athletes	2007 Black Female Student-Athletes	2007 White Female Student-Athletes	1999–2007 Black Female Student-Athletes Net Gains	1999–2007 White Female Student-Athletes Net Gains
Equestrian	0	246	4	667	4	421
Field Hockey	16	1508	32	1533	16	25
Golf	86	1303	83	1519	−3	216
Gymnastics	37	949	61	888	24	−61
Lacrosse	45	1648	44	1949	−1	301
Rowing	53	3225	101	4560	48	1335
Soccer	191	5470	479	6350	318	880
Swim/Diving	64	3916	69	4353	5	437
Tennis	192	1794	207	1878	15	84
Volleyball	463	3210	538	3422	75	212
Total:	1147	23269	1618	27119	501	3805

hockey female student-athletes were 48 times more likely to be White, and swimming female student-athletes were 63 times more likely to be White. Comparing the net gains of White and Black female student-athletes between 1999–2008 provides another means to assess racial equity in women's collegiate sports. Between 1999 and 2008, in the 10 women's varsity prep sports, White females experienced an overall increase in participation of 3,805 slots while Black females only gained 501 slots. Black female student-athletes only experienced 13% of the gains experienced by their White student-athlete peers.

The data supports the assertion that Black females have not benefited from Title IX, to the degree of White females, when it comes to collegiate athletic participation. We know there are a variety of socioeconomic reasons, beyond the small percentage of Black females in the general college population, for the absence of Black females from interscholastic and collegiate sports. Still advocacy, in its most potent form, should be capable of developing strategies to dispense of some of the movable barriers to sport experienced by females of color. In an age where gender-based differences in the number of collegiate nonrevenue sports participants, team expenditures and coaching salaries have significantly decreased why are our Black female student-athletes still so far behind?

DEMOGRAPHY OF TITLE IX ADVOCACY
WHITE OWNERSHIP AND BLACK AMBIVALENCE

The demography of Title IX refers to race and ethnicity of Title IX advocacy. Again, advocacy involves many things including petitions, testimonies, public hearings, alliance building, litigation, and legislation. While these activities are critical, so too is the composition of organizations that advocate for Title IX, the content of Title IX forums and the use of media experts in Title IX awareness raising efforts. The presence of the Black feminists who are interested sport is also critical to advocacy. However, Black feminist scholars and

Hispanic Female Student-Athletes

Former LPGA golfer Nancy Lopez used to be the only well-known female Hispanic athlete. Now young girls are more likely to know US softball player Lisa Fernandez, Olympic speed skater Jennifer Rodriguez, or LPGA golfer Lorena Ochoa. There is a reason for the small number of Latina sports role models—the lack of participation of Hispanic girls at the interscholastic and collegiate levels. In 2002 Hispanic females made up 2.6% all Division I female student-athletes (NCAA, 2008). However, in 2007 Latina's have made great strides. More Hispanic females compete in Division I equestrian (16), swimming and diving (141), and fencing (23) than do Black females. More-over, in lacrosse and field hockey the number of Black and Hispanic female student-athletes are virtually equal (NCAA, 2008). Hispanic females also have a unique set of barriers that should be included in the conversation:

- Standardized Test Scores
- Family Obligations
- Work Obligations
- Financial Constraints
- Gang Affiliations/Influences
- Early Teen Pregnancy
- Language Barriers

(Barracato, 2007)

activists first must temporarily reconcile the unflattering media representations, public emergence of Black lesbianism and lack of a captive audience that appreciates the benefits of sports before they can enter the game. This portion of the chapter will discuss the demography of Title IX advocacy with a particular emphasis on the role of White Advocates and Black Feminists. Again, the demography of advocacy includes many things, thus this section represents one of many perspectives on the demography of Title IX advocacy.

White Ownership

White females dominate the demography of Title IX, and its composition makes it difficult for key White stakeholders to empathize with issues impacting sports participation of women of color. The majorities of organizations engaged in ongoing Title IX advocacy are predominately White or have predominately White leadership. Major Title IX stakeholders include the American Association of Health, Physical Education, and Recreation (AAHPERD), Association of American Colleges and Universities, Women's Sports Foundation (WSF), National Women's Law Center (NWLC), Tucker Center for Research on Girls and Women in Sport, National Association of Collegiate Women's Athletic Administrators (NACWAA), The Institute for Diversity and Ethics in Sport (TIDES), Association for Gender Equity Leadership in Education, American Civil Liberties Union (ACLU), National Coalition for Women and Girls in Education (NCWGE), American Association of University Women (AAUW), Center for Women's Policy Studies, Young Women's Christian Association (YWCA), Amateur Athletic Union (AAU), National Association of Girls and Women in Sport, United States Soccer Federation, and Girls Incorporated.

The aforementioned organizations and coalitions have great influence in sports because they have stakeholders in crucial women's sport leadership positions, access to a large assortment of sports constituents, large membership bases and control of financial capital dedicated to women's sports. Diversity in amateur sports organizations is critical to increasing all aspects of Black female participation because these entities dictate problem definition, agenda setting, areas of Title IX research, the direction of revenue streams and the structure of intervention strategies.

Meertens and Pettigrew (1997) suggest that to redress inequalities social justice requires giving precedence, or at least equal weight, to the voice of the least advantaged groups. When speaking of Title IX-focused organizations their governing boards are an indicator in assessing the diversity of Title IX demography. Women and minorities hold 13% (five of 38) of the top positions at US national governing sport bodies and no Black men or women hold head positions (Lloyd, 2009). The National Association for Girls and Women in Sports (NAGWS), a prominent nonprofit organization located in Arlington, VA, is a distinguished Title IX alliance. The NAGSW 11-member board includes eight White women and three Black women; including a Black president, director of Diversity and Parliamentarian. The NAGSW president, a Black female tenured sport management professor, is renowned for her work on intercollegiate sports and the experiences of Black female athletes. Even so, there is no NAGWS initiative to improve the participation of Black females in sport, and there is no information on the organizational website that speaks to race and gender and its impact on Black female interscholastic or collegiate sports participation. The current 12-member executive board of Women Sports Foundation (WSF) includes 11 Whites and one Black in key leadership positions. Like NAGWS, WSF has not developed any initiatives specifically designed to positively affect the participation of women of color in interscholastic or collegiate sports. Lastly, the National Women's Law Center (NWLC) is a renowned legal force in the Title IX landscape, yet both co-presidents and all three vice-presidents are White females. Without key stakeholders, who have lived the counter stories of Black females, the voices of these athletes will not be fully audible on the national agenda.

Organizations and their leaders are critical to future enhancements in state and national Title IX legislation because they indirectly and directly oversee major efforts to convene Title IX discussions and the content of the conversations. In April 2007, the Stanford University Center for Ethics held a conference entitled *Title IX Today, Title IX Tomorrow: Gender Equity in College Athletics*. Of the 19 featured speakers on the conference program, only one presenter was Black. The conference themes for the *Title IX Today, Title IX Tomorrow* conference included commercialism, facts and fiction and evaluating the success of Title IX (Stanford University Center for Ethics, 2007). None of the subject matter was directly aimed at Black women in collegiate sports or increasing their participation. In March 2007, prior to the Women's Final Four in Cleveland (OH), McDonald Hopkins LLC Attorneys at Law sponsored *Title IX Academic & Legal Conference* during the *Girls & Women Rock: Celebrating 35 Years of Sport & Title IX*. Of the 11 members on the planning committee there were no Black females or males and among the 23 featured speakers only three were Black. Donna Lopiano, the keynote speaker at the *Girls & Women Rock* conference and then WSF president, alluded to the need to increase the sport participation rates of Black females, but she did not outline how to do so. Nonetheless, it is important to note that the *Title IX Academic & Legal Conference* did include a special session to honor three Black sports pioneers—professor Tina Sloan Green, Linda Green, Esq., and Dr. Alexander Alpha. Lastly, the leadership at the National Coalition for Women and Girls in Education (NCWGE) recently sent recommendations to improve educational opportunities for girls and women to then presidential candidate Barack Obama and 111th United States Congress. Yet again, none of the suggestions for athletics pertained to the need to improve the sport participation of females of color or provided insight into strategies for increased sport involvement by women of color. Henderson (1989) suggests, "it is not that Black women have nothing to say, but rather that they have had no say."

In addition to forums on Title IX and women in athletics, the media is a tremendous ally for Title IX advocates. Giving precedence, or at least equal weight, to the voice of the least advantaged Title IX target groups also involves their presence in media content. The Title IX experts interviewed by the media and the themes discussed with journalists are indicative of White female ownership of the Title IX agenda. For example, several US media outlets published stories documenting the 35th anniversary of Title IX, Title IX success stories, a potential 'midlife crisis' and future challenges. The barriers Black females confront in route to collegiate sports participation were neglected. For example, *The Chronicle of Higher Education* (2007) published a series of articles to commemorate the 35th anniversary of Title IX, including a section entitled, *What Are the Biggest Challenges Facing Gender Equity*? Of the eight Title IX advocates interviewed for the commentary four were males, four were females and none were Black. In 2007 *Sports Illustrated* also recognized the most influential people in the history of Title IX, however the article did not list one Black female who was not a former amateur or professional athlete (*Sports Illustrated*, 2007). In the same edition of *Sports Illustrated* Donna Lopiano penned a special commentary entitled *Title IX Is Succeeding*. Lopiano cited three key challenges for Title IX—budget allocations, shifting of financial resources away from Title IX compliance and the negative impact of government clarifications of Title IX (Sports Illustrated, 2007). Once again, none of the themes were directly or indirectly connected to the social, cultural, or economic barriers to sports participation for Black females. Neglecting these topics is an indicator of Whiteness. Whiteness, according to King and Springwood (2001) is a "practice, social space, tactic, a technology and strategy that is unified through privilege" and used "to create opportunity and access" (p. 399). As scholars we explore what it means to be Black, but we do not dedicate the same series of analyses to decoding the meaning attached to White skin color. Unfortunately, Whiteness prevails in society and in sport sociology, management, tourism, recreation and other sport-related scholarship.

Lastly, when assessing the demography of Title IX there is a distinction to be made between stakeholders whose rules result in unforeseen outcomes and shareholders who break agreed upon rules of fairness (Novak, 2000). One must ask the question if advocates are aware of the obvious racial disparities in women's sport participation, then why do they overlook the issues in organizational conversations, national meetings and international expert media commentary? This suggests a breach of the solidarity that supposedly characterizes the feminist sport movement.

White advocates have demonstrated a tendency to ignore racial issues that impact the sport socialization of Black female student-athletes and have chosen to extend "the gaze towards the politics of gender" (Evans, 1998). During the 5th Annual Black Athletes in America Forum Donna Lopiano then the president of the Women in Sports Foundation (WSF) declared race and gender are two separate issues that should be attacked "fervently, but separately" (Paule, 1995). In that forum Lopiano laid out a 16-point plan for increasing the sport participation of females of color. Fourteen years later, neither Lopiano nor the WSF have pursued or achieved any aspect of the plan. Tina Sloan Green, the current president of the Black Women in Sports Foundation, said "In order for us to get a power position, [White women] have to share power, and I think sometimes White women are more reluctant to share power than White men" (Hill, 2006, p. 28). Beverly Kearney, the University of Texas women's track coach, says the apparent disregard displayed by White advocates towards Black advocates has led to "a growing tension among African-American women who see race as the unwanted stepchild in the fight for equal rights on the playing fields" (Elliot, 1997).

Title IX and HBCUs	
HBCUs typically have more female students enrolled than male students, thus they tend to offer more women's sports to comply with the gender-equity requirements of Title IX. In 2008 the College Sports Council released a study that said 72 of 74 historically Black colleges and universities do not meet the proportionality standard of Title IX, the law that bans sex discrimination at schools receiving federal funds. At many HBCUs the number and percentage of females on campus outnumber the males. Title IX affects HBCUs in male and female locker rooms. In April 2009,	Delaware State became the last HBCU with a wrestling program to drop the sport. Since 1998, Norfolk State, Coppin State, Howard, Delaware State, and Morgan State have all dropped their men's wrestling programs. Some, like Howard, cut wrestling in order to comply with the strict proportionality requirement of Title IX. It is important to mention this story surfaced from an organization that advocates for issues based on Title IX and its "alleged" impact on men's sports.
	(http://www.delawareonline.com/article/20090427/SPORTS08/90427047)

Black Feminism and Sport Ambivalence

Earlier tenants of social justice theory were used to argue White women dominate the demography of Title IX advocacy, but there is virtually no theoretical framework that helps to explain why Black feminists have not argued more vigorously for racial and gender collegiate sports equity. Black feminist thought specializes in rearticulating the distinctive and self-defined standpoint of Black women (Collins, 2003). There is over 150 years of Black feminist thought in the literature, and the role of sport has very little presence (Douglas, 2002; Smith, 1999). The actuality—Black feminists have not embraced sports allows White women to hold a monopoly on the Title IX agenda. When referring to Black feminists I am referring to sport scholars, sports administrators, soccer moms, college students, coaches, and other women of color. The lack of commentary on sport by Black feminists is puzzling because several sociocultural challenges on their agenda, such as adolescent obesity, early parenthood and gang involvement, can be overcome if more Black adolescent females were involved in all levels of sport. Outside of Edwards (1999), Evans (1998), Corbett (2002), Greene and Sloan-Green (2006), Lattimier (2005), Alexander (1978) and a handful of Black female sport scholars, little has been written on sports social policy and Black females. Birrell (1990) writes, "The absence of commentary on sports by women of color is itself significant" (p. 185). This portion of the chapter will present three hypotheses for the deficiency in Black feminist involvement in Title IX sports advocacy including media representations, lesbianism and hypercompetitiveness in interscholastic and collegiate sports.

Media representations have constructed Black women as not feminine in order to legitimate the power and privilege of White heterosexuality (Douglas, 2002). There was a time when Black women could participate in sports and not fear sacrificing their femininity (Abney, 1999). However, today Black female athletes confront far more questions about their gender, femininity, sexuality and physical appearance when compared to their White female counterparts. Black females have been maligned in the mainstream media and projected as *less than* (Crenshaw, 1992; Douglas, 2002). Professional tennis superstars Venus and Serena Williams are a case study on unflattering and unfeminine media content related to Black female athletes. In 2001 Sid Rosenberg, a talk radio sports personality from *The Don Imus Morning Show*, called Venus Williams an animal and said that she and sister Serena had a better chance of posing nude for *National Geographic* than *Playboy* (Jet Magazine, 2001). Unflattering media depictions of Black female athletes date back to when they began to dominate in the handful of sports where they were allowed to compete. *Time Magazine* once reported that Althea Gibson, the first Black athlete to win a major tennis championship, was forced to take a test to see if her genetic make-up included an extra chromosome (Rhoden, 2007). The crude language used to describe Black female athletes physicality coincides with what Hall (1981) refers to as "ancient grammar" (p. 41). Questioning Black female athletes' femininity is one issue, however ridiculing their sexuality compounds the negative media images of female athletes of color.

Perhaps the public emergence of lesbianism among Black female collegiate student-athletes, college coaches and former college athletes has adversely affected Black feminist views of sport as a tool for the upward mobility. In the 1930s and 1940s lesbianism was not an issue in Black female sporting circles. Today the coming out of former Texas Tech basketball superstar Sheryl Swoopes (Granderson, 2006), the alleged inappropriate relationship involving former Louisiana State University women's basketball coach Pokey Chapman (Smith, 2007), and the accusations by the Penn State head women's basketball coach that a Black female player was a lesbian (Harris, 2006) have given lesbians in collegiate sports a cast of Black characters. Black mothers and their daughters may avoid organized sports because they are uncomfortable with female athletes who are lesbian or because they do not want to be perceived as a lesbian. In some Title IX literature, like Olson's work (1991), the trials of Black female athletes are inexplicably consolidated with the tribulations that accompany a lesbian lifestyle.

Is it plausible Black feminists do not participate in Title IX advocacy, via scholarship or otherwise, because they do not have faith that Black female mothers and daughters believe in the benefits of sport participation? Unfortunately, not all Black parents are fully invested in the physical and social benefits of sports for adolescent females. "Even today, I see the old mentality," says former Women's National Basketball Association (WNBA) player and current college coach Denise Graves, "that girls shouldn't do this, girls shouldn't do that, as if we don't have a future in athletics" (Murphy, 2009). Tina Sloan Green wrote, in an open letter to her daughter Traci, the head coach of the Harvard Women's Tennis Team, ". . . you and your brother Frankie are also privileged to have parents who understand and value the power of sports—and who always encourage and support your participation" (2007, p. 1). The notion of lack of parental investment in sports is not farfetched because many contemporary mothers of color did not have the opportunity to compete in sports due to household and family responsibilities, segregation or lack of resources.

Tina Sloan Green was successful as both a collegiate athlete and coach. Courtesy of Tina Sloan-Green

Is it plausible Black feminists do not write about Black adolescent female sport participation because they favor protecting the psychological well being of young Black females by de-emphasizing sport participation? It is thinkable that Black feminists anticipate that parents of Black adolescent females want to help their children avoid the hazards confronted by Black male student-athletes? Meaning Black parents may want their young Black daughters to avoid identity foreclosure (Miller & Kerr, 2000), the glorified self (Adler & Adler, 1989) and the coddling that is synonymous with some Black males competing in collegiate sports. In particular, feminists may want Black adolescent females to avoid pitfalls that can help to sidetrack or separate athletes from their academics. Likewise, parents of color may also want to help Black adolescent females avoid developing the scar tissue that can develop due to the hypercompetitiveness that characterizes many collegiate sports.

The negative aspects of the culture of athletics can be further exacerbated by ethnic differences between White and Black adolescent females. Ethnic dissimilarities can play out in several ways, but most readily through locker room norms and rituals that rule prep sports like soccer, volleyball, tennis, swimming, field hockey and the other country club sports. Black parents and adolescent females' lack of awareness of the norms, neutrality towards unfamiliar customs or inability to participate in rituals due to financial constraints can make sport participation less rewarding. Suggs (2001) suggests that in sports like soccer, Black females are further discouraged because they make up such a small percentage on interscholastic and collegiate teams and because there is a lack of appreciation for forms of Black female cultural expression. In country club sports like tennis, according to Isha Williams (the eldest sister of Venus and Serena) "there's just a nasty disrespect you see on some people's faces, . . . It's like they're not supposed to be there" (Cepeda, 2001, p. 184). Isha added that when the Williams sisters began playing in junior tennis tournaments some parents would tell their children, "Don't let that little Black girl beat you" (Cepeda, 2001, p. 184). There are several potential explanations for why Black feminists are not fully invested in Title IX advocacy, but it is not possible to present every plausible explanation or to try to speak for all Black women. The final portion of the chapter will explore the notion of social justice and how to ensure Title IX fulfills its promise to all female student-athletes.

SOCIAL JUSTICE AND WOMEN OF COLOR SPORT PARTICIPATION

Schram (1999) advises advocates deliberate both parts of the term social justice because it is a human creation, but the concept is also social. Schrams's view suggests White and Black advocates should be in constant collaboration to ensure Title IX benefits women of all ethnicities. White and Black feminists, advocates and sports enthusiasts appear to share the same overall goal to provide developmental supports and opportunities; however their energy, efforts, ideas and experiences have not co-existed in the most critical Title IX circles. Is it plausible that White female advocates fear Black female athletes will dominate the games if certain country club sports are further integrated? Perhaps Black female feminists resent White female athletes for their academic, athletic and professional advances that have come via Title IX. Whatever the case, the inequities will not be automatically alleviated by legal precedents. Instead, White and Black advocates must engage in collaboration and mutual aid (Sarvasy, 1992). Schram (1999) is clear that social justice cannot be legislated by some founding ethic that specifies the right normative standard for race and gender equity in collegiate athletics. Young's (1990) view of true social justice is an institutional condition that enables participation and overcomes oppression through self-development and determination, meaning social justice advocacy is more than handing out flyers and engaging in town hall meetings. Inherently, social justice advocacy must be shared, systematic, purposeful, and proactive and not reactive. The final component of this chapter will focus on five social justice advocacy strategies. Using a social justice advocacy framework allows ideas for increasing Black female sport participation to be grounded in theory and provides an objective lens for generating ideas to resolve the racial disparities in women's collegiate sports. Each strategy will be discussed in the context of issues raised earlier in the chapter with particular attention to how White and Black advocates can engage in shared responsibility.

REDEFINING THE PROBLEM AND QUESTIONING
THE WAY POLICY IS ADMINISTERED

Defining the specific shortfalls of Title IX, as they relate to Black female sport involvement, is paramount. Historically, the inadequacies of Title IX were defined using the universe of females to argue for more opportunities in sport, but future frameworks should spotlight the subpopulation of women of color disenfranchised from sport. Alpha Alexander (1978) affirmed that data on the status of women of color in sport ignites advocacy, and defining the problem requires data collection. What is the magnitude of the disparities among Black and White interscholastic and collegiate female student-athletes? Again, this chapter focuses on collegiate sports because in order to begin to address issues in collegiate sports first, we need to collect data and define problems in secondary schools. For instance, in the Prince Georges County, Maryland, (PGCPS) school system no females participate in lacrosse and only five females in the entire school system participate in golf (PGCPS, 2006). In light of such data Senator Mary Jo White (D—PA), in partnership with the Women's Law Project, introduced Senate Bill 890 or the Pennsylvania Equity in Interscholastic Athletics Disclosure Act (Women's Law Project, 2009). Senate Bill 890 requires Pennsylvania's public, charter, and private secondary schools, grades 7–12, to report the same gender sport participation information colleges report, including information sorted by race and ethnicity. New Mexico, Georgia, and Kentucky have signed similar legislation (Sloan-Green, 2009), and Maine introduced a similar bill in February 2009 (Murphy, 2009).

Collecting data on participation rates should not be a solely quantitative exercise. Data gathering also should include qualitative data. *Photo-voice*, or the use of pictures to tell a story, is an excellent way to advocate for change. Numbers accompanied by pictures of obese Black adolescents girls, snapshots of all-White girls lacrosse teams, images of pregnant Black females watching Black males play sports, while on their way to their way home to watch their siblings, and the like, provide a powerful story for advocates to communicate to stakeholders and shareholders.

Black feminists and white advocates should form alliances to "market" the data, once specific data is collected, on the subpopulation of Black females. Marketing the data will help stakeholders and shareholders understand the depth of the lack of sport participation of Black females. White advocates can be especially helpful when it comes to developing a media campaign ripe with public service announcements (PSAs) and media kits. White advocates can also help develop events and create public space to share the information on the lack of Black adolescent female sport participation. Likewise, White advocates can transport new data and problem definitions into their board meetings and conferences and via the Internet to help athletic administrators and national political figures understand the unique barriers confronting Black female student-athletes. The

Women in Sports Foundation (WSF), NCAA, and Women's Law Project are three prominent organizations with websites where little or no information exists on the circumstances of Black females in sports. Updated problem definitions will afford all Title IX advocates with the opportunity to craft culturally specific arguments that appeal to the diverse opinions of all shareholders in support of increasing women's sports participation.

Target Specific Political Systems

Advocates take aim at specific systems because sport or educational entities are not responding to people's needs. In this case, targeting specific political systems means creating alliances with organizations that represent the various segments of the Title IX political landscape. For example, Black advocates have increasingly begun to target the federal government, the NCAA, and initiatives developed by NCAA member institution sport administrators. Recently the Black Women in Sports Foundation (BWSF) partnered with the NCAA to produce two conversations on Black female sport participation. In May 2009, the BWSF joined forces with the NCAA to host a symposium entitled *Women of Color: Recruit, Retain, Results* in an effort to explore issues surrounding women of color in all aspects of collegiate athletics. During the summer of 2009, the BSWF, with NCAA funding, produced four *Next Step/Women of Color* forums designed to examine the role of women of color in collegiate sports and share grassroots perspectives to promote their inclusion. The forums were held at the University of the District of Columbia, Norfolk State University, Lincoln University, and Rutgers, the State University of New Jersey. The conversations ranged from women of color as college sports administrators, to barriers to inclusion to increasing the number of female sport administrators of color and female coaches of color in softball, golf, and volleyball.

Secondly, the BWSF has formed active alliances with the Minority Opportunities Athletics Association (MOAA) and sought input from the Congressional Black Caucus (CBC) in its effort to expand allies who share the goal of increasing sport participation, management opportunities, and coaching positions for females of color. Alliances with MOAA and the CBC are critical because each organization has political credibility within sport and government. The CBC and MOAA also have pre-existing audiences and relationships with entities that are capable of helping resolve inequities. MOAA and the CBC can raise awareness within their constituencies and their audiences are large and national in scope. In particular the BWSF has targeted the CBC in their attempt to revive the National Youth Sports Program (NYSP). It is a little known fact, outside urban communities, that NYSP was a critical sports and youth development resource for Black youth—especially for Black females. NYSP introduced kids in urban environments to nontraditional sports like tennis and volleyball and provided females with a forum to compete, in co-educational environments, against some of the best elementary and junior high male student-athletes. The BWSF recently invited the Honorable Emmanuel Cleaver II (Missouri, 5th District; US House of Representatives) and CBC member to a Minority Sports Organizations Coalition meeting during the 2009 NCAA national convention in Washington, DC (Minority Sports Organizations Coalition, 2009). These alliances can be fruitful if nonprofit organizations that advocate for Black female athletes understand how to yield a harvest from their collective efforts.

White advocates can train Black feminists and organizations that want to lobby for increasing sports participation of women of color. 501C3 nonprofit organizations interested in advocating for women of color in sports have certain limitations on the percentage of organizational activities entities can dedicate to lobbying. With restrictions on the lobbying activities of Black advocates, politically active organizations with White advocates can invite these nonprofit organizations to join their email campaigns, visits to politicians and annual advocacy events. In particular, nonprofit collaboration will allow Title IX advocates to further market the problem definition of Black female athletes and communicate data on the lack of participation. All social justice groups, including Black feminists, can utilize advanced training on how advocacy should translate into tangible results. White advocates can help Black feminists understand indicators of advocacy success and how to achieve and measure outcomes. Nonprofits led by seasoned White advocates can also help nonprofits led by Black advocates, further comprehend how juggle the agendas of alliances and meet the needs of most of their political friends.

Participatory Action Research (PAR)

Traditional research is needed, but participatory action research (PAR) research can truly help paint a more vivid portrait of inequities in female sport participation. PAR is a recognized form of qualitative research that focuses on the effects of the researcher's direct actions of practice on the improvement of the area of concern (Dick, 2002). Black scholar-activists are in an outstanding position to conduct PAR, but they need support from White advocates to develop strategies and add rigor to documentation efforts. For instance a high school teacher and women's field hockey coach, who work, in an urban area, might decide to collect data during a skill-building field hockey summer camp. Afterwards the teacher/coach might track the participants and document females of color who went on to play field hockey—whether it be in high school or college.

Greater participatory research by Black female sport advocates who operate grass-roots programs is sorely needed and visuals are effective and efficient. Projecting a photo-voice, or the use of photos to tell this story, can be especially helpful in contributing to agendas that include sport and youth development. Photo-voices on techniques for Black females acculturating into a sport, recruiting of women of color in prep sports or working with families who may devalue sport because of family obligations are needed. Photo voice is a constructive tool to document the benefits of student-athletes of color on Division I campuses, including Black female student-athletes who are active in the community. What if a lacrosse team presents at an inner city high school on the benefits of playing lacrosse and videotape girls of color trying the sport of lacrosse? The video could be a wonderful tool to inspire local and state officials to allocate funding to replicate collegiate inner city sports clinics through local government. In a sense coaches, student-athletes, and these teams become researchers who document their work in order assist advocates. Division I athletic teams who participate in this type of community service can inform their stakeholders, shareholders, and peers on strategies to incrementally increase sport participation of women of color.

White advocates, especially those who teach at the university level can partner with Black feminists, athletic teams, and advocacy organizations to publish qualitative and mixed methods scholarly articles. More in-depth and diverse research is needed to legitimize new problem definitions and lend credibility to participatory action research.

Engagement and Inclusiveness

As women of color, Black women should also include Hispanic women in their Title IX problem definition, agenda setting, marketing, and research. Hispanics may include Columbians, Mexicans, Puerto Ricans, and other females with a Hispanic influence. Again, Hispanic females accounted for 2.4% of all Division I female student athletes in 1999–2000 and 2.6% in 2000–2001. Rugby, an NCAA emerging sport, carried the highest percentage of Hispanic females (12.9) (NCAA, 2008). Latina student-athletes are increasingly present on college campuses thus they warrant inclusion in efforts to bring equity in athletics to all women. Corbett (2002) notes that in soccer, golf, rowing, and lacrosse there has been growth for Latinos (and not for Black females). The *2007 NCAA Gender Equity & Issues Forum* provided some insight into the challenges Hispanic student-athletes confront with regard to involvement in collegiate athletics. Language is a major barrier, but the forum also revealed the college application and financial aid processes present major barriers. In prep sports a smaller percentage of student-athletes receive full scholarships and must supplement their athletic financial aid, which presents another barrier to populations of color. On the collegiate level sport administrators and HBCUs have tried to engage the Hispanic community by reaching out to Latinas at local college fairs, open houses, and during Hispanic Heritage Day.

Currently, there is one Division I Hispanic female athletic director, Irma Garcia, at Saint Francis (NY) College. Organizations interested in expanding their constituency to include Hispanic females might start with recruiting Ms. Garcia, Denee Barracato, Gloria Nevarez, and other prominent Hispanic females in college sports and NCAA administration. Garcia, Barracato and Nevarez are all former student-athletes who understand the unique barriers to Hispanic female sport participation and they can constructively inform the problem definition, agenda setting and research objectives. From a grassroots perspective individuals and organizations that promote sports participation of females of color also should tap Hispanic churches to build alliances, especially those with parents and elders. The composition of the problem definition in Hispanic communities differs in some areas from the challenges confronted by Black females. The Latino groups and Hispanic churches should be tapped because the church stresses integration into new roles as a vital part of community and personal development. Nonetheless, Hispanic females are quickly becoming a prominent group in collegiate athletics, and their voice can only strengthen the collective speech of women of color.

Create Additional Space for Public Argumentation

Organizations like the BWSF, NCAA, Black Coaches Association (BCA), NACWAA, CBC, MOAA, and WBCA discuss sport in society issues. Public space at conferences, during professional development and in other settings needs to drastically increase. Each of the organizations mentioned above should seek to have a forum or featured speaker to discuss the involvement of females of color in college sports. Typically, conferences accept ideas from speakers with a desire to present. However, conference coordinators need to seek out speakers and earmark funding so their attendees can hear about and from females of color. The inclusion of scholars, collegiate coaches and administrators of color is wonderful; however, grandmothers, mothers, and daughters also need to be at the table. Black feminists can bring this group to the table through sorority gatherings, churches and parent/teacher/student associations. Bringing diverse groups to the table will expand the space for public argumentation at the middle and high school level, and this is where our work must begin. Lastly, the augmentation of public space also must be virtual. Social networking sites can help to create conversations and disseminate information. The BWSF currently has Myspace and Facebook pages. Part of BSWF's mission is to provide space where it is routine to recognize and celebrate Black female sport achievement (Greene & Sloan-Green, 2003).

CONCLUSION

Mutual engagement in mutual aid also will bring out mutual understanding and, hopefully, a change in the demography of Title IX social justice advocacy. Black female student-athletes who entered Division I schools in 1999 graduated at a federal rate of 66% or 16 percentage points higher than the federal graduation rate for Black female nonstudents-athletes. From grassroots perspective, Black adolescent females who participate in sports can maintain a healthy lifestyle, avoid early pregnancy, and decrease the likelihood of adolescent obesity. From an advocacy standpoint, Title IX will never achieve the ultimate goal of gender equity without achieving some degree of racial and gender equity. In order to achieve racial and gender equity Black feminists and White advocates must step-up their game and engage in shared responsibility when carrying out social justice advocacy.

STUDY QUESTIONS

1. What is social justice?
2. What are the five strategies for effective social justice advocacy?
3. Select two issues you feel impact sport participation of females of color and select two social justice advocacy strategies. Discuss pursuing some steps related to this strategy and how they will help address the issues.
4. Explore the unique abilities of Black advocates and White advocates and discuss additional ways they can collaborate to advocate for black females in sport.
5. If you were to create an initiative designed to increase women of color in sport, on or off the field, what might be your top three priorities?

SUGGESTED READINGS

Edwards, J. (1999). The Black female athlete and the politics if (in)visibility. *New Political Economy, 4*(2), 278–282.

Evans, T. M. (1998). In the Title IX race toward gender equity, the Black female athlete is left to finish last: The lack of access for the invisible woman. *Howard Law Journal, 42,* 105–137.

Fraser, N. (1996, Apr/May). Social justice in the age of identity politics: Redistribution, recognition, and participation. Lecture conducted as part *of The Tanner Lectures on Human Values* at Stanford University, Paulo Alto, California.

Hill, J. (2006). Black women in sports. *The Crisis,* 28–29.

Paule, A. (1995). We need to do more: How Title IX impacts women of color. Retrieved from http://www/womenssportsfoundation.org

Rand, S. (2006). Teaching law students to practice social justice: An interdisciplinary search for help through social work's empowerment approach. *Clinical Law Review, 13*(1), 459–504.

REFERENCES

Abney, R. (1999). African American women in sport. *The Journal of Physical Education, Recreation & Dance, 70*(4), 35–38.

Adler, P. A., & Adler, P. (1989). The gloried self: The aggrandizement and the constriction of self. *Social Psychology Quarterly, 52*(4), 299–310.

Alexander, A. (1978). *Status of minority women in the association of intercollegiate athletics for women* (Un-published master's thesis). Temple University, Philadelphia, PA.

Augenblick, J. G., Myers, J. L., & Anderson, A. B. (1997). Equity and adequacy in school funding. *The Future of Children, 7*(3), 63–77.

Barracato, D. (2007). (Personal communication, October 7, 2007).

Birrell, S. (1990). Women of color critical autobiography

& sport. In M. A. Messner & D. F. Suber (Eds.), *Sports, man and the gender order: Critical feminist perspectives* (pp. 185–200). Champaign, IL: Human Kinetics.

Butler, J., & Lopiano, D. (2003). The women's sports foundation report: Title IX and race in intercollegiate sport. *Women's Sports Foundation*. East Meadow, NY: Eisenhower Park.

Carrington, B. (1998). Sport, masculinity, and Black cultural resistance. *Journal of Sport and Social Issues, 22*, 275–298.

Cepada, R. (2001, June). Courting destiny. *Essence*, 182–184.

Cohen, D., de la Vega, R., & Watson, G. (2001). *Advocacy for social justice*. Bloomfield, CT: Kumarian Press Inc.

Collins, P. H. (2003). Toward an Afrocentric feminist epistemology. In Y. S. Lincoln & N. K. Denzin (Eds.), *Turning points in qualitative research: Tying knots in a handkerchief* (pp. 47–72). Blue Ridge Summit, PA: Alta Mira Press.

Collins, P. H. (1989). The social construction of Black feminist Tthought. *Signs: Journal of Women in Culture and Society, 14*(4), 745–773.

Corbett, D. (2002). *Title IX and women of color: Assessing Title IX: Past, present, and future*. A Title IX 30th Anniversary Symposium. University of Miami, Center for Research on Sport in Society.

Corbett, D., & Johnson, W. (2000). The African American female in collegiate sport: Sexism and racism. In D. Brooks & R. Althouse (Eds.), *Racism in college athletics: The African American athletes experience* (2nd ed., pp. 199–225). Morgantown, WV: Fitness Information Technology.

Crenshaw, K. (1992). *Whose story is it anyway? Feminist and antiracist appropriations of Anita Hill, in race-ing justice, en-gendering power: Essays on Anita Hill, Clarence Thomas, and the construction of social reality*. Toni Morrison (Ed.). New York: Pantheon Books.

Department of Labor (1988). Title IX of the Education Amendments of 1972 10 U.S.C §§ 1681–1688 Title 20—Education Chapter 38—*Discrimination based on sex or blindness*. Retrieved from http://www.usdoj.gov/crt/cor/coord/titleixstat.htm

Dick, B. (2002). *Action research: Action and research*. Retrieved from http://www.scu.edu.au/schools/gcm/ar/arp/aandr.html

Digest of Education Statistics. (2007). *Total enrollment in degree-granting institutions, by race/ethnicity, sex, attendance status, and level of student: Selected years, 1976 through 2004*. Retrieved from http:///nces.ed.gov

Douglas, D. (2002). To be young, gifted, Black, and female: A mediation on the cultural politics at play in representations of Venus and Serena Williams. *Sociology of Sport Online*. Retrieved from http://physed.otago.ac.nz/sosol/v5i2_3.html

Edwards, J. (1999). The Black female athlete and the politics if (in) visibility. *New Political Economy, 4*(2), 278–282.

Evans, T. M. (1998). In the Title IX race toward gender equity, the Black female athlete is left to finish last: The lack of access for the invisible woman. *Harvard Law Journal, 42*, 105–137.

Elliot, A. (1997, June 22). Title IX 25 years later—Minority women worry about which sports get support. *Seattle Times*, A11.

Engelhardt, H. T. (1989) Advocacy: Some reflections on an ambiguous term. *Children and Health Care: Moral and Social Issues*, 317–322.

Fraser, N. (1996, Apr/May). Social justice in the age of identity politics: Redistribution, recognition, and participation. Lecture conducted as part *of The Tanner Lectures on Human Values* at Stanford University, Paulo Alto, CA.

Fiegly, D. (2007). (Personal communication, October 17, 2007).

Goff, A. (2002). *Minority women often left out of Title IX mix*. Retrieved from http://www.ncaa.org

Granderson, L. Z. (2006). *Outside the arc*. Retrieved from http://sports.espn.go.com/wnba/news/story?id=2204322

Green, L. S., & Sloan-Green, T. (2007). Beyond tokenism to empowerment: The Black Women in Sport Foundation. In D. Brooks & R. Althouse (Eds.), *Diversity and social justice in college sports: Sport management and the student athlete* (pp. 313–332). Morgantown, WV: Fitness Information Technology.

Greenlee, C. T. (1997, April 17). Title IX: Does help for women come at the expense of African Americans. *Black Issues In Higher Education*, 24–27.

Hall, S. (1980). The whites of their eyes: Racist ideologies and the media. In G. Bridges & R. Brunt (Eds.), *Silver Lining: Some strategies for the eighties* (pp. 28– 52). London: Lawrence and Wishart.

Harris, J. (2006). *Standing up to persecution at Penn State*. Retrieved from http://lesbianlife.about.com

Harrison, L., Lee, A. M., & Belcher, D. (1999). Race and gender differences in sport participation as a function of self-schema. *Journal of Sport & Social Issues, 23*(4), 287–307

Henderson, M. G. (1989). *Speaking in tongues: Dialogics and dialectics and the Black woman writer's literary tradition, changing our own words*. New Brunswick, NJ: Rutgers University Press.

Hill, J. (2006). Black women in sports. *The Crisis*, 28–29.

Jet Magazine. (2001). *Fired White sportscaster apologizes for remarks about Venus and Serena Williams*. Retrieved from http://findarticles.com/p/articles/mi_m1355/is_4_100/ai_76513096/

Lattimer, C. (2005). *Track and basketball, is that all: An exploration of African-American women in intercollegiate athletics post Title IX*. Unpublished Paper, Princeton University, Princeton, NJ.

Lapchick, R. (2000, April). *Women of color in sports: Double jeopardy*. Retrieved from www.bus.ucf.edu/sport/

Lapchick, R. (2005, June). *The 2004 racial and gender report card*. College Sports.

Lopiano, D. (2007, June 22). *Room for improvement Title IX is succeeding, but there's still work to do*. Retrieved from http://sportsillustrated.cnn.com/2007/more/06/21/titleix.wsf/

Lloyd, J. (2009). *Diversity missing among leaders of USA Olympic sports*. Retrieved from http://www.usatoday.com/sports/2009-04-07-noc-boards-survey_N.htm

Mathewson, A. D. (1996). Black women and gender equity and the function at the junction. *Marquette Sports Law Journal, 6*(2), 239–266.

Meertens, R. W., & Pettigrew, T. F. (1997). Is subtle prejudice really prejudice? *Public Opinion Quarterly, 61*(10), 54–71.

Miller, P. S., & Kerr, G. A. (2003). The role experimentation of intercollegiate student athletes. *The Psychologist, 17*, 196–219.

Minority Sports Organizations Coalition. (2009, January 16). *Minutes of the minority sports organizations coalition*. NCAA Convention, Washington, DC.

Murphy, C. (2009). *Girls sports opportunities MIA in city schools*. Retrieved from http://womensnews.org

National Collegiate Athletic Association. (2008). 1999–2000—2007-2008. *Student-athlete ethnicity report*. Indianapolis, IN: Author.

Novak, M. (2000). Defining social justice. *First Things: A Monthly Journal of Religion and Public Life*, *108*, 11–13.

National Organization for Woman. (2009). *History*. Retrieved from http://www.now.org

Olson, W. (1991). Beyond Title IX: Toward an agenda for women and sports in the 1990s. *Yale Journal of Law and Feminism*, *3*, 105–151.

Paule, A. (1995). We need to do more: How Title IX impacts women of color. Retrieved from http://www/womenssportsfoundation.org

Prince Georges County Public Schools. (2006). *Prince Georges County Public Schools Title IX report for the National Women' Law Center*. Unpublished Report, Prince Georges County Public Schools, Prince Georges County, MD.

Rawls, J. (1999). *A theory of justice* (Revised Edition). New York, NY: Oxford University Press.

Rand, S. (2006). Teaching law Students to practice social justice: An interdisciplinary search for help through social work's empowerment approach. *Clinical Law Review*, *13*(1), 459–504.

Rhoden, W. (2007). The unpleasant reality for women's sports. *The New York Times*. Retrieved from http://select.nytimes.com/2007/04/09sports/09rhoden.html

Sarvasy, W. (1992). Beyond the difference versus equality policy debate: Postsuffrage feminism, citizenship and the quest for feminist welfare state. *Signs*, *17*(2), 329–362.

Schneider, R. L., & Lester, L. (2001). *Social work advocacy: A new framework for action*. Belmont, CA: Books/Cole.

Schram, S. F. (1999). *After welfare: The culture of postindustrial social policy*. New York, NY: New York University Press.

Scranton, P. (2001). *Beauty and business: Commerce, gender, and culture in modern America*. Oxford, UK: Routledge.

Sellers, R. M., Kupermic, G. P., & Dumas, A. (1997). The college life experiences of African American women athletes. *American Journal of Community Psychology*, *25*(5), 699–720.

Sloan-Green, T. (2007). *My letter to Traci*. Unpublished, Black Women In Sports Foundation, Philadelphia, PA.

Smith, M. (2007 April 12). *Pokey Chatman's assistant told LSU about relationship*. Retrieved on from http://www.aolnews.com/2007/03/12/pokey-chatmans-assistant-told-lsu-about-relationship/

Smith, Y. (1992). Women of color in society & sport. *Quest*, *44*(22), 228–250

Sports Illustrated (2007). *The most influential people in Title IX history*. Retrieved from http://sportsillustrated.cnn.com

Stanford Center on Ethics. (2007). *Title IX today, Title IX tomorrow: Gender equity in college athletics*. Retrieved, from http://ethics.stanford.edu

Suggs, W. (2001). Left behind. *Chronicle of Higher Education*, *48*(14), A35–A37.

Women's Law Center. (2006). Title IX and women's athletic opportunity: A nation's promise yet to be fulfilled. Published Paper, Women's Law Center, Washington, DC.

Women's Law Project. (2009). *Women's law project and Senator Mary Jo White team up to give Pennsylvania girls a sporting chance*. Retrieved from http://www.womenslawproject.org/press/PA_SB890_WLPPressRelease.pdf

Young, I. M. (1990). *Justice and the politics of difference*. Princeton, NJ: Princeton University Press.

Section VI: Racism, Media Exposure, and Stereotyping

Two themes feed this section: The first produces an overview of race relations with a focus on contemporary Whiteness theory, while the other depicts the effect of racism on stakeholder management issues in big-time NCAA sports programs—who gets what, when, and how?

Antiracism advocacy begins at the personal level with a desire to learn more about other racial minorities. In Chapter 14, Lawrence provides an overview of race relation theories with a focus on contemporary Whiteness theory and Whiteness studies, sharpening the concepts of race, racism, and discrimination to forge an understanding about "how power, Whiteness, White privilege, and the White athlete have had an effect on sports and the sport science literature." The study of White privilege permits the reader to more fully comprehend the interconnectiveness of racial identity, privilege, cultural values, masculinity, gender, nationalism, and dominate cultural beliefs. Lawrence believes her present journey as a White woman, athlete, and scholar mirrors the journey of a "color-affirming White" who is vested in promoting the concepts of social justice and fairness, especially in college athletics.

Singer's mission in Chapter 15 is to map a framework that can provide scholars, practitioners, and students who are interested in college sport with a tool for understanding and addressing the educational interests of the African American male athlete in the revenue-producing sports of football and men's basketball at predominantly White institutions of higher education. At the heart of the debate rests the question, to what degree are big-time college athletic programs willing to sacrifice the education experiences of student-athletes, especially African American males, to gain a greater market share on their investment? Singer suggests that "those who manage sport (i.e., coaches and administrators) must be more concerned with the benefits that prime beneficiaries (student-athletes) receive from the athletic department's existence and operations." He chastises them not only because of their fiscal gains via the commodification of the African American male body, but also for their disregard of policies and practices that might affect the overall welfare of these athletes. There is, after all, a moral duty to provide remedies to eradicate the condition contributing to exploitation of African American male student-athletes.

CHAPTER 14

Whiteness Studies in Sport: A 21st Century Perspective

SUZANNE MALIA LAWRENCE

Abstract

The focus of this chapter is on Whiteness theory and Whiteness studies and how they have been applied to the sport sciences. In the introduction an initial set of guiding questions for this chapter is articulated. Then the chapter begins with an overview of the current state of global race relations. A definition of terms chart is presented to assist with significant race relation concepts. The new world racial system is outlined in this section as well. Next, the emergence of Whiteness studies and the origin of the Whiteness theory are presented. The chapter then proposes concepts of White privilege, White power, whiteness as property, and the possessive investment of Whiteness. Next, an overview of the existing studies focusing on Whiteness in sport is displayed, which includes the following intriguing topics: White privilege in sport, White supremacy in sport, and Whiteness within sport media. A synopsis of the Whiteness studies in the sport science literature is offered in a useful table. The force of the White athlete is iterated and the White athlete perspective is offered. The overrepresentation of the White athlete is explored and specific statistics are outlined. The author, a White athlete, provides a personal narrative in regard to race and the experience of her own Whiteness. The chapter concludes with the implications of Whiteness in sport and Whiteness studies for 21st century sport scholars and practitioners.

Key Terms		
● race	●	Whiteness
● race relations	●	Whiteness theory
● White privilege		

"The reality, the depth, and the persistence of the delusion of White Supremacy in this country causes any real concept of education to be as remote, and as much to be feared, as change or freedom itself."
—*James Baldwin (1985)* The Price of the Ticket

INTRODUCTION

The significance of understanding current race relations cannot be underestimated for students studying the social and historical underpinnings of sport. Initially, a grasp of race relations will expose students to the racial and power dynamics that exist in the world and the arena of sport as well. Therefore, important concepts such as *race*, *racism*, and *discrimination* will be outlined in this chapter. These concepts are an integral part of understanding relationships among particular groups. Race, racism, and discrimination are the most fundamental mechanisms of hierarchical difference that shape the ordering of social relations as well as the allocation of life experiences and life chances (Zuberi, 2001). In efforts to stimulate an appreciation for whiteness studies in sport, *Whiteness theory* and *Whiteness studies* will be specifically outlined as well. The phenomenon of overlooking the White athlete is relevant to Whiteness in sport and will be explored. Important questions need to be posed such as, how often do you hear that the White athlete is overly represented in the sport of archery? And why is there a failure to focus on the large number of sports that the White athlete is overly represented in? The primary aim of the author is to encourage students to grasp how power, whiteness, White privilege, and the White athlete have had an impact on sports and the sport science literature. The following questions will be examined: a) What is the current state of global race relations?; b) What is Whiteness theory?; c) What is White privilege and how is it manifested in society?; d) What are the major findings in the Whiteness studies in sport literature?; e) Is the White athlete an underdog in most sports?; and f) How does Whiteness impact sports and the sport science literature?

Suzanne Malia Lawrence

21ST CENTURY RACE RELATIONS

According to Howard Winant (2006), a well-known American sociologist and race theorist, "The race concept is more problematic than ever before" (p. 987). The concept of *race* lacks an objective basis; "and yet the concept persists, as idea, as practice, as identity, and as social structure" (Winant, 2006, p. 986). Race involves socially constructed categorizations, which vary in configuration and salience over time (Collins, 2001). The practices of government play a primary role in the understanding and social effects of these categories. The 21st century represents a worldwide confusion and an anxiety about the political significance and meaning of race (Winant, 2002). "Race defines and organizes the world and its future, as it has done for centuries" (Winant, 2002, p. 17). Contemporary threats to human rights and social well-being cannot be managed without paying attention to issues of race (Winant, 2002). See Table 14.1 for key terms to assist with contemporary race relation terms.

Race Relations

The true nature of race relations "is a system of racial domination and exploitation based on violence, resulting in the suppression and dehumanization of an entire people over centuries of American history" (Steinberg, 2007, p. 16). The global political terrain, which is marked by post-colonalism, postapartheid, post civil rights movement, post

Table 14.1.	Key Terms
Term	**Definition**
Antifascism	A strong sentiment, which is opposed to a system of government marked by centralization of authority under a dictator and typically a policy of belligerent nationalism and racism.
Colorblind	A perspective in which emphasis is placed on treating each person as a unique individual, as opposed to an interchangeable member of a social category. The origins of this approach were based on ameliorating prejudice and claiming that the categorization process, hence the mere existence of different groups creates biased behavior (Wolsko, Park, Judd, & Wittenbrink, 2000).
Discrimination	A complex system of social relations, which involve subtle and overt actions "that serve to limit the social, political, or economic opportunities of particular groups" (Fredrickson & Knobel, 1982).
Exclusion/ Exclusionism	To prevent a particular group of people from being included, considered, or accepted; rejection.
Meritocracy /Meritocratic	A system in which advancement is based on individual ability or achievement.
Mobility	The movement of people, as from one social group, class, or level to another.
Power	A person, group, or nation having great influence or control over others.
Race	A population of people who are believed to be naturally or biologically distinct from other populations. Race categorizations are socially constructed based on the meanings people give to particular physical traits (Coakley, 2009).
Racism	A set of institutional conditions of group inequality and a set of beliefs holding that the subordinate racial group is biologically or culturally inferior to the dominant racial group (Bobo & Fox, 2003).
Racialized Groups	Groups of people that have been designated as distinct based on a shared race and these groups consist of people of color and/or minorities who are typically discriminated in society.
Stratification	To arrange or separate groups of people into castes, classes, or social levels.
Superexploitation/ Exploitation	Utilization of another person or group for selfish purposes.

Source: The American Heritage Dictionary of the English Language (4th ed.) (2000). See reference pages.

Cold War, and *antifascism*, has called into question White Supremacy like never before (Winant, 2002). The worldwide rejection of the former methods of racial hierarchy has linked antiracism to democracy more strongly than ever before (Winant, 2002). Due to White supremacy being fiercely contested, for the first time in modern history there is worldwide support for racial equality. Therefore, race relations existing in contemporary society involves a perpetual dichotomy; this is due to the fact that mobility among racialized groups is increasing. However, at the same time patterns of exclusion and superexploitation of these racialized groups persist (Winant, 2006). Postcolonial states (Sudan, South Africa, India) and national societies (United Arab Emirates, France, Spain, United States) have become more *racially democratic*; however, the 'life chances' of racialized groups have not drastically changed. (Life chances refers to the opportunities that individuals are afforded due to their racial backgrounds and nationalized settings.) These national societies have incorporated and normalized their racial conflicts (Winant, 2006). In many of these more "racially democratic" national societies the conditions of Blacks, Muslims, indigenous peoples, and undocumented migrants have actually worsened (Winant, 2006). For example, the post 9/11 mentality has caused many Muslims worldwide to be negatively stereotyped as terrorists and fanatics leaving them with fewer opportunities for improving their economic status and living conditions; also undocumented migrants are more stigmatized and less likely to get work therefore causing their living conditions to decline.

According to sociologists Bobo and Thompson (2006), "We as a society have normalized and, for the time being, largely depoliticized, a remarkable set of social conditions" (p. 447). They (2006) examined the United States and its use of incarceration for purposes of social control. Bobo and Thompson (2006) claimed the mechanisms of systematic racial injustices are more indirect, covert and implied than the mechanisms of racial bias evident in the past. Some examples of covert, racial injustices are when a person of color walks into a room and the first thing others notice is the color of his/her skin, or when a person of color is treated as a subordinate in a bank and his/her true identity is questioned. This claim explains the current state of race relations, at least in the US, and reminds us that racism has persevered in today's society; in addition, racial identities and injustices are less apparent and more indescribable than in the past (Winant, 2006).

New World Racial System

White supremacy has recreated itself as colorblind, nonracialist, and *meritocratic* (Winant, 2002). Therefore, a new colorblind racial system has emerged in which racial inequality can thrive, by depending on stereotypes and fears and resorting to *exclusionism* and scapegoating when politically necessary (Winant, 2002). According to Bobo (2001), "the death of Jim Crow racism has left us in an uncomfortable place, however; a state of laissez-faire racism" (p. 294). The reformed version of White supremacy perpetuates the so-called superiority of White mainstream values and at the same time maintains the racial equality that has been previously achieved. The idea here is that racial justice has already been largely achieved, which is extremely problematic. The colorblind concept in the US, the nonracialist sentiment of the South African Freedom Charter, the Brazilian ideals of racial democracy, and the racial differentialism of the European Union supposedly promote the idea that there is racial equality (Winant, 2002).

The racial politics of this new system has caused racial conflict and racial reform to be unstable, uncertain, and more variable than ever before (Winant, 2002). Even though the ideals of freedom, democracy, and human rights persist, the new system has implemented "a renewed racial complacency" (Winant, 2002, p. 18). There has been a shift to a dominant ideology of "laissez-faire racism" (Bobo, Kluegel, & Smith, 1997; Bobo & Smith, 1998). There has been a disappearance of overt racism, demands for segregation, support for governmentally enforced discrimination, and compliance to the idea that Blacks are categorically the intellectual inferiors of Whites (Bobo, 2001). The new racial system is guided by the nonracialist and colorblind argument that claims "race is less salient than before in determining life chances" (Winant, 2006, p. 989). However, according to Winant (2002), this argument could be a disguise for a reassertion of White privilege, White rule, and White cultural norms. There is reason for caution here, because the global racial situation is marked by tension and is not clearly defined (Winant, 2006). "There is political stagnation over some types of affirmative action, and persistent negative stereotyping of racial minorities; and a wide gulf in perceptions regarding the importance of racial discrimination remains" (Bobo, 2001, p. 294). A vision of racial justice has not been established and the memories of years of racial oppression remain. The problem remains; however, the depth of the problem is greatly debated and integration is accepted however, under very limited terms and in specific areas (Bobo, 2001). This new ideology includes negative stereotypes of Blacks, a tendency to lean towards the trend of individuality and stray away from structural accounts of racial inequality; and an unwillingness to see government actively work to demolish racial disparity (Bobo, 2001). This new mentality is a more subtle and covert form of racism, making it more challenging to confront; it is also more accountable to the "more fluid and permeable set of racial divisions in the social order" (Bobo, 2001).

According to Winant (2002), most likely the world will never get beyond race, nor transcend race. However, the world has an opportunity of overcoming the stratification, the hierarchy, the taken-for-granted injustice and inhumanity that very often accompanies the concept of race (Winant, 2002). The future of democracy depends on the concept of race and the meaning that is attached to it (Winant, 2002). Redefining *race* and *racism* is necessary now; new accounts of these concepts should address the emergent racial conditions of the 21st century.

WHITENESS THEORY AND STUDIES

Over the past decade, legal scholars (Harris, 1995) and social scientists (Jensen, 2000; Lewis, 2001a; Lipsitz, 1998; Roediger, 2002) began to analyze critically the concept of *Whiteness*. Whiteness studies are scholarly examinations of White privileges and exploration of the role Whiteness and White culture play in an increasingly multicultural society. It is important to note, that many of the studies conducted on whiteness are not grounded in the traditional definition of racism or White supremacy. *Whiteness theory*, which emerged out of these legal and social science scholarly investigations (Harris, 1995; Delgado & Stefancic, 1997; Roediger, 2002), treats Whiteness not as a biological category but as a social construction (Thompson, 1999). Whiteness theory is interdisciplinary; it does not agree on a single methodology or theoretical claim (Thompson, 1999). "Whiteness theory is intended to make White cultural and political assumptions and privileges visible so that whites do not assume that their own position is neutral or normal" (Thompson, 2001, p. 2). Whiteness theory views Whiteness as a political and cultural position, a position and an identity that are gained at the expense of people of color (Thompson, 2001).

Whiteness

According to Lipsitz (1998), "Whiteness is a social fact, an identity created and continued with all-too-real consequences for the distribution of wealth, prestige, and opportunity" (p. vii). Whiteness is a process, which cannot ever be fully captured and nailed down (Tochluk, 2008). "Whiteness is irregularly experienced and dynamic, always shifting and changing" (Tochluk, 2008, p. 23). According to Tochluk (2008), being White is normal or neutral but it also means we are an oppressor. "Whiteness symbolizes our history of slavery, the genocide of the Native American populations, racism, and the Ku Klux Klan" (Tochluk, 2008, p. 25). The White community is not comfortable with its own Whiteness because it aligns us with a shameful history, which we have no desire to be connected to (Tochluk, 2008).

Whiteness as Property and the Possessive Investment in Whiteness

According to Harris (1995), the construction of race and the emergence of Whiteness as property are grounded in racial domination. Harris (1995) described the relationship between race and property as follows: "It was not the concept of race alone that operated to oppress Blacks and Indians; rather, it was the intersection between conceptions of race and property which played a critical role in establishing and maintaining racial and economic subordination" (p. 277). Harris (1993) and Roediger (2002) also concluded that Whiteness fits and reinforces the concept of property. Harris (1993) wrote, "'Whiteness is a property,' is a longstanding idea which ought to pay off even if it is not so at the moment, it survives with distressing ease amid such hands, even as income inequities within Black, White, and Hispanic population have grown tremendously" (p. 12). Lipsitz (1998) claimed that both public policy and private prejudice have contributed to a racialized hierarchy in society and also created a "possessive investment in Whiteness" (p. vii). White Americans are encouraged to invest in whiteness, to remain connected to an identity that gives them resources, power, and opportunity (Lipsitz, 1998). Whiteness can be invested in like property and most White Americans do invest in it.

WHITE PRIVILEGE AND WHITE POWER

White privilege is an assemblage of benefits that have been given to people in society who have White skin (McIntosh, 1988). McIntosh (1989) examined White privilege and created a list of benefits associated with being White. A few examples of these benefits: a) being able to go shopping and not get followed or harassed, b) being able to turn on the television or open the newspaper and see people of their own race widely represented, and c) being able to succeed without being called a credit to their race. Sullivan (2006) discovered, among White people, a problematic denial of the existence of unconscious investments in White privilege and an explanation that this unconsciousness is innate to the human psyche.

White power has typically taken the form of White supremacy, which is defined by Fredrickson (1981). White supremacy "refers to the attitudes, ideologies, and policies associated with the rise of blatant forms of white or European dominance over 'nonwhite' populations. It involves making invidious distinctions of a socially crucial kind that are based primarily, if not exclusively, on physical characteristics and ancestry" (p. ix).

WHITENESS STUDIES IN SPORT

The study of whiteness (Lewis, 2001a; Lipsitz, 1998; Roediger, 2002) and White privilege (Jensen, 1999, 2000; McIntosh, 1988) represent new departures from traditional lines of race relations and sports research. King (2005) and other scholars (King, Leonard, & Kusz, 2007; McDonald, 2005) have suggested a broader dialogue about the epistemological and political problems and tensions accompanying sport studies scholarship about whiteness, especially in light of the mainstream and White-dominated representation and demographics of North American higher education (McDonald, 2005). Some sport science scholars are encouraging a discourse and study of Whiteness in sport that ex-

poses and interrogates contemporary power relations, racial performances, and struggles over
meaning (Brayton, 2005; Douglas, 2005; Erickson, 2005; Fusco, 2005; King, 2005; McDonald,
2005). King et al. (2007) claimed that many
manuscripts on race and sport have ignored
"the most fundamental feature of sporting
worlds since their crystallization in the 19th
century, that is, White power" (p. 3). Existing
studies of Whiteness in sport have focused on
White privilege, White Supremacy, and largely
on how Whiteness invades sport media.

This is a club where White athletes
are overly represented in the sport of
basketball. Courtesy of Suzanne Malia
Lawrence

White Privilege in Sport

Butryn (2002) and Long and Hylton (2002) investigated the concept of White privilege in
sport and its impact on race relations. Butryn (2002) studied White racial identity and
privilege in a sport psychology consulting environment and found a preliminary account
of White privileges specific to the applied sport psychology field. He (2002) presented
the details of a life-history interview with a White male sport psychology consultant. He
(2002) also depicted the outcome of a three-way conversation between himself, the consultant, and an African American sport psychology graduate student. Long and Hylton
(2002) examined personal identity of White athletes in the context of normalized, privileged Whiteness and demonstrated the processes by which these operate in sporting environments. They (2002) claimed, "Examining whiteness more closely should allow researchers to make it visible and open to discussion" (p. 1). Long and Hylton (2002)
postulated that understanding the construction of Whiteness produces an apparent com-
prehension of the processes of racism, hence an increased opportunity to disturb them.
Results also revealed indicators of White privilege in sport. An example of a privilege is
as follows: An athlete can express himself/herself in sport without people attributing it
to his/her "race" (Long & Hylton, 2002). Long and Hylton (2002) concluded that due to
the privileges endowed by Whiteness, moving in and out of athletic identities is in fact
easier for Whites than it is for Blacks.

White Supremacy in Sport

Douglas (2005) critiqued how dominant cultural meanings and values are expressed in
the atmosphere prevalent at sporting events. She (2005) studied the significance of the
atmosphere at two tennis tournaments in which Venus and Serena Williams (Black female athletes) were the primary competitors. The character and climate were witnessed
in efforts to understand how White racial fans are apprehended and communicated in
society. The fans booed Serena when she entered the stadium and during her introduction. Venus and Richard (father of Serena/Venus) were booed as they came into the stadium to watch Serena's match. During the match, fans cheered Serena's errors, booed
her points, and yelled during her serve, all of which are breaches in tennis etiquette.
Douglas (2005) concluded that the hostile nature of the climate (White fans) created
during the tennis tournaments is symbolic of the practices of discrimination and social
exclusion that manifest into racism.

Ferber (2007) explored the construction of Black masculinity and claimed that elements of White supremacy and the new racism are reinforced by representations of

Black male athletes. She (2007) examined the following question: Does the success of Black men in the arena of sports challenge this White supremacist construction of Black masculinity? Ferber (2007) indicated, "The success of Black men as athletes does little to challenge the systematic and institutionalized system of White supremacy" (p. 23). The success of Black male athletes is manipulated and rearticulated to support White Supremacy and White male privilege (Ferber, 2007). King (2007) in his overview of why sport matters to White power, claimed Eurocentrism and White Supremacy were central components in the invention of the Olympic Games. He (2007) reviewed interpretations of the 2006 Winter Olympics in Torino and verified that the interpretations lack the optimism of the earlier Olympic Games and they confirm racial characters and their limitations. King (2007) revealed that advocates of White power use the games "to recenter whiteness as a source of pride, marker of civilization, and expression of naturalized superiority" (p. 94).

Sports Media and Whiteness

Wheaton and Beal (2003) investigated media consumption by the alternative sport subculture. Within the subculture authentic status is based on assumptions of maleness and Whiteness, which makes it challenging for females and non-White participants to be included and accepted in the subculture (Wheaton & Beal, 2003). Cosgrove and Bruce (2005) postulated that the death of America's Cup sailor Sir Peter Blake helped to reframe notions of national character in New Zealand. Sir Blake was portrayed as a New Zealand hero representing a true national character. New Zealand's traditional national character has been linked to White masculinity, however, this has been recently contested (Cosgrove & Bruce, 2005). They (2005) concluded that as long as the centrality of Whiteness is under threat there would be an ongoing effort to recreate the traditional vision of nationalism in New Zealand.

Brayton (2005) analyzed the skateboard media and postulated that it fosters a continued critique of Whiteness. Due to White male rebellion there is a White resistance in skateboarding (Brayton, 2005). Brayton (2005) concluded that the skateboard media refuses middle-class Whiteness and replaces it with a renewed heteromasculinity that is informed by the Black other. Fusco (2005) researched how race and space intersect and how Whiteness through architecture and style of design can be found in North American and Canadian sport spaces. She (2005) demonstrated how discourses of Whiteness and other discourses of respectability, progress, reproduction, renewal, and reinvigoration are placed on the participants who use sport spaces.

Douglas and Jamieson (2006) analyzed print media accounts of Nancy Lopez's Ladies Professional Golf Association (LPGA) farewell tour. They (2006) claimed the media representations of Lopez are intertwined with new strategies of racialization that strengthen White power and White privilege. Walton and Butryn (2006) examined the relationship between Whiteness and men's US distance running. They (2006) critically reviewed print and electronic sources dealing with US distance running. Researchers (2006) concluded the media aims to normalize Whiteness within the larger story of US distance running.

In an interpretive case study, Hartmann (2007) focused on of the controversy that surrounded Rush Limbaugh's comments about Philadelphia Eagles quarterback Donovan McNabb. Hartmann (2007) argued that Limbaugh's comments were a classic example of how the discourse of Whiteness functions to assert the cultural normativity of the White group and establish its privilege. This normativity, this perceived universality and transcendence, allowed Limbaugh (Hartmann, 2007), as Dave Roediger (2002) has commented on the pundit's ill-fated television show, to "walk the tightrope between the un-

Table 14.2.	Whiteness Studies in Sport: Some Major Findings (2001–2012)	
Year	Scholar(s)	Major Finding
2001	Kusz	The representations of disadvantaged and victimized young White males within popular sport serve as powerful cultural messages that encourage viewers to deny the privileged position of Whiteness that these males hold.
2002	Butryn	There are preliminary accounts of White privileges specific to the applied sport psychology field.
2002	Long & Hylton	Due to the privileges endowed by Whiteness, moving in and out of athletic identities is in fact easier for Whites than it is for Blacks.
2005	Brayton	The skateboard media refuses middle-class Whiteness and replaces it with a renewed heteromasculinity, which is informed by the Black other.
2005	Cosgrove & Bruce	As long as the centrality of Whiteness is under threat there will be an ongoing effort to recreate the traditional vision of nationalism in New Zealand through the use of sport.
2005	Douglas	The hostile nature of the White fans perpetuated during the sporting events (tennis tournaments) is symbolic of the practices of discrimination and social exclusion that manifest into racism.
2006	Walton & Butryn	The media aims to normalize Whiteness within the larger story of US distance running.
2007	Hartmann	The institution of sport is supposed to be colorblind, but, the institution is invested in economic gain and White supremacy. Demographic and cultural dominance of Whites in sport and in society is prevalent.
2007	King	Advocates of White power use the Olympic games "to recenter whiteness as a source of pride, marker of civilization, and expression of naturalized superiority."
2007	Leonard	Student athlete identities were evidence of innocence in the Duke Lacrosse Case. People held denials of the possibility of guilt based on "player's whiteness, sport of choice, educational institution and class status."
2009	Butryn	Connect narratives to larger issues of pedagogy and possibilities as they coincide with an active, progressive, anti-racist mode of addressing sport psychology and whiteness.
2010	McDonald & Toglia	The practices surrounding the NBA dress code are embedded in an economic rationale frequently embraced in corporate cultures that reproduce whiteness.
2011	Rhodes	Media representations of boxing champions illustrate the way in which their "respectability" is asserted to broader conversations about a perceived growing "White underclass."
2012	Poniatowski & Whiteside	T.V. commentary displays White hockey players as having exceptional physical bodies, intellectual aptitude, and moral righteousness.

spoken and the largely unspeakable" (p. 54). Hartmann (2007) verified the demographic and cultural dominance of Whites in sport and society.

Leonard (2007) studied the Duke Lacrosse case and the numerous online bloggers who defended the White lacrosse players who were accused of rape at a college party. Leonard (2007) suggested the media and the online defenders reinvented a sentiment of White power and claimed another assault on White masculinity. Student-athlete identities were evidence of innocence because denials of the possibility of guilt were held based on "player's whiteness, sport of choice, educational institution, and class status" (Leonard, 2007, p. 25). Kusz (2007a) examined "a domestic White cultural nationalism" that emerged after the 9/11 attacks and how it relates to sport and politics. He (2007a) reviewed two powerful media stories: the *National Review* cover story on NASCAR and Pat Tillman's death and life. Kusz (2007a) argued that sport is being used in the media after 9/11 to express, naturalize, and obtain public approval of White cultural nationalism. See Table 14.2 above, titled: *Whiteness Studies in Sport: Some Major Findings (2001–2012)*, for a synopsis of studies conducted in the last ten years.

THE WHITE ATHLETE:
OVERLOOKED REPRESENTATION AND STEREOTYPES

Simply because African American athletes dominate the two most widely publicized sports of football (college/pro) and basketball (college/pro) there is a tendency to overlook the White athlete. In 2000, Harry Edwards responded to an article in *Sports Illustrated* magazine titled *Whatever happened to the White athlete?* (Price, 1997). Edwards (2000) claimed, "In 95% of American sports the White athlete is dominant" (p. 23). Kyle Kusz's (2007b) popular book titled *Revolt of the White athlete: Race, Media and the Emergence of Extreme Athletes in America* is a response to sports media cover stories outlining the so-called disappearance of the White athlete in American sports. Kusz (2007b) examined how sport discourses reproduce a central, normative, and superior position for White masculinity in American culture and society.

There is an overrepresentation of White athletes among most college sports, from archery to wrestling, in the National Collegiate Athletic Association (NCAA) (All Divisions I, II, & III). In the 2005–06 academic year 70.6% of all athletes were White men and 77.4% were White women (NCAA, 2005/2006). In the 2006–07 academic year 72.2% of all athletes were White men and 78.8% were White women (NCAA, 2006/2007) (see Table 14.3). These statistics indicate that White athletes representation in most NCAA sports is on the rise. White athletes are also overrepresented in the professional ranks of the National Hockey League (NHL): 98% White (Lapchick, 2003); Major League Baseball (MLB): 60% White; and Major League Soccer (MLS): 58% White (Lapchick, Martin, Kushner, & Brenden, 2005).

Even though the White athlete is still widely represented in a large variety of sports, most of the research on athleticism (Harpalani, 1998; Harrison & Lawrence, 2004; Miller, 1998; Sailes, 1996) has focused on the African American athlete. According to Harrison, Azzarito, and Burden (2004), "No known research has investigated this phenomenon from the European American perspective" (p. 7). Harrison et al. (2004) investigated White athletes' perspectives on the phenomenon of athletic "superiority" and found they experienced being stereotyped and discriminated against. White athletes reported they were steered away by their coaches and parents from collegiate/professional athletic dreams and encouraged to pursue their academic degrees (Harrison et al., 2004). According to Harrison et al. (2004), in terms of European athletic heroes, Western cul-

Table 14.3.	2006–2007 NCAA White Student Athlete Race Percentages for All Divisions I, II, & III	
Sport	% of White Men	% of White Women
Archery	88.9	73.9
Badminton	0.0	38.5
Baseball	87.1	N/A
Basketball	49.3	62.1
Bowling	96.6	43.1
Cross Country	79.8	80.4
Equestrian	100.0	94.5
Fencing	72.0	63.5
Field Hockey	N/A	92.3
Football	60.2	N/A
Golf	89.5	83.0
Gymnastics	80.6	82.1
Ice Hockey	90.7	88.5
Lacrosse	92.3	91.5
Rifle	91.9	85.8
Rowing	81.6	83.1
Rugby	89.7	75.5
Sailing	90.0	N/A
Skiing	88.9	92.2
Soccer	78.0	86.8
Softball	N/A	84.3
Squash	76.0	77.2
Swimming/Diving	85.6	88.5
Sync. Swimming	N/A	77.0
Team Handball	N/A	0.0
Tennis	71.3	75.1
Track, Indoor	70.0	70.4
Track, Outdoor	68.4	69.5
Volleyball	68.0	80.9
Water Polo	78.7	79.9
Wrestling	84.7	N/A
ALL SPORTS	72.2	78.8

NCAA Race & Ethnicity Report 2006–2007

ture has a fairly long tradition of attributing people's actions to internal causes (i.e., the athlete's own initiative and hard work). White athletes have somewhat been protected from the "God-given" talent stereotype that many Black athletes must face.

White Athletic Stereotypes

Sport science scholars, who focus on race relations, have studied the relationship between racial stereotypes and sport performance. Stone, Lynch, Sjomeling, and Darley (1999) found that framing an athletic task as diagnostic of negative racial stereotypes about Black or White athletes can impede their performance in sports. Findings indicated White participants performed worse than did control participants when the golf task was framed as diagnostic of "natural athletic ability." Stone (2002) examined the effects of stereotype threat on self-handicapping in White athletes and found when a sports test was framed as a measure of "natural athletic ability," White participants felt threatened about confirming the negative stereotype about poor White athleticism and practiced less before the test as compared to control groups.

RACE, WHITENESS, AND PRIVILEGE: MY PERSONAL NARRATIVE

As a White woman, an athlete, and a sport scholar, I understand the significance of acknowledging my own experience of Whiteness and identifying my assumptions in regard to sport. Several themes are figural in my experience of sport in regard to my race. The first theme involves my acknowledgment of difference and recognizing the attention that Black players paid my family and me. When I was 8 and my brother was 11, my brother played in an all Black basketball league through a local boys club located in the inner city. I first noticed that there were no other White players in the league. I also noticed how the other kids in the league would always pay close attention to my family and me. It seems as if they were always asking me questions about my Dad's car, about our house, and where we lived. I noticed how my family was the only family that came to the games.

A second theme that emerged consists of a sense of sympathy for the Black players and a fascination with the difference in cultures. We would always end up giving a player a ride home or taking him to dinner with us after the game. At the time, I really did not understand why their families were not at the games. However, I remember having great concern for some of the players. Ever since I can remember, both my brother and I played sports and there was always a lot of diversity. I learned a lot about my teammates' cultures and backgrounds from developing friendships with many of them. Even at a young age I knew my family had it well; I just did not know how well until much later. We actually had season basketball tickets for many years for the San Diego Clippers and San Diego State University Aztecs.

A third theme, which emerged during my undergraduate years, encompasses my curiosity about various issues, such as differences between White and Black athletes in academic goals, career aspirations, and received treatment. I played softball at a major NCAA Division I institution where I experienced the life of a student-athlete. Many of my close friends were African American student-athletes. I noticed that some of these athletes had aspirations to play professional sports; however, none of them demonstrated a desire to attend graduate school. I had aspirations to further my education and I wondered why they did not. Additionally, some of these athletes were very concerned about graduating with their bachelor's degree. I felt very confident about receiving my degree on time in only four years. There was a definite difference in what I call my *scholarly swagger* than that of my African American student-athlete friends. I also noticed the differential treatment that these athletes received in the academic counseling center. For example, the academic counselor would register these student-athletes for classes, whereas I had to register for my own classes. African American student-athletes had mandatory tutors for all classes, whereas I could simply request a tutor whenever I felt the need for it. These types of experiences made me wonder why African American student-athletes were treated differently but also if they were treated differently in other arenas, such as the practice field, the training room, and the classroom.

My experience in graduate school stimulated my fascination with race and difference. I was enrolled in a sport psychology doctoral program that had a cultural studies emphasis, which is where I learned about Whiteness, White privilege, and power. For my dissertation I explored African American athletes' experiences of race throughout their athletic careers. My role as a researcher opened my eyes to extreme cases of racism and exposed me to the realities of African American athletes. These experiences motivated me to pursue research studies exploring race and social justice issues.

As a White Female Scholar

Now that I study racism in sport, stereotypes surrounding White and Black athleticism, and experiences of White athletes, many of my colleagues who I conduct research studies with are passionate about these issues as well. First and foremost as a White female scholar, I am indebted to many of my Black colleague friends who have included me and reached out to me. They have assisted me to gain insight into my Whiteness; over the years they have included me in their conversations on race in sport and have shared their perspectives on White mainstream behavior. We share our stories of Whiteness or

White privilege with each other. Some of my colleagues have asked me to give them insight into the mentality of White folks. These conversations have helped me learn more about my perspective of my whiteness.

There are times when I am completely oblivious to my Whiteness and there are times when I am ultra-aware of my Whiteness. My experiences and conversations have fueled my curiosity for race, race in sport, and most of all made me fascinated with my own whiteness. This fascination has made me more aware of my privileges in society. However, it is important to remember I am still White and I still enjoy my privileges as a White woman in society. I realize I could never be completely aware of all my privileges. I have learned to accept that there will always be instances of power that I benefit from that I will be oblivious to.

WHITENESS, SPORT, AND APPLICATION: BEST PRACTICES IN THE 21ST CENTURY

The media uses the sport stage to perpetuate whiteness and negative stereotypes. Both scholars and practitioners in sport need to continue to expose the media practices of promoting whiteness and White Supremacy. Erickson (2005) explained, "Given the visual to the logic of whiteness, the politics of representation in sport, is a fertile place to disrupt this logic" (p. 394). This disruption would encourage the viewer to question one's relation to race (Erickson, 2005). Elite sport academies, such as tennis, golf, and gymnastic academies are typically dictated by Whites and White supremacy and their practices need to be exposed. Athletic organizations (e.g., elite sport academies, professional sport leagues, college athletic departments) and the entire institute of sport need to offer broader opportunity to all races and classes. As indicated by many sport science scholars, subcultures within sport are marginalized and losing power, there is a pressing need to level the playing field for these subcultures. Sport should empower all involved, not indirectly marginalize any group. These marginalized practices could have a negative influence on youth in sport. Youth will assume these practices are normal and acceptable and they will end up perpetuating unjust practices in sport and society, which benefits only one group, Whites.

Contrary to popular media messages, White athletes are not the underdog and are not underrepresented in most sports. White athletes are a force and will continue to be in force on all levels. The significance of the White athlete and how their presence influences power dynamics in sport should be addressed. The fact that only a few individuals are discussing the large number of sports that White athletes dominate needs to be examined. According to Kusz (2007b) sport discourses place White males in a superior position in American culture and society. White male athletes are in a dominant position in sport as well. The White athlete perspective needs to be exposed as well.

Athletes are a diverse group; applied sport practitioners need to be aware of how Whiteness and White power work within the arena of sport. Due to the diverse athlete population it is imperative that the focus on diversity training for athletic organization personnel (on all levels) continues and even increases in the very near future. Training should include the following topics: cultural awareness, dismantling racism, and power relations. The power relations training should focus on the following components: a) White power; b) Whiteness; c) White privilege; and d) hiring practices. Unfortunately, within collegiate and professional sport the primary positions of power such as owners, managers, athletic directors, and coaches consist of a limited amount of people of color.

Therefore, collegiate athletic department personnel and professional league administrators should be trained on hiring practices. The Black Coaches & Administrators (BCA) produces Hiring Report Cards each year for universities. The Institute for Diversity and Ethics in Sport (TIDES) produces The Racial and Gender Report Card for an assessment of hiring practices in coaching and sport management in professional and college sport; for reports see web links (http://bcasports.cstv.com & http://www.tidesport.org).

The study of Whiteness and sport as interdisciplinary scholarship should continue to work within and against traditional examinations of racism. Future investigations should focus on racial performances, power dynamics, and conflict involving media representations and discourses. Walton and Butryn (2006) suggested future investigations on "how representations of women differ from the entwined crises of whiteness and masculinity in narratives of US men's distance running, as well as in sport in general" (p. 24). King (2005) provided a relevant suggestion that sport studies scholars should focus on "racial projects in which individuals and institutions engage through sport: How do they practice and produce race? What do they do with it? How do they articulate with, reinforce, or resist dominant power relations?" (p. 405). We need more White sport science scholars to tell their own narratives of Whiteness and sport, especially those that are former athletes such as myself, Dr. Jay Coakley, Dr. George Sage, and Dr. Richard Lapchick. According to Erickson (2005), "In sport studies we have a privileged place to start the conversation by exposing the narratives that hide the insecurity of whiteness and move through the fantasy of desiring whiteness" (p. 394).

Given the current climate of the academy, which is dominated by White professors, scholars in most disciplines need to address the engrained power dynamics of society. These dynamics affect every societal institution and every individual. The sport sciences are dominated by White male professors, which make it significant to address issues of whiteness in classrooms and expose power dynamics within sport to students who study the sport sciences.

According to Roediger (2002), "Crossing over requires the steady, everyday work of organizing to fight against White privilege and against the miseries that make Whites settle for those privileges and encourage others to aspire to whiteness" (p. 240). We need to learn how to function more effectively and productively within the current system, which is infested with white power. Being aware of the White agenda will allow us to fight against White supremacy and oppressive acts and injustices. We need to heighten the level of consciousness for society and for sport professors, athletes, fans, practitioners, and researchers.

STUDY QUESTIONS

1. Describe the new world racial system.
2. What is Whiteness theory? From which field did the Whiteness theory originate?
3. Explain the concept of White privilege. How does White privilege apply to today's society?
4. How do the sports media perpetuate whiteness?
5. What are three major findings from the Whiteness studies in sport literature?
6. Describe the status of the contemporary White athlete.

SUGGESTED READINGS

Lipsitz, G. (1988). *The possessive investment in whiteness: How White people profit from identity politics.* Philadelphia, PA: Temple University Press.

McIntosh, P. (1988). White privilege and male privilege: A personal account of coming to see correspondences through work in women's studies. Working Paper No.189. Wellesley College Center for Research on Women, Wellesley, MA.

REFERENCES

Black Coaches Administrators (BCA). (2008). Retrieved from http://bcasports.cstv.com

Baldwin, J. (1985). *The price of the ticket.* London, UK: Michael Joseph Limited.

Bobo, L. (2001). Racial attitudes and relations at the close of the 20th century. In N. J. Smelser, W. J. Wilson, & F. Mitchell (Eds.), *America becoming: Racial trends and their consequences* (pp. 264–301). Washington, DC: National Academies Press.

Bobo, L., & Fox, C. (2003). Race, racism, and discrimination: Bridging problems, methods, and theory in social psychological research. *Social Psychology Quarterly, 66*(4), 319–332.

Bobo, L., Kluegel, J., & Smith, R. (1997). Laissez-faire racism: The crystallization of a kinder, gentler, anti-Black ideology. In S. Tuch & J. Martin (Eds.), *Racial attitudes in the 1990s: Continuity and change* (pp. 15–42). Westport, CT: Praeger.

Bobo, L., & Smith, S. (1998). From Jim Crow racism to laissez faire racism: The transformation of racial attitudes. In W. Katkin, N. Landsman, & A. Tyree (Eds.), *Beyond pluralism: Essays on the conception of groups and group identities in America* (pp. 182–220). Urbana, IL: University of Illinois Press.

Bobo, L., & Thompson, V. (2006). Unfair by design: The war on drugs, race, and the legitimacy of the criminal justice system. *Social Research, 73*(2), 445–472.

Brayton, S. (2005). "Black-Lash": Revisiting the "White Negro" through skateboarding. *Sociology of Sport Journal, 22*(3), 356–372.

Butryn, T. M. (2002). Critically examining White racial identity and privilege in sport psychology consulting. *The Sport Psychologist, 16,* 316–336.

Butryn, T. M. (2009). (Re)examining whiteness in sport psychology through autonarrative excavation. *International Journal of Sport and Exercise Psychology, 7*(3), 323–341.

Coakley, J. J. (2009). *Sports in society: Issues & controversies* (10th ed.). Boston, MA: McGraw Hill.

Collins, R. (2001). Ethnic changes in macro-historical perspective. In E. Anderson & D. S. Massey, *Problem of the century: Racial stratification in the United States* (pp. 13–46). New York, NY: Russell Sage Foundation.

Cosgrove, A., & Bruce, T. (2005). The way New Zealander's would like to see themselves: Reading White masculinity via media coverage of the death of Sir Peter Blake. *Sociology of Sport Journal, 22,* 336–355.

Delgado, R., & Stefancic, J. (1997). *Critical white studies: Looking behind the mirror.* Philadelphia, PA: Temple University Press.

Douglas, D. (2005). Venus, Serena, and the women's tennis association (WTA): When and where race enters. *Sociology of Sport Journal, 22*(3), 256–282.

Douglas, D., & Jamieson, K. (2006). A farewell to remember: Interrogating the Nancy Lopez farewell tour. *Sociology of Sport Journal, 23,* 117–141.

Edwards, H. (2000). The decline of the Black athlete: An interview with Harry Edwards. Interviewed by David Leonard. *Colorlines, 3,* 20–24.

Erickson, B. (2005). Style matters: Explorations of bodies, whiteness, and identity in rock climbing. *Sociology of Sport Journal, 22*(3), 373–396.

Ferber, A. L. (2007). The construction of Black masculinity: White supremacy now and then. *Journal of Sport and Social Issues, 31*(1), 11–24.

Fredrickson, G. M., & Knobel, D. T. (1982). A history of discrimination. In S. Thernstrom, A. Orlov, & O. Handlin (Eds.), *Prejudice: Dimensions of ethnicity* (pp. 30–87). Cambridge, MA: Harvard University Press.

Fredrickson, G. M. (1981) *White supremacy: A comparative study in American and South African history.* New York, NY: Oxford University Press.

Fusco, C. (2005). Cultural landscapes of purification: Sports spaces and discourses of whiteness. *Sociology of Sport Journal, 22*(3), 283–310.

Harpalani, V. (1998). The athletic dominance of African Americans—Is there a genetic basis? In G. Sailes (Ed.), *African Americans in sport* (pp.103–120). New Brunswick, NJ: Transaction.

Harris, C. (1993). Whiteness as property. *Harvard Law Review, 17,* 89–90.

Harris, C. (1995). *Whiteness as property.* New York, NY: The New York Press.

Lawrence, S. M., & Harrison, C. K. (2004). College students' perceptions, myths, and stereotypes about African American athleticism: A qualitative investigation. *Sport, Education and Society, 9,* 33–52.

Harrison, Jr. L., Azzarito, L., & Burden, Jr. J. (2004). Perceptions of athletic superiority: A view from the other side. *Race Ethnicity and Education, 7,* 149–166.

Hartmann, D. (2007). Rush Limbaugh, Donovan McNabb, and "a little social concern": Reflections on the problems of whiteness in contemporary American sport. *Journal of Sport and Social Issues, 31*(1), 45–60.

Jensen, R. (2000). White privilege shapes the US. In J. Ferrante & P. Brown (Eds.), *The social construction of race and ethnicity in the United States* (2nd ed.) (pp. 129–132). Upper Saddle River, NJ: Prentice Hall.

Jensen, R. (1999, July 4). More thoughts on why system of white privilege is wrong. *Baltimore Sun,* p. C-1. Retrieved from http://uts.cc.utexas.edu/ ~ rjensen/free lance/whitefolo.htm

King, C. R. (2005). Cautionary notes on whiteness and sport studies. *Sociology of Sport Journal, 22*, 397–407.

King, C. R. (2007). Staging the winter White Olympics: Or, why sport matters to White power. *Journal of Sport and Social Issues, 31*(1), 89–94.

King, C. R., Leonard, D. J., & Kusz, K. W. (2007). White power and sport: An introduction. *Journal of Sport and Social Issues, 31*(1), 3–10.

Kusz, K. (2001). "I want to be the minority": The cultural politics of young White males in sport and popular culture. *Journal of Sport and Social Issues, 25*, 390–416.

Kusz, K. (2007a). From NASCAR nation to Pat Tillman: Notes on sport and the politics of White cultural nationalism in post-9/11 America. *Journal of Sport and Social Issues, 31*(1), 77–88.

Kusz, K. (2007b). *Revolt of the White athlete: Race, media and the emergence of extreme athletes in America*. New York, NY: Peter Lang.

Lapchick, R. E. (2003). *Racial and gender report card*. Retrieved from http://www.tidesport.org

Lapchick, R. E., Martin, S., Kushner, D., & Brenden, J. (2005). *Racial and gender report card*. Retrieved from http://www.tidesport.org

Leonard, D. J. (2007). Innocent until proven innocent: In defense of Duke lacrosse and White power (and against menacing Black student-athletes, a Black stripper, activists, and the Jewish media). *Journal of Sport and Social Issues, 31*(1), 25–44.

Lewis, A. E. (2001). Whiteness studies: Past research and future directions. *African American Research Perspectives, 8*, 1–16.

Lipsitz, G. (1998). *The possessive investment in whiteness: How White people profit from identity politics*. Philadelphia, PA: Temple University Press.

Long, J., & Hylton, K. (2002). Shades of white: An examination of whiteness in sport. *Leisure Studies, 21*, 87–103.

McDonald, M. G. (2005). Mapping whiteness and sport: An introduction [Special issue, Whiteness and Sport]. *Sociology of Sport Journal, 22*(3), 245–255.

McDonald, M. G., & Toglia, J. (2010). Dressed for success? The NBA's dress code, the workings of whiteness and corporate culture. *Sport in Society, 13*(6), 970–983.

McIntosh, P. (1988). White privilege and male privilege: A personal account of coming to see correspondences through work in women's studies. Working Paper No. 189. Wellesley College Center for Research on Women, Wellesley, MA.

McIntosh, P. (1989). White privilege: Unpacking the invisible knapsack. *Peace & Freedom, July/August*, 10–12.

Miller, P. B. (1998). The anatomy of scientific racism: Racialist responses to Black athletic achievement, *Journal of Sport History, 25*(1), 119–151.

NCAA (2005/2006). *NCAA race & ethnicity report 2005–2006*. Indianapolis, IN: National Collegiate Athletic Association.

NCAA (2006/2007). *NCAA race & ethnicity report 2006–2007*. Indianapolis, IN: National Collegiate Athletic Association.

Poniatowski, K., & Whiteside, E. (2012). "Isn't he a good guy?": Constructions of whiteness in the 2006 Olympic hockey tournament. *Howard Journal of Communications, 23*(1), 1–16.

Price, S. L. (1997, December 6). Whatever happened to the White athlete? *Sports Illustrated, 87*(23), 32–51.

Roediger, D. R. (2002). *Colored White: Transcending the racial past*. Berkeley, CA: University of California Press.

Rhodes, J. (2011). Fighting for "Respectability": Media representations of the White, "Working-Class" male boxing "Hero". *Journal of Sport & Social Issues, 35*(4), 350–376.

Sailes, G. (1996). An examination of basketball performance orientations among African American males. *Journal of African American Men, 1*, 37–46.

Steinberg, S. (2007). *Race relations: A critique*. Stanford, CA: Stanford University Press.

Stone, J., Lynch, C. I., Sjomeling, M., & Darley, J. M. (1999). Stereotype threat effects on Black and White athletic performance. *Journal of Personality and Social Psychology, 77*(6), 1213–1227.

Stone, J. (2002). Battling doubt by avoiding practice: The effects of stereotype threat on self-handicapping in White athletes. *Personality & Social Psychology Bulletin, 28*, 1667–1678.

Sullivan, S. (2006). *Revealing whiteness: The unconscious habits of racial privilege*. Indianapolis, IN: Indiana University Press.

The American Heritage dictionary of the English language (4th ed.) (2000). Retrieved from http://www.bartleby.com/

The Institute for Diversity and Ethics in Sport (TIDES) (2008). Retrieved from http://www.tidesport.org

Thompson, A. (1999). Off White: Reading on race, power, and society. *Educational Studies, 30*(2), 141–160.

Thompson, A. (2001). *Summary of whiteness theory*. Retrieved from http://www.mccaugheycentre.unimelb.edu.au/__data/assets/pdf_file/0003/144660/Thompson_2001_2.pdf, pp. 1–5.

Tochluk, S. (2008). *Witnessing whiteness: First steps toward an antiracist practice and culture*. Lanham, MD: Rowman & Littlefield Education.

Walton, T. A., & Butryn, T. M. (2006). Policing the race: US men's distance running and the crisis of whiteness. *Sociology of Sport Journal, 23*, 1–28.

Wheaton, B., & Beal, B. (2003). Understanding lifestyle sport. *International Review for the Sociology of Sport, 38*, 155–176.

Winant, H. (2002). Race and globalization: The modern world racial system. *Souls, 4*(3), 17–30.

Winant, H. (2004). *The new politics of race: Globalism, difference, justice*. Minneapolis, MN: University of Minnesota Press.

Winant, H. (2006). Race and racism: Towards a global future. *Ethnic and Racial Studies, 29*(5), 986–1003.

Wolsko, C., Park, B., Judd, C. M., & Wittenbrink, B. (2000). Framing interethnic ideology: Effects of multicultural and colorblind perspectives on judgments of groups and individuals. *Journal of Personality & Social Psychology, 78*(4), 635–654.

Zuberi, T. (2001). *Thicker than blood: How racial statistics lie*. Minneapolis, MN: University of Minnesota

Stakeholder Management in Big-Time College Sport: The Educational Interests of the African American Male Athlete

JOHN N. SINGER

Abstract

There are several groups and individuals who have formal and informal relationships with college and university athletic departments, and who can affect and are affected by the organizational structures, policies, and activities of these athletic departments and their athletic programs, particularly football and men's basketball. This chapter draws from some of the stakeholder theory literature as well as elements of a critical race theory framework in efforts to provide scholars, practitioners, and students who are interested in college sport with an alternative conceptual and analytical tool for understanding and addressing the educational interests of the African American male athlete in the revenue-producing sports of football and men's basketball at predominantly White institutions of higher education (PWIHE). Although there are several stakeholder groups that have a stake or vested interest in the mission, purpose, and activity of these big-time college sport programs, the focus here is on the African American male in these particular sports for a couple reasons: a) these athletes were not regularly invited to participate in these athletic programs until these institutions acknowledged that it went against good financial policy to continue excluding them, and b) since their arrival on campus, these athletes, in particular, have been (and continue to be) academically and economically exploited for their athletic prowess to the detriment of other areas of development. This chapter will conclude with a discussion of some important research and practical implications related to stakeholder management in big-time college sport.

Key Terms			
●	African American males	●	exploitation
●	college athletes	●	stakeholder salience
●	critical race theory	●	systemic racism

Collegiate sport in America has become a showcase of African American talent. No longer denied athletic scholarships and opportunities at major colleges and universities, African Americans dominate the record books. Statistical leaders in categories such as rushing and receiving in football, scoring and rebounding in basketball, and sprints in track and field are, almost without exception in recent years, African Americans. . . . Their presence is required, it seems, for teams to compete, not to mention excel, in revenue-generating intercollegiate sports.

—Othello Harris (from Racism in College Athletics, 2nd ed., 2000, pp. 37–38)

INTRODUCTION

The integration of predominantly White institutions of higher education (PWIHE) in the midst of the 1954 *Brown v. Board of Education* decision that made racial segregation in public education illegal helped set the tone for the influx of African American athletes into the once segregated athletic programs at these PWIHE. Prior to this historic decision, a few African American male athletes competed on athletic teams at PWIHE, particularly in football (e.g., Paul Robeson at Rutgers University) and track and field (e.g., Jesse Owens at Ohio State University). However, these athletes were the exception, not the rule; they were expected to carry the load for their teams while being subjected to many forms of overt racism when not in competition (Harris, 2000). Events such as the 1966 national championship triumph of coach Don Haskin's Texas Western basketball team—which had an all Black starting line-up—over Adolph Rupp's all White and heavily favored Kentucky squad helped pave the way for the eventual full scale integration of college sport. According to the HBO documentary, *The Journey of the African American Athlete* (1996), the defining moment for African American athletes came in 1970 when the University of Southern California (USC) African American running back, Sam "Bam" Cunningham, ran for several yards in a victory over legendary coach, Paul "Bear" Bryant's all White Alabama squad. In the documentary, the late great, Eddie Robinson—who coached football at Grambling State University—discussed how, after the game, the Alabama fans, in response to Cunningham's incredible performance, were saying, "Get us one; get us one!" The following year, Alabama did indeed sign Wilbur Jackson, an African American running back to play football (Bernstein et al., 1996).

Since this time, the figurative flood gates have opened, and African American males have been invited in droves to participate in football, basketball, and track and field in these major big-time college sport programs (i.e., athletic departments that have the largest budgets, highest media visibility, largest fan bases, and the most competitive football and basketball programs) at PWIHE. Today, they constitute more than half of the players in the National Collegiate Athletic Association (NCAA) revenue-producing sports of men's basketball and football (Lapchick, Little, Lerner, & Mathew, 2009), and as alluded to in the epigraph at the beginning of this chapter, these athletes' presence is one of the primary reasons that these programs have become highly competitive and entertaining commercial enterprises. It is now commonplace for African American males to lead their teams to the NCAA men's basketball tournament (i.e., "March Madness") and bowl championship series (BCS) games in football. This kind of success on the basketball court and football playing field has led to great financial benefits via ticket and merchandise sales, corporate sponsorships, television and radio contracts, appearance fees for postseason play, monetary donations, and other gifts from alumni to the athletic department; it has also led to the enhancement of the reputation of the university (Donnor, 2005).

There is no doubt that the African American male basketball and football athletes have become a precious commodity that is crucial to the continuing commercial development and success of the college sport enterprise. But how much have African American male athletes benefited from their affiliation with big-time college sport programs? A small percentage has been fortunate to receive a professional sport contract and participate in the National Basketball Association (NBA) and National Football League (NFL) or other professional sport leagues throughout the world. And many have earned college degrees and gone on to pursue various career paths and opportunities inside and outside of the sport industry. However, in far too many instances, African American male athletes have exhausted their athletic eligibility with no degree to show for it, and very few marketable skills that are transferrable to the economy and workplace. Or in some tragic cases, they leave these teams before their eligibility is exhausted, drop out of school, and either stick around the college town where they were once a star athlete or go back to their hometowns (or elsewhere) and become engaged in activities that land them in prison or jail, or some other kind of trouble.

Some scholars have questioned the motives behind these PWIHE decision to recruit and invite African American athletes to campus (Davis, 1995; Donnor, 2005; Grant, 2003); the literature suggests that many African American males in these athletic programs today are victims of academic exploitation (Anderson & South, 2007; Benson, 2000; Edwards, 1983, 1984, 1985; Hawkins, 1999, 2001; Spigner, 1993) and economic exploitation (Brooks & Kim, 2007; Eitzen, 2003; Shropshire, 2000; Smith, 2007; Zimbalist, 1999), especially since many of them come to these campuses with questionable academic preparation and from economically disadvantaged backgrounds. In essence, these PWIHE and their athletic programs have been criticized for treating these athletes more as a commodity (focusing on their athletic prowess for commercial advantage and benefit), and less as students who need to be fully integrated into the academic and social culture of higher education and college sport (Davis, 2000). This would suggest that the educational interests of African American male football and basketball athletes have taken a back seat to the financial interests of those who oversee the operations of big-time college sport (NCAA and its member institutions).

In a provocative article that focuses on African American football athletes in major college sports, Jamel Donnor (2005) advanced critical race theory (CRT) pioneer Derrick Bell's (1980, 1992) interest convergence principle as an analytical tool for understanding the complex role of race in the educational experiences of these athletes. It is Donnor's contention that for

> African American males who possess the physical potential or talent to participate at the level of Division IA football, education no longer only serves their interests. Rather, the Black male student athletes' educational interests converge with the interests of other individuals and his institution. In other words, while a Black male football student athlete may be interested in receiving a college education and graduating (or playing professional football), other educational stakeholders such as football coaches and institutions of higher education may be more interested in the personal (i.e., cash bonuses for meeting academic incentives) and institutional advancement gained through association with or exploitation of the physical talents of these student athletes. (2005, p. 48)

Donnor (2005) utilized the legal literature to provide a deeper understanding of the educational experiences of African American male athletes in two ways: 1) by contextualizing their relationship to a PWIHE and the athletic department specifically, and 2) by presenting examples of personal and institutional practices that influence their educational opportunities. More specifically, Donnor discussed different lawsuits that were filed against PWIHE by two African American male athletes (i.e., Gregg Taylor, a football player at Wake Forest University; and Kevin Ross, a basketball player at Creighton University) and how each represented a case of educational malpractice or a breach of contract, especially given the binding agreement that exist between PWIHE and these athletes via the National Letter of Intent (NLI) that athletes sign and the athletic scholarship they receive in exchange for their participation in the athletic program. These particular cases and the implications they have for stakeholder management issues in big-time college sport will be discussed in a bit more detail later on in this chapter.

The purpose of this chapter is to draw from some of the stakeholder theory literature as well as elements of the CRT framework in efforts to provide scholars, students, and practitioners with a conceptual tool for understanding the significance of race (and racism) and the impact it has on stakeholder management issues in big-time college sport. Moreover and specifically, the goal is to provide some practical insights that could help to address some of the stakeholder management issues that are germane to the African American male football and basketball athlete in particular, and to other athletes in general. This specific focus on African American male athletes is not to suggest that a) there are not several other groups that have a stake or vested interest in the mission, purpose, and activity of these athletic programs, or b) other stakeholder groups (e.g., African American female athletes) are unworthy of our attention; however, the specific focus here is on African American male athletes in the revenue-producing sports (i.e., football and men's basketball) for a few reasons.

First and foremost, historically, the African American male in American society has been an emasculated individual, one whose opportunities and abilities to take on a leadership role in his family and community have been limited and inhibited by social systems (educational, societal, and cultural) and policies of oppression, prejudice, and disregard (Jenkins, 2006; Reese, 2000). Within the sport realm, however, the basketball court and football playing field has become one of a few spaces "where an African American man can be a man" (Harrison, Harrison, & Moore, 2002, p. 131). Related to this first point, African American males who lead and dominate on the football field and basketball court are essentially being exploited because they are recruited and admitted to these PWIHE primarily because of their physical prowess (Eitzen, 2003) and in many instances, although only a very small percentage of these football and men's basketball programs generate a net profit each year (Zimbalist, 2007), it is typically these programs that financially support nonrevenue-producing sports (e.g., golf, tennis, swimming and diving) that are overwhelmingly participated in by White middle and upper class students (Donnor, 2005). And finally, it is in the highly visible, commercialized sports of football and men's basketball where most of the acute problems pertaining to the educational experiences and opportunities of athletes are typically found. The structure, functions, and activities of these athletic programs sometimes make it difficult for athletes in these programs to balance the demands of sport participation with that of academic and other educational experiences (Comeaux, 2007; Singer, 2008).

The remainder of this chapter will focus on several things. First, a brief discussion of the major purpose for the establishment of competitive sports on the college campus is appropriate. This will help set the tone for a discussion on the educational interests of African American male athletes in particular, and other athletes in general. Second, a general overview of the stakeholder management literature will be provided, and more specifically, situated within the context of college sport. Third, elements of the CRT framework will be outlined and advanced as a way to demonstrate how issues of race and racism continue to permeate the management decision-making processes and practices in college sport. Furthermore, an attempt will be made to show how those who control college sport have been willing to sacrifice the well-being and educational interests of African American male athletes in favor of their own economic self-interests, and that the continued exploitation and subordination of African American male athletes (and other athletes) is sustained by those structural arrangements that promote white privilege and sustain the status quo. Finally, this chapter concludes with a brief discussion of some important implications for research and practice related to the management of stakeholder interests in big-time college sport.

THE EDUCATIONAL MISSION OF COLLEGE ATHLETICS: A CONTRADICTION?

In watching various sports programs on television and discussing the state of college athletics with various people, I have heard proponents of college athletics argue that college sport participation contributes greatly to the educational experiences of college athletes, and it supplements the academic values and the educational mission of the larger college or university of which it is a part. Depending on the level at which these institutions of higher education are involved in formal intercollegiate athletics, the validity of this assertion might be called into question by some people. At one extreme, college sport participation takes place at the Division III level, where the college athletes are an integral part of the student body, receiving no athletic scholarships for playing their sport. In these types of institutions, the athletic programs are primarily funded from general institutional accounts, competition is confined to teams within the region, and spectator attendance at games is typically small (Coakley, 2007; Sage, 1998).

At the other extreme, college sport participation takes place at the Division I level (now known as Football Bowl Subdivision [FBS]) where the college athletes typically receive athletic scholarships to compete at the highest, most competitive levels. Moreover, it is at this level where the challenges to succeed (i.e., pressure to win as a team, and to standout as an individual athlete), as well as the academic, social and leisure, and health and injury challenges are most pronounced for athletes (Coakley, 2007; Parham, 1993). In addition, although only a few athletic departments

Table 15.1	Top Ten NCAA Athletic Department Budgets	
School		**Budget**
1	Ohio State University	$104.7 million
2	University of Texas	$97.8 million
3	University of Virginia	$92.7 million
4	University of Michigan	$85.5 million
5	University of Florida	$82.4 million
6	University of Georgia	$79.2 million
7	University of Wisconsin	$78.9 million
8	University of Notre Dame	$78.2 million
9	Texas A&M University	$70.9 million
10	Penn State University	$70.5 million

Source: Retrieved from http://www.democraticunderground.com/discuss/duboard.php?az
Note. Given that these budgets are from the year ending in 2006 and accounting practices at schools on this list may vary, this list might not be 100% accurate and dollar figures might not be totally precise (they could actually be larger today); however, the schools listed here are typically among the top schools in terms of athletics budgets year in and year out; and according to most sources, Ohio State University has been at the top for several years (see Weinbach, 2007).

are actually profitable enterprises via their football and men's basketball programs (Zimbalist, 2007) many have astronomically high athletic budgets (see Table 15.1). Furthermore, a great bulk of the financial support and other resources that these athletic programs rely on is derived from stakeholders who are external to the college or university (e.g., the media, corporations, alumni, fans), and this creates a potential conflict of interest as it relates to whether these athletic departments choose to focus more on human development or commercial development.

There is a need to further understand the educational interests of African American student-athletes, especially in high-profile sports such as basketball and football, at predominantly white institutions of higher education.

Courtesy of Gary Lake

The NCAA is the preeminent sport governing body that oversees college sport at most levels, and as the commercial influence in college sport has continued to escalate, particularly at the highest level, the NCAA has struggled to successfully balance the goals of promoting and enhancing the marketability of collegiate sports while simultaneously maintaining the idea of amateurism and academic integrity (Anderson & South, 2007). As Anderson and South (2007) asserted, "The more successful the NCAA is in achieving one of these goals, the more difficult it becomes to achieve the other" (p. 78). Given that the NCAA and the athletic departments that are under its governance are considered to be a part of higher education, the mission and activities of these entities should reflect a primary focus on the educational interests of athletes, not the commercial interests of the individual institutions, regional conferences, national agencies, and other stakeholder groups.

According to the NCAA's website (http://www.ncaa.org), its core purpose is "to govern competition in a fair, safe, equitable and sportsmanlike manner, and to integrate intercollegiate athletics into higher education so that the educational experience of the student-athlete is paramount." Of particular note here is the NCAA's purported goal to make the educational experience of the athletes "paramount," meaning that it should be chief in importance and superior to all other things. The NCAA insists that through its member institutions, conferences, and national office staff the association shares a belief in and commitment to, among other things, the supporting role that intercollegiate athletics plays in the higher education mission; in general, the mission of institutions of higher education is to prepare students to become educated and enlightened citizens who are able to pursue meaningful careers and other opportunities in a rapidly changing, diverse world. Therefore, the question becomes, how well are athletics programs at Division I schools, in particular, contributing to this mission?

Given that students are the prime beneficiary (i.e., the group whose benefit is the primary reason for an organization's existence) of colleges and universities, and these institutions of higher education are the prime beneficiary of athletic departments (Chu, 1989), college athletes should be considered the prime beneficiary of athletic departments at these institutions. This is not to suggest that the prime beneficiary is the only important stakeholder group of big-time college sport. There are certainly other stakeholders that managers of college sport must show concern for if the organization is to sustain itself (financially and otherwise). However, it is argued in this chapter that those who manage college sport (i.e., coaches and administrators) must be most concerned with the benefits that the prime beneficiary receives from the athletic department's existence and operations. In this regard, those who control intercollegiate athletics should view athletes as the end to which they act or serve, and subsequent policies and practices should be designed in the interest of athletes and to benefit them. This is important, especially given that—as the NCAA has stated in its commercials—the overwhelming majority of the 400,000 or so athletes who participate in athletics at its member institutions will be "going pro in something other than sports."

THE STAKEHOLDER PERSPECIVE AND COLLEGE SPORT

Since the writing of Freeman's (1984) landmark book *Strategic Management: A Stakeholder Approach*, organizational theorists and management scholars have discussed and debated the stakeholder perspective and its relationship to the study of strategic management within organizations (see, for example, *Academy of Management Review*, 1999, 24[2]). Essentially, the stakeholder perspective is an organizational construct that focuses on the cooperative and competitive interests of multiple stakeholders of an organization, and the impact that management decisions have on these various stakeholder groups. A central purpose of the stakeholder approach has been to enable managers to understand stakeholders and strategically manage them (Frooman, 1999).

In order for managers to strategically manage the interests of various stakeholder groups they must identify and understand who the relevant stakeholders of the organization are (Preble, 2005). Freeman (1984) and Clarkson (1995) offered useful definitions of a *stakeholder*:

- A stakeholder is "any group or individual who can affect, or is affected by, the achievement of a corporation's purpose" (Freeman, 1984, p. vi).
- Stakeholders are "persons or groups that have, or claim, ownership, rights, or interests in a corporation and its activities, past, present, or future" (Clarkson, 1995, p. 106).

Freeman's (1984) definition highlights the two-way relationship between an organization and its stakeholders (Preble, 2005); on the one hand, stakeholders can impact whether or not an organization achieves its goals and objectives, and therefore, should be managed *instrumentally* (see Donaldson & Preston, 1995; Jones, 1995) if financial performance is to be maximized (Preble, 2005). On the other hand, an organization's operations and decisions can affect the well-being of stakeholders, and therefore, managers have a *normative* (see Hasnas, 1998; Langtry, 1994; Reed, 1999) duty or obligation to its stakeholders that is moral in nature (Preble, 2005). Clarkson's (1995) definition of stakeholders further highlights the importance of the normative approach to stakeholder theory because it identifies stakeholders based on their interest in the organization, regardless to the extent that the organization has an interest in them (Preble, 2005). In this regard, organizations should show a concern for all of its stakeholders because the interests of all stakeholders are of intrinsic value, meaning that each group merits consideration for its own sake (Donaldson & Preston, 1995).

In applying the stakeholder perspective to the organizational context of college sport, it is important to note that there are different types of stakeholder groups. Preble (2005) highlighted the differences between and importance of *primary*, *public*, and *secondary* stakeholders. Primary stakeholders have been described as individuals or groups who have a formal, official, or contractual relationship with an organization (Carroll, 1993), and as those individuals and groups whose affiliation with the organization is absolutely necessary for its survival (Clarkson, 1995). In this sense, the organization itself can be viewed as a system of primary stakeholders, a complex set of relationships between and among interest groups with varying agendas (Clarkson, 1995). For example, in a college athletic department the interactions between the coaching staff of the athletic teams and the athletes on these teams are absolutely critical to the existence and successful operation of the department. Both groups have a contractual relationship with the department, and without these groups, it would be next to impossible for these athletic departments to function. Further, as the labor force that actually produces the core sport product (i.e., the athletic competitions) on the courts and fields of play, athletes should be viewed and treated as the most important stakeholder group in college sport.

Public stakeholders are important because organizations depend on them to provide infrastructures and legal frameworks in which to operate. In college sport, the local communities in which these colleges and universities are located provide the underlying base and foundation that these institutions and their athletic programs need to fully function and operate. As the predominant sport governing body of intercollegiate athletics, the NCAA is also an important public stakeholder of college athletic departments because it essentially creates the rules, regulations, policies, and procedures that its member institutions must adhere to in order for their athletic teams to remain in good standing, and carry out the many activities that are necessary to remain functional and competitive (e.g., recruiting and offering athletic scholarships, being eligible for post-season play).

Secondary stakeholders are also important because they could influence or be influenced by the organization, even though they are not always engaged in direct transactions with the organization and are not necessarily essential to its survival (Clarkson, 1995). However, as Preble (2005) noted, while secondary stakeholders are not essential to the direct functioning of the organization, they can strongly influence how it is perceived by the public and various governmental entities, and thus, have a potentially major impact on the organization through the *interaction* of stakeholders (p. 410). In the case of college sport, the media has played a major role in contributing to the commercial success and visibility of many big-time programs (Coakely, 2007). For example, the NCAA's multibillion dollar contract with CBS to televise its "March Madness" basketball tournament, and ESPN's and other national, regional, and local networks' (television, radio, internet) decisions to air competitions, particularly in football and basketball, between the teams at these NCAA member institutions bears witness to the direct impact that secondary stakeholders such as the media can have on athletic departments. On the flipside, the media can also have a negative impact on athletic departments. For instance, when ESPN (e.g., "Outside the Lines") or HBO Sports (e.g., "Real Sports with Bryant Gumbel") decides to air special features on some of the indiscretions of these athletic programs (e.g., exploitation of athletes, recruiting violations and scandals) this has the potential to bring negative publicity to these programs and their personnel.

The preceding discussion provides some important definitions of what a stakeholder is and a general idea as to who some of the major stakeholders of college sport are and the impact they can have on an athletic department. What has not yet been discussed is stakeholder salience, i.e., the degree to which managers give priority to competing stakeholder claims (see Preble, 2005). Mitchell, Agle, and Wood (1997) presented a theory of stakeholder identification and salience in efforts to explain who and what really should count to managers (see Agle, Mitchell, & Sonnenfeld, 1999, for empirical support). According to these scholars, the factors that determine the salience of stakeholders are 1) possession of power, 2) legitimacy, and 3) urgency of claim. *Power* is a stakeholder's ability to influence an organization's behavior, regardless to whether or not they have a legitimate claim; *legitimacy* is a claim or imposition on the organization, based on a contractual or legal obligation, a moral right, an at-risk status, or a stakeholder having a moral interest in the harms and benefits generated by an organization's actions; *urgency* is the degree to which a stakeholder's claim calls for immediate attention (Preble, 2005).

Sport management scholars have insisted that those who are in management positions in college sport should be sensitive to and seek to gain a clear understanding of the priorities, perceptions, and preferences of important stakeholder groups (Chelladurai, 2005; Putler & Wolfe, 1999; Trail & Chelladurai, 2000; Wolfe & Putler, 2002). This literature has revealed a couple key points. First, just because individuals are in the same stakeholder group (e.g., college students, prospective college students, college athletes, faculty, alumni) does not mean they agree on the priorities (i.e., winning, athletic program revenue, education, ethics) that athletic departments should focus on (Putler & Wolfe, 1999; Wolfe & Putler, 2002). And second, some stakeholder groups (i.e., faculty and students), in line with the mission of higher education, believe developmental goals and processes are more important than the performance goals and processes in intercollegiate athletics (Trail & Chelladurai, 2000). The findings from this research are important to consider in reflecting on the interests of African American male athletes in big-time college sport because, although there certainly are common interests this stakeholder group might hold, we should not assume all members of this group will have the same preferences and priorities concerning their college sport experiences; moreover, there could be some variance within this stakeholder group in terms of their perceptions of what goals and processes managers of college sport should focus on.

The above-mentioned research by sport management scholars has provided insight into the perceptions and preferences of important stakeholder groups in college sport, but what's missing from this literature is a focus on issues of race, and how it impacts the educational interests of the prime beneficiary or most important stakeholder of college sport. It is for this reason that this chapter focuses specifically on the African American male athlete in football and men's basketball. It is important that researchers and practitioners focus on the interests of this particular group of athletes (as well as other athletes) because these stakeholders do have *legitimacy* by virtue of being a part of the student body and because they have a contractual relationship with these institutions via the NLI. Further, given the growing commercialism of college sport, and subsequently, the calls for reform by various stakeholder groups (e.g., Drake Group, the Knight Commission) to combat the exploitation of athletes, the college athlete, particularly in football and men's basketball, has an *urgency* of claim. And finally, although many people (including the athletes themselves) believe that the athletes have very little control over how big-time college sport is managed, this stakeholder group actually has the potential to impact the priorities of those who control college sport and what they pay attention to. However, it will take a collective effort on the part of athletes in order to have the *power* to bring about change to the current system, and this most likely will only happen if this group as a collective whole truly desires change.

As the prime beneficiary of college sport, athletes, particularly African American males in football and basketball, can certainly affect and be affected by big-time college sport. Moreover, this important stakeholder group does indeed have a vested interest in how things are organized and operated in these athletic departments and programs. Therefore, those who manage college sport (i.e., administrators and coaches) should not only be concerned with financial gain via the commodification of the African American male body. More importantly, however, they should be mindful of how their decision making regarding policies, rules, regulations, and procedures might impact the overall welfare of these athletes. In fact, it is argued in this chapter that—given the racism that has existed and continues to persist in college sport today (Brooks & Althouse, 2000; Davis, 1995) and the sometimes tumultuous journey that is in front and lies ahead of the African American athlete in these PWIHE today—these athletic programs have a moral duty and obligation to reassess and address how their structures, functions, and activities might be contributing to the negative exploitation of this particular stakeholder group. In this regard, an engagement with the critical race theory literature is helpful to any discussion pertaining to how the educational interests of African American male athletes should be managed.

CRITICAL RACE THEORY AND AFRICAN AMERICAN MALE ATHLETES

Critical race theory is a form of oppositional scholarship that originated in the 1970s from the work of legal scholars who were disenchanted with the stalled progress of traditional civil rights litigation to produce meaningful racial reform (Taylor, 1998). These scholars emphasized "the many ways that race and racism were fundamentally ingrained in American social structures and historical consciousness and hence shaped US ideology, legal systems, and fundamental conceptions of law, property, and privilege" (Lynn & Adams, 2002, p. 88). As an academic and activist movement that is interdisciplinary in nature and that crosses epistemological boundaries—drawing from traditions such as Marxism, feminism, post-structuralism, liberalism, cultural nationalism, and critical legal studies in efforts to provide a more complete analysis of "raced" people (Tate, 1997)—CRT scholars are unified by two common interests: 1) *understanding* how a regime of White supremacy and the subordination of people of color (in particular) have been created and maintained in American society and its social institutions, and 2) *changing* the bond that exists between the law and racial power. In this regard, CRT could be employed to better understand how the organizational structures, processes, and practices in college sport impact African American male athletes, and ultimately, utilized as a tool to change or alter the racist policies and activities in college sport that have a negative (and disproportionate) impact on the educational experiences of African American male athletes.

CRT has some core tenets or principles that are particularly relevant to the discussion on stakeholder management and the educational interests of the African American male athlete in big-time college sport at PWIHE. For one, CRT scholars have argued that given the historical social construction of race in this society and the role that US jurisprudence played in reifying conceptions of race (see Haney Lopez, 1996; Harris, 1993), White racism (i.e., "whiteness" is deemed superior, racial "otherness" is deemed as inferior) has become entrenched in society, and it is reproduced through routine as well as extraordinary customs, traditions, and experiences that critically impact the quality of life and opportunities of racial groups (Brown, 2003). The work of Brooks and Althouse in the previous editions of this book, *Racism in College Athletics* (1993, 2000) and law professor Timothy Davis (1995) speaks directly to this issue of how the embedded nature and permanence of racism in American society has impacted African American athletes and other stakeholder groups (i.e., African American coaches and administrators) in college sport.

Derrick Bell's (1980, 1992, 2004) interest-convergence principle is another tenet of CRT that is especially relevant to the discussion of stakeholder management and the educational interests of African American male athletes. Essentially, Bell's basic premise is that people in power (particularly Whites) are often, in theory, supportive of laws, equity-oriented policies, and practices that do not oppress and discriminate against racial "others" as long as they (i.e., Whites) do not have to alter their own ways, systems, and privileges of experiencing life. Bell (2004) discussed several examples throughout American history (e.g., *Brown v. Board of Education*) where racial policy making occurred because it served more in the interests of the nation and portions of its populace, not necessarily the interests of racial minorities who had been historically discriminated against. In this regard, from an interest-convergence perspective, allowing African American males into PWIHE to compete in football and basketball, and in some cases, advance to the professional sport level, was not antithetical to the benefits that whites would receive and the power that they would continue to maintain. In fact, providing some African American males with the opportunity to participate and have successful careers in college athletics painted a picture for some people (including African American male athletes) that these PWIHE had turned the corner in terms of moving beyond the racist policies and practices that had locked African Americans out of these institutions for so long (see Brown et al., 2003, for empirical support).

As alluded to and mentioned earlier in this chapter, the notion that PWIHE integrated their athletic programs for altruistic reasons is challenged by Donnor (2005), who utilized the legal literature and Bell's principle to demonstrate how African American males have been *exploited* for their athletic prowess while being simultaneously denied a real opportunity to receive a high quality education. In particular, Donnor (2005) focused on two lawsuits in his article to provide the basis of his argument. In *Taylor v. Wake Forest University* (1971), a former football athlete, Gregg Taylor, brought a wrongful termination lawsuit against the school alleging a breach of contract. Taylor's basic argument was that the team's practice and activities interfered with his academic progress (he had a 1.0 grade point average on a 4.0 scale at the end of the 1967 fall semester and football season), and therefore, he needed to leave the team to focus on his academic interests. He left the football program during his junior year after earning a 2.4 grade point average (GPA) (Wake Forest only required athletes to have a 1.85 GPA by the end of junior year), and consequently, his scholarship was terminated by the athletic department. It was Taylor's contention that the university had orally agreed that in the event of any conflict between educational achievement and athletic involvement, participation in athletic activities could be limited or eliminated to the extent necessary to assure reasonable academic progress. Unfortunately for Taylor, his case was dismissed because, according to the courts, he essentially failed to comply with the contractual obligations of his NLI with Wake Forest University; that is, when he refused to participate in athletics in the absence of injury or an excuse other than his academics or studies, he was in noncompliance with his contractual obligations.

Donnor (2005) emphasized several important points in regards to the significance of this case. First, the courts recognized that a contract existed between an athlete and an institution of higher education. Second, the case demonstrated an instance where this athlete's educational opportunity was negatively impacted by the affirmative conduct and competing interests on the part of the athletic department; moreover, it also uncovered the mediocre or low academic expectations that the athletic programs have for these athletes. Finally, it demonstrated how an athlete participating in major college sport can succeed academically despite the competitive interests of the institution, and how this African American male athlete, unlike most of his fellow peers, was able to recognize that his educational interests did not correspond with the competitive interests of the university's athletic department. Similarly, the story of Anton Gunn, a former football athlete who played at the University of South Carolina in the 1990s, is another example where an African American male athlete took action when he realized that his educational interests did not converge with those of the athletic program (i.e., he left the football team during his final year of eligibility because the time of practice conflicted with his class time and because coaches tried to discourage him from majoring in history; see Klein, 1998).

Donnor (2005) contended that most African American male athletes have, unfortunately, ignored or could not identify this convergence of interest until after their contracts with the athletic departments have expired. He highlighted the case of African American male basketball athlete, Kevin Ross, as a classic example of this. In *Ross v. Creighton University* (1990), Ross filed a lawsuit against the institution for alleged educational malpractice—educational malpractice claims assert that these institutions are obligated to educate students in a manner as to impart a minimum level of competence in basic subjects; furthermore, according to Donnor (2005), underpinning this assertion is this belief that institutions of higher learning have a moral duty or obligation to provide an education (i.e., they have an implied duty), and the plaintiff's actions are peripheral in the court's determination of the quality of education offered by the institution. This is an important point because Ross was a student who was recruited to the university to play basketball, despite the fact that he was grossly unprepared academically for college. It was reported that the athletic program was able to keep him eligible to play by enrolling him in courses that did not put him on track to graduate and earn a degree. Despite this, like Gregg Taylor's case, Ross's suit against his institution was unsuccessful because the courts basically claimed that Ross did not take responsibility for his own education by asserting the proper effort required to be educated.

Ross's situation is a classic case of how the athletic talent and academic development of an African American male athlete can be manipulated for the competitive interests of other educational stakeholders (Donnor, 2005). In addition, the tragic story of former high school, college, and professional football standout, James Brooks, is an excellent example of the far-reaching, negative impact that the educational system (i.e., K–16) can have on an athletically gifted and talented African American male. Despite the fact that he graduated from high school in 1977 and spent at least four years at Auburn University on a football scholarship, Brooks was functionally illiterate throughout his college career and he left the university in 1980 without a degree and continued to be unable to read during his time as a professional football player (see Downton, 2000, for more details). Similarly, the story of Dexter Manley—a former football standout at the college (at Oklahoma State University) and professional level who was illiterate as well—reveals how these African American male athletes' physical talent and academic development are manipulated for the competitive interests of the athletic program (see Randolph, 1989, for more details). My professional and personal experiences working with and mentoring African American male college athletes as an assistant coordinator of a summer bridge program, an academic mentor for student-athletes in a student-athlete support program, and as a college professor provides further support for this contention.

What the foregoing discussion should demonstrate is that historically football and men's basketball programs at PWIHE have entered into contractual relationships with African American male athletes, and in far too many instances, this subgroup of the prime beneficiary of college sport has gotten the proverbial short end of the stick. In other words, the interests (i.e., financial) of those who control college sport (i.e., coaches, athletic administrators, and external stakeholder groups) seem to have usurped the interests (particularly graduation, academic achievement, and other nonsport developmental opportunities) of the African American male athletes who have helped to build the college sport enterprise into what it has become today. Therefore, Donnor's (2005) use of the interest-convergence construct to make sense of the educational experiences of African American male athletes is timely because it can be "advanced as a way to highlight the past and current educational location of African American male student-athletes" (Donnor, 2005, p. 60). Further, it allows one to better understand how some of these athletes' precollegiate educational experiences (i.e., K–12 schooling) help contribute to their failure to take advantage of the contractual offerings of the college or university where they participate in athletics.

Finally, CRT's emphasis on the experiential knowledge of people of color in a society based on racial oppression and subordination is also important to the discussion of stakeholder management and the educational interests of African American male athletes in college sport. Providing a space for African American male athletes to tell their stories about their educational experiences is potentially empowering because it could allow them to critically reflect upon their social conditions and provide them with a voice that challenges the dominant discourse and stories that have been based on white norms and privileges in college sport. Dixson and Rousseau (2005) discussed the importance of voice and explained how personal narratives and stories can be used to challenge the dominant approach (i.e., numbers only, quantitative) to documenting inequity and discrimination in educational settings. They acknowledged that the stories of individuals might differ, but contended, "Although there is not one common voice, there is a common experience of racism that structures the stories of people of colour and allows for the use of the term voice" (Dixson & Rousseau, 2005, p. 11). Benson's (2000) and Singer's (2005, 2009) research with African American football athletes in big-time college sport programs provides support for these CRT scholars' assertion. This research allowed these athletes to speak freely and openly about the organizational structures, policies, rules, and regulations that impact their experiences and run counter to their educational interests.

CONCLUSION AND IMPLICATIONS

According to Anderson and South (2007), the marriage between higher education and college athletics is very likely to continue into the future, and as such, the relationship that has existed between these PWIHE and the African American male athlete in football and basketball will endure because the NCAA and its member institutions will continue to want the manpower that is needed to produce an entertaining product on the fields and courts in order to produce revenue, and African American athletes will want the experience and exposure necessary to get to the professional level in their respective sport. Given this reality and the fact that big-time college sport has become so entrenched and ingrained in the culture and fabric of higher education (Beyer & Hannah, 2000), it is important for those researchers and scholars who study and write about college sport and practitioners who manage college sport to think critically about the educational interests of the African American male athlete, as well as the interests of athletes from other racial, gender, and class backgrounds.

From a research perspective, there are a few avenues that scholars might consider. First, African American male athletes in particular, and college athletes in general, need to be given a voice or platform to express their concerns regarding their educational experiences and the impact that the college sport enterprise has on these experiences. From a CRT perspective, there is a need for an *African American male athlete epistemology for stakeholder management in college sport* to be considered. In the field of education, Beverly Gordon (1990) advanced the idea of an African American epistemology for educational theory and practice, where the actual experience of the African American community is the starting point. In a similar vein, it is argued here that the voices and actual experiences of the African American male athlete (past, present, and future) in big-time college sport be viewed as a starting point and alternative lens for looking at issues of stakeholder management in college sport as well as issues of college sport reform. This is not to suggest that all African American male athletes will speak with a singular voice; however, it does imply that a great deal can be learned by documenting the common and varied experiences of this important stakeholder group. In addition, perhaps the research process could encourage and empower these athletes to begin to take stock in their educational experiences, and as Donnor (2005) suggested, place their education at the forefront of their agendas as college athletes.

Second, scholars should not only analyze legal cases as Donnor (2005) did, but should also consider a critical race analysis of the policies, rules, and other documents that pertain to the structures, functions, and activities in college sport. In this regard, the NCAA rules manual and other documents should be carefully scrutinized; in addition, the mission statements and other documents and programs within athletic departments should also be analyzed and critiqued. In particular, the academic support programs in these athletic departments should become the subject of study for scholars. Spigner (1993) stressed the need for these institutions to refrain from the use of their academic support programs to consciously or subconsciously perpetuate institutional racism (e.g., focusing exclusively on keeping these athletes eligible to participate in football, but not focusing on helping them to graduate). Unfortunately, I have seen this scenario played out in some of my experiences working with African American male athletes who I have mentored as students in my classes or who participated in the summer bridge program that I worked in for three years. Smith's (2007) work on the deepening relationship between African American males and the institution of sport speaks to the need for this form of institutional racism to be properly addressed.

Finally, scholars might consider conducting research with African American male athletes at PWIHE as well as historically Black colleges and universities (HBCU) in efforts to document the stories of this important stakeholder of college sport in these vastly different educational and social contexts. From an interest-convergence perspective, it would be quite interesting to study any potential differences, especially when you consider both the potentially positive and negative effects that the integration of African American athletes into PWIHE could have had on the African American athlete. Why did some African American male athletes choose PWIHE over HBCU, or vice versa? What have the educational experiences been like for these athletes at these different types of institutions? What role did their property value (i.e., physical ability and athletic talent) play in whether or not these athletes were recruited to PWIHE? What impact did integration have on athletic programs at HBCU? Perhaps the answers to these and other questions might be helpful as scholars reflect on stakeholder management and the educational interests of African American male and other athletes in college sport.

From a practical standpoint, because CRT is a movement that emphasizes both an academic as well as an activist agenda it should be infused into the discussion of college sport reform issues. For example, one of the major reform groups (i.e., the Knight Commission) has done important work since the early 1990s, but has failed to directly, explicitly, and intentionally confront and address the issue of racial exploitation in college sport (Anderson & South, 2000). Although the Knight Commission and other secondary stakeholder groups have focused on issues that are pertinent to college athletes in general (see Benford, 2007 for details), this dialogue, for the most part, has neglected the issue of race and the impact it has on the educational interests of college athletes. The issue of race is very important to this discussion, especially when you consider that, dating back to the Civil Rights era, these PWIHE have, in a sense, raided HBCU for the athletic talent of the African American athlete; and today, it is the African American male athlete, in particular, at these PWIHE whose educational interests have taken a back seat to the competitive interests of these athletic programs. Therefore, those stakeholder groups that are genuinely concerned with college sport reform (e.g., special interest groups, academic support personnel, educators) should create partnerships and coalitions that tend to the educational interests of the African American male athlete in addressing the interests of all college athletes.

Related to the point above, these athletic departments at PWIHE should also strongly attempt to upgrade and improve their academic support programs by supporting and implementing programs designed specifically to address the unique needs of African American athletes at PWIHE. For example, initiatives such as the Majority of One program—which was founded and implemented by James Hall, a former athletic academic counselor in a big-time college sport program and current associate athletic director at another NCAA member institution—should be considered because programs like this were designed specifically to provide racial minority athletes with the support network necessary to succeed away from the fields and courts of play and to prepare them for life after sports (see Gammage, 2004). As another example, the "Scholar-Baller Paradigm" or program (see Chapter 10 of this text; Harrison & Boyd, 2007) should be considered because it combines the best elements of an academic, athletic, and social identity, and creates a synergy between education, sports, and entertainment that has real meaning to today's African American athlete in particular, and other college athletes in general.

Given their intimate relationship with athletes and the critical role they play in the educational experiences of their athletes (see Singer & Armstrong, 2001), coaches should be willing to embrace and support academic support programs and initiatives such as the ones mentioned above. While there perhaps are examples of coaches who do support such programs and initiatives and have a genuine interest in the educational experiences of their athletes, there are others who appear to be more concerned with their own self-interests (e.g., signing the next top recruiting class, securing a lucrative contract, winning games). In this regard, mechanisms for holding coaches accountable for how they go about addressing the educational interests of African American male athletes (and other athletes) need to be implemented. Because its primary purpose is to foster the growth and development of racial minorities at various levels of sport, organizations such as the Black Coaches and Administrators (BCA) should be involved in this process. The BCA should partner with other organizations in creating mandates to challenge its membership and coaching professionals throughout the NCAA to focus not only on the athletic development of their athletes, but also other aspects of athlete development (e.g., social, intellectual).

Finally, and most importantly, it is the ultimate responsibility of the African American male athlete himself to take charge of his own educational experiences and interests. College athletics in America has become such a highly commercialized entity to the point where it appears that athletes do not have much of a voice and very little input into policies that directly influence their educational experiences (Eitzen, 2003). Moreover, given that these individuals' athletic scholarships (i.e., being able to retain it from year to year) are not only riding on their ability to perform athletically at the highest levels, but also their ability to stay in good favor with the coaching staff, many are discouraged from speaking honestly and openly about those things that negatively impact their educational experiences. When you combine these factors with the reality that many African American male athletes seem only to be interested in the pursuit of a professional sport career, and therefore, take very little interest in other areas of personal and professional development during their time on these campuses, one begins to see and understand how forces at the structural and individual levels collide to create the many problems related to the educational experiences of African American male athletes.

This is why it is important for African American male and all other athletes in these big-time college sport programs to take charge of their educational interests by aligning themselves with programs, coalitions, alliances, and people that will enlighten and provide support for them during their time on campus. Furthermore, it is imperative that these athletes assess and evaluate their priorities and preferences by focusing on the true meaning of why they are on campus. To be sure, in a few cases, these tremendously gifted athletes view their time on campus (sometimes only one to three years) merely as a stepping stone to the NBA or NFL; in most cases, however, whether or not some of these athletes know, understand, or accept it, the college sport experience signals the end of their organized, highly institutionalized sport participation endeavors. In this sense, the ultimate responsibility lies on the shoulders of athletes to embrace this reality and utilize all of the resources at their disposal to reap the benefits from their experiences as important stakeholders of big-time college sport.

STUDY QUESTIONS

1. Identify the different types of stakeholder groups, and provide examples of each in big-time college sport. Further, discuss which ones are (or should be) most salient and why?

2. What are some of the potential advantages and limitations to using the interest-convergence principle to understand the integration of college sport and the educational experiences of African American athletes?

3. Discuss what is meant by "big-time college sport" and some strategies for managing the various stakeholder interests in this particular context. Be sure to provide examples of college and universities that you would classify as "big-time."

SUGGESTED READINGS

Beyer, J. M., & Hannah, D. R. (2000). The cultural significance of athletics in US higher education. *Journal of Sport Management, 14*, 105–132.

Donnor, J. K. (2005). Towards an interest-convergence in the education of African American football student-athletes in major college sports. *Race, Ethnicity and Education, 8*(1), 45–67.

Feagin, J. R. (2006). *Systemic racism: A theory of oppression.* New York, NY: Routledge.

Jenkins, T. S. (2006). Mr. Nigger: The challenges of educating Black males within American society. *Journal of Black Studies, 37*(1), 127–155.

Powell, S. (2008). *Souled out? How Blacks are winning and losing in sports.* Champaign, IL: Human Kinetics.

Preble, J. F. (2005). Toward a comprehensive model of stakeholder management. *Business and Society Review, 110*(4), 407–431.

Smith, E. (2007). *Race, sport and the American dream*. Durham, NC: Carolina Academic Press.

Taylor, E. (1998). A primer on critical race theory. *Journal of Blacks in Higher Education, 19*, 122–124.

REFERENCES

Agle, B. R., Mitchell, R. K., & Sonnenfeld, J. A. (1999). Who matters to CEOs? An investigation of stakeholder attributes and salience, corporate performance, and CEO values. *Academy of Management Journal, 42*, 507–525.

Anderson, A., & South, D. (2007). The academic experiences of African American collegiate athletes: Implications for policy and practice. In D. Brooks & R. Althouse (Eds.), *Diversity and social justice in college sports: Sport management and the student athlete* (pp. 77–94). Morgantown, WV: Fitness Information Technology.

Bell, D. (1980). Brown vs. Board of Education and the interest-convergence principle. *Harvard Law Review, 93*, 518–533.

Bell, D. (1992). *Race, racism, and American law*. Boston, MA: Little Brown.

Bell, D. (2004). *Silent covenants: Brown v. Board of Education and the unfulfilled hopes for racial reform*. New York, NY: Oxford University Press.

Benford, R. D. (2007). The college sports reform movement: Reframing the "edutainment" industry. *The Sociological Quarterly, 48*, 1–28.

Benson, K. F. (2000). Constructing academic inadequacy: African American athletes' stories of schooling. *Journal of Higher Education, 71*(2), 223–246.

Berstein, R., Farrell, L. D., Greenburg, R., Hutchinson, P. H., Reid, K. (Prods.) (1996). *The Journey of the African American Athlete* (TV), Home Box Office.

Brooks, D., & Althouse, R. (Eds.). (1993). *Racism in college athletics: The African American athlete's experience*. Morgantown, WV: Fitness Information Technology.

Brooks, D., & Althouse, R. (Eds.). (2000). *Racism in college athletics: The African American athlete's experience* (2nd ed.). Morgantown, WV: Fitness Information Technology.

Brooks, S. N., & Kim, L. J. (2007). The dilemmas and contradictions of "getting' paid." In D. Brooks & R. Althouse (Eds.), *Diversity and social justice in college sports: Sport management and the student-athlete* (pp. 295–309). Morgantown, WV: Fitness Information Technology.

Brown, T. N. (2003). Critical race theory speaks to the sociology of mental health: Mental health problems produced by racial stratification. *Journal of Health and Social Behavior, 44*, 292–301.

Carroll, A. B. (1993). *Business and society: Ethics and stakeholder management* (2nd ed.). Cincinnati, OH: Southwestern.

Chelladurai, P. (2005). *Managing organizations for sport and physical activity: A systems perspective* (2nd ed.). Scottsdale, AZ: Holcomb Hathaway.

Chu, D. (1989). *The character of American higher education and intercollegiate sport*. New York, NY: State University of New York Press.

Clarkson, M. B. E. (1995). A stakeholder framework for analyzing and evaluating corporate social performance. *Academy of Management Review, 20*(1), 92–117.

Comeaux, E. (2007). The student(less) athlete: Identifying the unidentified college student. *Journal for the Study of Sports and Athletes in Education, 1*(1), 37–43.

Daniels, O. C. B. (1987). Perceiving and nurturing the intellectual development of black student-athletes: A case for institutional integrity. *Western Journal of Black Studies, 11*, 155–163.

Davis, T. (1995). The myth of the superspade: The persistence of racism in college athletics. *Fordham Urban Law Journal, 22*, 615–698.

Davis, T. (2000). Race, law, and collegiate athletics. In D. Brooks & R. Althouse (Eds.), *Racism in college athletics: The African American athlete's experience* (pp. 245–265). Morgantown, WV: Fitness Information Technology, Inc.

Dixson, A. D., & Rousseau, C. K. (2005). And we are still not saved: Critical race theory in education ten years later. *Race, Ethnicity and Education, 8*(1), 7–27.

Donaldson, T., & Preston, L. E. (1995). The stakeholder theory of the corporation: Concepts, evidence, and implications. *Academy of Management Review, 20*, 65–91.

Donnor, J. K. (2005). Towards an interest-convergence in the education of African American football student-athletes in major college sports. *Race, Ethnicity and Education, 8*(1), 45–67.

Downton, J. (2000, January). The James Brooks illiteracy scandal: Auburn university's and the Cincinnati Bengals' secret little "problem" unveiled. *Black Issues in Higher Education, 16*(23), 18–20.

Edwards, H. (1983). Educating Black athletes. *The Atlantic Monthly*, August, 31–38.

Edwards, H. (1984). The Black 'dumb jock': An American sports tragedy. *The College Board Review, 131*, 8–13.

Edwards, H. (1985). Beyond symptoms: Unethical behavior in American collegiate sport and the problem of the color line. *Journal of Sport and Social Issues, 9*(3), 3–13.

Eitzen, D. S. (2003). *Fair and foul: Beyond the myths and paradoxes of sport* (2nd ed.). Lanham, MD: Rowman & Littlefield Publishers, Inc.

Freeman, R. E. (1984). *Strategic management: A stakeholder approach*. Boston, MA: Pitman.

Frooman, J. (1999). Stakeholder influence strategies. *Academy of Management Review, 24*, 191–205.

Gammage, R. (2004, May 11). Minority athletes join majority of one peer support program to prepare for life beyond sports. *onCampus, 38*(8). Retrieved from http://www.oncampus.osu.edu/article.php?id = 133

Gordon, B. M. (1990). The necessity of African-American epistemology for educational theory and practice. *Journal of Education, 172*(3), 88–106.

Grant, O. B. (2003). African American collegiate football players and the dilemma of exploitation, racism and education: A socio-economic analysis of sports law. *Whittier Law Review, 24*, 645–661.

Haney-Lopez, I. F. (1996). *White by law: The legal construction of race.* New York, NY: New York University Press.

Harris, C. (1993). Whiteness as property. *Harvard Law Review, 106*(8), 1707–1791.

Harris, O. (2000). African American predominance in sport. In D. Brooks & R. Althouse (Eds.), *Racism in college athletics: The African American athlete's experience* (2nd ed.) (pp. 37–52). Morgantown, WV: Fitness Information Technology.

Harrison, C. K., & Boyd, J. (2007). Mainstreaming and integrating the spectacle and substance of scholar-baller: A new blueprint for higher education, the NCAA, and society. In D. Brooks & R. Althouse (Eds.), *Diversity and social justice in college sports: Sport management and the student-athlete* (pp. 201–231). Morgantown, WV: Fitness Information Technology.

Harrison, L., Harrison, C. K., & Moore, L. N. (2002). African American racial identity and sport. *Sport, Education, and Society, 7*(2), 121–133.

Hasnas, J. (1998). The normative theories of business ethics: A guide for the perplexed. *Business Ethics Quarterly, 8*(1), 19–42.

Hawkins, B. (1999). Black student athletes at predominately White National Collegiate Athletic Association (NCAA) Division I institutions and the pattern of oscillating migrant laborers. *Western Journal of Black Studies, 23*(1), 1–9.

Hawkins, B. (2001). *The new plantation: The internal colonization of Black student athletes.* Winterville, GA: Sadiki Press.

Jenkins, T. S. (2006). Mr. Nigger: The challenges of educating Black males within American society. *Journal of Black Studies, 37*(1), 127–155.

Jones, T. M. (1995). Instrumental stakeholder theory: A synthesis of ethics and economics. *Academy of Management Review, 20*(2), 404–437.

Klein, F. C. (1998, September 25). Looking back, ex-lineman takes college sports to task. *The Wall Street Journal.*

Ladson-Billings, G., & Donnor, J. (2005). The moral activist role of critical race theory scholarship. In N. K. Denzin & Y. S. Lincoln (Eds.), *The sage handbook of qualitative research* (3rd ed.) (pp. 279–301). Thousand Oaks, CA: Sage.

Langtry, B. (1994). Stakeholders and the moral responsibilities of business. *Business Ethics Quarterly, 4*(4), 431–443.

Lapchick, R., Little, E., Lerner, C., & Mathew, R. (2009). *The 2008 racial and gender report card: College sports.* University of Central Florida, Orlando, FL: The Institute for Diversity and Ethics in Sport.

Lynn, M., & Adams, M. (2002). Introductory overview to the special issue critical race theory and education: Recent developments in the field. *Equity & Excellence in Education, 35*(2), 87–92.

Mitchell, R. K., Agle, B. R., & Wood, D. J. (1997). Toward a theory of stakeholder identification and salience: Defining the principle of who and what really counts. *Academy of Management Review, 22*(4), 853–886.

Parham, W. D. (1993). The intercollegiate athlete: A 1990s profile. *The Counseling Psychologist, 21*(3), 411–429.

Preble, J. F. (2005). Toward a comprehensive model of stakeholder management. *Business and Society Review, 110*(4), 407–431.

Putler, D. S., & Wolfe, R. A. (1999). Perceptions of intercollegiate athletic programs: Priorities and tradeoffs. *Sociology of Sport Journal, 16*, 301–325.

Randolph, L. B. (1989, October). Dexter Manley's incredible story: 'I broke down and started crying . . . how did I get through school when I couldn't read?' *Ebony.*

Reed, D. (1999). Stakeholder management theory: A critical theory perspective. *Business Ethics Quarterly, 9*(3), 453–483.

Reese, L. E. (2000). The impact of American social systems on African American men. In L. Jones (Ed.), *Brothers of the academy: Up and coming Black scholars earning our way in higher education* (pp. 191–196). Sterling, VA: Stylus Publishing.

Sage, G. H. (1998). *Power and ideology in American sport* (2nd ed.). Champaign, IL: Human Kinetics.

Shropshire, K. L. (2000). Compensation and the African American student-athlete. In D. Brooks & R. Althouse (Eds.), *Racism in college athletics: The African American athlete's experience* (pp. 267–277). Morgantown, WV: Fitness Information Technology.

Singer, J. N. (2005). Understanding racism through the eyes of African American male student-athletes. *Race, Ethnicity and Education, 8*(4), 365–386.

Singer, J. N. (2008). Benefits and detriments of African American male athletes' participation in a big-time college football program. *International Review for the Sociology of Sport, 43*(4), 399–408.

Singer, J. N. (2009). African American football athletes' perspectives on institutional integrity in college sport. *Research Quarterly for Exercise and Sport, 80*(1), 102–116.

Singer, J. N., & Armstrong, K. L. (2001). Black coaches' roles in the holistic development of student-athletes. *Academic Athletic Journal, 15*(2), 114–131.

Smith, E. (2007). *Race, sport and the American dream.* Durham, NC: Carolina Academic Press.

Spigner, C. (1993). African American student-athletes: Academic support or institutionalized racism? *Education, 114*(1), 144–150.

Tate, W. F. (1997). Critical race theory and education: History, theory, and implications. In M. Apple (Ed.), *Review of research in education* (pp. 191–243). Washington, DC: American Educational Research Association.

Taylor, E. (1998). A primer on critical race theory. *Journal of Blacks in Higher Education, 19*, 122–124.

Trail, G., & Chelladurai, P. (2000). Perceptions of goals and processes of intercollegiate athletics: A case study. *Journal of Sport Management, 14*, 154–178.

Weinbach, J. (2007, October 19). *Inside college sports' biggest money machine.* Retrieved from http://online.wsj.com/article/SB119275242417864220.html?mod

Wolfe, R. A., & Putler, D. S. (2002). How tight are the ties that bind stakeholder groups? *Organization Science, 13*(1), 64–80.

Zimbalist, A. (1999). *Unpaid professionals: Commercialism and conflict in big-time college sports.* Princeton, NJ: Princeton University Press.

Zimbalist, A. (2007, June 18). College athletic budgets are bulging but their profits are slim to none. *Street & Smith's SportsBusiness Journal, 26.*

Section VII: Diversity:
Beyond Black and White

This section contains two chapters that expand our view of the literature, discussing Hispanic/Latino student-athletes and the effect of international student-athletes involved in American intercollegiate sports programs and organizations.

Chapter 16 turns our focus toward the experiences of male Latino college football players. Historically, African American and Latino students were confronted by similar social conditions: discrimination, limited resources, health issues, lower high school and college graduation rates when compared to their White counterparts, and access to higher education via the junior/community college route. To an extent, by overcoming some barriers, Latinos have gained a level of success in the sport industry. Latino athletes made contributions to boxing, baseball, and professional football. Yet, much is still unknown about the academic and athletic experiences of Latino male and female student-athletes. Harrison, Ochoa, and Hernandez employ critical race theory (CRT) to understand Latino male student-athletes' access to resources and to a higher education that has enhanced their social and athletic identities in revenue sports such as football.

Success in intercollegiate athletics has long been a race among coaches to procure the best and most capable athletes for their respective teams, and thus, there is the need to identify and recruit athletic talent that extends beyond America's borders. In the final chapter of this new edition, Teed provides an analysis of migration patterns of international student-athletes, suggesting that college sport in America is grounded in the ever-increasing need to generate revenue to sustain the athletic corporation and pressure to produce successful athletic teams, including international players. Often noted by some critics is the extent to which international student-athletes are contributing to a reduction of playing opportunities for African Americans in some NCAA sports, but Teed shows that a majority of foreign athletes participate in tennis, soccer, indoor and outdoor track, hockey, and golf, sports that have not traditionally had a high participation of African Americans at the collegiate level. Teed concludes that "researchers may want to review the intersections of geography, economics, culture, and politics on the international student-athlete recruitment process."

CHAPTER 16

From the Turf to the Top:
Access to Higher Education by
Latino Male College Football Players

C. KEITH HARRISON, VANESSA OCHOA,
and MICHELLE S. HERNANDEZ

Abstract

The purpose of this paper is to examine the role and dilemma of the Latino male student-athlete in the revenue sport of intercollegiate football with implications for other sport experiences. First, the authors will briefly examine the existing higher education literature on Latinos in terms of access to and success in higher education. Second, the authors will provide a historical context of Latinos in sport. Third, the authors will apply critical race theory (CRT) to Latino male student-athletes across their social and athletic identities in revenue sports such as football. Lastly, the authors will explain the importance of qualitative research with respect to Latino male football student-athletes.

Key Terms	
• critical race theory	• mircoaggressions
• Latino	• social identity theory
• institutionalized racism	• athletic identity

INTRODUCTION

When 12-year-old Joe Kapp visited the University of California, Berkeley, he asked a teacher, "What do I have to do to play here?" The teacher responded, "You have to take college prep courses" (Craddock, 2005). Eventually Kapp, born in New Mexico and of Mexican descent, earned a basketball scholarship to attend the University of California, Berkeley in the late 1950s. As a Golden Bear on the basketball court, he earned many honors and the team won the 1959 National Collegiate Athletic Association (NCAA) championship. On the football field, Kapp further distinguished himself as a leader and tough opponent as quarterback of the team (Longoria, 1997). Kapp earned his college degree and played professionally in the National Football League (NFL) and the Canadian Football League (CFL) (Longoria, 1997; Fremont, 1998). Kapp recently established an organization to promote excellence in higher education (Craddock, 2005). Today, Kapp's story as a student-athlete, and as someone who enjoys motivating students to succeed in academics and athletics, arrives full circle to higher education as he continues to give back to those on college campuses.

A review of the literature on intercollegiate Latino student-athletes is needed in the study of higher education, especially in the revenue sport of football to move beyond the Black/White athlete binary. In this chapter, the authors will briefly examine the existing higher education literature on Latinos in terms of access to and success in higher education. Second, the authors will provide a historical context of Latinos in sport. Third, the authors will apply critical race theory (CRT) to Latino male student-athletes across their social and athletic identities in revenue sports such as football. Lastly, the authors will explain the importance of qualitative research related to Latino male football student-athletes, with an eye on the African American male athlete (Jordan & Denson, 1990).

The authors will use the term Latino to describe the ethnicity and cultural identity of the student-athletes discussed in this chapter. Over the years, many terms have gained or lost prominence in describing people who presently live in the United States but who have varied historical backgrounds and national origins, ranging from Central America and South America to the Spanish-speaking Caribbean. The word *Latino*, as it is used in this chapter, includes "Mexican Americans, Puerto Ricans, Cubans, and Latin Americans who are linked to US history through immigration, acquisition of lands, or political upheavals" (Macdonald & Garcia, 2003, p. 19). Federal and state governments created a census classification for Hispanics in the 1970s; however, "identity issues and census classification cause considerable challenges to historians of the Latino experience" (Macdonald & Garcia, 2003, p. 19). Reliable data on Latinos in higher education proves to be problematic (Macdonald & Garcia, 2003). This phenomenon provides a glimpse into the identity development of this student population. Thus, the following section will discuss existing literature on Latino access to higher education.

LEGACY OF ACCESS TO HIGHER EDUCATION: LATINOS ON CAMPUS

"From their earliest school years, African American and Latino students are consistently overrepresented in low-track, remedial, and special education programs" (Oakes & Lipton, 1996, p. 170). Academic excellence represents a particular challenge to these students based on a history of discrimination and lack of access in higher education. Student perceptions of the institution have a large impact on academic success (Hurtado, 1996; Washington, 1996). Institutionalized racism has further limited access to higher education (Washington, 1996) and intercollegiate leadership roles for these students (NCAA, 2004a), but has not entirely quashed it. Benson (2000) points to two main perspectives that outline the problem of persistent lack of academic achievement amongst minority student-athletes. The *deficit* model tends to leave the "impression that the poor performance is primarily their fault" (Benson, 2000, p. 224). The second approach (infrequently applied) invokes a connection between societal structures that maintain "prevailing social and economic order" (Benson, 2000, p. 225). The current system often appears to unjustly reward student-athletes with passing grades and limited faculty interaction or career planning after college (Benson, 2000). Equally disturbing is the sense among the athletes interviewed by Benson (2000) that faculty and coaches do not seem to care about the athletes beyond their "lip service" to academics (p. 232).

It has been shown that students will rise to the level of expectation by teachers and administrators. Both African American and Latino students are particularly susceptible to "stereotype threat" (Chickering & Gamson, 1987; Steele, 1997). Current research has begun yielding similar results for athletes. Padilla and Walker (1994) state that after the implementation of Proposition 48, which raised the academic standards for NCAA student-athletes beginning in the fall of 1986, academic indicators (e.g., GPA, graduation rates) improved. This policy spurred local districts to adopt college preparation curriculum that includes algebra II, chemistry, physics, English, and foreign language. The literature aimed at increasing academic success for ethnic minorities recommends many strategies already employed in many athletic departments. Therefore, school districts that emphasize a balance of academics and athletics may substantially increase the pool of students prepared for college.

Current statistics on Latino graduation rates are difficult to extrapolate from any one source. The high school graduation rate for Latinos reported at state level varies from 38% to 54%. The elusive figure depends on measuring tools and definition. In the recent past, the No Child Left Behind Act (NCLB) further exacerbated the situation for some by adding a high-stakes testing component to graduation requirements. Moreover, the state of bilingual education and the tracking of Latino students affect the quality of the academic experience of many of the students identified in this research. An observation of these converging factors reveals an unfortunate cycle of substantially limited access to higher education by Latinos.

The available evidence finds that many Latino students in higher education are first served by community colleges (Vigil Laden, 1999). On a collegiate level, when it comes to representation and graduation, the community colleges graduate more Latinos than other postsecondary institutions (Vigil Laden, 1999). Studying Latino football players at this level would be interesting in order to identify the factors for why they choose not to attend to four-year institutions. Hixson (1998a) interviewed a Latino student-athlete that cited several reasons for his playing football at the community college level (e.g., financial, academic). Studies on access to higher education by Black and Latino students (Mow & Nettles, 1996; Nora & Rendón, 1996; Allen, 1996) have found common characteristics necessary for persistence. These characteristics are often found in the successful community college system (Vigil Laden, 1999). Among those already mentioned, institutional commitment, cultural awareness, and resource allocation are extremely important to the graduation of ethnic minorities. Latinos with a doctorate are more likely to have graduated from a community college (Solórzano, Rivas, & Velez, 2005).

Ensuring Academic Success

The research shows consistent factors favorable to improving access and success at higher education for ethnic minorities. Hurtado (1996b) recommends careful attention to the sense of isolation many students experience. Latino students respond favorably to quality extracurricular activities and interactive faculty by achieving higher grade point averages and completing more degrees (Mow & Nettles, 1996). Additionally, Richardson and Skinner (1991) advocate for university approaches to multiculturalism that veer from a deficit model. At Texas Tech University, the Raiders Rojos alumni association fortified strong institutional interaction and encouraged a "space" on campus (Iber, 2001). This sense of space will contribute to the campus climate in both measurable and immeasurable ways on the well-being of Latino students. Athletic departments already support many of the strategies aimed at increasing academic success for minority students in general (Attinasi & Nora, 1996; Hurtado, 1996b). These strategies include services that provide better coping skills, time management, and leadership training.

Both Attinasi and Nora (1996) and Hurtado (1996a) identify key strategies for students to navigate campus life, including peer support. Treviño and Ewing (2004) recommend fostering positive experiences for all students of color by engaging students in meaningful ways. Engaging the student-athlete, and especially the student-athlete of color, would bring a dynamic element to this type of intergroup intersection because it's a view that remains unheard from and under the radar. Dr. Carpenter states in Hixson (1998b) that the emphasis on campus athletics

> Should be on the educational basis, and if it is tied to education, then the values of athletic participation are perhaps even more important for Latinos and other minorities than they are for non-minorities because the need for learning those skills of teamwork, decision-making, self-esteem, etc, are probably even more valuable to minority group members and even harder for them to come by elsewhere—all the more reason why minority group members benefit from sports participation. (p. 21)

Furthermore, in reference to such issues, the following section will briefly examine the history of Latinos in sport.

BRIEF HISTORY OF LATINOS IN SPORT

In the Latino community, sport often provided early vehicles to social change, economic independence, and political clout. In communities of color, sport participation and resulting community support has allowed venues and opportunity to pursue access to US institutions beyond higher education. Lomax (2004) discusses early actions by united African American and Latino professional baseball players to expose the injustice of racism. Traveling for away games, many of these players became incensed by the blatant racism when in the south during segregation. These players organized themselves and pressured owners to demand equal access to all facilities by Latinos and African Americans.

Over the last decade (Iber, 2001; Longoria, 1997), the history of Latinos in sport has focused on boxing and quality work by historians with their analysis of baseball (Burgos, 2007; Regalado, 1998). Santillán (2000) looks at sport as a method of cultural survival. As previously mentioned, sport unites communities. For communities that face political and economic impediments because of discrimination, sport may become a vehicle of access. Participation in sport allows marginalized communities to create a positive purpose and means of "community identity and political empowerment" (Santillán, 2000, p. 146).

Longoria (1997) clearly provides the definitive account of professional Latino football players. But of greater significance, at least in terms of this inquiry, is the historical presence of Latino student-athletes in higher education that emerges from the shadows. In this manner, Longoria's work (1997) serves as both the first historical account of Latinos in professional football and establishes a previously unseen sliver of the history of higher education. The narrative collection often includes first-person interviews and covers each Latino player from 1929–1970. The documentation demonstrates a Latino presence throughout the formation of professional football. Many of the athletes represented played professionally for both the NFL and CFL. Joe Kapp, the first Mexican player in a Super Bowl, led the 1969 Minnesota Vikings to Super Bowl IV. That Super Bowl game marked a new era for Latinos in professional football.

From gross analysis of the anecdotes and biographical accounts reviewed here, the authors noted regional and cultural similarities. Although snippets of the higher education experience were useful, a data table of graduation rates or major declaration would have further aided this review of the literature (see appendix). Instead, the researcher relied on consistent mention of either graduation or undergraduate major records for each student. This method revealed historical evidence that most of the players primarily participated in public four-year institutions, which would be akin to today's Division I-A institution. Many were from the southwest, primarily New Mexico, California, or Texas. Further cataloging these narratives in such a manner proved to be outside the scope of this investigation. Overall the text is an extremely well written account of the Latino presence on the gridiron. Longoria (1997) organizes the narratives in chronological order and accounts for much of his research through personal interviews. His methodology rested on the availability of athletic records kept by the university. The relatively small size of this slice of overall student enrollment may have contributed to a "grapevine" effect that enhanced the ability of Longoria (1997) to personally interview many of the subjects. As previously mentioned, the power of sport not

Former University of Southern California and Cincinnati Bengals offensive lineman Anthony Muñoz proved to be an early pioneer as a Latino playing major college football. He was inducted into the Pro Football Hall of Fame in 1998. Courtesy of USC Athletic Department

only brings communities closer together, but can also facilitate positive social change. With this in mind, the use of a theoretical framework can often be helpful in understanding the persistence of racial marginalization.

CRITICAL RACE THEORY (CRT) AND
THE LATINO MALE STUDENT-ATHLETE

Critical race theory is a valuable tool to help examine racial mircoaggressions and how they influence student-athletes of color (Solorzano, 2000). Pierce, Carew, Pierce-Gonzalez, and Wills (1978) describe mircoaggressions as a form of nonverbal racism or "put downs" against people of color (Pierce et al., 1978). Other researchers define racial microaggressions as acts of disregard as a result of Black-White interactions where people of color are regarded as inferior (Solorzano, 2000). Racial microaggressions continue to plague our society, spurring little investigation.

Social Identity

Social identity theory, first outlined by Tajfel (1982), has become the cornerstone to our understanding of student development. The body of literature on this topic now includes the discussion and experiences of ethnic minorities. Social development theory, according to Tajfel (1982), outlines the ways humans can connect to other humans. A fundamental component of this process remains the ability to connect as a group and to identify with a community. As such, the student-athlete often arrives on campus with a salient athletic identity and therefore a built-in niche in which to connect socially, academically, and athletically. Moreover, the athletic component of a university contains purposeful policy to implement these essential elements of NCAA Division I-A Intercollegiate Athletic (ICA) programs. For example, most sport programs require preseason practice, uniforms, and rigorous scheduling (often including significant travel), all of which legitimize a sense of community. While sport participation allows a sense of teamwork, individuality frequently thrives as well (Wolf-Wendel, Toma, & Morphew, 2001). Coleman (2000) found that athletes were more likely to be satisfied academically and socially than non athletes. Furthermore, Coleman (2000) cites various studies that link athletic involvement with positive interactions, skill and leadership development, and a positive effect on persistence. Athletic participation creates opportunities for athletes to know each other outside the classroom (Astin, 1993; Jordan & Denson, 1990; Wolf-Wendel, Toma, & Morphew, 2001). Thus, from the studies that discuss the link between athletic identity and social development, there remains a need for further examination at the intersection of social identity created by race, gender, and culture in the context of sport.

Athletic Identity

Benson (2000) examined the experiences of African American student-athletes who report low-academic expectations from the campus community. Her qualitative approach and research serve as a parallel to Latinos (Benson, 2000). Much like African American student-athletes, many Latino student-athletes academically outperform their non-athlete counterparts (Martin, 2006).

The athlete community does create a sense of community, but can become an island unto itself. This athletic island culture may be one explanation for high rates of underperformance among student-athletes (Adler & Adler, 1991; Bowen & Levin, 2003). Underperformance is defined here as "the phenomenon of a group's having a lower grade-point average (GPA) or in-class rank than would be predicted on the basis of pre-college achievement and other observable characteristics" (Bowen & Levin, 2003, p. 5).

The authors incorporate these explanations, with a focus on smaller Division III schools, as a starting point to further the discussion and ultimately to redirect the focus on Latinos who play Division I football. The higher education literature contains investigation of campus racial climates that document an "alienation from the mainstream of campus life, particularly acute among minority students on predominantly white campuses (Hurtado, 1996a, p. 286). Currently, a gap of inquiry exists on whether this sense of isolation experienced amongst Latino student-athletes has been exacerbated, neutralized, or minimized by athletic identity. Bowen & Levin (2003) build on the work of Steele (1997) in his study of "stereotype threat" when describing possible reasons for academic underperformance among student-athletes. Clearly, the subjective and qualitative experiences of the Latino male student-athlete would better inform researchers and practitioners in higher education and sport management.

LATINO MALE STUDENT-ATHLETES: THE NEED FOR QUALITATIVE DATA

The authors examined graduation rates, population (city and university) demographics, and enrollment rates for Latino student-athletes in intercollegiate football. Primary sources used by the authors include the United States Census (2000), the *Chronicle of Higher Education Almanac*, and a data set provided by the Paul Robeson Research Center for Academic and Athletic Prowess (2005). From these statistics, the authors make some general observations in order to determine the level of academic achievement among this subpopulation of students. Ochoa (2005) surmises that many young Latinos "utilize football as an extracurricular activity that acts as a driving force (maintaining grades simply to play on the team) to get through high school and for some as a ticket out of the barrio and into the university gates" (p. 2).

Many of the larger, public, four-year universities that have NCAA Division I-A sport programs are considered traditionally White institutions (TWIs). The overall representation of minorities remains low, but can vary widely according to geographical location and other factors. The authors will look at some of these other factors. According to statistics provided by the NCAA, Latinos in football number about 218 (NCAA, 2005b). This figure will undoubtedly grow as Latinos continue to grow in population. Studies on athletes in these types of institutions have been primarily focused on the Black/White para-

New York Jets quarterback Mark Sanchez was named the 2009 Rose Bowl MVP after leading the University of Southern California to a win in the postseason contest.
Courtesy of USC Athletic Department

digm and Lilly Cheng (1996) calls for this paradigm to shift to better "recognize diversity." Mow and Nettles (1996) provide two compelling reasons for this current emphasis on Black/White student intersections. Firstly, African Americans or Blacks have been surpassed by Latinos as the largest minority population in the United States and ever increasing in respect to college enrollments. Secondly, faltering academic progress among this population over the last decade has alarmed researchers, spurring an interest in explanations. Overall there is little research on athletic identity in general; therefore, minimal statistics or studies of Latino student-athletes in particular are available.

The universities of particular interest here are considered to be in the Pacific 12 Conference. A focus on the Pac-12 emerged from two reasons. First, two of six participating states have significant Latino populations (Arizona and California) and among the California participating institutions are four that are considered to have highly selective admissions processes. Listed here, they are Stanford University, University of California, Berkeley (Cal), The University of California at Los Angeles (UCLA), and the University of Southern California (USC). A table of participating universities can be found in the appendix. As an overview, the six states represented are Arizona, California, Oregon and Washington. The designation of Hispanic Serving Institution (HSI) provides some federal funding. In this conference, 10 institutions are four-year public universities and two are private four-year universities. Among the highly selective universities previously mentioned, Stanford and the University of Southern California are private. Cal and UCLA are also highly sought for admission and their football programs recruit heavily. Both Arizona with a 27.8% and California a 34.3% Latino demographic are high above the national average of 13.7%. The University of Oregon and Oregon State University also participate; however, their statewide Latino demographic falls below the national average at

9.2%. In Washington the Hispanic population represents 8.3%. For comparison purposes, the authors also provided statistics for the University of Texas, Austin, and the University of Texas, El Paso as both the state figures for Latino representation (34.2%) and minority enrollment (41.3%) are high. The University of Texas-Austin has a low participation rate of Latino student-athletes based on statewide Latino representation. UTEP has a high participation rate, but its graduation rate remains very low.

Latino student-athletes may or may not have different experiences in higher education than other more researched populations such as African Americans. This unique experience has value and deserves more inquiry to uncover these voices (Harrison & Lawrence, 2004; Leonard, 1998). A pilot study (Harrison, Ochoa, & Hernandez, 2006) with two Latino male student-athletes further illustrates some of the intersections and unique aspects of the Latino male student-athlete experience. These narratives are a precursor to the final section and both student-athletes were asked the following question pertaining to the below narratives: *Do you feel you challenged yourself to the best of your intellectual ability or did sports hinder you?*

> No, I did not challenge myself to the best of my ability because I believed without a shadow of a doubt that my career was going to be baseball, I felt was going to have a long distinguished baseball career and sometime end up in the baseball Hall of Fame. No one could convince me differently at that point. But I was fortunate that I didn't put all my eggs in one basket. I did study and did what I needed to do to graduate. Did I put all of my emphasis on academics? No, at that time I didn't. (Pilot 1)

> I don't think sports hindered it at all. I think that as an athlete, you think it does. But as you grow older, you realize it doesn't. It's more a mindset that you have, that you're above. Basically, you figure you do this for the school, okay, I got this, I mean I can get by a little bit here. You know? I mean it works that way. As far as pushing myself? No. That's one thing I do regret. It's not applying myself. Because, college was kind of easy. I could do very little and get by with Cs or Bs. And I was like wow, if I would have pushed myself, who says I couldn't have gotten As all the way through. And you know, that's just another setback. I'm never going that route again. You know what I mean? (Pilot 2)

CONCLUSION

The literature clearly states that with academic preparation, many Latinos succeed at rates equal to other successful populations (Mow & Nettles, 1996). Other research cited in this chapter reveals positive results when academics and athletics are thoughtfully blended together. Therefore, the "pipeline" becomes more than a system that flows, it becomes be a system that grows. In addition, the authors recommend that coaches and recruiters understand the cultural factors of Latino student-athletes. "When recruiting Latinos, you're not just recruiting the son/daughter, but the whole family" (C. Marin, personal communication, 2006).

Scholars in the area of higher education recommend positive peer pressure, mentoring, and higher expectations to ensure the academic success of all students. Intercollegiate athletics often already contain these elements implemented into the program. Student-athletes are expected to be eligible and this also helps students achieve their academic goals. The Latino student-athlete will need to be recognized but they do not necessarily need their own student services; rather, intercollegiate programs can incorporate larger university initiatives that create positive learning environments.

Division I football athletes are about the only pool of football players to be drafted into the National Football League (NFL). The lucrative career as a professional football player has been largely out of reach for the majority of student-athletes, as only a small percentage continue professional play. For Latino student-athletes this reality remains especially elusive (RGRC, Lapchick 2011). The culture of academics and athletics and the subsequent balance needed to maintain eligibility in a Division I setting may open opportunities for Latino students historically underrepresented at public four-year institutions.

Furthermore, the influence of athletics on university campuses across the United States has a history that dates back to the 1800s. Throughout the evolution of higher education, this influence has extended beyond the idea of extracurricular programs. Athletics often measure the pulse of the university and drive the campus culture. This may be particularly true at Division I institutions where football has become the uniting factor among university constituents including students, faculty, administrators, staff, and alumni. From a look at recent national demographics and the vision of higher education scholars, we see that Latinos are the fastest growing ethnic group on many campuses. Keys to success in responding to the increasing enrollments include increasing Latino faculty (Olivas, 1996). And by extension, this includes increasing Latino athletic personnel and leadership.

Finally, attending to the needs of Latino student-athletes necessitates an approach that recognizes the importance of culture and the historical role sports participation has provided in regard to access to higher education. Fostering positive experiences for all students-athletes of color by engaging them within a diverse group not only encourages an element of cross-race interaction, but also facilitates diverse practices, a crucial component to any environment in the 21st century (Treviño & Ewing, 2004). Lastly, a priority for higher educational institutions should be to include focus on the student in the *student-athlete*. Mark Sanchez was a first round and fourth overall draft pick of the New York Jets in the NFL, which is a great accomplishment. However, it should be highlighted to the public, and Latino males specifically, that he graduated from USC and went from the turf to the top with education as well as athletics.

STUDY QUESTIONS

1. List three issues common to both the public education system and higher education. Which legislation did the NCAA employ to raise student-athlete academic eligibility?

2. Which sport over the past decade has been the focus for Latino participation?

3. Two key benefits of athletics include . . . ?

4. Who is the first Mexican to play in a Super Bowl?

5. What does CRT stand for and how can it highlight Latino experiences?

6. Define the term *mircoaggressions*.

7. Name three high profile sports?

8. Name two US states with a Latino demographic above the national average of 13.7%?

SUGGESTED READINGS

Cunningham, G. B., & Sagas, M. (2004). Access discrimination in intercollegiate athletics. *Journal of Sport & Social Issues*, *29*(2), 148–163.

Hurtado, S., Milem, J., Clayton-Pedersen, A., & Allen, W. (1998). Enhancing campus climates for racial/ethnic diversity: Educational policy and practice. *The Review of Higher Education*, *21*(3), 279–302.

Lapchick, R. (2000). *Smashing barriers: Race and sport in the millennium*. Lanham, MD: Madison Books.

Lapchick, R. (2008). *Racial and gender report card*. Orlando, FL: University of Central Florida.

Longoria, M. (1997). *Athletes remembered: Mexicano/Latino professional football players, 1929–1970*. Tempe, AZ: Bilingual Review Press/Editorial Bilingüe.

Shropshire, K. L. (2004). Minority issues in contemporary sports. *Standford Law & Policy Review*, *15*, 189–211.

Steele, C. M. (1997). A threat in the air: How stereotypes shape intellectual identity and performance. *American Psychologist*. *52*, 613–629.

REFERENCES

Adler, P., & Adler, P. (1991). *Backboards and blackboards: College athletics and role engulfment.* New York, NY: Columbia University Press.

Allen, W. (1996). Improving Black student access and achievement in higher education. In C. Turner, M. Garcia, A. Nora, & L. Rendón (Eds.), *Racial and ethnic diversity in higher education* (pp. 269–279). Needham Heights, MA: Simon & Schuster.

Arizona Board of Regents. (2005). *Arizona State University: A new American university.* Tempe, AZ: Office of University Initiatives.

Astin, A. (1993). What matters in college. *Liberal Education*, *79*, 1–12.

Attinasi, Jr., L. (1996). Getting in: Mexican Americans' perceptions of university attendance and the implications of freshmen year experience. In C. Turner, M. Garcia, A. Nora, & L. Rendón (Eds.), *Racial and ethnic diversity in higher education* (pp. 189–209). Needham Heights, MA: Simon & Schuster.

Attinasi, Jr., L., & Nora, A. (1996). Diverse students and complex issues: A case for multiple methods in college research. In C. Turner, M. Garcia, A. Nora, & L. Rendón (Eds.), *Racial and ethnic diversity in higher education* (pp. 189–209). Needham Heights, MA: Simon & Schuster.

Benson, K. (2000). Constructing academic inadequacy: African-American athletes' stories of schooling. *Journal of Higher Education*, *71*(2), 223–246.

Bowen, W., & Levin, S. (2003). *Reclaiming the game: College sports and our educational values.* Princeton, NJ: University Press.

Brown, S., Santiago, D., & Lopez, E. (2003). Latinos in higher education: Today and tomorrow. *Change*, *35*, 40–46.

Burgos, A. (2007). *Playing America's game: Baseball, Latinos, and the color line.* Berkeley,CA: University of California Press.

Chickering, A., & Gamson, Z. (1987). Seven principles for good practice in higher education. New York, NY: Jossey-Bass.

Coleman, G. (2000). *Time out: Why aren't more Black and Latino female students participating in intercollegiate sports?* (Master's thesis). Massachusetts College of Liberal Arts. Eugene, OR: Microform Publications.

Craddock, B. (2005, March 23). Ex super bowl star backs college play: Quarterback visits Modesto to promote school among Latinos. *The Modesto Bee*, B3.

Fremont, R. (1998). The challenges of Hispanic student-athletes: Family, finances, and early experience. *Hispanic Outlook*, 12–13.

Gándara, P. (2005). Addressing educational inequities for Latino students: The politics of 'forgetting.' *Journal of Higher Education*, *4*, 295–313.

Harrison, C. K., & Herrera, R. (2004). *Data set: Latinos in Division I football.* Ann Arbor, MI: Paul Robeson Research Center for Academic & Athletic Prowess.

Harrison, C. K., & Lawrence, M. (2004). Female and male student athletes' perceptions of career transition in sport and higher education: A visual elicitation and qualitative assessment. *Journal of Vocational Education and Training*, *56*(4), 485–506.

Harrison, C. K., & Váldez, A. (2004). The uneven view of African American ballers. In C. K. Ross (Ed.), *Race and sport: The struggle for equality on and off the field. Essays by Scott Brooks . . . [et al]* (pp. 183–221). Jackson, MI: University Press.

Harrison, C. K., Ochoa, V., & Hernandez, M. (2006). *Latino male student-athletes: A qualitative Investigation.* Paper presented at the American Educational Research Association, San Francisco, California.

Hixson, A. (1998a). Life is more than a sport: A Latino athlete's case history. *Hispanic Outlook*, 24–27.

Hixson, A. (1998b). Researchers talk women, sports, and academia; Participation up, role models down. *Hispanic Outlook*, 14–20.

Hurtado, S. (1996a). The campus racial climate: Contexts

of conflict. In C. Turner, M. Garcia, A. Nora, & L. Rendón (Eds.), *Racial and ethnic diversity in higher education* (pp. 269–279). Needham Heights, MA: Simon & Schuster.

Hurtado, S. (1996b). Latino student transition to college: Assessing difficulties and factors in successful college adjustment. *Research in higher education, 37*(2), 135–157.

Hurtado, S., Milem, J., Clayton-Pedersen, A., & Allen, W. (1998). Enhancing campus climates for racial/ethnic diversity: Educational policy and practice. *The Review of Higher Education, 21*(3), 279–302.

Iber, J. (2001). Becoming raiders rojos. *West Texas Historical Association Year Book*, pp. 139–151.

Iber, J., & Regalado, S. (2007). Mexican Americans in sport: A reader on athletics and barrio life. College Station: Texas A & M Press Consortium.

Jones, L., Castellanos, J., & Cole, J. (2002). Examining the ethnic minority student experience at predominantly White institutions: A case study. *Journal of Hispanic Education, 1*, 19–39.

Jordan, J., & Denson, E. (1990). Student services for athletes: A model for enhancing the student-athlete experience. *Journal of Counseling & Development, 69*, 95–97.

Leonard II, W. (1998). *A sociological perspective of sport* (5th ed.). Boston, MA: Allyn and Bacon.

Lilly Cheng, L. (1996). Recognizing diversity: A need for a paradigm shift. In C. Turner, M. Garcia, A. Nora, & L. Rendón (Eds.), *Racial and ethnic diversity in higher education* (pp. 269–279). Needham Heights, MA: Simon & Schuster.

Lapchick, R. E. (2009). New study reveals marked improvements for the graduation rates forAfrican-American student athletes. *The Institute for Diversity and Ethics in Sport. University of Central Florida*, 1–4.

Lapchick, R. E. (2011). *Racial and gender report card.* Orlando, FL. University of Central Florida. The Institute of Diversity and Ethics in Sport (TIDES).

Lomax, M. (2004). Major League Baseball's separate-and-unequal doctrine: The African-American and Latino experience in spring training, 1946–1961. In C. K. Ross (Ed.), *Race and sport: The struggle for equality on and off the field. Essays by Scott Brooks . . . [et al]* (pp. 59–94). Jackson, MI: University Press.

Longoria, M. (1997). *Athletes remembered: Mexicano/Latino professional football players, 1929–1970.* Tempe, AZ: Bilingual Review Press/Editorial Bilingüe.

Macdonald, V. M., & García, T. (2003). Historical perspectives on Latino access to higher education, 1848–1990. In J. Castellanos & L. Jones (Eds.), *The majority in the minority: Expanding the representation of Latina/o faculty, administrators, and students in higher education* (pp. 14–43). Sterling, VA: Stylus Publishing.

Martin, B. (2006, April). *Examining non-cognitive variables and academic outcomes of academically driven African-American male student-athletes at highly selective division I Universities.* Paper presented at the meeting of the American Educational Research Association, San Francisco, CA.

Mow, S., & Nettles, M. (1996). Minority student access to, and persistence and performance in, College: A review of the trends and research literature. In C. Turner, M. Garcia, A. Nora, & L. Rendón (Eds.), *Racial and ethnic diversity in higher education* (pp. 189–209). Needham Heights, MA: Simon & Schuster.

National Collegiate Athletic Association. (2004a). *Graduation rates.* Retrieved from http://www.ncaa.org/grad_rates/2004/d1/DI.html

NCAA. (2004b). *History of academic reform.* Retrieved from http://www2.ncaa.org/academics_and_athletes/education_and_research/academic_reform/history.html

NCAA. (2005a). Defining reform. *The NCAA news online, dated February 14.* Retrieved from http://www2.ncaa.org/media_and_events/association_news/ncaa_news_online/2005/02_14_05/front_page_news/4204n02.html

NCAA. (2005b). *Division I statistics.* from http://web1.ncaa.org/d1mfb/mainpage.jsp

Nevárez, C. (2001). Mexican Americans and other Latinos in postsecondary education: Institutional influences. *Annual ERIC Digest*, 30–34. Charleston, WV: ERIC Clearinghouse on Rural Education and Small Schools.

Nora, A., & Rendón, L. (1996). Hispanic student retention in community colleges: Reconciling access with outcomes. In C. Turner, M. Garcia, A. Nora, & L. Rendón (Eds.), *Racial and ethnic diversity in higher education* (pp. 269–279). Needham Heights, MA: Simon & Schuster.

Oakes, J., & Lipton, M. (1990). *Making the best of school: A handbook for parents, teachers, and policymakers.* McGraw-Hill College.

Ochoa, V. (2005). *Touchdowns, passes, and 'ganas': A historical and contemporary analyses of Latino Collegiate and NFL players on and off the field.* Unpublished proposal, the University of California, Los Angles.

Olivas, M. (1996). Latino faculty at the border: Increasing numbers key to more Hispanic access. In C. Turner, M. Garcia, A. Nora, & L. Rendón (Eds.), *Racial and ethnic diversity in higher education* (pp. 376–389). Needham Heights, MA: Simon & Schuster.

Padilla, A., & Walker, L. (1994). The battle for control of college sports. *Chronicle of Higher Education.* Retrieved from http://chronicle.com

Pierce, C., Carew, J., Pierce-Gonzalez, D., & Wills, D. (1978). An experiment in racism: TV Commericals. In C. Pierce (Ed.), *Television and education* (pp 62–88). Thousand Oaks, CA: Sage.

Regalado, S. (1994). "Image is everything": Latin baseball players and the United States press. *Studies in Latin American Popular Culture, 13*, 101–115.

Regalado, S. (1998). *Viva Baseball!: Latin major leaguers and their special hunger.* Urbana, IL: University of Illinois Press.

Rendón, L. (1994). Validating culturally diverse students: Toward a new model of learning and student development. *Innovative Higher Education, 19*(1), 23–32.

Richardson, R. C., & Skinner, E. F. (1991). *Achieving quality and diversity: Universities in a multicultural society.* New York, NY: American Council on Education/Macmillan Publishing.

Santillán, R. (2000). Mexican baseball teams in the Midwest, 1916–1965: The politics of cultural survival and civil rights. *Perspectives in Mexican American Studies, 7*, 131–151.

Shulman, J., & Bowen, W. (2001). *The game of life: College sports and educational values.* Princeton, NJ: Princeton University Press.

Solórzano, D., Rivas, M., & Velez, V. (2005). Community

college as a pathway to Chicana/o doctorate production. *UCLA Chicano Studies Latino Policy & Issues Brief.* Retrieved from http://www.chicano.ucla.edu/press/siteart/LPIB_11June2005.pdf

Solórzano, D. (2000). Critical race theory, racial microaggressions, and campus racial climate: The experience of African American college students. *Journal of Negro Education, 69*, 1(2), 60–73

Steele, C. (1997). A threat in the air: How stereotypes shape intellectual identity and performance. *American Psychologist, June,* 613–629.

Tajfel, H. (1982). *Social identity in intergroup relations.* Boston, MA: Cambridge University Press.

The Chronicle of Higher Education. (2005). *Almanac.* Retrieved from http//:chronicle.com

Trevino, J., & Ewing, K. (2004). Fostering positive intergroup relations in the first year of college. In. L. Rendon, G. Mildred, & D. Person (Eds.), *Transforming the first year of college for students of color. The first year experience monograph series no. 38* (pp. 67–76). Columbia, SC: University of South Carolina.

US Census. (2000). State and county quick facts. Retrieved from http//:quickfacts.census.gov

Vigil Laden, B. (1999). Two-year Hispanic-serving colleges. In B. Townsend (Ed.), *Two-year colleges for women and minorities: Enabling access to the baccalaureate* (pp. 151–194). Independence, KY: Routledge.

Washington, M. (1996). The minority student in college: A historical analysis. In C. Turner, M. Garcia, A. Nora, & L. Rendón (Eds.), *Racial and ethnic diversity in higher education* (pp. 69–83). Needham Heights, MA: Simon & Schuster.

Wolf-Wendel, J., Toma, D., & Morphew, C. (2001). There's no "I" in "team": Lessons from athletics on community building. *The Review of Higher Education, 24*(4), 369–396.

Authors' Note: This chapter is dedicated to Mr. Dan Guerrero; Dr. Liberato Mukul, MD; Mr. Thomas Sauceda; Mr. Alex Toyos; Mr. Matthew Hicks; and Mr. Arnold Vasquez.

Appendix A

Institution	Div. I Latinos[1]	Grad. Rate %[2]	HSI[3]	Latino Pop. % (City)[4]	Minority Representation % (campus)[5]
Overall					
NCAA Division I	218	46	N/A	N/A	N/A
Pacific 12 (Pac-12) Conference					
University of Arizona	10	43-b	✔	35.7	22.3
Arizona State University	4	100-a	3	17.9	
University of California, Berkeley	2	50-a	3	9.7	50.9
University of California, Los Angeles	3	67-a	3	46.5	
University of Oregon	4	100-a		6.8	14.1
Oregon State University	2	67-a		8.0	
University of Southern California	3	50-a		46.5	N/A
Stanford University	4			4.6	
University of Washington	3	33-b		5.3	20.7
Washington State University	1	100-a		—	
Big 12					
University of Texas, Austin	6	0-a	3	30.5	38.3
Texas Tech University	7	100-a	3	27.5	
Conference USA					
University of Texas, El Paso	12	20-b	3	76.6	38.3

Note: In Column 3, values for N (a. 1–5, b. 6–10, c. 11–15, d. 16–20. e > 20). Statistics provided are for only student-athletes receiving athletics aid, utilizing the four-class average 1997–2001.

1. Raw data. *Source:* Herrera & Harrison (2004)

2. *Source:* Division I statistics (NCAA (2004)

3. Hispanic-Serving Institution, 3 = associate member. This designates more than 10% Latino total enrollment except UTEP which has more 25% Latino enrollment

4. Latino population by city. *Source:* US Census (2000)

5. Statewide Minority enrollment 4-year public university. *Source: The Chronicle of Higher Education Almanac* (2005)

CHAPTER 17

Migration of the International Student-Athlete into the NCAA

KENNETH C. TEED

Abstract

Success in intercollegiate athletics has long been a race among coaches to procure the best and most capable athletes for their respective teams. The arms race that we call the NCAA is based greatly on the win-loss records of the coaches and respective teams. The inordinate pressure to justify large program costs and revenue generation leads many athletic teams to procure the best talent in their sports on a global basis rather than a regional or continental traditional method. The purpose of this book chapter is to provide the student with a more detailed insight into this complex sociological and competitive business process. Data presented here will allow the reader to better understand the factors that surround the recruitment and sociological implications that involve the acquisition of the international athlete.

Key Terms			
•	diversity	•	NCAA
•	equity in athletics	•	social justice
•	economic impact	•	student-athlete
•	international	•	tuition costs

THE BUSINESS OF INTERCOLLEGIATE SPORTS

Sport in the United States has been thought to be a $213 billion per year impact on the economy (Broughton, Lee, & Nethery, 1999). Intercollegiate sports, as a social institution, also provides the university with a large revenue influx in terms of student fees, alumni donations, and direct sport operations, to include TV revenue, to the coffers of the university and athletic department. The ability of the university to promote athletic success is important as this drives many of the vicarious brand loyalty programs and also highlights the ability to promote a winning identity.

The ability to be successful in intercollegiate athletics allows some institutions to have a more national brand. The obvious resultant effects for increase in alumni support are

Table 17.1	Athletic Department's Top 10 Revenue			
Rank	School	US Dollars	Year	Total for Year 2004
1	Texas	$47,556,281	2004	
2	Tennessee	$46,704,719	2004	
3	Ohio State	$46,242,355	2004	
4	Florida	$42,710,967	2004	
5	Georgia	$42,104,214	2004	
6	Alabama	$39,848,836	2004	
7	Notre Dame	$38,596,090	2004	
8	Michigan	$38,547,937	2004	
9	LSU	$38,381,625	2004	
10	Auburn	$37,173,943	2004	$417,866,967

Rank	School	US Dollars	Year	Total for Year 2006
1	Ohio State University	$104,700,000	2006	
2	University of Texas	$97,800,000	2006	
3	University of Virginia	$92,700,000	2006	
4	University of Michigan	$85,500,000	2006	
5	University of Florida	$82,400,000	2006	
6	University of Georgia	$79,200,000	2006	
7	University of Wisconsin	$78,900,000	2006	
8	University of Notre Dame	$78,200,000	2006	
9	Texas A&M University	$70,900,000	2006	
10	Penn State University	$70,500,000	2006	$840,800,000

Rank	School	US Dollars	Year	Total for Year 2008
1	Texas	$120,300,000	2008	
2	OSU	$118,000,000	2008	
3	Florida	$106,000,000	2008	
4	University of Michigan	$99,000,000	2008	
5	University of Wisconsin	$93,500,000	2008	
6	Pennsylvania State University	$91,600,000	2008	
7	Auburn University	$89,300,000	2008	
8	University of Alabama	$88,900,000	2008	
9	University of Tennessee	$88,700,000	2008	
10	Oklahoma State University	$88,600,000	2008	$983,900,000.00

sometimes overshadowed by the increase in student enrollment and substantial increased incoming student SAT scores (Toma & Cross, 1998; McCormick & Tinsley, 1987). Winning has demonstrable effect on the status, perception, and operation of any university. Question: Would anyone really know about Gonzaga University without the success of their basketball team? The name recognition for NCAA Sweet Sixteen and Final Four times is extremely high. Viewership and the $600 million per year sponsorship (just one sponsor: CBS Sports) allow for a more robust appreciation of the stakes of a successful athletic program.

The growth of intercollegiate sports has been rapid and expensive. Table 17.1 displays the top revenue producing athletic departments in the United States for 2004, 2006, and 2008. It is important to note that the cumulative revenue over the top 10 schools from 2004 has risen from $417 million to $840 million (2006) to $983 million (2008) in less than four years. The University of Texas football program (2007–08) brought in $72,952,397 in one year ("Top revenue," 2009). In 2008–09, The University of Texas produced a grand total of $138,459,149 in revenue with 652 athletic participants (529 unduplicated roster spots) (The Equity in Athletics Data Analysis Cutting Tool, n.d.). It is important to note that $1,322,467 was spent on recruiting.

THE GROWTH OF SPORTS: VALUATION OF SPORTS (Revenue Sports)

Every year *Forbes* undertakes a financial valuation of the top collegiate basketball programs in the US. Table 17.2 displays the 2008–09 rankings (Schwartz, 2009). Table 17.2 shows the top 10 financially ranked basketball teams in the NCAA. The top 10 teams are valued to be worth between $16.1 and $25.9 million. The operating income ranges from $9.6 to $16.4 million per annum. It is clear that this is the tip of the iceberg. This does not reflect any of the alumni contributions and support that the schools collects from other interest groups. The sale of university (bookstore) logo t-shirts, cups, hats, etc., are not always accurately reflected in valuation studies. These extra-income sources are very significant, especially during an athletic championship level season. The ability to maintain and be successful in intercollegiate athletics is a very large economic undertaking. It is critical to understand the amount of money that is being spent on intercollegiate athletics each year. This investment typically is only successful when the school's athletic teams are successful (revenue based teams). Success on the athletic field is highly dependent on the type and quality of the athletes that are recruited to participate for the school. While the recruitment costs and scholarship (talent) costs are controlled by NCAA regulation, the salary of the coach is not. The greatest increase in revenue sport expenses is the cost of the head coach and their staff (Wolverton & Lipka, 2005). The payment of $2 million per year for a head coach is not that uncommon.

Table 17.3 reflects the 2008–09 NCAA basketball Division I financial data that shows the gross revenue, expenses, profit, and margin data. A total of just over $1 billion was generated in revenue ($1,076,708,738) with $795,651,053 in expenses that translates to $281,057,685 of profit. Please note this is over *all* Division I men's basketball teams. Table 17.3 shows the top 30 teams and the Final Four teams from the 2010 NCAA men's basketball tournament. It is important to note that the top 30 teams' profit ranged from $5 million to almost $17 million, with only one school (Duke) showing a loss on $11.8 million in revenue.

It is important to understand that intercollegiate sport is not only big business, it is extremely big business. The ability of each intercollegiate athletic sport program to remain competitive depends on its ability to win. The maxim that success breeds success is still

Table 17.2 — Forbes' Top Basketball Programs

Rank	School	Value	Operating Income
1	University of North Carolina, Tar Heels	$25.9 million	$16.4 million
2	University of Kentucky, Wildcats	$25.4 million	$16 million
3	University of Louisville, Cardinals	$24.1 million	$16.6 million
4	Indiana University, Hoosiers	$22.3 million	$16.1 million
5	University of Kansas, Jayhawks	$21.7 million	$12.9 million
6	University of Arizona, Wildcats	$21 million	$12 million
7	University of Illinois, Fighting Illini	$19.6 million	$12.8 million
8	Duke University, Blue Devils	$16.8 million	$6.6 million
9	University of Maryland, Terrapins	$16.7 million	$10.8 million
10	Ohio State University, Buckeyes	$16.1 million	$9.6 million

Table 17.3 — 2008–2009 NCAA Division I Men's Basketball Team Revenues

	Revenue	Expenses	Profit	Margin
Total:	**$1,076,708,738**	**$795,651,053**	**$281,057,685**	**26.10%**
University of Louisville	25,494,904	8,625,245	16,869,659	66.20%
University of North Carolina at Chapel Hill	19,852,544	7,488,429	12,364,115	62.30%
University of Arizona	17,524,360	6,132,352	11,392,008	65.00%
Syracuse University	16,817,122	7,784,244	9,032,878	53.70%
Ohio State University-Main Campus	16,115,419	4,697,478	11,417,941	70.90%
University of Kansas	15,737,145	8,219,362	7,517,783	47.80%
Michigan State University	15,592,500	9,031,373	6,561,127	42.10%
Indiana University-Bloomington	15,173,264	6,946,942	8,226,322	54.20%
University of Wisconsin-Madison	14,900,715	5,446,455	9,454,260	63.40%
University of Kentucky	14,773,034	8,615,726	6,157,308	41.70%
The University of Texas at Austin	14,770,278	7,891,661	6,878,617	46.60%
University of Illinois at Urbana-Champaign	14,507,336	4,772,399	9,734,937	67.10%
University of Arkansas Main Campus	14,391,769	6,636,416	7,755,353	53.90%
Marquette University	13,446,395	10,306,548	3,139,847	23.40%
University of Minnesota-Twin Cities	12,956,390	5,113,345	7,843,045	60.50%
The University of Tennessee	12,576,715	5,464,911	7,111,804	56.50%
Duke University	11,842,009	13,873,859	-2,031,850	-17.20%
University of California-Los Angeles	11,775,932	6,996,960	4,778,972	40.60%
University of Pittsburgh-Pittsburgh Campus	11,100,032	5,337,512	5,762,520	51.90%
Oklahoma State University-Main Campus	11,052,293	5,166,055	5,886,238	53.30%
North Carolina State University at Raleigh	10,914,295	3,747,426	7,166,869	65.70%
University of Maryland-College Park	10,793,864	4,891,205	5,902,659	54.70%
University of Florida	10,016,431	8,107,121	1,909,310	19.10%
Georgia Institute of Technology-Main Campus	9,746,695	4,411,839	5,334,856	54.70%
Georgetown University	9,700,309	7,405,214	2,295,095	23.70%
West Virginia University	9,632,187	5,963,760	3,668,427	38.10%
University of Iowa	9,423,886	4,443,481	4,980,405	52.80%
Northwestern University	9,328,062	3,720,715	5,607,347	60.10%
Butler University (Ranked 145 in total Revenue)	1,729,756	1,729,754	2	0.00%

= Final four 2010

Coach	Conference	Prev. Rank	City	Population
Roy Williams	ACC	1	Chapel Hill, NC	489,200
Billy Gillispie	SEC	2	Lexington, KY	454,210
Rick Pitino	Big East	3	Louisville, KY	1,248,000
Tom Crean	Big Ten	tie 6th	Bloomington, IN	185,050
Bill Self	Big 12	8	Lawrence, KS	114,970
Russ Pennell	Pac-10	4	Tucson, AZ	988,390
Bruce Weber	Big Ten	tie 6th	Champaign-Urbana, IL	222,630
Mike Krzyzewski	ACC	5	Durham, NC	489,200
Gary Williams	ACC	17	Washington, DC	4,211,740
Thad Matta	Big Ten	10	Columbus, OH	1,766,930

true today as it was 50 years ago. Remaining successful in sport depends on the ability to recruit and develop quality athletic talent. The turnover in college coaching in high profile programs is directly related to a *win now* mentality. This translates into recruiting athletes that can have an immediate impact. There is strong pressure to win and win immediately.

Pressure to Win

Coaches have long lamented that their futures were inextricably tied to the mental maturity of the 18-year-old athlete. Athletic scholarship football typically allows for 85 scholarships to be awarded across four to five years of athletic participation. Each year this number is around 20–22 scholarships about which each school must make very important decisions regarding their needs and what can be obtained from the student athlete talent pool. In the US there are roughly 600,000 high school football players who participate annually. This number is drastically reduced to about 60,000 intercollegiate football players. In the NCAA big time football conferences there are 119 schools that vie for a Division I or BCS championship. The shear amount of attrition means that coaches must be very selective in the 20–22 athletes they select every year. Coaches are always mindful that their job security is directly linked to each recruiting class.

As revenues for bowl games are dictated by conference affiliation, they are also having their foundations in win-loss records. Each team to be bowl eligible must have six wins. Further, the expectations to be in the top 25 and also to beat the hated *rival* are among many of the external pressures that come to bear upon a high revenue sport coach.

Salaries of Coaches

It is no longer the case that the football or basketball coach is the highest paid university employee; they are now the highest paid employees in the state. Salaries that are approaching $4 million for a head football coach often come with very large expectations. These high revenue sports have adapted to the business practices that come with high pressure recruiting. Most, if not all, schools now employ a director of recruiting that is part of the coaching staff. The pressure to win is not only in the domain of the revenue sports now the management metrics to determine success in the nonrevenue sports is the team's record or national ranking. More and more the single greatest criterion of success is the win-loss record. All coaches understand that to consistently win you must recruit talent that you can develop or use right away.

RECRUITING DOMESTICALLY AND THE RECRUITMENT OF THE INTERNATIONAL ATHLETE

The international recruitment of labor and specialized talent is not a new phenomenon. Beaverstock (1996, 2004, 2005) and Salt (1992, 1997) provide detailed insight into the area of labor migration. Elliot and Maguire (2008); Maguire (1988, 1990, 1996); Miller, Lawrence, McKay, and Rowe (2001); and Miller, Rowe, McKay, and Lawrence (2003) provide a sound foundation to better understand the transnational recruitment of athletes. It is John Bale who provides the most seminal work on international student athlete recruitment. Bale's (1991) book entitled the *Brawn Drain* is the pioneering landmark study of the recruitment of international athletes to the NCAA (US). Bale's work details the geographic and sociological understanding of how and why foreign student athletes participate in US universities (Bale, 2004; Bale & Maguire, 1994; Bale & Sang, 1996). Bale

highlights the need for foreign athletes. Vern Wolfe (collegiate track coach) said "In general when you recruit in the United States you're looking for an athlete you can develop. If you're bringing in a foreign runner you look for someone who can help right away" (Bale, 1991, p. 98). Among many of the topics that Bale brings to the table, his explanation of the dimensions of global recruiting (Chapter 3) and recruiting tactics and the migration decision (Chapter 5) provide a unique and very valuable insight in the recruitment of the international athlete to the NCAA. It is important to understand how coaches view talent recruitment (at the NCAA level) at the regional, national, and international level.

Recruiting the Talent Pool Regionally

The ability to maintain a successful athletic program is predicated on the recruitment of high level athletic talent, and successful coaches that work as part of a very effective management team to procure those blue chippers who will increase their chances of winning. Very sophisticated models and data are now available for coaches to review. Every state has a list of their Top 20 players as well as All-Star teams that are well advertised. Historically, football and basketball programs always started with "home cooking" or local athletes to ensure a competitive team. The ability to develop local or intra state football athletes was and still is a mandate

Gilbert Tuhabonye left his native country of Burundi and later became an NCAA Division II All-American runner at Abilene Christian University. Courtesy of Holly Reed Photography

to provide summer camps and the development of a relationship with the regional football coaches. In fact, many coaches were almost duty bound to offer the best player in the state a scholarship regardless of their perception about the viability of the student-athlete due to the pressure that surrounds the home town crowd. As college sports have increased, many of these local products are now susceptible to the allures of more media driven athletic teams. It has been long suggested that Duke University does not rebuild, they re-load when it comes to recruiting the best basketball talent in the country. It has been suggested that most major top level/tier schools have deemphasized regional recruiting. It is still very much part of the community relations with the town, but resource limitations on money and scholarships tend to suggest that coaches recruit from the top players in the state or nation.

Recruiting the Talent Pool Nationally

The sign that a high revenue sport has reached the upper echelons of the NCAA indicates a movement away from traditional regional of in-state recruitment to a more national or football/basketball rich talent pool. The advancement of high school level combines and talent evaluation services that rank and order high school prospects in all major and some nonrevenue sports has become common place in the NCAA Division I intercollegiate athletic department(s). The annual competition for 20–25 football and perhaps 3–4 basketball athletes has created a recruiting frenzy at the Division I level. Extensive regulations on travel and contact with potential athletic talent have been created by the NCAA. In fact, every Division I major sport recruiter must complete a Compliance exam in order to be eligible to recruit. The drive to locate and sign quality nationally ranked players has led some coaches to pursue alternative avenues for talent. International level sport talent is located in other countries have provided a fertile field to recruit athletic talent to participate at the highest levels of sport in the US.

Recruiting the Talent Pool Internationally

International student athlete recruitment is not a new idea. In fact there were 66 Canadians playing Division I men's basketball in 2010 (Berman, 2010). The 2010 men's basketball championship featured 68 players from 33 countries. Out of a field of 65 teams, 39 teams had at least one foreign player; Canada (11) and Australia (7) had the most players in the men's tournament (Hein, 2010). It is evident that top quality talent can be found across the globe that can compete at the highest levels. The ability to seek out and recruit this talent is not without pitfalls and obstacles. Many people in the coaching ranks have stated that the recruitment of foreign players is becoming more and more a

Advantages	Disadvantages
Inexpensive	Distance (not always face to face)
Athlete(s) may be older	Be perceived as not taking US students
More experience	Language problems
Talent level is high due to excess of athlete(s)	Cultural mores
May have higher or more rigorous education	Perception of US culture

Although this list is not exhaustive or conclusive, it does highlight a number of salient issues that are involved in the recruitment of international athletes.

bureaucratic process. Beyond language barriers there are academic equivalency issues and accreditation translation considerations. Bale, in his work, cites a number of recruiting tactics, and he also expands upon the migration (athletic) decision. The ability for a NCAA coach to recruit foreign players is perceived to be easier or less expensive than competing against other schools in the US. The development of a pipeline has been found to be the most successful route to garner the best international players. The ability to foster a relationship with the athlete's coach and former athletes (non-US) that are from that country appear to be a very successful method of acquiring athletes.

NCAA Data 2007–2008

A tally of all the foreign student athletes and US athletes who have participated in the NCAA for the academic year 2007–2008 is found in Table 17.4. There were a total of 432,255 athletes who competed across the three divisions of the NCAA. Foreign athletes represented 16,440 (415,815 US athletes) for a total of 3.80% of all athletes in the NCAA. It is important to note that 60% of all foreign athletes competed in Division I. This was

Table 17.4   Foreign and US Athlete Participants in the NCAA from 2007–2008

2007–08 Student-Athlete Race/Ethnicity Estimated Frequencies of Nonresident Aliens

Sport	Division I Men	Division I Women	Division II Men	Division II Women	Division III Men	Division III Women	Total Men	Total Women
Archery	0	0	0	0	0	0	0	0
Badminton	0	0	0	0	0	5	0	5
Baseball	138	N/A	147	N/A	36	N/A	321	N/A
Basketball	380	294	222	133	104	49	706	476
Bowling	0	5	0	3	0	0	0	8
Cross Country	273	273	114	98	65	53	452	424
Equestrian	0	7	0	1	0	2	0	10
Fencing	20	30	5	3	7	6	32	39
Field Hockey	N/A	128	N/A	7	N/A	9	N/A	144
Football	145	N/A	59	N/A	26	N/A	230	N/A
Golf	345	302	218	83	42	11	605	396
Gymnastics	9	51	0	1	0	0	9	52
Ice Hockey	504	256	8	0	388	141	900	397
Lacrosse	60	30	44	7	34	36	138	73
Rifle	0	1	2	0	0	0	2	1
Rowing	0	202	0	19	0	12	0	233
Rugby	0	0	0	0	1	3	1	3
Sailing	2	0	0	0	2	8	4	8
Skiing	41	41	12	9	4	6	57	56
Soccer	688	399	765	300	462	91	1,915	790
Softball	N/A	83	N/A	63	N/A	42	N/A	188
Squash	20	16	0	0	45	36	65	52
Swimming/Diving	301	283	89	69	42	29	432	381
Sync. Swimming	N/A	9	N/A	2	N/A	1	N/A	12
Team Handball	0	0	0	0	0	0	0	0
Tennis	1,013	992	511	370	123	102	1,647	1,464
Track, Indoor	460	689	101	89	67	40	628	818
Track, Outdoor	495	687	125	110	79	47	699	844
Volleyball	22	279	8	169	42	56	72	504
Water Polo	30	34	12	3	1	0	43	37
Wrestling	5	N/A	58	N/A	4	N/A	67	N/A
Total	4,951	5,091	2,500	1,539	1,574	785	9,025	7,415

2007–08 Student-Athlete Race/Ethnicity Estimated Frequencies of US Citizens

Sport	Division I Men	Division I Women	Division II Men	Division II Women	Division III Men	Division III Women	Total Men	Total Women
Archery	0	12	0	0	0	0	0	12
Badminton	0	0	0	0	0	22	0	20
Baseball	10,195	N/A	8,601	0	11,588	N/A	29,908	N/A
Basketball	5,119	4,727	4,768	4,291	7,194	6,251	16,990	15,130
Bowling	10	245	0	146	0	71	10	460
Cross Country	4,453	5,311	2,985	3,054	5,124	5,126	12,444	13,438
Equestrian	0	684	0	184	5	520	5	1386
Fencing	352	373	42	46	231	236	625	650
Field Hockey	N/A	1,791	0	564	N/A	3,278	N/A	5,622
Football	25,658	N/A	15,764	0	22,812	N/A	63,720	N/A
Golf	2,960	2,047	2,278	974	3,064	1,087	8,272	4,081
Gymnastics	319	1,070	0	92	34	268	353	1,423
Ice Hockey	1,632	837	218	52	2,156	1,007	3,999	1,890
Lacrosse	2,507	2,317	1,258	919	5,134	3,594	8,881	6,792
Rifle	133	130	19	17	56	29	207	173
Rowing	1,273	5,239	26	465	964	1,360	2,257	7,033
Rugby	0	26	0	45	79	110	79	179
Sailing	210	N/A	18	0	300	N/A	528	N/A
Skiing	210	236	100	87	257	224	566	547
Soccer	5,556	7,955	4,801	5,344	10,660	9,383	20,880	22,524
Softball	N/A	5,285	0	4,905	N/A	6,964	N/A	17,003
Squash	153	130	0	0	301	262	453	389
Swimming/Diving	3,670	5,155	1,080	1,392	3,632	4,691	8,351	11,193
Sync. Swimming	N/A	62	0	12	N/A	30	N/A	104
Team Handball	0	0	0	0	0	0	0	0
Tennis	2,680	2,891	1,619	2,004	3,533	3,825	7,797	8,651
Track, Indoor	9,231	10,944	3,772	3,504	7,339	5,965	20,269	20,324
Track, Outdoor	10,266	11,230	5,052	4,451	8,161	6,682	23,389	22,253
Volleyball	456	4,650	238	4,020	604	6,045	1,280	14,558
Water Polo	575	670	75	184	269	301	909	1,149
Wrestling	2,646	N/A	1,318	0	2,344	N/A	6,283	N/A
Total	90,264	74,017	54,032	36,752	95,841	67,331	238,831	176,984

Table 17.5 Foreign and US Athlete Participants in the NCAA from 2007–2008

Type of Athlete	Count	Percentage
Total Non Resident Athletes	16,440	3.8
Total US Athletes	415,815	96.2
Total Athletes	432,255	100

Table 17.6 Non-US Athletes Over All Three NCAA Divisions by Gender

	Division I Men	Division I Women	Division II Men	Division II Women	Division III Men	Division III Women	Total Men	Total Women
Total	4,951	5,091	2,500	1,539	1,574	785	9,025	7,415	16,440

Table 17.6	Distribution of Foreign Players by Division (NCAA)
Division	**Percentage of All Foreign Players**
Division I	61.1
Division II	24.6
Division III	14.3

Table 17.8	Breakdown of Foreign Athletes by Gender
Gender	**Percentage**
Male	54.8
Female	45.2

followed by 24.56% in Division II and 14.34% in Division III. Gender equality is closest at the Division I level with more women recruited than men. Overall men represent 54.8% and women account for 45.2% of all foreign athletes that participate in the NCAA. Interestingly, in cross-country, fencing, swimming-diving, tennis, outdoor track, and volleyball women are very equal to and in some cases far surpass the recruitment of men overall. There appears to be a distinct gender and division pattern for international athletes.

Percentage of Foreign Athletes by NCAA Sport

Table 17.9 retains an accounting of all NCAA athletes by citizenship and by sport. Tennis (3,111), soccer (2,705), outdoor track and field (1,543), indoor track & field (1,446), ice hockey (1,297), and golf (1,001) account for 75% of *all* recruited foreign athletes. These sports seem to foster the greatest magnitude or interest for the recruitment of foreign athletes. An analysis of the ratio of foreign players to US players by sport revealed that ice hockey (18.05), tennis (15.91), squash (12.20), synchronized swimming (10.34), skiing (9.22), golf (7.50), soccer (5.87), fencing (5.27), swimming-diving (10.34), and water polo (3.74) had the greatest percentage of foreign to US athletes. It would appear that this clustering of foreign athletes in each sport would indicate a sport-specific pipeline of athletes that would be identifiable by their nationality. Further research as to country and affiliation would provide more specific data on the migratory pattern.

Economic Costs of Athletic Scholarships

The economic costs of providing NCAA scholarships to 3.8/4.0% of the NCAA athletes depend on a number of factors. The type of school that athletes attend, such as private school versus public school, will determine tuition and other academic costs. Typically a NCAA scholarship includes tuition, room and board plus books/fees. Based on the type of academic program and institution the tuition/fee costs will vary greatly. As reported by the College Board, the 2009–2010 average tuition for public universities was $15,213 for in-state and $26,741 for out-of-state tuition. Private school tuition was $35,636. This amount includes tuition, room and board; it does not include books or other fees. Presented in Table 17.9 are the public in-state, public out-of-state and private school data. Costs for foreign athletes can range from $250 million to $585 million US dollars per year. US athletic scholarships can cost between $6 to $14 billion US dollars annually. (*Please note: Not all NCAA athletes are on paid scholarship and these numbers are a rough order of magnitude*)

A review of just two sports, ice hockey and tennis, that have the two highest levels of foreign athletes 18.05% and 15.91%, respectively, account, for between (approximately) $65 to $156 million tuition, room, and board. This does not account for facility, coaching and other overhead costs that are underwritten by the resident school. It is very in-

Table 17.9		Distribution of Foreign Athletes by Sport and Cost of Tuition/Room and Board					

Total Non-US Tuition	Total US Tuition	Sport	% Non-US to US	Rank	$15,213 In-State Tuition	$26,741 Out-of-State Tuition	$35,636 Private School
3,111	16,448	Tennis	15.91	3	$47,327,643	$83,191,251	$110,863,596
2,705	43,404	Soccer	5.87	8	$41,151,165	$72,334,405	$96,395,380
1,543	45,642	Track, Outdoor	3.27	17	$23,473,659	$41,261,363	$54,986,348
1,446	40,593	Track, Indoor	3.44	14	$21,997,998	$38,667,486	$51,529,656
1,297	5,889	Ice Hockey	18.05	2	$19,731,261	$34,683,077	$46,219,892
1,182	32,120	Basketball	3.55	12	$17,981,766	$31,607,862	$42,121,752
1,001	12,353	Golf	7.50	7	$15,228,213	$26,767,741	$35,671,636
876	25,882	Cross Country	3.27	16	$13,326,588	$23,425,116	$31,217,136
813	19,544	Swimming/Diving	3.99	10	$12,368,169	$21,740,433	$28,972,068
576	15,838	Volleyball	3.51	13	$8,762,688	$15,402,816	$20,526,336
321	29,908	Baseball	1.06	25	$4,883,373	$8,583,861	$11,439,156
233	9,290	Rowing	2.45	19	$3,544,629	$6,230,653	$8,303,188
230	63,720	Football	0.36	29	$3,498,990	$6,150,430	$8,196,280
211	15,673	Lacrosse	1.33	23	$3,209,943	$5,642,351	$7,519,196
188	17,003	Softball	1.09	24	$2,860,044	$5,027,308	$6,699,568
144	5,622	Field Hockey	2.50	18	$2,190,672	$3,850,704	$5,131,584
117	842	Squash	12.20	4	$1,779,921	$3,128,697	$4,169,412
113	1,113	Skiing	9.22	6	$1,719,069	$3,021,733	$4,026,868
80	2,058	Water Polo	3.74	11	$1,217,040	$2,139,280	$2,850,880
71	1,275	Fencing	5.27	9	$1,080,123	$1,898,611	$2,530,156
67	6,283	Wrestling	1.06	26	$1,019,271	$1,791,647	$2,387,612
61	1,776	Gymnastics	3.32	15	$927,993	$1,631,201	$2,173,796
12	104	Sync. Swimming	10.34	5	$182,556	$320,892	$427,632
12	528	Sailing	2.22	20	$182,556	$320,892	$427,632
10	1,391	Equestrian	0.71	28	$152,130	$267,410	$356,360
8	470	Bowling	1.67	21	$121,704	$213,928	$285,088
5	20	Badminton	20.00	1	$76,065	$133,705	$178,180
4	258	Rugby	1.53	22	$60,852	$106,964	$142,544
3	380	Rifle	0.78	27	$45,639	$80,223	$106,908
0	12	Archery	0.00		$0	$0	$0
0	0	Team Handball	0.00		$0	$0	$0
16,440	415,815	Total	0.00		$250,101,720	$439,622,040	**$585,855,840**

Table 17.10		Summary Table of US vs. Foreign Athletes' Economic Costs		

Type	Athletes	In-State Tuition/ Room and Board	Out-of-State Tuition/ Room and Board	Private School Tuition/ Room and Board
		$15,213	$26,741	$35,636
Foreign	16,440	$250,101,720	$439,622,040	$585,855,840
US	415,815	$6,325,793,595	$11,119,308,915	$14,817,983,340

teresting that only 230 foreign athletes are recruited for men's football as compared to 63,720 US athletes. The economic cost for foreign players is very little considering the revenue generation that accompanies the Division I Bowl Championship Series payout schedule. The economics of sports that do not generate a large amount of money (non-revenue) may be in the realm of the non-US athlete. Nationalism and protectionism concerns aside, the traditional American sports of baseball, basketball, and football do not come close to the percentage of US to foreign athletes. Cultural relevancy and economics appear to be aligned.

FURTHER RESEARCH

It would be valuable to collect data on which countries come to the US for opportunities to participate in NCAA athletics. An analysis of the trend would more than likely develop a better understanding of the "pipeline" that creates avenues of migration to the US. It would be mutually advantageous to the NCAA and foreign-born players to better understand the multi-cultural racial dynamics that come into play when different races seek to achieve and compete in their respective sport. Tracking length of stay and measuring the developmental process that differing racial groups experience would be beneficial study projects. A more complete understanding of how people assimilate and accommodate in athletics could provide far-reaching data that could be used to advantage. Finally, it would be valuable to measure US students who go to school and/or compete abroad. The comparison of the US experience as a minority in other cultures would bear much fruit.

CONCLUSION

International student athletics and their migration to the NCAA is a very difficult and complex subject area. The sport business of the NCAA is a very large and complex model that is predicated on one simple fact: Winning is profitable and competing is very expensive. The ability to be competitive at any level of sport is dependent on quality athletic performance. The notion of developing student athletes from a single geographical region with volunteer or low paid professionals is a thing of the past. The win now culture is prevalent and pervasive in the NCAA. The ability for intercollegiate athletic programs to be successful immediately is very financially important. The race to procure the best coaches and athletes is an ongoing off the field battle ground. Perception of victory and ultimately overall success is predicated on the foundational ability to recruit top quality athletic talent. International athletic talent has historically been one way to be successful in intercollegiate athletics.

STUDY QUESTIONS

1. How has the growth of NCAA sports affected the influx of international athletes?

2. How would you describe the growth of the NCAA sport business model? Please refer to all contributory factors. How does this contribute or not contribute to a more diverse student body?

3. What is the *Pressure to win* Why is this important? How is this different than any other profession or industry? What makes college sports special as a business? As a profession? As a field for advancement?

4. How much does the cost of scholarships impact your decision about the value of international athletes? Is it fair for the NCAA and member schools to give money to non-US student athletes?

5. Is the economic impact really that great? What do you think is an appropriate amount?

6. Should the NCAA and its member schools increase the level and number of international athletes? Would this make the US more competitive in other Olympic sports?

SUGGESTED READINGS

Bale, J. (1991). *The brawn drain: Foreign student-athletes in American universities.* Urbana, IL: University of Illinois Press.

Bale, J. (2004). Three geographies of Africa footballer migration: Patterns, problems and postcoloniality. In G. Armstrong & R. Giulianotti (Eds.), *Football in Africa: Conflict, conciliation and community* (pp. 229–246). Basingstoke, UK: Palgrave Macmillian.

Elliot, R., & Maguire, J. (2008). "Getting caught in the net": Examining the recruitment of Canadian players in British professional ice hockey. *Journal of Sport and Social Issues, 32*(2), 158–176.

McGovern, P. (2002). Globalization or internationalization? Foreign footballers in the English league, 1946–95. *Sociology, 36*(1), 23–42.

REFERENCES

Bale, J. (1991). *The brawn drain: Foreign student-athletes in American universities.* Urbana, IL: University of Illinois Press.

Bale, J. (2004). Three geographies of Africa footballer migration: Patterns, problems and postcoloniality. In G. Armstrong & R. Giulianotti (Eds.), *Football in Africa: Conflict, conciliation and community* (pp. 229–246). Basingstoke, UK: Palgrave Macmillian.

Bale, J., & Maguire, J. (Eds.). (1994). *The global sports arena: Athletic talent migration in an interdependent world.* London, UK: Frank Cass.

Bale, J., & Sang, J. (1996). *Kenyan running: Movement culture, geography and global change.* London, UK: Frank Cass.

Beaverstock, J. V. (1996). Subcontracting the accountant! Professional Labour markets, migration, and organisational networks in the global accountancy industry. *Environment & Planning A., 28*, 303–326.

Beaverstock, J. V. (2004). "Managing across borders": Knowledge management and expatriation in professional service legal firms. *Journal of Economic Geography, 4*, 157–179.

Beaverstock, J. V. (2005). Transnational elites in the city: British highly skilled inter-company transferees in New York City's financial district. *Journal of Ethnic and Migration Studies, 31*(2), 245–268.

Berman, Z. (2010, March 21). At the top of their game north of the border. *The Washington Post*, D5.

Broughton, D., Lee, J., & Nethery, R. (1999). The answer: $213 billion. *Street & Smith's SportsBusiness Journal, 2*(35), 23–29.

Elliot, R., & Maguire, J. (2008). "Getting caught in the net": Examining the recruitment of Canadian players in British professional ice hockey. *Journal of Sport and Social Issues, 32*(2), 158–176.

The Equity in Athletics Data Analysis Cutting Tool. (n.d.). Department of Education. Retrieved from http://ope.ed.gov/athletics/

Hein, D. (2010). *International players in 2010 NCAAs— East college basketball event rich in Europeans, Africans.* Retrieved from http://news.suite101.com/article.cfm/international-players-in-2010-ncaas—-east-a213513

Maguire, J. (1988). The commercialization of English elite basketball 1972–1988: A figurational perspective. *International Review for the Sociology of Sport, 23*(4), 305–322.

Maguire, J. (1990). More than a sporting touchdown: The making of American football in England 1982–1990. *Sociology of Sport Journal, 7*(3), 213–237.

Maguire, J. (1996). Blade runners: Canadian migrants, ice hockey and the global sports process. *Journal of Sport and Social Issues, 21*(3), 335–360.

McCormick, R. E., & Tinsley, M. (1987). Athletics versus academics? Evidence from SAT scores. *The Journal of Political Economy, 95*(5), 1103–1116

McGovern, P. (2002). Globalization or internationalization? Foreign footballers in the English league, 1946–95, *Sociology, 36*(1), 23–42.

Miller, T., Lawrence , G., McKay, J., & Rowe, D. (2001). *Globalization and sport.* London: Sage.

Miller, T., Rowe, D., McKay, J., & Lawrence, G. (2003). The over-production of US sports and the new international division of cultural labour. *International Review for the Sociology of Sport, 38*(4), 427–440.

Salt, J. (1992). Migration processes among the highly skilled in Europe. *International Migration Review, 26*, 484–505.

Salt, J. (1997). *International movements of the highly skilled*. Paris: OECD, International Migration Unit Occasional Paper Number 3.

Schwartz, P. (2010). *Most valuable college basketball teams*. Retrieved from http://www.forbes.com/2010/03/16/most-valuable-college-basketball-teams-business-sports-college-basketball.html

Toma, J. D., & Cross, M. E. (1998). Intercollegiate athletics and student college choice: Exploring the impact of championship seasons on undergraduate applications. *Research in Higher Education, 39*(6), 633–661

Top revenue producers in college athletics. (2009, June 15). *Street & Smith's SportsBusiness Journal*. Retrieved from http://www.sportsbusinessdaily.com/Journal/Issues/2009/06/20090615/SBJ-In-Depth/Top-Revenue-Producers-In-College-Athletics.aspx

Wolverton, B., & Lipka, S. (2005, December 28). Knight commission to fight high salaries and recruiting pressures. *The Chronicle of Higher Education*, A.28

Conclusion
The African American College Sport Experiences: Beyond Race, Gender, and Social Class

DANA BROOKS and RONALD ALTHOUSE

"Freedom is never voluntarily given by the oppressor. It must be demanded by the oppressed."

—Martin Luther King, Jr.

The third edition of *Racism in College Athletics* expands and broadens the discussion of racism, exploitation, and other forms of social injustice in college athletics as articulated in the first two editions. Previous *Racism in College Athletics* texts (1993, 2000) discussed a wide range of topics including an historical analysis of racism in college athletics, African American student-athlete recruitment and retention inequality in the form of different graduation rates, racial imbalance in coaching and managerial positions, the intersection of racism and sexism, and an analysis of racism and prospects for change.

This new edition provides the reader with a critique and discussion about the concepts of diversity, power, privilege, multiculturalism, and globalization of college athletics and its effect on the African American college sport experiences. Social and historical analysis of the literature indicate political, social, and economic factors still have a considerable impact on the playing and experiences (on and off the field) of African American student-athletes (males and females).

We include discussion about the intersection of hip hop culture and sports, the historical contributions of historically Black colleges and universities (HBCUs), sport contributions of community and junior colleges to the African American experience, and a look at the impact of foreign student-athletes on college campuses. As editors, we benefitted from the conviction among these contributing scholars that it is still appropriate to look at the problems found in sports for African Americans (men and women) and other ethnic minorities who participate at various levels of NCAA college sports.

Such conviction is ever present in Lumpkin's, "Critical Events: Historical Overview of Minorities (Men and Women) in College Sports" (Chapter 1). Her project was framed by three objectives: first, why few African American athletes initially were allowed to compete at some predominantly White colleges; second, how African American athletes were treated on predominantly White college campuses over time, and specifically how this treatment has changed; and third, to acquire an understanding of the notable achievements of African Americans in football, basketball, and track and field, despite the disparate treatment they had to endure.

Readers are invited to learn about the struggles and barriers that African American athletes (males and females) had to endure in order to gain access to college and professional sports. The author showed us the social, political, and economic conditions that impacted these HBCU campuses and how, in spite of conditions, these schools provided many African American athletes with quality education and, in some cases, with access to outstanding athletic opportunities. The HBCUs rallied community support, employed nurturing and caring faculty, and offered quality educational experiences across the many academic disciplines.

In spite of the academic and athletic accomplishments of the men and women competing at HBCUs, particularly from 1900–1954 during America's "separate but equal" era of legalized oppression, Lumpkin notes that, "besides being denied opportunities to play, African American athletes had to deal with other discriminatory practices too." Among the practices noted: (1) exclusion from All-American football status, (2) "gentleman's agreements," (3) African American exclusion from postgame social activities following athletic competitions, and (4) racial profanity on and off the playing fields.

Lumpkin takes time to chronicle the contributions of African Americans during the Olympic Games of this time period. She highlights some remarkable achievements of George Poage (1904 Olympian and the first African American to win an Olympic medal), John Taylor (1908 Olympic games), William Hubbard (1924 Olympics), Eddie Tolan (1932 Olympics), Ralph Metcalfe (1932, 1936 Olympics), and Jesse Owens (1936 Olympics—four gold medals). Of equal importance, she hails the contributions of African American women to track and field, and particularly the unique role that HBCUs played in providing women with the opportunity to participate in college athletics when White America's colleges failed them entirely.

From 1946–1965, the number of African Americans playing college sports grew rapidly. However, with increased participation, Lumpkin notes, came persistent discrimination in the form of Jim Crow laws, which galvanized an unwillingness among Southern states to comply with the 1954 Supreme Court ruling of *Brown v. Board*. This oppression prompted refusal by many Southern college athletic teams to compete against integrated college teams from the North, promoted racial stereotyping, and certainly contributed to an absence of African American college head coaches and administrators.

The 1960s and 1970s saw outright opposition from Black student-athlete's in their fight for civil rights and expressed their desire to experience academic success in college and in the marketplace. Racial conflict and turmoil manifested itself on college campus across the country, so that virtually any outstanding athletic achievements during this period must be understood in the context of a racially divided America. Lumpkin writes, "Illustrations of the disparate treatment experienced by African Americans attending predominantly Caucasian institutions have included poor academic support, academic marginalization, harsh discipline, positional stacking based on speed, quickness, and jumping ability, quotas, and social segregation." Attention was focused on the extent to which African Americans (men and women) were afforded equal outcome of educational and sporting experiences on the college campus.

Looking toward the future, the chapter suggests that in an age of increasing sports commercialization, those key powers coming together to forge big-time college sports, namely the NCAA and college officials, must address the academic issues facing all student-athletes on the college campuses, and any proposed changes in policies governing NCAA college athletes must be based on the proposition of the student-athlete concept. College athletics has become a business, such that athletes are perceived by many merely as a commodity. Thus, with this in mind, what can be done to reduce the perceived exploitation of African American student-athletes? What can be done to enhance the educational experiences of student-athletes? And how do we structure college athletics to provide greater opportunities for African Americans to achieve head coaching, administrative, and other leadership roles in college athletics?

"Historically Black colleges and universities' Athletics and Sport Programs: Historical Overview, Evaluations, and Affiliations" (Chapter 2), and "The Journey of the Black Athlete on the HBCU Playing Field" (Chapter 3), written by Hodge, Collins, and Bennett III, give us an appreciation of Black student-athletes' experiences on HBCUs campuses. HBCUs gave us fields of elite, talented African American student-athletes (men and women) in football (e.g., Bob Hayes, Florida A&M University; Steve McNair, Alcorn State University), basketball (e.g., Earl Monroe, Winston-Salem State University), and track and field (e.g., Wilma Rudolph, Tennessee State University). These talented HBCUs student-athletes have gone on to distinguish themselves professionally, including sports.

Chapter 3 describes in some detail the sporting experience of African American student-athletes and, especially, their experiences on HBCU campuses as compared to their White counterparts. One of the landmark and comprehensive studies conducted in 1989 (AIR) compared the experiences of Black and White student-athletes (across various NCAA levels and HBCUs) and found notable differences between the various groups in their ACT/SAT scores, high school GPA, lack of control of their lives, and experiences of racial isolation. As our authors updated this research they also found that Black student-athletes continue to have negative social and educational experiences as compared to their White counter parts.

In an effort to more fully explore the social experiences of Black student-athletes, the authors employ the critical race theory, race-based stereotypes, perception about fairness, consequences of racial policies and race neutrality, racial diversity, and racial identity. Accordingly, HBCUs are facing some very important challenges that may have an effect on the future experiences of Black men and women who attend these institutions. HBCUs must continue to offer a socially and culturally rich environment, thus providing a climate for athletic and academic success. HBCUs should remain a portal by which Black high school boys and girls gain access to higher education. Similarly, HBCUs provided an arena by which student-athletes are afforded the opportunity to play sports at the college level, recognizing that not all participants will pursue a professional sports career.

Data supports that both HBCUs and all NCAA level institutions need to work harder to increase student-athlete graduation rates. Other issues that generate perennial candidates for consideration are recent NCAA policies and guidelines (i.e., specifically, academic performance and graduation success rates); the unique mission and educational role of HBCUs; uneven support of Title IX compliance and gender equity; and, also accreditation standards.

The authors realized America's financial crisis has had an impact on the athletic programs located on HBCUs campuses, but tight-fisted budgets and longtime fiscal austerity is nothing new for many HBCUs. Negative impact has included the inability to hire and retain high paid coaches, to build and renovate athletic facilities, and to purchase needed equipment, or all of these in some cases. In an attempt to guarantee new sources of revenue, HBCUs are scheduling athletic events with more predominantly white institutions and increasing marketing and promotion efforts.

The question was asked, "Why are so many students failing to complete their educational journey at many HBCUs?" Socio-cultural factors such as family stability and pre-college academic preparation seem to be strong predictors for Black male athletes. The authors write, and we concur, that "largely absent from the existing research base are studies that persistently evaluate the academic and social experiences and graduation rates with respect to Black student-athletes (men and women) at historically Black institutions of higher education."

Hodges et.al., arguably claim the second Morrill Act (1890) was the genesis of the growth of HBCUs in America (Chapter 2). Today, the majority of the HBCUs are located in America's southern states. These historians focus on the development of sports on various HBCUs campuses, briefing us on the nature of racism imposed on sport programs within HBCUs' segregated competition. Realize that it took the NCAA at least a decade after the *Brown v. Board* decision to accept HBCU member institutions, but once it did, the exodus of Black athletes to predominantly White institutions appears to have contributed to the drain of athletes (i.e., access to scholarships, access to better facilities, college prominence/name visibility for the student-athletes).

At its peak, football comprised almost 47% of all male student-athletes on HBCU campuses, while the highest percentage of female student-athletes participated in track and field (indoor/outdoor—29%) and basketball (almost 24%). Title IX has had an effect on athletic participation for females, and especially, today, continues to challenge compliance with regard to Title IX's controversial proportionality standards. Finally, the inconsistent level of competition as well as the variable quality of performance is evident from the fragmented array of conferences and divisions that are unequal partners, pegging their weaknesses and affecting conference statuses.

"The Transformation and Rise of the African American College Coach" by Tucker, Hall, and Johnson begins on the campuses of HBCUs tracking the careers of such coaches as Eddie Robinson, Arnett Mumford, Clarence "Big House" Gaines, and Jake Gaither whose legendary careers gained notoriety and fame for their coaching prowess and leadership, and gives tribute to the stellar teaching contributions of John McLendon (three-time NAIA Coach of the Year) and Edwin Bancroft Henderson (Civil Rights Advocate and "Father of Black Basketball"). Still, amidst these achievers, Tucker et al. must insist that the struggle for social justice and inclusion in the college sports marketplace is still a dream deferred for most coaches (men and women) of color.

Black coaches were faced with awesome barriers as they attempted to integrate the ranks of predominately White college campuses. In order to critique the NCAA member institutions' hiring and retention practices relative to NCAA college coaches and administrative positions, Tucker et.al., discuss coaching roles and coaching mobility patterns of African American coaches. Building on the work of Mintzberg (1973), the chapter focuses discussion on three roles of effective sport administrators: informational (spokesperson), interpersonal (leader), and decision-maker (resource allocator). Additionally, the authors believe it is also important to understand the unique role and duties of Black coaches as father figures, that is, as a mentor and spiritual guide. Previous research of coaching mobility patterns suggests relevance of factors such as racism, sexism, level of education, previous head coaching experience, effect of stacking, and leadership attributes (Brooks & Althouse, 1996). Brooks and Althouse's (2000) examination of coaching models and career mobility patterns found variables such as organizational effectiveness, athletic program success, occupational subcultures, and fit were also tied to the mobility process.

For Tucker and colleagues, "coaching mobility largely depends upon networking," and it's not difficult to agree with them that access to "network ties" is an important component to gaining access and upward mobility in the marketplace. However, the question is not how do African Americans develop old boy or old gal recruiting networks, but rather that more opportunities are given to minorities. In the current workplace environment promoting the values of diversity may and can be an effective way of combating and promoting discrimination in intercollegiate athletics.

There still appear to be many challenges facing African American (males and females) as they pursue head college coaching careers. The social justice advocacy work of the Black Coaches & Administrators (BCA; formerly the Black Coaches Association) and the dedication of Richard Lapchick continue to shed light of inequality of hiring practices still in existence on college campuses. Tucker and colleagues suggest colleges may want to implement the Rooney Rule, thus requiring colleges to interview at least one minority candidate when filling a head coaching position. We believe the idea is worthy of additional discussion and debate. This is particularly noteworthy given the more recent practice of some NCAA institutions to adopt the *coach-in-waiting* concept, thus by-passing the traditional search and screen process for new hires.

The focus of the essays in Section II is on recruitment, retention, and NCAA rules and regulations with regard to minorities. For more than a century, the partnership between academia and athletics has been neither healthy nor stable. In "NCAA Academic Regulations: Impact on Participation Rates for African American Males" (Chapter 5), Martin, Gragg, and Kramer II tackled the historical debate about the relationship between academics and athletics on the college campus. Critics have argued that intercollegiate sport had had a negative effect on academic performance and has basically corrupted higher education. Others have argued that the notion of student-athlete is a contradiction and, in fact, implies African American male athletes who enter the college rank with lower entrance skills (i.e., score of standardized test, lower GPA) than their White counterparts; thus, they have a greater possibility of not graduating with their classes.

Historically, the leadership of the NCAA along with other higher education associations has made attempts to regulate academic priorities that have often have created barriers particularly for the successes of African American student athletes. By the 1970s there was a public outcry for more education accountability of the nation's college athletic programs. The demand for institutional accountability led the NCAA to pass Proposition 48, launching a succession of policies to assure academic integrity and standards at the college level.

Martin and colleagues remind the readers of the academic and physical prowess of early African American student-athletes: William Henry Lewis (Amherst College) and Paul Robeson (Rutgers University). Lewis and Robeson represent the ideal balance between academics and athletics to the extent both individuals were able to endure the social conditions of the day, yet remained committed to pursuing their academic goals.

More than ever before, the African American male college athlete is inundated with images of a highly commercial, profitable college scholarship and professional sport contract. The entrance to college became a means to professional sports, rather than access to a quality education. The authors of this chapter point out that since professional sport integration, the notion of academic importance within the African American community has deteriorated. Martin and colleagues warn parents and college administrators that they must fight against what is perceived as a climate of *anti-intellectualism*, racial stereotypes regarding the academic performance of African American student-athletes.

The historical evolution of freshman NCAA eligibility standards reaffirms the belief of academic performance differences between student-athletes and nonathlete students. The road to academic reform dates to the 1944 Sanity Code (elimination of athletic scholarships). The 1.6 Rule (1965) was another earlier attempt to predict academic success based on a predicted grade point average. In 1982, Proposition 48 was established to have uniform standardization of entrance standards, emphasizing grade point average (GPAs and SAT scores) to project future postsecondary academic success.

Proposition 48 met with opposition; its critics claimed the purpose of the legislation was to reduce the number of African American college student-athletes. While that may not have been the intent of Proposition 48, African American male athletes were often declared ineligible to participate. Initially, Proposition 48 also had a negative impact on African Americans who attended HBCUs. Thus, later, Proposition 16 was offered as a means to address the voiced concerns. The unique nature of Proposition 16 provided the student-athlete with a sliding-scale whereby a student-athlete could offset a low SAT/ACT score with a higher GPA. Unfortunately, both Proposition 48 and 16 continued to have a negative effect on participation rates of African American student-athletes. The court systems were not immune from the NCAA academic standards debate. In fact, the outcomes of the various court decisions resulted in a change to Proposition 16, allowing more weight to be given to high school GPAs.

Today, according to the authors, the debate between stronger academic requirements, initial high school core course requirements, and continuing eligibility rules for student-athletes remains contested ground. The implementation of the 40/60/80 Rule, graduation success rate (GSR), and the academic progress rate (APR) are manifestations of this debate. At least on the surface, the ultimate goal of legislation is to ensure student-athletes, especially minority students, have higher graduation rates. The chapter ends on a cautionary note, suggesting that we await in-depth information and full disclosure regarding participation rates until we decide about the academic success of African American athletes.

Tackling the issues surrounding "Academic Integrity and the Plight of the African American Student-Athlete," Corbett refocused the concerns addressed in Chapter 5 by presenting us an understanding of the current academic state of affairs for African American students who are athletes in higher education. From the outset, Corbett tells us that even as overt discrimination has lessened, racism continues. Since college presidents, faculty, alumni and booster clubs are stakeholders in intercollegiate academic reform, addressing the negative stereotypes connected with the academic performances of African American athletes is the kernel of a movement to regain academic integrity.

The key indicators that athletic departments and university administrators use as measures of academic success are academic progress rates, retention and graduation rates, and disparities between African American and White student-athletes are an increasing concern to the academic communities that provide the educational experiences of African American students who are athletes. The author believes academic disparities, representing academic exploitation, remains one of the most critical issues facing African-American student-athletes. Recent and past occurrences of low graduation rates, academic scandals, and the frequency with which African American athletes leave higher education institutions in mediocre, if not poor academic standing have eroded the public's trust in the educational benefits of sports participation at the collegiate level.

Throughout the chapter, Corbett is able to document differences in academic performance between racial groups. The National Collegiate Athletic Association instituted various academic reform initiatives such as Proposition 48 (1986) and Proposition 16 (1995) to help reduce racial differences in educational performances in the classroom. More recently, the academic performance rating (APR) was created to represent efforts to strengthen student-athletes' academic performance prior to and during the academic career of the student-athletes, concluding with graduation from college. Finding the right balance between intercollegiate athletics and the academic goals of higher education is no easy task, but it is one that must be achieved if African American students are to experience gains in student learning and academic performance. Corbett's arguments, supported by the work of Martin, Gragg, and Kramer II, concede the belief, and we concur, the NCAA should continue to explore new policies and practices to enhance the educational experiences for student-athletes on the college campus.

"Community and Junior College Athletic Programs: New Models for Success—Transition from Junior/Community College to Four-Year Institution" (Chapter 7) by Althouse and Brooks begins discussion about the playing and coaching experiences of ethnic minorities, particularly African Americans youth who attended these institutions. Junior and community colleges in America, embracing their open door policy, provide a vehicle by which ethnic minorities often gained access to four-year colleges/universities. By and large, students attend junior and community colleges for a variety of reasons (e.g., skill development, certification, and transfer to a four-year institution). Furthermore, some junior colleges also afforded students the opportunity to play athletics at this level and, hopefully, transfer their talent to a four-year college.

The historic development of athletic programs in two-year institutions, similar to the impact of athletics at four-year institutions, have perennially debated issues concerning the alignment of athletics within the educational mission of the institutions. Those who do not favor sports programs are apt to see junior colleges sports as farm systems yielding quick-fixes for coaches afflicted with winning at all costs. The chapter reflects how intercollegiate juco sports were shaped as they adapted to big-time collegiate athletics in the context of NCAA policy and rules.

Since 1939, within the charter of the National Junior College Association (NTCAA), the number of two-year institutions continued to expand. In the past decade, athletics was found at 58% of all two-year colleges. Guided by research dealing with the internal and external benefits to student-athletes and their colleges as a result of intercollegiate athletics at the community college level (Castaneda, 2004), we know that sports are very important on many of these campuses, and for rural-serving campuses particularly. On many rural campuses, sport is a student body attraction and also handles the "missing male" problem. Over time and given the influx of freshmen and first-year student-athletes at the community college level, concern has been voiced regarding the academic qualifications of athletes to attend college. In addition, the lay public and sport scholars voiced a concern about the apparent low graduation rates of these students.

The academic reform movement in the form of Proposition 48 adopted by the NCAA (1986–1987) also had an impact on student-athletes, especially minorities, who attended community colleges. Anderson and South (2000) stated the junior/community colleges were not governed by this NCAA legislation. Given this fact, and an open door policy at the community college level, Althouse and Brooks write, "No matter which path one chooses to trace the experiences of students in junior colleges, the issues of the student-athletes subsequently transferring from or to other four-year colleges and institutions have been a continuing concern for study about national standards and practices."

Looking toward the future, community colleges will remain valuable resources to help meet local community workforce demands, and they will also remain significant educational institutions for ethnic minorities to gain access to higher education. Community college coaches and administrators must continue to be cognizant of how NCAA academic standards legislation impacts community colleges and be willing to seek internal and external financial support to enhance the mission of the institution, including seeking financial aid for student-athletes, and provide all student-athletes the opportunity to complete their AA degrees and certification, if appropriate. There are numerous external forces (e.g., Title IX legislation, NCAA legislation) and internal factors (e.g., budget for athletic teams, facilities and equipment, geographical localities of the institution and mission) that will continue impacting the future community college athletic programs in America.

Section III focuses on the effect of gender and race in collegiate sports. Jackson's "The Impact of Title IX on HBCU Campuses," (Chapter 8) traces the passage of the Educational Amendment Act of 1972 (Title IX), focusing its impact on women's athletic programs at HBCU institutions. This makes an excellent addition to Chapters 2 and 3 in this book.

What do nationally known athletic programs at recognized HBCUs such as Florida A&M University, Howard University, and Jackson State University share in common with each other? Jackson reports that these three stellar schools failed to meet Title IX compliance under prong one (proportionality), and they are not alone among HBCUs in America today. There are 104 documented HBCUs, and women's enrollment is about 61% of the undergraduates, which means, of course, a serious problem in meeting prong one (proportionality) compliance requirements, and finding prong two (continuing history of expansion) too hard to meet because of budgetary constraints. Most HBCUs are too small to cope with budget constraints; the largest only has an undergraduate enrollment rate of 3,000 students.

Jackson provides us with an understanding of the challenges that HBCUs face in relation to Title IX legislation, Title IX enforcement cases, and the use of the three-prong test to measure Title IX compliance. Jackson writes, "The problems facing HBCUs, as compared to other colleges and universities, is that enrollment for males at HBCUs is decreasing and enrollment for females is increasing." As a result of this trend, "in order to meet Title IX compliance, 39% of HBCUs' athletic budgets should go to male athletes and 61% for female athletes." College administrators are faced with what can be done to increase the number of African American males to attend HBCUs? If this trend is not reversed, it will be very difficult for HBCUs to meet the proportionality prong of students under Title IX.

Many athletic departments at HBCUs, due to budget constraints and other factors, are also unable to document efforts to add sports or to expand athletic programs. Jackson states, "Until the recent trends are reversed and more African American males are entering colleges and universities, Title IX compliance will remain an issue for HBCUs." On a more positive note, Jackson believes HBCUs can prove compliance with Title IX if they can fully and effectively accommodate the interest and abilities of the underrepresented gender. The key to determining the interests and abilities of individuals is to develop an appropriate instrument and methodology. The clincher, of course: Should HBCUs be forced to meet Title IX compliance by using prong one (proportionality) and two (continuing history of expansion), or should the NCAA allow HBCUs the ability to use surveys to measure compliance?"

Abney's "The Glass Ceiling Effect for African American Women Coaches and Athletic Administrators," (Chapter 9) complements Chapter 4, which explored the "dreams deferred, principally among African American males aspiring to coaching careers, and Jackson's concerns over proportionality and compliance with Title IX as a particular perplexing problem facing HBCU institutions.

The chapter undertakes as its mission an investigation of the social, economic, and political impact of the glass ceiling effect on the ability of African American females to gain access to NCAA head coaching and other administrative positions in intercollegiate athletics. It is what she says it is. Since 1972 the number of women participating in college sports has continued to increase, while at the same time the number of African American women in NCAA leadership positions continues to lag far behind.

With the passage of various forms of federal legislation (i.e., Title IX, Civil Rights Act of 1991), one would have anticipated an increase in the number of women holding leadership positions within college athletics, but data does not support this expectation. Abney contends the glass ceiling effect is partially responsible; however, building the ranks of African American women in athletic department decision-making positions will require a change in the organizational mind-set. Those in positions to hire must be committed and sensitive to diversifying the ranks of college coaches and athletic administrators. NCAA employment data consistently reveals that African American women are underrepresented in leadership positions (i.e., coaches, athletic directors, compliance officers).

Acosta and Carpenter's (2010) recent report reveals that the number of women's teams per school is the highest it has ever been, indicating that about four of 10 head coaches of women's teams are females, and so are about 57% of the paid assistants. Interestingly, more women are found in administrative ranks then at any time since the mid-1970s, but the percentage of African American women or women of color is unexplored and unclear. To shatter the glass ceiling will require change in the workplace culture so as to provide positive and proactive measures to be taken by college administrators to ensure African American women are afforded the opportunity to apply for vacant positions. The chapter concludes, "The commitment by the NCAA to establish a rule to insure that institutions interview at least one minority candidate for coaching and athletic administrative positions would not only constitute an acknowledgement that a problem or glass ceiling exists, but strategies are being implemented to provide opportunities for minorities to reach and shatter the ceiling."

Section IV offers two chapters exploring pop culture and African American student-athletes. First, Harrison and Sutton's Chapter 10, "Cracking Their World: Utilizing Pop Culture to Impact Academic Success of Today's Student-Athlete" offers a refreshing look at the intersection of pop culture, athletic participation, and academic success. The authors introduce concepts focusing notions of self-affirmation, like the cultural concept of *cool* and *cool pose* to help understand and appreciate the African American male culture and media images. This sets the stage for two very important questions: Is it possible to create more balance and synergy between the player and his/her academic performance as a student in American higher education? If so, how can academic institutions and individual stakeholders proactively implement programs and strategies to utilize pop culture to improve academic performance?

It's proposed that pop cultural contributes to a student-athlete's ideas about, and consumption patterns relating to, academic achievement and athletic motivation, in which the student athlete's choices are deemed either cool or un-cool. Because perceptions are highly subjective, they can be correct or they can be incorrect in terms of the message being sent or the intent of the sender. Harrison and Sutton argue it is important to convince African American male student-athletes that staying in school is cool. They currently believe there is the perception that staying in school and studying is un-cool. If elements can be perceived as cool, then the choices become successful. If they are not perceived to be cool, they are often ignored and finally close because of that perception of not being the cool place or the cool thing.

This is a serious challenge for 21st century athletic departments that still operate with a traditional cultural model and that sometimes fail to understand the importance of using relevant concepts and beliefs to challenge student-athletes to compete in the classroom and encourage student-athletes to take pride in their academic performance versus barely remaining eligible. The authors speak to a need to "crack this world" or break this perceived perception by many African American males.

In an attempt to alter behaviors and perceptions, the authors highlighted the success of the Scholar-Baller Program as "an innovative and culturally relevant approach to academic performance and intellectual recognition through pop culture." The Scholar-Baller Program was conducted on several colleges and community colleges in America. The authors reported a positive effect (e.g., increased GPAs) of this initiative with is primary mission to "increase academic performance and cultural motivation of today's student-athletes with a particular focus of African American male student-athletes."

In closing, the authors introduce the concept of *educationalism* to the reader. In essence, the authors of this chapter want to make the readers more fully aware of the intersection between education, commerce, sport, and entertainment. Harrison and Sutton provide a list of 10 items that are perceived as "cool" and are tied to academic success (e.g., sneakers associated with cool people, being respected for who you are as an individual is cool).

Chapter 11, "Coaching Hip Hop Athletes, Confronting Double Doses of Hypermasculinity" by Smith, presents a ground-breaking discussion about the relationship between the hip hop culture and college athletics. At first glance, hip hop and college athletes may seem unrelated, but throughout the chapter, Smith provides a convincing argument of the synergy between the two elements.

During the past decade or two, some of America's most talented and highly visible professional athletes have been products of hip hop culture (e.g., Allen Iverson, Shaquille O'Neal, Kobe Bryant). Likewise, athletic departments and many businesses have begun to embrace hip hop for its cultural and economic benefits. Smith proposes that it would be wise for college coaches to understand and appreciate the relationship between sports and hip hop culture and understand the functional nature of each to society.

The author's depiction of the relationship between hip hop and hypermasculinity in sports, economics, and power helps the reader to understand why Smith insists that "hip hop and sports as distinct social systems are more symmetrical with each other than either of them are with mainstream culture. Part of the symmetry between hip hop and sports includes the way each system develops language, generates esteem, and orders social relationships." Any discussion of hip hop culture and sports would not be complete without the consideration of women in hip hop, since hip hop transcends gender and begins to build a foundation in which African American women are valued for their strength.

In closing, the author encourages high school and college coaches to embrace hip hop culture, "specifically, coaches dealing with hip hop athletes are likely to be more successful, not by feigning understanding and adoption of hip hop music and culture, and certainly not by treating hip hop as a less culture, but by respecting its normative order."

Section V examines race, gender, and fan support. Chapter 12, "Alumni Support, Ethnicity, and Fan Loyalty" by Althouse, Brooks, Dean-Crowly, and Dotson, provides a unique analysis of the extent to which former student-athletes, and especially ethnic minorities and women, contribute financially to their alma maters.

The authors begin with a brief review of the development of intercollegiate athletics in America, from its beginning as activities organized by the student body into a multimillion dollar sports enterprise. While America's intercollegiate sports are an enormous enterprise, its driving force is concentrated in NCAA Division I-A athletic departments and their programs. Financing intercollegiate athletics is complicated by the fact that costs are usually fixed, but the revenues streams are highly variable. Almost invariably, the issue is whether the system is sustainable. Thus, the need for athletic administrators to garner additional external funding to support the athletic mission is simultaneously under siege and conspicuously self-justifying. Most college athletic programs have turned to alumni (i.e., former student-athletes and alumni and friends of the university) to support the athletic department activities and programs. Many athletic programs are run as independent, profit-driven enterprises. Critics argue that the separation that exists between academic and athletic communities means that virtually all athletic department fundraising efforts are directed at raising money specifically for sports, rather than for the institution generally.

The relative independence of athletic associations and other athletic fundraising groups on college campuses provides some insight into the link between the athletic department and the institution on matters of fundraising. In other words, even if indirect benefits in the form of brand name recognition existed, without disclosure of the entire institutional fundraising record, athletic fundraising creates a clear competing interest with academic and other educational priorities where limited financial resources exist.

The question of whether alumni/nae support the current emphasis on sports in colleges and universities yields interesting, if uneven results. Clearly, we need to learn more about specific strategies for appealing to women graduates as legitimate donor constituencies. During 2008–2009, Black males constituted 24.8% and Black females constituted 16% of *all* NCAA Division I sport participants. Hispanic male and female participation rates consisted of 4% and 3.9%, respectively. During the same time period, White male participation rates were 63.8% and White female participate rate data were 71.3% (NCAA, 1999–2000—2008–09). After further investigation, Althouse et al. noted, "There exists some antidotal evidence to support that former student-athletes, now professional athletes, do give back to their alma mater." To date, few researchers have investigated the extent to which ethnic minorities, particularly African-American student-athletes, actively contribute financial assistance back to their athletic program upon graduation.

Chapter 13, "Title IX and Black Female Student-Athletes: Increasing Sports Participation Through Shared Advocacy," by Gill Jr. and Sloan-Green provides an insiders account of the race, gender, and sport literature. Title IX (enacted in 1972) has had an effect, increasing the number of women participating in high school and college athletics. However, "concern remains over the scarcity of Black females in collegiate athletics," most particularly, according to Gill Jr. and Sloan-Green, lending to the diminished level of Black female student-athletes in "country club sports" (e.g., golf, lacrosse, tennis, rowing). As a whole, analysis of NCAA race and gender data shows, "Black female student-athletes have not benefited to the degree of White female student-athletes." From an advocacy standpoint, Title IX will never achieve the ultimate goal of gender equity without achieving some significant degree of racial and gender equity. Given the shortfall encountered with the impact of demography on Title IX (e.g., suburban v. urban sports), mutual engagement in mutual aid, accordingly, also will bring out mutual understanding and hopefully a change in the demography of social justice advocacy.

As veterans of social justice advocacy for Black women in sport, Gill Jr. and Sloan-Green marshal a collection of stakeholder advocacy organizations (e.g., Women's Sport Foundation, AAHPERD, Tucker Center for Research on Girls and Women in Sport) committed to promoting social justice and diversity in college athletics. What has been missing from such discussions is the consistent lack of Black females in leadership positions on the governing boards where policy, strategies, and priorities are established for the Title IX advocacy organization. In their judgment, Black females were not and are not proactive in advocacy efforts. One possible explanation may be a desire to deemphasize sport participation; another might be the expense associated with achieving a quality higher education.

Given this scenario, Gill Jr. and Sloan-Green ask, "if advocates are aware of the obvious racial disparities in women's sports participation, then why do they overlook this issue in organized conversation, national meetings, and international expert media commentary?" Their answer, not so subtly: "In order to achieve racial and gender equity Black feminists and White advocates must step up their game and engage in shared responsibility when carrying out social justice advocacy."

Chapter 14 opens Section VI, which focuses on racism, media exposure, and stereotyping. When Lawrence tackled the task of pinning-down "Whiteness Studies in Sport: A 21st Century Perspective," she joined a group of highly regarded sport science scholars interested in understanding "how power, whiteness, White privilege, and the White athlete have had an impact on sports and the sport science literature." Her work provided us a perspective on race relation theories (race, racism, and discrimination) with her focus on contemporary whiteness theory and whiteness studies.

Lawrence begins with a critique of the status of race and race relations in a global market place with an understanding of colorblind perspectives on diversity and racial complacency. Actually, sports discourses, accordingly, place White males in a superior position in American culture and society. Contrary to popular media, White athletes are not the underdog and are not underrepresented in most sports. In an age of "diversity," Lawrence contends overt racism and segregation has been replaced, far more subtly, with various forms of discrimination associated with race.

The study of whiteness is connected with White theory which, Lawrence posits, had its onset in the legal profession. White male athletes are in a dominant position in sport as well. Being aware of the White agenda will allow opposition to White supremacy and oppressive acts and injustices. The literature in her chapter defines Whiteness in terms of prestige, privilege, and as property rights. Understanding the nature of White privilege, White supremacy, and social media in the context of sports permits us to more fully comprehend the interconnectiveness of racial identity, privilege, cultural values, masculinity, gender, nationalism, and dominate cultural beliefs. Thus, bluntly stated, being White offers the individual privilege and power. Lawrence concludes the study of Whiteness and White privilege "represents new departures from the traditional line of race relations and sport research."

Lawrence's present journey as a White woman, athlete, and scholar represents an individual seeking to conceptualize her own life experiences in the context of interactions with the African American community, family members, other student-athletes, and life as a PhD degree student. She writes, "My role as a researcher opened my eyes to extreme cases of racism and exposed me to the realities of African American athletes. These experiences motivated me to pursue research studies exploring race and social justice issues."

In 1993, sport science scholar Carol Oglesby asked the question, "Where is the White in the Rainbow Coalition?" Oglesby believed racism was initially created by White people and challenged the White population to work hard to resolve the opposition and strife it brought into civil society. Similar to Lawrence's position, Oglesby channels her remarks to White people, career educators, and professionals involved in athletics. Antiracist advocacy begins at the personal level with a desire to learn more about other racial minorities; hopefully, becoming "a White individual (color affirming White) who is committed to building an equitable, racially diverse network of relationships" (p. 260). Lawrence is one of those "color affirming Whites" who dedicated her professional academic career to promoting the concepts of social justice and fairness, especially in college athletics.

Chapter 15, "Stakeholder Management in Big-Time College Sport: The Educational Interest of the African American Male Athlete," by Singer provides an exceptional analysis of the African American male experiences in college sports through the lens of the Critical race theory and stakeholder management theory.

The author provide extensive literature depicting the impact of racism on stakeholder management issues in NCAA Division I competition (e.g., recruitment, retention, and graduation rates of African American male student-athletes). At the heart of the debate rests the question, to what degree are big-time college athletic programs willing to sacrifice the education experiences of student-athletes, especially African American males, to gain a greater market share on their investment.

A common theme found throughout the various chapters in this book is the perceived contradiction of terms such as *student-athlete* and *educational mission of college athletics*. Singer argues that "those who manage sport (i.e., coaches and administrators) must be more concerned with the benefits that prime beneficiaries (student-athletes) receive from the athletic department's existence and operations." Reflecting on the educational experiences of African American student-athletes, Brooks and Althouse (1996) wrote, "commercial forces imposing an incompatible condition on the experiences of collegiate African Americans: the academic and economic exploitative nature of big-time college sports played out in the academic-athletic conflict" (p. viii).

Singer's introduction of the concepts of stakeholders, stakeholder identification, and salience (i.e., power and legitimacy) will assist sport management scholars and students in better understanding how various priorities (e.g., salaries, financial assistance for support units) are established within the athletic department.

Singer concedes, "The stakeholder group does indeed have a vested interest in how things are organized and operated in these athletic departments and programs. Therefore, those who manage college sport (i.e., administrators and coaches) should not only be concerned with financial gain via commodification of the African American male body; but more importantly, they should be mindful of how their decision-making regarding policies, rules, regulations, and procedures might impact the overall welfare of these athletes." While the literature continues to acknowledge the existence of racism in college athletics, Singer voices the opinion that athletic programs have a moral duty to provide remedies to eradicate these factors and conditions contributing to the exploitation of stakeholders (i.e., African American male student-athletes).

Singer concludes his chapter by encouraging scholars to use critical race theory and stakeholder management theory to better gauge the experiences of the African American male student-athletes on HBCUs and on the campuses of predominantly White institutions of higher education.

Examining other diversity issues is the intent of Section VII. "From the Turf to the Top: Access to Higher Education by Latino Male College Football Players" (Chapter 16), by Harrison, Ochoa, and Hernandez, turns our focus on the sport experiences of male Latino college football players. This chapter represents a departure from the issues focused on the college experiences of African American male and female student-athletes, although only a limited research has focused on this very important area of study.

Historically, African American and Latino students were confronted by similar social conditions such as discrimination, lack of access to resources, health issues, lower high school and college graduation rates when compared to their White counterparts, and access to higher education via the junior/community college route. To some extent, overcoming these social, cultural, political, and economic barriers, Latinos have enjoyed a level of success in the sport industry.

Latino athletes, historically, made contributions to boxing, baseball, and professional football; yet, much is still unknown about the academic and athletic experiences of Latino male and female student-athletes. Harrison and colleagues urge sport scientists to develop tools grounded in sound theories to systematically analyze the sport experiences of this growing population in America.

The final chapter in the book (Chapter 17), "Migration of the International Student-Athlete," by Teed, provides an analysis of migration patterns of international student-athletes. The historical evaluation of college sport in America is grounded in the ever-increasing need to generate revenue to sustain the athletic corporation and pressure to produce successful athletic teams.

Teed writes, "The ability to maintain a successful athletic program is predicated on the recruitment of high level talent and successful coaches who work as part of a very effective management team to produce those blue chippers who will increase their chances of winning." The need to identify and recruit athletic talent extends beyond America's borders. The author is able to identify several advantages (e.g., inexpensive, more experience) and weaknesses (e.g., language barriers, perceived as not taking USA students) with the recruitment of international student-athletes. An issue relevant to this book is the extent to which international student-athletes are contributing to a perceived reduction in the number of playing opportunities for African Americans in some NCAA sports. Teed cites data indicating that a majority of foreign athletes participate on tennis, soccer, indoor and outdoor track, hockey, and golf teams. African American NCAA student-athletes (men and women) tend to have a higher percentage of participation in basketball, football, and track and field. A more comprehensive analysis and understanding of the migration patterns of foreign student-athletes is needed. Researchers may want to review the intersections of geography, economics, culture, and politics on the international student-athlete recruitment process.

In part, the ending of this volume is revealed at its beginning, within the Foreword written by Floyd Keith. Currently the president of the Black Coaches & Administrators, Keith opens the third edition with a brief manifesto of intentions in his statement: "Minorities Are Separate and Unequal: A Look at Minority Hiring Practices in Collegiate and Professional Athletics." The BCA, according to Keith, apparently has both a moral and social responsibility to maintain an annual Hiring Report Card for intercollegiate football and for the benefit of sport in general. The Hiring Report Card uses the power of public exposure as its source of accountability. Such action will also bring renewed attention to similar studies with regard to women's basketball and athletics director searches. In light of these intentions, Keith, nonetheless, expresses some doubts about whether such potential public acknowledgement is strong enough by itself to make a significant change. Indeed, it may be that a NCAA version of the Rooney Rule or a Title VII lawsuit the answer?

Mindful of the fact that each separate NCAA institution hires its own coaches, not much seems to be happening to increase diversity among coaches when left in the hands of each individual institution. Perhaps legal filing of a strong qualifying Title VII case against a visible institution would change the status quo of collegiate searches and then a more forceful realization of the legal implications with regard to Title VII would press toward the equality needed in the intercollegiate hiring landscape. The merits of bringing a Title VII test case forward might at least force the NCAA's member institutions to consider a best practices model like the NFL's Rooney Rule. We can only hope the effort to resolve the lack of minority coaches at the collegiate level catches up with the need to end this social injustice.

REFERENCES

Abney, R. (1988). The effects of role models and mentors on career patterns of African American women coaches and athletic administrators in historically African American and historically White institutions of higher education. Unpublished doctoral dissertation, The University of Iowa, Iowa City.

Acosta, R. V., & Carpenter, L. J. (2010). *Women in intercollegiate sport: A longitudinal study thirty-three year update (1977–2010)*. Retrieved from http://www.acostacarpenter.org

Anderson, A., & South, D. (2000). Racial differences in collegiate recruitment, retention and graduation rates. In D. Brooks & R. Althouse (Eds.), *Racism in college athletics: The African American athlete's experience* (2nd ed., pp. 155–169). Morgantown, WV: Fitness Information Technology.

Brooks, D., & Althouse, R. (Eds.) (1993). *Racism in college athletics: The African American athlete's experience*. Morgantown, WV: Fitness Information Technology.

Brooks, D., & Althouse, R. (1996). The African American resource directory. Morgantown, WV: Fitness Information Technology.

Brooks, D., & Althouse, R. (Eds.) (2000). *Racism in college athletics: The African American athlete's experience* (2nd ed.). Morgantown, WV: Fitness Information Technology.

Brooks, D., & Althouse, R. (Eds.). (2000). African American head coaches and administrators: Progress but . . . . . . ? In D. Brooks & R. Althouse (Eds.), *Racism in college athletics: The African American athlete's experience* (2nd ed., pp. 85–117). Morgantown, WV: Fitness Information Technology.

Castaneda, C. (2004). *A national overview of intercollegiate athletics at public community colleges*. Meridan, MS: MidSouth Partnership for Rural Community Colleges. Retrieved from http://www.msgovt.org/files/castaneda.pdf

Oglesby, C. (1993). Issues of sport and racism: where is the white in the rainbow coalition? In D. Brooks & R. Althouse (Eds.), *Racism in college athletics: The African-American athlete's experience* (pp. 251–267). Morgantown, WV: Fitness Information Technology.

Index

About the Editors

Ronald Althouse is a professor of sociology, a past chairperson of the Department of Sociology and Anthropology, and director of the Survey and Research Center at West Virginia University. He received his MA and PhD in sociology from the University of Minnesota. Althouse's research interests and publications have focused on worker's risk and worker's health, health care delivery, and health systems. He has contributed to the literature on athletic participation and is committed to efforts focused on social justice in sports. In his leisure time, he enjoys bicycling and jazz, and is an avid science fiction reader.

Dana Brooks is a professor and dean at West Virginia University College of Physical Activity and Sport Sciences. He received his AA degree from Hagerstown Junior College, BS from Towson State University, and MS and EdD from West Virginia University. He has published and presented nationally and internationally in the area of sport sociology. Brooks is also co-author of *Diversity and Social Justice in College Sports*. He has authored or co-authored manuscripts that have appeared in *Quest*, *Sports Management Review*, *Journal of Strength and Conditioning Research*, *Journal of Physical Education and Recreation*, and *The Journal of African American Men*. He teaches "African Americans in Sport" and "Sociology of Sport." His numerous honors and awards include Dean's Recognition Award from the College of Health Professions, Towson University Alumni Association; Martin Luther King, Jr., Achievement Award, WVU Center for Black Culture and Research; WVU Social Justice Award; and the Martin Luther King "Living the Dream" Award, State of West Virginia. Brooks is a fellow in the National Academy of Kinesiology and served as president of the American Alliance for Health, Physical Education, Recreation and Dance. He recently was awarded the Lifetime Achievement Award from Hagerstown Community College.

About the Authors

Robertha Abney is an associate professor in the Department of Sport Management at Slippery Rock University. She has distinguished herself as a leading writer, presenter, and authority in the area of women and minorities in leadership roles in sport. Abney has served as president of the National Association for Girls and Women in Sport (NAGWS).

Robert A. Bennett III, MA, is a PhD candidate in the Department of History and a doctoral fellow in the Todd A. Bell National Resource Center on the African American Male at The Ohio State University. His scholarship interests focus on African American history, with a concentration on African American political and social activism in the 20th century.

Frankie G. Collins, PhD, is an assistant professor in the Department of Health Sciences (Physical Education) at South Carolina State University. His scholarship interests include issues pertaining to high school physical education teachers' attitudes and understandings about culturally relevant pedagogy and teaching African American male students within urban schools, equity and diversity within sport and physical education contexts, mentoring new faculty and at-promise students, and K–16 professional development.

Doris R. Corbett is a professor and director of the School of Health, Physical Education, and Leisure Services (HPELS) at the University of Northern Iowa and is professor emeritus of sport studies and former chairperson in the Department of Health, Human Performance & Leisure Studies at Howard University. A former president of AAHPERD and member of the International Olympic Committee Sport for All Commission, Corbett's research interests focus primarily on sport and human rights, ethics and moral reasoning in sport, and race and gender issues in sport.

Andrea Dean-Crowley, MA, works as a special projects and development coordinator at the Manuel H. Johnson Center for Political Economy at Troy University.

D. Lyn Dotson, JD, is the vice president for Development at the WVU Foundation and an adjunct faculty member in the Department of Political Science at West Virginia University, where he earned his law degree. He previously served as WVU's associate dean at the College of Law and as assistant vice president for Institutional Advancement.

Emmett L. Gill, Jr. is an assistant professor at North Carolina Central University (NCCU) and the director of the Student-Athletes Human Rights Project. Gill has worked in athletics at Rutgers University, the University of Maryland, the United States Military Academy Prep School, and NCCU. He has taught graduate level courses on collegiate sports and university life, counseling student-athletes, and ethics in sports.

Derrick L. Gragg is the athletics director at Eastern Michigan University (EMU). A former collegiate wide receiver at Vanderbilt, Gragg earned his doctorate in higher education administration from the University of Arkansas. He has published articles and editorials on intercollegiate athletics as well as a nationwide study on sports-related gambling. He is a former member of the NCAA's Minority Opportunities & Interests Committee and in 2008–09 earned the Black Coaches & Administrators Administrator of the Year Award.

Chevelle Hall, PhD, is the department chair of Health, Physical Education and Recreation at Hampton University.

Michelle S. Hernández, MEd, is a doctoral candidate in higher education at the University of Denver. Her research focuses on the social, political, historical, and structural inequities that disproportionately and negatively affect underrepresented students.

Samuel R. Hodge, PhD, is a professor in the College of Education and Human Ecology at The Ohio State University. He was a recipient of the 2011 E. B. Henderson Award from the American Alliance for Health, Physical Education, Recreation and Dance (AAHPERD). His scholarship focuses on diversity, disability, and social justice in education and sport.

C. Keith Harrison is an associate professor and associate director of the DeVos Sport Business Management Program at the University of Central Florida. He is the founder of the Paul Robeson Research Center for Academic and Athletic Prowess, an author and principal investigator for the Black Coaches & Administrators' Hiring Report Card Study (2003–2009), and president and co-founder of Scholar-Baller.

Cryshanna A. Jackson, PhD, is an assistant professor in the Department of Political Science at Youngstown State University. Jackson's research interests focus on public polices pertaining to social equity, civil rights, and gender equality.

Wardell Johnson, PhD, is an associate professor in the Department of Exercise & Sports Sciences at Eastern Kentucky University. His teaching interests include issues in athletic administration, legal issues in sport and human resources, management, and leadership and student development issues.

Floyd Keith is the executive director of the Black Coaches & Administrators. A former collegiate football coach, Keith has been honored by numerous organizations as a coach and administrator. The National Consortium for Academics and Sports awarded him the "2007 Giant Steps Award for Coaching"; *Sports Illustrated* recognized him as one of "The 101 Most Influential Minorities in Sports" in 2004; and *Black Enterprise* magazine listed him as one of the "50 Most Powerful Blacks in Sports" in 2005.

Dennis A. Kramer II is a doctoral candidate within the Institute of Higher Education at the University of Georgia. He also is the Senior Research and Policy Analyst for the Policy Division at the Georgia Department of Education. Previously, he served as the research and policy fellowship position for the Knight Commission on Intercollegiate Athletics and co-edited a 2010 monograph with Dr. J. Douglas Toma titled *The Uses of Intercollegiate Athletics: Opportunities and Challenges in Positioning Universities*. His research focuses on the application of advanced econometric and quasi-experimental analyses on policy evaluation and the role of athletics in the postsecondary organizations and decision-making.

Suzanne Malia Lawrence is a professor in the Graduate Physical Education Program at Azusa Pacific University (APU). Lawrence's research interests include the racial experiences of White/Black athletes, career transition of college athletes, stereotypes surrounding athleticism, academic achievement of college athletes, and the lived experience of her participants/students.

Angela Lumpkin, PhD, is a professor in the Department of Health, Sport, and Exercise Sciences at the University of Kansas, where she previously served as dean of the School of Education. She has authored or co-authored 22 books. She has served as president of the National Association for Sport and Physical Education, been selected as an American Council on Education Fellow, and served as distinguished visiting professor at the United States Military Academy.

Brandon E. Martin, EdD, is a senior associate athletics director for administration at the University of Oklahoma. Martin is also an adjunct professor in both the Rainbolt College of Education and the African and African American Studies Department at the University of Oklahoma. In 2005, he earned the National Association of Academic Advisors for Student Athlete Excellence in Research Award.

Vanessa Ochoa, PhD, is director of *iComunidad*—First-Year Experience Program at Mount St. Mary's College (MSMC) in Los Angeles and an adjunct professor in the sociology department. Her research interests include issues of equity and access for Latina/o students into higher education by focusing on how counseling programs at the high school and collegiate level can better serve the needs of first-generation Latina/o students.

John N. Singer, PhD, is an assistant professor in the Department of Health and Kinesiology at Texas A&M University. His research focus is in the area of diversity and social justice, with a keen focus on race in organized school sport settings. Singer was named a Montague Teaching Scholar in the Texas A&M University Center for Teaching Excellence in 2009. In 2008, he served as a co-investigator on a research grant with the National Collegiate Athletic Association (NCAA) that focuses on "diversity best practices" in college athletic departments.

Tina Sloan-Green is co-founder and president of the Black Women in Sport Foundation. She is a professor emeritus in the College of Education at Temple University. She became the first African American head coach in the history of women's intercollegiate lacrosse, and from 1973–1992 she led Temple to a 207-62-4 record, three national championships, and 11 consecutive NCAA Final Four appearances. A co-author of two books, Sloan-Green received Lifetime Achievement Awards from the National Association of Collegiate Women Athletic Administrators and the National Women's Lacrosse Coaches Association in 2008.

Andre L. Smith is an associate professor of law at Widener Law School in Wilmington, Delaware, where he teaches administrative law and federal taxation. His publications include, *Other Peoples' Property: HipHop's Inherent Clashes with US Property Laws and its Rise as Global Counter Culture*, in the University of Virginia Sports and Entertainment Law Journal; *Do NFL Signing Bonuses Carry A Substantial Risk of Forfeiture Pursuant to Section 83 of the Internal Revenue Code?*, in the Seton Hall Sports and Entertainment Journal; *Reparations and Taxation*, in the Pittsburgh Tax Review; and *Consumer Boycotts Versus Civil Litigation* in the Howard University Law Journal.

William A. Sutton is a professor of management and founding director of the University of South Florida's Sport and Entertainment MBA Graduate Program. In this role, Sutton teaches courses in sport marketing and sales and promotional management in sport, and serves as the internship coordinator for the program. Sutton is also the founder and principal of Bill Sutton & Associates, a consulting firm specializing in strategic marketing and revenue enhancement for clients including the NBA, NHL, Orlando Magic, New York Yankees, Phoenix Suns, Charlotte Bobcats, Pittsburgh Pirates, and Cleveland Indians.

Kenneth C. Teed is a senior research scholar at The George Washington University School of Business and is an active consultant in the field of sport management. He also has wide-ranging interests, from IOC marketing to the development of Title IX and worked on the Equity in Interscholastic Athletics Disclosure Act report to Congress.

Delano Tucker, PhD, is a professor and past chair of the Department of Health, Physical Education and Exercise Science at Norfolk State University. He previously served as a department chair, assistant athletic director, and faculty representative at Coppin State University. A former collegiate athlete and coach, Tucker was the first minority head coach in swimming and gymnastics in the Fairfax Public School System. He is a retired Major US Army Medical Service Corp.